D1416341

READINGS IN RUSSIAN HISTORY

Readings...

IN RUSSIAN HISTORY

COMPILED AND EDITED BY WARREN B. WALSH

Professor of History and Chairman of the Board
of Russian Studies at Syracuse University.

Enlarged Edition

SYRACUSE UNIVERSITY PRESS
1950

Copyright 1948 and 1950

BY

SYRACUSE UNIVERSITY PRESS

TO

ELIZABETH CANTRIL WALSH

Preface

Among the problems brought by the growing interest in the history of Russia, one of the most vexing is the lack of readings suitable to supplement lectures and textbooks. Few libraries can boast of their Russian collections and even those which are well supplied qualitatively frequently lack the quantity to care for the increasing demand. Moreover, many of the most desirable books have long been out of print and are virtually irreplaceable when wear and tear forces their withdrawal from circulation. It is the purpose of this anthology to aid in the solution of this problem by making an integrated collection of usable materials readily available.

Although suggestions have been solicited and followed the final choice of materials has been mine, and I am somewhat painfully aware that my selections will not satisfy everyone. Some explanation of the criteria used in making the choices would seem to be in order.

History means to me primarily the story of people. Governments rise and fall, laws are promulgated and forgotten, treaties are signed and broken—but the people are always there. I have therefore been at pains to seek out reports of the social norms and values of the various periods— how the people lived, how they fed and clothed themselves, their habits, their customs and their prejudices. "People" include tsars and princelings as well as the masses, and in an autocracy the characteristics and actions of the autocrat and his associates are obviously of great importance in the lives of many. I have therefore included descriptions and records which reveal some aspects of the personalities and policies of the rulers. Institutions also form a part of the norm and value patterns so some selections deal with the institutions of serfdom, the state, the administration and the church. Art, letters, military campaigns, laws, diplomatic interchanges and certain other matters, although certainly parts of the norms and values, have been omitted because of space limitations.

Two other criteria have also been kept in mind: first, that the selection should have some intrinsic interest and value which would contribute toward an understanding of Russian history; and, second, that the material should not be readily available elsewhere. It was this latter consideration which led to picking the February Revolution as the stopping place of the anthology, and also to the relative briefness of the last section. The reader's attention may be called to: F. A. Golder, *Documents of Russian History;* to the various publications of the Hoover Library such as J. Bunyan and H. H. Fisher, *The Bolshevik Revolution, 1917-1918;* to the collected works of

Lenin; and especially to Sir Bernard Pares' definitive study of this period, *The Fall of the Russian Monarchy*. I have excluded much excellent and pertinent material because I did not wish to duplicate these books.

As to the mechanics of the anthology, each selection is preceded by a short editorial statement, printed in italics, concerning the author or the general setting. All translations, unless otherwise indicated, are my work. Each part of the book has a suggested bibliography under the heading of "Additional Readings." I have excluded from these all the sources from which selections are printed and all foreign language books. I have included some periodical material and numerous historical or otherwise pertinent novels. Page or chapter assignments are given for most of the citations.

All copyrighted material has been used with the express permission of the copyright holder. The full source is given in the introductory material of each selection. I am grateful to those authors and publishers who have permitted the use of their material.

Finally I wish to express here my appreciation to all who have helped in making this book, including my students in Russian history whose reactions over a period of years to my "Assigned Readings" gave me valuable clues as to the interest and usefulness of many passages.

WARREN B. WALSH

January 1948.

Foreword

When the first edition of this book was published I assumed that the tremendous quantities of material dealing with Soviet Russia made another anthology for that period somewhat superfluous. It has been pointed out, however, that certain types of material are not generally available and that these *Readings* would be more useful to many people if they contained selections dealing with the period after 1917. When the generous response to the original edition made it possible to enlarge the second without increasing the price of the book it was decided to concentrate on the Soviet period and upon the development of the Leninist program and party during the last years of the old regime. This supplement therefore contains only three items not directly linked to those two themes. The three exceptions were included because they complement certain selections in the main portion of the anthology.

The criteria of selection generally followed those described in the Preface except for one thing. Much less attention is paid in the Supplement to descriptions of social norms and values because it is believed that most libraries will have an adequate sampling of the many travelers' accounts, eye-witness stories, and polemics which have been printed about the Soviets. That is the reason for the omission of reports by such familiar figures as: Chamberlin, Ward, Dallin, Davies, Strong, Kravchenko, Duranty, the Webbs, and others. Since many of the basic documents — such as the constitutions, reports on the Five Year Plans, treaties and agreements, the speeches and pronouncements of Stalin and his associates — have been printed in many forms and are generally available, they are not included in this collection.

The "Note on Transliterations and Spellings" holds good for the Supplement as does the description of the mechanics of the anthology as given in the Preface.

The Leninania which are identified as being in the Central Lenin Museum were reproduced in facsimile in, *Lenin (V. I. Ulyanov)* which was published by the Soviet State Publishing House of Political Literature in 1939. I am responsible for all translations which are not specifically accredited. All copyright material has been used by arrangements with the owners.

I regret that it is not feasible to attempt to name here all the persons whose suggestions and encouragement made this edition possible. I am their debtor in many ways, and I hope that they will not take it amiss that, of them all, I single out for specific mention Dr. William A. Miller, Director of Syracuse University Press. His friendly understanding, his sympathetic help, his unfailing courtesy and forbearance, and his unflagging support since the beginning of this book have contributed greatly to its success.

WARREN B. WALSH

A Note on Transliterations and Spellings

There has never been a uniformly accepted system of transliteration of Russian words and names. Variations due to national habits, current styles, and personal idiosyncrasies of spelling are manifold and sometimes puzzling. To have achieved uniformity within this anthology would have involved numerous alterations in almost every selection, a process which seemed neither feasible nor desirable. Uniformity has therefore been sought only in the editorial comments and titles; the transliterations and spellings of the originals have not been changed.

Contents

* Indicates primary source material.

Part IV. The Reigns of Alexander I and Nicholas I

* Indicates primary source material.

CONTENTS

* Indicates primary source material.

PART VI. THE ROAD TO REVOLUTION

* Indicates primary source material.

Contents of the Supplement

* Indicates primary source material.

* Indicates primary source material.

Part I: ANCIENT AND MEDIEVAL TIMES

The Legendary Account: The Chronicle of Nestor

The Chronicles, which are the earliest written records of Russian history, appear to date from the 11th century A.D. The most authoritative, complete and earliest of the Chronicles to have survived is The Lavrentyesky Spisok, *dating from 1377 and so called after the Monk Lawrence who copied it. The second oldest is called* Ipatsky Spisok, *after the Ipatsky Monastery where it was found. The main part of both these Chronicles is an historical compilation, "The Tale of By-gone Years" which was long thought to be the work of the Monk Nestor and was known as* The Chronicle of Nestor. *It is now generally held to be a compilation of the work of many men.*

The following excerpts are free translations, somewhat adapted, from an early, uncorrected version. The source is: Louis Paris, La Chronique de Nestor. *Traduite en francais d'apres l'edition imperiale de Petersbourg, manuscrit de Koenigsberg.* Paris, 1834.

THE BEGINNINGS. Let us begin our story. After the flood the three children of Noah: Sem, Cham, and Japhat divided the world among them. Sem occupied the East: Cham, the middle part; and Japhat received the North and the Southwest. In the portion belonging to Japhat there lived the Russian, the Chudes, and many other people.

After the fall of the tower of Babel and the confusion of tongues, the sons of Japhat occupied the countries of the West and North. From the descendants of Japhat came those who took the name of Slavs. They established themselves near the Danube in the countries of the Egri and the Bulgars. Some of these Slavs were scattered over the earth, and they have taken the names of those places where they established themselves, for example, those who populated the frontiers of Moravia call themselves Moravians; others, Czechs. The Serbs and the Kroats are also Slavs. Among those Slavs who lived along the Dnieper, some took the name of Poles, others that of Dreviliens (because they lived in the forest) others that of Dregovich (who established themselves between the Pripet and the Dvina) thus the language of the Slavs was dispersed. As to the alphabet, that was not born until later.

THE ANCIENT ROAD. There is a road which runs from Varangia to Greece, and another which goes from Greece to the Lovat; and one which returns from the Lovat by a route across the Great Lake Ilmen. From this [inland] sea flows the Volkhov which enters into the great lake of the Neva. The Neva empties into the Sea of the Varangians [the Baltic]. From this sea one can go to Rome and from Rome, also by sea, even to Constantinople. From Constantinople, one can go by way of the Black Sea into which flows the River Dnieper. The Dnieper rises in the forests of Volkhov and flows to the south; while the Dvina which has its source in the same forests flows to the north and empties into the Varangian Sea; from these same forests, the Volga flows to the west. From this sea one can go from Russia to Bulgaria by way of the Volga; to Varangia by way of the Dvina; from the Varangians to Rome, and from Rome to the farthermost possessions of Cham. The Dnieper with its three mouths empties into the Black Sea, which is called the Sea of the Russians.

THE THREE PRINCES. During the years 6386, 6369, and 6370, [from 860-862] the Varangians crossed the Sea. This time the people who had already submitted to them refused to pay them tribute longer, and wished to govern themselves, but there was no sense of justice among them. One family raised itself against the others, and this foolishness brought frequent disaster. They therefore decided among themselves, "Let us seek a Prince who will govern us and who will give us justice." In order to find him, the Slavs crossed the Sea and sought him among the Varangians. The Chudes, the Slavs, the Krivichs and other peoples together spoke thus to the princes of Varangia: "Our country is large and has everything in abundance except that we lack order and justice; come take possession and govern us." Three Varangian brothers together with their families went, in effect, to occupy Slavonia. They settled among the Slavs, and in the country they built the city of Ladoga. The eldest of the three, Rurik, set up his residence along the banks of the river of that name. The second, Sineous, set up his house in the regions of the Blanc. The third, Trouvor, at Isbosk. That part of Russia was later called Novgorod by the Varangians, but the residents of that country, before the arrival of Rurik, had been known only by the name of Slavs.

There were among the Varangians, two men, Askold and Dir, who were not of the royal family but were important nobles. Without the King's permission, they left with some of their companions and went into the countryside and penetrated along the Dnieper even to Constantinople. Along the way they discovered a city situated on a mountain and they asked, "Whose city is that?" The response was made, "It belonged once to three brothers, Kii, Shchechek, and Choriv, who built it, but actually we who live there pay tribute to the Khazars." Askold and Dir then conquered the city and established themselves there, attracting to them a large number of the Varangians.

THE YEAR 6496 [988]. [The Grand Prince Vladimir having, according to the ancient chroniclers, studied all sorts of religions, determined upon the adoption of Christianity. He was perhaps helped to this decision by his desire to marry a Greek princess who made his baptism a prerequisite. After his baptism, he imposed similar baptism upon his people. The words of the Chronicle follow.]

Vladimir made known throughout his village: "Those who day after to-morrow do not appear on the bank of the river, rich or poor, will be considered as rebels and traitors." The day following Vladimir accompanied by the priests, those of the empress and those of Kherson, went to the Dnieper, where there was gathered an innumerable crowd of men who entered into the water, some up to the neck, others only to the chest. The children stayed on the bank and were covered with water; some plunged into the river. Others swam here and there while the priests read their prayers. And this formed a spectacle tremendously curious and beautiful to see. At last, when all the people were baptized, each returned to his home.

THE YEAR 6534 [1026]. Yaroslav after having rebuilt his army approached Kiev and concluded a peace with his brother Mstislav. They divided the Russian territory along the Danube river. Yaroslav took the Western part, and Mstislav the rest. The two princes, reconciled, then dwelt in peace and brotherly friendship. The civil wars and internal rebellions were stopped, and the country knew a rebirth of tranquility.

THE YEAR 6535 [1027]. The third son of Yaroslav was born, and received the name Sviatoslav. The year following there was seen in the sky an extraor-dinary sign: it was the figure of a serpent, and this sign was noticed by all the world.

THE YEAR 6537 [1029]. General tranquility.

A Modern Account: The Early Peoples of the Russian Plain

The early Chronicles were a mixture of fact, legend, tradition and various sorts of political and ecclesiastical propaganda. Only the most expert can disentangle them and read them correctly, and even the experts disagree about them. Here is a recent scholarly account of the early peoples of the Russian plain, written by the late Ales Hrdlicka, an outstanding American anthropologist. The source is: Ales Hrdlicka, The Peoples of the Soviet Union. War Background Studies # 3. Washington, D.C.: The Smithsonian Institution, 1942. Pp. 2-10. (Slightly abridged.)

THE PEOPLING OF RUSSIA. Prehistory. — Up to the middle of the Quaternary period or Ice Age, the vast stretches of European as well as Asiatic Soviet Union were still devoid of human occupation. According to present-day evidence, it was only during the Mousterian or Neanderthal phase of man.

and later, that sparse human contingents began to spread over the more southern parts of these regions. At the end of the last glaciation or soon thereafter the early comers had reached the Crimea, other southern parts of European Russia, and as far at least as Uzbekistan, where recently (1938) the Leningrad anthropologist Okladnikov found in a cave, with Mousterian implements, the remains of a Neanderthal child. Farther east, along the upper Yenisei, Angara, and Lena Rivers and in the Lake Baikal region, occur the remains of later, upper paleolithic and highly interesting neolithic populations, the latter offering close resemblances to some of the American Indians. Upper paleolithic and especially neolithic men reached also over a large part of the European as well as the more southern Asiatic portions of the country.

Early and later historical data. — From the time of the neolithic men to the dawn of historical times, both the European and Asiatic parts of what is now the Soviet Union were extensively although sparsely peopled, and there began taking place in the more southern parts of the country in Europe and Siberia some large-scale displacements.

About 600 B. C., the European region of what was to become Russia comprised the area now occupied by Finland, Karelia, Estonia, Livonia, the higher Volga, and the main central regions, peopled sparsely by the "Finno-Ugrians," a somewhat Mongoloid stock speaking Finno-Ugrian (Uralo-Altaic) dialects, and connected with the original Hun, Magyar, Turcic and other related elements of Asia. At the same time the region that is now southern Russia, aside from some older tribes such as the Cimmerians and Taurids, was occupied by partly nomadic (east), partly sedentary and agricultural (west) tribes known to the old Greeks collectively as "Scythians." The more eastern nomadic parts of this loose complex were doubtless Tatar, the sedentary western portions probably early Slavic. Lithuania, then occupying the territory that after the thirteenth century became Eastern Prussia, had an old and probably already mixed European population of its own, while Poland was always essentially Slav.

It was in these earliest historical times also that the Greeks established a number of trading posts and small colonies along the southern coasts of the territory, particularly in the Crimea, the names and remains of which exist in those parts to this day.

In the Arctic regions lived the Mongoloid forefathers of the Lapps, and farther east the Samoyeds.

In the Asiatic portion of the present Soviet Union, over the southern steppes, roamed the Tatars, Kirghiz, and related groups; while more to the south were the Turkmenian and related central Asiatic aggregations.

In Siberia, the neolithic population had passed apparently into the numerous paleo-Asiatic groups, and well before the beginning of the Christian era these were being pushed northward by the Mongol groups from farther south. This large movement of peoples, of which there are many evidences, resulted in many displacements, leading perhaps even to immigrations into the American continent.

As to earlier movements of peoples over what are now the European Soviet territories, many details are lost or obscure. Facilitated by the vast unobstructed grassy southern flats, many such movements occurred, some of much importance. These movements were from all directions except from the Arctic and the northeast, but particularly from the east westward, from the south northward, and eventually from the west eastward.

The "drives" from the east were those by more or less powerful groups of the Mongoloid nomads from the less hospitable Asiatic regions, where the climate was becoming drier. The invaders were the descendants of the old nomadic "Scythians," now known as the Hun, Bolgar, Magyar, Ugrian, Avar, Polovetz, Tatar, and Mongol, and their incursions plagued eastern and even central Europe from the fourth to the thirteenth centuries and even later. They overran generally parts of what is now Ukrainia, and some reached as far as Poland, eastern Germany, and Pannonia (a larger part of which became "Hun-land, Hungary"). The Huns under Attila penetrated in fact as far as northern France, where in 451 on the "champs de Chalôns," near the Marne, they suffered a fatal defeat.

The advances from the south were made by the Greeks, Venetians, Genoese, Khazars, and Turks; those from the northwest by the Goths, Varangians (Swedes), and Germans; and from the west by the Slavs, who eventually spread over wide areas, with later immigrations of varying magnitude of Jews, Germans, Poles, Czechs, and Rumanians. The more important of these processes deserve more detailed attention.

MOVEMENTS OF PEOPLES IN EUROPEAN RUSSIA. THE SCYTHIANS. The peoples of what are now the European parts of the Soviet Union first began to be better known as a result of the famous march into their country of Darius Hystaspes — the first "Napoleon" — about 512 B. C., and more especially through the writings of Herodotus, about 450 B. C. Of those populations that were mainly of Asiatic origin, by far the most prominent were the "Scythians," whose territory embraced practically the whole present southern Russia below about 50° N. latitude. Peoples of related origin covered the country from the Urals to Finland, and from the Volga to the Baltic. They were subdivided into numerous tribes and differed somewhat in blood, but all belonged to the Turkish, Tataric, Finno-Ugrian, and Laplandic subdivisions of the great Ural-Altaic stock of Asia. All these peoples, including the Scythians proper, had in common more or less marked Mongoloid features, many were nomadic or semi-nomadic, none originally being strictly agricultural, and except where they were in prolonged contact with other peoples, such as in the case of the Scythians with the Greeks, the Bolgars with the Khazars, or the Finns with the Scandinavians, their culture was of a primitive order.

The term "Scythians" deserves a few comments. Owing to their warlike qualities and the direct intercourse with them by the earlier Greeks, few "barbaric" nations of the pre-Christian era have been more discussed and few peoples since have given rise to more speculation as to their ethnic identity. On the basis of present historical and archeological knowledge it may safely be said that the early Greeks applied the term "Scythians" not to a race, but to a mass or conglomerate of peoples, partly nomadic and partly agricultural, who occupied the southern part of Russia when the Greeks began to explore and colonize the coasts of the Black Sea. The main strains of the more eastern nomadic Scythians were undoubtedly Tatar and Turkic. To the west of the Borythenes (Dneiper), however, and particularly in present Volhynia, Bukovina, and Galicia, the principal and possibly exclusive element of the population from the earliest times was of European extraction, and this stock it seems could in the main have been no other than Slav. To it belonged tribes such as the "Neuri" (Nestor, the earliest Russian historian, mentions "Norici, who are the same with the Slavs"), the Alazones or Halizones (which in Russian would be Galitshani, from which Galicia received its name), and probably the Borysthenitae husbandmen.

The Scythians claimed to have roamed over or occupied for many centuries the country in which they were found by the Greeks. As shown by their customs described by the Greeks, and by the remains of their culture uncovered by archeological exploration, they were not wholly barbaric people; and contrary to what may be observed regarding later Tatar tribes, their warlike activities were directed mainly toward Persia and Asia Minor rather than toward Europe. It was to avenge their invasion of Medea and Persia that Darius undertook his memorable incursion into their country. Crossing the Hellespont into Thrace and proceeding then northward to and across the Danube, he reached as far as the "Oarus" River (supposed to have been the Volga, but more probably the Dnieper), only to find his great effort against the nomads quite futile. He finally barely escaped with the famished remnants of his army back across the Danube.

THE GOTHS. The first of the historic invasions into Scythia is that of the Goths, . . .

The Goth sovereignty in southwestern Russia was not an occupancy of a waste region by a new race. The territories in question were peopled, even though not densely, and remained so after the Goth domination; and their sedentary population was not Goth but in all probability Vendic or Slav, though there are also mentioned the Callipidae (Gepidae), the Alans, and Heruli, may have been some of Alpine and some of Nordic extraction.

The Goths were warlike northerners, who invaded Scythia in some force and brought with them their families. Owing to their favorable original geographical position and their sea activities, they were more advanced in general culture and especially in military art and equipment than the inland populations, who were being only slightly affected by the rest of the world. As a consequence of all this the northmen found no great difficulty in over-running large areas occupied by the sedentary as well as the nomadic tribes, which had little political unity and no adequate powers of resistance. Some such tribes could even be employed against others, though of their own blood, and the invader finished by becoming the ruler. There are ample illustrations of similar processes elsewhere, such as many centuries later on the American continent, in Mexico and Peru. But the invaders, though they may create a state under their own banners, are seldom strong enough to give the conquered people their language, and though their name may remain, as happened later in Bulgaria and Rumania, the conquerors them-selves disappear, either by being driven out or more commonly through amalgamation with the old population. Thus the Goths who gave way before the Huns were merely the usurping and then the ruling class, through their military organization; and when this power was overcome and they were driven westward, they left little behind them that would permanently affect the type of the indigenous populations. Moreover, they doubtless carried with them, in their families, households, and the army, many elements and perhaps even whole groups of the indigenous people.

THE HUNS. The great Hun invasion which overcame and drove out the Goths and which was one of the most sustained and serious of the Asiatic incursions of all times, obliterated Scythia and disorganized the whole region of the present Ukrainia and Bessarabia. The nomadic Scythians apparently receded to Asia; at all events they vanished completely as a power and entity. They left thousands of kourgans or burial mounds over southern Russia, though some such mounds may have been made also by other people.

The Hun swarm came from beyond the lower Don and Volga. In blood they were of Tatar or "Ugrian" derivation. Their language, like that of all the native population east of the Slav Russia, belonged to the Ural-Altaic. Contemporary accounts show them to have been typical Mongoloid nomads. From southern Russia they extended their incursions over most of western Europe. Soon after their defeat in France their dread chief Attila died, the power which they had established in Pannonia and central Europe rapidly crumbled, their confederates, among whom were some of the Germans and even Ostrogoths, broke away, and what remained of the horde, no longer able to hold its ground, retraced its steps eastward and was lost to sight. Exactly what effect this Hun invasion and occupation had on the population of southern Russia and central Europe is difficult to gauge, but it was probably mainly that of destruction or dispersion.

THE KHAZARS. What remained of the population in southern Russia-to-be after the Hun invasion now became gradually infiltrated with a new ethnic unit, the Khazars. The Khazars, according to many indications, were of Caucasian or anterior Asian extraction, and were related to the Georgians and Armenians. There were with them, however, also the so-called "black Khazars," who have not yet been identified. Their history in southeastern Russia extends over a considerable period of time — to the eleventh century. Between 600 and 950 the territory they controlled is said to have spread from the Caspian Sea to the Don and later even into the Crimea. They were relatively civilized people, who built small towns and engaged extensively in sea trade, which earned them the name of the "Phoenicians" of the Caspian and Black Seas. In the earlier part of the seventh century their power was such that they compelled the agricultural Slavs of the Dnieper and even those of the more northern regions to pay tribute. About 740 they accepted Judaism. But during the ninth and tenth centuries they were slowly outnumbered by the Russians, and in the eleventh century they practically disappear from the stage. Remnants of them probably still exist under different name or names in the Caucasus.

TURKISH AND TATAR TRIBES. The Khazar occupation of the regions which now form southeastern Russia was, however, far from uniform, dense, or continuously peaceful. The waves of incursion of the Turkish and the Tatar tribes from farther east followed at greater or shorter intervals, and over approximately the same roads — the broad open steppes traversed before by the Huns. Some of these invasions it is not necessary to enumerate in detail. The more important ones were those of the Bolgars in 482, of the Avars in 557, and those of the Polovtsi (Kumans), Ugri (Magyars), Pechenegs, and related tribes, in the ninth and tenth centuries. Whatever the name under which they came, they were all of the Tatar or of Turkish extraction, with some admixtures. All were more or less nomadic and destructive, bent mostly on spoliation, but in the case of the major movements also on penetration toward the richer more central and southern parts of Europe, rather than on the conquest of Russia and the establishment there of a permanent new home; though some, such as the Polovtsi, Pechenegs, and others, became for a longer or shorter period settled in the territory. Taken collectively, these invasions resulted in a great retardation of the settlement of the southern parts of Russia. The hordes did not colonize or mix readily except through captives, and although remnants of them and mixtures were left, they made no very great impression on the sedentary population of the region.

THE SLAVS Meanwhile, from as early as the time of Herodotus, the Greeks began to hear of tribes such as the Budini, which reached far eastward in the future Russia, and may have been Slav, for the root of the term is evidently Slavonic. Later on, in the fourth century, according to Jordanes, the historian of the Goths, Hermanric conquered the Veneti, or Vends, which was the earlier generic name for the Slavs, the term "Slav" not appearing until after the close of the fifth century. In Jordanes' time, or about the middle of the sixth century A. D., the "populous race of the Veneti dwell near the left ridge of the Alps [Carpathians] which inclines toward the north, and, beginning at the source of the Vistula, occupy a great expanse of land. Though their names are now dispersed amid various clans and places, yet they are chiefly called Sclaveni and Anti. The abode of the Sclaveni extends from the city of Noviodunum and the lake called Mursianus to the Danaster, and northward along the Vistula. The Anti, who are the bravest of these peoples dwelling in the curve of the sea of Pontus, spread from the Danaster [Dniester] to the Danaper [Dnieper] rivers that are many days' journey apart." In another section of the work of the same author we read that these people "though off-shoots from one stock, have now three names, that is, Veneti, Anti, Sclaveni." And "they now rage in war far and wide, in punishment for our [i.e. Goth] sins," though once "all were obedient to Hermanric's commands."

During the ninth and tenth centuries many Slav settlements or outposts are mentioned in Russia, by Arab traders mainly, as far north as the "Tchoud" country (Estonia), and as far west as the region between the Don and the Volga. Since the sixth and seventh centuries also there are historical data indicating extensive and in a large measure uninterrupted Slav population reaching from the Balkans to Pomerania, and from Bohemia and the Elbe over Poland, Galicia, and what is now eastern Germany, and western Russia. This population is subdivided into numerous "families," tribes, or nations, which form as yet no great units. The term "Slavs" (from sláva, glory; slavit, to glorify), applied to these people, originated probably from their frequent usage in personal names of the terminal "slav," as in Jaroslav, glorifying the spring, Mstislav, extolling revenge, Boguslav, praising God, etc., which at that time was common to the whole people. Their earlier history and origin are lost in the mists of uncertainty, and their western contingents, except in language, were not clearly differentiated from the Germanic tribes. Tacitus evidently comprised all of them in his "Germania." They bore as yet none of the names by which they later became distinguished.

The Early Slavs: Soviet Reports

Soviet archeologists have been extremely diligent in their investigations of the pre-historic remains of their Slavic and other ancestors. The results of their studies have not been generally available to the West because few of their reports have been translated into English. The following selection is adapted from a synthesis of the more recent findings of Soviet archeologists. The source is: P. Tretyakov, "Archeological Studies on the Origin of the Eastern Slavs." VOKS Bulletin, # 6. Moscow, 1945. Pp. 21-28, passim.

The problem of the ethnogeny of the Slavs takes us, first and foremost, to the Ukraine, to the area of the Middle Dnieper, where Soviet archaeologists have made many very important discoveries.

Studies of Tripolye and the Bronze Age carried out on the territory of the Ukrainian S. S. R., have confirmed the statement that the territory along the middle course of the Dnieper and the vast spaces between the Dnieper and the Danube were regions of ancient East European agriculture. Unless this is taken into account, there can be no understanding of the numerous phenomena in the subsequent historical life of Eastern Europe, and, in particular, the origin of the Slavs. It is quite obvious that the ancient agricultural tribes of Eastern Europe were one of the sources from which the Slavs stemmed.

At the beginning of our era the so-called culture of "burial fields" was widespread in the area of the middle Dnieper and the Northern Carpathians. These were for a long time considered to be of Slavic origin, and research work carried on by Soviet and foreign archaeologists during the last few years has confirmed the correctness of this viewpoint. Evidently, at the threshold of our era, and as a result of both internal social-economic processes and the shifting of different tribes in the Black Sea Area and Central Europe which had begun at that time, an active cultural and ethnic consolidation had further proceeded among the different tribes in the vast area from the Dnieper to the upper reaches of the Danube, a consolidation which embraced the descendants of Scythian agricultural tribes, the tribes of the Vistula basin, and probably some of the Dacian tribes from the Carpathians. This body of ancient Slavic tribes had been in existence for several centuries and is genetically linked with the Slavic tribes of the end of the first and the beginning of the second millennium of our era.

There is now no longer any doubt about the ties that existed between the tribes of the "burial fields" in the middle Dnieper and the Scythian agricultural tribes. The earliest "fields" discovered by Soviet archaeologists show that the people to whom they belonged continued to have an almost completely Scythian culture. Particularly striking in this connection is the material provided by the "field" which was recently discovered at Korchevaty, near Kiev. Here, alongside of vessels characteristic of the early "burial fields," real Scythian ceramics have been found. Only in the beginning of our era, under the influence of the provincial-Roman culture, the tribes of the "fields" changed considerably, and continued to exist in their new form up to the fifth-sixth centuries and, in some western regions, even longer. "Fields" of the Roman era have been discovered and explored during the last twenty years in several places of the Ukraine.

All this archaeological material provides serious grounds for regarding the agricultural tribes of Scythian times as the most important unit from which stemmed the Dnieper Slavs. This is confirmed by various other factual data.

Ancestors of the Eastern Slavs were found not only in the area of the middle Dnieper, but to the north as well. Byelorussian archaeologists have for a number of years been engaged in a study of previously almost unknown ancient settlements of the upper Dnieper. Similar settlements have been explored in the basin of the River Desna. These likewise give an extremely convincing picture of the uninterrupted development of local culture. It has also been found that even among the early settlements it is possible to distinguish an extensive group bearing traces of ties with the Scythian Dnieper settlements, and in later time close ties and common features with the tribes of the "burial fields."

At the same time, considerable differences have been observed between the cultures of the upper Dnieper tribes and those of the Southeastern Baltic and the Volga area. Thus, Soviet archaeology has put forward and is proving the thesis that the basic territory of Slavic ethnogeny in Eastern Europe probably includes in its bounds not only the middle but also the upper Dnieper area.

The problem of identifying Anti antiquities is extremely difficult indeed. The middle of the first millennium of our era was marked by the settlement of large masses of barbarians in areas around the Black Sea and the Carpathians. Goths, Huns, Avars, and Bulgarian tribes—all of them left traces of their sojourn in the area round the Black Sea. Archaeology, however, in adopting new methods of research, is gradually clearing up this complex picture and is already on the way to solving the problem. The culture of the Anti is no longer a riddle.

In the first place, new excavations and the study of the materials previously obtained have proved that the people who inhabited the area on the right bank of the Dnieper during the period of the Anti, were the same as those who inhabited this area previously, during the era of the "burial fields." Their culture, however, had lost the provincial-Roman traits peculiar to the tribes of the "burial fields," and had acquired a more original character. The reason for this will become clear if we recall the invasion of the Black Sea area by the Hunnish tribes, which had for long isolated the Dnieper

Slavs from the Black Sea and at the same time assisted in the establishment of closer ties between tribes of the middle Dnieper and inhabitants of the northern belt. The migration of the nomads had also resulted in a considerable shifting to the west and north of the ancient Slav population from the woodlands and steppelands on the left bank of the Dnieper.

Secondly, it has become quite clear that the Anti tribes were bearers of a comparatively well developed culture, which had imbibed the century-old heritage of the ancient Black Sea and Dnieper areas. There is no doubt that the Anti practised field agriculture and stock breeding, were skilled in metal working, while their jewelry is amazing for its highly developed craftsmanship. Unfortunately, there is not a single settlement of the Anti era which has yet been studied by means of archaeological excavations.

There is reason to believe that besides the numerous small settlements scattered along the rivers of the right bank of the Dnieper, the Anti also had large settlements which were prototypes of the future towns of Kiev Russ.

Further, in spite of the fact that Anti antiquities on the Southern Bug and the Dniester have not been studied at all, all material available enables us to assert that the historical and cultural life of the Anti tribes had its centre not in the West, but in the East, along the Dnieper, — the most important artery of the economic, cultural, and, probably, political life of the Anti. Moreover, the Dnieper territory around Kiev and especially to the south of it was of particular importance in the Anti period. It is here that most objects dating back to the Anti period have been discovered.

And, finally, the study of the traces of Anti culture and in the culture of Kiev Russ enables us to speak of the existence of strong genetic ties between them. Thus it becomes clear that Kiev Russ was not so much the beginning of the full-blooded political life of the Eastern Slavs as the result of the long road which they had already traversed.

Kiev Russ, however, was not merely a continuation of the Anti period. Russ of the ninth-tenth centuries represented a phenomenon considerably more complex, in whose formation other groups of Eastern Slavs besides the Anti, took an active part.

It would be absolutely wrong to follow the old tradition and place a sign of equality between the Anti and the Eastern Slavs as a whole. At present, when it is being ascertained that the sphere of Slavonic ethnogeny in Eastern Europe had not been limited to the Scythian Dnieper and that other tribes besides those of the "burial fields," formed part of the ancient East Slavonic tribes, it is possible to form a clear picture not only of the Anti group, but also of the other groups of Eastern Slavs. Moreover, it appears that tribal formations among Eastern Slavs had been known even in the Anti period. These were subsequently mentioned in the chronicles of the eleventh-twelfth centuries.

The Anti tribes themselves were not a completely homogeneous ethnic group. As a result of archaeological excavations carried out during the past few years, a special group has begun to be defined in the region of Kiev Polesie, which differed somewhat from the tribes residing farther south, along the Dnieper and in the basin of the Rossi. Doubtless, the tribes residing to the west also had their peculiar features, but the abundance of blank spaces on the archaeological map of Slavonic history in the Ukrainian S. S. R. hinders us from differentiating the Anti group. We can, however, speak with absolute certainty of the differences between the Anti group and the Slavs mentioned in the Northern Chronicles.

Pre-revolutionary archaeology had at its disposal only a few memorials relating to the Slavs who had populated the left bank of the Dnieper. These were settlements along the upper course of the river Sula, near the town of Romny, which had been studied by N. E. Makarenko. At present we possess archaeological data from the Desna and the Sejm. In the course of the past few years, research work has been carried on in settlements located along the upper and middle courses of the Vorskla. It has been found that in all this vast territory traces exist of a homogeneous Slavonic culture of the second half of the first millennium of our era, a very typical culture, which had taken shape outside the periphery of the Black Sea area, outside the routes of the "great migration of peoples." The economic and social life of the "Romny" tribes was much more primitive than those of the Anti. But, beginning with the seventh-eighth centuries, these tribes began to appear on the historical arena as an active political force. Archaeological researches have shown that precisely during these centuries there began the migration of Slavonic tribes from the basin of the Desna and the Sejm, south and southeast, to the basin of the Donets and the Don; this migration terminated in the settlement of the Slavs in the Lower Don and the Taman, and was marked in Byzantium by the appearance of the Black Sea of the Ross-Russ. No doubt exists as to the tremendous role played by the southwestern tribes in the formation of the ancient Russian State. The ancient necropolises of Kiev and Chernigov bear witness to the fact that both the descendants of the Anti and the emigrants from the left bank of the Dnieper had populated these cities. At the same time these two ethnic elements have been found both in ordinary and in rich burial places.

In the middle of the first millennium of our era, another group of Eastern Slavs appeared along the upper course of the Oka — the Vyatichi. Their habitations are marked both by peculiar settlements and burial mounds with special structures for burning corpses. Archaeological field excavations carried on after the revolution along the Oka, in the area around Kaluga, as well as in the Tula and the Orel Regions, greatly assisted in the study of this group.

Almost completely unexplored as yet are the ancient Slavonic memorials in the basin of the River Sozh. But there is every reason to believe that here too, in the land of the Radimichi, a peculiar Slavonic culture is to be found beginning with the second half of the first millennium of our era.

These three groups: the Severiane, the Vyatichi and the Radimichi, as has been proved by archaeological data, had common traits which distinguished them not only from the Anti tribes, but from the Slavonic tribes which inhabited the upper parts of the Dnieper, the Dvina and the Volga, as well as the Valdai Plateau. . . .

Various archaeological data also provide information concerning the migration of the Slavs northward — to the Volkhov and the Luga, as well as eastward, to the lands of the Volga Meri. New archaeological researches outline the routes of this colonization which began in the seventh-eighth centuries in the north, and somewhat later on the Volga — in the eighth-ninth century. A clear picture has also been provided of the significance of the Volga trade route to the east, a more ancient route than the Baltic-Dnieper route.

And finally, the least known at the present time are the ancient Slavonic memorials of the lands inhabited by the Dregovichi. However, the study of the settlements located in the southern districts of Byelorussia have resulted in the discovery of certain traits peculiar to the local Slavonic culture.

In their attempt to penetrate to the depths of the East Slavonic past, former historians always proceeded from the theory of a single Slavonic culture, regarding the East Slavonic tribes as a homogeneous body in regard to the social order, culture and economy. Contemporary archaeology, which now actually deals with traces of the real Slavonic past, holds different views. While Slavs of the second half of the first millennium of our era possessed characteristic traits which on the whole distinguished them sharply from Leto-Lithuanian, North Chud, the Volga tribes and the nomads of the steppes, within the East Slavonic tribes themselves numerous local differences existed both of a cultural-ethnic character and with regard to different rates of historical development, primarily in the north and south. This makes comprehensible to archaeologists the apparent contradictions in the descriptions of Eastern Slavs, given by Arabian and other ancient authors who had dealings with Slavs from the most varied regions.

On the middle Dnieper and the regions on the right bank of the Dnieper, Slavonic tribes had evidently done away with the clan order as far back as the first centuries of our era. The territorial commune (verv) was their prevailing form of social relations. Its economic basis consisted of field agriculture, comparatively developed crafts, and barter. The Roman coin represented a very important element in the economic life of the forefathers of the Anti tribes, who had undoubtedly conducted extensive trade with peoples from the Black Sea area. Information gleaned from Byzantine authors with regard to the economic and social life of the Anti supports this.

Things had been quite different in the north. While in the Black Sea area, during the first centuries before and after our era historical development had been rapid, in the north, life continued to preserve its ancient rhythm. In the middle of the first millennium of our era a patriarchal clan order held sway along the tributaries of the Dnieper and the upper Oka. Small fortified settlements, patriarchal nests similar to the upper Volga settlements, on the River Sonokha, were the basic form of settlements. They practised the most primitive forms of agriculture (by clearing plots in the forests); an important place in their economy, beside agriculture and stock raising, was fishing and hunting.

Gradually they took up metal working. Their trade with remote countries was very inconsiderable and had hardly any effect on the social and economic life of the northern tribes.

After the sixth century of our era, the picture began to change considerably. The tribes of the right bank of the Dnieper, having reached the highest stages of the primitive communal order under complicated and difficult conditions imposed by the invasion of the Huns, the Balkan Wars, their struggle against the Avars and the Bulgarian tribes, had, as it were, slackened their development, accumulating strength for the future. As a result of the Balkan events of the fifth-seventh centuries, the centre of political life had evidently shifted to the west of the Dnieper, where a tribal union of the Dulebs arose which is presumed to have had the form of a primitive state. Unfortunately, archaeological science is as yet unable to say anything about the Dulebs, or about their archaic state, for archaeological remains along the Western Bug are still waiting to be explored.

During the same period, other East Slavonic tribes had been experiencing a period of rapid economic and social development as though in pursuit of their southern brothers. On the basis of archaeological material, it is possible to state that in the territory of the upper Dnieper, in the basin of the Desna and the upper Volga, Slavonic tribes had in the course of the sixth-eighth centuries been gradually abandoning the clan order; the territorial commune was becoming the prevailing form of social order. So far the paths of this process are far from clear, but one thing is certain — that a tremendous role was played by the transfer from ancient primitive agriculture to field agriculture, and by the development of crafts and barter. Archaeologists are well aware of the fact that precisely during these centuries the ancient forms of fortified settlements began to disappear and were replaced by huge new settlements. An example of these can be seen in the remarkably preserved material of the Voronezh settlement of the eighth-tenth century, studied by P. P. Efimenko. During this period, too, the first iron ploughshares and other implements of field agriculture put in their appearance; from being a meat-providing beast, the horse became a draught animal and little by little the use of horse meat was discontinued.

It was in a situation such as this that there began the above-mentioned migration of the northern Slavonic tribes to the Volkhov and the Volga, to the lands of the ancient Meri, and, what was particularly important, to the south and the southeast; to the Don, the Donets and the Taman. This was due to the fact that at this particular time the northern Slavs had reached the same order of life as that which two centuries earlier had forced the Anti to migrate southward. They had now become interested in fertile lands.

In this way, by the eleventh-twelfth centuries, different groups of Eastern Slavs had to a considerable degree reached the same stage of development with regard to their social, economic and cultural life, and had become still more consolidated ethnically. Thus, in the course of centuries, the ground had been prepared among Eastern Slavs for the appearance of the Kiev State.

The Novgorod Chronicle: Selected Annals

The most important, as well as the best known, of the basic written sources of early Russian history is The Chronicle of Novgorod. *The following selection consists of samples taken from the Chronicle, exemplifying the various types of entries from the 11th through the 15th centuries. The translation was made by Robert Michell and Nevill Forbes. The source is: Robert Michell and Nevill Forbes, (Translators)* The Chronicle of Novgorod, 1016- 1471. *Camden Third Series. Vol. 25. London: The Camden Society, 1914. Passim et seriatim. Whenever possible English terms have been substituted for the Russian words which were retained in the Michell and Forbes translation. These substitutions are indicated by brackets.*

A.D. 1016. A.M. 6524. [There was] a fight at Lyubets, and [the sons of Vladimir] won; and Svyatopolk fled to Poland. And at that time Yaroslav was keeping many Varangians in Novgorod, fearing war; and the Varangians began to commit violence against the wives of the townsmen. The men of Novgorod said: 'We cannot look upon this violence,' and they gathered by night and fell upon and killed the Varangians in Poromon's Court; and that night [Prince] Yaroslav was at Rakomo. And having heard this, [Prince] Yaroslav was wroth with the townsfolk, and gathered a thousand soldiers in Slavno, and by craft falling on those who had killed the Varangians, he killed them; and others fled out of the town. And the same night Yaroslav's sister, Peredslava, sent word to him from Kiev, saying: 'Thy father is dead, and thy brethren slain.' And having heard this, Yaroslav the next day gathered a number of the men of Novgorod, and held an [assembly] in the open air, and said to them: 'My beloved and honourable [bodyguard], whom yesterday in my madness I slew, I cannot now buy back even with gold.' And thus he said to them: 'Brethren! my father Volodimir is dead, and Svyatopolk is [Prince] in Kiev; I want to go against him; come with me and help me.' And the men of Novgorod said to him: 'Yes, [Prince], we will folllow thee.' And he gathered 4,000 soldiers: there were a thousand Varangians, and 3,000 of the men of Novgorod; and he went against him.

And Svyatopolk having heard this, gathered a countless number of soldiers, and went out against him to Lyubets and encamped there in the open country with a number of soldiers. And Yaroslav having come, halted on the bank of the Dnieper; and they stood there three months, not daring to come together (i.e. in conflict). Svyatopolk's [General] by name of Wolf's Tail, riding along the river-bank, began to reproach the men of Novgorod: 'Wherefore have you come with that builder of wooden [houses]?

'You are carpenters, and we shall make you build houses for us.' And the Dnieper began to freeze. And one of Yaroslav's men was on friendly terms with Svyatopolk. And Yaroslav sent one of his attendants to him by night, and he spoke to him. And this is what he said to him: 'What dost thou advise to be done now? There is but little mead brewed, and the [bodyguard] is large.' And that man said to him: 'Say thus to Yaroslav, if there is little mead, but a large [bodyguard], then give it in the evening.' And Yaroslav understood that he was advising him to fight at night; and that evening Yaroslav with his troops crossed the other bank of the Dnieper, and they pushed the boats away from the bank, and prepared to make battle that night. And Yaroslav said to his [bodyguard]: 'Put a mark on you, wind your heads in kerchiefs.' And there was a terrible fight, and before dawn they conquered Svyatopolk, and Svyatopolk fled to the Pecheneg people.

And Yaroslav went to Kiev, and took his seat on the throne of his father Volodimir. And he began to distribute pay to his troops: to the [elders] ten [half pounds of silver each], to the [foot soldiers] one [half pound of silver] each, and to all the men of Novgorod ten each, and let them all go to their homes.

A.D. 1066. A.M. 6574. Vseslav came and took Novgorod, with the women and children; and he took down the bells from St. Sophia—Oh great was the distress at that time!—and he took down the church lustres.

A.D. 1067. A.M. 6575. They defeated Vseslav at Nemiza. The same year they captured him in *Russia*.

A.D. 1068. A.M. 6576. The wrath of God came on us; the Polovets people came and conquered the Russian Land. The same year the men of Kiev rescued Vseslav from prison. The same year Svyatoslav defeated the Polovets people near Snovsk, and Izyaslav fled to Poland.

A.D. 1093. A.M. 6601. Vsevolod died; and Svyatopolk took his seat in Kiev. The same summer the Polovets people defeated Svyatopolk and Mstislav at Trepol.

A.D. 1107. A.M. 6615. The earth trembled on February 5.

A.D. 1109. A.M. 6617. The water was high in the Dnieper, the Desna and the Pripet. And they finished the refectory in the Pechersk monastery. The same year a church was founded at Kiev by Prince Svyatopolk.

A.D. 1111. A.M. 6619. Svyatopolk, Volodimir and David and the whole Russian Land to a man went against the Polovets people and defeated them and took their children, and rebuilt the fortified towns of Surtev and Sharukan.

At the same time the Lower town at Kiev was burnt, as well as Cherigov, Smolensk and Novgorod. The same year Ioan, Bishop of Chernigov, died. The same year Mstislav went against Ochela.

A.D. 1124. A.M. 6632. On the 11th day of August before evening service; the sun began to decrease and it totally perished; oh, there was great terror and darkness! There were stars and the moon; then it began to re-appear and came out quickly in full; then all the city rejoiced.

A.D. 1135. A.M. 6643. [Mayor] Miroslav went from Novgorod to make peace between the people of Kiev and those of Chernigov, and he came back without having achieved anything; for the whole Russian Land was in great disorder; Yaropolk called the men of Novgorod to his side; and the [Prince] of Chernigov to his; and they fought, and God helped the son of Oleg with the men of Chernigov and he cut up many of the men of Kiev and others they captured in the month of August. And this was not the whole of the evil; the Polovets people and everyone began to muster fighting men.

The same year, Vsevolod with [Arch-Bishop] Nifont founded a stone church of the Holy Mother of God in the Market Place.

The same year, Irozhnet founded a church to St. Nicholas in Yakov Street. The same year in the winter, [Arch-Bishop] Nifont with the best men went into Russia, and found the men of Kiev and the men of Chernigov ranged against each other, and a quantity of troops; and by the will of God they were reconciled. And Miroslav died before the return of the [Arch-Bishop] in January 28; the Bishop came on February 4. And they gave the [Mayor]-ship in Novgorod to Kostyantin Mikultsits.

A.D. 1141. A.M. 6649. On April 1 there was a very marvellous sign in the sky; six circles, three close about the sun, and three other large ones outside the sun, and stood nearly all day.

The same year they came from Vsevolod from Kiev for his brother Svyatoslav to take him to Kiev; 'and receive my son as your [Prince],' he said. And when they sent the Bishop and many best men for his son, they said to

Svyatoslav: 'Thou wait for thy brother, then thou shalt go:' but he, fearing the men of Novgorod, 'whether they are going to deceive me,' fled secretly in the night; Yakun fled with him. And they took Yakun on the [river] Plisa, and having brought him hither with his brother Procupi, they nearly did him to death, having stripped him naked, as his mother bore him, and they threw him down from the bridge; but God saved him, he waded to the bank, and they beat him no more, but took from him 1,000 [half pounds of silver] and from his brother 100 [half pounds of silver], likewise they took from others; and they exiled Yakun with his brother to the Chud people, having chained their hands to their wives from Novgorod, and kept them by him in favour. And Vsevolod was wroth, and he detained all the emissaries and the Bishop and the Merchants.

And the people of Novgorod went without a [Prince] nine months; and they summoned Sudila, Nezhata and Strashko from Suzhdal, who had fled from Novgorod on account of Svyatoslav and Yakun; and they gave the [Mayor]-ship in Novgorod to Sudila; and they sent to Suzhdal for. Gyurgi to be [Prince] and he did not go, but sent his son, Rostislav, who had been before.

The same year Rostislav went on the throne at Novgorod, on November 26.

A.D. 1177. A.M. 6685. Gleb, [Prince] of Ryazan, died in captivity in Volodi-mir. At the same time [Prince] Mstislav was blinded, with his brother Yaropolk, by their Uncle Vsevolod, and he let them go into Russia. And the two blind [men,] being led with rotting eyes, when they reached Smolensk they came to Smyadino into the Church of the Holy Martyrs Boris and Gleb; and there forthwith the Grace of God and of our Holy Sovereign Lady the Mother of God and of the newly manifested holy Martyrs Boris and Gleb descended on them and there they saw clearly. The same year in the autumn the Nerev end from Ivankova took fire and five churches were burnt down. And in the winter [Prince] Mstislav with his brother Yaropolk came to Novgorod, and the men of Novgorod set Mstislav on the throne, and Yaropolk in Novitorg, and Yaroslav in Volok-Lamsk, and thus they arranged [things] according to their will.

A.D. 1203. A.M. 6711. Rurik with the sons of Oleg and the heathen Polovets people, with Kontsyak and Danila Byakovits captured Kiev, on January 1, St. Vasili's Day; and whomever their hands reached, whether monk or nun, priest or priest's wife, these they led off to the heathen; and all foreign merchants and foreigners of every country shut themselves up in the churches, and they granted them their lives; but their merchandise they divided with them by halves; but everything in the monasteries and in all the churches, all valuables and ornaments and ikons the pagans tore off and carried away into their own land; and they set fire to the town. Then, too, the Russian [Princes] Rurik, Roman, Mstislav and many others [Princes] went against the Polovets people. And then the winter was very cruel; and they took much plunder and drove away their herds. The same year Roman sent Vyacheslav ordering him to have Rurik shorn [a monk]. The same year the sons of Oleg defeated the Lithuanians, and did to death seven hundred and a thousand of them. The same year Miroshka; [Mayor] of Novgorod died, he was shorn in St. Georgi's, and then they gave the [Mayor]-ship to Mikhalko Stepanits. The same year for our sins all the horses died in Novgorod and in the villages so that it was not possible to go anywhere for the stench.

A.D. 1210. A.M. 6718. The men of Novgorod with [Prince] Volodimir and [Mayor] Tverdislav, having pursued and found the Lithuanians in Khodynitsy, killed them.

The same year Vsevolod went against Ryazan and said to them: 'Come to me and my son Yaroslav over the Oka to deliberate.' And they went over to him and there he seized them all; and sent troops; and took all their wives and children, and set fire to their town; and thus he distributed them about the towns. The same winter [Prince] Mstislav Mstislavits came against Torshok, and seized Svyatoslav's courtiers and put the [Mayor] in chains and whoever could lay hands on their goods [took them;] and he sent to Novgorod: 'I bow down to St. Sophia and to the tomb of my father and to all the men of Novgorod; I have come to you having heard of the violence [done you] by the [Prince;] and I am sorry for my patrimony.' Having heard this the men of Novgorod sent for him with great honour: 'Come, [Prince] to the throne.' And they sent Svyatoslav with his men in the Arch-Bishop's court until the settlement with his father. Mstislav came to Novgorod and they set him on his father's throne, and the men of Novgorod were glad; and Mstislav went with the whole army against Vsevolod, and they were at Ploskeya and Vsevolod sent to him: 'Thou art son to me and I father to thee; let go Svyatoslav with his men; and all that thou hast confiscated, make good, and I will let go the merchants and merchandise.' And Mstislav released Svyatoslav and his men and Vsevolod released the merchants and their merchandise; they both of them kissed the Cross and took peace, and Mstislav came to Novgorod.

A.D. 1238. A.M. 6746. The wife of Semen Borisovich made a monastery at the Church of St. Paul. That same year foreigners called Tartars came in countless numbers, like locusts, into the land of Ryazan, and on first coming they halted at the river Nukhla, and took it, and halted in camp there. And thence they sent their emissaries to the [Princes] of Ryazan, a sorceress and two men with her, demanding from them one-tenth of everything; of men and [Princes] and horses—of everything one-tenth. And the [Princes] of Ryazan, George Ingvor's brother, Oleg, Roman Ingvorevich, and those of Murom and Pronsk, without letting them into their towns, went out to meet them to Voronazh. And the [Princes] said to them: 'Only when none of us remain then all will be yours.' And thence they let them go to Yuri in Volodimir, and thence they let the Tartars at Voronazh go back to the Nukhla. And the [Princes] of Ryazan sent to Yuri of Volodimir asking for help, or himself to come. But Yuri neither went himself nor listened to the request of the [Princes] of Ryazan, but he himself wished to make war separately. But it was too late to oppose the wrath of God, as was said of old by God, to Joshua the son of Nun, when leading them to the promised land, then he said: 'I shall before you send upon them perplexity, and thunder, and fear, and trembling.' Thus also did God before these men take from us our strength and put into us perplexity and thunder and dread and trembling for our sins. And then the pagan foreigners surrounded Ryazan and fenced it in with a stockade. And [Prince] Yuri of Ryazan, shut himself in the town with his people, but [Prince] Roman Ingorovich began to fight against them with his own men. Then [Prince] Yuri of Volodimir sent Yeremei as *Voyevoda* with a patrol and joined Roman; and the Tartars surrounded them at Kolomno, and they fought hard and drove them to the ramparts. And there they killed Roman and Yeremei and many fell here with the [Prince] and with Yeremei. And the men of Moscow ran away having seen nothing. And the Tartars took the town on December 21, and they had advanced against it on the 16th of the same month. They likewise killed the [Prince] and *Knyaginya,* and men, women and children, monks, nuns and priests, some by fire, some by the sword, and violated nuns, priests' wives, good women and girls in the presence of their mothers and sisters. But God saved the Bishop, for he had departed the same moment when the troops invested the town. And who, brethren, would not lament over this, among those of us left alive when they suffered this bitter and violent death? And we, indeed, having seen it, were terrified and wept with sighing day and night over our sins, while we sigh every day and night, taking thought for our possessions and for the hatred of brothers.

But let us return to what lied before us. The pagan and godless Tartars, then, having taken Ryazan, went to Volodimir, a host of shedders of Christian blood. And [Prince] Yuri went out from Volodimir and fled to Yaroslavl, while his son Vsevolod with his mother and the [Arch-bishop] and the whole of the province shut themselves in Volodimir. And the lawless Ismaelites approached the town and surrounded the town in force, and fenced it all round with a fence. And it was in the morning [Prince] Vsevolod and [Arch-bishop] Mitrofan saw that the town must be taken, and entered the Church of the Holy Mother of God and were all shorn into the monastic order and into the strictest monastic order, the Prince and the *Knyaginya,* their daughter and daughter-in-law, and good men and women, by [Arch-bishop] Mitrofan. And when the lawless ones had already come near and set up battering rams, and took the town and fired it on Friday before Sexagesima Sunday, the [Prince] and *Knyaginya* and [Arch-bishop], seeing that the town was on fire and that the people were already perishing, some by fire and others by the sword, took refuge in the Church of the Holy Mother of God and shut themselves in the Sacristy. The pagans breaking down the doors, piled up wood and set fire to the sacred church; and slew all, thus they perished, giving up their souls to God. Others went in pursuit of [Prince] Yuri to Yaroslavl. And [Prince] Yuri sent out Dorozh to scout with 3,000 men; and Dorozh came running, and said: 'They have already surrounded us, [Prince].' And the [Prince] began to muster his forces about him, and behold, the Tartars came up suddenly, and the [Prince,] without having been able to do anything, fled. And it happened when he reached the river Sit they overtook him and there he ended his life. And God knows how he died; for some say much about him. And Rostov and Suzhdal went each his own way. And the accursed ones having come thence took Moscow, Peryaslavl, Yurev, Dmitrov, *Volok*, and Tver; there also they killed the son of Yaroslav. And thence the lawless ones came and invested Torshok on the festival of the first Sunday in Lent. They fenced it all round with a fence as they had taken other towns, and here the accursed ones fought with battering rams for two weeks. And the people in the town were exhausted and from Novgorod there was no help for them; but already every man began to be in perplexity and terror. And so the pagans took the town, and slew all from the male sex even to the female, all the priests and the monks, and all stripped and reviled gave up their souls to the Lord in a bitter and a wretched death on March 5, the day of the commemoration of the holy Martyr Nikon, on Wednesday in Easter week. And there, too, were killed Ivanko the [Arch-bishop] of Novitorg, Yakim Vlunkovich, Gleb Borisovich, and Mikhailo Moisievich. And the accursed godless ones then pushed on from Torshok by the road of Seregeri right up to Ignati's cross, cutting down everybody like grass, to within 100 and [66 miles] of Novgorod. God, however, and the great and sacred apostolic cathedral of St. Sophia, and St. Kyuril, and the prayers of the holy and orthodox [Arch-bishop], of the faithful [Princes] and of the very reverend monks of the hierachical [assembly], protected Novgorod. And who, brothers, fathers, and children, seeing this, God's infliction on the whole Russian Land, does not lament? God let the pagans on us for our sins. God brings foreigners on to the land in his wrath, and thus crushed by them they will be reminded of God. And the internecine war comes from the prompting of the devil: for God does not wish evil amongst man, but good; but the devil rejoices at the wicked murder and bloodshed. And any other land which has sinned God punished with death of famine, or with infliction of pagans, or with drought, or with heavy rain, or with other punishment, to see whether we will repent and live as God bids; for He tells us by the prophet: 'Turn to me with your whole heart, with fasting and weeping.' And if we do so we shall be forgiven of all our sins. But we always turn to evil, like swine ever wallowing in the filth of sin, and thus we remain; and for this we receive every kind of punishment from God; and the invasion of armed men, too, we accept at God's command; as punishment for our sins.

A.D. 1311. A.M. 6819. The men of Novgorod went in war over sea to the country of the [Germans], against the Yem people, with Prince Dmitri Romanovich, and having crossed the sea they first occupied the Kupets river, they burned villages, and captured people and destroyed the cattle. And there Konstantin the son of Ilya Stanimirovich was killed by a column that went in pursuit. They then took the whole of the Black river, and thus following along the Black river they reached the town of Vanai and they took the town and burned it. And the [Germans] fell back into the [citadel:] for the place was very strong and firm, on a high rock, not having access from any side. And they sent with greeting, asking for peace, but the men of Novgorod did not grant peace, and they stood three days and three nights wasting the district. They burned the large villages, laid waste all the corn-fields, and did not leave a single horn of cattle; and going hence, they took the Kavgola river and the Perna river, and they came out on the sea and returned all well to Novgorod.

The same spring, on May 19, a fire broke out at night in Yanev Street, and forty less three houses were burnt and seven people. Then in the night of June 28 Glebov's house in Rozvazha Street caught fire, and the Norev quarter was burnt, on one side so far as the fosse, and on the other beyond Borkov Street; and the Church of SS. Kosma and Demyan was burnt, also that of St. Sava, and forty churches were damaged by fire and several good houses. Oh, woe, brethren, the conflagration was fierce, with wind and hurricane! And wicked and bad men having no fear of God, seeing peoples run, plundered other men's property. Then on July 16 a fire broke out at night in the Ilya Street, and here likewise was a fierce conflagration with a high wind, and crashing noise; the market place was burnt, and houses up to Rogatitsa Street, and the churches burnt were—seven wooden churches: St. Dmitri, St. Georgi, S.S. Boris and Gleb, St. Ioan Ishkov, St. Catherine, St. Prokopi, and of Christ; and six stone churches were damaged by fire, and the seventh was the Varangian Church. And accursed men likewise having no fear of God, nor remembering the judgement of God, and having no pity for their fellows, plundered other people's property. Repay them, Lord, according to their deeds!

The same year they took the [Mayor]-ship from Mikhail and gave to Semen Klimovich. The same year [Arch-bishop] David erected a stone church at the gate of the Nerev quarter, to St. Volodimir.

A.D. 1327. A.M. 6835. The same winter a very great force of Tartars came, and they took Tver and Kashin and the Novi-torg district, and to put it simply, laid waste all the Russian Land, God and St. Sophia preserved Novgorod alone, and [Prince] Olexander fled to Pleskov, and his brother Kostyantin and Vasili to Dadoga. And the Tartars sent envoys to Novgorod, and the men of Novgorod gave them 2,000 in silver, and they sent their own envoys with them, with numerous presents to the [Generals].

A.D. 1349. A.M. 6857. The King of Cracow with a large force seized the country of Volynia by deceit, and did much injury to the Christians, and he converted the sacred churches to the Latin service hated of God.

A.D. 1379. A.M. 6887. The same year the Tartars came into the Russian Land, against the [Great Prince] Dmitri. And the [Prince] went out against them, and it was on the Ovosha river, and there both forces met and God aided the Great Prince, and the Tartars turned shoulder and fled. The same year they founded two stone churches: one to the Holy Mother of God in the Mikhalitsa [Street] and the other to the Holy Frola and Lavra in Lyudogoshcha Street.

The same year the Lithuanian [Prince] Yuri Narimantovich came to Novgorod.

A.D. 1380. A.M. 688. The same year, in the month of August, news came to the [Great Prince] Dmitri and to his brother [Prince] Volodimir from the Horde that the pagan race of Ishmaelites was rising against the Christians; for there was some weak man *Tsar* among them, and [Prince] Mamai was controlling all their affairs and he was savagely enraged against the [Great Prince] and all the Russian Land.

And having heard this, that a great Tartar force was coming against him, the [Great Prince] Dmitri Ivanovich gathered many soldiers and went against the godless Tartars, trusting in the mercy of God and in His Immaculate Mother, the Mother of God, the eternal Virgin Mary, calling to his aid the honourable Cross. For he entered their country beyond the Don, and there was there a clean field at the mouth of the river Nepryadva, and there the pagan Ishmaelites had ranged themselves against the Christians. And the Moscovites, of whom many were inexperienced, were frightened and in despair for their lives at sight of the great numbers of Tartars, others turned to flight, forgetful of the Prophet's saying that one shall reap one thousand, and two shall move ten thousand, if God does not abandon them.

And the [Great Prince] Dmitri with his brother Volodimir ranged their troops against the pagan Polovets people, and raising their eyes humbly to heaven, and sighing from the depth of their hearts, said, in the words of the psalm: 'Brothers, God is our refuge and our strength.' And both forces immediately met, and there was a fierce battle for a long time, and God terrified the sons of Hagar with an invisible might, and they turned their shoulders to wounds, and they were routed by the Christians, and some were struck down with weapons, and others drowned in the river, a countless number of them.

And in the encounter [Prince] Fedor Belozerski was killed, also his son [Prince] Ivan; and other [Princes] and captains went in pursuit of the aliens.

The godless Tartars fell from dread of God and by the arms of the Christians; and God raised the right hand of the [Great Prince] Dmitri Ivanovich and of his brother [Prince] Volodimir Andreyevich for the defeat of the aliens.

And this was because of our sins: the aliens take up arms against us, that we might renounce our wrong-doings and hatred of our brethren, from our love of silver, and from wrong judging and violence; but God is merciful and man-loving; He is not angry with us utterly, and is not at enmity for ever.

A.D. 1420. A.M. 6928. The men of Novgorod began to trade with silver coins, and sold the [Swedish copper coins] to the Germans, having traded with them nine years.

A.D. 1432. A.M. 6940. The Russian [Princes] Vasili Vasilievich and Yuri Dmitrievich came away from the Horde; *Tsar* Mahmed gave the title of [Great Prince] over the whole Russian Land to [Prince] Vasili Vasilievich.

A.D. 1434. A.M. 6942. [Prince] Yuri Dmitrievich seized the town of Moscow and took his seat as [Great Prince].

And the same year, in the spring, on April 1, in Holy week, the [Great Prince] Vasili Vasilievich came to Novgorod.

A.D. 1441. A.M. 6949. The same winter the Metropolitan Isidor returned to Russia from the Eighth [Assembly] in Rome, and began calling himself *Legatos* from the rib of the Apostolic seat of Roman power, and Roman Metropolitan: he also began the naming of the Pope of Rome in his services, and other new things which we had never heard since the baptism of the Russian Land; and he ordered Russian priests to perform his service in the Polish churches, and chaplains to serve in Russian churches. But Lithuania and Russia did not support this.

A.D. 1445. A.M. 6953. The same winter the [Great Prince] Vasili went against the Tartar *Tsar* Mahmed; many Christians died from cold, others were slain by the Tartars who laid waste the country. But God aided the [Great Prince] Vasili, and the Tartars fled, others being slain.

Bread was dear in Novgorod, and not only this year but during ten whole years: one [half-rouble] for two [baskets]; sometimes a little more, sometimes less; sometimes there was none to be bought anywhere. And amongst the Christians there was great grief and distress; only crying and sobbing were to be heard in the streets and market place, and many people fell down dead from hunger, children before their parents, fathers and mothers before their children; and many dispersed, some to Lithuania, others passed over to Latinism, and others to the *Besermeny* and to the Jews, giving themselves to the traders for bread.

At the same time there was no law or justice in Novgorod; calumniators arose and turned obligations and accounts and oaths to falsehood; and began to rob in the town and in the villages and districts; we were exposed to the rebukes of our neighbours, who were around us. There was much confiscation, frequent demands for money, throughout the districts, with weeping and anguish and with outcries and curses on all sides against our seniors and our town: because there was no grace in us, nor justice.

The Tatars: A 13th Century Description

Although Tatar troops had defeated those of the Russian princes in 1228, this had been only a reconnaissance in force and the Tatars had withdrawn without attempting to follow up the victory. They returned in 1236, however, and within less than four years brought all the Russian principalities, except Novogorod, under their dominion. Tatar control of the Russian lands lasted almost two and one-half centuries and had very important, far-reaching consequences. The following description of the Tatars was written in 1243. The source is: Richard Hakluyt, The Principal Navigations, Voyages, Traffiques and Discoveries of the English Nation. *Ten vols. New York: E. P. Dutton & Co., 1927. Vol. 1, pp. 91–93.*

But concerning their maners and superstitions, of the disposition and stature of their bodies, of their countrey and maner of fighting &c, he protested the particulars following to be true: namely, that they were above all men, covetous, hasty, deceitfull, and mercilesse: notwithstanding, by reason of the rigour and extremitie of punishments to be inflicted upon them by their superiors, they are restreined from brawlings, and from mutuall strife and contention. The ancient founders and fathers of their tribes, they call by the name of gods, and at certaine set times the doe celebrate solemne fèasts unto them, many of them being particular, & but foure onely generall. They thinke that all things are created for themselves alone. They esteeme it none offence to exercise cruelty against rebels. They be hardie and strong in the breast, leane and pale-faced, rough and hug-shouldred, having flatte and short noses, long and sharpe chinnes, their upper jawes are low and declining, their teeth long and thinne, their eye-browes extending from their foreheads downe to their noses, their eies inconstand and blacke, their countenances writhen and terrible, their extreame joynts strong with bones and sinews, having thicke and great thighes, and short legs, and yet being equall unto us in stature: for that length which is wanting in their legs, is supplied in the upper parts of their bodies. Their countrey in olde time was a land utterly desert and waste, situated far beyond Chaldea, from whence they have expelled Lions, Beares, & such like untamed beasts, with their bowes, and other engines. Of the hides of beasts being tanned, they use to shape for themselves light but yet impenetrable armour. They ride fast bound unto their horses, which are not very great in stature, but exceedingly strong, and mainteined with little provender. They used to fight constantly and valiantly with javelins, maces, battle-axes, and swords. But specially they are excellent archers, and cunning warriers with their bowes. Their backs are slightly armed, that they may not flee. They withdraw not themselves from the combate, till they see the chiefe Standard of their Generall give backe. Vanquished, they aske no favour, and vanquishing, they shew no compassion. They all persist in their purpose of subduing the whole world under their owne subjection, as if they were but one man, and yet they are more then millions in number. They have 60000. Courriers, who being sent before upon light horses to prepare a place for the armie to incampe in, will in the space of one night gallop three dayes journey. And suddenly diffusing themselves over an whole province, and surprising all the people thereof unarmed, unprovided, dispersed, they make such horrible slaughters, that the king or prince of the land invaded, cannot finde people sufficient to wage battell against them, and to withstand them. They delude all people and princes of regions in time of peace, pretending that for a cause, which indeed is no cause. Sometimes they say, that they will make a voyage to Colen, to fetch home the three wise kings into their owne countrey; sometimes to punish the avarice and pride of the Romans, who oppressed them in times past; sometimes to conquere barbarous and Northern nations; sometimes to moderate the furie of the Germans with their owne meeke mildnesse; sometimes to learne warlike feats and stratagems of the French; sometimes for the finding out of fertile ground to suffice their huge multitudes; sometimes againe in derision they say that they intend to goe on pilgrimage to S. James of Galicia. In regard of which sleights and collusions certain undiscreet governors concluding a league with them, have granted them free passage thorow their territories, which leagues notwithstanding being violate, were an occasion of ruine and destruction unto the foresayd governours &c.

Kliuchevskii on Kievan Rus

The greatest of all Russian historians, and one of the great historians of the world was Professor Vasilii O. Kliuchevskii. All students of Russian history are greatly indebted to him and to his Kurs Russkoi Istorii *(A Course of Russian History.) This five volume work covers in detail the domestic history of Russia from the beginnings to the accession of Catherine II. It was Kliuchevskii's purpose to tell the social and economic history of the Russian people, and he ignored all other aspects. The following selections are from the only English translation of his work. The source is: Vasilii O. Kluchevsky (C. J. Hogarth, translator)* A History of Russia. *Five volumes. New York: E. P. Dutton and Co., 1911–1931.*

The first section deals with the beginnings of Kiev; the second, describes Kievan Rus at the height of its power. (Vol. I, pp. 71–73, 87–89.)

THE BEGINNINGS. Kiev stood in the position, not only of principal advanced post in the defence of the country against the Steppes, but also of central export depot for Russian trade. These two facts alone were bound to prevent the city from remaining a mere Varangian principality after falling into Varangian hands, as did the principalities of the same kind which arose about at the same period at Novgorod, Izborsk, and Bieloe Ozero, as well as, later, at Polotsk and Turov. Trading connections with Byzantium and the Arabic East, as well as with the markets of the Black Sea, the Sea of Azov, and the Caspian, not only turned the popular industry towards exploitation of the forest wealth of the country, but also concentrated upon Kiev the country's most important commercial traffic. To make, however, that traffic secure it was indispensable to have inviolable frontiers and free passage along the rivers of the Steppes, as well as, at times, to bring armed pressure to bear upon foreign markets for the securing of advantageous terms in them. All this could be attained only by the united forces of the *whole* of the Eastern Slavonic tribes, and this circumstance entailed forcible impressment into the service of those tribes which lived at a distance from the principal trade-routes and so had no inducement to support the Kievan Princes of their own free will. For that reason both foreign sources and our own have a good deal to say about the warlike operations of the first rulers of the Principality. The researches of the great authority Vassilievski into the biographies of Saints George of Amastris and Stephen of Surozh have proved, beyond all practical doubt, that the first half of the ninth century saw Rus already raiding the coasts—even the southern coasts—of the Black Sea. Nevertheless, it was not until the time of the Patriarch Photius that Rus ventured to attack Constantinople itself. Previous to that event Photius had heard reports of an important change having begun in Rus—a change which had its origin in

Kiev. In a rescript concerning the Russian attack upon Constantinople, as well as in an encyclical letter, he says that the Russians, who had hitherto been wholly unknown and "of no account," had suddenly become "most renowned and glorious" after that deed of daring. Such valour, he explains, must have been inspired in that people through the fact that it had recently subjugated the tribes which lived around its territory, so that the success had made it "boundlessly proud and bold." This means that, as soon as ever the great Varangian Principality of Kiev was formed, it organised a concentration of the forces of the whole country, and so brought about the first Russian enterprise undertaken for a common end—that end being the securing of trade relations.

Such were the conditions the combined action of which brought the great Principality of Kiev into being. At first this State formed merely one of the many *local* Varangian principalities, since Askold and his brother Dir originally settled there simply as Varangian *Konings* whose activities were limited to protecting the province attached to the city from foreign foes and to supporting its trade interests; while Oleg, who followed in their footsteps, only continued their work. To that work, however, the military-industrial position of Kiev soon communicated a wider importance. The province attached to the city shut off from the south the whole of the country bordering upon the Baltic-Greek trade route—an area having trade interests identical with those of Kiev itself. Consequently it was not long before the other Varangian principalities and town-provinces of Rus were driven, willy-nilly, to unite themselves under the authority of the Kievan Prince, until the federation thus formed acquired the importance of a Russian State. This process of federation was necessitated by the political and economic dependence upon Kiev in which the various petty Varangian principalities and town-provinces had been placed by the downfall of the Chazar power in the Steppes.

In view of these facts I do not think that the arrival of Rurik in Novgorod can properly be regarded as the beginning of the Russian Empire, seeing that there arose there, when he came, but a local, as well as only a very short-lived, Varangian principality. No; the Russian Empire was founded through the deeds of Askold and, after him, Oleg at Kiev. From Kiev it was, and not from Novgorod, that the political federation of Russian Slavdom originated, and it was the petty Varangian state which those two Vikings there founded that constituted the first germ of that union of all the Slavonic and Finnish tribes which may be looked upon as having been the primal form of the modern Russian Empire.

APOGEE. Thus we see that the early Kievan Princes continued the policy originated before their time by the fortified trading towns of Rus—namely, the policy of maintaining trade relations with overseas markets and protecting the frontiers and trade-routes of the country from the nomads of the Steppes.

Having now described the policy of the early Kievan Princes, let us sum up its results, as well as touch upon the composition of Rus in the middle of the eleventh century. By that time the Kievan rulers had carved out for themselves a wide expanse of territory, of which Kiev was the political centre. The population of their dominions was of mixed composition, since there had gradually become absorbed into the Principality not only the whole of the Eastern Slavonic tribes, but also a certain number of the Finnish—the latter comprising the Tchudes of Bielozersk and the Baltic, and the Meres of Rostov and Murom. Among these Finnish tribes Russian towns had arisen at an early date, such as Yuriev (now Dorpat) among the Tchudes of the Baltic, and Murom, Rostov, and Bielozersk among the more easterly tribes of that race. The three towns last mentioned were founded earlier than Yuriev, which was called after Yaroslav's Christian name of Yuri (George)—the town of Yaroslav on the Volga (also built in Yaroslav's time) representing his titular appellation. In this manner the Principality of Kiev had come to stretch from Lake Ladoga in the north to the river Rhos in the south, and from the Kliazma in the east to the head of the Western Bug in the west. Galicia—the ancient home of the Chrobatians—can scarcely be counted, since in the tenth and eleventh centuries it was disputed territory between Rus and Poland. Both the lower course of the Oka (the upper course of which formed part of the eastern frontier of Rus) and the lower portions of the Dnieper, the Eastern Bug, and the Dniester seems to have lain outside the then territory of the Prince of Kiev, but on his eastern flank he still retained the ancient colony of Tmutorokan, connection with which was kept up by way of the left tributaries of the Dnieper and of the rivers discharging into the Sea of Azov.

This huge territory, then, with its vast heterogeneous population, formed the Principality of Kiev, or State of Rus. Yet the State of Rus did not yet constitute the State of the Russian *nation*, for the reason that the Russian nation had not yet come into existence. All that had been accomplished in that direction was that the ethnographical elements had been prepared out of which, by a long and difficult process, the Russian nation was eventually to be compounded. Meanwhile those various heterogeneous elements were mixed together in mechanical fashion only, since the moral tie of Christianity was slow in its working, and had not yet succeeded in embracing even the whole of the Slavonic tribes of the country (the Vatizes, for instance, not becoming Christianised until the beginning of the twelfth century). Of the mechanical ties connecting the various sections of the population the chief was the State system of administration, with its *posadniki, dan,* and taxes. With the nature and origin of the authority wielded by the Prince who stood at the head of that administration we are already acquainted, and know that he derived his authoritative status from those Varangian captains of city companies who first began to appear in Rus during the ninth century, and whose original functions were to protect the trade, the Steppe trade-routes, and the oversea markets of Rus, in return for certain payment from the native Slavonic population. In time, however, the lust of conquest, as well as contact with foreign political forms, caused certain borrowed features to creep into the character of the authority of these mercenary Princes, with the result that their authority ended by becoming the supreme governmental power. During the tenth century, for instance, we frequently find the Prince styled "Kagan" or "Khan"—a title borrowed from his Chazar suzerain; while Ilarion does the same by Vladimir, in a laudatory work on that Prince which he composed at about the middle of the eleventh century. With the coming of Christianity, however, there set in a new trend of political ideas and relations in Rus, and it was not long before the recently created priesthood imported from Byzantium the notion that a soverign ruler is appointed of God to establish and maintain the internal order of his state equally with its external security. Consequently we find Ilarion writing that "Prince Vladimir did often and amicably commune with his holy fathers the bishops, to the end that he might learn of them how to establish law among a people which had not long known God." The Ancient Chronicle also describes Vladimir as conferring with the bishops, and being told by them that he ought to punish robbers, "seeing that he had been appointed of God to deal retribution unto the wicked and favour unto the good."

RUSSKAIA PRAVDA. *The first legal code of ancient Russia was the* Russkaia Pravda. *After examining in detail its origin and composition, Professor Kliuchevskii summed it up in the following description. (Kluchevsky, op. cit., vol. 1, pp. 163–164.)*

Such are the main features of the *Russkaia Pravda* as illustrative of the basic, ruling interests and motives in the life of the Russian community of Kievan days. The Code is first and foremost an exposition of the rights of capital. Upon labour, upon the manifestation of human energy, it looks as upon the mere instrument by which capital is created. All the most important legal processes which it formulates have to do with capital; all its most stringent injunctions are directed rather against acts detrimental to capital than against those inimical to the security of the person. In it, capital furnishes not only the means of restitution in civil and criminal offences, but likewise the basis of its whole system of penalties and indictments. The individual is looked upon not so much as a member of the community as a possessor or a non-possessor, a producer or a non-producer, of capital. If he were neither a possessor nor a producer of that commodity he lost his right to freedom and to the civil qualifications of a citizen. For the same reason a woman's life was valued at twenty *grivni* only, or "half *vira*." Yet capital, in those days, was extremely costly. For short-date loans no exact rate of monthly interest is to be found prescribed in the Pravda, but for loans of one year or upwards an article fixes the annual rate at fifty per cent. Vladimir Monomakh alone attempted to modify this usurious system, by ordaining that interest should in no case be suffered to accumulate to the amount of more than one-half of the original principal, and that such interest should be recoverable only during the first two years of the loan—after which period nothing but the principal could be sued for, and even that under pain of forfeiture if the lender should be proved to be demanding more than his two years' interest. At the same time, for loans which it was expressly agreed to spread over three or more years he allowed interest, throughout, of forty per cent. Little attention, however, seems to have been paid to these restrictive enactments, for, although we read that Bishop Niphont of Novgorod charged his questioners to denounce usury among the laity, and to instruct them to exact only "merciful" interest of from three to five *kuni* in the *grivna*, we find that Monomakh had not long been dead before "merciful" interest was once again being assessed at the rate of from sixty to eighty per cent.—half as much, or nearly twice as much, as the legal rate! In fact, it was not until the thirteenth century, when the great trading towns were beginning to lose their importance as a factor in the industrial life of the people, that the clergy at last found it possible to insist upon "light" interest being charged—i.e. interest of three *kuni* or seven *riezani* in the *grivna*, or at the rate of from twelve to fourteen per cent. This fact, combined with the hard, *bourgeois* character of the *Pravda*, points clearly to the social centre whence the jurisdiction originated which served as the basis of the Code. That centre was the great trading town. Consequently, study of the civil order of the period, as revealed in the pages of the *Pravda*, brings us face to face again with the force which did so much to establish the political order of the period—namely, the force represented by the great trading town and its *vietché*. This force, then it was which, combined with capital, determined both the civil and the political order of the eleventh and twelfth centuries.

DECLINE. *In the following passage, Professor Kliuchevskii offers his interpretation of the reasons for the decline and fall of the Kievan state. The final paragraphs summarize his conclusions as to the most important consequences of this change. (Kluchevsky, op cit., vol. 1, pp. 182–202, passim. Adapted.)*

Two radical changes in Russian life are embraced within the period from the beginning of the thirteenth century to approximately the middle of the fifteenth—namely, the transference of the bulk of the Russian population from the basin of the Dnieper to the region of the upper Volga, and the substitution of the hereditary prince of the Appanage for the great trading town as the chief organizing and directing agency of the political and economic orders of the country. Undoubtedly the migratory movement originated in the social disintegration of Kievan Russ. To that circumstance many and complex factors contributed.

The middle of the twelfth century saw conditions enter into operation which were bound, sooner or later, to militate against the social order and economic well being of Kievan Russ. Hitherto, to judge from the condition of the upper classes, a high level of material affluence, citizenship, and general culture had been attained by the community, since the ruling factor in the popular industry—namely foreign trade—had served both to preserve the life of the people from isolation and stagnancy and to bring great wealth into the country.

This great wealth, however, belonged only to the upper side of the picture. Let us look at the under side—at the condition of the lower classes. The economic prosperity of Kievan Russ depended for its maintenance upon slavery—a system which, toward the close of the twelfth century, attained immense proportions. Not only wealth in trade, but also wealth in land was dependent upon the slave traffic because the original title to the soil was based upon the settlement and exploitation of the land by the slaves. The idea of the right to own land may be looked upon as deriving directly from slave ownership. Gradually the peasantry were added to the class of personal possessions. This makes it additionally clear the social system and the economic prosperity of Kievan Russ were maintained only at the cost of the enslavement of the lower classes, and that the amenities of life enjoyed by the upper strata of the community entailed the legal debasement of the lower.

It was this legal and economic disparity between the upper and lower strata of the community which constituted the first of the conditions disruptive of the social and economic order of Kievan Russ, inasmuch as the social order found no support among the common people, but made itself felt among them only through its disadvantages.

The second disruptive condition was the multitude of the princely feuds, the third, and even more potent one, was the attacks upon Russ by a barbarian people of the Steppes named the Polovtsi. With that barbarian race Russ maintained a stubborn struggle during the whole of the eleventh and twelfth centuries. As we read the ancient chronicles record of those days, there rises before us a vivid picture of the desolation to which the Steppe regions of Russ became reduced. This struggle between the Russians and the Polovtsi— a struggle lasting for nearly two centuries—was not without its place in European history at large; for while the West was engaged in crusades against the forces of Asia and the Orient, and a similar movement was in progress in the Iberian Peninsula against the Moors, Russ was holding the left flank of Europe. Yet this historical service cost her dear, since not only did it dislodge her from the old settlements on the Dnieper, but it caused the whole trend of her life to become altered.

From the middle of the twelfth century onwards, then, the three adverse conditions specified (namely the legal and economic debasement of the lower orders of the community, the feuds of the princes, and the attacks of the Polovtsi) caused Kiev to become depopulated, and the whole region of the middle Dnieper to fall to waste. The exodus from Kievan Russ took two different directions, and flowed into different streams. One tended towards the West—towards the region of the western Bug, the upper portions of the Dniester, and Vistula, and the interior districts of Galicia and Poland. Hence a certain proportion of the population of southern Russ and the Dnieper returned to the very locality which their forefathers had left in the 7th century. The depopulation which began in the twelfth century was completed during the thirteenth by the Tartar invasions. For a long period thereafter the provinces of ancient Russ, once so thickly peopled, remained in a state of desolation.

With regard to the other of the two streams of immigration, its trend was north-eastwards, towards the regions of the rivers Ugra, Oka, and Volga.

All the results in question may be narrowed down to one central fundamental fact—namely, that the Russian nationality, gradually compounded during the first period of our history, became sundered during the second, according as the bulk of the Russian population was forced to retreat northwards to the region of the Oka and upper Volga. There, sheltered in the fastnesses of central Russ, it preserved its nationality intact, and slowly recovered its strength until finally it was able to return from the Dnieper and the south-west, there to rescue from foreign influence and the foreign yoke the small remnant of Russian population which had remained behind.

The Appanages

The Appanage Period in Russian history has been generally regarded as a transitional stage between the decline of Kiev and the rise of Muscovy. The prime exponent of this interpretation was Professor Kliuchevskii, whose views on it are set forth in the following selection. (Kluchevsky, op. cit., vol. 1, pp. 249–271, passim. Adapted.)

Formerly the Russian land had been accounted the common heritage of the whole princely stock, which, in its turn, had been the collective wielder of the ruling power in that heritage, while the individual princes, as participaters only in the collective ruling power, had been temporary holders only of their provinces.

Yet that power had never contained the least trace of the idea of a prince's right to own territory *as* land—of such a right, that is to say, as would naturally accrue to the private owner of an estate. Ruling their principalities either in order of seniority or by agreement both among themselves and with the provincial capitals, the princes had always exercised supreme rights of *government* in their domains; yet neither they as a body nor any cf them as an individual had ever applied to their provinces those means of disposing of the same which would have accrued to them had they possessed any actual right of *ownership*. That is to say, they had never proceeded to sell, mortgage, give away in dowry, or bequeath, their temporary spheres of rule. In the North, however, although the region of Rostov was the common *otchina* of the whole of Vsevolod's stock, it did not remain their *collective, joint otchina,* but became split up into a number of principalities altogether separate from and independent of one another—territories which were looked upon as the personal and devisable property of their several rulers, who governed the free population therein as overlords, and administered their territories as private owners possessed of all the rights of disposal of the same which would naturally arise out of absolute ownership. Such rule as that was appanage rule in its purest form and most complete development: which form and development were attained only in the heritage governed by Vsevolod's successors during the thirteenth, fourteenth, and fifteenth centuries. Thus, in the appanage system, the wielder of the governing power was the *individual,* not the *stock,* while princely rule became divided, and, losing none of its ancient supreme rights, acquired also such rights as would attach to private, personal ownership. It is in that combination that we must seek for an explanation of the fact that local conditions contributed both to this division of princely rule in the *otchina* of Vsevold's successors and to the rise of the idea of an appanage being the personal property of its ruler.

Thus we see that the appanage system rested upon two bases—a geographical and a political. That is to say, it was created by the joint action of the nature of the country and of the process of colonisation. Let us sum up those factors. (1) The physical features of the region caused the process of colonisation to give rise to small river provinces, isolated from one another, and serving as a ready-made basis for political division of the land—i.e. for its disintegration into appanages. In other words, the appanages of the thirteenth and fourteenth centuries were river basins. (2) Colonisation of the country usually brought the first prince of an appanage face to face, not with a ready-made community, but with a desert wild which needed settlement and organisation before it could contain one. Hence, the idea of a prince as the personal owner of his appanage was the juridical outcome of his significance as its first settler and organiser.

The community was becoming dissolved into small local communes — each man departing to his petty plot of land, to confine his ideas and relations to his own narrow interests or to such ties as chance and his nearest neighbours imposed upon him. A state relies for its support upon lasting common interests and broad social ties, and therefore either becomes impossible under such a disintegrated, relaxed order of life as I am now describing or adopts forms and methods of action foreign to its nature. With the population, it becomes divided up into small units, in whose organisation the elements of a state order find themselves intermingled; in happy promiscuity, with the norms of private right. In Western Europe such a condition of society gave rise to feudalism. On the Upper Volga it provided the basis of the appanage system.

Such were the principal results of the appanage system. They may be summed up by saying that the working of the system caused Northern Rus to undergo ever-increasing political disintegration and to become bereft even of her former slender ties of political unity; that that disintegration, in its turn, rendered the princes continually more and more impoverished; that, in proportion as that occurred, they shut themselves up more and more in their *otchini,* and became estranged from one another; and that, in proportion as they became estranged from one another, they converted themselves, according to their several ideas and interests, into private rural seigniors, and, losing altogether their role of overseers of the public weal, lost also their territorial sense. These results of the system were of great importance in the subsequent political history of Northern Rus, for they paved the way for conditions favorable to political reunification. When at length a strong ruler arose from among the mass of petty impoverished appanage princes, he encountered among them, it is true, a total absence of support for his unificatory ideas, and so was forced to take advantage of their mutual estrangement and incapacity for common action in order to subdue them each in turn; yet, on the other hand, the prince-unifier found in the local communities at large such utter indifference to the petty, semi-barbarous rulers with whom those communities were connected by only the slenderest of ties that he was able to annex them, one by one, without evoking in them any rising in support of their respective princes. All this helps us to determine the importance of the appanage system in our political history, and to show us that it was through its own results that the downfall of the system came. Its very nature, indeed, rendered it less capable of self-defence than its predecessor, the rota system, had been, and therefore the more easy to destroy in order to rear upon its ruins a unified state. Hence the appanage system of rule represents, in our history, a transitional political form which enabled the Russian land to pass from mere *national* unity to *political* unity. The story of that passage is the story of the Principality of Moscow.

Additional Readings

Pares, Bernard, *A History of Russia*. Fifth edition. New York: Alfred A. Knopf, 1947. Pp. 3-73.

Tompkins, Stuart R., *Russia Through the Ages From the Scythians to the Soviets*. New York: Prentice-Hall, Inc., 1940. Pp. 8-98.

Vernadsky, George, *History of Russia*. New York: New Home Library, 1944. New Haven: Yale University Press, 4th edition, 1939. Pp. 1-50.

Goodall, George (ed.), *Soviet Russia in Maps — Its Origins and Development*. London: George Philip & Sons, Ltd., 1942. U.S. distributor: Denoyer-Geppert Co., Chicago. Pp. 2, 3, 10, 11, 14, 15, 27.

Martin, John S. (ed.), *A Picture History of Russia*. New York: Crown Publishers, 1945. Pp. 1-30.

Sumner, B. H., *Short History of Russia*. New York: Reynal & Hitchcock, 1943. Chap. 1.

Kerner, Robert J., *The Urge to the Sea*. Berkeley: U. of California Press, 1942. Chaps. 1 and 2.

Elnett, Eleanor, *Historic Origin . . . of Family Life in Russia*. New York: Columbia University Press, 1926. Chap. 1.

Nowak, Frank, *Medieval Slavdom and the Rise of Russia*. New York: Henry Holt & Co., 1930. Pp. 3-8, 35-54.

Rambaud, Alfred, *Russia*. Many editions. Vol. 1, Chaps. 1-11.

Frederiksen, O. J. (ed.), Hrushevsky, M., *History of Ukraine*. New Haven: Yale University Press, 1941. Chaps. 1-6.

Allen, W. E. D., *The Ukraine: A History*. Cambridge: Cambridge University Press, 1941. Chaps. 1 and 2.

Karpovich, M. M. (ed.), Miliukov, P., *Outlines of Russian Culture*. Three volumes. Philadelphia: University of Pennsylvania Press, 1941. Vol. 1, chap. 1; vol. 2, chap. 1.

Curtin, Jeremiah, *The Mongols: A History*. Boston: Little, Brown & Co., 1908.

Platonov, S. F. (E. Aronsberg, tr.; F. A. Golder, ed.), *History of Russia*. New York: Macmillan, 1929. Pp. 1-124.

Kluchevsky, V. O. (C. J. Hograth, tr.), *History of Russia*. Five volumes. New York: E. P. Dutton, 1911-1931. Vols. 1 and 2.

Vernadsky, G., *Ancient Russia*. (Vol. 1 of *A History of Russia* by G. Vernadsky and M. M. Karpovich). New Haven: Yale University Press, 1943. Chap. 8.

Peisker, J., "The Expansion of the Slavs," *Cambridge Medieval History*. Vol. 2, chap. 14.

Part II: THE RISE OF MUSCOVY

The Pomestie System

One of the distinguishing features of the rise of Muscovy was the development of a new system of land tenure based upon state service. In the following passage Professor Kliuchevskii sketches the growth of this "Pomestie System" and its results. The source is: V. O. Kluchevsky, A History of Russia. Vol. 2, pp. 121–148. (Very much abridged and adapted.)

By the term Pomiestie System, I mean the system of obligatory military service as a condition of land tenure, which became established in the Muscovite Empire during the 15th and 16th centuries. At the base of the system lay the *Pomiestie,* which was a portion of land conferred upon a member of the official class either in return for military service performed, or in order to secure the performance of military service in the future. The possession of the pomiestie was temporary and personal which distinguished it from the otchina, or absolutely owned, hereditary state. Like everything else in the Moscovite empire, pomiestie tenure originated during the Appanage period. It developed from the land tenure enjoyed by household servitors under the old Appanage princes, and was distinguished from the former only by the fact that pomiestie tenure was conditioned by military and household service alike. This distinction begins with the middle of the 15th century. There was an immense and systematic allotment of pomiestie estates during the latter half of the 15th century, and in the 16th century it was a frequent occurrence for members of the official class to be allotted pomiestia wholesale. The further Russian settlement was pushed forward toward the Steppes, the more did pomiestie tenure take the place of otchina proprietorship.

The 16th century saw service of the state become a corporate, hereditary, obligation from which no member of the upper classes was exempt save by special action of Tsar. Also there began a system whereby service liability devolved from father to son. A member of the official class usually entered the service of the state on attaining his 15th year. Subsequently — if his early career warranted the step — he was allotted a pomiestie.

The first direct result of pomiestie development was the gradual extinction of the private, non-service, hereditary estate (otchina). These estates ceased to be private, and became conditional properties. As soon as military service became obligatory upon individuals in virtue of land tenure, there arose an idea that he who served should own land; as also (a natural corollary to the first idea) that he who owned land should serve. The second direct result of pomiestie development was an artificial increase in private land ownership. The third, was the creation of local agrarian corporations of the nobility. These had a joint responsibility for the discharge of the obligation of state service, and took an active part, through their deputies, in local government. The fourth result was the rise of a new stratum in the official class — a stratum to which we might give the title of service-land owning proletariat. The last direct result was an important change in the position of the peasant population. It must be remembered that the conquest of Kazan and Astrakhan opened up enormous additional expances of virgin land to Russian agricultural labor. Civil servants were transferred to these lands and acquired there pomiestie estates. Police restrictions were employed to further the peopling of those lands by the peasants. We may with some reason suppose that it was on these virgin pomiestia that the first length was forged of the chain which eventually bound the peasant into serf bondage.

Herberstein's "Notes on Russia" (1517 and 1526)

The Baron Sigismund von Herberstein went as Ambassador to the Court of the Grand Prince Basil Ivanovich (Basil III) in 1517 and again in 1526. His Rerum Moscovitarum Commentarii *is the first authentic description of Muscovy based upon personal residence and experience by a European observer. It is accounted a major source for the period. The following brief excerpts will give the flavor of von Herberstein's work as well as some description of Muscovy and its people. The source is: Major, R. H. (Translator and Editor),* Notes Upon Russia: Being a Translation of the Earliest Account of that Country, entitled Rerum Moscovitarum Commentarii, by the Baron Sigismund von Herberstein. *Two volumes. London: The Hakluyt Society, 1851–2. Vol. 1, pp. 95-6, 105-6; vol. 2, pp. 131-2.*

All confess themselves to be Chlopos, that is, serfs of the prince. Almost all the upper classes also have serfs, who either have been taken prisoners, or purchased; and those whom they keep in free service are not at liberty to quit at their own pleasure. If any one goes away without his master's consent, no one receives him. If a master does not treat a good and useful servant well, he by some means gets a bad name amongst others, and after that he can procure no more domestics.

This people enjoy slavery more than freedom; for persons on the point of death very often manumit some of their serfs, but they immediately sell themselves for money to other families. If the father should sell the son, which is the custom, and he by means become free or be manumitted, the father can sell him again and again, by right of his paternal authority. But after the fourth sale, the father has no more right over his son. The prince alone can inflict capital punishment on serfs or others.

Every second or third year the prince holds a census through the provinces, and conscribes the sons of the boyars, that he may know their number, and how many horses and serfs each one has. Then he appoints each his stipend, as has been said above. Those who have the means to do so, fight without pay. Rest is seldom given them, for either they are waging war against the Lithuanians, or the Livonians, or the Swedes, or the Tartars of Cazar; or if no war is going on, the prince generally appoints twenty thousand men every year in places about the Don and the Occa, as guards to repress the eruptions and depredations of the Tartars of Precop. He generally summons some also every year by rotation out of his provinces, to fill the various offices in his service at Moscow. But in war time, they do not serve in annual rotation, or by turns, but each and all are compelled, both as stipendiaries and as aspirants to the prince's favour, to go to battle.

• • •

The testimony of one nobleman is worth more than that of a multitude of low condition. Attorneys are very seldom allowed: every one explains his own case. Although the prince is very severe, nevertheless all justice is venal, and that without much concealment. I heard of a certain counsellor who presided over the judgments being apprehended, because in a certain case he had received bribes from both parties, and had given judgment in the favour of the one who had made him the largest presents: when he was brought to the prince he did not deny the charge, but stated that the man in whose favour he had given judgment was rich, and held an honourable position in life, and therefore more to be believed than the other, who was poor and abject. The prince revoked the sentence, but at length sent him away with a laugh unpunished. It may be that poverty itself is the cause of so much avarice and injustice, and that the prince knowing his people are poor, connives at such misdeeds and dishonesty as by a predetermined concession of impunity to them.

The poor have no access to the prince, but only to the counsellors themselves; and indeed that is very difficult. *Ocolnick* holds the place of a praetor or judge appointed by the prince, otherwise the chief counsellor, who is always near the prince's person, is so called. *Nedelsnick* is the post of those who summon men to justice, seize malefactors and cast them into prison; and these are reckoned amongst the nobility.

Labourers work six days in the week for their master, but the seventh day is allowed for their private work. They have some fields and meadows of their own allowed them by their masters, from which they derive their livelihood: all the rest is their master's. They are, moreover, in a very wretched condition, for their goods are exposed to plunder from the nobility and soldiery, who call them Christians and black rascals by way of insult.

A nobleman, however poor he might be, would think it ignominious and disgraceful to labour with his own hands; but he does not think it disgraceful to pick up from the ground and eat the rind or peeling of fruits that have been thrown away by us and our servants, especially the skins of melons, garlic, and onions; but whenever occasion offers, they drink as immoderately as they eat sparingly. They are nearly all slow to anger, but proud in their poverty, whose irksome companion they consider slavery. They wear oblong dresses and white peaked hats of felt (of which we see coarse mantles made) rough from the shop.

. . .

The prince often honours his guests by sending them dishes and drink. He never meddles with matters of serious moment during dinner; but when the dinner is over, it is his custom to say to the ambassadors, "Now you may depart." When thus dismissed, they are escorted back to their hotels by the same persons who had conducted them to the palace, who state that they have orders to remain with them in the hotel, to make merry with them. Silver goblets, and various other vessels containing liquor, are then produced, and all strive to make each other drunk; and very clever they are in finding excuses for inviting men to drink, and when they are at a loss for a toast to propose, they begin at last to drink to the health of the emperor and the prince his brother, and after that to the welfare of any others whom they believe to hold any position of dignity and honour. They think that no one ought or can refuse the cup, when these names are proposed. The drinking is done in this fashion. He who proposes the toast takes his cup, and goes into the middle of the room, and standing with his head uncovered, pronounces, in a festive speech, the name of him whose health he wishes to drink, and what he has to say in his behalf. Then after emptying the cup, he turns it upside down over his head, so that all may see that he has emptied it, and that he sincerely gave the health of the person in honour of whom the toast was drunk. He then goes to the top of the table and orders many cups to be filled, and then hands each man his cup, pronouncing the name of the party whose health is to be drunk, on which each is obliged to go into the middle of the room, and, after emptying his cup, to return to his place. He who wishes to escape too long a drinking-bout, must pretend that he is drunk or sleepy, or at least declare that, having already emptied many cups, he cannot drink any more; for they do not think that their guests are well received, or hospitably treated, unless they are sent home drunk. It is common practice for nobles and those who are permitted to drink mead and beer, to observe this fashion.

Chancelour's Description of Muscovy in the 16th Century

The Englishmen, Sir Hugh Willoughby and Richard Chancelour, were sent out in 1553 by the Muscovy Company of England to search for a northeast passage to Asia. Willoughby and all his people perished, but Chancelour made his way into the White Sea and to the shores of Muscovy. With the permission of John the Dread, he and his party made their way to Moscow where they were well received by the Tsar. The following selection is taken from Chancelour's description of John and his realm. The source is: Hakluyt, Principal Navigations, etc. Vol. 1, pp. 254–266, passim.

The booke of the great and mighty Emperor of Russia, and Duke of Moscovia, and of the dominions orders and commodities thereunto belonging: drawen by Richard Chancelour.

FORASMUCH as it is meete and necessary for all those that minde to take in hande the travell into farre or strange countreys, to endevour themselves not onely to understande the orders, commodities, and fruitfulness thereof, but also to applie them to the setting foorth of the same whereby it may incourage others to the like travaile: therefore have I nowe thought good to make a briefe rehearsall of the orders of this my travaile in Russia and Muscovia, and other countreys thereunto adjoyning; because it was my chance to fall with the North partes of Russia before I came towards Moscovia, I will partly declare my knowledge therein. Russia is very plentifull both of land and people, and also welthy for such commodities as they have. They be very great fishers for Salmons and small Coddes: they have much oyle which wee call treine oyle, the most whereof is made by a river called Duina. They make it in other places, in seething of salte water. To the North parte of that countrey are the places where they have their Furres, as Sables, marterns, greese Bevers, Foxes white, black, and redde, Minkes, Ermines, Miniver, and Harts. There are also a fishes teeth, which fish is called a Morsse. The takers thereof dwell in a place called Postesora, which bring them upon Hartes to Lampas to sell, and from Lampas carie them to a place called Colmogro, where the hie market is holden on Saint Nicholas day. To the West of Colmogro there is a place called Gratanove, in our language Novogorode, where much fine Flaxe and Hempe groweth, and also much waxe and honie. The Dutch marchants have a Staplehouse there. There is also great store of hides, and at a place called Plesco: and thereabout is great store of Flaxe, Hempe, Waxe, Honie; and that towne is from Colmogro 120 miles.

There is a place called Vologda; the commodities whereof are Tallowe, Waxe, and Flaxe: but not so great plenty as is in Gratanove. From Vologda to Colmogro there runneth a river called Duyna, and from thence it falleth into the sea. Colmogro serveth Gratanove, Vologda and the Mosco with all the countrey thereabout with salte and saltfish. From Vologda to Jeraslave is two hundreth miles: which towne is very great. The commodities thereof are hides, and tallowe, and corne in great plenty, and some Waxe, but not so plentifull as in other places.

The Mosco is from Jeraslave two hundreth miles. The countrey betwixt them is very wel replenished with small Villages, which are so well filled with people, that it is wonder to see them: the ground is well stored with corne which they carie to the citie of Mosco in such abundance that it is wonder to see it. You shall meete in a morning seven or eight hundred sleds comming or going thither, that carrie corne, and some carie fish. You shall have some that carie corne to the Mosco, and some that fetch corne from thence, that at the least dwell a thousand miles off; and all their carriage is on sleds. Those which come so farre dwell in the North partes of the Dukes dominions, where the cold will suffer no corne to grow, it is so extreme. They bring thither fishes, furres, and beastse skinnes. In those partes they have but small store of cattell.

The Mosco it selfe is great: I take the whole towne to bee greater then London with the suburbes: but it is very rude, and standeth without all order. Their houses are all of timber very dangerous for fire. There is a faire Castle, the walles whereof are of bricke, and very high: they say they are eighteene foote thicke, but I doe not believe it, it doth not seeme, notwithstanding I doe not certainely know it: for no stranger may come to viewe it. The one side is ditched, and on the other side runneth a river called Moscua which runneth into Tartarie and so into the sea called Mare Caspium: and on the North side there is a base towne, the which hath also a bricke wall about it, and so it joyneth with the Castle wall. The Emperour lieth in the castle, wherein are nine fayre Churches, and therin are religious men. Also there is a Metropolitane with divers Bishops. I will not stande in description of their buildinges nor of the strength thereof because we have better in all points in England. They be well furnished with ordinance of all sortes.

The Emperours or Dukes house neither in building nor in the outward shew, nor yet within the house is so sumptuous as I have seene. It is very lowe built in eight square, much like the olde building of England, with small windowes, and so in other poynts.

Now to declare my comming before his Majestie: After I had remained twelve daies, the Secretary which hath the hearing of strangers did send for me, advertising me that the Dukes pleasure was to have me to come before his Ma. with the kings my masters letters: whereof I was right glad, and so I gave mine attendance. And when the Duke was in his place appointed, the interpretour came for me into the utter chamber, where sate one hundred or moe gentlemen, all in cloth of golde very sumptuous, and from thence I came into the Counsaile chamber, where sate the Duke himselfe with his nobles, which were a faire company: they sate round about the chamber on high, yet so that he himselfe sate much higher then any of his nobles in a chaire gilt, and in a long garment of beaten golde, with an emperial crowne upon his head, and a staffe of Cristall and golde in his right hand, and his other hand halfe leaning on his chaire. The Chancelour stoode up with the Secretary before the Duke. After my dutie done and my letter delivered, he bade me welcome, & enquired of me the health of the King my master, and I answered that he was in good health at my departure from his court, and that my trust was that he was now in the same. Upon the which he made me to dinner. The Chancelour presented my present unto his Grace bareheaded (for before they were all covered) and when his Grace had received my letter, I was required to depart: for I had charge not to speake to the Duke, but when he spake to me. So I departed unto the Secretaries chamber, where I remayned two houres, and then I was sent for againe unto another place which is called the golden palace, but I saw no fayrer then it in all poynts: and so I cam into the hall, which was small and not great as is the Kings Majesties of England, and the table was covered with a tablecloth; and the Marshall sate at the ende of the table with a little white rod in his hand, which boorde was full of vessell of golde: and on the other side of the hall did stand a faire cupborde of plate. From thence I came into the dining chamber, where the Duke himselfe sate at his table without cloth of estate, in a gowne of silver, with a crowne emperiall upon his head, he sate in a chaire somewhat hie: There sate none neare him by a great way. There were long tables set round about the chamber, which were full set with such as the Duke had at dinner: they were all in white. Also the places where the tables stoode were higher by two steppes then the rest of the house. In the middle of the chamber stoode a table or cupbord to set plate on; which stoode full of cuppes of golde: and amongst all the rest there stoode foure marveilous great pottes or crudences as they call them, of golde and silver: I thinke they were a good yarde and a halfe hie. By the cupborde stoode two gentlemen with napkins on their shoulders, and in their handes each of them had a cuppe of gold set with pearles and precious stones, which were the Dukes owne drinking cups: When he was disposed, he drunke them off at a draught. And for his service at meate it came in without order, yet it was very rich service: for all were served in gold, not onely he himselfe, but also all the rest of us, and it was very massie: the cups also were of golde and very massie. The number that dined there that day was two hundred persons, and all were served in golden vessell. The gentlemen that waited were all in cloth of gold, and they served him with their caps on their heads. Before the service came in, the Duke sent to every man a great shiver of bread, and the bearer called the party so sent to by his name aloude, and sayd, John

Basilivich Emperour of Russia and great Duke of Moscovia doth reward thee with bread: then must all men stand up, and doe at all times when those wordes are spoken. And then last of all he giveth the Marshall bread, whereof he eateth before the Dukes Grace, and so doth reverence and departeth. Then commeth the Dukes service of the Swannes all in pieces, and every one in a severall dish: the which the Duke sendeth as he did the bread, and the bearer sayth the same wordes as he sayd before. And as I sayd before, the service of his meate is in no order, but commeth in dish by dish: and then after that the Duke sendeth drinke, with the like saying as before is tolde. Also before dinner hee changed his crowne, and in dinner time two crownes; so that I saw three severall crownes upon his head in one day. And thus when his service was all come in hee gave to every one of his gentlemen waiters meate with his owne hand, & so likewise drinke. His intent thereby is, as I have heard, that every man shall know perfectly his servants. Thus when dinner is done hee calleth his nobles before him name by name, that it is wonder to heare howe he could name them, having so many as he hath. Thus when dinner was done I departed to my lodging, which was an hower within night. I will leave this, and speake no more of him nor his houshold: but I will somewhat declare of his land and people, with their nature and power in the wars. This Duke is Lord and Emperour of many countreis, & his power is marveilous great. For he is able to bring into the field two or three hundred thousand men: he never goeth into the field himselfe with under two hundred thousand men: And when he goeth himselfe he furnisheth his borders all with men of warre, which are no small number. He leaveth on the borders of Liefland fortie thousand men, and upon the borders of Letto 60 thousand men, and towarde the Nagayan Tartars sixtie thousand, which is wonder to heare of: yet doeth hee never take to his warres neither husbandman nor marchant. All his men are horsemen: he useth no footmen, but such as goe with the ordinance and labourers, which are thirtie thousand. The horsemen are all archers, with such bowes as the Turkes have, and they ride short as doe the Turkes. Their armour is a coate of plate, with a skull on their heads. Some of their coates are covered with velvet or cloth of gold: their desire is to be sumptuous in the field, and especially the nobles and gentlemen: as I have heard their trimming is very costly, and partly I have seene it, or else I would scarcely have beleeved it: but the Duke himselfe is richly attired above all measure: his pavilion is covered either with cloth of gold or silver, and so set with stones that it is wonderfull to see it. I have seene the Kings Majesties of England and the French Kings pavilions, which are fayre, yet not like unto his. And when they bee sent into farre or strange countreys, or that strangers come to them, they be very gorgious. Els the Duke himselfe goeth but meanly in apparell: and when he goeth betwixt one place and another hee is but reasonably apparelled over other times. In the while that I was in Mosco the Duke sent two ambassadours to the King of Poleland, which had at the lest five hundred horses; their sumptuousnes was above measure, not onely in themselves, but also in their horses, as velvet, cloth of golde, and cloth of silver set with pearles and not scant. What shall I farther say? I never heard of nor saw men so sumptuous: but it is no dayly guise, for when they have not occasion, as I sayd before, all their doing is but meane. And now to the effect of their warres: They are men without al order in the field. For they runne hurling on heapes, and for the most part they never give battell to their enemies: but that which they doe, they doe it all by stelth. But I beleeve they be such men for hard living as are not under the sun: for no cold wil hurt them. Yea and though they lie in the field two moneths, at such time as it shall freese more then a yard thicke, the common souldier hath neither tent nor any thing else over his head: the most defence they have against the wether is a felte, which is set against the winde and weather, and when Snowe commeth hee doth cast it off, and maketh him a fire, and laieth him down thereby. Thus doe the most of all his men, except they bee gentlemen which have other provision of their owne. Their lying in the fielde is not so strange as is their hardnes: for every man must carie & make provision for himselfe & his horse for a moneth or two, which is very wonderful. For he himselfe shal live upon water & otemeale mingled together cold, and drinke water thereto: his horse shal eat green wood, & such like baggage, & shal stand open in the cold field without covert, & yet wil he labour & serve him right wel. I pray you amongst all our boasting warriors how many should we find to endure the field with them but one moneth. I know no such region about us that beareth that name for man & beast. Now what might be made of these men if they were trained & broken to order and knowledge of civill wars? If this Prince had within his countreys such men as could make them to understand ye things aforesaid, I do beleeve that 2 of the best or greatest princes in Christendome were not wel able to match with him, considering the greatnes of his power & the hardnes of his people & straite living both of people and horse, and the small charges which his warres stand him in: for he giveth no wages, except to strangers. They have a yerely stipend & not much. As for his own countrey men every one serveth of his owne proper costes and charges, saving that he giveth to his Harcubusiers certaine allowance for powder & shot: or else no man in all his country hath one pennie wages. But if any man hath done very good service he giveth him a ferme or a piece of lande; for the which hee is bound at all times to bee readie with so many men as the Duke shall appoynt: who considereth in his mind what that lande or ferme is well able to finde: and so many shall he bee bound to furnish at all and every such time as warres are holden in any of the Dukes dominions. For there is no man of living, but hee is bound likewise, whether the

Duke call for either souldier or labourer, to furnish them with all such necessaries as to them belong.

Also, if any gentleman or man of living do die without issue male, immediately after his death the Duke takes his land, notwithstanding he have never so many daughters, and peradventure giveth it foorthwith to another man, except a small portion that he spareth to marrie the daughters with all. Also if there be a rich man, a fermour, or man of living, which is striken in age or by chance is maimed, and be not able to doe the Duke service, some other gentleman that is not able to live and more able to doe service, will come to the Duke and complayne, saying, your Grace hath such an one, which is unmeete to doe service to your Highnes, who hath great abundance of welth, and likewise your Grace hath many gentlemen which are poore and lacke living, and we that lacke are well able to doe good service, your Grace might doe well to looke upon him, and make him to helpe those that want. Immediately the Duke sendeth forth to inquire of his wealth: and if it be so proved, he shall be called before the Duke, and it shall bee sayd unto him, friend, you have too much living, and are unserviceable to your prince, lesse will serve you, and the rest will serve other men that are more able to serve. Whereupon immediately his living shal be taken away from him, saving a little to find himselfe and his wife on, and he may not once repine thereat: but for answere he will say, that he hath nothing, but it is Gods and the Dukes Graces, and cannot say, as we the common people in England say, if wee have any thing; that it is Gods and our owne. Men may say, that these men are in wonderful great awe, and obedience, that thus one must give and grant his goods which he hath bene scraping and scratching for all his life to be at his Princes pleasure and commandement. Oh that our sturdie rebels were had in the like subjection to knowe their duety towarde their Princes. They may not say as some snudges in England say, I would find the Queene a man to serve in my place, or make his friends tarrie at home if money have the upper hand. No, no, it is not so in this countrey: for hee shall make humble sute to serve the Duke. And whom he sendeth most to the warres he thinketh he is most in his favour: and yet as I before have sayde, he giveth no wages. If they knewe their strength no man were able to make match with them: nor they that dwel neere them should have any rest of them. But I thinke it is not Gods will: For I may compare them to a young horse that knoweth not his strength, whome a little childe ruleth and guideth with a bridle, for all his great strength: for if hee did, neither childe nor man could rule him. Their warres are holden against the Crimme Tartarians and the Nagaians.

I will stand no longer in the rehearsall of their power and warres. For it were too tedious to the reader. But I will in part declare their lawes, and punishments, and the execution of justice. And first I will begin with the commons of the countrey, which the gentlemen have rule on: And that is, that every gentleman hath rule and justice upon his owne tenants. And if it so fall out that two gentlemens servants or tenaunts doe disagree, the two gentlemen examine the matter, and have the parties before them, and soe give the sentence. And yet cannot they make the ende betwixt them of the controversie, but either of the gentlemen must bring his servant or tenant before the high judge or justice of that countrey, and there present them, and declare the matter and case. The plaintiffe sayth, I require the law; which is graunted: then commeth an officer and arresteth the party defendant, and useth him contrarie to the lawes of England. For when they attach any man they beate him about the legges, untill such time as he fineth suerties to answere the matter: And if not, his handes and necke are bound together, and he is led about the towne and beaten about the legges, with other extreme punishments till he come to his answere: And the Justice demaundeth if it be for debt, and sayth: Owest thou this man any such debt? He will perhaps say nay. Then sayth the Judge: art thou able to denie it? Let us heare how? By othe sayth the defendant. Then he commandeth to leave beating him till further triall be had.

Their order in one point is commendable. They have no man of Law to pleadeth his owne cause, and giveth bill and answere in writing: contrarie to the order in England. The complaint is in maner of a supplication, & made to the Dukes Grace, and delivered him into his owne hand, requiring to have justice as in his complaint is alleaged.

The duke giveth sentence himself upon all matters in the Law. Which is very commendable, that such a Prince wil take paines to see ministration of justice. Yet notwithstanding it is wonderfully abused: and thereby the Duke is much deceived. But if it fall out that the officers be espied in cloking the trueth, they have most condigne punishment. And if the plaintife can nothing proove, then the defendant must take his othe upon the crucifixe whether he bee in the right or no. Then is demanded if the plaintife be any thing able further to make proofe: if hee bee not; then sometimes he will say, I am able to proove it by my body and hands, or by my champions body, so requiring the Campe. After the other hath his othe, it is graunted as well to the one as to the other. So when they goe to the field, they sweare upon the Crucifixe, that they bee both in the right, and that the one shall make the other to confesse the trueth before they depart foorth of the field: and so they goe both to the battell armed with such weapons as they use in that countrey: they fight all on foote, & seldome the parties themselves do fight, except they be Gentlemen, for they stand much upon their reputation, for they wil not fight, but with such as are come of as good an house as themselves. So that if either partie require the combate, it is granted unto them, and no champion is to serve in their roome: wherein is no deceit: but otherwise by champions there is. For although they take great othes upon them to doe the battell truely, yet is the contrary often seene: because the common champions have none other living. And as soone as the one party hath gotten the victory, hee demandeth the debt, and the other is carried to prison, and there is shamefully used till he take order. There is also another order in the lawe, that the plaintife may sweare in some causes of debt. And if the partie defendant be poore, he shalbe set under the Crucifixe, and the partie plaintife must sweare over his head, and when hee hath taken his othe, the Duke taketh the partie defendant home to his house, and useth him as a bond-man, and putteth him to labour, or letteth him for hier to any such as neede him, untill such time as his friends make provision for his redemption: or else hee remaineth in bondage all the dayes of his life. Againe there are many that will sell themselves to Gentlemen or Marchants to bee their bond-men, to have during their life meate, drinke and cloth, and at their comming to have a piece of mony. Yea and some will sell their wives and children to bee bawdes and drudges to the byer. Also they have a Lawe for Fellons and pickers contrary to the Lawes of England. For by their law they can hang no man for his first offence; but may keepe him long in prison, and oftentimes beate him with whips and other punishment: and there he shall remaine untill his friends be able to bayle him. If he be a picker or a cut-purse, as there be very many, the second time he is taken, he hath a piece of his Nose cut off, and is burned in the forehead, and kept in prison till hee finds sureties for his good behaviour. And if he be taken the third time, he is hanged. And at the first time he is extremely punished and not released, except hee have very good friends, or that some Gentleman require to have him to the warres: And in so doing, he shall enter into great bonds for him: by which meanes the countrey is brought into good quietnesse. But they be naturally given to great deceit, except extreme beating did bridle them. They be naturally given a hard living as well in fare as in lodging. I heard a Russian say, that it was a great deale merrier living in prison then foorth, but for the great beating. For they have meate and drinke without any labour, and get the charitie of well disposed people: But being at libertie they get nothing. The poore is very innumerable, and live most miserable: for I have seene them eate the pickle of Hearring and other stinking fish: nor the fish cannot be so stinking nor rotten, but they will eate it and praise it to be more wholesome then other fish or fresh meate. In mine opinion there be no such people under the sunne for their hardnesse of living. Well, I will leave them in this poynt, and will in part declare their Religion. They doe observe the lawe of the Greekes with such excesse of superstition, as the like hath not bene heard of. They have no graven images in their Churches, but all painted, to the intent they will not breake the comandement: but to their painted images they use such idolatrie, that the like was never heard of in England. They will neither worship nor honour any image that is made forth of their owne countrey. For their owne images (say they) have pictures to declare what they be, and howe they be of God, and so be not ours: They say, Looke how the Painter or Carver hath made them, so we doe worship them, and they worship none before they be Christened. They say we be but halfe Christians because we observe not part of the olde law with the Turks. Therefore they call themselves more holy than us. They have none other learning but their mother tongue, nor will suffer no other in their countrey among them. All their service in Churches is in their mother tongue. They have the olde and newe Testament, which are daily read among them: and yet their superstition is no lesse. For when the Priests doe reade, they have such tricks in their reading, that no man can understand them, nor no man giveth eare to them. For all the while the Priest readeth, the people sit downe and one talke with another. But when the Priest is at service no man sitteth, but gagle and ducke like so many Geese. And as for their prayers they have but little skill, but use to say As bodi pomele: As much to say, Lord have mercy upon me. For the tenth man within the land cannot say the Pater noster. And as for the Creede, no man may be so bolde as to meddle therewith but in the Church: for they say it shoulde not bee spoken of, but in the Churches. Speake to them of the Commandements, and they will say they were given to Moses in the law, which Christ hath nowe abrogated by his precious death and passion: therefore, (say they) we observe little or none thereof. And I doe beleeve them. For if they were examined of their Lawe and Commaundements together, they shoulde agree but in fewe poynts. They have the Sacrament of the Lords Supper in both kindes, and more ceremonies then wee have. They present them in a dish in both kindes together, and carrie them rounde about the Church upon the Priestes head, and so doe minister at all such times as any shall require. They bee great offerers of Candles, and sometimes of money, which wee call in England, Soule pense, with more ceremonies then I am able to declare. They have foure Lents in the yeere, whereof our Lent is the greatest. Looke as we doe begin on the Wednesday, so they doe on the Munday before: And the weeke before that they call The Butter weeke: And in that weeke they eate nothing but Butter and milke. Howbeit I beleeve there bee in no other countrey the like people for drunkennesse. The next Lent is called Saint Peters Lent, and beginneth alwayes the Munday next after Trinitie sunday, and endeth on Saint Peters even. If they should breake that fast, their beliefe is, that they should not come in at heaven gates. And when any of them die, they have a testimoniall with them in the Coffin, that when the soule commeth to heaven gates it may deliver the same to Saint Peter, which declareth Lent beginneth fifteene dayes before the later Lady day, and endeth on our Lady Eeven. The fourth Lent beginneth on Saint Martins day, and endeth on Christmas Even: which Lent is fasted for Saint Philip, Saint Peter, Saint Nicholas, and Saint Clement. For they foure be the principall and greatest Saints in that countrey. In these Lents they eate neither Butter, Egges, Milke, nor Cheese; but they are very straitely kept with Fish, Cabbages, and Rootes. And out of their Lents, they observe truely the Wednesdayes and Fridayes throughout the yeere: and on the Saturday they doe eate flesh. Furthermore they have a great number of Religious men: which are blacke Monks, and they eate no flesh throughout the yeere, but fish, milke and Butter. By their order they should eate no fresh-fish, and in their Lents they eate nothing but Coleworts, Cabbages,. salt Cowcumbers, and other rootes, as Radish and such like. Their drinke is like our peny Ale, and is called Quass. They have service daily in their Churches; and use to goe to service two houres before day, and that is ended by day light. At nine of the clocke they goe to Masse: that ended, to dinner: and after that to service againe: and then to supper. You shall understand that at every dinner and supper they have declared the exposition of the Gospel that day: but howe they wrest and twine the Scripture and that together by report it is wonderfull. As for whoredome and drunkennesse there be none such living: and for extortion, they be the most abhominable under the sunne. Nowe judge of their holinesse. They have twise as much land as the Duke himselfe hath: but yet he is reasonable even with them, as thus: When they take bribes of any of the poore and simple, he hath it by an order. When the Abbot of any of their houses dieth, then the Duke hath all his goods moveable and unmoveable: so that the successour buieth all at the Dukes hands: and by this meane they be the best Fermers the Duke hath. Thus with their Religion I make an ende, trusting hereafter to know it better.

"Of Muscovie"

One of Chancelour's pilots, Clement Adams, also wrote an account of what he had seen and learned about Russia. The following excerpts from his narrative supplement that written by Chancelour. (Hakluyt, op. cit., vol. 1, pp. 285, 292.)

NOVOGORODE. Next unto Mosco, the Citie of Novogorode is reputed the chiefest of Russia: for although it be in Majestie inferior to it, yet in greatnesse it goeth beyond it. It is the chiefest and greatest Marte Towne of all Moscovie: and albeit the Emperours seate is not there, but at Mosco, yet the commodiousnesse of the river, falling into that gulfe, which is called Sinus Finnicus, whereby it is well frequented by Marchants, makes it more famous than Mosco it selfe. This towne excels all the rest in the commodities of flaxe and hempe: it yeeldes also hides, honie, and waxe. The Flemings there sometimes had a house of Marchandize, but by reason that they used the like ill dealing there, which they did with us, they lost their privileges, a restitution whereof they earnestly sued for at the time that our men were there. But those Flemings hearing of the arrivall of our men in those parts, wrote their letters to the Emperour against them, accusing them for pirats and rovers, wishing him to detaine, and imprison them. Which things when they were knowen of our men, they conceived feare, that they should never have returned home. But the Emperour beleeving rather the Kings letters, which our men brought, then the lying and false suggestions of the Flemings, used no ill intreatie towards them.

Of the forme of their private houses, and of the apparell of the people.

The common houses of the countrey are every where built of beames of Firre tree: the lower beames doe so recieve the round holownesse of the uppermost, that by the meanes of the building thereupon, they resist, and expell all winds that blow, and where the timber is joined together, there they stop the chinks with mosse. The forme & fashion of their houses in al places is foure square, with streit and narrow windoes, whereby with a transparent casement made or covered with skinne like to parchment, they receive the light. The roofes of their houses are made of boords covered without with ye barke of trees: within their houses they have benches or griezes hard by their wals, which commonly they sleepe upon, for the common people knowe not the use of beds: they have stooves wherein in the morning they make a fire, and the same fire doth either moderately warme, or make very hote the whole house.

The apparell of the people for the most part is made of wooll, their caps are picked like unto a rike or diamond, broad beneath, and sharpe upward. In the maner of making whereof, there is a signe and representation of nobilitie: for the loftier or higher their caps are, the greater is their birth supposed to be, and the greater reverence is given them by the common people.

John the Dread and his Court

As a direct result of the Willoughby-Chancelour Expedition and the negotiations between England and Russia which grew out of it, Queen Mary sent one Osep (Joseph) Napea as ambassador to John's court. A portion of one of Napea's reports is given below. (Hakluyt, op. cit., vol. 1, pp. 420–425, passim.)

The 14 of September, 1557, we were commanded to come unto the Emperour, and immediatly after our comming we were brought into his presence, unto whom each of us did his duetie accordingly, and kissed his right hand, his majestie sitting in his chaire of estate, with his crowne on his head, and a staffe of goldsmiths worke in his left hand well garnished with rich and costly stones: and when we had all kissed his hand and done our dueties, his majestie did declare by his interpreter that we were all welcome unto him, and into his countrey, & thereupon willed us to dine with him: that day we gave thanks unto his majestie, and so departed untill the dinner was readie.

When dinner time approached, we were brought againe into the Emperours dining chamber, where we were set on one side of a table that stoode over against the Emperours table, to the end that he might wel behold us al: and when we came into the foresayd chamber, we found there readie set these tables following.

First at the upper end of one table were set the Emperour his majestie, his brother, & the Emperour of Cazan, which ts prisoner. About two yardes lower sate the Emperour of Cazan his sonne, being a child of five yeeres of age, and beneath him sate the most part of the Emperors noble men.

And at another table neere unto the Emperours table, there were set a Monke all alone, which was in all points as well served as the Emperour. At another table sate another kind of people called Chirkasses, which the Emperour entertaineth for men of warre to serve against his enemies. Of which people and of their countrey, I will hereafter make mention.

All the tables aforesayde were covered onely with salt and bread, and after that we had sitten a while, the Emperour sent unto every one of us a piece of bread, which were given and delivered unto every man severally by these words: The Emperour and great Duke giveth the bread this day, and in like manner three or foure times before dinner was ended, he sent unto every man drinke. All the tables aforesayd were served in vessels of pure and fine golde, as well basons and ewers, platters, dishes and sawcers, as also of great pots, with an innumerable sorte of small drinking pottes of divers fashions, whereof a great number were set with stone. As for costly meates I have many times seene better: but for change of wines, and divers sorts of meads, it was wonderfull: for there was not left at any time so much void roome on the table, that one cuppe more might have bin set, and as far as I could perceive, all the rest were in the like maner served.

In the dinner time there came in six singers which stood in the midst of the chamber, and their faces towards the Emperor, who sang there before dinner was ended three severall times, whose songs or voices delighted our eares little or nothing.

The Emperour never putteth morsell of meate in his mouth, but he first blesseth it himselfe, & in like maner as often as he drinketh: for after his maner he is very religious, & he esteemeth his religious men above his noble men.

This dinner continued about the space of five houres, which being ended, and the tables taken up, we came into the midst of the chamber, where we did reverence unto the Emperors majestie, and then he delivered unto every one of us with his own hands a cup of mead, which when every man had received and drunke a quantity thereof, we were licenced to depart, & so ended that dinner. And because the Emperour would have us to be mery, he sent to our lodging the same Evening three barrels of meade of sundry sortes, of the quantitie in all of one hogshed. . . .

The Emperors majestie useth every yeare in the moneth of December, to have all his ordinance that is in the citie of Mosco caried into the field which is without the Suburbs of the citie, and there to have it planted and bent upon two houses of Wood filled within with earth: against which two houses there were two faire white markes set up, at which markes they discharge all their ordinance, to the ende the Emperour may see what his Gunners can doe. They have faire ordinance of brasse of all sortes, bases, faulcons, minions, sakers, culverings, cannons double and royall, basiliskes long and large, they have sixe great pieces whose shot is a yard of height, which shot a man may easily discerne as they flee: they have also a great many of morter pieces or potguns, out of which pieces they shoote wild fire.

The 12 of December the Emperors Majestie and all his nobility came into the field on horsebacke, in most goodly order, having very fine Jennets & Turkie horses garnished with gold & silver abundantly. The Emperors majestie having on him a gown of rich tissue, & a cap of skarlet on his head, set not only with pearles, but also with a great number of rich and costly stones: his noble men were all in gownes of cloth of gold, which did ride before him in good order by 3. & 3. and before them there went 5000 harquebusiers, which went by 5 and 5 in a rank in very good order, every of them carying his gun upon his left shoulder, and his match in his right hand, and in this order they marched into the field where as the aforesayd ordinance was planted.

And before the Emperors majestie came into the field, there was a certaine stage made of small poles which was a quarter of a mile long, and about threescore yardess off from the stage of poles were certaine pieces of ice of two foot thicke, and six foote high set up, which ranke of ice was as long as the stage of poles, and as soone as the Emperors majestie came into the field, the harquebusiers went upon the stage of poles where they setled themselves in order. And when the Emperors majestie was setled where he would be, and where he might see all the ordinance discharged and shot off, the harquebusiers began to shoot off at the banke of ice, as though it had bin in any skirmish or battel, who ceased not shooting, untill they had beaten all the ice flat on the ground.

After the handguns, they shot off their wild fire up into the aire, which was a goodly sight to behold. And after this, they began to discharge the smal pieces of brasse, beginning with the smallest and so orderly bigger and bigger, untill the last and biggest. When they had shot them all off, they began to charge them againe, and so shot them al off 3 times after the first order, beginning with the smallest, and ending with the greatest. And note that before they had ended their shooting, the 2 houses that they shot unto were beaten in pieces, & yet they were very strongly made of Wood and filled with earth, being at the least 30 foote thicke. This triumph being ended, the Emperour departed and rode home in the same order that he came foorth into the field. The ordinance is discharged every yeare in the moneth of December, according to the order before mentioned.

. . .

Every yeare upon the 12 day they use to blesse or sanctifie the river Moscua, which runneth through the citie of Moco, after this maner.

First, they make a square hole in the ice about 3 fadoms large every way, which is trimmed about the sides & edges with white boords. Then about 9 of the clocke they come out of the church with procession towards the river in this wise.

First and foremost there goe certaine young men with waxe tapers burning, and one carying a great lanterne: then follow certaine banners, then the crosse, then the images of our Lady, of S. Nicholas, and of other Saints, which images men carie upon their shoulders: after the images follow certaine priests to the number of 100 or more: after them the Metropolitan who is led betweene two priests, and after the Metropolitan came the Emperour with his crowne upon his head, and after his majestie all his noble men orderly. Thus they followed the procession unto the water, & when they came unto the hole that was made, the priests set themselves in order round about it. And at one side of the same poole there was a scaffold of boords made, upon which stood a faire chaire in which the Metropolitan was set, but the Emperours majestie stood upon the ice.

After this the priests began to sing, to blesse and to sense, and did their service, and so by that time that they had done, the water was holy, which being sanctified, the Metropolitan tooke a litle thereof in his hands, and cast it on the Emperour, likewise upon certaine of the Dukes, & then they returned againe to the church with the priests that sate about the water: but that preasse that there was about the water when the Emperor was gone, was wonderful to behold, for there came above 5000 pots to be filled of that water: for that Muscovite which hath no part of that water, thinks himselfe unhappy.

And very many went naked into the water, both men and women and children: after the preasse was a litle gone, the Emperours Jennets and horses were brought to drinke of the same water, and likewise many other men brought their horses thither to drinke, and by that means they make their horses as holy as themselves.

All these ceremonies being ended, we went to the Emperour to dinner, where we were served in vessels of silver, and in all other points as we had bene beforetime.

A Tatar Attack

The Crimean Tatars in 1571 successfully attacked and burned the city of Moscow. The first of the following accounts of this incident is from a letter written at the time; the second, from the famous report by Giles Fletcher. The source for both is: Hakluyt, op. cit., vol. 2, pp. 135, 136, 315.

The Mosco is burnt every sticke by the Crimme the 24. day of May last, and an innumerable number of people: and in the English house was smothered Thomas Southam, Tofild, Waverley, Greenes wife and children, two children of Rafe, & more to the number of 25. persons were stifeled in our Beere seller: and yet in the same seller was Rafe, his wife, John Browne, and John Clarke preserved, which was wonderfull. And there went into that seller master Glover and master Rowley also: but because the heate was so great, they came foorth againe with much perill, so that a boy at their heeles was taken with the fire, yet they escaped blindfold into another seller, and there, as God's will was, they were preserved. The Emperour fled out of the field, and many of his people were caried away by the Crimme Tartar: to wit, all the yong people, the old they would not meddle with, but let them alone, and so with exceeding much spoile and infinite prisoners, they returned home againe. What with the Crimme on the one side, and his crueltie on the other, he hath but few people left. . . .

The greatest and mightiest of them is the Chrim Tartar, (whom some call the Great Can) that lieth South, & Southeastward from Russia, and doth most annoy the country by often invasions, commonly once every yere, sometimes entring very farre within the inland parts. In the yere 1571 he came as farre as the citie of Mosco, with an armie of 200000 men, without any battel, or resistance at al, for that the Russe Emperor (then Ivan Vasiliwich) leading forth his armie to encounter with him, marched a wrong way. The citie he tooke not, but fired the suburbs, which by reason of the buildings (which are all of wood without any stone, brick, or lime, save certaine out roomes) kindled so quickly, and went on with such rage, as that it consumed the greatest part of the citie almost within the space of foure hours, being of 30 miles or more of compasse. Then might you have seene a lamentable spectacle: besides the huge & mighty flame of the citie all on light fire, the people burning in their houses and streetes, but most of all of such as laboured to passe out of the gates farthest from the enemie, where meeting together in a mighty throng, & so pressing every man to prevent another, wedged themselves so fast within the gate, and streets neere unto it, as that three rankes walked one upon the others head, the uppermost treading downe those that were lower: so that there perished at that time (as was said) by the fire & the presse, the number of 800000 people or more.

Oprichnina: the Classic Interpretation

Kasimerz Waliszewski wrote prolifically and brilliantly, if not always accurately about Russian history. His ten monographs, based upon extensive research, deal with the major persons and events from the time of John the Dread through that of Alexander I. This selection is from: Waliszewski, K. (Lady Mary Loyd, Translator), Ivan the Terrible. Philadelphia: J. B. Lippincott Co., 1904. Pp. 240–246.

On December 3, 1564, a Sunday, Ivan had all his treasures, his money, his plate, his gems, his furniture, and his ikons, packed on to waggons, and, followed by a huge train, many boïars chosen out of various towns, and his whole Court and household, he left his capital with his second wife, Maria Temrioukovna, a half-savage Circassian, as violent and passionate as himself. For some time, nobody in Moscow heard anything of him, and no man knew whither he had betaken to the village of Kolemskoié, where bad weather detained him for a fortnight. He then spent some days at Taïninskoié, another village in the neighbourhood of Moscow, and near the Troïtsa, and finally took up his quarters in a suburb of the little town of Alexandrov, north of Vladimir. There he revealed the motives and object of his unwonted exodus. On January 3, a courier reached Moscow with a letter from the Tsar to the Metropolitan. In it the monarch, after dwelling at length on the misdeeds of the *voievodes* and officials of every degree, and the clergy, upper and lower, declared he had 'laid his anger' on them all, from the greatest to the least. This was what was called the *Opala*, a sort of ban, which placed all those affected by it in a state of disgrace and incapacity to perform any active function, whether about the Court or in the service of the State. At the same time Ivan announced his determination to leave the Empire and establish himself 'wherever God should counsel him to go.' There was something contradictory in the terms of the message. The Tsar was abdicating, then? And yet he used his authority to punish his subjects. But this message, again, was accompanied by another, addressed to the merchants and 'the whole Christian population of Moscow,' and its contents were to the effect that, as far as they were concerned, the Tsar had no cause of complaint, nor any feeling of displeasure.

What was the meaning of it all? Probably people knew that as partially then as they do now. But so accustomed were the Russians of that day to riddles, that they did not hesitate as to the course they should pursue. The Tsar, displeased with a certain section of his subjects, was meditating some dark design against them, the nature of which would not be revealed till its effects made themselves felt. What was apparent at the present moment was merely the usual setting of the scene. Obediently all men prepared to bear their part in the coming comedy. The boïars betrayed the correct amount of emotion, the populace rose up, shouted aloud, and was much affected. The merchants offered money, the most eloquent fashion of proving their share in the general feeling, and the Metropolitan was called upon to intercede with the Sovereign. Ivan was entreated not to forsake his people, but to rule as best pleased him, and mete out such treatment as he deemed fit to those of whom he thought he had reason to complain. A deputation took its way to Alexandrov, and the Tsar allowed himself to be mollified, but he made his own conditions; he intended to keep all traitors and rebels in disgrace, to put some to death, and confiscate their fortunes, and he would not go back to Moscow till he had organized his *Opritchnina*.

This, in the common parlance of that day, was the name applied to the dowry paid to the wives of the great Princes. At banquets, certain special dishes which the amphitryon kept in front of himself, and the contents of which he divided amongst his chief guests, were called *Opritchnyié*. And a particular class of peasants settled on the lands belonging to certain monasteries were known as *Opritchniki* (from *opritch*, a part). Let my readers now cast their minds back to the ukase of October 10, 1550, which gave the district of Moscow a territorial and political constitution of its own, and settled a selection of *sloojilyié lioodi*, taken from every rank of the nobility and every province of the Empire, within its borders. Without any essential modification of the existing order of things, solely by virtue of this transplanting process and of a change in the nature of the tenure, Ivan had summoned the men just transplanted to form the nucleus of a court, an administration, and an army, all reorganized on a new basis. The *Opritchnina* of 1565, in its fundamental idea, was neither more nor less than the extension and wider application of this original plan.

Ivan now divided his Empire into two parts. One of these was to preserve its ancient organization and its ancient government—in other words, the *voiévodes*, lieutenants, bailiffs, and *Kormlenchtchiki* of every kind were to carry on the administration as it had been carried on hitherto, a college presided over by two boïars taking the place of the Supreme Council as the centre of the various services. The other part, which comprised various portions of the country, a certain number of towns, and several quarters of the capital city, was converted into a sort of dowry or appanage, which the Tsar kept for himself, and on which, with a thousand boïars or boïars' sons, chosen by himself, he was about to follow up the experiment of 1550.

I must insist here on the scope of this experiment, which may be summed up in two principal features: the transformation of the freehold properties into fiefs, and the removal of owners from one holding to another. To take the proprietor of an hereditary freehold, subject to no charges of any kind, to tear him out of the corner of the soil on which, for centuries past, his fortune and importance had sprouted, grown, and struck their roots; to part him from his natural adherents, break off all his natural connections, and, having thus uprooted him, isolated him, and removed him from his own sphere, to set him down elsewhere, as far as possible from his native place, to give him another property, but on a life interest, and on terms exacting service, and the payment of the usual taxes from him, and thus to make a new man of him, a man without a past, without backing, defenceless—this was the constitution of the system. So, at least, we may suppose, for Ivan never revealed his secret. But, though the fact has hitherto passed unnoticed, the evident connection between the two decrees, that of 1550 and that of 1565, does indicate a *system*, and all we know of the two measures, of their character and their application, is in favour of the correctness of the conjecture I have adopted, after the example of Monsieur Platonov, who seems to me to have approached nearest to the truth ('Essays on the History of the Political Disturbances of the Sixteenth and Seventeenth Centuries,' St. Petersburg, 1899, i. 137, etc.), and Monsieur Milioukov, whom I am inclined to think a little further removed from it ('Essays on the History of Russian Culture,' 1896, i. 147, etc.), by his determination to see nothing, either in Ivan's reforms or in Peter the Great's, except financial expedients.

Ivan's horizon was certainly wider than this. During his lifetime, and even after his death, silence has been kept, by superior order, concerning all this undertaking. Questions on the subject must have been foreseen when an embassy from the Tsar went into Poland in 1565. Muscovite diplomacy was in the habit of providing against possible indiscretions by foreseeing such inquiries, and dictating the replies beforehand. Thus, if the envoys were asked what the *Opritchnina* was, they were to answer, 'We do not know what you mean. There is no *Opritchnina*. The Tsar is living in the place of residence he has been pleased to choose, and such of his servants as have given him cause for satisfaction are there with him, or are settled close by; the others are a little farther off—that is all. If peasants, who know nothing about anything, talk about an *Opritchnina*, people should not listen to them.' The same orders were given to other embassies, in 1567 and 1571 ('Collections of the Imperial Society of Russian History,' vol. lxxi., pp. 461, 777).

But facts began to speak in their turn. The part of the Empire originally given up to the *Opritchnina* was gradually increased till it comprised a good half of the Tsar's dominions, and till the *Opritchniki* number 5,000, instead of 1,000, men. In 1565, the provinces of Vologda, Oustioug, Kargopol, Mojaïsk, and Viazma were added; in 1566, all the Stroganov properties; in 1571, part of the province of Novgorod. Each fresh extension was accompanied by a distribution of freehold lands or fiefs, taken from their original possessors. These received territorial compensation exchange, the *Opritchnina* who had been substituted for themselves on their old holdings—unless, indeed, they had the good luck to be received into the *Opritchnina* without undergoing expropriation or exile. And the districts claimed by the *Opritchnina* in the central provinces were just those in which the remnants of the old appanage system were largest and strongest. It laid its hand, thus, on the hereditary patrimonies of the Dukes of Rostov, Starodoub, Souzdal, and Tchernigov. It swallowed up, too, the territories 'beyond the Oka.' The ancient inheritance of yet another group of appanaged Princes—the Odoiévski, the Vorotynski, and the Troubetskoï. Some of these, Prince Feodor Mikhaïlovitch Troubetskoï, Prince Nikita Ivanovitch Odoiévski, allowed themselves to be enrolled under the banners of the new system, and proved its zealous servants. The rest were forced to migrate. Thus, in exchange for Odoiév, Prince Michael Ivanovitch Vorotynski received Starodoub-Riapolovski, some hundred miles further west. Other landowners in that country were given lands in the districts near Moscow, round Kolomna, Dmitrov, and Zvenigorod.

One instance will suffice to show the practical consequences of this moving to and fro. Out of 272 freehold domains in the district of Tver, the proprietors of 53 gave the State no service of any sort or kind; some of these were the lieges of Prince Vladimir Andreiévitch, the Tsar's cousin, the others owed service to descendants of the old appanaged Princes, one to an Obolenski, another to a Mikoulinski, or a Mstislavski, a Galitzine, a Kourliatev, or even to some plain boïar. The *Opritchnina* altered all this. It brought about a general devolution of everything that was owed on the one and only master who had set himself in the place of all the others. At the same time it suppressed the local military bodies, thanks to which the Tsar's unruly vassals frequently made themselves more dangerous to him than to his foes; it proclaimed the law of individual service, and over all the country its rule affected, it established a system of direct and indirect taxation levied for the benefit of the Treasury.

Swayed, too, by economic and financial considerations which I do not dream of denying, it most particularly sought to obtain possession of the towns along the great trade routes of the Empire, and to this change of system—this is worth observing—the traders affected were by no means opposed. The representatives of the English company craved admission to it as a favour. The Stroganovs followed the same course. The only roads between the capital and the frontier which escaped the *Opritchnina's* attention were those running southward, through Toula and Riazan, and these were probably omitted because no apparent advantage was to be derived from their inclusion.

It is only with the greatest difficulty that any full inventory of the territories annexed by the *Opritchnina* has been drawn up, for documents precise enough to serve as a foundation for the calculation do not exist. It seems to have ended by comprising a great slice of the central and northern provinces, bailiwicks, and towns, and of the coast as well (*pomorié*, all the districts of the *Zamoskovié* (Moscow region), all the regions 'beyond the Oka,' and two districts (*piatiny*) out of the five which constituted the province of Novgorod—those of Obonéjé and Biéjetsk. The *Opritchnina*, the northern boundaries of which thus rested on the 'great ocean-sea,' as it was called in those days, cut cornerwise into the territory handed over to the old system, the *Ziémchtcina* (*ziémia*, land), as it was called, while it ran southward as far as the Oka, eastward towards Viatka, and westward up to the Lithuanian-German frontier. The provinces of Perm, Viatka, and Riazan on the east, and the dependencies of Pskov and Novgorod, with the frontier towns, Vielikié-Louki, Smolensk, and Siéviérsk, on the west, were not included in the new organization. Southwards the two zones of the *Ziemchtchina* were connected by the Ukraine and by wild steppes (*dikoié pole*).

In the centre of the country, as I have just said, the *Opritchnina* only affected certain localities, and the bailiwicks, towns, and town quarters under its jurisdiction were mingled in unimaginable and indescribable confusion with those of the *Ziemchtchina*. But of the important towns, the old system only kept Tver, Vladimir, and Kalouga, and it may be said generally speaking, to have been pushed back towards the far ends of the Empire. This was a reversal of the history of Rome, which assumed immediate authority over her most distant provinces, so as to draw the steel-clad circle of her legions round the heart of the Empire.

Towards the year 1572, the *Opritchnina* lost its original name. It was then called the Court (*dvor*). At that moment it already possessed all the characteristics of a regularly constituted State organization, and in its working, indeed, it preserved all the administrative forms of the old system, so much so that it is not easy to discover, from any document of that period, which of the two branches thus wedded together has issued it. In principle the *Opritchnina* did not even suppress the *Miestnitchestov:* it simply forbade the application of that system within its own borders. Its action and that of the *Ziemchtchina* ran on parallel and concerted lines, and both possessed a common centre in the Offices of War and Finance. *Diaks* attached to these two branches of the Government overlooked the distribution of the business connected with each. It seems probable, at least, that affairs followed this course, for the coexistence and concerted labours of the two sets of officials are an established fact, which suffices to destroy the legend of an *Opritchnina* confined to the duties of a mere political police force. In 1570, authentic documents show us the *Opritchnina* and the *Ziémchtchina* summoned to deliberate, through their respective representatives—all of them boïars—on questions connected with the Lithuanian frontier. The discussions were held separately, but an agreement was reached. There is no trace of any enmity or conflict. That very same year, and the next, detachments furnished by both organizations went campaigning together against the Tartars, and perfect harmony appears to have reigned between them.

The solution of the problem confronting Ivan furnished by the *Opritchnina* was certainly not wholly satisfactory. What was needed was something which would have annulled the twofold contradiction which afflicted his whole Empire: a contradiction in politics arising out of the fact that the historical march of events had endued the Sovereign with an absolute power founded on a democratic basis, which he was obliged to exercise through an aristocracy; a social contradiction resulting from the fact that this same Sovereign, in his quest of fresh food for the growing ambitions of his Empire, and to insure it, was forced into making over his productive class, bound hand and foot, to the arbitrary will of his non-producers, his 'men who serve,' his soldiers, and his tax collectors.

As far as the destruction of the aristocratic element is concerned, the *Opritchnina* proved a failure. But it shook it sorely, and Ivan's plan probably did not go beyond this result. Apart from the great and mighty lords it enrolled, and by enrolling disarmed them, only an elect few of the aristocratic class escaped, such as Prince Ivan Feodorovitch Mstislavski and Prince Ivan Dmitriévitch Biélski, both of them placed at the head of the *Ziémchtchïna*— two inoffensive utility actors. It destroyed all the political importance of the class, and the effect of this was to be manifest, even after Ivan's death, in the preponderating part played by parvenus created by him, such as Zakharine and Godounov. Others of his subjects, of yet humbler extraction, peasants, Cossacks, Tartars, recruited in increasing numbers to fill the gaps caused by his confiscations and wholesale executions, not to mention his *transplantings,* ended by forming a comparatively numerous body, and a powerful weapon for levelling and democratic purposes. 'My father's boïars, and my own have learnt to be traitors,' wrote Ivan to Vassiouchka Gria noï, 'so we have resolved to call on you, vile varlets, and from you we expect fidelity and truth!' Vasiouchka replied: 'You are like unto God! You make a little man into a great man!'

This revolution—for a revolution it certainly was—could not be accomplished without some kind of struggle. Everywhere, in the lowest classes, where it broke bonds that were centuries old, in the towns and country places, into which it introduced strange elements, on the great landed properties which it divided up, calling a new agricultural and industrial proletariat into existence, it wounded innumerable feelings and interests. I have already shown how, by destroying the ancient administrative autonomy of the peasants, now made subject to their new proprietors in all those matters as to which they had hitherto dealt directly with the State, it contributed, indirectly, to the establishment of serfdom. It had a more immediate effect in quickening the current of emigration amongst the elements thus disaggregated, and hastening, through the increase of the calls made on them, the exhaustion of the resources dependent on those elements. From this point of view, Ivan's undertaking is open to much blame, and his conflict with Poland was soon to demonstrate the weak side of a work in other respects useful, and no doubt even necessary. Its execution was attended by excesses of various sorts, which cannot fail to attract severe judgment. But the historian cannot regard the *Opritchnina* from one point of view only. . . .

An Evaluation of the Reign of John the Dread

This evaluation of the results of John's reign is typical not only of M. Waliszewski's dashing style, but also of his keen insight and original approach. The source is: Waliszewski, op. cit., pp. 394–399.

The massacres ordered by Ivan have been notoriously exaggerated by his enemies and his detractors, the first egging on the second. Kourbski mentions the *entire destruction* of families—such as the Kolytchev, the Zabolotski, the Odiévski, the Vorotynski—all of which appear in the inventories of the following century. The gaps created in the ranks of the aristocracy by emigration were certainly much larger, and even so they were not entirely emptied. Ivan's conduct in this particular was not dictated by any fixed principle, and he himself endeavoured to ensure the future of three great houses—the Mstislavski, the Glinski, and the Romanov—whose fidelity seemed guaranteed by lack of connections in the country, by a material state of dependence, or by family relationships. The two first-named families had just arrived from Lithuania, and the last was related to the Sovereign's own house.

The principal factors in the weakening of the aristocratic element were economic causes and political measures. In the course of the sixteenth century, as a result of the condition of debt to which everybody had been reduced, landed property began to crumble away of itself in the boïars' hands. In the registers kept by a moneylender of that period, named Protopopov, is a list of noble names, and the archives of the Monastery of St. Cyril afford proof of the continuance of this state of things. In 1557 Prince D. D. Oukhtomski, whose credit with such persons as Protopopov had probably become exhausted, sold the monks a village, with twenty-six hamlets round it, for 350 roubles; three years later he received 150 roubles, and gave up possession of four more outlying places. At about the same time the community acquired a large property, also belonging to this family, and in 1575 it received another lot of meadows, 'for Masses'; so that, in one way or another, the whole of the Oukhtomski properties passed into the same hands (see Rojkov, 'Agriculture . . . in the Sixteenth Century,' 1899, p. 396).

Now, this financial distress amongst the great families was the direct consequence of the new political system, and the obligations it had cast upon them. Universal service implied residence at Court, or near it, even if it did not imply active military service or the performance of some official function or other. When the nobles had lived on their family properties they had found it hard enough to draw a scanty income from them. Once they left them, they were very soon ruined. Thereupon came the Opritchnina—that is to say, wholesale dispossession under the conditions I have already described— and this dealt the position, economic and political, of the persons concerned its death-blow. Ivan's system of guarantees increased the effect of emigration twofold—nay, a hundredfold, seeing that for every fugitive there were from ten to a hundred persons who had to pay for him. Except for the Stroganovs, you will not find a single instance of a large fortune in the aristocratic class which escaped this other form of massacre. If in the present day some few authentic descendants of Rurik and Guédymine, such as the Troubetzkoïs, the Galitzines, the Kourakines, the Soltykovs, the Boutourlines, still possess some worldly wealth, their opulence only dates from the eighteenth century, and from the favours of some Empress.

And thus a class which already differed from the Western aristocracies, in that the feudal principle was entirely absent from it, was completely and democratically levelled. The hierarchy of the service did indeed create new titles and fresh prerogatives, guaranteed by the *miéstnitchestvo*, but these were not corporative elements in the Western signification of the term. They rather tended to break up the family and reduce it to atoms, on which the hold of the absolute power continued, and grew perpetually stronger.

This revolution, which had seemed destined to benefit the popular element, brought it nothing but the bitterest fruit. The new system was a house of two stories, both built on the same plan. The officials were upstairs, the serfs below, and slavery everywhere. But in this matter all Ivan the Terrible did was to complete or carry on that which had been the Moscow programme for two centuries past, and the *Opritchnina* itself, was no more than an extension of the policy applied by the Tsar's predecessors to all their conquered towns and territories. It was a sort of colonization backwards. As to colonization in the normal direction, it continued to depend on private enterprise; but Ivan opened a wider field for it.

Westwards his expansive policy failed. It would not be just to cast all the responsibility for this on him. If Peter the Great, when he took the same road 150 years later, had found his way barred by a man like Batory, instead of by a madman like Charles XII., the result of the Battle of Poltava might have been very different. Eastward, Kazan, Astrakan, and Siberia make up a noble score in Ivan's favour.

From the economic point of view, the conquest of Kazan did not result in the immediate advantages that might have been expected from it. The trade of that place, which the Tartars had exaggerated in their desire to induce the Sultan to retake possession of the town, was a disappointment to the English merchants. Ivan did not fail to seek compensation elsewhere. When he offered the Swedish traders a free passage through his dominions, even for going to India, he stipulated for a similar privilege for his own subjects, in their enterprises, existing or to be undertaken, with Lübeck and even with Spain. In 1567 the chroniclers mention the departure of Russian merchants for Antwerp and London, and in 1568 English authorities mention the presence on the banks of the Thames of two such Muscovites, Tviérdikov and Pogoriélov, who were taken to be Ambassadors. They performed both offices, no doubt, and devoted their endeavours partly to diplomacy and partly to mercantile affairs.

The development of industry in Ivan's time was rather superficial; the field was widened by the annexation of the eastern provinces. The acquisition of the Lower Volga favoured the development of fisheries. There were ninety-nine establishments of this kind at Péréiaslavl in 1562. After the occupation of the banks of the Kama by the Stroganovs, and the discovery of salt-mines near Astkrakan, the salt-works there attained great importance.

Ivan's financial policy does not call for praise. It may be summed up as a series of expedients, all savouring more or less of robbery. Fletcher mentions several of these. Governors of provinces were treated with the utmost tolerance till they had gorged themselves with plunder, when they were forced to give up the spoil. The same system was applied to monasteries, which were allowed to heap up wealth in the same way. There were temporary seizures or monopolies of certain forms of produce or merchandise, thus made to bring in very large profits. Fines were imposed on officials for imaginary offences. The English diplomat tells an almost incredible story about a capful of *live flies* demanded on his way from the Moscow municipality.

The taxes themselves were managed in the most senseless manner that could have been devised. Generally speaking, every fresh need resulted in the imposition of a fresh tax, and there never was the smallest care as to fitting the burdens to the means of those who had to bear them, nor the slightest prudence as to killing the goose that laid the golden eggs. By the time the end of the reign was reached, the bird's laying-powers were very nearly exhausted.

The interests best served by the conquest of Kazan and Astrakan were those of the Church, whose borders were thus enlarged. Gourii, first Archbishop of Kazan, made a good many converts among the Tartars; but this triumph of orthodox proselytism was counterbalanced, till the close of Ivan's reign, by the prolonged resistance of the paganism still existing in the interior of his dominions, and especially in certain districts in the province of Novgorod. As to the Tsar's attempts at religious reform, which he soon abandoned or only carried on in a most perfunctory fashion, they produced no appreciable result at all, and the intellectual and moral condition of the clergy was in no way altered by them.

Yet, from a more general point of view, there was a visible increase in the intellectual life of the country. Though the schools planned in 1551 never were anything but plans, though printing did not get beyond the stage of rudimentary attempt, the author of the letters to Kourbski did none the less witness a certain upward trend of ideas, which took their flight out of the narrow walls of the cloister and the confined circle of religious discussion into the world of secular thought. This beginning of the secularizing process was one of the great conquests of Ivan's reign.

On the other hand, Ivan, even in his international dealings, could not or would not break with certain barbarous traditions which harmonized but ill with progress such as this. Just as in past times, envoys sent to his Court were often treated as if they had been prisoners of war, and the fate of his genuine prisoners of war continued to be lamentable. The happiest thing they could expect was to be sold or given to the monasteries as serfs. Occasionally they were simply thrown into the water. In 1581, Ivan gave orders that when the Swedish 'tongues'—in other words, the persons belligerents or non-belligerents, taken with a view to obtaining information—had served their purpose, they were all to be killed. Polish and Swedish captives were used as current coin in the exchanges arranged by Tartar merchants on the Constantinople markets.

But as he stood, with all his faults and vices, his errors and his crimes, his weaknesses and his failures, Ivan was popular, and his was a genuine popularity, which has stood the twofold test of time and of misfortune. This, too, is a result. In the cycle of the historic songs of Russia, the Tsar holds the place of honour, and is shown in by no means repulsive colours; he is open to every feeling of humanity—severe, but just, and even generous. True, indeed, his sacerdotal majesty lifts him up so high and surrounds him with such an aureole of glory that no critic would dare to lay his hand upon him. But we feel that, in spite of that, all the popular sympathies are with him. When he indulges in savage orgies over the corpses of the vanquished Tartars, or hands one of his boïars over to the executioner on the merest hint of suspicion, the masses are on his side; they applaud the carnage, and rejoice in their master's joy. Even when they cannot applaud, they shut their eyes respectfully, religiously, and cast a mantle of decent fiction over that which makes their consciences revolt. The populace will not admit that the Tsar killed his own son. The Tsar of the *bylines* bestows a noble reward on Nikita Romanovitch, who at the peril of his own life, saves that of the victim; for the moment the order was given the Sovereign had repented. This Tsar has some weaknesses, indeed; he is apt to be choleric, and his first instinct is not always his best. Under the walls of Kazan, whither the intentional anachronism of the poets has already brought Ermak and even Stenka Razin, Ivan taxes his artificers, who have been too slow about blowing up a mine, with treason, and threatens them with the gallows. The chiefs, cowards in this case, as always, according to the popular historians, shelter themselves behind their subordinates. But one young soldier speaks boldly in defence of his fellows, the mine blows up, and the Tsar acknowledges his own mistake and the merit of the humble hero. Passing into the conquered town, Ivan spares the Tsarine Helen, who comes out to meet him bearing bread and salt, and is content with having her baptized by force and thrust into a convent. But he has the eyes of the Tsar Simeon, who shows less goodwill and greater dignity, torn out of his head; and here again, the populace applauds the victor.

This is the theory of morals peculiar to the period to which Ivan's name is attached. The ideal it evolves is one of material greatness and brute force— a twofold postulate to which the Russian race has proved itself ready to sacrifice everything else, end pursued, and the extent of the sacrifice it has entailed. In this other dream, Tsar and people both had their part, and they were to make it a living reality on the day when Peter took Ivan's place, and completed the incarnation which gave birth to modern Russia. But when Ivan died, this work was in the embryonic stage. His labour had been one of destruction, more especially, and he had no time to build up again. Still less had he ensured the continuity of his effort. The legacy left his country by the luckless adversary of Batory, the murderer of the Tsarevitch, his own heir, was a war with Poland and a state of anarchy. The germ was there, too, of a fresh inroad by the rivals of the Slavonic West, destined, under the shelter of the false Dmitri, to reach Moscow itself, and of a triumphant return of the aristocratic oligarchy, which, favoured by the general crumbling of the unfinished edifice, was to recover its old advantages. This was to be the history of the seventeenth century. But Peter the Great was not to guard his inheritance any better against future risks; and yet, after a fresh eclipse, Catherine was to come, even as he had come. The strength was there still, increased materially and tempered morally—the imperishable pledge of a mighty future.

Oprichnina: A Marxist Interpretation

Ablest of the Marxist historians was Professor Mikhail Nikolaevich Pokrovskii who became actively associated with the Bolsheviks at the time of the 1905 Revolution. Forced to emigrate, Pokrovskii lived in exile from 1908 to 1917 and during the period wrote his chief historical work, A History of Russia from the Earliest Times. *After the Bolshevik Revolution he became a very powerful leader in the People's Commissariat of Education and was responsible for the persecution of some of his non-Bolshevik professional colleagues. As editor, archivist and bureaucrat he was the dominant figure in Soviet historiography until his death in 1932. Not long thereafter the Party line changed and Pokrovskii and his school were condemned as "Trotskyite agents of fascism" and "enemies of the people."*

The following excerpt presents a Marxist interpretation of the struggle between Ivan Grozny (John the Dread) and his boyars. It is presented here by way of contrast to the more familiar accounts. The source is: M. N. Pokrovsky, (J. D. Clarkson and M. R. M. Griffiths, Editors and Translators), History of Russia. *New York: International Publishers, 1931. Pp. 142–150.*

There is nothing more unjust than to deny that there was a principle at stake in Ivan's struggle with the boyars or to see in this struggle only political stagnation. Whether Ivan IV was himself the initiator or not—most probably he was not—yet this "oprichnina" was an attempt, a hundred and fifty years before Peter's time, to found a personal autocracy like the Petrine monarchy. The attempt was premature, and its collapse was inevitable; but he who ventured it unquestionably ranked above his contemporaries. The "warriors' " road lay over the dead body of old Muscovite feudalism, a fact which made the "warriors" progressive, whatever the motives that immediately guided them. The old votchinas within the realm were now the only source of land at the expense of which middling pomestye landholding might expand, the tsar's treasury, the only source of money capital. But to enjoy either it was necessary to take into their own hands the power that was in the hands of a hostile group, which held it not only with all the tenacity of secular tradition but also with all the force of moral authority. Peresvetov might have the audacity to declare that politics is higher than religion, "justice" than "faith," but his rank-and-file partisans would not have countenanced such a sentiment, much less have expressed it, and still less have acted upon it. The coup of January 3, 1565, was an attempt, not to infuse a new content into old forms, but to set up new forms alongside the old and, without touching old institutions, so to act that they might serve merely as a screen for new men who did not have the right to enter these institutions as actual masters. Peter was bolder; he simply seated his officials in the boyar duma and called it the Senate, and every one made the best of it. But by Peter's time the boyars were in the eyes of all already a "riven and falling tree." A hundred and fifty years earlier the tree had, it is true, begun to lose its foliage, but its roots were still firmly fixed in the ground and were not to be torn out at the first wrench.

Denying to the "oprichnina" significance in principle, historians have, on the other hand, depicted its appearance in most dramatic form. How Ivan the Terrible, on an unusually solemn expedition, suddenly left for Alexandrovsk (they generally explain the location of this mysterious place that so unexpectedly bobs up in Russian history), how from there he began to exchange letters with the "people" of Moscow, and what effect this produced—all this of course, you have read many times, and there is no need to repeat the story. In fact, like everything in the world, the event was much more workaday. Alexandrovsk had long been Ivan's summer residence; in the chronicle we constantly find him there in the intervals between military campaigns and his very frequent trips through the Muscovite provinces, on pilgrimage and for economic purposes. The suddenness of his departure is considerably weakened by the fact that Ivan IV took with him all his valuable movables—all the "holy things, icons and crosses, with gold and precious stones adorned," his gold and silver vessels, his whole wardrobe and his whole treasury, and mobilised his whole guard—"the nobles and knights selected from all the towns, whom the sovereign had taken to be with him." All these preparations could not have been made in one day, or in two—especially since the tsar's courtiers were ordered to "go with wives and with children." Setting forth, Ivan did not disappear somewhere for a whole month; the Muscovites knew very well that the tsar celebrated the day of Nicholas the Miracle-Worker (December 6) at Kolomensk, that on Sunday, the 17th, he was at Taininsk, and that on the 21st he arrived at Troitsa to spend Christmas. In a word, this was the customary itinerary of his trips to Alexandrovsk, except for the passing visit at Kolomensk, explained by the thaw and the overflow of the rivers, unusual in December. While the fact that matters moved so swiftly at Moscow—on the 3rd the courier arrived with the tsar's letter, on the 5th the embassy from Moscow was already at Alexandrovsk—clearly shows that the month had not been wasted, that while the tsar was travelling, his partisans had been carefully preparing the dramatic effect that so beguiles modern historians. If during this month Ivan the Terrible really grew grey and aged by twenty years, as foreigners relate, it was, of course, not because he had been quaking all this time for the success of his unexpected "prank," but because to break with the whole past was not an easy thing for a man reared and educated in a feudal environment. Peter was born in a different environment, and from childhood was accustomed to think and act without reference to custom. Ivan in his thirty-fifth year had to smash everything; that was something to grow grey over. That material strength lay in his hands, that the external, so to speak, physical success of the coup was assured for the tsar and his new counsellors,—this was so evident to all that we find not the least attempt at resistance on the part of the old counsellors. And, of course, not because in their servility they did not dare think of resistance; flight from the tsar of all the Orthodox to the service of the Catholic king of Poland-Lithuania was a leap incomparably greater than would have been an attempt to repeat what Andrew of Staritsa had done only thirty years before when he raised the pomeshchiks of Novgorod against the Moscow government. But now the boyars would have had no one to raise against their foes; the pomeshchiks were siding with Alexandrovsk, and the Moscow townsmen were now siding with the pomeshchiks, not with the boyars. The gosts, the merchants, and "all Orthodox Christendom of the city of Moscow," in answer to the gracious letter of the tsar, which was read at an assembly of the higher Muscovite merchantry, "in order that they might retain no doubt, that there was no wrath upon them and displeasure," unanimously replied that they "stand not for the sovereign's evildoers and traitors and themselves destroy them." And in the embassy despatched to Alexandrovsk, along with bishops, abbots, and boyars, we find gosts, merchants, and even simple "common people," who, it would seem, had no place at all in a matter of state. The Moscow townsmen gave up their allies of yesterday. For negotiations with them, in all probability, the future *oprichniks* had needed a whole month, and their decision definitely tipped the scales to the side of the coup. What evoked this decision is easily determined from the sequel; commercial capital itself was associated with the oprichnina, and this promised advantages that no amount of protection from the Princes Shuisky could counter-balance. Soon after the coup we find merchants and gosts acting as official agents of the Muscovite government both at Constantinopole, and in Antwerp, and in England—in all the "seaboard states," toward which they yearned so much; and they were all equipped not only with all sorts of safe-conducts, but also with *"bologodet"* (subsidy) from the tsar's treasury. "Into the oprichnina fell all the chief (trade) routes, with a great part of the towns located along them," says Prof. Platonov; and here he gives a very convincing list of these towns. "Not for nothing did the English who had business with the northern provinces beg to be taken into the oprichnina: not for nothing did the Stroganovs seek to be included; commercial-industrial capital, of course, needed the support of the administration that controlled the country and, as is evident, did not fear the horrors attendant upon our conception of the oprichnina." Why should capital fear what it itself had helped to create?

Just as the "reforms" had been the work of a coalition of the bourgeoisie and the boyars, the coup of 1564 was carried out by a coalition of the townsmen and the petty vassals. This explains, in all probability, one peculiarity in the tsar's letter as read at Moscow which hitherto has not attracted great attention but possesses great interest. In form the coup was an act of self-defence on the part of the tsar against his great vassals, who "had begun to betray." But these "treasonous matters" are mentioned very obscurely and only at the end of the letter. On the other hand, the document develops three points in detail. First, the conduct of the boyars during the minority of Ivan IV—"who committed treasons and caused losses to his realm before he the soverign reached maturity." Second, that the boyars and voevodas "seized upon the soverign's lands" and, holding great pomestves and votchinas, by unlawful means gathered great wealth. This motif, taken straight from Peresvetov, envisaged a quite definite fact, which had already led to a partial confiscation of votchina lands three years before the coup. On January 15, 1562, Ivan IV "decreed with the boyars (not with 'all the boyars'!): whatever old votchinas are in the possession of the princes of Yaroslavl, Starodub, Rostov, Tver, Suzdal, Obolensk, Beloozero, Vorotynsk, Mosalsk, Trubetsk, Odoev, and *other serving princes,* those princes shall not sell nor exchange their votchinas." The right of these men to dispose of their lands had been reduced to a minimum; they could bequeath estates only to their sons. If there were no sons, the votchina reverted to the sovereign, who did what was necessary—"ordered his soul," *i.e.,* dealt out lands to the Church for prayers for the soul of the deceased, allotted a portion "for life" to his widow, dowries

for his daughters, etc. What is more, the sovereign confiscated, without compensation, all votchinas of this category that had been sold fifty or twenty
but not less than ten years before the publication of the edict. The basis for
such an extraordinary measure was that under decrees even of the times of
Ivan III and of Vasily III, father of Ivan the Terrible, princes' votchinas
might be sold only with the licence of the grand prince: a new landholder
meant a new vassal and, in accordance with widespread feudal custom, not
peculiar to Russia, the suzerain must be asked for his consent. Votchina lands
were simply treated as the sovereign's, and arbitrary disposal of them as
embezzlement of treasury property. Finally, the third point made in the
letter—it, too, occurs in Peresvetov—is the aversion of the boyars to an active
foreign policy; they "did not wish to take care of all Orthodox Christendom"
and did not wish to defend Christendom against the Crimea, and Lithuania,
and the Germans. These were all themes popular among wide masses, and
those who read or heard the proclamation did not. of course, stop to question
why in his thirties the tsar had a mind to punish the boyars for sins and faults
committed in the days of his youth. Had it been a palace coup organised from
above, these demagogic methods would, of course, be very strange; but the
point is that in December, 1564—January, 1565, as in 1547, and as in the
'thirties under the Shusikys, the masses of the people were on the stage and
must be addressed in a language they could understand.

Yet the content of this proclamation, as of any other, by no means defined
the current policy of those who published it. When business negotiations
began between Ivan the Terrible and the Moscow deputation that had come
to Alexandrovsk, the tsar put forward demands relevant to the immediate
causes of the coup, demands that had nothing to do with recollections of the
days of his youth. In these demands two aspects must be distinguished. In
the first place, Ivan insisted on fulfilment of the promise, given freely by
the merchantry of Moscow and subscribed to by the terror-stricken boyars
and officials left in Moscow, namely, to surrender his foes to him uncondition-
ally. In fulfilment of this demand in February of the same year (the negotiations had taken place, we shall remember, at the beginning of January) a
number of boyars of old princely families were executed, others given the
tonsure, still others banished for life to Kazan with their wives and children,
while the property of all of them was confiscated. Banishments and executions
at once gave into Ivan's hands a supply of land probably sufficient to remunerate the immediate participants in the coup d'état. To secure them a money
salary the tsar and grand prince decreed that *for his expenses* a hundred
thousand rubles (about 5,000,000 rubles gold, according to the reckoning of
Professor Klyuchevsky) be taken from the treasury of the land. From this
aspect the coup was only the affair of a small circle, but Ivan was serving
the interests of a class. Not all the pomeshchiks could be satisfied out of the
proceeds of a few banishments and a small appropriation from the treasury

chest. The form devised to satisfy the "warriors" was as old-fashioned as the content of the change effected was new. In the state the sovereign could not give orders without his boyars, the suzerain without his curia; but on his "domain," in his court economy, he was as absolute as was any votchinnik at home. Conversion of half the state, and the wealthiest part of it at that, into the sovereign domain made it possible to hold sway over a vast territory without consulting the feudal aristocracy. Without violating the decrees of 1550, he might here do all that he liked, not only without the assent of "all the boyars" but without that of even a single boyar; the right of the boyar college did not, of course, extend to the sovereign's court management. And for the tsar's court, now increased to colossal proportions, a very old name was at first chosen; the tsar demanded that "from his realm be set apart an *oprichnina.*" This was the name given to the estates in former times portioned out to widowed princesses "for life." Later there came into use the more accurate and newer term, *dvor* (court). In its arrangements this "dvor" was an exact copy of an old sovereign's votchina, so exact that one modern scholar has even doubted whether the oprichnina had any institutions of its own, or whether new men were not simply seated in the old institutions along with the old "clerks," for management of "oprichnina" (select) matters. While effecting a genuine revolution, the creators of the oprichnina apparently strove to conceal all juridical traces of it, and we cannot but see in this fact a conscious purpose, issuing from the same impulses as were reflected in the tsar's proclamation that we analysed above. The people needed a scapegoat, and they were assured that the coup was directed against individual persons, however numerous, the old order remaining inviolate.

The sovereign's dvor began to expand enormously, but it never came to embrace the whole country, and the *zemshchina,* which administered all that remained outside the limits of the oprichnina, was more than merely decorative. The best study of the territorial composition of the oprichnina has been made by Professor Platonov; we shall therefore describe it in his words. "The territory of the oprichnina," says this scholar, "taking form gradually, in the 1570's comprised the towns and townships lying in the central and northern parts of the state. . . . Resting to the north on the 'great sea-ocean,' the lands of the oprichnina cut into the zemshchina like a wedge, dividing it in two. On the east were left to the zemshchina the Perm and Vyatka towns, the Low country and Ryazan; on the west the border towns 'of the German frontier' (Pskov and Novgorod), 'of the Lithuanian frontier' (Veliky Luki, Smolensk, and others), and the Seversk towns. To the south these two zones of the 'zemshchina' were connected by the frontier towns and the 'wilderness.' The Moscow North, the Littoral, and two of the Novgorod pyatinas the oprichnina ruled integrally; in the central provinces its lands were interspersed with those of the zemshchina in a patchwork that is as hard to understand as to describe," but that can nevertheless be characterised in a general way. "In the oprichnina administration," says Professor Platonov in another passage, "were gathered the *old appanage lands*." The goal toward which the law of 1562 had striven, by inches and within legal bounds, was attained three years later, all at once and by a revolutionary road; the most valuable part of the territory of the Muscovite state, together with the greatest commercial-industrial centres, became immediately an appanage of the sovereign where, unrestrained by the old boyars, the men of the "Peresvetov party" now began to hold sway. The old authority retained the worst and poorest regions; it is curious that just as Kazan had become a place of exile, so the newly-conquered lands in the west were now willingly ceded to the "men of the zemshchina." The Novgorodin "knights" from the Obonezh and Bezhets pyatinas, when these were taken into the oprichnina, received pomestyes around Polotsk, on the recently annexed and very insecure Lithuanian lands.

The tsar's edict, even in the brief résumé preserved in the official Moscow chronicle (like a great part of the official documents of this stormy time, the original edict on the oprichnina has not come down to us), states quite distinctly in whose favour and for what proximate goal all this shuffling of lands was effected. "And to give to the sovereign in the oprichnina princes and nobles and knights, of court and town, 1,000 head, *and to them to give pomestyes in those towns which he took into the oprichnina*," says the chronicle. Modern historians have seen in this something in the nature of the establishment of a corps of gendarmes charged with the detection of domestic sedition, the protection of the tsar, and the defence of the realm. But tempting as is this analogy, one must not yield to it. Police work, and that alone, has always been the task of gendarmes; not they—there were too few of them for that— but the standing army has constituted the material support of the government. The oprichniks represented something quite different. The detachment of a thousand knights really constituted a corps of ten or twelve thousand men, inasmuch as each appeared for service with several armed bondsmen. Not a single large landholder, even among the former appanage princes, could have such a retinue; even two or three together of the very greatest probably would not have raised so many men. Besides this mounted detachment there were in the oprichnina infantry as well—"and he ordered the *streltsy* to be to him especially," says the chronicler. To cope with a "domestic foe" such a force would have been more than sufficient; the grand prince of Moscow was now, in his single person, the very greatest of the Muscovite feudatories. The oprichnina army was a logical corollary to the oprichnina dvor of the sovereign, and, it must be added, the very possibility of forming this dvor had been conditioned by the existence of such an army; for the novelty of this part of the edict was not the appearance close to the tsar of a "thousand heads" but the quartering of them on lands unceremoniously taken from other holders—"and the votchinniks and pomeshchiks who are not to be in the oprichnina (the sovereign) bade to be removed from these towns." A detachment of a thousand had long existed, even from 1550, and in the coup of January 3, 1565, it had played exactly the same role as did the Paris garrison in the coup of December 2, 1851. This tsar's guard, founded, as we shall recall, by the boyar government as a concession to the upper crust of the pomeshchik masses, had become a powerful weapon in the struggle of the pomeshchik class against the boyars themselves. Only by its closeness to the tsar is to be explained the fact that "base-born" now standing around him dared so audaciously to raise their hands against their feudal lords of yesterday, and in the tsar's train this "picked" thousand, moving "after the tsar with men and with horses, with all service attire," was, of course, the most imposing part. In all probability, all of them, with the exception of a few individuals, were taken into the oprichnina corps, so that actually the latter represented nothing new. And as before, so also after 1565, along with its military and police significance it continued to have political significance; there entered it the "better," *i.e.*, the most influential, elements of the local bodies of nobles. As Klyuchevsky has explained in detail, they did not while in the tsar's guard lose contact with the local communities; in other words, they were the political leaders of the pomeshchik class, and distribution of oprichnina lands to them signified nothing else than that along with the old, boyar-votchina state, now more than cut in half, there arose a new, noble-pomestye state.

Clear proof that the coup meant merely the establishment of a new class régime, of which the tsar's personal authority was only a tool, and not the personal emancipation of Ivan from the boyar tutelage that had trammelled him, is the singular assembly that was held in Moscow in the summer of the following year (1566). On June 28, 1566, the Tsar and Grand Prince Ivan IV of All Rus "spoke" with Prince Vladimir of Staritsa, with his archbishops, bishops, and the whole "Holy Synod," with all the boyars and officials, with the princes, with the knights and military servitors, "and with the gosts, and with the merchants, and with all trading men." The subject of this conversation was a truce proposed by the Polish-Lithuanian government on the basis of *uti possidetis*. Thus, it was proposed that Ivan the Terrible renounce his original goal, the seizure of all Livonia. In essence, the question was put: is it worth while to keep on fighting? And it is significant that Ivan and his new government did not presume to decide this question upon their own responsibility but referred it to the judgment of all those in whose name they ruled. It would, of course, be very naïve to imagine that this "zemsky sobor of 1566," the first sobor whose existence is historically indisputable, even remotely resembled modern popular representative bodies; the very worst of them, if only in theory, speaks in the name of the "people," a concept alien to feudal Europe. Mediaeval assemblies, both in Russia and in the West, represented, not the people but "estates," *états, Stände*. From this point of view the important point about the sobor of 1566 was the rôle of two "estates" whose political importance had hitherto scarcely been openly recognised—the petty vassals or "nobility," and the bourgeoisie. Quantitatively the pomeshchiks even constituted a majority of this assembly. The Livonian War had been decided on by the boyars, unwillingly and under pressure from below, and now they were asking the "warriors" and the "trading folk" whether this war should be continued. Between 1557 and 1566 lay a wide gulf. The details of the debates at the sobor, assuming there were debates, have not come down to us. The one-day sobor was, of course, not summoned to learn the opinions of those assembled; the pomeshchiks and the merchants were summoned because their opinions were already known, and it was hoped that the authority of their voices would reinforce the authority of the declarations of Muscovite diplomacy. The sobor was, in essence, a ceremonial façade; the real negotiations took place, of course, before the sobor met and, apparently, by no means inspired the government with the confidence breathed by the solemn speeches at the sobor itself. The sobor decided to continue the war, come what might; but in fact *negotiations* were continued and a few years later terminated in a truce on the conditions proposed by the Poles. The suzerain Ivan needed the formal promise of his new, extensive vassalage to "die for the sovereign on horseback" in case of war, and of the trading men to give their last red cent if need be. This promise Ivan received, and on their speeches the military-serving and the trading men kissed the cross. Whether or not to make the fullest use of this promise was the business of the government, which was, of course, guided by the views of its supporters, but these views were not ascertained at the sobor.

Russia at the time of Boris Godunov

One of the most famous descriptions of Russia by a foreign observer was written by Giles Fletcher who went to Moscow as the ambassador of Queen Elizabeth of England. Western and Russian historians both count Fletcher's The Russe Commonwealth *as a first class source. Fletcher arrived at Moscow in 1588, four years after the death of John the Dread. The weak Feodor was on the throne, but the real power was in the hands of the nobles, especially Nikita Romanov and Boris Godunov. The excerpt from* The Russe Commonwealth *which follows was taken from Hakluyt, op. cit., vol. 2, pp. 284–301, passim.*

The description of the countrey of Russia, with the bredth, length, and names of the Shires.

The whole Countrey being nowe reduced under the government of one, conteineth these chiefe Provinces or Shires. Volodmer, (which beareth the first place in the Emperours stile, because their house came of the Dukes of that Countrey) Mosco, Nisnovogrod, Plesko, Smolensko, Novogrod velica (or Novogrod of the low Countrey) Rostove, Yaruslave, Bealozera, Rezan, Duyna, Cargapolia, Meschora, Vagha, Ustuga, Ghaletsa. These are the naturall shires perteyning to Russia, but farre greater and larger then the shires of England, though not so well peopled. The other Countreys or provinces which the Russe Emperours have gotten perforce added of late to their other dominion, are these which followe, Twerra, Youghoria, Permia, Vadska, Boulghoria, Chernigo, Oudoria, Obdoria, Condora, with a great part of Siberia: where the people though they be not naturall Russes, yet obey the Emperour of Russia, and are ruled by the Lawes of the Countrey, paying customes and taxes, as his owne people doe. Besides these he hath under him the kingdomes of Cazan and Astracan, gotten by conquest not long since. As for all his possession in Lituania (to the number of 30. great Townes and more,) with Narve and Dorp in Livonia, they are quite gone, being surprised of late yeeres by the Kings of Poland and Sweden. These Shires and Provinces are reduced all into foure Jurisdictions, which they call Chetfyrds (that is) Tetrarchies, or Fourthparts.

The whole Countrey is of great length and breadth. From the North to the South (if you measure from Cola to Astracan which bendeth somewhat Eastward) it reacheth in length about 4260. verst, or miles. Notwithstanding the Emperour of Russia hath more territorie Northward, farre beyond Cola unto the River of Tromschua, that runneth a hundred verst, welnigh beyond Pechinga, neere to Wardhouse, but not intire nor clearely limited, by reason of the kings of Sweden and Denmarke, that have divers Townes there, as well as the Russe, plotted together the one with the other: every one of them clayming the whole of those North parts as his owne right. The breadth (if you go from that part of his territorie that lyeth farthest Westward on the Narve side, to the parts of Siberia Eastward, where the Emperour hath his garrisons) is 4400. verst or thereabouts. A verst (by their reckoning) is a 1000. pases, yet lesse by one quarter then an English mile. If the whole dominion of the Russe Emperour were all habitable, and peopled in all places, as it is in some, he would either hardly holde it all within one regiment, or be over mightie for all his neighbour Princes.

OF THE SOILE AND CLIMATE. The soyle of the Countrey for the most part is of a sleight sandie moulde, yet very much different one place from another, for the yeeld of such things as grow out of the earth. The Countrey Northwards towards the parts of S. Nicholas and Cola, and Northeast towards Siberia, is all very barren, and full of desert woods by reason of the Climate, and extremitie of the colde in Winter time. So likewise along the River Volgha betwixt the Countreys of Cazan, and Astracan: where (not withstanding the soyle is very fruitfull) it is all unhabited, saving that upon the river Volgha on the Westside, the Emperour hath some fewe Castels with garisons in them. This happenth by meanes of the Crimme Tartar, that will neither himselfe plant Townes to dwel there, (living a wild and vagrant life) nor suffer the Russe (that is farre off with the strength of his Countrey) to people those parts. From Vologda (which lyeth almost 1700. verst from the port of S. Nicholas downe towards Mosco, and so towards the South part that bordereth upon the Crimme, (which conteineth the life space of 1700. verst or there abouts) is a very fruitfull and pleasant Countrey, yeelding pasture, and corne, with woods and waters in very great plentie. The like is betwixt Rezan (that lyeth Southeast from Mosco) to Novogrod and Vobsko, that reach farthest towards the Northwest. So betwixt Mosco, and Smolensko, (that lyeth Southwest towards Lituania) is a very fruitfull and pleasant soile.

The whole Countrey differeth very much from it selfe, by reason of the yeere: so that a man would marveile to see the great alteration and difference betwixt the Winter, and the Summer Russia. The whole Countrey in the Winter lieth under snow, which falleth continually, and is sometime of a yard or two thicke, but greater towards the North. The Rivers and other waters are all frosen up a yard or more thicke, how swift or broade so ever they bee. And this continueth commonly five moneths, viz. from the beginning of November till towardes the ende of March, what time the snow beginneth to melt. So that it would breede a frost in a man to looke abroad at that time, and see the Winter face of that Countrey. The sharpenesse of the aire you may judge of by this: for that water dropped downe or cast up into the aire congealeth into yce before it come to the ground. In the extremitie of Winter, if you holde a pewter dish or pot in your hand, or any other mettall (except in some chamber where their warme stoaves bee) your fingers will friese fast unto it, and drawe off the skinne at the parting. When you passe out of a warme roome into a colde, you shall sensibly feele your breath to waxe starke, and even stifeling with the colde, as you drawe it in and out. Divers not onely that travell abroad, but in the very markets, and streetes of their Townes, are mortally pinched and killed withall: so that you shall see many drop downe in the streetes; many travellers brought into the Townes sitting dead and stiffe in their Sleds. Divers lose their noses, the tips of their eares, and the bals of their cheekes, their toes, feete, &c. Many times (when the Winter is very hard and extreeme) the beares and woolfes issue by troupes out of the woods driven by hunger, and enter the villages, tearing and ravening all they can finde: so that the inhabitants are faine to flie for safegard of their lives. And yet in the Sommer time you shal see such a new hiew and face of a Countrey, the woods (for the most part which are all of firre and birch) so fresh and so sweete, the pastures and medowes so greene and well growen, (and that upon the sudden) such varietie of flowers, such noyse of birdes (specially of Nightingales, that seeme to be more lowde and of a more variable note then in other Countreys) that a man shall not lightly travell in a more pleasant Countrey.

And this fresh and speedy growth of the Spring there seemeth to proceede from the benefite of the snow: which all the Winter time being spread over the whole Countrey as a white robe, and keeping it warme from the rigour of the frost, in the Spring time (when the Sunne waxeth warme, and dissolveth it into water) doeth so throughly drench and soake the ground, that is somewhat of a sleight and sandie mould, and then shineth so hotely upon it againe, that it draweth the hearbes and plants foorth in great plentie and varietie, in a very short time. As the Winter exceedeth in colde, so the Sommer inclineth to over much heat, specially in the moneths of June, July and August, being much warmer then the Sommer aire in England.

The Countrey throughout is very well watred with springs, rivers, and Ozeraes, or lakes. Wherein the providence of God is to be noted, for that much of the Countrey being so farre inland, as that some part lieth a thousand miles and more every way from any Sea, yet it is served with faire Rivers, and that in very great number, that emptying themselves one into another, runne all into the Sea. Their lakes are many and large, some of 60. 80. 100. and 200. miles long, with breadth proportionate.

The chiefe Rivers are these, First, Volgha, that hath his head or spring at the roote of an Aldertree, about 200. verst above Yaruslave, and groweth so bigge by the encrease of other Rivers by that time it commeth thither, that it is broad an English mile and more, and so runneth into the Caspian sea, about 2800. verst or miles of length.

The next is Boristhenes (now called Neper) that divideth the Countrey from Lituania, and falleth into the Euxin sea.

The third Tanais or Don, (the ancient bounder betwixt Europe and Asia) that taketh his head out of Rezan Ozera, and so running through the Countrey of the Chrim Tartar, falleth into the great Sea, lake, or meare, (called Maeotis) by the Citie of Azov. By this River (as the Russe reporteth) you may passe from their Citie Mosco to Constantinople, and so into all those parts of the world by water, drawing your boate (as their maner is) over a little Isthmus or narrowe slip of land, a few versts overthwart. Which was proved not long since by an Ambassadour sent to Constantinople, who passed the River of Moscua, and so into another called Ocka, whence hee drew his boat over into Tanais, and thence passed the whole way by water.

The fourth is called Duyna, many hundred miles long, that falleth Northward into the bay of S. Nicholas, and hath great Alabaster rockes on the bankes towards the sea side.

The fifth Duna, that emptieth into the Baltick sea by the towne Riga.

The sixth Onega, that falleth into the Bay of Solovetsko 90. verst from the port of S. Nicholas. This River, below the towne Cargapolia, meeteth with the River Volock, that falleth into the Finland Sea by the towne Yama. So that from the port of S. Nicholas into the Finland sea, and so into the Sound, you may passe all by the water, as hath bene tried by the Russe.

The seventh Suchana, that floweth into Duyna, and so into the North sea.

The eight Ocka, that fetcheth his head from the borders of the Chrim, and streameth into Volgha.

The ninth Moscua, that runneth thorow the Citie Mosco, and giveth it the name.

There is Wichida also a very large and long river that riseth out of Permia, and falleth into Volgha. All these are rivers of very large streames, the least to be compared to the Thames in bignesse, and in length farre more, besides divers others. The Pole at Mosco is 55. degrees 10. minutes. At the port of S. Nicholas towards the North 63. degrees and 50. minutes.

The native commodities of the Countrey.

For kindes of fruites, they have Apples, peares, plummes, cherries, red and blacke, (but the blacke wilde) a deene like a muske millian, but more sweete and pleasant, cucumbers and goords (which they call Arbouse) rasps, strawberies, and hurtilberies, with many other beries in great quantitie in every wood and hedge. Their kindes of graine are wheat, rie, barley, oates, pease, buckway, psnytha, that in taste is somewhat like to rice. Of all these graines the Countrey yeeldeth very sufficient with an overplus quantitie, so that wheate is solde sometime for two alteens or ten pence starling the Chetfird, which maketh almost three English bushels.

Their rie is sowed before the Winter, all their other graine in the Spring time, and for the most part in May. The Permians and some other that dwell farre North, and in desert places, are served from the parts that lye more Southward, and are forced to make bread sometimes of a kinde of roote (called Vaghnoy) and of the middle rine of the firre tree. If there be any dearth (as they accompted this last yeere Anno 1588. wheat and rie being at 13. alteens, or 5. shillings five pence starling the Chetfird) the fault is rather in the practise of their Nobilitie that use to engrosse it, then in the Countrey it selfe.

The native commodities of the Countrey (wherewith they serve both their owne turnes, and send much abroad to the great enriching of the Emperor, and his people) are many & substantiall. First, furres of all sorts. Wherein the providence of God is to be noted, that provideth a naturall remedie for them, to helpe the naturall inconvenience of their Countrey by the cold of the Climat. Their chief furres are these, Blacke fox, Sables, Lusernes, dun fox, Martrones, Gurnestalles or Armins, Lasets or Miniver, Bever, Wulverins, the skin of a great water Rat that smelleth naturally like muske, Calaber or gray squirrel, red squirrel, red & white fox. Besides the great quantitie spent within ye Countrey (the people being clad al in furres the whole winter) there are transported out of the Countrey some yeeres by the merchants of Turkie, Persia, Bougharia, Georgia, Armenia, and some other of Christendom, to the value of foure or five hundred thousand rubbles, as I have heard of the merchants. The best Sable furre groweth in the countrey of Pechora, Momgosorskoy and Obdorskoy, the worser sort in Siberia, Perm, & other places. The blacke foxe and red come out of Siberia, white and dunne from Pechora, whence also come the white wolfe, and white Beare skin. The best Wulverin also thence and from Perm. The best Martrons are from Siberia, Cadam, Morum, Perm, and Cazan. Lyserns, Minever, and Armins, the best are out of Gallets, and Ouglits, many from Novogrod and Perm. The Beaver of the best sort breedeth in Murmonskey by Cola. Other common furres and most of these kindes grow in many, and some in all parts of the Countrey.

The second commoditie is of Waxe, whereof hath bene shipped into forreigne countreys (as I have heard it reported by those that best know it) the summe of 50000. pood yeerely, every pood conteyneth 40. pound, but now about 10000. pood conteyneth 40. pound, but now about 10000. pood a yeere.

The third is their Honie, whereof besides an exceeding great quantitie spent in their ordinary drinkes (which is Mead of all sorts) and their other uses, some good quantitie is caried out of the countrey. The chiefe encrease of hony is in Mordua and Cadam neere to the Cheremissen Tartar: much out of Severskoy, Rezan, Morum, Cazan, Dorogobose, and Vasma.

Fourthly, of Tallow they afoord a great waight for transportation: not onely for that their countrey hath very much good ground apt for pasturage of cattell, but also by reason of their many Lents and other fastes: and partly because their greater men use much waxe for their lights, the poorer and meaner sort birch dried in their stoaves, and cut into long shivers, which they call Luchineos. Of tallow there hath bene shipped out of the Realme a few yeeres since about 100000. pood yerely, now not past 30000. or thereabouts. The best yeeld of tallow is in the parts and territories of Smolensko, Yaruslave, Ouglits, Novogrod, and Vologda, Otfer, and Gorodetskey.

An other principall commoditie is their Losh and Cow hide. Their Losh or Buffe hide is very faire and large. Their bull and cowe hide (for oxen they make none, neither yet weather) is of a small sise. There hath bene transported by merchants strangers some yeres 100000. hides. Now it is decreased to 30000. or thereabouts. Besides great store of goates skinnes, whereof great numbers are shipped out of the countrey. The largest kinde of Losh or Buffe breedeth about Rostove, Wichida, Novogrod, Morum, and Perm. The lesser sort within the kingdome of Cazan.

An other very great and principall commoditie is their Trane oyle, drawen out of the Seal fish. Where it will not be impertinent to shewe the maner of their hunting the Seal, which they make this oyle of: which is in this sort.

Towards the ende of Sommer (before the frost beginne) they goe downe with their boates into the Bay of S. Nicholas, to a cape called Cusconesse or Foxnose, where they leave their boates till the next spring tide. When the Sunne waxeth warme toward the spring, and yet the yce not melted within the Bay, they returne thither againe. Then drawing their boates over the sea yce, they use them for houses to rest and lodge in. There are commonly about 17. or 18. fleete of them, of great large boates, which divide themselves into divers companies, five or sixe boats in a consort.

They that first finde the haunt, fire a beacon, which they carry with them for the nonce. Which being espied by the other companies, by such among them as are appointed of purpose, they come altogether and compasse the Seales round about in a ring, that lie sunning themselves together upon the yce, commonly foure or five thousand in a shoale, and so they invade them every man with his club in his hand. If they hit them on the nose, they are soone killed. If on the sides or backe they beare out the blow, and many times so catch and holde downe the clubbe with their teeth by maine force, that the partie is forced to call for helpe to his fellowes.

The maner of the Seals is when they see themselves beset, to gather all close together in a throng or plumpe, to sway downe the yce, and to breake it (if they can) which so bendeth the yce that many times it taketh the sea water upon it, and maketh the hunters to wade a foote or more deepe. After the slaughter when they have killed what they can, they fall to sharing every boate his part in equall portions; and so they flay them, taking from the body the skin, and the lard or fat with all that cleaveth to the skin. This they take with them, leaving the bodies behind, and so go to shore. Where they digge pits in the ground of a fadome and an halfe deepe, or thereabout, and so taking the fat or lard off from the skinne, they throw it into the pit, and cast in among it hoat burning stones to melt it withall. The uppermost and purest is sold, and used to oile wool for cloth, the grosser (that is of a red colour) they sell to make sope.

Likewise of Ickary or Cavery, a great quantitie is made upon the river of Volgha out of the fish called Bellougina, the Sturgeon, the Severiga and the Sterledey. Whereof the most part is shipped by French and Netherlandish merchants for Italy and Spaine, some by English merchants.

The next is of Flax and Hempe, whereof there hath bene shipped (as I have heard merchants say) at the port of Narve a great part of 100. ships small and great yerely. Now, not past five. The reason of this abating and decrease of this & other commodities, that were wont to be transported in a greater quantitie, is the shutting up of the port of ye Narve towards the Finland sea, which now is in the handes and possession of the Swedes. Likewise the stopping of the passage overland by the way of Smolensko, & Plotsko, by reason of their warres with the Polonian, which causeth the people to be lesse provident in mainteining and gathering these and like commodities, for that they lacke sales. For the growth of flaxe the province of Vobsko, and the countrey about is the chiefe and onely place. For Hempe Smolensko, Dorogobose and Vasma.

The countrey besides maketh great store of salt. Their best salt is made at Stararovse in very great quantitie, where they have great store of salt wels, about 250. verst from the sea. At Astracan salt is made naturally by the sea water, that casteth it up into great hils, and so it is digged downe, and caried away by the merchants and other that wil fetch it from thence. They pay to the Emperor for acknowledgement or custome 3.d. Russe upon every hundred weight. Besides these two, they make salt in many other places of the Realme, as in Perm, Wichida, Totma, Kenitsma, Solovetsky, Ocona, Bombasey, and Nonocks, all out of salt pits, save at Solovetsky, which lieth neere to the sea.

Likewise of Tarre they make a great quantitie out of their firre trees in the countrey of Duyna and Smolensko, whereof much is sent abroad. Besides these (which are all good and substantiall commodities) they have divers other of smaller accompt, that are naturall and proper to that countrey: as the fish tooth (which they call Ribazuba) which is used both among themselves, and the Persians and Bougharians that fetch it from thence for beads, knives, and sword hafts of Noblemen and gentlemen, and for divers other uses. Some use the powder of it against poison, as the Unicornes horne. The fish that weareth it is called a Morse, and is caught about Pechora. These fish teeth some of them are almost 2. foote of length, and weigh 11. or 12. pound apiece.

In the province of Corelia, and about the river Duyna towards the North sea, there groweth a soft rocke which they call Slude. This they cut into pieces, and so teare it into thin flakes, which naturally it is apt for, and so use it for glasse-lanthorns and such like. It giveth both inwards and outwards a clearer light then glasse, and for this respect is better then either glasse or horne: for that it neither breaketh like glasse, nor yet will burne like the lanthorne. Saltpeter they make in many places, as at Ouglits, Yaruslave & Ustiug, and some smal store of brimstone upon the river Volgha, but want skil to refine it. Their iron is somewhat brittle, but a great weight of it is made in Corelia, Cargapolia, & Ustiug Thelesna. Other mine they have none growing within ye realme.

Their beasts of strange kinds are the Losh, the Ollen, the wild horse, the beare, the wolvering, or wood dog, the Lyserne, the Beaver, the Sable, the Martron, the blacke and dunne fox, the white Beare towards the sea coast of Pechora, the Gurnstale, the Laset or Minever. They have a kinde of Squirrell that hath growing on the pinion of the shoulder bone a long tuft of haire, much like unto feathers with a far broader taile then have any other squirrels, which they move and shake as they leape from tree to tree, much like unto a wing. They skise a large space, & seeme for to flie withal, and therefore they cal them Letach Vechshe, that is, the flying squirrels. Their hares and squirrels in Sommer are of the same colour with ours, in Winter the hare changeth her coate into milke white, the squirrel into gray, whereof commeth the Calaber.

They have fallow deere, the roe bucke, & goats very great store. Their horses are but smal, but very swift & hard, they travell them unshod both winter and Sommer, without all regard of pace. Their sheepe are but smal & beare course & harsh wool. Of foule they have divers of the principal kinds: First, great store of hawks, the eagle, the gerfaulcon, the slightfaulcon, the goshawk, the tassel, the sparhawk, &c. But the principal hawke y^t breedeth in the country, is counted ye gerfaulcon. Of other foules their principal kinds are the swan tame & wilde, (whereof they have great store) the storke, the crane, the tedder of the colour of a feasant, but far bigger & liveth in the firre woods. Of feasant and partridge they. have very great plentie. An owle there is of a very great bignesse, more ugly to behold then ye owles of this country, with a broad face, & eares much like unto a man.

For fresh water fish, besides the common sorts (as carpe, pikes, pearch, tench, roach, &c.) they have divers kinds very good and delicate: as the Bellouga or Bellougina of 4. or 5. elnes long, the Ositrina or Sturgion, the Severiga and Sterledy somewhat in fashion and taste like to the Sturgion, but not so thicke nor long. These 4. kinds of fish breed in the Volgha, and are catched in great plenty, and served thence into the whole Realme for a great food. Of the Roes of these foure kinds they make very great store of Icary or Caveary as was said before.

They have besides these that breed in the Volgha a fish called the Riba bela, or white salmon, which they accompt more delicate then they do the red salmon, whereof also they have exceeding great plentie in the Rivers Northward, as in Duyna, the river of Cola, &c. In the Ozera or lake neere a towne called Perislave, not far from the Mosco, they have a smal fish which they cal the fresh herring, of the fashion, and somewhat of the taste of a sea-herring. Their chiefe townes for fish are, Yaruslave, Bealozera, Novogrod, Astracan, and Cazan: which all yeeld a large custome to the Emperour every yeere for their trades of fishing, which they practise in Sommer, but sende it frozen in the Winter time into all parts of the Realme.

THE CHIEFE CITIES OF RUSSIA. The chiefe cities of Russia are Mosco, Novogrod, Rostove, Volodomer, Plesko, Smolensko, Jaruslave, Perislave, Nisnovogrod, Vologda, Ustiug, Colmogro, Cazan, Astracan, Cargapolia, Columna. The city of Mosco is supposed to be of great antiquitie, though the first founder be unknowen to the Russe. It seemeth to have taken the name from the River that runneth on the one side of the towne. Berosus the Chaldean

in his 5. booke telleth that Nimrod (whom other prophane stories cal
Saturne) sent Assyrius, Meduc, Moscus, & Magog into Asia to plant colonies
there, and that Moscus planted both in Asia and Europe. Which may make
some probabilitie, that the citie, or rather the river whereon it is built,
tooke the denomination from this Moscus: the rather because of the climate
or situation, which is in the very farthest part & list of Europe, bordering
upon Asia. The Citie was much enlarged by one Ivan or John, sonne to
Daniel, that first changed his title of duke into King: though that honor continued not to his posterity: the rather because he was invested into it by
the Popes Legate, who at that time was Innocentius the 4. about the yeere
1246. which was very much misliked by the Russe people, being then a part
of the Easterne or Greeke Church. Since that time the name of this city
hath growen more famous, & better knowen to the world: insomuch that
not only the province, but the whole Countrey of Russia is termed by some
by the name of Moscovia the Metropolite city. The forme of this City is
in maner round with 3. strong wals, circuling the one within the other, &
streets lying betwene, whereof the inmost wall, and the buildings closed
within it (lying safest as the heart within the body, fenced and watred
with the river Moscua, that runneth close by it) is all accompted the Emperors castle. The number of houses (as I have heard) through the whole
Citie (being reckoned by the Emperor a little before it was fired by the
Crim) was 41500. in all. Since the Tartar besieged and fired the towne
(which was in the yere 1571.) there lieth waste of it a great breadth of
ground, which before was wel set and planted with buildings, specially that
part on the South side of Moscua, built not long before by Basilius the
Emperor for his garison of souldiers, to whom he gave priviledge to drinke
Mead, and beere at the dry or prohibited times, when other Russes may
drinke nothing but water, and for that cause called this new city by the
name of Naloi, that is skinck or poure in. So that now the city of Mosco
is not much bigger then the city of London. The next in greatnes, & in a
maner as large, is the citie Novograd: where was committed (as the Russe
saith) the memorable warre so much spoke of in stories of the Scythians
servants, that tooke armes against their masters: which they report in
this sort: viz. That the Boiarens or gentlemen of Novograd & the territory
about (which only are souldiers after the discipline of those countreis) had
war with the Tartars. Which being wel performed & ended by them, they
returned homewards. Where they understood by the way that their Cholopey
or bondslaves whom they left at home, had in their absence possessed their
townes, lands, houses, wives and all. At which newes being somewhat
amased, and yet disdeining the villany of their servants, they made the more
speed home: and so not far from Novograd met them in warlike maner
marching against them. Whereupon advising what was best to be done,
they agreed all to set upon them with no other shew of weapon but with

their horse whips (which as their maner is every man rideth withal) to put them in remembrance of their servile condition, thereby to terrifie them, & abate their courage. And so marching on & lashing al together with their whips in their hands they gave the onset. Which seemed so terrible in the eares of their villaines, and stroke such a sense into them of the smart of the whip which they had felt before, that they fled altogether like sheepe before the drivers. In memory of this victory the Novogradians ever since have stamped their coine (which they cal a dingoe Novogrodskoy currant through al Russia) with the figure of a horsman shaking a whip aloft in his hand. These 2. cities exceed ye rest in greatnes. For strength their chiefe townes are Vobsko, Smolensko, Cazan, & Astracan, as lying upon the borders. But for situation Jaruslave far exceedeth the rest. For besides the commodities that the soile yeeldeth of pasture and corne, it lieth upon the famous river of Volgha, & looketh over it from a high banke very faire & stately to behold: whereof the towne taketh the name. For Jaraslave in that tongue signifieth as much as a faire or famous banke. In this towne (as may be ghessed by the name) dwelt the Russe kind Vladimer sirnamed Jaruslave, that maried the daughter of Harald king of England, by mediation of Sveno the Dane, as is noted in the Danish story about the yere 1067.

The other townes have nothing y^t is greatly memorable, save many ruines within their wals. The streets of their cities and townes in stead of paving are planked with fir trees, plained & layd even close the one to the other. Their houses are of wood without any lime or stone, built very close and warme with firre trees plained and piled one upon another. They are fastened together with dents or notches at every corner, & so clasped fast together. Betwixt the trees or timber they thrust in mosse (whereof they gather plenty in their woods) to keep out the aire. Every house hath a paire of staires that lead up into the chambers out of the yard of streat after the Scottish maner. This building seemeth far better for their countrey, then that of stone or bricke; as being colder & more dampish then their wooden houses, specially of firre, that is a dry & warme wood. Whereof the providence of God hath given them such store, as that you may build a faire house for 20. or 30. rubbles or litle more, where wood is most scant. The greatest inconvenience of their wodden building is the aptnesse for firing, which happeneth very oft & in very fearful sort, by reason of the drinesse and fatnes of the fir, that being once fired, burneth like a torch, & is hardly quenched til all be burnt up.

Boris Godunov

Fedor, second son and successor of John the Dread, was incompetent to rule. Ambitious boyars plotted to displace or succeed him and the power was seized temporarily by the boyar, Nikita Romanov, uncle of Fedor. Upon

Nikita's death, authority passed to another boyar, Fedor's brother-in-law, Boris Godunov who had been one of John's chief agents. Godunov, tsar in fact, succeeded to the title after Fedor's death in 1598. His reign is the prelude to the Time of Troubles.

The following brief characterization of Godunov is translated from the writings of the French novelist and historian, Prosper Mérimée. The work from which it was taken was based mainly upon Russian sources. The source is: Mérimée, P., Episode de l'histoire de Russie—Les faux Demetrius. Paris: Levy Freres, 1854. Pp. 26–29.

His ambition was immoderate, but patient. His habit was to temporize and the Russian negotiations with Sweden, Turkey and Poland which took place under his administration give proof of this. Always he advanced slowly but firmly toward his goal, taking care never to risk a false step. Moreover, it is entirely probable that the goal was not at first clear to him. If it is true that he had the young Demetrius killed, it is not necessarily also true that he aspired to the throne from that moment; but the heir-presumptive, trained by his enemies, and under a prince as feeble as Fedor, would one day be able to thwart his plans and ruin his power. Absolute master of the tsar, safely sheltered behind this phantom sovereign, Boris had too much sense to hasten the moment when the last tsar of the Varangian dynasty should go to his grave.

That event had long been foreseen and it was, in fact, astonishing that Fedor, ill from infancy, lived so long. Boris had long been preparing himself for the extinction of the dynasty. All public officials were his creatures; the streltsi, and the clergy were, so to speak, in his hands, and he was accustomed to think of himself as the sole head of the state. The people, who all hated him, believed in his skill and his luck; and it was an established opinion that empire could not descend to a more resourceful leader. Finally, Fedor himself regarded Boris as his inevitable successor and seemed to designate him as such to the nation. Not long before his death Fedor presented to Boris a chest filled with relics, saying: "Place your hands upon these holy relics, Regent of the Orthodox People. Rule with wisdom. You will achieve all your aims, but you will find that on this earth all is vanity and deception."

Like Richard III and other ambitious men, Boris made a show of refusing the crown when it could not in fact escape from him. Before Fedor's death, the Regent forced the Boyars' Council and the important officials to take the oath of allegiance to Irene [the tsarina and Boris' sister]. But whether because of disgust with the world, or because of a secret order of her dying husband, or because of the instigation of her brother, Irene announced her intention of entering a convent. As for Boris, he haughtily declared that he wanted to abandon the affairs of state and live in retirement — knowing full well that he would not have to do so. Several times the nobility, the provincial deputies, and the clergy with the patriarch at their head, threw themselves at his feet and tearfully begged him to rule over Russia. They competed for the honor of persuading him, or rather each saw clearly the necessity for proving his devotion to Boris and as a Russian annalist said, "those who were not able to weep moistened their eyes with saliva."

The people, frightened by rumors of a Tatar invasion, joined the nobility in urging the favorite to accept his destiny. Mothers threw their suckling babies before him. A countless multitude surrounded the monastery to which Boris had retired and answered each of his refusals with wails of despair. "Have pity on me," said Boris weeping — for he could command his tears, "have pity, do not make me the victim of the throne."— But this pretended resistance came to an end. Boris granted what he had always intended to grant on the ground that he was called to the throne by the will of the nation. Amidst the general enthusiasm, only the Shuiskis [rival boyars, one of whom, Basil, later became tsar] were lukewarm or even somewhat opposed; Boris never forgot that.

The Time of Troubles

The following narrative and analysis of the events following upon the failure of the dynasty was written by Professor Kliuchevskii. The source is his History of Russia *(Hogarth translation), vol. 3, pp. 47–52, 57–59, 86–90.*

To explain the causes of the Period of Troubles is to point out the circumstances which brought it about and the conditions which so long maintained it in being. Of the circumstances which conduced to the Period we already know. They were the violent and mysterious ending of the old dynasty, and its artificial resurrection in the person of various pretenders. Yet the circumstances which conduced to the upheaval, as well as its profound inward causes, attained their force only because they sprouted on a favourable soil which had been worked by the assiduous, though improvident, efforts both of Ivan IV. and of Boris Godunov during the time that the latter was chief administrator of the State under Tsar Theodor. That soil was the depressed, mystified attitude of the community — an attitude which had been created by the enormities of the *Oprichnina* and the secret intrigues of Godunov.

The course of the Period reveals also its causes. The Period was evoked by a fortuitous incident — by the cutting off of the old dynasty. Whether due to force or to nature, the extinction of a family, of a stock, is a phenomenon almost daily to be observed among us. In private life it excites little notice, but the foreclosure of a whole dynasty is a very different matter.

At the close of the sixteenth century an event of this kind in Russia led to political and social struggle: to a struggle at first *political* — i.e. for a form of rule — and, subsequently, to a struggle *social* — i.e. to a feud between different classes of the community. In this upheaval a clashing of political ideas was accompanied by a contest of economic conditions; while, as the forces which stood behind the ever-changing Tsars and the ever-aspiring pretenders, we see the various social *strata* of the Muscovite Empire. Each class was for a Tsar or a would-be Tsar of its own. Such Tsars and candidates were the standards under which the different political aspirations (which, behind them, the different classes of the Russian community) marched. The disturbance began with the aristocratic intrigues of the "great boyars," who rose against the unlimited powers of the new Tsars, and was continued with the political aspirations of the *dvoriane* — the guards' corps — of the capital, who took up arms against the oligarchic schemes of the "great boyars" in the name of political freedom for the military caste. The rising of the metropolitan *dvoriane* was followed by one of the provincial *dvoriane,* who had a mind to rule the country. These, in turn, attracted to their standard the non-official classes of the provinces (who were against a State order of *any* kind), in the name of personal emancipation — i.e. of anarchy. Each of these stages in the upheaval was accompanied by the interposition of Cossack and Polish offscourings of the Muscovite and Lithuanian Empires, who seized upon the unsettled state of the Russian land as an excuse to come from their lairs on the Don, the Dnieper, and the Vistula, and to rob and pillage at their ease. At first, in view of the imminent disruption of the community, the boyars tried to unite all classes on behalf of a new State order; but, unfortunately, that order did not conform to the ideas of the other classes in the community. Next, an attempt was made to avert the catastrophe by artificially recreating the late defunct dynasty (hitherto the only factor which had served to curb dissension) in the hope of reconciling the divergent interests of the several classes in the person of a pretender. In fact, pretendership was resorted to as a means of escape from the warring of those interests. When the attempt proved unsuccessful, even on second trial, there seemed to remain no political tie, no political interest, which could avert the disruption of the community. Yet that disruption never came about: only the State order tottered. Though the political fastenings of the social system burst asunder, there remained the stronger clamps of nationality and religion to preserve the fabric. Slowly, but surely, educating the population which they ravaged, Cossack and Polish bands forced the mutually hostile classes of Russian society to combine, not on behalf of a State Order, but on behalf of the national, religious, and civic security which was menaced by those Cossacks and Poles. Thus, though the upheaval derived its strength from universal social dissension, it reached its end through the fact that the entire community was forced to enter upon a struggle with the extraneous forces — alien and destructive to Russian nationality — which had ventured to intrude themselves into the domestic feud.

Thus we see that the course of the Period of Troubles very clearly reveals two of the conditions which maintained it. Those two conditions were pretendership and social discord. To them we must look for guidance to the principal causes of the unrest. Already I have had occasion to point out one misapprehension in the political consciousness of the Muscovites — namely, the misapprehension that, though, as the union of a nation, a State can belong to none but the nation itself, both the Muscovite Tsar and the Muscovite people looked upon the Muscovite Empire as the hereditary manor of the princely dynasty from whose property it had developed. In this manorial-dynastic view of the Empire I see one of the fundamental causes of the Troubled Period. The misapprehension to which I have referred was bound up with a certain poverty or immaturity of political ideas, since the latter were altogether divorced from the elemental working of the national life. In the public conception the Muscovite Empire was still understood only in the old appanage sense — i.e. in the sense of being the estate of the Muscovite Tsars, the family property of Kalita's stock, by whom that property had been directed, extended, and consolidated during a space of three centuries. In reality the Empire was a union of the Great Russian race. True, men's minds had grasped the idea of the Russian land as an integral entity, but those minds had not risen to the idea of the nation as a union of State. The real ties of that union were still the free-will and the interests of the lord of the Imperial Manor. To this it may be added that such a manorial view of the State was no dynastic claim of the Muscovite Tsars, but a part of the political thought of the day, as inherited from the appanage period. At that time a State was looked upon in Russia as the *otchina* or heritable property — the manor — of the Tsar of a given dynasty; and if the average Muscovite citizen of those days had been told that the authority of the Tsar was also the Tsar's obligation or duty, and that, in administering the nation, the Tsar also served the State and the public weal, such a statement would have seemed to the hearer a confusion of ideas, a sheer anarchy of thought. This enables us to understand the conception of the relation of the Tsar and the nation to the State which the then Muscovite population had worked out for itself. That conception was the view that the Muscovite Empire wherein the Muscovite population had its being was the Empire of the Muscovite Emperor, and not of the Muscovite, the Russian, nation. The two inseparable ideas in the matter were, not the State and the nation, but the State and a lord of that State who belonged to a given dynasty. It was easier for Moscow to imagine an Emperor without a people than an

Empire without an Emperor. This view found characteristic expression in the political life of the Muscovite nation. When a people, hitherto associated with its Government through the idea of the welfare of the State, becomes dissatisfied with the ruling authority, on seeing that such authority does not properly safeguard the public welfare, it usually rises against it. Similarly, when servants or lodgers who are associated with a master or a landlord through temporary and conditional amenities perceive that they have ceased to receive those amenities they usually quit his establishment. Yet, when rising against authority, a people seldom also abandons its State, since it looks upon that State as one with itself; whereas a servant or a lodger who is dissatisfied with his master or his landlord ceases to remain in the house of the latter, for the reason that he (the servant or the lodger) does not look upon that house as his own. The population of the Muscovite Empire acted rather as servants or lodgers who are dissatisfied with their landlord than as citizens who rebel against a Government. They murmured against the acts of the authority which ruled them; yet never once during the time that the old dynasty was still alive did they allow popular dissatisfaction to attain the point of rebelling against the authority itself. On the contrary, the Muscovite nation ended by devising a special form of political protest. Malcontents who could not stomach the existing order of things did not *rise* against it, but simply *left* it — "wandered afar," i.e. departed out of the State. The Muscovite of the age seemed to feel that he was only a temporary sojourner in the Empire — a mere chance, removable inmate of another man's house. In the event of his finding the position irksome he considered it possible to leave the uncongenial landlord, yet never quite to reconcile himself to the idea of *rebelling* against that landlord, or of establishing another *régime* in the mansion. Thus the central knot of all relations in the Muscovite Empire was, not the thought of the popular weal, but the person of a member of a given dynasty; and a State order was considered possible only under a Tsar of that particular dynasty. Consequently, when the dynasty came to an end and the State appeared to be no man's property, men felt at a loss, and, abandoning their old conceptions of who or where they were, took to roaming afield, and living in anarchistic fashion. They felt themselves to be anarchists against their will and through an obligation which, though calamitous, was also inevitable: and since no one was to blame for this state of affairs, they felt it incumbent upon them to run amok.

The next event was the election of a Tsar by a *Zemski Sobor* or Territorial Council. Yet the very novelty of such an election by such a body caused it to be looked upon as an insufficient justification for a new power in the State. Thus it gave rise to doubt and alarm. The Council's decree announcing its choice of Boris Godunov shows, in itself, that the Council had foreseen what men would say of the electors who were responsible — namely, that "we do stand apart from them (the electors), in that they have appointed a Tsar unto themselves." At the same time, we find the document dubbing anyone who so expressed himself "both foolish and accursed." Also, in a lengthy pamphlet of 1611 it is related that the author of the script was vouchsafed a miraculous vision wherein he was informed that God Himself would show who was to rule the Russian State, and that any ruler whom the State might appoint on its own account "would never be Tsar." In short, never during the course of the Period of Troubles did men grow accustomed to the idea of an elected Sovereign. They thought that such a ruler could not be Tsar at all—that the only true, legal Tsar must of necessity be a born, hereditary scion of the line of Ivan Kalita. Consequently they strove by every manner of means to connect their elected Sovereign with that line — both by juridical devices, by a stretching of genealogical points, and by rhetorical exaggeration. Thus, Boris Godunov, when elected, was greeted by clergy and people as "hereditary Tsar" ("they offered unto him greetings touching his *otchina*, the State"); while Vassilii Shuiski, though formally limiting his own power, was none the less described in official documents as *Samoderzetz* or "Autocrat" (after the manner of the title usually ascribed to the old *born* Tsars of Moscow). In view of this unyielding bent of governing circles, the phenomenon of an elected Tsar on the throne must have seemed to the masses of the people less the result of political necessity, however pressing, than something akin to an infringement of the laws of nature. To the masses an elected Tsar would seem as grave an irregularity as an elected father or an elected mother. Consequently simple minds were powerless — were intellectually unable — to fit the idea of a "true Tsar" either to Boris Godunov or to Vassilii Shuiski — still less to the Polish King's son, Vladislav. In such rulers they could see only usurpers, while, on the other hand, even a single sign of a "born Tsar" in the person of a newcomer, however unknown his origin, was sufficient to quiet their dynastic conscience, and to inspire them with respect. The Period of Troubles ended only when the nation had succeeded in finding a Tsar whom it could connect by birth, however indirect, with the extinct line of Sovereigns. Tsar Michael established himself on the throne less through the fact that he was the candidate of the country and of the people at large than through the fact that he turned out to be nephew of the concluding Tsar of the old dynasty. Such a doubt as to the efficacy of popular election as a regular source of supreme power was the condition which, more than all others, nourished the unrest of the period: which doubt proceeded from a rooted belief that, properly, such a source could only be hereditary, proprietary succession in a given dynasty. Consequently as the first derivative cause of the upheaval which arose from the basis just expounded we must name this inability to adopt the idea of an elected Sovereign.

· · ·

At the close of 1611 the Muscovite Empire presented a spectacle of universal and complete disruption. The Poles had taken Smolensk; a second Polish force had burnt Moscow and entrenched itself within the surviving walls of the Kremlin and the Kitaigorod; the Swedes had occupied Novgorod, and put forward one of their princes as a candidate for the Muscovite throne; the murdered second false Dmitri had been succeeded, in Pskov, by a third pretender, a man named Sidorka; and the first expeditionary force of provincial *dvoriane* had, on the death of Liapunov, been broken up near Moscow. Meanwhile the country lacked an administration. The *Boyarskaia Duma,* which had assumed the lead on the downfall of Tsar Shuiski, effaced itself when the Poles took the Kremlin, and was succeeded by a small band of boyars, headed by Prince Mstislavski. Its centre lost, the Empire began once more to dissolve into constituent portions, since each town now acted practically alone, or only in conjunction with other towns. Thus the State became formed into a sort of amorphous, coagulated federation. At length proclamations issued from the Troitski Monastery by the Archimandrite Dionysius and the Abbot Abraham aroused the people of Nizhni Novgorod to combine under their *starosta* or prefect, a butcher named Minin; and to their call, again, responded the State servitors, urban *dvoriane,* and "sons of boyars" of the district—men who, for the most part, had lost, in the general disturbance, both their posts, their emoluments, and in many cases, their *pomiestia.* For this section Minin found a leader in the person of Prince Dmitri Michaelovitch Pozharski, and thus the second expeditionary force of *dvoriane* was formed. In warlike qualities it in no way excelled the first, though it was well equipped with funds collected by the burghers of Nizhni Novgorod and certain allied towns, at some sacrifice to themselves. After four months spent in preparation it advanced upon Moscow, and was reinforced *en route* by additional bands of State servitors, who begged to be taken on, in the hope of receiving future grants of land. Before Moscow there was also posted a body of Cossacks, under Prince Trubetskoi, which represented a remnant of the first expeditionary force. Yet to the provincial *dvoriane* these troopers seemed stranger individuals even than the Poles: with the result that when Trubetskoi sent the *Dvoriane* an offer of co-operation they returned him the answer, "Of a surety we stand not with thy Cossacks!" Soon, however, it became manifest that without Cossack support nothing could be done; and, true enough, throughout a three months' investment of Moscow, nothing whatever of importance issued as the result. Although Pozharski's force comprised in its ranks over forty prominent officers of good service names, only two of his subordinates distinguished themselves, and they were not State servitors at all. The two referred to were the monk Palitsin and the butcher Minin. At Pozharski's request the former of these persuaded the Cossacks to lend their support, at a decisive moment, to the Russian *dvoriane:* while the latter distinguished himself by begging of

Pozharski some three or four companies, and then, with their aid, effecting a successful attack upon a small detachment of Poles which, under a *hettman* named Chotkeivitch, was making for the Kremlin with supplies for its beleaguered compatriots. Minin's daring exploit put some heart into the *dvoriañe* of the expedition, and encouraged them to force Chotkeivitch to retire, after the Cossacks had duly prepared the way. Next, in October 1612, the Cossacks took the Kitaigorod by storm; but, for their part, the *dvoriañe* could not make up their minds to attack the Kremlin, and it fell only through the fact that at length the handful of Poles who were in possession of it were compelled by hunger—hunger which had brought them to the pitch of cannibalism — to surrender of their own accord. Again, it was Cossack *atamans*, not Muscovite *voievodi*, who repelled King Sigismund from Volokolamsk when he was making for Moscow in order to restore the city to Polish hands, and forced him to return home. In short, we see this expeditionary force of provincial *dvoriañe* giving yet a second proof during the Period of Troubles that this class was incapable of the very work which was at once its professional calling and its State obligation.

. . .

This was owing to the fact that the storms of that Period had done immense harm both to the industrial position of the nation and to the moral attitude of the Russian community. In fact, the country was in a state of utter ruin. Certain foreigners who visited Moscow soon after the accession of Michael (to be precise, in 1615), have bequeathed to us a terrible picture of burned and wasted *sela* and *derevni* wherein the deserted huts were choked with corpses which had not yet been removed, and from which the stench compelled even travellers in the winter time to spend the night in the open air. Everywhere persons who had survived the Period of Troubles were wandering about; the whole civil order had been thrown out of gear, and all human relations were now plunged in confusion. Consequently it took a prolonged series of efforts to re-establish order, to collect the wanderers, to resettle them in their old habitations, and to restart them in the daily routine from which they had been ousted by the upheaval. Also, from Michael's day there have come down to us not a few cantonal lists or "tenth books" and agrarian registers or "writers' books" which give us a clear picture of the then industrial position of the service-landowning and peasant sections of the population, since in those records we find particulars of the economic reconstruction of the Muscovite Empire and nation during the first reign of the new dynasty. First of all we note a change in the composition of the rural peasant population, which served as the principal source of the State's income. Registers of the sixteenth century indicate that amount of substance divided the peasantry into two classes — namely, *krestiañe* and *bobili*. Bobili were much the same as *krestiañe*, except either that they possessed less means and cultivated smaller plots than did *krestiañe* or that they held no arable land at all, but merely homesteads. During the sixteenth century the number of *krestiañe* considerably exceeded that of *bobili*, but from agrarian registers of Michael's day we see that, after the Period of Troubles, quite a different relation became established, and that in some places the proportion of *krestiañe* to *bobili* even came to be reversed—the latter either rising to numerical equality with the former or coming to constitute an actual majority over them (thus, in the cantons of Bielaev, Mtzensk, and Elets the cantonal estates of the local State servitors had come, in 1622, to comprise 1187 *krestiañe* and 2563 *bobili*). Hence it follows that the Period of Troubles forced an immense number of *krestiañe* either to abandon altogether their tillage plots or to curtail the extent of those plots. Also, the increase in the number of *bobili* means that there took place also an increase in *pustota* or waste land; nor can it be regarded as an exceptional instance that a register of the period tells us that, in one district of the canton of Riazan, the local *pomiestia* or service estates contained, in 1616 twenty-two times as much waste land as cultivated. Again, in the works of the monk Palitsin—an excellent monasterial landlord, and a man who was thoroughly acquainted with the industrial position of his country—we find a curious confirmation of this wholesale abandonment of land; for he writes that, during a three years' failure of the harvest in Boris' reign, many persons nevertheless had enormous quantities of stale grain stored in their barns, that threshing-floors were filled to overflowing with straw and hay, and that on these accumulations of old stocks the writer and others subsisted throughout the fourteen years of the Troubled Period, when "to plough and to sow and to reap men did forbear, for the reason that the sword did for ever lie over them." This item testifies both to the great development of agriculture before the Troubled Period and to the decline of that industry during the epoch in question. The recasting of rural industry, coupled with the change in the industrial composition of the rural population of which I have been speaking, must have told heavily upon private landownership, more especially in the matter of the industrial position of the provincial *dvoriañe*. Let me cite a few *data* which I have culled at random from certain cantonal "tenth books" for the year 1622, when the traces of destruction had become obliterated. The fitness for service of the military class depended upon the productiveness of that class's property and the number and comparative affluence of the *krestiañe* who had settled its *otchini* and *pomiestia*. Thus, in the canton of Bielaev, *otchini* constituted 1/4 of all the estates belonging to *dvoriañe* in that district; in the canton of Tula they constituted rather more than 1/5; in the canton of Mtzesk, 1/17; in the canton of Elets, 1/157; and in the canton of Tver—even among the *vibor* (the wealthiest *stratum* of provincial *dvoriañe*)—1/4. The pomiestia of cantonal *dvoriañe* were also, for the most part, very small, and but sparsely settled with peasantry. For instance, an average-sized *pomiestie* in the canton of Tula comprised only 135 *dessiatini* of arable land; in that of Elets, only 124; in that of Bielaev, only 150; and in that of Mtzesk, only 68. Also, in the four cantons just named the number of taxpaying agriculturists (both *krestiane* and *bobili*) averaged only two souls to every 120 dessiatini of *pomiestie* land; or one to every 60. Yet it must not be supposed that all this tillage was actually worked by *krestiane* or *bobili*. Only a small portion of it was so worked, and even of that not all was actually in cultivation. Thus, in the canton of Tver we find the estate of a wealthy *dvorianin*-councillor—an estate made up of 900 *dessiatini* of *otchina* and *pomiestie* land—being worked only to the extent of 95 *dessiatini;* whereof the owner himself cultivated 20 dessiatini with his domestic staff, while the remaining 75 *dessiatini* were leased to 28 *krestiane* and *bobili,* who resided in 19 homesteads. Thus each such homestead had attached to it, in round figures, 4.6 dessiatini. Indeed, peasant tillage on anything of a large scale was a very rare phenomenon indeed. On the other hand, Elets and certain other cantons of the South contained not only many *dvoriane* who, owning no land at all, possessed (as *odnodvortsi* or "one-homesteaders") but a manor-house to which there were neither *krestiane* nor *bobili* attached as tenants, but also many *pusto-pomiestnie* (owners of waste *pomiestia*) who could not boast even of an establishment of that kind. Thus, among the 878 *dvoriane* and "sons of boyars" registered in the canton of Elets we note there to have been 133 landless proprietors and 296 "one-homesteaders" and proprietors of waste *pomiestia*. Indeed, it was not an uncommon thing for a *dvorianin* altogether to abandon his *otchina* or *pomiestie,* and then either to join the Cossacks, to become a bond-slave or servant in some boyaral or monastic establishment, or (if I may quote the phrase employed by a "tenth book") to "fall to wallowing in taverns." The greater became the decline of service landownership, the greater became the necessity of increasing the allotments of monetary salaries to State servitors, if the service efficiency of that class was ever to be restored. Again, increase of salaries led to an increase in the agrarian taxation which fell upon the peasantry alone: and since such taxation was assessed according to area of tillage, the *krestianin* soon found himself unable to bear the ever-growing weight of his imposts, and forced to curtail his arable plot until it had come to pay less. Of this the consequence was that the Treasury found itself in a circle from which there was no escape.

Finally, the Government's internal difficulties were augmented by a profound change in the moral attitude of the nation. The new dynasty was called upon to deal with quite a different community to the one which the olden Tsars had ruled. The alarms of the Troubled Period had exercised such a disruptive effect upon the political adjustment of the people that, from the accession of the new dynasty until the close of the seventeenth century, we see each several class engaged in ceaseless complaints concerning its misfortunes, its growing impoverishment and ruin, and the abuses of the powers that were — engaged in complaints, that is to say, concerning grievances which it had always suffered, yet against which it had never before protested. This dissatisfaction grew until, by the close of the century, it had come to be the dominant note in the attitude of the masses. From the storms of the Troubled Period the nation issued more impressed with and irate with its lot than it had ever been before. It had lost that political long-suffering which had made such an impression upon foreign observers of the sixteenth century; it was anything but the resigned, obedient instrument in the hands of the Government which it had formerly been. This change found expression in a phenomenon which until now we have not remarked in the life of the Muscovite Empire — namely, in the phenomenon that the seventeenth century constitutes, in our history, a period of popular uprisings. It is all the more unlooked-for a phenomenon in that it manifested itself under Tsars who, to judge from their personal qualities and the form of their policy, seem the less to have justified it.

The Rising of Minin and Pozharsky

Perhaps the most dramatic incident of the Time of Troubles was the national rising against the Poles led by Kuzma Minin and Prince Pozharsky. The first of the two following accounts of this rising appeared originally in a textbook of Russian history which was used in Russian high schools during tsarist days. The second is taken from the textbook now being used in Soviet high schools. The contrasts and the similarities in the two versions are both interesting and significant. Notice how the Soviet account stresses the part played by the "humble people" and by the non-Russian groups. Notice also that it does not mention the role of the church.

The source for the first is: Sergei F. Platonov (E. Aronsberg, translator) History of Russia. New York: The Macmillan Co., 1929. Pp. 162–163. The source of the second version is: A. M. Pankratovoi (Editor), Istoriia SSSR. (History of the USSR.) Three volumes. Moscow, 1943. Vol. 1, pp. 164–165.

The leadership in this national movement belongs to the city of Nizhni-Novgorod and to its patriotic citizen, Kozma Minin Sukhoruk. In September, 1611, he persuaded his fellow citizens to appropriate one third of the annual income of each house owner for the purpose of raising an army. When the money was raised Prince Dmitri Mikhaelovich Pozharski was appointed to organize the militia. The next move was to persuade the neighboring cities to follow a similar policy. In their correspondence the citizens of Nizhni-Novgorod made it clear that the army was to be used against the Poles and the Cossacks. In the course of the autumn and winter of

1611-12 many other cities in addition to Nizhni-Novgorod put their forces under Pozharski and entrusted their funds to Minin. The Cossacks in Moscow regarded this as an insurrectionary movement and prepared to crush it. In the Spring of 1612 Pozharski moved his forces to Iaroslavl on the Middle Volga and summoned a national assembly of the clergy, boyars and representatives of the cities. At Pozharski's request, this assembly assumed both the civil and the military government of the country. It planned at first to elect a tsar and then order a march on Moscow. Circumstances, however, necessitated a change in plan.

In July, 1612, a report reached Iaroslavl that Sigismund was sending reenforcements to Moscow, and, to prevent their entrance to the city, Pozharski hurried towards the capital. The Cossacks were so hostile that it was necessary to camp some distance from them. At first they tried to assassinate Pozharski, but when that failed they became alarmed, and more than half of them, together with Zarutski and Marina Mniszech, fled to Astrakhan. The remaining Cossacks, under Prince Trubetskoi, attempted to come to terms with Pozharski. Before these negotiations were concluded the Polish reenforcements came up and attacked Pozharski. In this bloody battle the Cossacks were at first little more than spectators but when they finally got into the fight the Poles were repulsed. After this victory Trubetskoi and Pozharski consolidated their departments and officials into a single government and did "all things in common." On October 22 the Russians took Kitaigorod, just outside of the Kremlin and four days later the Polish garrison exhausted by hunger and fighting, surrendered to Pozharski. Moscow was once more free. To commemorate this great event, the army erected the Kazan Cathedral on the Red Square.

* * * * *

The first uprising, composed mostly of gentry and Kossacks, was crushed in the Fall of 1611, but the struggle of the Russian people against the Polish usurpers was not weakened. At the head of the newly organized peoples' army stood the humble tradesman, Kuzma Minin, martial leader of the people in the old land of Nizhni Novgorod. He summoned the people with a passionate appeal to rise in defense of their fatherland without sparing their liberty, their lives or their property. The humbly-born took an oath, vowing to obey their leaders, to give money to pay soldiers and not to spare themselves. At Minin's suggestion the command of this peoples' army was entrusted to Prince Dmitri Mikhailovich Pozharski, already famous for his victory over the Poles before Moscow, where he had been wounded.

From Nizhni Novgorod appeals were sent to neighboring cities, asking them to join against the enemy to free their native land, and to send men, weapons and money. They aroused all the region from the Northern Sea to

Riazin. The Poles in Moscow were very much alarmed at the news of the gathering of this great peoples' army. The reactionary boyars, frightened at the popular rising, tried to persuade the people to subordinate themselves to the Polish King Wladislaw, but this appeal of the boyars was unsuccessful.

Early in the Spring of 1612 the peoples' army marched from Nizhni Novgorod to Iaroslavl. The people along the way greeted the army with delight. Townspeople gave money, and from other places came new detachments of militia. The army stayed for four months at Iaroslavl. While they were there, they created a national assembly and established departments to manage different branches of the government. The leaders of the army, Minin and Pozharsky, planned only the military operations.

This peoples' army was composed of numerous heterogeneous units; in it marched landlords from various towns, trades people, *streltsi,* Kossacks and peasants. Besides Russians — Tatars, Maritians, Chuvash and others took part in the rising.

While the main body of the expedition remained at Iaroslavl, detachments were sent into different sections, liberating many parts of the country from Polish forces and also from those Kossacks who served the Second False Dmitri and did not acknowledge the national government.

In various places the people themselves carried on the struggle against the Polish forces. The Poles, who did not know the country, ruthlessly compelled some peasants to serve them as guides. Not a few of these guides, at the sacrifice of their lives, led the Polish troops into impenetrable forests or into the arms of Russian forces. To this time of such great deeds belongs the heroic behavior of a peasant of Kostroma, Ivan Susanin, whom the Polish nobility compelled to guide them. Ivan Susanin led the Polish detachment into a dense forest and was there struck down by the nobility.

At the end of August 1612, the leaders led the expedition to Moscow. Hetman Zarutski, who had gone over to the side of the Poles, fled to the Kossack regions of the south. The remaining Kossacks, wishing neither to join the expedition nor to impede it, stayed at Moscow under Prince D. T. Trubetski. At the time the expedition marched toward Moscow, a Polish army, under the command of Hetman Khodkevich, hastened to the assistance of the Poles (in the Kremlin) with arms and provisions. Khodevich's forces were not less numerous than those of Minin and Pozharsky and he threw them all against the expeditionary troops. The Poles made a sally from their base at Moscow. The situation of the expedition was very difficult. Each day the struggle was more violent. The expedition took part in hand to hand fighting. Part of the Kossack hundreds of Trubetski did not wait for his authorization but joined the expeditionary forces and with them threw back the Poles. The Poles resumed the attack. They violently forced their way through to the crossing of the Moscow River. Then Kuzma Minin, joining with Pozharsky and four troops of Kossacks, crossed the river and violently attacked the Poles on the plain. The Poles could not withstand the attack and fled to their fortified camp. All the wagon trains (four hundred wagons with provisions) were captured by the victors. The remainder of the Polish troops deserted. The Polish detachments occupying Moscow were left without weapons or supplies; the Poles suffered severe hunger. On October 26th, 1612, the Poles surrendered. Moscow was free.

Church and State in Early Russian History

As even the Bolshevik historians have finally been forced to recognize, the Orthodox Church was a powerful and important factor in the creation and the development of the Russian state and society. The following selection is an excellent summary of the relations of church and state in the sixteenth century, together with a brief sketch of their historical connections. The source is: Karpovich, Mikhail M., "Church and State in Russian History," The Russian Review. *Vol. 3, No. 3, pp. 10–20 (Spring, 1944.) Pp. 10–14.*

In the early sixteenth century an acute struggle was going on within the ranks of the Orthodox Church in Muscovy. The immediate issue was the question of church land possession. Like the Western church during the Middle Ages, the Russian Church had accumulated, in the course of the previous centuries of its existence, enormous wealth in land which for the most part belonged to the monasteries. It was against this state of affairs that a small but determined group of church reformers raised the voice of protest. Known as the "Trans-Volga Elders," the protestants were grouped around the hermitage of Sorsk, a center of ascetic monasticism, highly respected for the purity of life and the devotional zeal of its members. They had for leader a remarkable man — Nilus of Sorsk, himself an ascetic and a mystic, a man of deep convictions and of a great strength of character. The Trans-Volga Elders, who also were referred to as the "noncovetous" monks, loudly called upon the church to give up its worldly possessions in order to achieve the Christian ideal of poverty and humility. In their eyes, a truly monastic life and management of big land estates were fundamentally incompatible.

On the other side stood the so-called "Josephites," by far the larger of the two groups, and one that enjoyed the support of the church hierarchy. To them the material wealth of the church was one of the indispensable conditions for the proper performance of its functions. The head of this faction, Joseph of Volokolamsk (hence the name of the Josephites) was the abbot of one of the richest and most influential monasteries in Muscovy. Throughout the sixteenth century this monastery played the part of a "nursery of bishops," and many of the most prominent hierarchs of the period had received their training there. Profoundly different from Nilus of Sorsk in character and outlook, Joseph too was a remarkable man, in his own way. An outstanding church administrator, he defended the retention by the monasteries of their land possessions on purely utilitarian grounds. One of his typical arguments was that the poor monasteries could not attract the better class of people, and these were needed for the building up of an educated and influential hierarchy.

Behind this controversy over the problem of church lands lay a more fundamental difference between two distinct religious types. The Josephites stood for a strict adherence to tradition, emphasized the importance of the ritual and were inclined towards a literal interpretation of religious texts. The followers of Nilus represented the spiritual trend in Russian Christianity, assigning first place to personal piety and assuming a much more liberal attitude towards the dogma and tradition.

Of particular importance was the difference between the two groups with regard to the problem of Church and State relationship. The Josephites wanted the Russian Church to be in an intimate and indissoluble alliance with the State. Preaching a doctrine of absolute loyalty to the secular power, they expected in return a full measure of state support and protection for the Church. In particular, they did not hesitate to invoke the assistance of the secular arm in the suppression of heresies. The Trans-Volga Elders differed sharply from the Josephites on this point. With a degree of tolerance surprising for their time, they rejected compulsion in matters of faith. Those who strayed away from the path of true Christianity should be brought back by persuasion, not by force. The realm of the Church, unlike that of the State, was one of spirit, and in the solution of its problems only spiritual methods could be used. Therefore, it would be better for the State not to interfere with the Church, just as the clergy should refrain from interfering in politics.

The Russian government of the period was bound to be vitally interested in this controversy within the Church. It was particularly concerned with the problem of church lands. Precisely at that time the Moscow rulers were engaged in reorganizing the system of national defense in their dominions. The new system was based on the principle of military service in return for land grants, and the government needed a sufficiently large land fund at its disposal. This is why it viewed the growth of church landownership with some alarm, and why at times it even contemplated secularization of church estates. With regard to this issue the government found itself in agreement with the followers of Nilus of Sorsk who, as is known, demanded the voluntary relinquishment by the church of its worldly possessions. And yet it could not enter into an alliance with the Trans-Volga Elders because of the other tenets held by that group. The spirit of individual freedom in which they approached the religious problems, their liberal attitude towards those deviating from Orthodoxy, and, above all, their endeavor to protect the Church from state interference and control, were hardly compatible with the centralizing and absolutist tendencies of the rising Russian autocracy. On the contrary, the government was in full sympathy with the traditionalism of the Josephites, their strict adherence to Orthodoxy, and, in particular, their advocacy of a close alliance between Church and State.

And so, a sort of unwritten concordat was concluded between the Moscow government and the leading faction of the Russian Church. For the time being, the government gave up its plan of secularizing the church estates, limiting itself to enacting legislation that tended to prevent their further growth, and in return it received the unqualified allegiance of the church hierarchy. With governmental support, the opposition movement within the Church was effectively silenced, and the Josephites achieved a complete victory over their antagonists. Under their leadership, the Orthodox Church finally became, by the middle of the sixteenth century, the official national Church of Russia, thus winning a position that it was destined to hold until the Revolution of 1917.

II

At that time the Russian Church already had over five centuries of existence behind it. In the course of this long period it played a great and creative part in the history of Russian culture and the State. Not only did it control the spiritual life of the people, being the only educational agency in the country, but it also became the chief guardian and exponent of the slowly growing idea of national unity. When, in the later part of the Middle Ages, the princes of Moscow undertook the political unification of Russia, it was the Church that rendered them the most determined and particularly effective support. It contributed to the rise of the Tsardom of Moscow by lending it its own moral prestige and, in the persons of some of its outstanding representatives, it took a direct part in the work of national consolidation. Moreover, it supplied the young Russian monarchy with a ready-made theory of divinely ordained royal absolutism which it borrowed from its spiritual parent, the Church of the Byzantine Empire.

One could expect that in virtue of this contribution the Church would emerge an equal partner in the alliance between Church and State in Russia. And yet, in reality, almost from the outset the Church became a subordinate member of the alliance, with the State firmly retaining full measure of control. In a large degree, the very nature of political theories preached by the clergy was responsible for such a result. True, in Byzantium there existed a doctrine which emphasized the equality of the spiritual and the secular power and envisaged a harmonious balance between the two, and that doctrine, too, found its way into Russia. But on the whole the main tradition of the Byzantine Empire was that of the imperial domination over the Church, and it was this tradition that was particularly familiar to the Russian hierarchs. At any rate, neither in Byzantium nor in Russia did the Church as a whole ever exhibit either a strong tendency to assert the supremacy of the spiritual power over the secular, or such a tenacity in defending itself against the encroachments of the State as were characteristic of the Roman Catholic Church in the West.

Of even greater importance were, perhaps, the specific conditions of Russia's historical development. In comparison with the relatively slow progress of royal absolutism in Western Europe, the Russian autocracy succeeded in establishing itself in a surprisingly short period of time. It arose in the process of a rapid territorial expansion of the Tsardom of Moscow, under the constant pressure of foreign menace, and it consolidated its position within the country before any of its potential domestic rivals could become strong enough to successfully challenge its supremacy. Unlike Western European absolutism, the rising Russian monarchy did not have to face either a fully developed and firmly established feudal system, or (after the early fall of the city-republic of Novgorod) any strong and prosperous urban communes. The Russian Church merely shared the fate of other social forces in the country. In spite of its riches and its privileges, it too had not developed into an independent feudal body, and in the end, it succumbed under the sway of the Tsar's autocratic power in the same way as did the other social groups and organizations.

In the early centuries of its existence the Russian Church remained in canonical dependence on the mother Church in Byzantium, and its head had to be appointed or at least confirmed in office by the Patriarch of Constantinople. Gradually, however, this dependence grew weaker and weaker, and since the destruction of the Byzantine Empire by the Turks in 1453, the Russian Church, to all practical purposes, became an independent national Church. This independence was given formal sanction with the elevation, in 1589, of the Russian Metropolitan to the dignity of the Patriarch of Moscow, recognized as an equal by the other Eastern Patriarchs. In the process of this gradual emancipation from canonical dependence on Constantinople, the practice was established of electing first the Metropolitan and then the Patriarch of Moscow at a Russian Church council. Theoretically, the Church was free in the choice of its head, but there is enough evidence to show that from the outset the elections were controlled by the State. It became customary to submit the names of the candidates for the Tsar's preliminary approval.

No wonder, therefore, that as a rule the Patriarch was not and could not feel himself to be the Tsar's equal. During the whole seventeenth century, there were only two cases when it was otherwise, but both these cases can be viewed as exceptions proving the rule.

The first of these cases was that of Patriarch Philaret (1619-33) who was the virtual co-regent with Tsar Michael (the first of the Romanovs) and was officially recognized as such. But, in addition to his outstanding ability and personal prestige, Philaret owed his exalted position to the fact that he was the Tsar's father. Two decades later a similar position was attained by Patriarch Nikon who, for a while, also acted as the Tsar's co-regent and was given the use of the sovereign title. This time the exaltation of the Patriarch was due to the remarkable ascendency that Nikon had succeeded in gaining over the mind of Tsar Alexis. Nikon, however, began to lose ground the moment he ceased to enjoy the personal favor of the Tsar. Significantly, the cause of his ruin was precisely his uncompromising insistence on the prerogatives of his office, in which, in the opinion of the Tsar, he overstepped the boundaries of the permissible. Practically alone of all the Russian hierarchs, Nikon attempted to advance in Russia the medieval Western doctrine of the supremacy of the spiritual over the secular power, but in this he was not supported by the Church. Finally he was deposed by a church council and died in disgrace. His fall might be viewed as a prelude to the final subordination of the Russian Church to the State, which took place in the reign of Peter the Great.

Additional Readings

Pares, *History*   Pp. 73–147

Tompkins, *Russia*   Pp. 99–145

Vernadsky, *History*   Pp. 51–66

Martin, *Picture History*   Pp. 31–63

Nowak, *Medieval*   Pp. 54–62

Rambaud, *Russia*   Vol. 1, Chaps. 12–18

Bury, J. B., "Russia, 1462–1682," *Cambridge Modern History.* Vol. 5, Chap. 16

Bain, R. Nisbet, *Slavonic Europe.* Cambridge: The University Press, 1908.

Graham, Stephen, *Ivan the Terrible.* New Haven: Yale University Press, 1933.

Hrushevsky (Frederiksen. ed.), *History*   Chap. 8

Allen, *Ukraine*   Chap. 3

Kerner, *Urge*   Chap. 4

Platonov, *History*   Pp. 125–167

Kluchevsky, *History*   Vol. 3

Tolstoi, A. (J. Curtin, tr.), *Prince Serebryani.* New York: Dodd, Mead & Co., 1892

Curtiss, J. S., *Church and State in Russia. The Last Years of the Empire, 1900–1917.* New York: Columbia U. Press, 1940. Pp. 1–15.

Part III: THE SEVENTEENTH AND EIGHTEENTH CENTURIES

The Growth of Serfdom

The author of the following selection was Professor of Public Law in the University of Moscow in the late nineteenth century. He was deprived of that post by the government, despite his distinction as a scholar, on the ground that he was politically unreliable. He later was active in the Constitutional Democratic Party.

Economic serfdom was already established in Russia by the Time of Troubles, but legal serfdom did not come into existence until the Code of 1649. In the following selection, Professor Kovalevsky sketches the origins and growth of the institution. The source is: Kovalevsky, M., Modern Customs and Ancient Laws of Russia *(Being the Ilchester Lectures for 1889–90).* London, 1891. Pp. 209–219. *(Slightly abridged.)*

An account of the origin, growth, and abolition of serfdom in Russia might easily be made to fill volumes, so vast and so various are the materials on which the study of it is based. But for the purpose now in view, that of bringing before your notice the general conclusion to which Russian historians and legists have come as to the social development of their country, perhaps a single lecture will suffice. In it I cannot pretend to do more than present to you those aspects of the subject on which the minds of Russian scholars have been specially fixed of late years.

Among the first to be considered is the origin of that system of personal servitude and bondage to the land in which the Russian peasant lived for centuries. An opinion long prevailed that this system was due solely to the action of the State, which, at the end of the sixteenth century, abolished the freedom of migration previously enjoyed by the Russian peasant and bound him for ever to the soil. This opinion, which would have made Russian serfdom an institution quite apart from that of the serfdom of the Western States of Europe, has been happily abandoned, and consequently its development becomes the more interesting, in so far as it discloses the action of those economic and social forces which produced the personal and real servitude of the so-called villein all over Europe.

The first point to which I desire to call your attention is the social freedom enjoyed by the Russian peasant in the earlier portion of mediaeval history. The peasant, then known by the name of *smerd*—from the verb *smerdet,* to have a bad smell—was as free to dispose of his person and property. He had the right to appear as a witness in Courts of Justice, both in civil and in criminal actions; he enjoyed the right of inheriting—a right, however, which was somewhat limited by the prevalence of family communism—and no one could prevent him from engaging his services to any landlord for as many years as he liked, and on terms settled by contract. Lack of means to buy a plough and the cattle which he needed for tilling the ground very often led the free peasant to get them from his landlord on condition that every year he ploughed and harrowed the fields of his creditor. It is in this way that an economic dependence was first established between two persons equally free, equally in possession of the soil, but disposing the one of a larger, the other of a smaller capital. The name under which the voluntary serf is known to the Pravda, the first legal code of Russia, is that of *roleine zakoup;* this term signifies a person who has borrowed money on condition of performing the work of ploughing (ralo means the plough) so long as debt remains unpaid.

The frequent want of the simplest agricultural implements, was also probably the chief cause, which induced more than one Russian peasant to prefer the condition of a sort of [share-cropper], whose rent, paid in kind, amounts to a fixed proportion of the yearly produce, to that of a free shareholder in the open fields and village common. The prevalence in ancient Russia of the same rude and elementary mode of farming is established by numerous charters and contracts, some of which are as late as the end of the seventeenth century, whilst others go back to the beginning of the sixteenth. It would appear that previous to that date such contracts were not put into writing, apparently on account of the small diffusion of knowledge. We are therefore reduced to the necessity of presuming the existence of these contracts solely because the intrinsic causes which brought them into existence in the sixteenth century had been in operation for hundreds of years before. The peasant, on entering into such a contract, took upon himself the obligation of paying back in the course of time the money which had been lent to him—the *serebro,* silver, according to the expression used in contemporary documents. From the name of the capital intrusted to them (the serebro) arose the surname of *serebrenik,* which may be translated silver-men, under which peasants settled on a manor were generally known; their other being *polovnik,* or men paying half of their yearly produce to the lord, although as a rule their payments did not amount to more than a quarter. So long as his debt remained unpaid the share-cropper was obliged to remunerate the landlord by villein service performed on the demesne lands of the manor. According to the German writer Herberstein, who visited Russia in the seventeenth century, the agricultural labour which the serebrenik performed for the lord very often amounted each week to a six-days' service, at any rate in summer. Contracts still preserved also speak of other obligations of the serebrenik. Such, for instance, were the obligations of cutting wood and of forwarding it on their own carts to the manor-house, and of paying certain dues on the occasion of the marriage of the peasant's daughter. Custom also required the peasant to make certain presents to his lord at Christmas and Easter, or at some other yearly festival, such for instance as that of the Assumption of the Blessed Virgin.

The peasant who chose to settle on the land of a manorial lord got the grant of a homestead in addition to that of land, and this was the origin of a sort of house-rent called the *projivnoe,* which as a rule amounted yearly to the fourth part of the value of the homestead.

As to the land ceded by the landlord to the settler who wished to live on his manor, its use became the origin of another special payment, the *obrok,* which represented a definite amount of agricultural produce. The obrok was often replaced by the obligation of doing certain fixed agricultural labour on the demesne land of the manor.

As soon as the peasant had repaid the money borrowed from the manorial lord, and had discharged all the payments required from him for the use of his land and homestead, he was authorized by custom to remove wherever he liked, of course giving up to the squire his house and his share in the open fields of the manor. At first this right of removal could be exercised at any period of the year, but this being found prejudicial to the agricultural interests of the country certain fixed periods were soon established, at which alone such a removal was allowed. Usually the end of harvest was fixed as the time when new arrangements could be entered into with regard to future agricultural labour without causing any loss to the interests of the landlord. Not only in autumn, however, but also in spring, soon after Easter, manorial lords were in the habit of permitting the establishment of new settlers on their estates, and the withdrawal of those peasants who expressed a desire to leave.

The first *Sudebnik,* the legal code published by Ivan III, in 1497, speaks of the festival of Saint George, which according to the Russian calendar falls on the 26th of November, as a period at which all removals ought to take place. Those peasants who had not been fortunate enough to free themselves from all obligations to the manor by this period were obliged to remain another year on its lands; he who was unable to repay the lord the sum borrowed was reduced to the same condition as that of the insolvent farmers of the Roman ager publicus, who, according to Fustel de Coulanges, saw their arrears of debt changed into a perpetual rent called the canon, and their liberty of migration superseded by a state of continual bondage to the land they cultivated. No Russian historian has shown the analogy existing between the origin of the Roman colonatus and that of Russian serfdom so clearly as Mr. Kluchevsky, the eminent professor of Russian history in the University of Moscow. It is to him that we are indebted for the discovery of the fact that centuries before the legal and general abolition of the right of free migration a considerable number of peasants had thus ceased to enjoy that liberty.

Such was the case of those so-called "silver-men from the oldest times," (viz., *starinnii serebrenniki*) who during the sixteenth century were already deprived of the right of free removal. from no other cause but the want of money, so that the only condition on which they could withdraw from the manor on which they were was that of finding some other landlord willing to pay the money they owed, and thereby acquiring the right to remove them to his own manor.

So long as the Russian power was geographically limited to the possession of the central provinces in the immediate neighbourhood of Moscow, and so long as the shores of the Volga and Dnieper suffered from almost periodical invasions of the Tartars, the Russian peasant who might wish to leave a manor could not easily have procured the land he required; but when the conquests of Ivan III, and Ivan the Terrible had reduced to naught the power of the Tartars, and had extended the Russian possessions both to the East and to South, the peasants were seized with a spirit of migration, and legislation was required to put a stop to the economic insecurity created by their continual withdrawal from the manors of Inner Russia to the Southern and Eastern steppes. It is, therefore, easy to understand why laws to prevent the possibility of a return of peasant migration were first passed, at least on a general scale, at this period. It is no doubt true that, even at the end of the fifteenth century, to certain monasteries were granted, among other privileges, that of being free from the liability of having their peasants removed to the estates of other landlords. A charter of the year 1478 recognises such a privilege as belonging to the monks of the monastery of Troitzko-Sergievsk, which is, according to popular belief, one of the most sacred places in Russia. The financial interests of the State also contributed greatly to the change. The fact that the taxpayer was tied to the soil rendered the collection of taxes both speedier and more exact. These two causes sufficiently explain why, by the end of the sixteenth century, the removal of peasants from manor to manor had become very rare.

The system of land endowments in favour of the higher clergy and monasteries, and also of persons belonging to the knightly class, had increased to such an extent that, according to modern calculation, two-thirds of the cultivated area was already the property either of ecclesiastics or of secular grandees. It is therefore easy to understand why, during the sixteenth century, the migratory state of the Russian agricultural population came to be considered as a real danger to the State by the higher classes of Russian society. The most powerful of the nobles and gentry did their best to retain the peasants on their lands. Some went even farther, and by alleviating the burdens of villein-service, and securing a more efficent protection for them from administrative oppression, induced the peasants who inhabited the lands of smaller squires to leave their old homes and settle on their manors. It was in order to protect the small landowners from this sort of oppression that

Boris Gudonov, the all-powerful ruler of Russia in the reign of Theodor Ivanovitch, promulgated a law, according to which every one was authorised to insist on the return of a peasant who left his abode, and that during the five years next following his departure. This law was promulgated in 1597. As no mention is made in it of the right previously enjoyed by the peasants of removing from one manor to another on St. George's Day, this law of 1597 has been considered by historians as the direct cause of the introduction of the so-called "bondage to the soil" (*krepostnoie pravo*). Such was certainly not its object. The right of migration on the Day of St. George was openly acknowledged by the laws of 1601 and 1602. The bondage of the peasant to the soil became an established fact only in the year 1649, when the new code of law, the so-called Ulozhenie, refused to any one the right to receive on his lands the peasant who should run away from a manor, and abolished that limit of time beyond which the landlord lost the right to reclaim the peasant who had removed from his ancient dwelling.

The number of serfs rapidly increased during the second half of the seventeenth and the eighteenth centuries, owing to the prodigality with which the Czars and Emperors endowed the members of the official class with lands, in disregard often of the previous occupation by free village communities, the members of which were forced to become the serfs of the persons who received the grant. It is in this way that Catherine II., for instance, during the thirty-four years of her reign, increased the number of serfs by 800,000 new ones, and that Paul I., in a period of four years added 600,000 to the number, which was already enormous.

Before the reign of Catherine, serfdom was almost unknown in Little Russia, where it had been abolished by Bogdan Chmelnitzky, soon after the separation of Little Russia from Poland, and in the Ukraine (the modern Government of Kharkov), where it had never before existed. In 1788 she revoked the right hitherto enjoyed by the peasants of these two provinces to remove from one manor to another. The same right of free removal was abolished a few years later in the "Land of the Don Kossacks" and among the peasants of the Southern Governments, called New Russia (Novorossia).

Class War: Bolotnikov's Rebellion

During the Time of Troubles, Ivan Bolotnikov led a rising of the unprivileged and underprivileged against the tsar and the richer boyars. This was a real class war of the "have-nots" against the "haves" and Soviet historians have not failed to emphasize the incident. The following account with its Marxist-Leninist explanation of Bolotnikov's failure is from a recent Soviet textbook. The source is: Shestakov, A. V. (Editor), A Short History of the USSR. Moscow, 1938. Pp. 55–56.

Ivan Bolotnikov, the Peasants' Leader. The peasant revolt continued under the reign of Shuisky. At this time an energetic leader named Ivan Bolotnikov rose among the peasants. Bolotnikov had formerly been a serf to one of the boyars and had fled from him. He had been to Turkey and Italy, and had seen a great deal. He was a gifted military leader, and the peasants, minor serving men and Cossacks rallied to him in large numbers. He collected an army in the south, and in 1606 marched on Moscow to overthrow the boyar tsar, Vasili Shuisky, and to put a "good" tsar in his place.

In the towns and villages along the line of march the rebels captured the tsar's officials, exterminated the boyars and pomeshchiks, laid waste to their estates and destroyed the houses of the rich merchants. Detachments of small landowners, who were discontented with the tyranny of the boyars and with the boyar tsar, Shuisky, also joined Bolotnikov's army.

Bolotnikov laid siege to Moscow. The small landowners who had joined Bolotnikov soon realized that his victory would weaken the power of the landlords. During a battle outside of Moscow these landlord detachments betrayed Bolotnikov and deserted to the side of the boyars and Tsar Shuisky. Bolotnikov's army was defeated.

Bolotnikov retreated, first to Kaluga and then to Tula, in order to prepare for another attack on Moscow. Shuisky with a large army besieged Bolotnikov in Tula. The rebel army defended itself heroically, but suffered defeat. This is not surprising. The peasants at that time had no such ally and leader as the working class. Besides, the peasants themselves lacked political consciousness. They did not fight againt tsarism and landlordism, but against the bad tsar and the bad landlords. They wanted a "good" tsar and "good" landlords.

In the winter of 1607 Ivan Bolotnikov was taken prisoner by the boyars. They put out his eyes and then took him to the river and drowned him in a hole in the ice. The conditions of the defeated peasantry became still worse. Shuisky issued new decrees increasing the state of bondage of the serfs. These decrees gave the landlords the right to search for and bring back fugitive peasants for a period of fifteen years from the time of their escape. The peasant revolts continued.

Revolts in the Towns

The following selection is also from Shestakov, op. cit., pp. 59–61.

Revolts in the Towns. After the death of Tsar Michael Romanov, his son Alexei become tsar of Muscovy. By his order a heavy salt tax was introduced in 1646. This tax roused the anger of the people. Fearing a rebellion, Tsar Alexei repealed the tax. But the tax was not the only trouble. Even after it was repealed the people of Moscow rose against their oppressors. In 1648 the people of Moscow caused a "riot," as popular rebellions were called at that time. The people well remembered the wrongs inflicted upon them by the tsar's servants and officials. They demanded that the chief of these officials be surrendered to them for punishment.

The tsar promised to fulfill the demands of the rebels, but he sent his horsemen against them, who beat them with whips and trampled upon them with their horses. Then the crowds of people wrecked the houses of the most hated of the boyars and tsarist officials and killed a number of them. The rebellion was crushed by the tsar's troops. In that year, 1648, rebellions in other towns were also crushed. After this, the tsar assembled the representatives of the boyars, landlords and merchants in what was known as the Zemsky Sobor. In 1649 they passed a law granting the landlords the right to search for and bring back fugitive peasants no matter how long since they had escaped. The peasants were made complete serfs. A census was taken of all villages and peasant households. It became very difficult for a fugitive peasant to hide anywhere. At that time, also, handicraftsmen and small traders were forbidden to move from one town to another without permission.

In the towns the handicraftsmen lived in special districts called *slobodas,* according to their occupation. For example, there was a Tanners' Sloboda, Potters' Sloboda, Gunsmiths' Sloboda, etc. There were many such slobodas in Moscow, which was the largest city in the country. The narrow crooked streets of these slobodas in Moscow were lined with small houses with two or three tiny windows.

The handicraftsmen earned little. Their lives were very hard; they were robbed by the voyevodas and merchants.

The revolts of the handicraftsmen and town poor continued. These revolts assumed particularly large dimensions in Pskov and Novgorod in 1650. They were joined by the peasants. Tsar Alexei had to send a large army to suppress the revolts.

The town poor rose in rebellion also in subsequent years. For example, a great revolt broke out in Moscow in 1662. In suppressing this revolt the tsar's soldiers killed and drowned in the River Moscow several thousand rebels.

Russia, Poland and Ukraine

The word "Ukraine" is derived from the phrase "ot kraina" which means "at the border" and the lands so designated were literally at the borders of both Russia and Poland. A bitter struggle for the control of these borderlands has gone on for centuries. One of the great heroes of Ukrainian national history is the Cossack Bogdan Khmelnitski who led a revolt against the Poles in the mid-seventeenth century. Russia was soon involved and Khmelnitski's movement, ironically, led directly to the annexation of Ukraine by Russia.

The two stories of this which follow offer a contrast in both style and interpretation. The shorter is from Shestakov, op. cit., pp. 62–64 and is an example of recent Soviet historiography. The source of the longer and more balanced account is: Rambaud, Alfred, (L. D. Lang, Translator) Russia. Two volumes. New York: F. P. Collier & Sons, 1902. Vol. 1, pp. 274–282.

BOGDAN KHMELNITSKY AND THE UKRAINIAN PEASANT WAR AGAINST THE POLISH PANS. Beginning with the 13th century the Ukraine gradually passed under the yoke of the Polish and Lithuanian pans. The latter transformed all the peasants into serfs. Even slight offences by their serfs they punished with death. In some of the Polish manors permanent gallows were erected. The Poles forcibly compelled the Ukrainian people to adopt their religion.

In Poland, and in Byelorussia, too, the peasants groaned under the tyranny of the pans. The serfs fled from the pans to the Dniepr, where they built small fortifications below the Rapids and called the place *Zaporozhskaya Sech*, or the Zaporozhye Cossacks. In other places, in the Ukrainian towns and villages, lived the town Cossacks. The town Cossacks as well as the Zaporozhye Cossacks were organized in regiments. Their chiefs were elected by the Cossacks. These chiefs were called hetmans.

The peasants and Cossacks frequently rose in rebellion against the Polish rulers. Even the rich Cossacks were discontented with the Poles because they robbed the land, and because of their oppression.

In 1648 a great rebellion of Cossacks and peasants broke out against the Poles. This rebellion was led by a rich town Cossack named Bogdan Khmelnitsky.

Bogdan Khmelnitsky sent his people disguised as beggars and monks to the villages of the Ukraine to rouse the peasants for the struggle against the pans. Soon the peasants rose in rebellion in all parts of the Ukraine and Byelorussia. The rebels began to wreck the mansions of the pans. The latter were compelled to split up their forces in order to fight Khmelnitsky and the rebel peasants. Khmelnitsky succeeded in defeating the Polish troops and in capturing their chief leaders.

The news of Khmelnitsky's victories rapidly spread throughout the Ukraine, Byelorussia and Poland. The peasants rallied to Khmelnitsky's standard in large masses. One of the most outstanding of the peasant leaders was Maxim Krivonos. Khmelnitsky, however, did not want to give the peasants freedom. He himself was a landlord and owned serfs. He started negotiations with the Poles and concluded a treaty with them which granted many concessions to the Cossacks. The Poles promised to pay the Cossacks regular salaries, to supply them with arms, and not to deprive them of their liberties.

The Polish pans deceived Khmelnitsky, however, and failed to carry out their promises. Then Khmelnitsky went to war against the Poles again.

THE UKRAINE JOINS RUSSIA. There seemed to be no prospect of the war coming to an end. The Poles were devastating the country. In order to extricate himself from his difficult position, Khmelnitsky, in 1654, concluded a treaty with Tsar Alexei of Moscow, who professed the same religion as he. In accordance with the treaty Ukraine became subject to Russia. The Cossack elders received the rights which formerly they had tried to obtain from Poland. The peasants of the Ukraine were released from the oppression of the pans. No one was now forcing an alien religion upon them. But the fact that the Ukraine was joined to Russia did not free the toilers of the Ukraine from the oppression of their elders and Hetmans.

To assist Khmelnitsky, the tsar made war upon Poland. The war ended with the annexation by Russia of all the lands on the left bank of the Dnieper and of the city of Kiev.

. . .

We have seen that Little Russia [Ukraine], after many partial risings, only awaited a chief to break out into a general insurrection. This chief was found in Bogdan Khmelnitski,—a brave, clever, energetic, and even educated Cossack. He was owner of Soubbotovo, near Tchigirine, and had been ill-treated and imprisoned by one of his neighbors, the Pole Tchaplinski, who also seized on Khmelnitski's son, a boy of ten years, and had him whipped in the public streets by his men. Khmelnitski could obtain no redress, either for himself or for his countrymen, against the Jews and the taxes. King Vladislas is said to have told him that the senators would not obey him, and, drawing a sword on paper, he handed it to Bogdan, observing, "This is the sign royal: if you have arms at your sides, resist those who insult and rob you; revenge your wrongs with your swords, and when the time comes you will help me against the pagans and the rebels of my kingdom." In the Polish anarchy of that date it is quite possible that the king may have held this language, and himself placed the sword in the hands of those whom he could not protect. Vladislas acknowledged Bogdan ataman of the Zaporogues, and in return Bogdan promised him the following year a body of 12,000 men.

Konetspolski, the gonfalonier of the Crown, and Potocki, tried to get rid of Bogdan, but he fled to the Zaporogues, and then passed over to the Khan of the Crimea, and returned to the heroes of the Dnieper with a Mussulman army. To Tatars and Zaporogues were soon added all the malcontents of Little Russia. Cossacks and people were alike determined to finish with it. Bogdan defeated the Polish generals Potocki and Kalinovski; first at the "Yellow Waters," where the registered Cossacks abandoned the Polish banners after having stabbed their hetman Barabbas, and then at Korsoun, where the Poles lost 8000 men and 41 guns. The two generals fell into the hands of Bogdan, who delivered them to the Khan of the Crimea. This double victory was the signal of a general insurrection. The orthodox clergy everywhere preached a crusade against the Jesuits and Uniates, and everywhere the peasants rose against the Polish or Polonized *pans*. The castles were demolished, the governors put to death. The Jews were in a sad strait. According to a popular song they only asked one thing—to be allowed "to escape in their shirts beyond the Vistula, abandoning their wealth to the Cossacks, and promising to teach their children to live honestly, and to covet no more the land of the Ukraine" (1648).

At this critical moment for Poland, King Vladislas died, and the Diet met at Warsaw for the new election, with all its accustomed turbulence. At this news the revolt in Little Russia increased. Wherever the nobles could defend themselves they gave back cruelty for cruelty. Jeremiah Vichnevetski, a powerful Polonized Russian lord, took a town belonging to him by assault, and exercised the most horrible reprisals. "Make them suffer," he cried to the executioners, "they must be made to feel death;" and his Cossack prisoners were impaled. The Cossacks, who in the absence of a king expected justice from no one, broke out more violently than ever. Khmelnitsky pursued his course of success; he defeated the Poles near Pilava, and penetrated into Gallicia as far as Lemberg, a rich, half-Jewish city, which had to pay a war indemnity. He was besieging Podmostié when he learned that John Casimir was elected in the place of his brother Vladislas. The new king at once sent envoys to negotiate his submission. The commissioners promised him satisfaction for his own grievances and those of the Cossacks on condition that the insurgents were abandoned to them. "Let the peasants return to their ploughs, and the Cossacks alone bear arms," said the Poles. Bogdan could neither abandon the Cossacks, who would not hear of the register, nor the country people, whose revolt had given him the victory, to be again placed, as was proposed, under the yoke of the *pans*. "The time for negotiations is past," he said to the commissioners; "I must free the whole Russian nation from the yoke of the Poles. At first I took up arms for my own injuries—now I fight for the true faith. The people will stand by me as far as Lublin, as far as Cracow; I will not betray them." The war continued, and Bogdan summoned the Khan of the Crimea to his aid, and marched to meet the Polish army, commanded by the king in person. John Casimir found himself at Zborovo surrounded by the innumerable cavalry of the enemy. It would have been all over with him had he not purchased the defection of the Khan of the Crimea by a large sum, and the promise of an annual tribute. The Khan then retired, recommending his ally to the clemency of the king. Khmelnitski was driven to treat; the register was re-established, but the number of Cossacks enrolled was raised to 40,000; Bogdan was recognized hetman of Little Russia, and the town of Tchigirine assigned to him as a residence. It was agreed that there should be neither Crown troops nor Jews in the localities inhabited by the Cossacks, and no Jesuits where orthodox schools existed. The Metropolitan of Kief was to have a seat in the senate of Warsaw.

What Bogdan had foreseen when he refused to treat really happened; the treaty could not be executed. The number of fighting men who had taken part in the election exceeded 40,000—were those in excess to be relegated to the work of the fields, to the seignorial *corvée?* The people had helped the Cossacks, were they then to be surrendered to their *pans?* Bogdan soon found himself involved in inextricable difficulties: on one side he violated the treaty by enrolling more than 40,000 men in his register; on the other hand, if he executed it, he would have to begin by inflicting death on the rebels. He wore out his popularity in performing this ungrateful task. He preferred to take up arms, accusing the Poles of having broken certain clauses of the treaty. This war was less successful than the first; the Khan of the Crimea, who a second time came to the aid of the Cossacks, a second time betrayed them, and the Cossacks were beaten at Berestechtko. The conditions of the Peace of the White Church (*Belaïa Tcherkof*) were more severe than those of the first peace. The number of registered Cossacks was reduced to 20,000; and 20,000 more, thus finding themselves excluded from the army, were thrown back upon the people. The greater part chose rather to emigrate to Russian soil, to wander to the Don, or to live by brigandage on the Volga.

A peace such as this was only a truce, and the Cossacks were certain to break it as soon as they could find an ally. Bogdan wrote to entreat the Tzar to take Little Russia under his protection. The Government of Alexis had sought for some time a pretext for rupture with Poland. The Polish Government, in writing to the Tzar, had not used the full royal title. Moscow never missed an opportunity for remonstrance; Warsaw assured them that it was pure inadvertence. "Then," said the Russians, "an example must be made of the guilty." No example was made, and the diminution of title was used at every interchange of notes. The Court of Russia kept up this *casus belli*, waiting for a moment to profit by it; this was found in the appeal of Khmelnitsky. The Estates were convoked, and to them were reported the repeated insults to his Tzarian Majesty, and the persecution of the true faith in Little Russia. It was added, that the Little Russians, if repulsed by the Tzar, would have to place themselves under the protection of the Sultan. On this occasion the Estates declared for war. Alexis sent the boyard Boutourline to receive the oath of the hetman, the army, and the people of Little Russia.

It was time that the Tzar decided. Bogdan, betrayed a third time by the Khan, had been defeated at Ivanetz on the Dniester, but on the receipt of the news from Moscow he called the General Assembly at Peréiaslavl to announce to them the fact. "Noble colonels; *esauls*, and centurions, and you army of Zaporogues, and you orthodox Christians," cried the hetman, "you see it is no longer possible to live without a prince. Now we have four to choose from: the Sultan of Turkey, the Khan of the Crimea, the King of Poland, and the Tzar of orthodox Great Russia, whom for six years we have not ceased to entreat to become our Tzar and lord. The Sultan is a Mussulman; we know what our brethren the orthodox Greeks suffered at his hands. The Khan is also a Mussulman, and our alliances with him have brought us nothing but trouble. It is needless to remind you of what the Polish *pans* have made us endure. But the Christian and orthodox Tzar is of the same religion as ourselves. We shall not find a better support than his. Whoever thinks ótherwise may go where he likes—the way is open." The air rang with applause, the oath demanded by Boutourline was taken, and an embassy set out for Moscow, to ask the maintenance of Ukrainian liberties. The Tzar freely granted all their conditions: the army was to be raised permanently to the number of 60,000; the Cossacks were to elect their hetman; the rights of the *schliachta* and the towns were to be maintained; the administration of the towns and the imposition of taxes were to be entrusted to the natives; the hetman was to have the right of receiving foreign ambassadors, but was to signify the fact to the Tzar; and he was forbidden, without special leave, to receive the envoys of Turkey and Poland.

In May 1654 the Tzar Alexis solemnly announced in the *Ouspienski Sobor* that he had resolved to march in person against his enemy the King of Poland. He commanded that in this campaign no occasion should be given for the generals to dispute precedence. The Polish voïevodes affirm that on this occasion "Moscow made war in quite a new way, and conquered the people by the clemency and gentleness of the Tzar." This humanity, so well timed in a war of deliverance, contributed greatly to the success of the Muscovites. Polotsk, Mohilef, and all the towns of White Russia opened their gates one after the other, and Smolensk only resisted five weeks (1654). The following year the Prince Tcherkasski defeated the hetman Radziwill and began the conquest of Lithuania proper; Wilna, the capital, Grodno, and Kobno, fell successively. During this time Khmelnitski and the Muscovites invaded Southern Poland and took Lublin. All the East resounded with the Russian victories: it was said at Moscow that the Greeks prayed for the Tzar and refused obedience to any but an orthodox emperor, and that the Hospodars of Wallachia and Moldavia implored Alexis to take them under his protection.

Poland seemed reduced to the last extremity; and there was still a third enemy to fall on her. Charles X., King of Sweden, arrived and captured Posen, Warsaw, and Cracow, the three Polish capitals. This conflict of ambition was, however, the salvation of the *pospolite;* the Swede threatened the Russian conquests, and claimed Lithuania. He entered into relations with Khmelnitski, who forgot the oath he had taken; it was Charles XII, and Mazeppa enacted half a century before. The Tzar Alexis feared he had only shaken Poland to strengthen Sweden, and would not risk the reunion of these two formidable monarchies under the same sceptre. He hastened to negotiate with the Poles, who promised to elect him after the death of their present king; then he turned his arms against Sweden. The latter was the heir on the Baltic of the Livonian Order. Alexis trod in the steps of Ivan the Terrible; like him, his successes were rapid, but they as rapidly evaporated in smoke. He took Dünaburg and Kokenhusen, two old castles of the Knights; but the Russians besieged Riga in vain, and succeeded no better at Oréchek or Kexholm. The occupation of Dorpat terminated the first campaign (1656); after that, hostilities languished, and Alexis concluded a truce of twenty years, which secured him Dorpat and a part of his conquests. The affairs of Poland and Little Russia became, however, so terribly complicated, that the truce became the Peace of Cardis, by which Alexis abandoned all Livonia (1661).

The hetman Khmelnitski had more than once given his new sovereign cause for discontent. In spite of his oath, he had negotiated with Sweden and Poland. In fact, now that he had got rid of his former master, he did not want to become the vassal of a new sovereign, but to create a third Slav State between Poland and Russia, and to remain its independent sovereign. This hope was shared by the Cossacks. They had revolted against Poland because the king was weak and could not make himself respected by the aristocracy; they feared the Tzar of Muscovy would be only too strong. All government, all authority, was a burden to the free Cossack.

Bogdan, however, kept up the appearances of submission. His death was the signal of disorder. Vygovski, chancellor of the Cossack army, took the mace of the hetman, but Martin Pouchkar, the *polkovnik* of Pultowa, and the Zaporogues, refused to recognize him. Vygovski, Pouchkar, and the Zaporogue ataman denounced each other at Moscow. Vygovski caused Pouchkar to be assassinated, and made advances to Poland, to secure himself an ally against the Tzar; he also applied to the Khan of the Crimea, and defeated Prince Troubetskoï at Konotop; but after the retreat of the Khan, the majority of the Cossacks declared for Moscow, and obliged the rebel to fly to Poland. George Khmelnitski, son of the liberator, was elected hetman.

The troubles of Little Russia revived the courage of the Poles. They succeeded in expelling the Swedes, and refused to execute the treaty of Moscow. The war recommenced, and the Russians were unfortunate. The very extremity of their misfortunes seemed to have bound the Poles together. After some slight successes, one Russian army was defeated at Polonka by the voïevode Tcharnetski, the conqueror of the Swedes; another, commanded by the boyard Cheremetief and the hetman George Khmelnitski, allowed itself to be surrounded near Tchoudnovo by the Tatars and Poles, and being deserted by the Cossacks, was forced to lay down its arms. In the north they lost Wilna and the whole of Lithuania.

Khmelnitski, had become a monk. Teteria, his successor, had done homage to the king; but the country on the left bank of the Dnieper refused to recognize him as hetman, and elected Brioukhovetski, who was devoted to Russia. John Casimir crossed the river, and was on the point of reconquering the whole Ukraine; but having been repulsed at the siege of Gloukhof, he lost all his best troops through hunger and cold in the steppes of the desert. The two empires were exhausted by a war which had already lasted ten years. The whole of Poland had been overrun by Swedes, Russians, and Cossacks. Russia had no longer money with which to pay her army, and she had recourse to a forced currency, by which a bronze coinage was given the fictitious value of silver. Everywhere were heard bitter complaints of the famine. At Moscow a riot broke out against the Miloslavskis, the kinsmen of the Tzarina, and the multitude marched to the palace of Kolomenskoé to drag them out by force. The soldiers had to fire on the rebels, and 7000 of them were killed or taken.

Notwithstanding all this, neither the Poles nor the Russians would lay down arms without being assured the possession of all that they had conquered with so many sacrifices. Poland was now attacked by two new misfortunes—the revolt of Prince Lubomirski, who had some grievance against the queen, and the death of Teteria, whose successor, Dorochenko, went over to the Sultan, and by so doing involved the Government in a war with both Turks and Tatars. It was necessary to treat with Russia, and a thirteen years' truce was concluded at Androussovo. Alexis renounced Lithuania, but kept Smolensk and Kief on the right bank of the Dnieper, and all the Little Russian left bank (1667).

The treaty with Poland did not give peace to Little Russia. Neither the Dnieper Cossacks nor the Don Cossacks could exist under the obedience and regularity essential to a modern State. The more Russia became civilized and centralized, the more she became separated from the men of the Steppe; the further the frontier of this civilized Russia advanced to the South, the nearer approached the inevitable conflict. The reign of Alexis, troubled at first by the revolts of the Muscovite cities, was now vexed by the revolts of the Cossacks.

The hetman Brioukhovetski was a devoted adherent of Russia, but he was surrounded by many malcontents. As usual, the people had not got all they had hoped by the revolution; he saw, however, in the absolute authority of the Tzar, a bulwark against the Little Russian oligarchy of the *starchina* and the *polkovniks,* and against the turbulence of the Cossacks. "God," he said to the latter, "has delivered us from you; you can no longer pillage and devastate our houses." The Cossacks and the *starchina,* or in other words, the military and aristocratic party, were still more displeased to see the Muscovite voïevodes establish themselves in the towns. The Republic of the Zaporogues already feared that it had given itself a master. Methodius, Metropolitan of Kief, encouraged the resistance of a party of the clergy who wished to remain subject to the Patriarch of Constantinople, and not to be transferred to the Patriarch of Moscow. It was Methodius who organized the rebellion; he made advances to the hetman, who opened a negotiation with Dorochenko, the ataman of the right bank, who promised to resign his office and to recognise as chief of Little Russia the man who would deliver her. The weak Brioukhovetski allowed himself to be persuaded, and at the Assembly of Gadatch, in 1668, it was decided to revolt against the Tzar, and to take the oath to the Sultan, as the men of the right bank had already done. Two voïevodes and 120 Muscovites were put to death. A short time after, Brioukhovetski was slain by order of Dorochenko, who became hetman of both banks. But of the two parties which divided Little Russia, the party of independence or the Polish and Turkish Party, and the party of Moscow, the latter was predominant on the left bank. It did not hesitate to make terms with the Tzar, and, at the price of a few concessions, a second time submitted to him entirely. Mnogogrechnyi, the new hetman, took up his abode at Batourine.

The right bank had no reason to pride itself on the policy to which it was committed by Dorochenko. It became the theatre of a terrible war between Turkey and Poland, and was cruelly ravaged by Mahomet IV. Abandoned for a moment by the weak King Michael Vichnevetski, it was conquered by his energetic successor, John Sobieski. The left, or Muscovite bank, had less to suffer, although the Sultan claimed it equally as his own possession, but the inhabitants had only to fight with their old enemies the Tatars.

Razin's Rebellion

The third major revolt of the seventeenth century was that of Stepan (Stenko) Razin. The first excerpt is from Rambaud, loc. cit., pp. 281–282. The second is from Shestakov, op. cit., pp. 64–66.

The Cossacks of the Don at this period were, on the whole, tolerably quiet; but one of their number, Stenko Razine, overturned all Eastern Russia. The immigration of Cossacks of the Dnieper, expelled from their native land by war, had created a great famine in these poor plains of the Don. Stenko assembled some of these starved adventurers, and formed a scheme for the capture of Azof; but on being hindered by the *starchina* of the Dontsi, he turned towards the East, towards the Volga and the Jaïk (Oural). His reputation was wide-spread; he was said to be a magician, against whom neither sabre, balls, nor bullets could prevail, and the brigands of all the country crowded to his banner. He swept the Caspian, and ravaged the shores of Persia. The Russian Government, powerless to crush him, offered him a pardon if he would surrender his guns and boats stolen from the Crown. He accepted the offer; but his exploits, his wealth acquired by pillage, and his princely liberality created him an immense party among the lower classes, and among the Cossacks and even the *streltsi* of the towns. The lands of the Volga were always ready for a social revolution, hence the success of Razine, and later of Pougatchef. There brigands were popular and respected; honest merchants, come to the Don for trading purposes, and learning that Stenko had begun the career of a pirate, did not hesitate to join him.

In 1670, Stenko having spent all the money he had gained by pillage, went up the Don with an army of vagabonds, and thence crossed to the Volga. All the country rose on the approach of a chief already so famous. The inhabitants of Tzaritsyne opened their gates to him. A flotilla was sent against him, but the sailors and the *streltsi* surrendered, and betrayed to him their commanders. Astrakhan revolted, and delivered up its two voïevodes, one of whom was thrown from the top of a bell-tower. Ascending the Volga, he took Saratof and Samara, and raised the country of Nijni-Novgorod, Tambof, and Pensa. Everywhere in the Russia of the Volga the serfs revolted against their masters—the Tatars, Tchouvaches, Mordvians, and Tcheremisses against the domination of Russia. It was a fearful revolution. In 1671 Stenko Razine was defeated, near Simbirsk, by George Baratinski. His prestige was lost; he was pursued into the steppes, arrested on the Don, and sent to Moscow, where he was executed (1671).

His death did not immediately check the rebellion. The brigands still continued to hold the country. At Astrakhan, Vassili Ouss governed despotically, and threw the archbishop from a belfry. Finally, however, all these imitators of Razine were killed or captured, the Volga freed, and the Don became as peaceful as the Dnieper.

. . .

The peasants who fled to the south, to the banks of the River Don and its tributaries, formed large Cossack settlements which were called *stanitsas*.

There was no equality among the Cossacks of the Don in the middle of the 17th century. Some of the Cossacks had seized the best lands, accumulated property, began to trade, and became rich. Others remained poor. The poor Cossacks either had to go into bondage to the rich Cossacks, or to obtain their livelihood by robbery. The tsar's voyevodas hunted down the fugitives and returned them to the landlords. The poor Cossacks hated the Moscow landlords bitterly. They were roused to rebellion by the Cossack Stepan Razin.

A foreign traveller, who was in Muscovy at that time, described Razin as follows: "He is of majestic appearance and noble bearing; proud of feature, tall in stature, his face slightly pock-marked. He possessed the ability to inspire fear and love."

Stepan Razin rallied large masses of poor people to his standard. He was elected ataman, or chief. Many Cossacks and other people who were enraged against the tsar's voyevodas and the landlords joined him.

In the spring of 1670, Razin, at the head of an army of 7,000 men, attacked Tsaritsin on the Volga (now called Stalingrad) and captured that town. Here the tsar's soldiers, the *Streltsi,* came over to his side. Then he marched on Astrakhan and captured that town after a siege of two days. The rich merchants, boyars and the tsar's officials were put to death by the Cossacks. Razin threw the voyevoda of Astrakhan from the belfry of the church. In Astrakhan Razin's followers elected administrators from among the Cossacks.

With the munitions captured in Astrakhan, Razin moved up the Volga. He captured cities and wreaked vengeance on the tsar's voyevodas and officials. He sent messengers among the peasants to call upon them to join his ranks.

In response to Razin's call, the peasants rose in rebellion, killed their landlords, burned down the manors, and joined Razin's army in whole detachments. The peoples of the Volga, the Chuvash, Tatars, Mordovians and Maris, marched with the Russian peasants. The fact that they spoke different languages did not hinder them. Their hatred for the tsar and the landlords united them into one common family.

The tsar and the landlords gathered their army and regiments of mercenary foreign soldiers and marched against Razin. Razin found it hard to contend against these well-armed forces. He gave them battle near Simbirsk. Razin was wounded. His army was defeated. With a small detachment he managed to retire to the Don. But the rich Cossacks of the Don captured him and surrendered him to the tsar. The tsar pronounced the following sentence on him: "Put him to a cruel death."

Razin was executed in Moscow in 1671.

Tsar Alexei dealt cruelly with the rebel peasants. Thousands of the rebels were hacked to pieces, whipped to death and hanged on gallows. The peasant revolt was crushed.

During the Razin rebellion, as was the case during Bolotnikov's rebellion, the peasants did not have an organized working class for their reliable ally. Nor did they understand the aim of the rebellion; they could wreck the landlords' mansions and kill the landlords, but they did not know what to do further, what new order to introduce.

This was the cause of their weakness.

Pre-Petrine Contacts with the West

Peter the Great has been so publicized as "the westernizer of Russia" that earlier Russian relations with western Europe are often forgotten or ignored. Peter's efforts at westernization were spectacular, but as the following excerpts show, western contacts and influences did not originate with him. The source of the first excerpt is: Rambaud, Russia, vol 1, pp. 255–289, passim. The second is taken from: Schuyler, E., Peter the Great, Emperor of Russia. A Study of Historical Biography. Two volumes. New York: Charles Scribner's Sons, 1890. Vol. 1, pp. 199–207, slightly abridged. (On Schuyler, see below.)

In May 1614, Ouchakof and Zaborovski had been sent to ask help from Holland in men and money. The Dutch gave them a thousand gulden, but said that they had themselves only lately ended a great war, that they could give the Tzar no substantial aid, but would do their utmost to induce the King of Sweden to make peace. Alexis Ziousine had been despatched to London in June 1613; he was ordered to narrate all the excesses committed by the Poles in Moscow, and to say to King James, "After the destruction of Moscow, the Lithuanians seized your merchants—Mark the Englishman, and all the others—took away all their wares, subjected them to a rigorous imprisonment, and ended by massacring them." If by chance he discovered that the English were aware that it was not the Poles, but the Cossacks and the lower classes who had put Mark to death and seized on the merchandise, he was to have other excuses ready. The Tzar entreated help in money to pay the men-at-arms, and not in soldiers, as he could give them no pay. They would think themselves happy if the King of England would send the Tzar money, provisions, powder, lead, sulphur, and other munitions, to the value of about 100,000 roubles; but would content themselves with 70,000 roubles' worth, or in case of absolute necessity with 50,000. James received the envoy and his suite courteously, informed them that he was aware of the wrongs the Poles and the Swedes had inflicted on them, and ordered them three times following to cover themselves. The Russians declined to do this. "When we see thy fraternal love and lively friendship for our sovereign, when we hear thy royal words which glorify our prince, and contemplate thine eyes thus close at hand, how can we, *kholopys* as we are, put our hats on our heads at such a moment?"

In August 1614, the year following this embassy, there appeared at Moscow John Merrick, who had for long traded with the holy city, but who came this time as ambassador from James I., qualified with full powers, as prince, knight, and gentleman of the bedchamber. In an interview with Prince Ivan Kourakine he began by demanding, on the part of the English merchants, a direct communication with India by the Obi, and with Persia by the Volga and Astrakhan. Kourakine alleged that this route was unsafe, that Astrakhan had only lately been delivered from Zaroutski, and that numerous brigands still infested the Volga. When security should be established, they would open the question with King James. They then passed to the subject of mediation. John Merrick declared that the King of England had assembled his Parliament to consider the best means of helping the Tzar, but that the Parliament had as yet decided nothing, and that he had no instructions on this head. "But," said Kourakine, "can you not assure us that your sovereign will send us help in the spring?" "How can I guarantee it? The journey is long, and there is no way save that by Sweden. . . . I believe, however, he will give you aid." Merrick, having contented himself with causing the Russians to hope, returned to commercial matters: liberty of trade by the Obi and the Volga, concessions of iron and jet mines on the Soukhona, concessions of territory about Vologda for new establishments, &c. The Russian boyards continued to expatiate on the difficulty of the situation, and John Merrick went to Novgorod to negotiate with the Swedes, where he was joined by the envoys of Holland. Gustavus Adolphus, King of Sweden, had obtained some successes over the voïevodes, but he had not contented the Novgorodians, nor been able to take Pskof. The kings of Denmark and Poland were his enemies, and he may have felt a presentiment of the splendid career that awaited him in Germany. He consented to open a congress, and in 1617 concluded with Russia the Peace of Stolbovo, by which he received an indemnity of 20,000 roubles, and kept Ivangorod, Iam Koporié, and Oréchek (Schlüsselburg), but ceded Novgorod, Roussa, Ladoga, and some smaller places.

Russia had begun at last to be a European nation. Everywhere her political or commercial alliance was sought. Gustavus Adolphus, who was making preparations to play his part as the champion of Protestantism in Germany, wished to assure himself of the friendship of Russia against Poland. He represented to Michael, with much truth, that the Catholic League of the Pope, the King of Poland, and the house of Hapsburg were as dangerous to Russia as to Sweden; that if Protestantism succumbed it would be the turn of Orthodoxy, and that the Swedish army was the outpost of Russian security. "When your neighbor's house is on fire," writes the King, "you must bring water and try to extinguish it, to guarantee your own safety. May your Tzarian majesty help your neighbors to protect yourself." The terrible events of late years had only too well justified these remarks. The intrigues of the Jesuits with the false Dmitri, and the burning of Moscow by the Poles, were always present to the memory of the Russians. A treaty of peace and commerce was concluded with Sweden, and a Swedish ambassador appeared at the Court.

England had rendered more than one service to Russia. In her pressing need James I. had lent her 20,000 roubles, and British mediation had led to the Peace of Stolbovo. John Merrick considered he had the right to demand that Russia should open to English commerce the route to Persia by the Volga, and to Hindostan by Siberia. The Tzar consulted the merchants of Moscow. They unanimously replied that such a concession would be their ruin, for they could never hope to rival the wealthier and more enterprising English. They were, however, ready to sacrifice their interests to those of the empire, if the dues paid by the foreigners were essential to the treasury. John Merrick declined to pay any dues, and the negotiation was broken off. They paid him, however, the 20,000 roubles, as he assured them the King had need of them for the help of his son-in-law, the Elector Palatine.

In 1615 the Tzar sent an envoy into France, to announce to Louis XIII. his accession to the throne, and to ask his aid against Poland and Sweden. In 1629 there appeared at Moscow the ambassador Duguay Cormenin, who was commissioned to solicit for French commerce what had been refused to English trade—free passage into Persia. He also spoke of a political alliance. "His Tzarian majesty," he said, "is the head of Eastern countries and the orthodox faith; Louis, King of France, is the head of Southern countries; and the Tzar, by contracting a friendship and alliance with him, will get the better of his enemies. As the Emperor is closely allied to the King of Poland, the Tzar must be allied to the King of France. These two princes are everywhere glorious; they have no equals either in strength or power; their subjects obey them blindly, while the English and Brabançons are only obedient when they choose. The latter buy their wares in Spain, and sell them to the Russians at a high price, but the French will furnish them with everything at a reasonable rate." This negotiation for the first Franco-Russian treaty spoken of in history had no result. As to the route to Persia, it was refused by the boyards, who said that the French might buy the Persian merchandise from the Russians.

Western influence made considerable progress during this reign. The merchants entreated that access into the interior might be forbidden to those strangers whose rivalry was their ruin; but the latter were, on the contrary, so necessary to the State and to the general progress that they had to be invited into the country by all possible means. Under Michael, more foreigners than ever came into Russia. Vinius the Dutchman established foundries at Toula for guns, bullets, and other iron weapons. Marselein the German opened similar ones on the Vaga, the Kostroma, and the Cheksna. Privileges were granted to other foreign merchants or artisans, and the only condition imposed on them was not to conceal the secrets of their industries from the inhabitants of the countries. This is another point of resemblance between this reign of reform and that of Henri IV., who also summoned to his kingdom Flemish, English, and Venetian artisans. One European import did not however, find favor in Russia—the usage of tobacco was forbidden, and snuff-takers had their noses cut off.

Learned men were also sought from Europe. Adam Olearius of Holstein, a celebrated astronomer, geographer, and geometer, was invited to Moscow. Already the Academy of Sciences of Peter the Great was foreshadowed. A cosmographical treatise was translated from Latin into Russian. The Patriarch Philarete had established at Moscow an academy where Greek and Latin, the languages of the Renaissance, were taught. The Archimandrite Dionysius of Troïtsa, who had distinguished himself in the struggle with the Poles, undertook to correct the text of the Slavonian books—a hazardous enterprise, which cost Dionysius himself a short period of persecution. Native historians continued to re-edit their chronicles, and Abraham Palitsyne, cellarer of Troïtsa, narrated the famous siege of the convent.

During this reign, when Russia was trying to assimilate herself to Europe, diplomacy naturally took rapid strides. Muscovy had entered into more or less close relations with all the Courts of the West.

In 1645, Alexis sent Gerasimus Doktourof to notify his accession to the King of England, Charles I. The Russian envoy arrived in England in the midst of the Revolution. Being received at Gravesend with great honors and the firing of guns by the company of merchants that traded with Russia, he at once inquired "where was the king?" They replied, they did not know exactly where he was, because for three or four years there had been a great civil war, and instead of the king they had now the Parliament, composed of deputies from all the orders, who governed London as well as the kingdoms of England and Scotland. "Our war with the king," said the merchants, "began for the sake of religion, when he married the daughter of the King of France. She, being a Papist, persuaded the king into various superstitious practices; it was by her counsel that the king instituted archbishops and called in the Jesuits. Many people, in order to follow the example of the king, made themselves Papists too. Besides this, the king wished to govern the kingdom according to his own will, as do the sovereigns of other States. But here, from time immemorial, the country has been free: the early kings could settle nothing: it was the Parliament, the men who were elected, that governed. The king began to rule after his own will, but the Parliament would not allow that, and many archbishops and Jesuits were executed. The king, seeing that the Parliament intended to act according to its own wish, as it had done from all time, and not at all according to the royal will, left London with the queen, without being expelled by anyone, saying that they were going away into other towns. Once out of London, he sent the queen to France and began to fight us, but the Parliament was the stronger. The Parliament is composed of two *palaty* (chambers): in one of them sit the boyards, in the other the men elected by the commons—the *sloujilié lioudi* and the merchants. Five hundred men sit in the parliament, and one orator speaks for all."

These lessons in the English Constitution could not penetrate the brain of the Russian envoy. He only recognized the king, and persisted, according to the text of his instructions, in trying to deliver his letters of credit to the king himself. "Hast thou a letter from thy sovereign, and a mission to the Parliament?" they asked him. He replied, "I have neither a letter nor a mission to the Parliament. Let the Parliament send me immediately before the king, and give me an escort, carriages, and provisions. Let the Parliament present me to him—it is to him that I will speak." His demand was naturally refused, and he wished instantly to leave for Holland, but this was not allowed.

The following year Charles I. was brought a prisoner into London. Doktourof insisted on being presented to him. His request was ill-timed. "You cannot be brought before him," they said to him; "he no longer governs anything." Doktourof then refused a dinner given to him by the Russian Company, and only yielded when the dinner was served at his own house. The Parliament, however, did not wish to interrupt the friendly relations with Russia.

Doktourof was summoned before the House of Lords on the 13th of June. At his entrance all the "boyards" took off their hats, and Lord Manchester, the "chief boyard," rose. Then Doktourof, to the general consternation, made the following speech:—"I am sent by my sovereign to your king, Charles King of England. I have been sent as a courier (*gonets*) to negotiate important affairs of State, which offer great advantages to both sovereigns and to all Christendom, and may help to maintain peace and concord. It is the 13th of June, and, since I arrived in London on the 26th of November last, I have never ceased to show you the letter of the Tzar and to beg you to allow me to go before the king. You have kept me in London without permitting me either to have an interview with the king or to return to the Tzar; and yet in all neighboring countries the route is free to all ambassadors, envoys, and couriers of the Tzar."

Manchester replied that they would explain to the Tzar by letter their reasons for acting thus. They gave him a chair, and the English "boyards" likewise seated themselves; and he began to look about the House, of which he gives a minute description in his report. He was then conducted to the House of Commons, and the dignitaries came to meet him preceded by the royal sceptre. He renewed his declarations, and then retired ceremoniously. In June 1646 he left England much discontented. Alexis could understand no more of the English Revolution than his envoy. He maintained, like Catherine II., the cause of kings against the liberty of the subjects. In May 1647 he received at Moscow Nawtingall, envoy of Charles I., who denounced the captivity of the king, and said Charles would see with pleasure the English Company deprived of its privileges, and everyone allowed to trade freely with Russia. Alexis listened to his request, and granted him, as aid to the king 30,000 *tchetverts* of corn, out of the 300,000 that were asked of him. But the English merchants settled in Russia accused Nawtingall of imposture, saying that the king's letter was apocryphal, and that the dog he had brought as a present to Alexis had never been bought by Charles I. Nawtingall was expelled in disgrace, and avenged himself by accusing his compatriots of a project of attacking Arkhangel, and of pillaging the Russian merchants. His honors as ambassador were then given back to him, but he quitted Russia.

When Alexis heard of the execution of Charles I., he published the oukase of June 1649, which, as a punishment to the regicides, forbade the English merchants to live in the cities of the interior, and confined them to Arkhangel. The Tzar furnished help in money and corn to Charles, Prince of Wales, who in 1660 became Charles II., and resumed relations with him when he ascended the throne of the Stuarts.

THE GERMAN SUBURB AT Moscow. Although foreigners came to Russia from the earliest period, yet it was not until the time of Ivan III. that they arrived in great numbers. That prince received foreign artists and artisans so well that numbers of Italian architects, engineers, goldworkers, physicians, and mechanics hastened to Moscow. His marriage with the Greek Princess Sophia Palaeologos gave rise to new and more frequent relations with Italy, and he several times sent to Rome, Venice, and Milan for physicians and men of technical knowledge. It was in this way that the Cathedral of the Assumption came to be built by Aristotle Fioraventi of Bologna, that of St. Michael the Archangel by Aleviso of Milan, and the banqueting hall of the palace, and the walls and the gates of the Kremlin by other Italian architects. German miners, too, came, or were sent by Matthew Corvinus, King of Hungary, and some of them discovered silver and copper mines in Siberia.

Ivan IV, the Terrible, appreciated foreigners, and invited large numbers of them into Russia. But, besides this, it was during his reign in 1558, that an English expedition penetrated into the White Sea, and the trade with England began, which soon took great proportions, and brought to Russia many English merchants. After the conquest of Livonia and portions of the southern shore of the Baltic very many prisoners of war were sent to Moscow, and elsewhere in the interior of Russia, and were never allowed to return to their own country.

Under Ivan's son Theodore, and Boris Godunof, the intercourse with western Europe constantly increased. Favours were given, not only to the English merchants, but also to Dutchmen and Danes, to immigrants from Hamburg and the Hanse Towns. Godunof invited soldiers and officers as well as physicians and artisans. His children were educated with great deviations from Russian routine. He even thought of marrying his daughter to a Danish prince, and, when at his country estate, was fond of the society of foreigners. The so-called False Demetrius had very great inclinations toward foreigners. This was very natural, for he had been educated in Poland, and had seen the advantages of western culture. Polish manners prevailed at his court; he was surrounded by a guard of foreign soldiers; he protected all religions, especially the Catholic; he urged Russians to travel abroad, and so willingly received foreigners that a Pole, in writing about the immigration of so many foreigners into Russia, said: "For centuries long it was hard for the birds even to get into the realm of Muscovy, but now come not only many merchants, but a crowd of grocers and tavernkeepers." Under the Tsar Theodore, son of Ivan the Terrible, there were, according to Fletcher, about 4,300 foreigners in the Russian service, most of them Poles and Little Russians, but still about 150 Dutchmen and Scotchmen. In the reign of Boris Godunof, the foreign detachment in the army was composed of twenty-five hundred men of all nationalities. . . .

In the beginning of the sixteenth century, the Grand Duke Basil established the residence of his foreign body-guard, consisting of Poles, Germans and Lithuanians, on the right bank of the river Moskva, outside the town, in a place called Naleiki, in order, as Herberstein said, that the Russians might not be contaminated by the bad example of their drunkenness. Later on, this district became inhabited by Streltsi and the common people, and the Livonian prisoners of war were established by Ivan the Terrible on the Yauza, near the Pokrof gate. When Demetrius was so desperately defended by his foreign body-guard, that a Livonian, Wilhelm Furstenberg, fell at his side, the Russians said: "See what true dogs these Germans are: let us kill them all"; and during the Troublous Times, the foreigners in Moscow were subject to constant attacks from the Russians. Persecutions were organised against them, as at other times and places against the Jews. There was not a popular commotion in which threats, at least, were not made against them, and during one of the attacks the whole foreign quarter was burnt to the ground. After this, the foreigners lived within the walls, and for a while enjoyed the same privileges as Russian subjects, adopting their dress and their habits. Livonian prisoners of war had, even before the Troublous Times, made their way within the town, and had built a church or two. For some reason they incurred the wrath of the Tsar, were driven from their houses, and their property was plundered. . . .

When affairs became more settled under the Tsar Alexis, by a decree of 1652 there was a systematic settling of all foreigners in a suburb outside the town; the number of the streets and lanes was set down in the registers, the pieces of land, varying from 350 to 1,800 yards square, were set apart for the officers, the physicians, the apothecaries, the artisans and the widows of foreigners who had been in the Russian service. This suburb, which was nicknamed by the Russians Kukui, now forms the north-eastern portion of the city of Moscow, intersected by the Basmannaya and Pokrofskaya streets, and still contains the chief Protestant and Catholic churches. It is fairly depicted to us in one of the drawings made by the artist who accompanied Meyerberg's embassy in 1661. As the houses were of wood, and surrounded by gardens, this suburb had all the appearances of a large and flourishing village.

Reutenfels, who was in Russia from 1671 to 1673, estimated the number of foreigners in the country as about 18,000. Most of them lived in Moscow, but a large number inhabited Vologda, Archangel and other towns where there was foreign trade, as well as the mining districts.

The residence of the foreigners in a separate suburb naturally enabled them to keep up the traditions and customs of Western Europe much more easily than if they had mingled with the Russians. They wore foreign clothing, read foreign books, and spoke, at least in their households, their own language, although they all had some acquaintance with the Russian tongue, which sometimes served as a medium of communication with each other. The habitual use of a few Russian words, the adoption of a few Russian customs, conformity to the Russian dress and ways of thinking on some points, was the most they had advanced toward Russianisation. Rarely did they change their faith to advance their worldly prospects, although the children of marriages with Russians were brought up in the Russian church. In general, they held close to their own religion and their own modes of education. They kept up a constant intercourse with their native countries, by new arrivals, and by correspondence with their friends. They imported not only foreign conveniences for their own use, but also received from abroad the journals of the period, books of science and history, novels and poems. Their interest in the politics of their own lands was always maintained, and many and warm were the discussions which were caused by the wars between France and the Low Countries, and the English Revolution. In this way, the German suburb was a nucleus of a superior civilisation.

The influence of the foreign residents in Russia was especially seen in the material development of the country. The Russians were then, as they are now, quick to learn and ready to imitate. A Pole, Maszkiewicz, in the time of the False Demetrius, remarked that the metal and leather work of the Russians after Oriental designs could scarcely be distinguished from the genuine articles. Foreigners understood this quality of Russian workmen, and frequently endeavoured to keep their trades as a monopoly for themselves. We know that Hans Falck, a foreign manufacturer of bells and metal castings, sent away his Russian workmen when engaged in the delicate processes, in order that they might not learn the secrets of the art. The Government found it necessary, in many cases, to make contracts with foreign artisans that they should teach their trades to a certain number of Russian workmen. It was the Englishman John Merrick, first merchant and subsequently ambassador, who was one of the earliest to teach the Russians that it was better for them to manufacture for themselves than to export the raw materials. He explained to the boyars how people had been poor in England as long as they had exported raw wool, and had only begun to get rich when the laws protected the woollen manufacturers by insisting on the use of wool at home, and especially on the use of woollen shrouds, and how greatly the riches of England had increased since the country began to sell cloth instead of wool. It was in part through his influence that a manufactory of hemp and tow was established near Holmogory. In a similar way, paper-mills, glass-factories, powder-mills, saltpeter-works, and iron-works were established by foreigners. A Dane, Peter Marselis, had important and well-known iron-works near Tula, which were so productive that he was able to pay his inspector three thousand rubles a year, and had to pay to his brother-in-law, for his share, twenty thousand rubles.

We can see the relative value of this, when we remember that, at that time, two to two and a half quarters of rye could be bought for a ruble, and that, twenty years later, the salary of General Gordon, one of the highest in the Russian service, was only one thousand rubles a year; while the pastor of the Lutheran church in Moscow in 1699 received annually only sixty rubles. Concessions for copper mines were also given to Marselis and other foreigners, and the Stroganofs, who possessed such great and rich mining districts on the frontier of Siberia, constantly sent abroad for physicians, apothecaries, and artisans of all kinds.

It has already been said that the foreigners in Russia were not too well pleased with the ease with which the Russians learned their trades; neither did this please foreign Governments. The famous Duke of Alva said that it was "inexcusable to provide Russia with cannon and other arms, and to initiate the Russians into the way war was carried on in Western Europe, because, in this way, a dangerous neighbour was being educated." Sigismund, King of Poland, did his best to hinder the intercourse which sprang up between Moscow and England, and wrote to Queen Elizabeth that "such commercial relations were dangerous, because Russia would thus receive war material; and it would be still worse if Russia, in this way, could get immigrants who should spread through the country the technical knowledge so necessary there. It was in the interest of Christianity and religion to protest against Russia, the enemy of all free nations, receiving cannon and arms, artists and artisans, and being initiated into the views and purposes of European politics."

It was natural that, with constant and increasing intercourse with foreigners, the Russians should adopt some of the customs which the strangers had brought with them. For a long time the foreigners were greatly laughed at for eating salads, or grass, as the peasants called it, but this habit gradually spread. In the early part of the seventeenth century, the Dutch introduced the culture of asparagus, and garden roses were first brought by the Dane, Peter Marselis. The use of snuff and of smoking tobacco was speedily acquired, much to the horror of all right-thinking and orthodox people, who saw in this a plain work of the devil; for was it not said in the Bible: "Not that which goeth into the mouth defileth a man; but that which cometh out of the mouth, this defileth a man." Many Russian nobles even adopted foreign clothes, and trimmed their hair and beard. Nikita Romanof, the owner of the boat which Peter found at Ismailovo, wore German clothes while hunting, for which he was sharply reprimanded by the Patriarch; and the conduct of Prince Andrew Koltsof-Masalsky, in cutting his hair short, in 1675, caused so much displeasure that the Tsar Alexis issued an ukase, forbidding, under heavy penalties, the trimming of one's hair or beard, or the wearing of foreign clothes. This decree soon fell into desuetude, and at the time of which we are speaking, foreign clothes and foreign habits were not at all uncommon among the Russians of the higher ranks. Even Peter himself occasionally wore foreign dress, and was severely blamed by the Patriarch for daring to appear in such costume at the death-bed of his mother. . . .

One of the most important steps in civilisation introduced by foreigners was the letter-post. Postal communications had previously existed in the interior of the country, but, even for Government purposes, they were very slow, and nearly all letters were sent by private hand, or by a chance messenger. It was in 1664 that a decree of the Tsar Alexis gave a Swede named John privileges for the organisation of an international letter-post, and in 1667 the first postal convention was made with Poland. John of Sweden was succeeded by Peter Marselis, the Dane, and he by Andrew Vinius, who first received the title of Postmaster of His Majesty the Tsar, and was ordered to conclude postal conventions with the neighbouring States. The institution of the post-office did not please all Russians ·as much as it did the foreigners, and, if we may judge from the continued existence of a censorship, is still looked upon with a certain degree of suspicion. The Russian political economist, Ivan Pososhkof, writing in 1701, complains: "The Germans have cut a hole through from our land into their own, and from outside people can now, through this hole, observe all our political and commercial relations. This hole is the post. Heaven knows whether it brings advantage to the Tsar, but the harm which it causes to the realm is incalculable. Everything that goes on in our land is known to the whole world. The foreigners all become rich by it, the Russians become poor as beggars. The foreigners always know which of our goods are cheap and which are dear, which are plentiful and which are scarce. Thereupon they bargain, and know immediately how much they are obliged to pay for our goods. In this way trade is unequal. Without the post, both sides would be ignorant of the prices and the stock of goods on hand, and no party would be injured. Besides, it is a very bad thing that people know in other countries everything that happens in ours. This hole, then, should be shut up — that is, the post should be put an end to; and, it seems to me, it would be very sensible not to allow letters to be sent, even through messengers, except with a special permission each time from the proper authorities."

Peter the Great

One of the best biographies of Peter was written by Eugene Schuyler, an American diplomatic and consular official. Based upon very extensive research, Schuyler's biography is accurate and so sound that while later biographies have supplemented it they have not supplanted it, and few of them are as entertaining. The following excerpts deal with Peter's boyhood, his journey to western Europe and his reforms. The source is: Schuyler, Peter the Great, vol. 1, pp. 103–109, 274–286; vol. 2, pp. 348–352, 369–379 (somewhat abridged).

BOYHOOD. During the early period of Sophia's regency, Peter was left very much to himself. But as his name was used in all public documents he was required to sign many of them, and he seems to have performed this part of his duty with punctuality and accuracy. He had also to go to Moscow, on occasions of ceremony, to take part in the reception of foreign ambassadors, and to be present at state banquets, and at the ceremonies and processions on religious festivals. The Polish envoy, in his report on affairs at Moscow, stated that Sophia was exceedingly fond of her brother Peter, and was endeavouring to put the state in good condition in order to hand the Government over to him when he became old enough. The sincerity of her attachment to Peter we may be allowed to doubt, but she at least manifested no open ill-will to him, and indeed, there are several entries in the books of the court of her favourable disposition to him. Thus, in July, 1684, she presented him with some diamond clasps, buttons and stars. With his brother Ivan, Peter was always on the best of terms, and especially so after the Government had become settled. Van Keller, writing in 1683 of Peter's residence in the country, says: "The natural love and intelligence between the two Lords is even better than before. God will it long continue so."

So much was Peter's mind set on military objects, and on playing at soldiers, that even a day or two after the first riot of the Streltsi, we hear of his sending down to the arsenal for drums, banners and arms. The troubles of the Dissenters and of Prince Havansky naturally kept him from indulging the full bent of his inclinations in the country, and for the rest of the year he was detained in Moscow by official duties. Early in 1683, however, we find him ordering uniforms, banners, and wooden cannon, all of which were immediately furnished by the authorities, and as soon as he was able to go into the country, to Preobrazhensky and to the Sparrow Hills, messengers came almost daily to the Kremlin for lead, powder and shot. On his eleventh birthday — in 1683 — he was allowed for the first time to have some real guns, with which he fired salutes, under the direction of a German artilleryman named Simon Sommer, who had recently come from foreign parts, and was a captain in the regiment of General Shepelof. After this he was allowed small brass and iron cannon; and that he might indulge his taste for music as well as for military pastime, musicians — especially drummer-boys — were selected for him from the different regiments. About that time — July, 1683 — a German traveller, named Engelbert Kampfer, passed through Moscow on his way to Astrakhan, and, in his diary, which still exists in manuscript in the British Museum, tells of his reception at the Russian court, as acting secretary for the Swedish Envoy, Fabricius: —

"Here we got off our horses, and, handing our swords to a servant, walked up some steps and passed through a building magnificent with gilded vaults, and then through an open stone passage, again to the left, and through an anteroom in the audience hall, the floor of which was covered with Turkish carpets, where we came to the 'piercing eyes' of their Tsarish Majesties. Both their Majesties sat, not in the middle, but somewhat to the right side of the hall, next to the middle column, and sat on a silver throne like a bishop's chair, somewhat raised and covered with red cloth, as was most of the hall. Over the throne hung a holy picture. The Tsars wore, over their coats, robes of silver cloth woven with red and white flowers, and, instead of sceptres, had long golden staves bent at the end like bishops' croziers, on which, as on the breast-plate of their robes, their breasts and their caps, glittered white, green and other precious stones. The elder drew his cap down over his eyes several times, and with looks cast down on the floor, sat almost immovable. The younger had a frank and open face, and his young blood rose to his cheeks as often as anyone spoke to him. He constantly looked about and his great beauty and his lively manner — which sometimes brought the Muscovite magnates into confusion — struck all of us so much that had he been an ordinary youth and no imperial personage we would gladly have laughed and talked with him. The elder was seventeen, and the younger sixteen years old. When the Swedish Envoy gave his letters of credence, both Tsars rose from their places, slightly bared their heads and asked about the king's health, but Ivan, the elder, somewhat hindered the proceedings through not understanding what was going on, and gave his hand to be kissed at the wrong time. Peter was so eager that he did not give the secretaries the usual time for raising him and his brother from their seats and touching their heads: he jumped up at once, put his own hand to his hat and began quickly to ask the usual question: 'Is his royal Majesty, Carolus of Sweden, in good health?' He had to be pulled back until the elder brother had a chance of speaking."

It was evident that Peter must have been a large, healthy boy, if when he was only eleven he appeared to Kampfer and the Swedish mission to be sixteen.

It is interesting to compare with this the account of Johann Eberhard Hovel, who in the next year, 1684, came on a mission from the Emperor Leopold I. Peter was at that time ill with the measles — an illness which excited considerable alarm among his partisans — and was unable to receive. Hovel, therefore, saw no one but the Tsar Ivan. He says that when the health of the Emperor was asked about, the Tsar was so weak from long standing that he had to be supported by his two chamberlains, who held up his arms, and he spoke with a very weak and inarticulate voice. General Gordon, who was received a few days later, January 22, had tried to put off his reception in order to see both the Tsars at once; but as he was obliged to leave soon for his command at Kief, was received only by Ivan and Sophia. According to his account, Ivan was sickly and weak, and always looked toward the ground. He said nothing himself, and all the questions were put through Prince Golitsyn. This was just after the marriage of Ivan with Praskovia Soltykof, of a distinguished family. This marriage Hovel, as well as many other people, considered to be a plot on the part of Sophia to obtain heirs from the elder brother, and thus get rid of the claims of Peter, whom he calls "a youth of great expectancy, prudence, and vigour." Considering, however, that Ivan, in spite of the infirmities of his eyes, his tongue and his mind, was in fairly good health, it was the most natural thing in the world that his friends should desire him to marry. Later in the same year, in June, Laurent Rinhuber, a doctor of medicine, coming from Saxony, was received at court, and was granted an audience by the Tsars. He says: "Then I kissed the right hand of Peter, who, with a half-laughing mouth, gave me a friendly and gracious look and immediately held out to me his hand; while the hands of the Tsar Ivan had to be supported. He is a remarkably good-looking boy, in whom nature has shown her power; and has so many advantages of nature that being the son of a king is the least of his good qualities. He has a beauty which gains the heart of all who see him, and a mind which, even in his early years, did not find its like."

In the autumn of the same year, 1684, Peter had another attack of illness, which was more severe than the measles and which caused great alarm. His recovery excited universal joy, more especially in the foreign quarter of Moscow. There were many banquets and feasts in honour of his convalescence, and Prince Boris Golitsyn, the cousin of the Chancellor and the chief adviser of Peter, together with other Russians of that party, dined with the Dutch minister, and caroused till a late hour. A year later, in September, 1685, Van Keller writes: —

"The young Tsar has now entered his thirteenth year: nature develops herself with advantage and good fortune in his whole personality; his stature is great and his mien is fine; he grows visibly, and advances as much in intelligence and understanding as he gains the affection and love of all. He has such a strong preference for military pursuits that when he comes of age we may surely expect from him brave actions and heroic deeds, and we may hope that some day the attacks of the Crim Tartars will be somewhat better restrained than at present. This was the noble aim always set before the ancestors of the young Tsar."

The military exercises of Peter brought him into constant contact with German officers at Moscow, for all the best officers and even soldiers were foreigners, and it was necessary to draw on the German suburb for the officers and instructors for the new regiment which was organised, at the end of 1683, for Peter's amusement. The first man who was enrolled as a soldier in the regiment was Sergius Bukhavastof, one of the grooms of the palace, and Peter was so much struck with his readiness, and so much pleased with the formation of this regiment, that long afterward he ordered the Italian artist Rastrelli, then a favourite in St. Petersburg, to cast a life-size statue of him as the first Russian soldier. Other volunteers soon presented themselves, and Peter himself enlisted as bombardier, for which duty he had an especial fancy, and then passed through the various grades until he became colonel and chief of the regiment. Among the other volunteers were Yekim Voronin and Gregory Lukin — at whose deaths, during the siege of Azof, Peter grieved greatly, "as he and they had been brought up together" — and Alexander Menshikof, the future favourite. This was the beginning of the celebrated Preobrazhensky Regiment, even now the first regiment of the Imperial guard, and of which the Emperor is always the chief. The name Preobrazhensky was given to it first because it was formed and quartered at the palace and village of Preobrazhensky, or the Transfiguration, which, in turn, took their name from the village church. Peter and his friends called this regiment, and others which were afterwards formed, "the guards," but the common name for them at Moscow was the Potishnie Koniukhi — i.e. "Amusements Grooms," or "Troops for Sport."

The number of volunteers for this regiment increased so rapidly that the village of Preobrazhensky could not hold them all, and it was necessary to quarter some of the soldiers in the adjoining village of Semenofsky, where another regiment called the Semenofsky Regiment grew up. All the young nobles who desired to gain Peter's good graces followed his example by enrolling themselves in one of these regiments. Thus, Prince M. M. Golitsyn, the future Field Marshal, began his service as drummer in the Semenofsky Regiment, and Ivan Ivanovitch Buturlin served up to the rank of major in the Preobrazhensky Regiment.

Peter entered upon his military exercises with such zest that they ceased to be mere child's play. He himself performed every exercise, giving himself no rest night or day. He stood his watch in turn, took his share of the duties of the camp, slept in the same tent with his comrades, and partook of their fare. There was no distinction made between the Tsar and the least of his subjects. When his volunteers became proficient in their discipline, he used to lead them on long marches in the neighbourhood of his country home, and went at times even as far as the Trinity Monastery at Kaliazin. As his followers were armed, these marches were in the nature of campaigns, and the troops, such as they were, were under strict military discipline, and were regularly encamped at night with the usual military precautions. In 1685, when Peter was thirteen years old, he resolved on something further, and, in order to practise the assault and defence of fortifications, began to construct a small fortress on the banks of the Yauza, at Preobrazhensky, the remains of which are still visible on the edge of the Sokolniki wood. This fort, probably at the suggestion of one of the German officers, was called Pressburg. It was built with a considerable amount of care, timber was drawn for the purpose from Moscow, and its construction took the greater part of the year. Peter named it with great ceremony, leading a procession from Moscow which included most of the court officials and nobles. All this, as has been said, brought Peter into very close relations with the foreign suburb, and the foreigners in Moscow were fond of social amusements, always accompanied, according to their habits, with beer, wine, and tobacco. Peter, who was precocious, both physically and mentally, took his full share in these entertainments and on the return feasts he gave it may be imagined that there was no stint of drink. With such society Peter gained not only knowledge of men and of the world, but his inquiring mind led him to be curious about many subjects which rarely before had troubled the head of a Russian Prince. Without regard to rank or position, he was always glad to make the acquaintance of those from whom he could learn anything, and was especially attracted by all that was mechanically curious.

Frequently, for amusement, he used to hammer and forge at the blacksmith's shop. He had already become expert with the lathe, and we have documentary evidence to prove that he had practically learnt the mechanical operation of printing as well as the binding of books. We can believe that the Electress Charlotte Sophia did not exaggerate when, in 1697, in describing her interview with Peter, she said that he "already knew excellently well fourteen trades."

All this was a school for Peter; but do not let us be led astray by the word school. Peter's military education was such as he chose to give himself, and entirely for his own amusement. There was nothing in it similar to the regular course of military training practised in a cadet school. Peter was only too glad to escape from the nursery and house to the amusements of the street and the fields. Although we know that in the Russia of that day the intellectual development of a youth did not at all keep pace with his physical growth, and that when a lad was grown to the stature of a man, he immediately assumed the duties and responsibilities of a man, though in mind he might be still a child; yet there was generally the semblance of discipline. The way in which Peter seems to have slipped through the hands of his instructors, tutors and guardians shows not only his strong self-will, but the disorganisation of his party, and the carelessness of his family. Such a training may have been useful, and, indeed, it was useful to Peter; at all events it was better than nothing; but in no sense of the term can it be considered education. This Peter himself, in later life, admitted, and the Empress Elizabeth tells how, when she was bending over her books and exercises, her father regretted that he had not been obliged or enabled to do the same.

One more word with regard to Peter's military amusements. There were, as we have said, mere amusements, and had not the regularity or the plan which subsequent chroniclers and anecdote-writers ascribe to them. In playing at soldiers, Peter followed his natural inclination, and had in his head no plan whatever for reorganising or putting on a better footing the military forces of his country. The reorganisation of the Russian army, indeed, grew out of the campaigns and exercises at Preobrazhensky; but it was not until real war began that Peter saw of what service these exercises had been to him and to others, and found that the boy-soldiers could easily be made the nucleus of an army. . . .

THE WESTERN JOURNEY. The Tsar's feeling was so strong with regard to what might be learnt about ship-building in foreign countries that, after he had sent off many of his subjects to study the trade, he resolved to go himself. Without ascribing to this journey all the importance which Macaulay gave to it when he said, "His journey is an epoch in the history, not only of his own country, but of ours, and of the world," we must admit that it was a remarkable event, and one fraught with much consequence. Since the exiled Izyaslav visited the court of the Emperor Henry IV., at Mainz, in 1075, no Russian ruler had ever been out of his dominions. Peter's journey marks the division between the old Russia, an exclusive, little known country, and the new Russia, an important factor in European politics. It was also one of the turning points in the development of his character, and was the continuation of the education begun in the German suburb. In one way, it may be said that Peter's appearance in the German suburb was really more startling, and of more importance, than his journey westward, for that journey was the natural consequence and culmination of his intercourse with foreigners at Moscow.

This sudden and mysterious journey of the Tsar abroad exercised the minds of Peter's contemporaries no less than it has those of moderns. Many were the reasons which were ascribed then, and have given since, for this step. There was even a dispute among the students of the University of Thorn as to the motives which had induced the Tsar to travel. Pleyer, the secret Austrian agent, wrote to the Emperor Leopold that the whole embassy was "merely a cloak for the freedom sought by the Tsar, to get out of his own country and divert himself a little." Another document in the archives at Vienna finds the cause of the journey in a vow made by Peter, when in danger on the White Sea, to make a pilgrimage to the tombs of the Apostles St. Peter and St. Paul, at Rome. According to Voltaire, "He resolved to absent himself for some years from his dominions, in order to learn how better to govern them." Napoleon said: "He left his country to deliver himself for a while from the crown, so as to learn ordinary life, and to remount by degrees to greatness." But every authentic source gives us but one reason, and the same. Peter went abroad, not to fulfil a vow, not to amuse himself, not to become more civilised, not to learn the art of government, but simply to become a good shipwright. His mind was filled with the idea of creating a navy on the Black Sea for use against the Turks, and his tastes were still, as they had always been, purely mechanical. For this purpose, as he himself says, and as his prolonged residence in Holland shows, he desired to have an opportunity of studying the art of shipbuilding in those places where it was carried to the highest perfection, that is, in Holland, England, and Venice.

In order to give the Tsar greater freedom of action, and to save him from too much formality and ceremony, which he exceedingly disliked, an attempt was made to conceal the purpose of his journey by means of a great embassy, which should visit the chief countries of Western Europe, to explain the policy of Russia toward Turkey, and to make whatever treaties it was found possible, either for commercial purposes or for the war against the Turks. The embassy consisted of three extraordinary ambassadors, at the head of whom was General Lefort. Besides the other rewards he had received for the campaigns against Azof, he had been given the honorary title of Governor-General of Novgorod. The other ambassadors were the Governor-General of Siberia, Theodore Golovin, who had already distinguished himself by the treaty of Nertchinsk with the Chinese; and the Governor of Bolkhof, Prokop Voznitsyn, a skilful and experienced diplomatist. In the suite of the ambassadors were twenty nobles and thirty-five others, called volunteers, who, like those previously sent, were going abroad for the study of shipbuilding. Among these was the Tsar himself. These volunteers were chiefly young men who had been comrades of Peter in his play regiments, in his boat-building, and in his campaigns against Azof. Among them may be particularly remarked Alexander Menshikof and Alexis Golitsyn, two Golovins, Simeon Naryshkin, and the Prince Alexander Bagration of Imeritia. Including priests, interpreters, pages, singers, and servants of various kinds, the suite of the embassy numbered as many as two hundred and fifty persons. The Tsar himself travelled under the strictest incognito. It was forbidden to give him the title of Majesty — he was always to be addressed simply as *Min Her* Peter Mikhailof — and it was forbidden, under pain of death, to mention his presence with the embassy.

During the absence of the Tsar, the government was entrusted to a regency of three persons — Leo Naryshkin, Prince Boris Golitsyn, and Prince Peter Prozorofsky, who were given supreme power. Prince Ramodanofsky was charged with maintaining order in Moscow, and he had verbal instructions to follow up, in the severest way, the slightest movement of discontent or rebellion. The boyar Shein, assisted by General Gordon, had charge of the defence of the southern frontier on the side of Azof, while Prince Jacob Dolgoruky succeeded the boyar Sheremetief in charge of the defences against the Tartars on the frontier of Little Russia, and was ordered to get galleys ready for the siege of Otchakof in the spring of 1698. Sheremetief, who had already served two years in that country, obtained leave of absence and permission to travel abroad.

Preparations were nearly finished for the departure of the embassy, when an unexpected delay occurred. Gordon expressed it thus in his diary: "A merry night has been spoiled by an accident of discovering treason against his Majesty." The Colonel of the Streltsi, Ivan Zickler, of foreign birth or extraction, and two Russian nobles of high rank, Alexis Sokovnin and Theodore Pushkin, were accused of plotting against the life of the Tsar. They were accused on the testimony of Larion Yelisarof, who was one of the denunciators of the alleged plot against Peter's life in 1689, when he took refuge at Troitsa. In all probability there was no plot whatever, but simply loose and unguarded talk between discontented men. Zickler had always been well treated by the Princess Sophia and Shaklovity, but when he saw the preponderance on the side of Peter he went to Troitsa and made denunciations. He did not, however, receive the reward and favour which he expected, but on the contrary, was looked upon askance, and had recently been sent to Azof. He was naturally irritated against the Tsar, and in unguarded moments probably expressed his feelings too strongly. Sokovnin was a virulent dissenter, and the brother of two ladies well known for their opposition to the Patriarch Nikon, and their encouragement of dissent in the reign of Alexis — Theodora Morozof and the Princess Avdotia Urusof. He was therefore opposed to many of Peter's innovations; and his father-in-law, Matthew Pushkin, who had been appointed Governor of Azof, had excited the anger of the Tsar because he had refused to send his chlidren abroad. Theodore Pushkin was one of the sons, and had uttered vague threats of revenge in case the Tsar should have his father whipped to death for his refusal, for rumours to that effect were being industriously circulated. Torture produced confessions of various kinds, and among them repetitions by Zickler of the old accusations against the Princess Sophia. The prisoners were speedily condemned, and were beheaded on the Red Place, after having their arms and legs chopped off. Their heads were exposed on stakes. The confessions of Zickler, and the renewed accusations against his sister Sophia, excited Peter's mind against the whole of the Miloslavsky family, and in his rage he even went to the length of taking up the body of Ivan Miloslavsky — who had been dead fourteen years — of dragging the coffin by swine to the place of execution, and of placing it in such a position that the blood of the criminals spurted into the face of the corpse.

Even at this time there was much popular discontent and hostile criticism of Peter. Not all of those who saw that reforms were absolutely necessary approved his measures and his conduct. A rumour was spread that the Tsar Ivan had publicly proclaimed to all the people: "My brother does not live according to the Church. He goes to the German suburb, and is acquainted with Germans." There was talk, too, of the way in which Peter had abandoned his wife and family, and family affairs probably caused the quarrel between Leo Naryshkin and the Lopukhins, the relatives of Peter's wife. What exactly happened is not known, but Peter Lopukhin, the uncle of the Tsaritsa and the Minister of the Palace, was accused of bribery and extortion, and for this, or some other cause, was exiled, together with his brothers, one of them the father of the Tsaritsa. A report was circulated among the common people, and was widely believed, that Peter had assisted with his own hands in applying the torture to his wife's uncle. One man, the monk Abraham, dared to make himself the exponent of the popular feeling, and presented to Peter a petition in which he made mention of the abandonment of his wife, of the relations which he had formed in the German suburb, and of the bad feeling which had been excited by the Tsar lowering himself to work at boats, and to appear on foot in the triumphal procession, instead of taking his proper place. As was natural, the petition gave rise to a trial; Abraham was sent to a distant monastery, and three other men who were implicated were punished with the knout, and sent to Azof.

When these trials were completed, the embassy set out, on March 20, 1697. It was intended to go first to Vienna, then to Venice and Rome, then to Holland and England, and to return by the way of Königsberg. The trouble in Poland, consequent on the interregnum, made travelling through that country dangerous, and the only way in which Vienna could be reached was by a roundabout journey through Riga, Königsberg, and Dresden. The plan was therefore changed.

The first experience of the Tsar in a foreign country was an unfortunate one. The Governor of Pskov, who had been ordered to make the arrangements for Peter's journey through Livonia, had neglected to say in his letter to Eric Dahlberg, the Governor of Riga, how many persons accompanied the embassy. Dahlberg replied, asking that, while he would do his best, he hoped they would overlook some inconveniences, as a great famine was unfortunately reigning in the country. Major Glazenap was sent to the frontier to escort the embassy, but Peter was so impatient, and travelled so fast, that they arrived at the frontier before the proper arrangements had been made to receive them. They therefore found no conveyances, and were obliged to go on to Riga in the carriages brought from Pskov, and trust to their own provisions. A short distance from Riga, light carriages and an escort were waiting for them, and they were ceremoniously received in the town with a military parade, while a guard of fifty men was placed near their lodgings. The next day the ambassadors sent two of their nobles to thank the governor for his kindness, and a return visit was paid by one of his adjutants. Immediately afterward, Peter wrote to Vinius that they "were received with great honour, and with a salute of twenty-four guns, when they entered and left the fortress." Unfortunately, the embassy was detained at Riga for a whole week by the breaking up of the ice on the Düna, which made crossing impossible. Peter preserved his incognito, and went out to see the town. His military curiosity naturally led him to inspect the fortifications and measure the width and depth of the ditches, when he was somewhat rudely ordered away by the sentinel. Discontented at this, a complaint was made, and the governor apologised, assuring Lefort that no discourtesy was intended. Lefort was satisfied, and said that the sentinel had merely done his duty. It must be remembered that Riga was a frontier town, that Livonia was an outlying province of Sweden, and that the embassy was not accredited to the Swedish court. Dahlberg was coldly, formally polite; he did all that propriety demanded, but nothing more. He knew perfectly well that the Tsar was with the embassy, but he respected his incognito. As the ambassadors did not pay him a visit in person, he did not pay a personal visit to the ambassadors. Nothing was done in the way of amusement or diversion for the Tsar, besides the first reception. The ambassadors were left to pay for their lodgings and their provisions, and to get on as best they might. They paid high prices for everything, but times were hard, and the people naturally tried to make the most they could out of the distinguished strangers. As there was nothing to be seen, either in a military or naval way, as there were no feasts or amusements of any kind prepared for him, Peter became bored, especially as he was anxious to continue his journey. He left the rest, ventured across the river in a small boat, and remained waiting two days on the other side. In a letter to Vinius, of April 18, he says: "Here we lived in a slavish way, and were tired with the mere sight of things." Nevertheless, the embassy took its leave with all form and ceremony, and crossed the river on a vessel carrying the royal flag of Sweden, and with a salute. When it was necessary to find a pretext for a war with Sweden, the reception at Riga was made one of the reasons, and even in 1709, when the siege of Riga was undertaken, Peter, after throwing the first three bomb-shells into the town, wrote to Menshikóf: "Thus the Lord God has enabled us to see the beginning of our revenge on this accursed place." We should add here that Peter's feelings about his reception at Riga probably increased with time. In other countries where he went, there was a sovereign with a court, and although, in a certain way, the Tsar was incognito, yet he was privately and familiarly received and entertained. It was unfortunate for him that his first venture was in an outlying province, the tenure of which was not too secure, and in a commercial rather than in an aristocratic city.

Mitau is now a dull provincial town, and the Hebrew signs on the street corners show the great Jewish population. Its greatest object of interest to travellers is the old Ducal Castle, almost entirely rebuilt in the last century, with its reminiscences of the residence and sudden departure of the exiled Louis XVIII., and with the mummified body of the Duke John Ernest Biren (the lover of the Empress Anne, and the ancestor of the Sagan family), which lies in its coffin attired in velvet and ruffles, but by some malice lacking the tip of the nose. In 1697 Mitau was the capital of the little Duchy of Curland, which maintained a semi-independence by becoming a fief of the Polish crown. The reigning Duke, Frederic Casimir, was an old friend of Lefort. It was with him that Lefort had served in Holland. Although he was poor, he did everything that he could to make the time pass pleasantly for Peter and for the embassy. Here the Tsar consented to give up in part his incognito, made visits to the Duke, and received them in return. A week was quickly passed in amusement and pleasure, but even with this Peter found time to exercise himself in a carpenter's shop.

From Mitau Peter proceeded to Libau, where he was detained by bad weather for a week, until he finally took passage on a small ship going to Pillau, the port of Königsberg. During his stay at Libau, he passed for the skipper of a Russian privateer, though he was able to give no satisfactory explanation to an acquaintance, who frequently met and drank with him in a small beer-shop, as to why it was a privateer, and not a merchant vessel that he commanded. Besides the beer-house, Peter often visited an apothecary's shop, and wrote to Vinius that he had seen there "a wonder which was ordinarily considered untrue, a real salamander preserved in spirits in a bottle," which he had taken out and held in his hand. The embassy proceeded by land. The Tsar went by sea, to avoid passing through Polish territory.

Blomberg, whom we have already cited about the election of Patriarch, met the embassy in Curland, and says of their entertainment: "Open tables were kept everywhere, with trumpets and music, attended with feasting and excessive drinking all along, as if his Tsarish Majesty had been another Bacchus. I have not seen such hard drinkers; it is not possible to express it, and they boast of it as a mighty qualification." Of Lefort's drinking he remarks: "It never overcomes him, but he always continues master of his reason." Leibnitz, writing from private information received from Königsberg, says much the same thing: "Lefort drinks like a hero; no one can rival him. It is feared that he will be the death of some of the Elector's courtiers. Beginning in the evening, he does not leave his pipe and glass till three hours after sunrise, and yet he is a man of great parts."

Frederick III., Elector of Brandenburg, then on the eve of transforming himself into the first King of Prussia, was greatly interested to know whether the Tsar was really with the embassy, and beside sending a secret agent into Curland to find out, he gave directions about the treatment of the embassy, in case it were simply intending to pass through his dominions, or in case it were directed also to him. Peter was therefore met at Pillau by an officer who proffered the hospitality of the Elector, but an answer was returned that there was no person of distinction on board, except the Prince of Imeritia, and that no visits could be received. A similar occurrence took place at the mouth of the Pregel, and it was not until Peter arrived at Königsberg itself that he was willing to allow himself to be known to the elector. After taking small lodgings in a street on the Kneiphof, he went out in a close carriage, late at night, and paid a visit to the Elector, entering the palace by a private staircase. The interview lasted for an hour and a half, and the sovereigns were mutually pleased. Although, in order to keep his incognito, Peter refused to receive a return visit, yet he saw the Elector several times again, and was entertained by him at his country house, witnessed a bear-fight, and appeared at a hunting party. His curiosity and vivacity, his readiness to be pleased, and his appreciation of the manners and habits of the country, made a favourable impression. He astonished by his natural capacity and his dexterity, even in playing the trumpet and the drum.

The embassy arrived eleven days after Peter, and was splendidly received. Great advantages were expected to Brandenburg from an intimacy with Russia, and the Elector, therefore, spared no money. Peter's visit is said to have cost him 150,000 thalers. Under the skilful guidance of Lefort and Von Besser, all ceremonial observances were strictly complied with, and, for the first time in the history of Russian missions abroad, there was no unseemly wrangling over points of precedence and etiquette. The members of the embassy appeared officially in Russian costume, although they wore foreign dress in private. The Elector told the Tsar afterwards that he had hard work to keep from laughing, when, according to custom, he had to ask the ambassadors how the Tsar was, and whether they had left him in good health. Peter had just before been standing at the window to see the entry of the embassy, and was well satisfied. At a supper given in honour of the ambassadors, great pleasure was caused by the fireworks, one piece representing the Russian arms, and another the victory at Azof.

The two rulers were so well disposed towards each other, that a treaty of friendship was speedily concluded. The Elector was greatly desirous that there should be inserted an article of alliance for mutual defence and protection; but the Russians were too cautious for this, and although the treaty contained clauses giving additional privileges to merchants, especially as regarded the Persian trade, and for the surrender of criminals and deserters, yet the Elector had to be satisfied with a verbal agreement and oath "not to let a favourable occasion escape of being useful to each other by giving each other their mutual help, as far as possible, against all their enemies, but particularly against the Swedes."

On June 20, after nearly a month's stay, Peter went to Pillau, with the intention of taking ship directly to Holland, for he found it more convenient to defer his visit to Vienna till his return. Before leaving, he sent a ruby of large size as a present to his host. At Pillau he was detained three weeks longer, by the necessity of watching affairs in Poland, where the interregnum consequent on the death of Sobieski had produced more than the usual trouble. The threatened intervention by the French, to support the Prince de Conti on the Polish throne, would have been greatly against the interest of Russia. The Tsar occupied his leisure with active and thorough studies in artillery, under the guidance of the chief engineer of the Prussian fortresses, Colonel Steitner von Sternfeld, who gave him a certificate of remarkable progress and knowledge.

An unfortunate incident, arising from Peter's hasty temper, marked the conclusion of his stay. He had remained a day longer to celebrate his name's-day, and had expected the Elector to visit him. He had even made some fireworks for the occasion. Frederick had been obliged to go to Memel, to meet the Duke of Curland, and therefore sent Count von Kreyzen and the Landvogt von Schacken to present his compliments and his regrets. Peter was childishly vexed, and in his disappointment at not being able to show his fireworks, vented his rage on the envoys. We took it amiss that they had left the room after dinner to "refresh themselves" after their journey, and had them brought back. Looking "sourly" at Count von Kreyzen, he remarked in Dutch to Lefort, that "The Elector was very good, but his counsellors were the devil." Then, thinking he saw a smile steal over the face of Kreyzen, who was about to retire, he rushed at him, cried, "Go! go!" and twice pushed him backwards. His anger did not cool until he had written to his "dearest friend," the Elector, a letter half of complaint and half of apology.

Instead of going by sea from Pillau to Holland, Peter went no farther than Colberg, as he was fearful of falling in with the French squadron, which was said to be escorting the Prince de Conti to Poland. From that place he travelled by land as speedily as possible, stopping only to look at the famous ironworks near Ilsenburg, and to ascend the Brocken for the view.

The journey of the Tsar produced as much commotion and excitement in the minds of curious people of that time as did those of the Sultan and

Shah in our own day. Among those most anxious to form a personal acquaintance with the Tsar were the philosopher Leibnitz, who had long been interested in the widowed Electress of Hanover, granddaughter of James I. of England, and her daughter Sophia Charlotte, wife of the Elector of Brandenburg. Sophia Charlotte was on a visit to her mother, and had therefore missed the visit of Peter to Königsberg, though she had had full accounts of it from a constant correspondent. Leibnitz was unable at this time to see the Tsar, but the two Electresses, attended by several young princes and members of their court, made a hasty journey from Hanover to Koppenbrügge, through which they found Peter was to pass. They invited him to sup with them, but it took a discussion of an hour to persuade him to accept, and he did so only on the assurance that he would be received in the simplest way. He finally succeeded in avoiding the curious eyes of the attendants, and in getting into the supper-room by the back staircase. After supper there was a dance, and the party did not separate until four in the morning. Perhaps the princesses can tell their own story best. Sophia Charlotte says in a letter:

"My mother and I began to pay him our compliments, but he made Mr. Lefort reply for him, for he seemed shy, hid his face in his hands, and said: *'Ich kann nicht sprechen.'* But we tamed him a little, and then he sat down at the table between my mother and myself, and each of us talked to him in turn, and it was a strife who should have it. Sometimes he replied with the same promptitude, at others he made two interpreters talk, and assuredly he said nothing that was not to the point on all subjects that were suggested, for the vivacity of my mother put to him many questions, to which he replied with the same readiness, and I was astonished that he was not tired with the conversation, for I have been told that it is not much the habit in his country. As to his grimaces, I imagined them worse than I found them, and some are not in his power to correct. One can see also that he has had no one to teach him how to eat properly, but he has a natural, unconstrained air which pleases me."

Her mother wrote, a few days afterwards:

"The Tsar is very tall, his features are fine, and his figure very noble. He has great vivacity of mind, and a ready and just repartee. But, with all the advantages with which nature has endowed him, it could be wished that his manners were a little less rustic. We immediately sat down to table. Herr Koppenstein, who did the duty of marshal, presented the napkin to his Majesty, who was greatly embarrassed, for at Brandenburg, instead of a table-napkin, they had given him an ewer and basin after the meal. He was very gay, very talkative, and we established a great friendship for each other, and he exchanged snuff-boxes with my daughter. We stayed, in truth, a very long time at table, but we would gladly have remained there longer still without feeling a moment of *ennui*, for the Tsar was in very good humour, and never ceased talking to us. My daughter had her Italians sing. Their song pleased him, though he confessed to us that he did not care much for music.

"I asked him if he liked hunting. He replied that his father had been very fond of it, but that he himself, from his earliest youth, had had a real passion for navigation and for fireworks. He told us that he worked himself in building ships, showed us his hands, and made us touch the callous places that had been caused by work. He brought his musicians, and they played Russian dances, which we liked better than Polish ones.

"Lefort and his nephew dressed in French style, and had much wit. We did not speak to the other ambassadors. We regretted that he could not stay longer, so that we could see him again, for his society gave us much pleasure. He is a very extraordinary man. It is impossible to describe him, or even to give an idea of him, unless you have seen him. He has a very good heart, and remarkably noble sentiments. I must tell you, also, that he did not get drunk in our presence, but we had hardly left when the people of his suite made ample amends."

In another letter she says: —

"I could embellish the tale of the journey of the illustrious Tsar, if I should tell you that he is sensible to the charms of beauty, but, to come to the bare fact, I found in him no disposition to gallantry. If we had not taken so many steps to see him, I believe that he would never have thought of us. In his country it is the custom for all women to paint, and rouge forms an essential part of their marriage presents. That is why the Countess Platen singularly pleased the Muscovites; but in dancing, they took the whalebones of our corsets for our bones, and the Tsar showed his astonishment by saying that the German ladies had devilish hard bones.

"They have four dwarfs. Two of them are very well-proportioned, and perfectly well-bred; sometimes he kissed, and sometimes he pinched the ear of his favorite dwarf. He took the head of our little Princess (Sophia Dorothea, ten years old), and kissed her twice. The ribbons of her hair suffered in consequence. He also kissed her brother (afterwards George II. of England, then sixteen years old). He is a prince at once very good and very *méchant*. He has quite the manners of his country. If he had received a better education, he would be an accomplished man, for he has many good qualities; and an infinite amount of natural wit."

ADMINISTRATIVE REFORMS. Every time that the Tsar returned from a prolonged absence he found the administration of Russia in such a state that it was necessary to begin at once a series of trials and executions. The contrast, in this respect, between Russia and Sweden is striking. The King was absent from Sweden for fourteen years, communication with him was often difficult and interrupted, the country suffered greatly from the war, yet the regular machinery of government went on as before. In Russia, on the contrary, if the Tsar were away for a year or less, the administration became thoroughly disorganised. So far Peter had succeeded in pulling down better than in building up. He had set about this latter task several times, and now that the war was practically finished, it was necessary for him to be in earnest over it. In order to understand the state of affairs when the Tsar returned from Paris, we must go back for a few years and trace the course of the civil administration. As the negotiations for peace will still go on slowly for three years, we can the more readily turn from foreign to internal affairs.

The Senate, as we remember, was created by the Tsar on the eve of the campaign of the Pruth, in order to take his place in the internal administration of the country, and to govern during his absence. In its hands were concentrated all the powers of government of every kind. As was natural, things did not at once work smoothly. Ramodanófsky, the Governor of Moscow, had a bitter quarrel with the Senate for usurping his powers and interfering with his jurisdiction — a quarrel ending only with his death in 1713. His successor, Soltykóf, having been appointed through the influence of the senators, succeeded better; but he in turn got into a quarrel with his vice-governor and had to be changed, and under his successor Dolgoruky the disputes with the Senate began again. The Governor of Kazán complained that, while the Senate interfered in everything, it had not sufficient knowledge on which to base its decisions. His provinces were too heavily taxed because they were thought to be rich, and they had now become so poor that it was with difficulty anything could be got from them. The Tsar himself complained bitterly of the waste of time. He wrote frequent letters to "Messieurs the Senate," scolding them as one would a child or a careless servant. He reminds them of their oath of office, he tells them that they have made themselves a laughing-stock, once expresses the suspicion that they have been bribed, and threatens to hold them to strict accountability on his return. He tells them that "loss of time is like death, as hard to return as a life that is ended." He orders them while in session not to converse about matters not pertaining to the service, especially not to have idle talk or jests, "for the Senate represents the person of his Majesty." Nothing was to be done except with the consent of the whole Senate, and nothing transacted at home or privately. Everything must be written out and recorded, and no outsiders must be introduced into the Senate. The slowness of business in other departments of the Government naturally affected that of the Senate. Decrees frequently remained unattended to. In order to prevent this, Basil Zótof was in 1715 appointed a General Inspector of Decrees. It was his duty to watch over their execution and see that there were no delays. Three years later we find him complaining that the Senate pays no attention to his remonstrances, destroys his reports, transacts business without him, and does not hold regular sessions nor keep registers of all the business; that the returns are neither properly nor regularly sent from the provinces, that fines and forfeitures are not collected, that in three years nearly a million and a half of rubles remain unpaid, that fines had been imposed to the amount of 31,657 rubles, of which 3,368 only had been received, the rest having been either postponed, remitted, or not collected. Probably the Senate would not have done even as well as this, had not Prince Jacob Dolgorúky been appointed first Senator in 1712, and had he not immediately, so to speak, taken possession of that body. We remember the curious reports of his mission to France in 1687. He had been taken prisoner at the battle of Narva, and had after eleven years succeeded in escaping from Sweden. Shrewd, crafty, of violent prejudices, obstinate, and strong-willed, he could not but impose himself on his weaker colleagues, if only by force of lungs. Menshikóf was the only man who dared face him. Frank to an excess, he dared tell the truth to the Tsar, on many occasions when the truth was disagreeable. Many amusing anecdotes are told of his obstinacy.

An important change was made in the constitution and sphere of the Senate in 1718 by the institution of colleges, or, as we call them, boards of commissioners. The division of business among the old *Prikazes* or departments had come about a good deal by chance. Through the general changes, especially through the interference of the Senate, these departments had fallen into confusion, and business had been transferred at will from one to the other. This created additional delay. It was necessary to find something to take their place. Naturally, in the present turn of affairs, the first question was, How are these things done abroad? and in Stockholm and Vienna the business of the State was managed by colleges. This idea was proposed to the Tsar as long ago as 1698 by Dr. Francis Lee, but no particular attention had been paid to his proposals. In 1715 Heinrich Fick, formerly in the service of the Duke of Holstein, who had been recommended by Bassewitz to General Weyde, was secretly sent to Sweden to obtain accurate information of the constitution and working of the colleges in that country. He sent a series of reports, which were for a long time accredited to Leibnitz, who certainly had the same general idea, and had indeed, although a year later, proposed it to the Tsar. In one of these reports the functions of the colleges are compared to the works of a watch, "where one wheel brings another into movement," a comparison which naturally pleased the Tsar. The great difficulty of introducing such a system of wheels into Russia was to find the proper men to work them, and it was thought at first that recourse must be had to foreigners. For this purpose General Weyde, in the same year, was instructed to hire learned foreigners, skilled in jurisprudence and administration. Veselófsky in Vienna had similar orders.

He was to search especially for persons speaking Slavonic languages, one from each college at Vienna, and at the same time was to ask the Jesuit School at Prague to translate certain books, which would be of use to the new administration. There seems, however, to have been very few who were willing to go to Russia in such capacity; and therefore, in August, 1717, an effort was made to find Swedish prisoners of war who had learnt Russian well enough, and had other necessary qualities, to take service. Finally, in 1719, with the same end in view, thirty or forty Russians were sent to Königsberg to study German and jurisprudence.

At the end of 1717 the plan had made such progress that nine colleges were instituted, although it was only in 1720 that they got into thorough working order. These colleges or commissions were those of Foreign Affairs, Revenue, Expenditure, Control, Justice (including Internal Affairs), War, Admiralty, Commerce, and Mines and Manufactures; under the presidency respectively of Count Golófkin, Prince Dimítri Golítsyn (the Governor of Kief), Count Musin-Puskin, Prince Jacob Dolgorúky, Count Matvéief (who had finished his diplomatic career), Prince Menshikóf, Admiral Count Apráxin, Tolstói, and General Bruce. All the presidents — who were equivalent to Ministers — were Russian, with the exception of General Bruce in the College of Mines and Manufactures, there being no Russian fit for the place. The vice-presidents were all foreigners, except Baron Shafirof in the College of Foreign Affairs. The whole institution was so un-Russian that several colleges even bore foreign names, as *Kammer, Staats-Control, Justitz Collegium, Berg Collegium*. The presidents appointed councillors, assessors, writers, translators, &c., of whom a small fixed number could be foreigners. All business was to be transacted in full meeting of the members, as in the Senate, and the presidents were also to have seats in the Senate itself. These new wheels at first revolved very badly, and stopped one another more than they put one another in motion. In the College of Foreign Affairs, the vice-president did not wish to sit and discuss with persons whom he called the creatures of Count Golofkin. In others there were disputes, as was very natural between the Russians and the foreigners. That these institutions worked badly can be seen readily enough from the protocols of their sessions, and it did not escape the notice of all foreigners. Vockerodt, a competent contemporary, says: "It was soon shown that there had been too much haste, and that in the transaction of business there was more confusion to be expected than good order and promptitude. The chanceries in the provinces, from which business must come to the colleges in St. Petersburg, still remained on the old footing, and although instructions were sent to them how they must forward their reports and accounts, the old Russian clerks could not understand them, and thus caused much disorder. The Russian councillors in the colleges, even if they understood the concerns of their country, still could not immediately get a clear idea of the new method, and the Germans were seldom

able to show them, partly because they did not understand the Russian
language, and partly also because the Swedish forms were as little known to
them. Therefore the Tsar in 1722 was obliged to make a second change in
his new colleges, to dismiss most of the foreigners, and to put the colleges
themselves, though still keeping the German names, on a footing which came
considerably nearer the old one, and indeed did not differ from it in anything
except the number of members, which hindered rather than advanced the
prompt transaction of business, since no member was allowed to work at home
or read over the case except in full session, and then give his vote, and that
in those chanceries where there were accounts of revenue and expenditure
proper books were kept in the commercial style."

. . .

ECONOMIC REFORMS. "The Tsar, pitying the peoples of his realm, zealous
to root out unjust, disastrous, general burdens and crafty thefts from the State
treasury, having ascertained that great falsifications and thefts are increasing
the public burdens and injuring the interests of the State, and that by this
many people of every station, but most of all the peasants, are becoming
impoverished and ruined," &c., &c. So began one of the Tsar's decrees in
1713; but the Tsar really knew very little of the sufferings of the people.
Indeed, how could he? What were the Russian serfs at that time, that anyone should interest themselves in them except as mere draft animals, machines
for labour, and objects of taxation? The revenue of Russia which for 1709
had been calculated at 3,026,128 rubles had risen in 1725 to 10,186,707 rubles,
the ruble having depreciated fifteen per cent. in value. At the end of Peter's
reign the regular army numbered 210,000 men, and the fleet contained forty-
eight ships of the line and eight hundred smaller vessels, manned by 28,000
men. This result could not have been reached without immense and oppressive
taxation, and, as we have already seen, nearly everything possible was taxed.
Besides that, the recruiting and the way it was carried on, the building of
St. Petersburg, the construction of the fortresses, the digging of canals, and
the opening of harbours had cost the lives of hundreds of thousands of men.
To escape harsh treatment and death many more had run away. Strahlenberg
tells us that to escape the oppression of the tax officials, who collected the
taxes in the times of the year worst for agriculture, and seized the draft
horses of the peasants, at least a hundred thousand men had fled to Poland,
Lithuania, Turkey, and the Tartars. Others say two hundred thousand. The
figures may be doubted, but the general fact remains true. Whole villages
ran away to the frontiers or hid in the woods. As the maintenance of a large
army rendered both men and money necessary, the pursuit of the fugitive
serfs, and of unwilling and runaway conscripts, was carried on diligently
throughout the whole of Peter's reign. All other means of raising revenue
proving insufficient, even the monopolies of trade producing unsatisfactory

results, recourse was had to a poll-tax—imposed on males only—which fell chiefly on the peasants, as the nobles, the clergy, and their families, the inhabitants of the Baltic provinces, the Bashkirs and the Lapps were exempted from it. This amounted to 120 kopeks per head on the inhabitants of towns, 114 kopeks on the crown and church peasants, the odnodvórtsi, or peasant proprietors, and the inhabitants of the Kuraine, and 74 kopeks on the other taxpayers. The census ordered in 1719 to regulate the imposition of the poll-tax served to strengthen greatly the bonds of serfage. There had been hitherto a legal distinction between household slaves and serfs or peasants attached to the soil, but the department of serfage, charged with the registration of slaves and the maintenance of this distinction, had been abolished in 1704, and consequently all the peasants were inscribed indiscriminately on the census lists as serfs, became thenceforth the absolute property of the landed proprietors, and could be bought and sold. As the proprietors were made responsible for the poll-tax and the furnishing of recruits, it is easy to understand what power they were given over these wretched labourers. The laws establishing manufactures introduced a new kind of serfdom, where the peasant was separated from the land, and rendered a simple slave attached to a manufactory. To be sure, a decree was issued in 1721 forbidding the sale of serfs as such without land—the theory of Russian law being that, when land was sold, the serfs naturally went with it—but even in this very decree there was added "should such sale be absolutely necessary, they should be sold by families and not individually." Pososhkóf, himself a peasant and a contemporary of Peter, shows throughout his economical treatise how great was the oppression of the peasantry, and how little it was known to the Tsar. Foreigners, however, perceived it. Vockerodt wondered at the patience of the oppressed people, and questioned "whether some patriot will not arise before one expects, and find means to bring the complaints and sighs of the subjects to the steps of the throne." Weber, in a ciphered despatch to the Elector of Hanover, says: "Everything in this realm will have a fearful end, because the sighs of so many million souls against the Tsar rise to heaven, and the glowing sparks of rage concealed in every man lack nothing but a fair wind and a conductor." The real history of the Russian people at this time is, however, only to be found in the archives of the Secret Tribunal of Preobrazhénsky, and in the memoirs of traditions of the dissenters in the north and east.

The poll-tax had the merit of being simple and easily collected; but it replaced a tax on arable land, much better in principle, which had existed from the earliest times, was in thorough conformity with Russian ideas, and had been gradually developed and was capable of still further development and improvement. The inequality and injustice of the poll-tax—or tax on *souls,* as it was technically called— struck contemporaries. Pososhkóf opposed it, and recommended a land-tax. He thought this could not be permanent, and that the money spent on the census was therefore wasted. Two years after Peter's death Catherine appointed a commission to find means for diminishing the poll-tax, or substituting for it a land or house-tax. Her death put an end to the project.

In spite of the great increase of revenue and the constant economy practised by the Tsar, yet—owing to wars as well as bad harvests—the treasury was sometimes so low that it was necessary to recur to extraordinary measures, such as are now practised only in Turkey. In the winter of 1723 the Government officials were paid in furs and other Government wares instead of money. It was not so easy then for the Government to contract loans. A subsequent decree says that "when money is absolutely necessary, and when no other way of raising it is found, the sum must be deducted proportionally from the salaries of the officials, spiritual as well as temporal, except foreign artisans and soldiers and sailors." A few months later, besides raising the excise on spirits and the price of stamped paper, one-fourth was deducted from the pay of all officials, and the rations of officers were either reduced by half or withheld altogether.

In endeavoring to find ways of improving the revenues and of increasing the general well-being of the country, Peter was certainly in earnest and energetic. In some respects he was an adherent of the mercantile or protective theory, as far as he understood it; but it requires a strong imagination to find any real or consequent system in his commercial policy. He did things as they occurred to him. If when travelling abroad he saw something which he thought useful for Russia, he at once adopted it, without further thought as to whether its introduction was easy or not. Hence many trials which were soon abandoned, many measures which contradicted each other. Peter himself admitted that there was no branch of administration which he found so difficult to understand as economy and commerce. When the Dutch resident was pressing for a new commercial treaty, and had met with nothing but delay, Osterman at last said: "Between ourselves, I will tell you the whole truth. We have not a single man who understands commercial affairs at all. But I can assure you that the Tsar is now occupying himself with this matter." As concerns the accumulation of precious metals, the policy of Peter would certainly satisfy the most rigid adherent of the mercantile system. In 1714 he forbade the exportation of silver. The next year this order was repeated. Four years later, merchants who crossed the frontier were searched to see whether they took with them ducats, specie, thalers, or silver, and the coin was confiscated. Not even silver or copper small money was allowed to go out of the country. In 1721, a proposition had been made by the Mining College, and approved by the Tsar, that worked or unworked silver should never be exported. This decree was repeated two years later, with the addition of the punishment of death for its violation. None of these did any good, for the exportation of precious metals constantly increased. In those days the system of the easy transfer of money by paper had not reached its present development. The import of gold and silver was not only allowed, but Peter tried to increase it by freeing it from duty. At the same time it was not allowed to introduce any small Russian coin, on the ground that it would probably be counterfeit. Russians were not permitted to sell their wares to foreigners for Russian money, but must receive always foreign money. Peter even said that he would heartily thank the man who could show him how to keep money in the country, and many decrees say nearly the same thing.

The measures for the improvement of the economical condition of Russia had reference chiefly to mining, manufactures, and the regulation of commerce. Very little attention was paid to agriculture, which was apparently thought to be such a natural and simple condition of man that it needed none. One decree, however, orders the grain to be reaped with scythes and not with sickles, and the peasants were commanded, under heavy penalties for disobedience, to use hoes of new construction. Tobacco culture was introduced into the south, efforts were made to increase the production of flax and hemp, and it was forbidden to burn the grass in the steppes. To improve the wool shepherds introduced from Silesia, and sheep farmers, especially in Little Russia, were ordered to tend their flocks on the Silesian plan. An attempt was also made to improve the breed of horses in the south. To forests, as we have seen, the Tsar paid much more attention, but chiefly because he needed the trees for shipbuilding. The wilful destruction of forests, or even sometimes the necessary use of trees for timber, was forbidden by a series of severe decrees, in which the penalty of death was frequently threatened. On the Neva and the shore of the Finnish Gulf, as a warning, gallows were built every five miles, on which offenders against the forest laws were at once strung up. In St. Petersburg itself a birch grove stood on the site of the present bazaar. When, in spite of all laws, many inhabitants cut wood there, Peter resolved to hang every tenth man among the guilty and to knout the rest, but this severity was fortunately alleviated at the request of Catherine. Immense quantities of timber were used by the Government itself. So much went to the construction of the harbour works at Reval and Baltic Port, the latter of which was left unfinished, that Vockerodt said they had ruined the forests of Livonia and Esthonia and in 1720 Peter wrote to Repnin to forbid the export of wood from Pernan because the forest was disappearing.

In a decree of 1723 Peter thus explains the causes of the slow development of manufactures. "Either our decrees are not accurately observed, or there are few people who wish to go into the business. Manufacturers too are ruined by goods brought from abroad. For instance, a peasant discovered a dye called 'Florence lake.' I had artists try it. They said that it was only inferior to the Venetian, and quite equal to the German; some said even better. A good deal of it was made, and no other manufacturers also complain. Therefore it is necessary to look after this sharply and to communicate with the College of Commerce and, if it does not look after it, then to protest to the Senate and state the matter to us, for other nations greatly envy our manufactories and try by all means to ruin them by bribery, as many examples show. That there are few people wishing to go into business is true, for our people are like children, who never want to begin the alphabet unless they are compelled to by their teacher. It seems very hard to them at first, but when they have learnt it they are thankful. So in manufacturing affairs we must not be satisfied with the proposition only, but we must act and even compel, and help by teaching, by machines, and other aids, and even by compulsion, to become good economists. For instance, where there is fine felt we should compel people to make hats, by not allowing the sale of felt unless a certain number of hats are made." Always force, always compulsion. Peter seems to have found no better way for dealing with even such a delicate matter as commerce, where people are governed entirely by their own interests, and where a slight fear of loss, especially if caused by Government interference, counteracts an almost certain hope of profit. Force was of little avail to promote Russian industry. High import duties, bounties, privileges and monopolies did more, but Russian manufactures never took a high rank in Peter's day nor indeed for long after.

On the whole the constant Government intereference, the prohibitions of exports and imports, so suddenly and frequently established, changed, and withdrawn, the minute regulations, the paternal supervision, did more harm than good to Russian trade, and lessened instead of increased the wealth of the country. Many interests were sacrificed in these commercial experiments. Thus in 1701 two foreigners were commissioned to make hats in the German style out of beaver skins and wool, and the exportation of the raw material or its sale to foreigners was forbidden, though only two years before two Dutchmen had been given a twelve years' privilege for the purchase and exportation of wool. In 1705 woolen factories were doing so well that Peter wrote to Menshikóf: "They are making cloth, and this business is making good progress, and God gives excellent results, so that I have made a caftan for myself for the holidays." In 1715 he hoped that in five years' time there would be cloth enough made to stop the importation, and in 1718 he ordered that the uniforms for all the soldiers in garrison should be made out of Moscow cloth. Another decree of the same year ordered "the servants of the Boyars to wear livery or clothes of cloth of Russian manufacture and not foreign, the same to be the rule for the lower class of townspeople, who must in future content themselves with soldier's cloth. If there is not enough cloth for the Boyars' servants, than let them use serge, double if necessary. Either diminish the gold galloon or forbid it altogether, for it is beginning to be a habit to wear much of it, whence there is a loss not only to private people but also to the State, for the English are richer than we, and do not wear much of it." About the same time the use of gold and silver stuffs was forbidden during the war. Old stuffs could be worn out but no new could be made. The importation of gold lace and stuffs worked with gold and silver was forbidden, but their manufacture was allowed at St. Petersburg to not more than 2,200 pounds of silver in one year, and later still the importation was again permitted. The importation of serge was forbidden, as well as of stockings, the latter to encourage a Frenchman who had started a factory at Moscow. The hemp and flax industries went through a number of vicissitudes. With his idea of exporting only manufactured products and not raw material, Peter forbade the exportation of hemp and flax seed, the great staples of Russia, except in the shape of oil. The oil, however, was so bad that none would buy it, and the prohibition of export was removed. At the same time he was trying to extend by compulsion the culture of flax and hemp. The course of trade too was arbitrarily changed. At times all the flax and hemp must be sent to St. Petersburg; at others part could be sent to Archangel; at others still it must all be sold to the Government. To encourage honesty an admixture of stones in a bale of hemp was punished with death. The needs of the Fleet were so great that the manufacture of sail cloth took good proportions. The Government factories were nearly ruined by bad management, and it became necessary to give them into private hands. In 1712 the Tsar forbade the weaving of the narrow linen commonly used in Russia, and, with entire forgetfulness of the fact that the home market is the most important, for the sake of a possible export to England and her colonies, ordered all linen to be made at least a yard wide. The narrow linen made after that date was to be confiscated, and the informer was promised ten kopeks for each ell of linen he discovered. In 1718 this prohibition was withdrawn, and linen of all widths was allowed to be made; but again there was a change, and the export of narrow linen was forbidden (as if indeed it would have been exported without a demand for it). In spite of this paternal care, the linen industry languished. When long after, in 1762 and 1764, the restrictions on trade were removed, the export of flax and hemp increased, and they now constitute nearly one-fifth of the whole export. In order to encourage the manufacture of silk, Baron Shafirof and Tolstói were given a privilege for the manufacture of silk goods. The importation from abroad was entirely forbidden, and no European silk could even be worn, and they had the right of importing Asiastic raw silk free of duty; yet the business went on so badly that a limited importation (100,000 rubles) without duty of foreign silk goods was allowed to them for two years, in order to set the factory going again. The prospect, however, was so poor that they sold their privilege to private merchants for 20,000 rubles. One of the chief exports of Russia at that time was leather. In 1716 at least

five million pounds were brought to Archangel for shipment, and its quality
had long been famous. But the Tsar was dissatisfied with it on the ground
that it was not sufficiently durable and waterproof, and with the best of
intentions did what he could to break up the trade. In 1715 he forbade the
manufacture of Russian leather, and ordered it henceforth to be made on the
German·plan, to teach which a sort of tanning-school was opened at Moscow,
master-workmen being sent from Reval, who instructed the Russians, from
the factories of the interior. If after two years of trial anyone made leather
on the old system he was to be sent to Siberia and his property confiscated.
The mining industry fared better owing to the great richness of the ores
discovered in the Ural. Mining privileges were given to Nikíta Demídof,
the blacksmith of Tula, in 1702, who set to work vigorously and became·so
rich that, on the birth of the Tsarévitch Peter, he presented him with a
hundred thousand rubles as "tooth-cutting money." In 1720 he was ennobled. The Stróganofs increased their already great fortune in the same
region, and Alexander Stróganof was created a Baron in 1712. Even the
Government mines prospered under the excellent management of General
Hennin and Basil Tatístchef.

The general state of the country was not such as to encourage either
manufacturers or merchants. The officials had been so long accustomed to
look down upon the trading classes as low sorts of beings, that they made no
scruples of harassing them and seizing their property. The large factories
which were started by great nobles with the assistance of the State were safe,
but the smaller ones frequently suffered from exactions and irregularities,
and dared not complain. The safest way was to obtain the protection of some
powerful person, but this after a time was strictly forbidden. Thus we find
that many wealthy merchants had got themselves registered as servants of
the Princess Natalia, or even of the Tsaritza Catherine; and when they were
obliged to go back to their shops, they complained that the taxes were such
that they were unable to live and carry on their trade as before. We may
judge how necessary such protection sometimes was, from the case of the
merchant Bogomólof, who was a well-known and rich man in Moscow; had
much silver, gold, and jewels; had given much to the construction of a
monastery where he hoped to be buried; had lent money to various high
placed personages; and among others, had been on friendly terms with Prince
Boris Golítsyn, who frequently visited him. One day Sergius, son of Boris,
came to visit Bogomólof; and, finding him alone with a young nephew,
ordered all the servants out of the house, sent him off to a monastery in the
country, forced him to become a monk, and in fact robbed him of all his
property.

It is almost useless to recount the vain attempt to introduce the German
system of guilds among the Russian workmen, in which all laws and lessons

of historical development were disregarded. Yet the old Russian *artel*—a sort of mutually-guaranteeing, mutually-protecting company of artisans—lay ready to hand, waiting only for development. Nor need more particular mention be made of the hundreds of Russian artisans sent abroad by the Government to learn trades. Many found it pleasanter to stay where they were. Of those who returned, the majority, finding themselves isolated among their countrymen, soon fell back into the old ways.

Prince Menshikov

Among Peter's boon companions, none was more favored than Menshikov whom the Tsar raised to great power. During the reign of Catherine I, he was the power behind the throne and aspired to be more, affiancing his daughter to Peter II. But when Peter II came to power, he stripped Menshikov of his powers, honors and titles and exiled him to Siberia. The following description of Menshikov is from a contemporary source: Manstein, General, Memoirs of Russia, Historical, Political and Military from the Year MDCCXXVII to MDCCXLIV. (Introduction by David Hume.) *London, 1770. Pp. 10–13.*

The general opinion on the origin of Menzikoff is, that his father was a peasant, who had placed him, at Moskow, with a pastry-cook, and that he carried about little pies, singing along the streets; that the Emperor Peter I. having stopped to speak to him, he had pleased him with the wit and liveliness of his repartees. Upon this he put him servant to Monsieur Le Fort; thence he took him about his own person, and by degrees made his fortune.

Others again say, that his father was an officer in the service of the Czar, Alexis Michaëlowitz, and that as it is not extraordinary to see gentlemen serve in stables of the Czar, Menzikoff had also been employed in them, in quality of one of the head-grooms: that Peter having often spoke to him; had taken notice of the wit and shrewdness of his answers, insomuch that he took him out of the stables, and placed him as a more immediate attendant on himself; when, observing great talents in him, he had, in a few years, raised him to the first posts in the empire.

I have always thought the first of these opinions the nearest to the truth; for it is certain, that he was of an obscure birth, and that he began with being a common servant; after which the Emperor placed him as a private soldier in the first company of regular troops, which he raised under the appellation *preprovojdenie*. [Preobrazhenskii] Peter I. having thence taken him about his person, gave him his entire confidence, in such a manner, that, on many occasions, Menzikoff governed Russia with the same despotism as his master.

His credit had, however, been greatly diminished during the last years of the reign of Peter I. and it is believed, that if that Emperor had lived some months longer, there would have been changes at court, and in the ministry.

By the following character, any one may decide which preponderated, the good or the bad qualities of Prince Menzikoff.

He was strongly attached to his master, and to the maxims of Peter I. for civilizing the Russian nation; affable and polite towards strangers; that is to say, with such as did not pretend to have more wit than himself; neither did he misbehave to those of the Russians who showed submission to him. He treated all who were his inferiors with gentleness, never forgetting a service done him. Brave withal, he gave, on occasions of the greatest dangers, incontestable proofs of the necessary personal courage. Wherever he had once taken a friendship, he continued a zealous friend.

On the other hand, he was possessed with a boundless ambition; he could not endure a superior or an equal, and less yet one that he could suspect of pretending to surpass him in understanding. His avarice was insatiable. He was an implacable enemy. He did not want for natural wit; but having had no education, his manners were rather coarse. His avarice had led him into several disagreeable explanations with Peter I. who had sometimes condemned him to pay arbitrary fines: notwithstanding which, there was found, on his imprisonment, the value of three millions of rubles, in jewels, in plate, and ready money.

He had a son and two daughters: she who had been betrothed to the Emperor died, before her father, in exile; the other was married, under the reign of the Empress Anne, with the General Gustawus Biron, brother to the Duke of Courland, and died in the beginning of the year 1737. The son is major in the guards. So long as his father was in favor and prosperity, all the world allowed him a great deal of wit, though he was but a child; since the disgrace and death of his father, there are few persons in the whole empire of Russia that have less than he.

Menzikoff, who, from the lowest condition, had been raised to the highest stations of life, would have finished his career with honor, if he had not been so infatuated with ambition, as to seek to place his posterity on the throne of Russia. It is the same rock against which all the favorites that followed him have struck, and sunk like him, as will hereafter be shown.

The Empress Anne

Following the death of Peter II, the State Council, which was dominated by the Dolgoruki and Golitzin families, met to choose a sovereign and sought to use this opportunity to limit the autocratic power to the advantage of the nobility. Their choice fell upon Anne of Courland, niece of Peter I, to whom they offered the throne provided she would accept certain limitations. Anne first accepted the offer with its strings attached and then, sure of the crown, thanks to the support of other nobles, renounced the conditions. The following account of this abortive palace revolution is from Manstein, op. cit., pp. 26–35, passim.

The council of state, the senate, and such of the principal generals of the army as were than at Moscow, assembled immediately after the decease of Peter II. and sat in close committee in a chamber of the palace of Kremlin. The high-Chancellor Goloskin announced to the assembly the death of the Emperor, and as soon as he had done speaking, the Prince Demetrius Michaelowitz Gallitzin got up, and said, that *"since, by the demise of Peter II. the whole male line of Peter I. was extinct, and that Russia had suffered extremely by despotic power, to the prevalance of which the great number of foreigners brought in by Peter I. had greatly contributed, it would be highly expedient to limit the supreme authority by salutary laws, and not to confer the imperial crown on the new Empress that should be chosen, but under certain conditions;"* concluding with putting the question to the whole assembly, whether *"they did not approve this proposal?"* They all assented to it, without any of the least opposition. Upon which the Prince Basilius Loukitsch Dolgoroucki proposed the duchess dowager of Courland; alleging, that as the crown was now falling to female, it was but just to prefer the daughter of the Czar Iwan, the elder brother of Peter I. to those of this Emperor; that though the duchess of Mecklenburgh was the eldest, it was to be considered that she was married to a foreign Prince, whereas the Duchess of Courland was actually a widow, and, not being above thirty-six years of age, might marry, and give heirs to Russia.

The true reason, however, for preferring the duchess of Courland was, that she being at Mittau, the remoteness of that place would afford time for firmer establishment of the republican system.

All the votes then united in her favor, and it was agreed, that the Council of State, which was at that time constituted of seven members, of whome the majority were the Dolgorouckis or their relations, should have the whole power, and the assembly framed the following articles:

1st. That the Empress Anne was to reign only in virtue of the resolves, upon deliberation of the privy-council.

2d. That she should not declare war nor make peace on her own authority.

3d. That she would not lay any new tax, or bestow any post or place of consequence.

4th. That she would punish no gentleman with death unless he was duly convicted of his crime.

5th. That she should not confiscate anyone's property.

6th. That she should not alienate or dispose of any lands belonging to the crown.

7th. That she should not marry, nor choose an heir, without asking, upon all these points, the consent of the privy-council.

The assembly then chose three members to notify to the Empress her accession to the throne, and to propose to her the conditions under which she should reign.

In the instructions given to the deputies, it was enjoined to them, to require of the Empress that she should sign the above articles, and that she should not bring her favorite with her to Moscow, Biron, gentleman of the chamber.

. . .

The council of state imagined they had sufficient precaution against the restoration of despotic government, having exacted from the whole army an oath, that it would not serve the Empress but conjointly with the senate. Moreover, before the assembly broke up, they had forbidden, under pain of death, the acquainting the new Empress of any thing that had been debated and resolved. She was not to receive advice of her election, and of the conditions under which she was to mount the throne, but at first hand from the deputies.

. . .

The Empress consented, without making any difficulty, to the signing of whatever the deputies presented to her on the part of the privy-council. She did not even oppose the leaving her favorite behind her at Mittau, and got immediately in readiness to set out for Moscow.

Her Majesty came on the 20th of February to a village called All Saints, situated two leagues from Moscow, where she stopped for five days. As soon as she was arrived there the high-chancellor, at the head of the members of the privy-council, repaired thither, and presented her with the ribbon of St. Andrew, and star, in a gold bason. As soon as the Empress saw it, she said, "it is true, I had forgot to put the order on;" and taking it with her own hands out of the bason, she made one of her attendants put it on her, without suffering any members of the privy-council to help her on with it; and when the high-chancellor was beginning to harangue her, she stopped him, and prevented his going on.

On the same day she appointed the Prince Soltikoff, a very near relation to the mother of the Empress, lieutenant-colonel of the guards. This was the first act of authority she took since her accession to the throne. The rest of her conduct, after her arrival at Moscow, gave many members of the council and of the senate reason to think that she was satisfied with the restrictions laid upon despotic power. She signed anew all that the council of state required, and affected to submit cheerfully to all the conditions.

Her secret conduct was very different from this her public one. Her favorite, whom, at the requisition of the council, she had left behind, was arrived at Moscow; and she took all the pains imaginable to form a strong party. She tried to engage the guards, by her liberality to those who daily did duty about her person. In short, she left no arts or managements unemployed towards effectuating her purpose of creating misunderstandings among the members of the council of state. Everything succeeded to her wish. It had been remarked to them, that the family of the Dolgorouckis, and its connections, would be the only persons that would be benefited by the smallness of the Empress's influence; that they had tied up her hands only to establish the more firmly the power which they had acquired under Peter II; that there were already of that family many of the members of the privy-council, and of the senate; that, little by little, the number would go on augmenting; and that they ought to reflect on the conduct of that family, after the death of the late Emperor, at which time they had aspired to transmit the imperial crown to their family, in which not having been able to succeed, they had not given up the hope of bringing it about in time, by their circumscription of the supreme power.

Neither was it omitted the instilling a mistrust into the lesser nobility, which is very numerous in Russia, by giving them to understand, that none of them stood any chance of obtaining any preferment of the least consequence, while the council of state should have all the power in their hands; as each member would make a point of procuring the most considerable employments for his respective relations and creatures; and that, properly speaking, they would be slaves of the council: whereas, if the Empress was to be declared sovereign, the least private gentleman might pretend to the first posts of the empire, with the same currency as the first Princes: that there were examples of this under Peter I when the greatest regard was paid to true merit; and that if that Prince had done acts of severity, he had been obliged to it; besides, that the lesser nobility had nowise suffered by him; on the contrary, they had recovered their consequence under his reign.

Such hints thrown out, with proper discretion, did not fail of producing the expected effect. The guards, who, even to the private soldiers, are constituted of hardly any but the nobles of the country, formed meetings. Several hundreds of country-gentlemen assembled at the houses of the Princes Trubetszkoi, Boraitinski, and Kzerkasky, as being those in whom they had the greatest confidence, and who were in the interest of the Empress. These did not fail of animating them more and more, till, on the 8th of March, they judged them ripe for the point at which they wanted them. It was then that these Princes, at the head of six hundred gentlemen, went to wait on the Empress; and having obtained an audience, entreated of her to order the council of state and the senate to assemble for the examination of certain points touching the regency. The Empress having consented, she ordered, at the same time, Count Soltikoff, lieutenant-general and lieutenant-colonel of the guards, to have all the avenues well guarded, and not to permit any one to go out of the palace. The guards were also commanded to have their pieces loaded with ball; and special care was taken to acquaint all those who came to court, of the precautions which had been ordered.

While these arrangements were taking, the council of state and the senate were assembled. The Empress gave orders that both these bodies should appear before her. These Princes then having repaired to the presence-chamber, or hall, with the canopy; the count Mattweof, advancing towards her Majesty, spoke, and said, That he was deputed by the whole nobility of the empire to represent to her, that she had been, by the deputies of the council of state, surprised into the concessions she had made; that Russia having for so many ages been governed by sovereign monarchs, and not by council, all the nobility entreated her to take into her own hands the reins of government; that all the nation was of the same opinion, and wished that the family of her Majesty might reign over them to the end of time.

The Empress, at this speech, affected great surprize: "How?" (said she) "was it not then with the will of the whole nation that I signed the act presented to me at Mittau?" Upon which the whole assembly answered, "No." At this she turned towards Prince Dolgoroucki, and said to him, "How came you then, Prince Basilius Loukitch, to impose on me so?" She then ordered the high-chancellor to go and bring her the writings which she had signed. This being done, she made him read them with an audible voice; and at each article she stopped him, and asked if such an article was for the good of the nation. The assembly having to all and each of these constantly answered "NO;" she took the deeds out of the hands of the high-chancellor, and tore them, saying, "These writings then are not necessary." She declared at the same time, "That as the empire of Russia had never been governed but by one sole monarch, she claimed the same perogative as her ancestors had had, from whom she derived her crown by right of inheritance, and not from the election of the council of state, as they had pretended; and that whoever should oppose her sovereignty should be punished as guilty of high treason." This declaration was received with applause, and nothing was heard all over the town but acclamations and shouts of joy.

Russian Intervention in Poland

Active Russian intervention in Polish domestic affairs began long before Catherine the Great effected the partitioning of that unhappy nation. The Empress Anne, for example, supported her candidate for the Polish crown (the Elector of Saxony) by armed invasion of Poland. Here is a contemporary account of the start of that adventure. The source is: Manstein, op. cit., pp. 66–69.

The disturbances of Poland began with the year 1733. The King, Augustus II. who had repaired to Warsaw to hold a diet extraordinary, died there the 11th of February. The archbishop of Gnezen, primate of the kingdom, took the regency, and convened the diet of convocation, in which it was unanimously stipulated to give the exclusion to all foreign Princes, and to elect none but a *piaste,* or native nobleman.

The courts of Vienna and of Petersburgh at first much approved of this resolution of the diet, and gave orders to their embassadors to express their satisfaction at it to the republic, but to add, at the same time, that they could never suffer King Stanislaus to be chosen, who had been, by the result of a diet, declared incapable of the crown. These two courts were, at that time, very far from a disposition in favor of the Elector of Saxony: on the contrary, there had for some years, prevailed so great a coolness in them towards him, as was not unlikely to have brought on a war, if the death of the King had not prevented it. As to the court of Vienna, the cause of dispute was, that he had not only refused to sign the Pragmatic Sanction, but had even entered into a close connection with France against the interests of the house of Austria. As to Russia, its motives of discontent were, the King's not having acted according to the views of the court of Petersburgh in the affairs of Courland; besides which, the primate, and a part of the nobility, who had suspected the King of designs upon the liberty of Poland, had applied to Russia, imploring its assistance in case of his undertaking any thing against the republic.

Affairs soon changed aspect. The new Elector of Saxony found means to appease the court of Vienna, by signing the Pragmatic Sanction; and as to Russia, he promised to conform to the will of the Empress with regard to the affairs of Courland so that both courts united to procure him the crown of Poland. Their embassadors had orders to declare, especially to the primate, that they would recognize no other King of Poland than the Elector of Saxony, and that her Russian Majesty would support the election of that Prince with all her forces, in case of the republic's not taking such a resolution with a good grace.

The court of Petersburgh had caused two bodies of troops to be assembled, the one in Ukraine, on the frontiers of Lithuania, the other in Livonia, upon those of Courland. In the mean while, France had spared neither pains nor money to get King Stanislaus elected. The primate, and the greatest part of the nobility, seeing that the Russians signified their commands to them in the tone of masters, and that the point insisted on was nothing less than such a compulsion to receive the law from foreign powers as totally destroyed the *liberum veto*, which was the great essential of the Polish liberty, united in favor of Stanislaus. They wrote accordingly to France to hasten his departure, that he might come to Poland in time enough to be present at the proclamation.

The diet of election began on the twenty-fifth of August, and continued, though often not without violent contestations, till the twelfth of September, when Stanislaus Leckzinski was, for the second time, elected King of Poland, unanimously by all the gentlemen who were at the *kola*, or field of election. This Prince had arrived on the ninth, and had kept *incognito* in the house of the French ambassador. The primate, and all the nobility of his party, now imagined that they had triumphed over all opposition, and were in hopes, that though the courts of Vienna and Petersburgh might not be pleased with their procedure, they could never, however, carry the point of overturning the act of almost the whole nation.

The courts of Vienna and Petersburgh had been duly informed of the schemes of France, and cabals of the primate. The Empress of Russia had caused to be played off all the springs of policy imaginable, to embarrass and retard the election of Stanislaus, in the hope that, by gaining time, the Elector's party would increase, and that he might be chosen King without the necessity of coming to an open rupture. Her ambassadors at Warsaw had orders to spare neither fair promises nor money to weaken the French party. She wrote to the states of Lithuania, and made a mention to them of the concern she took in the maintenance of the liberty of the republic. Her aim was to persuade the senators of the grand dutchy to detach themselves from Poland. She did not, however, entirely succeed. There were but a few who came into a separation, and retired on the other side of the Wistula, to a village called Praag. The bishops of Cracovia, of Posnania, the Princes Wiesnowiski, and some others, were of the number, which altogether appeared but a small one in comparison of the rest of the nobility. And yet it was these that gave the first impulse to the whole machine, and placed Augustus III. on the throne of Poland. Some of the separatists had aspired to the crown for themselves, but finding that they could not succeed, they united to procure it for the Elector of Saxony, rather than suffer it quietly in the possession of King Stanislaus.

They wrote to Petersburgh, and requested the protection of Russia against the primate and the French party. The Empress, who only wanted a pretext for sending troops into Poland, could not have wished a fairer one than the being called in by the Poles themselves. Upon this, she sent orders to Count Lacy to enter Lithuania, at the head of twenty thousand men. On receipt of them, he advanced in hasty marches towards Warsaw, in the hope that he should arrive in time enough to hinder the proclamation of King Stanislaus. But the primate had taken his measures too well. In the meanwhile, the malcontent nobility went out to meet Count Lacy, and on the thirtieth of September came along with him to the banks of the Wistula. They proposed passing the river, and to repair directly to the field of election, but the Poles of the contrary party had broke down all the bridges, as soon as Stanislaus had retreated to make himself master of the town of Dantzick.

Not to lose time then, they proceeded to the election of the Elector of Saxony, near the village of Comiez, upon the same field, where Henry of Valois (the Third of France) had been chosen. It was on the fifth of October that this great affair was determined, on the eve of the day fixed to be the last of the diet of election. About fifteen senators and six hundred gentlemen were present at it.

A Palace Revolution

Just before her death, the Empress Anne named the infant Ivan as her successor under the regency of Biron, Duke of Courland. The latter plotted to secure the throne for his family by the marriage of his son to the Princess Elizabeth. One of Biron's associates, Marshal Münnich, was disappointed in his hopes of preferment and entered into a plot against the regent. The outcome was the disposal of Biron in favor of Ivan's mother, Anne. This coup d'etat, typical of the "Reign of the Women" is described by Manstein who took part in it. The source is: Manstein, op. cit., pp. 268–273.

When the marshal was returned from court, he told his aid-de-camp general, the lieutenant-colonel de Manstein, that he should have occasion for his service the next day, very early in the morning. Accordingly, at two, after midnight, he sent for him. They both got into a coach together by themselves, and repaired to the winter-palace, where the Emperor and his father and mother were lodged after the death of the Empress. The marshal and his aid-de-camp entered the apartment of the Princess, by the door of the wardrobe. There he made madamoiselle Mengden, lady of honor, and favorite of the Princess, get up. When Munich had explained himself to her, she went in and waked their Highnesses; but it was the Princess alone that came out to him. They had but a moment's talk. The marshal ordered Manstein to call all the officers who were on guard at the palace, for the Princess to speak to them. These being come, her Highness represented in a few words to them the injuries which the regent made the Emperor, herself, and her husband suffer; adding, that as it was impossible, and even shameful, for her to endure such insults any longer, she was resolved to have him apprehended, and had given marshal Munich the commission of it; so that she hoped that the officers would be so good as to follow all his orders, and assist him to the best of their power. The officers made not the least difficulty of obeying the Princess in whatever she required of them; upon which, giving them her hand to kiss, and embracing them all, they went down the stairs with the marshal, and got the guard under arms.

Count Munich told the soldiers what was in agitation; and all, with one accord, answered him, That they were ready to follow him wherever he would lead them. They were ordered to load their muskets, and an officer with forty men were left on guard with the colors. The other eighty marched with the marshal to the summer-palace, where the regent still resided.

About two hundred paces from this house, this troop halted, and the marshal sent Manstein to the officers of the regent's guard to acquaint them of the Princess Anne's intention: they made no more difficulty than the others had done, and even offered their assistance to seize the duke, if it was necessary.

Upon this, the marshal told the same lieutenant-colonel Manstein, to put himself, with an officer, at the head of twenty men, to enter the palace, to seize the duke; and in case of his making any the least resistence, to massacre him without mercy.

Manstein entered the palace; and not to make too much noise, he made the detachment follow him at a distance. All the centinels suffered him to pass in without any opposition; for, as he was personally known to all the soldiers, they imagined he might be sent to the duke upon some affair of consequence, so that he crossed the guards, and got as far as the apartments, without any difficulty. But as he did not know the particular room in which the duke lay, he was all on a sudden extremely embarrassed where to go, so as to avoid all noise and suspicion, neither would he ask any one the question, though he met with some servants who were waiting in the ante-chamber. After some moments meditation, he resolved to keep advancing through the apartments, in the hope he should at length find out the apartment he was seeking. And so it happened in fact; for, after he had gone through two chambers, he was come to a door that was locked; luckily for him, this was a folding door, and the servants had neglected to fasten it, by sliding the bolts at the top and bottom, so that he easily forced it open. In the chamber, he found a great bed, in which the duke and duchess were lying, buried in a profound sleep. Not even the noise he had made in forcing open the door had waked them. Manstein having got close to the bed, drew the curtains, and desired to speak with the regent. Upon this, both started up in a surprise, and begun to cry out aloud, judging rightly enough that he was not come to bring them any good news. Manstein happening to stand on the side on which the duchess lay, the regent threw himself out of bed, on the ground, certainly with an intention to hide himself under the bed; but this officer springing quickly round to the other side, threw himself upon him, and held him fast embraced till the guards came in. The duke having at length got upon his legs again, and wanting to disengage himself from their hold, distributed blows with his double fist to the right and left; to which the soldiers made no return but with strokes from the but-end of their muskets; and throwing him down again on the floor, they crammed a handkerchief into his mouth, and bound his hands with an officer's sash; then they led him, naked as he was, to the guard-room, where they covered him with a soldier's cloak, and put him into a coach of the marshal's, that was waiting for him. An officer was placed in it by the side of him, and he was carried to the winter-palace.

While the soldiers were struggling with the duke, the duchess was got out of bed in her shift, and, running after him as far as into the street, when a soldier took her in his arms, and asked Manstein, what he should do with her. He bid him carry her back to her chamber; but the soldier not caring, it seems, to take the trouble of it, threw her down on the ground, in the midst of the snow, and there left her. The captain of the guard, finding her in this piteous condition, made her clothes be brought to her, and reconducted her to the apartments she had always occupied.

As soon as the duke was thus on the way to the winter-palace, the same colonel, Manstein, was sent to seize his younger brother, Gustavus Biron, who was then at Petersburgh. He was lieutenant-colonel of the Ishmaëlow regiment of guards. But this expedition required somewhat more of pre-cautionary measures than the first; for Gustavus Biron was beloved in his regiment, and had a guard of it in his house, consisting of a serjeant and twelve men. And, accordingly, the centinels made at first some resistance, but they were soon laid hold of, and threatened with death if they made the least noise. After which, Manstein went into the bedchamber of Biron, and made him get up, telling him, that he had an affair of great consequence to impart to him. Having then drawn him to the window, he acquainted him with his orders of arrest. Biron wanted to open the window, and began to cry out; but he was instantly let to know that the duke was seized, and under confinement, and that himself would be killed on the least resistance. The soldiers, who had waited in the adjoining room, came in directly, and satisfied him that there was nothing for him but to obey. They gave him a furred cloke, put him into a sledge, and he too was carried to the winter-palace.

At the same time colonel Koneingsfelt, one of the adjutants of the marshal, who had joined him when he was returning with the duke, was sent back to apprehend count Bestucheff.

As for the duke, he was put into the room of the officers of the guard. His brother and count Bestucheff had each a separate room, where they remained till four o'clock in the afternoon, till the duke, with all his family (except his eldest son, who was then sick, and who staid till his recovery at Petersburgh) were carried to the fort of Schluiselburgh. The other two prisoners were sent to places at a small distance from the capital, where they were kept till after their examination.

As soon as the duke was seized, order was sent to all the regiments that happened to be then at Petersburgh, to be put under arms, and to assemble round the palace. The Princess Anne then declared herself Grand-Duchess of Russia, and regent of the empire during the minority of the Emperor. She at the same time put on the collar of the order of St. Andrew, and every one took a new oath of fidelity, in which the Grand-Duchess was mentioned by name, which had not been done in that imposed by the regent. There were none that did not make great demonstrations of joy, at seeing themselves delivered from the tyranny of Biron; and from that moment everything was quiet. Even the piquets were taken away, which the duke of Courland had posted in the Streets to prevent commotions during his regency; and yet there were some, who, at the very moment of that event, prognosticated that it would not be the last revolution; and that those who had been the most active in bringing this about, would be the first that would be overset by another. Time has shown that they were not in the wrong.

Elizabeth Seizes the Throne

Following the seizure of Biren by General Münnich, Princess Anne became regent. Münnich resigned in March, 1741, leaving confusion worse confounded and Sweden took advantage of Russia's weakness to declare war upon her. The only hope of the patriotic Russian nobility seemed to be Peter's younger daughter, Elizabeth. Urged and aided by the Guards, Elizabeth made a successful coup d'etat on December 6, 1741. The account which follows was written by "a learned man, an accomplished linguist, but a mediocre historian." It gives, however, a vivid picture of the palace revolution which made Elizabeth an empress. The source is: Bain, R. N., The Daughter of Peter the Great. A History of Russian Diplomacy and of the Russian Court under the Empress Elizabeth Petrovna, 1741–1762. New York: E. P. Dutton and Co., 1900. Pp. 50–61.

On December 6th, 1741, La Chetardie, the French Ambassador at St. Petersburg, wrote as follows to Amelot, the French Minister of Foreign Affairs, as to the prospects of a *coup d'etat* in favour of the Tsarevna Elizabeth: "An outbreak, the success of which can never be morally certain, especially now that the Swedes are not in a position to lend a hand, would, prudently considered, be very difficult to bring about, unless it could be substantially backed up." That very same evening, Elizabeth, without any help from without, overthrew the existing government in a couple of hours, a circumstance carefully to be borne in mind, as many historians, rashly relying on certain ex-post-facto statements by La Chetardie, have credited that diplomatist with a leading part in the revolution which placed the daughter of Peter the Great on the Russian throne. As a matter of fact La Chetardie, beyond lending the Tsarevna 2,000 ducats instead of the 15,000 she demanded of him, took no part whatever in the actual *coup d'etat,* which was as great a surprise to him as it was to everyone else. The merit and glory of that singular affair belong to Elizabeth alone.

It must also be observed that, from the first, Elizabeth had taken a much saner view of the situation than any of her foreign advisers, and all along, despite much fear and faltering, she seems to have never been without the comforting persuasion that her courage would rise to the level of her necessities. Thus, when the Swedish Minister, Nolcken, suggested that she should rally all her partisans and arrange everything before hand, even to the choosing of a leader for the enterprise, she objected, very pertinently, that the inveterate distrust with which every Russian regarded every other Russian, rendered any such combination impossible. To even attempt it would be sufficient to ruin everything. It were far better, she said, to win over her partisans one by one, and make each of them believe that he was contributing equally to the glory of the enterprise. To prevent any jealousy, moreover, she meant to head the Guards herself when the moment for action arrived. "I know very well," she concluded, "that you suspect me of weakness, but I will not be false to my blood, I will show myself worthy to be the daughter of Peter the Great." Yet nearly twelve months had elapsed since these brave words were spoken, and still nothing had been done. Elizabeth's vacillation was intelligible enough, it is true. The least evil which she knew would befall her in case of failure, was lifelong seclusion in a monastery, and this to a Princess "who," to use Mr. Finch's elegant expression, "had not an ounce of nun's flesh about her," was the most terrible prospect in the world. She was ready to endure much before risking such a contingency, but a point was reached at last beyond which even her endurance refused to go.

On Dec. 4th, the Tsarevna and most of the Foreign Ministers attended a crowded reception at the Winter Palace. The Regent, who appeared to be unusually perturbed that evening, withdrew early into an inner chamber, and shortly afterwards Elizabeth was summoned to her presence. No sooner did the Grand Duchess perceive her cousin than she exclaimed: "Matushka! what is this I hear of you? They tell me that you are in correspondence with the enemies of our country, and that your doctor is intriguing with the French Minister."—Elizabeth protested, with well-feigned astonishment, that this was the first she had heard of it, adding that she knew her duty better than to break the oath she had sworn to the young Emperor. But the Regent was not so easily mollified, "Madam," said she, adopting a harder tone, "I am about to request the King of France to recall M. de la Chetardie, and I must therefore request you never again to receive him at your house."—"Never again!" exclaimed Elizabeth, piqued in her turn. "I might refuse to see him once or twice perhaps, but to promise never to see him again is impossible."— "But I insist upon it!" cried Anne.—"My cousin," retorted Elizabeth, "you are Regent, and have but to command to be obeyed. Surely it would be much simpler if you were to order Count Ostermann to tell La Chetardie expressly not to visit me any more."—By this time both Princesses were growing warm, and had raised their voices, and while the Regent had recourse to threats, Elizabeth took refuge in tears. At the sight of her cousin's distress, the Regent was herself visibly affected, and the agitated ladies finally composed their quarrel in each other's arms, Elizabeth swearing eternal fidelity, and the Regent professing implicit faith in her loyalty. Nevertheless this scene seems to have at last opened the eyes of the Tsarevna to the imminence of her danger. She knew very well that the indolent and foolishly good-natured Regent would never have taken such a high hand with her unless prompted to do so, and she rightly suspected the hand of Ostermann in the affair. She was confirmed in her suspicions next day by another still more significant event. On the morning of Dec. 5th, the Government issued orders to all the regiments of the Guards in the capital to hold themselves in readiness to march to the seat of war within four-and-twenty hours, as the Swedish general, Levenhaupt, was reported to be advancing rapidly towards Viborg. This however, was a mere pretext. Ostermann was well aware that Levenhaupt was still in his cantonments at the other end of Finland; the manoeuvre was simply intended to render Elizabeth defenceless, and there can be little doubt that the astute old Minister intended to arrest the Tsarevna as soon as the Guards were gone.

That same night, at about 10 o'clock, a hurried and anxious conference was held at the Tsarevna's house, after Lestocq, her surgeon, had reconnoitered the town and made certain that all the lights in the Winter Palace and in Ostermann's house had been extinguished. The only persons present besides Lestocq, were the Princess's Kammerherr, Michael Ilarionovich Vorontsov; her old music-master, Herr Schwarz; her favourite, and future husband, Alexius Razumovsky, and Alexander and Peter Shuvalov, two of the gentlemen of her household. No monarch ever had more devoted servants than these men were to prove to Elizabeth; but they were, all of them, subaltern spirits who looked to their mistress to take the initiative, and now, at the supreme moment, it seemed as if she were about to yield to a sudden fit of panic, for she began to expatiate on the dangers they were likely to run. "Truly, Madam," replied Vorontsov, "the affair demands no little daring, but where shall we look for it if we cannot find it in the blood of Peter the Great?" At these words the Tsarevna recovered her sangfroid, and turning to Lestocq, ordered him to send at once for the twenty most resolute grenadiers of the Guard, whom he had already bought with the ducats of the French Ambassador, and, upon their arrival between eleven and twelve, they were admitted into the presence of the Tsarevna, and she asked them point-blank if she could absolutely rely upon their fidelity. "Yes, Matushka! we are ready to die for you," they exclaimed, whereupon she bade them withdraw for a moment, and, flinging herself down before an ikon of the Saviour, made a solemn vow to God that if her enterprise succeeded, she would never sign a death-warrant as long as she lived. Then rising from her knees and taking a cross in her hand, she went out to the soldiers and said: "If God be merciful to us and to Russia, I will never forget your devotion. Go now to the barracks, assemble your comrades with all speed and secrecy, and await my arrival, I will be with you immediately." When they had gone she returned to her oratory, and remained on her knees in silent prayer for nearly an hour, till Lestocq, growing anxious, reminded her of the danger of further delay, and handed her the insignia of the order of St. Catherine (a decoration cherished by her as having been instituted in honour of her beloved mother), which she put on forthwith, and a silver cross, which she concealed about her person. He also persuaded her to wear a mail cuirass beneath her clothes, escorted her to a sledge which was already waiting at the door, and took his seat himself by her side, while Vorontsov and one of the Shuvalovs mounted up behind, and Razumovsky remained in the house to keep order. It was close upon two o'clock in the morning when they set off on their adventurous drive through the silent snow-covered streets of the city to the Preobrazhensky Barracks, where nearly two hundred of the Guards were already awaiting them. Immediately on dismounting, Elizabeth snatched a spontoon from one of the soldiers, and led the way into the messroom, ordering first of all, however, that all the drums in the barracks should be slit up, so that nobody could give the alarm. The men crowded after her, and when they were all assembled, she exclaimed: "My children, you know whose daughter I am! It is my resolve this night to deliver you and all Russia from our German tormentors. Will you follow me?"—"Matushka!" they cried enthusiastically, "we will follow thee to the death, and as for the *nyemtsui*, we will cut them to pieces!" —"Nay, my children," replied Elizabeth, "if you hurt a hair of their heads, I will not go one step with you. There must be no bloodshed. What we are going to do we do simply for the benefit of our country."—Having thus restrained their savage zeal within due limits, she knelt down, all present following her example, and producing her silver cross, held it aloft and exclaimed: "I swear before Heaven to die for you, will you swear to die for me?"—"We swear!" thundered the Grenadiers.—"Then let us go!" cried the Tsarevna, rising, "and remember, my children, whatever befall, no bloodshed!"—By this time her escort of grenadiers had swelled to nearly 400, all of them with bayonets screwed on and grenades in their pockets. Her first care was to despatch well-mounted messengers to the barracks of the Semenovsky and Ismailovsky Guards, bidding the soldiers assemble before her house as speedily as possible, and there await further orders; then, at the head of the Preobrazhensky Regiment, she proceeded on her way to the Winter Palace where the Regent was reposing in absolute security. As she passed through the grand avenue of the Nevsky Prospect on her way thither, she had the persons of the Vice-Chancellor, Count Golovkin and Baron Mengden, who resided there, secured in their beds, and, on arriving at the end of the avenue leading to the Admiralty, she sent three separate detachments of grenadiers to arrest Count Ostermann, his three brothers-in-law the Streshnevs, all of whom were generals, and Field Marshal Münnich who lived at the other end of the city. At this point, moreover, in order to stimulate the zeal of her men, she descended from her sledge, and walked on foot in their midst, but the grenadiers soon perceiving that their "Matushka" had much difficulty in keeping pace with them, lifted the by no means ethereal form of their little mother on to their shoulders and so carried her the remainder of the distance, to the gates of the Winter Palace.

The guards in the barracks of the Winter Palace were surprised in their slumbers, and Elizabeth did not allow them a moment's time for reflection. "Wake up, my children!" she cried, "and listen to me. You know who I am, and that the crown belongs to me of right. Will you follow me?"—Most of the men responded with shouts of devotion, but four subaltern-officers and one private hesitated, and she ordered them to be arrested on the spot. Her command was not only instantly obeyed, but was even in danger of being exceeded, for the loyal grenadiers in their fiery zeal would have bayoneted their lukewarm comrades there and then, had not the Princess struck up their weapons with her pike. The backsliders having been safely secured, Elizabeth proceeded, like a prudent general, to marshal and distribute her forces for the final assault. Despatching numerous small detachments of her grenadiers to guard all the staircases and other exits, she ascended the grand staircase at the head of the remainder of the party, after once more solemnly adjuring them to use no violence. The guards in front of the Grand Duchess's apartments made no resistance, and Elizabeth entering the bedroom, found Anne Leopoldovna asleep in bed with Julia Mengden by her side. "Awake, my sister!" cried Elizabeth, gently shaking the slumbering ex- Regent, who started up exclaiming: "What, is it you, Sudaruinya?" Then perceiving the helmets of the grenadiers behind the Princess, she guessed the truth and quietly submitted, merely begging that no harm should be done to her children, and that she should not be separated from her friend Julia. Elizabeth assured her cousin that neither she nor her children had anything to fear, and she bade the grenadiers convey the Grand Duchess to her own litter. The persons of the infant Tsar and his lately born sister, Catherine, were then secured, and they were both brought in to Elizabeth. Taking them in her arms, she kissed them both, exclaiming: "Poor children, it is not you, but your parents, who are to blame." They were then placed, with their nurses, in a second sledge and driven to Elizabeth's own palace, she following closely behind them in her own sledge with Anna Leopoldovna and Julia Mengden. The seizure and abduction of the ex-Regent and her children had been effected in less than half an hour, indeed so smoothly, swiftly and noiselessly had the whole revolution proceeded, that, as late as eight o'clock the next morning, very few people in the city, except the confederates, were aware that Elizabeth Petrovna had, during the previous night, been raised to the throne of her father, on the shoulders of the Preobrazhensky Grenadiers.

On regaining her mansion, Elizabeth despatched Lestocq, Vorontsov and Schwarz to all parts of the city, to summon the notables, civil and ecclesiastical, to her presence. The Commander-in-Chief, Field Marshal Lacy, was one of the first to be advertised of the change. "To which party do you belong?" enquired the emissaries of the Tsaritsa. "To the party in power," responded the prudent old Irishman, without the slightest hesitation, and he immediately hastened to Elizabeth's mansion in order to place his services at the disposal of the new Empress. He found her surrounded by the chief dignitaries of the realm, holding her first council, the immediate results of which were a new oath of Allegiance and a skilfully worded manifesto, the joint production of the lately recalled ex-Minister, Alexius Bestuzhev, and Count Brevern, Ostermann's private secretary, who had already deserted his life-long benefactor, to the effect that her Majesty, moved by the prayers of her faithful subjects, had accepted the throne in order to put an end to the prevalent confusion caused by the late government. At eight o'clock the oath and manifesto were ready, the Council rose, and the Empress, after declaring herself Colonel of the three regiments of the Guards, and investing herself with the insignia of St. Andrew, appeared in the midst of the distinguished mob which was already thronging her ante-chambers, and received the congratulations of the nobility, gentry and high officials with a gracious *bonhomie* which won every heart. Then, despite the Arctic severity of the weather, she ordered the windows to be thrown open, stepped out on the balcony, and showed herself to the people who crowded the square below. She was received with a loud burst of enthusiasm, the like of which had not been heard in St. Petersburg since the death of Peter the Great.

After sufficiently gratifying the curiosity of the populace, Elizabeth retired to rest for a short time, and then proceeded in state to the Winter Palace, which had, in the meantime, been prepared for her reception. The din of salvoes from the citadel, and the still louder roar of the joyous multitude that thronged the line of route, marked her triumphal progress. Indeed so dense was the throng that the Court dignitaries had to leave their carriages and fight their way into the Palace, on foot. After hearing a Te Deum at the Imperial chapel, in the midst of her grenadiers, whose captain, at their urgent petition, she had consented to become, the Empress held a reception. The new oath was then administered to the Guards and to all the civil, military and ecclesiastical functionaries, and couriers were despatched to all parts of the realm announcing her Majesty's happy accession.

The confederates and adherents of the new sovereign were rewarded with a promptness and a liberality only to be expected of the most bountiful of Princesses; the favourites, Peter and Alexander Shuvalov, were made Generals and Colonels in the Guards; Alexius Razumvosky became a Lieutenant-Colonel and a Kammerherr, and Lestocq was made the Empress's first body-physician, a Privy Councillor and Director of the College of Medicine, with a salary of 7,000 rubles. He also received her Majesty's portrait set in brilliants worth 20,000 rubles. Twelve thousand rubles were distributed among the soldiers of the Preobrazhensky Regiment, which received at the same time the title of the Imperial Body Guard, with a new uniform; and nine thousand rubles were distributed among the soldiers of the Semenovsky and the Izmailovsky Regiments respectively. All the officers of these regiments were raised in rank, the very corporals becoming captains, while each private was made a lieutenant, ennobled and gratified with a small estate. All persons proscribed for political offences during the last two reigns were recalled to Court and restored to favour. Conspicuous among them was the aged Field Marshal Vasily Vladimirovich Dolgoruki, one of the victims of Anne's cruelty, who was released from his dungeon at Narva, where he had languished for ten years, to preside over the War Office. Moreover, he and his family had their estate restored to them, and their wives and daughters were appointed to considerable posts near the Empress's person, along with the female relations of their old rivals, the Golitsuins. Biren also was released, but, by the advice of La Chetardie, he was forbidden the Court and ordered to live quietly on an estate which was bestowed upon him, with an honourable maintenance.

Yet this bloodless revolution, this pleasing picture of a liberated nation rejoicing around the idolized monarch of its choice, was not without its sinister touch of tragedy, and chief among its victims was the man to whom, next after Peter the Great, belongs the honour of having laid the foundations of modern Russia. Ostermann could indeed expect little mercy from a Princess whom all his life long he had consistently neglected and despised. Perhaps Elizabeth's good nature might ultimately have got the better of her resentment, but La Chetardie was constantly at her elbow to keep alive her wrath against the most formidable enemy of the French system in Russia, and so the illustrious statesman was sacrificed. At first he so far abased himself as to address a couple of appealing letters to the Empress, which were treated as "very mean and paltry performances"; but during the subsequent farcical proceedings, dignified with the name of a trial, before a tribunal presided over by the personal enemies of the accused, he comported himself with a quiet resignation not without dignity.

The Empress Elizabeth

The following detailed description of Elizabeth and some of her associates was written by R. Nisbet Bain. The source is: Bain, Daughter of Peter the Great, *pp. 134–145. (Somewhat abridged.)*

Elizabeth Petrovna, although no longer the ravishing, exquisite madcap, "always on the hop," whom grave diplomatists judicially pronounced to be the most exquisite creature in existence, was still one of the most handsome, one of the most fascinating women in Europe. Lord Hyndford described her in her 38th year as "worthy of the admiration of all the world." Catherine II tells us that at forty her somewhat puissant, but marvellously well-proportioned, figure appeared to admiration in male attire, while all the movements of the stately Tsaritsa were so graceful that one could gladly have gazed upon her for ever. Nothing else in the room seemed worth looking at when she was gone. Her once brilliant complexion, indeed, now needed the assistance of cosmetics; but her large blue eyes, "so like a merry bird's," were as brilliant as ever, while her luxuriant hair, of the richest auburn hue, was the crowning charm of a singularly majestic and imposing liveliness. But her salient, her most irresistible attraction was a natural kindliness expressing itself in a ready courtesy, an impulsive sympathy, which came straight from the heart. La Chetardie frequently alludes to her as debonaire, and that delightful word exactly describes her. She was gentle, affable, and familiar with all who approached her, yet always with a due regard to her dignity, and her playful gaiety was without the slightest tinge of malice. It was good to be with her, folks said. She seemed to radiate joyousness. Catherine II also possessed a charm of manner which was well-nigh irresistible, but with her benevolence was always more or less a matter of profound calculation. It was not so with Elizabeth. To make people happy was a necessity of her nature; she loved to see smiling faces around her, and considered that distress of every kind had an imperative claim upon her. Her horror of bloodshed made the very idea of war hateful to her, and she wept bitterly at the news of every victory won by her arms. She took care that her soldiers were so well-clad that casualties from stress of weather were almost unknown, and on receiving intelligence of the earthquake at Lisbon, she offered to rebuild part of the city at her own cost, though she had no diplomatic relations with Portugal. We have seen how at the beginning of her reign, she resolved to abolish capital punishment. The Ukaz to that effect was, by the advice of her Ministers, never promulgated, lest malefactors should multiply; but she took care to commute every capital sentence as it came before her. Again, when Peter Shuvalov submitted to her his codification of the Russian laws, which bristled with cruel and vexatious fiscal penalties, the Empress indignantly declared that it was "written not with ink, but with blood," and refused to sign it. One of her most engaging qualities was her fondness for young people, children especially, and all little folk were passionately devoted to her. She also very frequently gave children's parties, eighty to ninety little couples sitting down to supper with their governors and governesses at separate tables. The Princess Dashkova tells us that she took "the affectionate interest of a good godmother" in the private affairs of the youth and maidens of her Court, and, match-maker as she was, repeatedly helped struggling young lovers out of their pecuniary difficulties. On one occasion, the Princess, then a mere child, was so affected by the tone of maternal tenderness with which the Empress congratulated her on her engagement, that she burst into tears, whereupon Elizabeth, tapping her gently on the shoulder and at the same time kissing her cheek, said with a smile: "Come, come, my child; compose yourself, or all your friends will fancy I have been scolding you." For, like most warm-hearted people, the Tsaritsa had a naturally quick and impetuous temper, and, when fairly roused, would scold and bully for an hour at a time, without stopping to pick her words, till she grew purple in the face. Yet when the paroxysm was over, she was as radiant as ever; never bore the slightest resentment, even under the most trying circumstances; and the words "Vinovata, Matushka!" uttered with becoming contrition, always disarmed her. And if hasty and choleric, she was also just, equitable, and a great peacemaker. It is one of her chief glories that, so far as she was able, she put a stop to that mischievous contention of rival ambitions at Court, which had disgraced the reigns of Peter II, Anne and Ivan VI, and enabled Foreign Powers to freely interfere in the domestic affairs of Russia. Her Ministers had not only to serve her, but to live in harmony with one another. We have already seen how she protected the Bestuzhevs against Lestocq and Trubetskoi, and how she would not sacrifice Vorontsov to Bestuzhev; we shall see presently how, for a long time, she held the balance equally between the Chancellor's party and the Shuvalovs.

Nevertheless this bright picture has its darker side. One of the chief faults imputed to the Empress Elizabeth is her indolence. Lord Hyndford, on one occasion, complains of "this lady's mortal backwardness in all sorts of business or anything that requires one moment's thought or application," and although there is much of exaggeration, there is also something of truth, in this accusation. No doubt, as Solovev justly observes, her backwardness was not always due to indolence, but to a conscientious endeavour to consider doubtful questions from every possible point of view, and it is quite certain that, under the pressure of emergency, she took infinite pains to disentangle truth from falsehood, and would decide nothing till she had quite satisfied her own mind as to the subject in debate. It must also be remembered that, even judged by the low standard of her own age, she was very ignorant, and therefore obliged to lean a good deal upon the opinions of others. But, after making every possible allowance, we cannot altogether acquit her of neglect of affairs. Frequently she left the most important documents unread and unsigned for months together, and Bestuzhev used bitterly to complain that she would not attend to business without a great deal of coaxing. There was the less excuse for her, moreover, because she had always plenty of time upon her hands. Literature naturally had no attraction for a Princess who regarded all reading (except the perusal of devotional books printed in very large type) as injurious to health. And then she lived in such a haphazard way. She had no fixed times for lying down or getting up, and her meals were uncertain and irregular. A large portion of each day was spent in gossiping in her private apartments with her favourite women, Maura Egorovna Shuvalova, Anna Karlovna Vorontsova, Nastasia Mikhailovna Izmailovna, and a certain Elizabeth Ivanovna, a mysterious and not altogether reputable old lady whom the Tsaritsa frequently employed on dark and dubious errands, and whom the witty Stroganov therefore dubbed "Le ministere des affairs étranges," in contradistinction to the Grand Chancellor, who was "Le ministere des affaires étrangeres." Her devotions, however, for she rigorously observed the innumerable feast and fast days of the Orthodox Church, occupied no small part of her leisure. In the summer she hawked and hunted, and, in winter, took horse exercise in the vast covered riding-school built in the reign of Anne for the favourite Biren. She was an excellent shot, a fearless and graceful rider, and could, in her best days, outwalk the strongest of her guardsmen. Nor was she altogether without æsthetic tastes, being passionately fond of music and the drama, and taking a great interest in architecture. No other Russian Sovereign ever erected so many churches, and the celebrated Winter Palace, Rastrelli's masterpiece, was built under her supervision, though she did not live long enough to inhabit it.

But building was by no means her most costly pastime. For every hundred rubles she expended on the permanent embellishment of her capital, she wasted a thousand on the transitory pleasures of her Court. Lavish to the verge of extravagance, and loving pomp and show with all the ardour of a sensuous, semi-barbarous Oriental, it was the great delight of Elizabeth Petrovna to pose as the majestic central figure of brilliant assemblies and gorgeous pageants, and her court was indisputably the most splendid in Europe. Her cousin Anne, before her, had indeed astonished foreigners by the gorgeousness of her appointments, but Anne's crude and bizarre magnificence lacked the veneer of grace, elegance and refinement which characterized the court of Elizabeth. For, though in many respects a Russian gentlewoman of the old school, and intensely patriotic, Elizabeth Petrovna was far more intelligent and receptive than Anne Ivanovna, and, especially where her pleasures were concerned, borrowed freely from the luxuries of the Western civilization. Hence the accusation of reckless extravagance so often and so justly brought against her by Prince Shcherbatov and other laudatores temporis acti. Sir Cyril Wych, as early as 1742, when Elizabeth was still comparatively economical, described the Court of St. Petersburg as the most expensive in Europe, and protested that his allowance could not meet even current expenses. This extravagance manifested itself principally in the habiliments, equipages, retinue and banquets of the gentry and nobility, the Empress herself setting the example in this respect. She is said to have changed her clothes half-a-dozen times a day, and although she lost 4,000 dresses at the great Moscow conflagration of 1747, fifteen thousand more were found in her wardrobes after her death, most of which had only been worn once. And the Empress took care that her courtiers should live up to this high standard of display. At the wedding of the Grand Duke Peter, all public officials were given a year's salary in advance that they might be able to make a brave show on the occasion, and a special ukaz laid down sumptuary regulations for the pageant. Every member of the first and second class in the table of grades was to have two heydukes and not less than eight lacqueys attached to each of his carriages, and as many more as he could afford. But the jeunesse dorée of Peterhof and Tsarkoe Selo needed little prompting. Their natural vanity and luxuriousness met the Tsaritsa's wishes half way. It soon became the ambition of every young Russian noble to outshine his neighbour, and at last even the most expensive galloon was generally looked down upon as common and vulgar. Sergius Naruishkin, accounted the greatest dandy of the age in Russia, won great favour by going to the wedding of the Grand Duke, in a carriage inlaid all over, even to the wheels, with crystal mirrors, and wearing a caftan ablaze with jewels, the back of which was made to imitate a tree, the trunk being represented by a broad golden hand in the middle of his body, while the branches were indicated by lines of silver running up the sleeves to the wrists, and the roots by similar lines running down to the knees of the breeches. The immensely wealthy Ivan Chernuishev, who had travelled widely and did more than any other man to import foreign luxury into Russia, used to order twelve suits at a time, and the very liveries of his pages were of cloth of gold. Yet even he could not compete with Count Alexander Razumovsky and his brother Cyril. The elder Razumovsky was the first to wear diamond buttons, buckles and epaulets; while Count Cyril, on being appointed Grand Hetman of the Cossacks, departed for Glukhov, the seat of his Government, where he lived in regal state, with an immense retinue which included a bodyguard, a troupe of actors, and half-a-dozen French cooks, including the famous chef, Barridian, who received a salary of 500 rubles (£125), and was considered even superior to Duval the chef of Frederick the Great. On one occasion Cyril bought up 100,000 bottles of wine, including 6,800 bottles of the best champagne, then a fashionable novelty, which he freely distributed among his friends. Far less generous was Chancellor Bestuzhev, whose immense cellar was, after his death, given by Catherine II to Prince Orlov, who sold it for an incredible sum. Prince Shcherbatov instances it as a sign of the degeneracy of the times, that pineapples and English horses were first introduced into Russia, at enormous expense, by Peter Shuvalov, who lived so recklessly that he left behind him a million rubles' worth of debts, although his standing income for years was 400,000 rubles (£100,000). Peter Shuvalov was particularly proud of the magnifience of his dessert; his brother Alexander, on the other hand, boasted that he was the chief propagandist of champagne in Russia. Then there was Field Marshal Stephen Apraksin who had hundreds of suits of clothes, a jewelled snuff-box for every day in the year, and required more than five hundred horses to drag his private baggage when he took the field against the King of Prussia; and Count Peter Borisovich Sheremetev, the richest man in the Empire, whose dresses were heavy with gold and silver, and who always went about surrounded by a whole army of domestics almost as brilliantly attired as himself. It is recorded of him that he kept such an ample table that once, when the Empress and her by no means tiny court looked in upon him unawares, he was able to entertain them all sumptuously with what was actually provided for the use of his household on that particular day. The lesser nobles naturally imitated the magnates, and the result was a rapid declension from the simplicity of the old Russian mode of life, and a growing fondness for costly and unnecessary exotic luxuries which ministered to vanity and dissipation with often the most serious consequences. This was bad enough, but still worse remained behind, for the Court of Elizabeth was not only the most extravagant, it was also the most licentious in Europe, and for this also the Empress must be held primarily responsible.

The Emancipation of the Nobles

On the death of Elizabeth in December 1761(O.S.) the crown went to her nephew, Peter, who as Tsar Peter III proved himself wholly incompetent to rule. Early in his reign, Peter freed the nobility from the obligation of state service which had been laid upon them by Peter the Great. This action was,

of course, very popular with the nobility and Catherine, whose power depend-
ed upon the favor of this group, reaffirmed and extended the grant by her
Charter of the Gentry in 1785. The following selection is an excerpt from
the ukase of Peter III. The source is: Tooke, William, The Life of Catherine
II, Empress of all the Russias. *(First American Edition.) Two volumes.*
Philadelphia, 1802. Vol. I, pp. 513–515.

WE PETER III, &c. The troubles and inconveniences experienced by the wise sovereign, our late dear grandsire, Peter the Great, of immortal memory, in his endeavours for the good of his country, and for procuring his subjects a competent knowledge, as well in military discipline, as in civil and political affairs, are known to all Europe, and the greater part of the globe.

In the attainment of this end, he found it necessary to begin by convincing the Russian nobility, which is the first body of the state, of the immense advantages possessed by the nations well versed in the sciences and the arts, over those people who continue benighted in ignorance and sloth. The state of things at that time imperiously demanded, that he should oblige his nobility to enter the military service, and engage in civil functions; that he should send them to travel into foreign countries, that they might get a tincture of the useful arts and sciences, and therefore he established, in his own country, schools and academies, that the seeds of these his salutary regulations, might be cherished in their growth, and more speedily matured. The nobility had the less reason to complain of the constraint thus laid upon them, as, independently of the utility, both public and private, that naturally resulted from it, it was their duty to concur with the wishes of an emperor to whom they were under so many obligations.

The execution, of these projects seemed at first to be attended with the utmost difficulty. They were intolerable to the nobility, who saw themselves obliged to abandon a soft and indolent life, to quit their dwellings, to serve in war and in peace, and to enrol their children for future services. Several members of their body withdrew from the service, and were therefore deprived of their estates, which were confiscated, and that for the best of reasons. They rendered themselves criminal towards their country, which they basely deserted.

These excellent ordinances, though at the beginning inseparable from certain methods of constraint, have served as a model to all the successors of Peter the Great, and especially to our dear aunt, the empress Elizabeth Petrovna, of glorious memory; who determined to follow the example of her father, encouraged, by a special protection, the advancement of the arts and sciences. Of this we are now reaping the fruits; and every impartial man will agree, that they are considerable. Manners have been improved;

minds indifferent to the happiness of the country have been roused from their fatal lethargy, and have habituated themselves to reflect on the public welfare; zeal in the service is augmented; generals, already valiant, are become experienced; intelligent ministers; enlightened magistrates; in a word, patriotism, love and attachment to our person, activity in all offices and posts, and every generous sentiment, are now the happy lot of the Russian nation. For all these reasons, we have judged it to be no longer necessary to compel into the service, as hitherto has been the practice, the nobility of our empire.

In consideration whereof, in virtue of the full power to us granted by God, and of our imperial especial grace, we grant to the Russian nobility, from this moment and forever, in the name of all our successors, permission to take service in our empire, as well as in all those of the European powers in alliance with us; and to this end we have given the following ordinance as a fundamental law, &c.

[Then follow nine articles concerning the terms on which liberty of resignation, of travelling abroad, of entering the service, &c. may be asked for and granted: concluding thus:]

Granting as we do, graciously and to perpetuity, to our nobility this franchise, making it a fundamental and unalterable law, we promise them equally on our imperial word, and in the most solemn manner, to observe the present ordinance sacredly and irrevocably, in all its tenor, and to maintain the prerogatives therein expressed. . . . Our successors on the throne ought not to alter it in any manner. The execution of our said ordinance being the principal support of the imperial throne, we hope that from gratitude for this benefit, the Russian nobility will serve us faithfully and zealously; and that, instead of withdrawing from our service, will enter it with eagerness, and that they will carefully educate their children. . . . We therefore command all our faithful subjects, and true sons of the country, to despise and avoid those who have wasted their time in idleness, and who have not educated their children in the useful sciences, as people who have never had the public good at heart, who shall have no access to our court, nor be admitted to the publick assemblies and the national festivities.

Given at St. Petersburg, Feb. 18, 1762.

Catherine's Coup d'etat: the report of the British Ambassador

Catherine the Great had no legal right to the Russian throne. She came to power through a successful coup d'etat against her husband, Peter III. The coup was originally planned to take place at Elizabeth's death, but that event found the conspirators unready. The arrest of one of them and the fear of complete discovery precipitated the coup in 1762. It was a palace revolution, made by some of the nobles among whom the most prominent were the Orlov brothers. The following account of the event was sent to London by the British agent in St. Petersburg. The source is: Collyer, A. D. (Editor), The Despatches and Correspondence of John, Second Earl of Buckinghamshire, Ambassador to the Court of Catherine II, 1762-1765. Two volumes. Published for the Royal Historical Society. London: Longmans, Green and Co., 1900/01. Vol. 1, pp. 60–63.

MR. KEITH TO MR. GRENVILLE. St. Petersburg: July 12, 1762. I have the honour to transmit to you the manifesto published by authority, with the translation, in which you will see that great stress is laid upon the shameful peace concluded with their enemy, notwithstanding which, as Baron Goltz, who attended the Emperor to the last, was returning to town, he was met on the road by M. Alsuffiew, who, by order of the Empress, assured him that he had nothing to fear, and that he might either return to Oranienbaum for a day or two, or proceed to Petersburg, a proper escort being appointed to attend him at either place; but he, choosing the town, is now at his house here in perfect freedom, and, what is most remarkable, M. Alsuffiew assured him that the Empress was perfectly well disposed towards cultivating his Prussian Majesty's friendship. The Hetman was, I hear, with General Villebois and M. Panin, the great Duke's Governor, the principal persons in bringing about this revolution, and under them the brothers Orlow were the most trusted and the most active; but the most singular circumstance of the whole is that the place of rendezvous was the house of the Princess Dashkow, a young lady not above twenty years old, daughter to Count Roman Larevonetz Woronzow, sister to the late favourite Elizabeth, and niece to the Chancellor. It is certain that she bore a principal share in contriving and carrying on the conspiracy, from the beginning to the conclusion of it.

Of all men the Hetman seemed to possess the greatest share of the unfortunate Emperor's affection, and two days before his fall he dined at Marshal Rosamowsky's country house, and was, upon that occasion, received and served with the greatest marks of duty, zeal, and attachment on the part of both brothers; and when he returned to Oranienbaum the Hetman went straight to Peterhof to concert matters with the Empress. It is a dispute what part the Chamberlain, Shouvalow, had in this affair.

On Friday evening, before the Empress left the town, she despatched an officer to bring back Count Bestucheff to Petersburg, and it is thought he will have a considerable share in the administration. In the meantime M. Panin is the person that takes most upon him, though both the Chancellor, Count Woronzie, and the Vice-Chancellor, Prince Galitzing, continue in their places; the former came to town on Friday evening, and, going directly to Court, was tolerably well received and promised the Empress's protection. However, at his own desire he had two officers of the Guards put about him for the first two days, but now they are taken off, and he goes on in the functions of his office. His lady was not at Court till Sunday (having continued with the Emperor till the end, and having even been at Cronstadt with him), and when she kissed the Empress's hand she took off her riband of St. Catherine, and, offering it to her Imperial Majesty, said she had never asked for it, and now laid it at her feet; but the Empress most obligingly took it, and with her own hand put it again over the Countess Woronzow's shoulder.

With regard to the motives of this Revolution, it is plain that the taking away the Church lands was the principal, joined to the neglect of the clergy. The next was the severe discipline which the Emperor endeavoured to introduce amongst the troops, especially the Guards, who had been accustomed to great idleness and licence, and the discontent amongst them was heightened by the Resolution his Imperial Majesty had taken of carrying a great part of that corps into Germany with him in his expedition against Denmark, which was a measure disagreeable to the whole nation, who stomached not greatly their being drawn into new expenses and new dangers for recovering the Duchy of Schleswig, which they considered a trifling object in itself, and entirely indifferent to Russia; and this after the Emperor had just sacrificed the conquests made by the Russian arms (and which might have been of great importance to this Empire) to his friendship for the King of Prussia, which however, their desires of peace would have made them not only put up with, but approve. Several other little circumstances, greatly exaggerated and artfully represented and improved, contributed to the fall of this unhappy Prince, who had many excellent qualities, and who never did a violent or cruel action in the course of his short reign; but who, from an abhorrence to business, owing to a bad education and the unhappy choice of favourites who encouraged him in it, let everything run into confusion, and by a mistaken notion he had conceived of having secured the affections of the nation by the great favours he had so nobly bestowed on them after his first mounting the throne, fell into an indolence and security that proved fatal to him.

To conclude, not only I, but several persons of sense and discernment thought they could perceive latterly in this Prince a considerable change from what he was for some months after his accession, and that the perpetual hurry in which he lived, and the flattery he met with from the vile people about him, had in some measure affected his understanding.

I must own that I had no apprehension that this Revolution would happen so soon, but I was always of opinion that if he left his dominions he ran a great risk of never returning to them, and for that reason I made use of every means I could think of to divert him from that expedition. Sometimes by insinuations to himself, and sometimes by representing the danger to others who had the honour to approach his person — whether they did their duty on this point, particularly Prince George, I cannot say; but if they did, the event has shown that it was all to no purpose.

Catherine's Coup: Her Own Account

This account of the palace revolution which brought Catherine to the Russian throne is in her own words. It is an excerpt from her letter of August, 1762 to Stanislaw Poniatowski, her lover whom she later made King of Poland. The source is: Bain, R. Nisbet, Peter III, Emperor of Russia. The Story of a Crisis and a Crime. New York: E. P. Dutton and Co., 1902. Pp. 191–197.

. . . It is six months ago since my accession to the throne was first put in hand. Peter III. had lost the little wit he had. He ran his head against everything. He wanted to break up the Guards, and with that intent led them out to war; he meant to substitute for them the Holstein troops which were to have remained in town. He wanted to change his religion, marry Elizabeth Vorontsov and shut me up.

The day of the celebration of the peace with [Prussia,] after having publicly insulted me at table, he ordered my arrest the same evening. My uncle, Prince George, got this order retracted, and from thenceforth I lent an ear to the propositions which had been made to me [ever] since the death of the Empress [Elizabeth.]

The [original] design was to seize him in his apartments and shut him up as was done with the Princess Anne and her children. He went off [however] to Oranienbaum. We were sure of a great number of the captains of the Guards. The fate of the secret was in the hands of the three brothers Orlov. . . . They are extremely determined people and much beloved by the common soldiers, having served in the Guards. I am under great obligation to these people, all Petersburg is my witness.

The minds of the Guards were made up and at last 30 to 40 officers and 10,000 of the common soldiers were in the secret. There was not a traitor to be found among them during the three weeks [before the revolution,] there were four separate parties among them, whose chiefs met together as an executive; the real secret was in the hands of the three brothers. Panin wanted the revolution to be in favour of my son, but they would not consent anyhow.

I was at Peterhof, Peter III. was making merry and dwelling at Oranienbaum. It had been agreed that in case of treason, his return should not be proclaimed. Their zeal for me did what treason might have done. On the [27th July, O. S.] a report spread among the troops that I was arrested.

The soldiers began to stir, one of our officers calmed them. Then a soldier went to a captain called Passek, chief of one of the [four] parties, and told him that it was certainly all up with me, he assured him he had news [to that effect]. This soldier, alarmed about me, then went to another officer, who was not in the secret, and told him the same thing. Alarmed to hear that an officer had sent away this soldier without arresting him, he posted off to his major. The major caused Passek to be arrested — and the whole regiment was instantly agog. The report [of this affair] was sent the same night to Oranienbaum. All our conspirators were alarmed. They immediately resolved to send the second brother Orlov to me to bring me into town, and the other two [Orlovs] secured the town, telling everybody I was coming.

The Hetman [Razumovsky,] Volkonsky and Panin were in the secret. I was sleeping calmly at Peterhof at 6 o'clock in the morning of the 28th [July O. S.] The day had been a very disturbing one for me as I knew all that was going on. [Suddenly] Alexius Orlov enters my room and says quite gently: "It is time to get up; all is ready for your proclamation." I demanded some details. "Passek is arrested," said he. I hesitated no longer. I dressed myself quickly without making my toilet and got into the carriage which he had brought with him. Another officer, dressed up as a valet, was at the carriage door, a third met us some versts from Peterhof.

Five versts from the town I met the elder Orlov with the younger Prince Bariatinsky. Orlov gave up his carriage to me, for my horses were done up, and we got out at the barracks of the Ismailovsky Regiment. [At the gates] were only twelve men, and a drummer, who began sounding an alarm, when the soldiers came running out, kissing me, embracing my hands and feet and clothes, and calling me their deliverer. Then they began swearing allegiance to me. When this had been done, they begged me to get into the carriage, and the priest, cross in hand, walked on in front. We went [first] to the [barracks of the] Semenovsky Regiment, but the regiment came marching out to meet us, crying, Vivat! Then we went to the church of Kazan, where I got out. Then the Preobrazhensky Regiment arrived, crying, Vivat! "We beg your pardon," they said to me, "for being the last. Our officers stopped us, but here are four of them whom we have arrested to shew you our zeal. We want what our brothers want." Then the horse-guards arrived frantic with joy, I never saw anything like it, weeping and crying at the deliverance of their country. . . . I went to the new Winter Palace where the Synod and the Senate were assembled. A manifesto and a form of oath were hastily drawn up. Then I went down and received the troops on foot. There were more than 14,000 men, guards and country regiments. As soon as they saw me they uttered cries of joy which were taken up by an innumerable crowd. I went on to the old Winter Palace to take [my] measures and finish [the business,] there we took counsel together, and it was resolved to go to Peterhof, where Peter III. was to have dined with me, at their head. All the great roads had been occupied and rumours came in every moment.

I sent Admiral Talisin to Cronstadt [to secure that fortress.] Then the Chancellor Vorontsov arrived to reproach me for my departure [from Peterhof;] they took him off to church to swear him in. Prince Trubetskoi and Count Shuvalov also arrived from Peterhof in order to collar the regiments and kill me. They were taken off to swear the oaths without the least resistance.

After having sent off our couriers and taken every precaution, towards 10 o'clock in the evening I put on a uniform of the Guards. Having been proclaimed Colonel, with inexpressible acclamations, I took horse and we left only a very few of each regiment behind to protect my son, whom we left in town. I set out at the head of the troops, and we marched all night towards Peterhof. On reaching a little monastery on the way, the Vice-Chancellor arrived with a very flattering letter from Peter III. I had forgotten to say that on leaving town, three soldiers of the Guards, sent from Peterhof to distribute a manifesto among the people, came to me and said: "Here! take what Peter III. has entrusted us with, we give it to you. We are very glad of the opportunity of joining our brethren."

After the first letter came a second, the bearer whereof, General Michal Ismailov, threw himself at my feet and said: "Do you take me for an honest man?" On my replying, "Yes!" "Well," says he, "it is pleasant to have to do with sensible folk. The Emperor offers to resign. I will bring to you [a form of abdication] after a very few alterations. I will save my country from a civil war without any difficulty."

I charged him with this commission, and off he went to accomplish it. Peter III. abdicated, at Oranienbaum, in full liberty, surrounded by 5000 Holsteiners, and came with Elizabeth Vorontsov, Gudovich and Ismailov to Peterhof, where, to protect his person, I gave him five officers and some soldiers. . . . Thereupon I sent the deposed Emperor to a remote and very agreeable place called Ropsha, 25 versts from Peterhof, under the command of Alexius Orlov, with four officers and a detachment of picked, good-natured men, whilst decent and convenient rooms were being prepared for him at Schlusselburg. But God disposed otherwise. Fear had given him a diarrhœa which lasted three days and passed away on the fourth; in this [fourth] day he drank excessively, for he had all he wanted except liberty. Nevertheless, the only things he asked me for were his mistress, his dog, his Negro and his violin; but for fear of scandal [sic] and increasing the agitation of the persons who guarded him, I only sent him the last three things.

The hemorrhoidal colic which seized him affected his brain: two days he was delirious, and the delirium was followed by very great exhaustion, and despite all the assistance of the doctors, he expired whilst demanding a

Lutheran priest. I feared that the officers might have poisoned him, so I had him opened, but it is an absolute fact that not the slightest trace of poison was found inside him. The stomach was quite sound, but inflammation of the bowels and a stroke of apoplexy had carried him off. His heart was extraordinarily small and quite decayed. . . .

It would take a whole book to describe the conduct of each of the leaders. The Orlovs brilliantly distinguished themselves by their faculty of ruling the minds of men, by their prudent audacity, by [their attention to] great and petty details, and by their presence of mind. They have a great deal of common-sense and generous courage. They are enthusiastic patriots, very honest folk, passionately attached to my person and united as never brothers were united before. There are five of them in all, but only three were here. . . . The Princess Dashkof, younger sister of Elizabeth Vorontsov, though she would like to attribute to herself all the honour [of the affair,] being acquainted with some of the chiefs, was looked upon askance because of her parentage, and being but 19 had no authority at all, and although she pretends that she was the chief intermediary all along, yet the real fact is that everyone had been in [direct] communication with me six months beforehand, before she even knew their names. But she has a meddlesome humour together with a great deal of ostentation, and our principal men hate her exceedingly. It was only a few feather-brains who let her into the secret and told her all they knew, which was very trumpery. Nevertheless, they say that Ivan Ivanovich Shuvalov, the lowest and most cowardly of men has written to Voltaire that a woman 19 years old, has changed the government of this Empire. I beg of you to undeceive this great writer. Five months before she knew anything it was necessary to conceal from the Princess Dashkov [the nature of] the modes of communication between myself and others, and during the last four weeks she was told as little as possible.

The strength of mind of Prince Bariatinsky, who concealed the secret from his dearly beloved brother, the late Emperor's adjutant . . . deserves praise.

In the Horse-Guards, an officer named Chitrov, aged 22, and an under officer, 17 years old, named Potemkin, directed everything with discernment, courage and energy.

That is pretty much the history of this affair and I assure you that everything was done under my direct personal orders. At the last moment I hurried up because the departure [of the Emperor] for the country prevented the execution [of the plot,] and everything had been ripe for a fortnight.

The late Emperor, when he heard of the tumult in town, was prevented by the young women of his suite from following the advice of old Field Marshal Münnich, who advised him to throw himself into Cronstadt, or set off for the army with a few followers. When he *did* go in his galley to Cronstadt the fortress was already ours in consequence of the good conduct of Admiral Talizin, who caused General Devier to be disarmed, this Devier being already on the spot on the Emperor's behalf when Talizin arrived. An officer of the port, on his own initiative, threatened to fire point-blank at the galley of this unfortunate Prince.

At last, then God has brought everything to pass according to His predisposition. The whole thing is rather a miracle than a fact foreseen and arranged beforehand, for so many felicitous combinations could not have coincided unless God's hand had been over it all.

. . . Be assured, too, that hatred of foreigners was the leading principle of the whole affair, and that Peter III. himself passed for a foreigner.

Adieu, there are some very strange situations in this world."

Catherine's Accession Manifesto

Catherine announced her usurpation of power by the following manifesto which she had printed and distributed in St. Petersburg. The source is: Tooke, Life of Catharine II, vol. 1, pp. 518–519.

By the grace of God, Catharine II, empress and autocratrix of all the Russias, &c.

All true sons of Russia have clearly seen the great danger to which the whole Russian empire has actually been exposed. First, the foundations of our orthodox Greek religion have been shaken, and its traditions exposed to total destruction; so that there was absolutely reason to fear, that the faith which has been established in Russia from the earliest times, would be entirely changed, and foreign religion introduced. In the second place, the glory which Russia has acquired at the expense of so much blood, and which was carried to the highest pitch by her victorious arms, has been trampled under foot by the peace lately concluded with its most dangerous enemy. And lastly, the domestic regulations, which are the basis of the country's welfare, have been entirely overturned.

For these causes, overcome by the imminent perils with which our faithful subjects were threatened, and seeing how sincere and express their desires on this matter were; we, putting our trust in the Almighty and his divine justice, have ascended the sovereign imperial throne of all the Russias, and have received a solemn oath of fidelity from all our loving subjects.

St. Petersburg, June 28, 1762.

Herzen's Estimate of Catherine

Alexander Herzen was one of the most famous of the nineteenth century non-Marxist socialists of Russia. By virtue of his beliefs, he was early forced into exile, and spent most of his adult life away from his native land. From his exile he edited the famous underground newspaper, The Bell (Kolokol). He also wrote profusely, and was instrumental in founding the Free Russian Press in London. The following excerpt is from his introduction to the Memoirs of the Empress Catherine II. *The source is:* Memoirs of the EMPRESS CATHERINE II Written by Herself. With a Preface by A. Herzen. *New York: D. Appleton and Company, 1859. Pp. 13–16.*

And now, after all that has been said, let the reader picture to himself what must have been the nature of the medium into which destiny had cast this young girl, gifted, as she was, not only with great talent, but also with a character pliant, though full of pride and passion.

Her position at St. Petersburg was horrible. On one side was her mother, a peevish, scolding, greedy, niggardly, pedantic German, boxing her ears, and taking away her new dresses to appropriate them to her own use; on the other, the Empress Elizabeth, a coarse and grumbling virago, never quite sober, jealous, envious, causing every step of the young Princess to be watched, every word reported, taking offence at everything, and all this after having given her for a husband the most ridiculous Benedict of the age.

A prisoner in the palace, she could do nothing without permission. If she wept for the death of her father, the Empress sent her word that she had grieved enough. "That her father was not a king, that she should mourn him longer than a week." If she evinced a friendship for any of her maids of honour, she might be sure the lady would be dismissed. If she became attached to a faithful servant, still more certain was it that that servant would be turned away.

Her relations with the Grand Duke were monstrous, degrading. He made her the confidante of his amorous intrigues. Drunk from the age of ten, he came one night in liquor to entertain his wife with a description of the graces and charms of the daughter of Biren; and as Catherine pretended to be asleep, he gave her a punch with his fist to waken her. This booby kept a kennel of dogs, which infested the air, at the side of his wife's bed-chamber, and hung rats in his own, to punish them according to the rules of martial law.

Nor is this all. After having wounded and outraged nearly every feeling of this young creature's nature, they began to deprave her systematically. The Empress regards as a breech of order her having no children. Madame Tchoglokoff speaks to her on the subject, insinuating that, *for the good of the state,* she ought to sacrifice her scruples, and concludes by proposing to her a choice between Soltikoff and Narichkine. The young lady affects simplicity and takes both — nay, Poniatowsky into the bargain, and thus was commenced a career of licentiousness in which she never halted during the space of forty years.

What renders the present publication of serious consequence to the imperial house of Russia is, that it proves not only that this house does not belong to the family of Romanoff, but that it does not even belong to that of Holstein Gottorp. The avowal of Catherine on this point is very explicit — *the father of the Emperor Paul is Sergius Soltikoff.*

The Imperial Dictatorship of Russia endeavours in vain to represent itself as traditional and secular.

One word before I close.

In perusing these Memoirs, the reader is astonished to find one thing constantly lost sight of, even to the extent of not appearing anywhere — it is *Russia and the People.* And here is the characteristic trait of the epoch.

The Winter Palace, with its military and administrative machinery, was a world of its own. Like a ship floating on the surface of the ocean, it had no real connection with the inhabitants of the deep, beyond that of eating them. It was the *State for the State.* Organized on the German model, it imposed itself on the nation as a conqueror. In that monstrous barrack, in that enormous chancery, there reigned the cold rigidity of a camp. One set gave or transmitted orders, the rest obeyed in silence. There was but one single spot within that dreary pile in which human passions reappeared, agitated and stormy, and that spot was the domestic hearth; not that of the nation — but of the state. Behind that triple line of sentinels, in those heavily ornamented saloons, there fermented a feverish life, with its intrigues and its conflicts, its dramas and its tragedies. It was there that the destinies of Russia were woven, in the gloom of the alcove, in the midst of orgies, *beyond* the reach of informers and of the police.

What interest, then, could the young German Princess take in that *magnum ignotum,* that people *unexpressed,* poor, semi-barbarous, which concealed itself in its villages, behind the snow, behind bad roads, and only appeared in the streets of St. Petersburg like a foreign outcast, with its persecuted beard, and prohibited dress — tolerated only through contempt.

It was only long afterwards that Catherine heard the Russian people seriously spoken of, when the Cossack Pougatcheff, at the head of an army of insurgent peasants, menaced Moscow.

When Pougatcheff was vanquished, the Winter Palace again forgot the people. And there is no telling when it would have been again remembered had it not itself put its masters in mind of its existence, by rising in mass in 1812, rejecting, on the one hand, the release from serfdom offered to it at the point of foreign bayonets, and, on the other, marching to death to save a country which gave it nothing but slavery, degradation, misery — and the oblivion of the Winter Palace.

This was the second memento of the Russian people. Let us hope that at the third it will be remembered a little longer. A. Herzen. London, *November 15th,* 1858.

The British Ambassador Describes Catherine

The Earl of Buckinghamshire, British Ambassador to Catherine's Court, sent his government two descriptions of the Empress. The first was written soon after his arrival in St. Petersburg in 1762; the second, shortly before his departure from there in 1765. The source is: Collyer, op. cit., vol. 1, pp. 100–104 and vol. 2, pp. 273–276.

Her Imperial Majesty is neither short nor tall; she has a majestic air, and possesses that happy mixture of dignity and ease which at once enforces respect and sets men at their ease. Formed with a mind and a body capable of acquiring every accomplishment, and enforced retirement gave her more leisure to cultivate them than is usually allotted to princes, and qualified her, as she charmed the eye in gay society, to delight the understanding in more serious moments. This period of constraint, which lasted several years, and the agitation of mind and continual fatigues which she has undergone since her accession, have deprived her charms of their freshness. Besides, she has never been beautiful. Her features were far from being so delicately and exactly formed as to compose what might pretend to regular beauty, but a fine complexion, an animated and intelligent eye, a mouth agreeably turned, and a profusion of glossy chestnut hair produce that sort of countenance which, a very few years ago, a man must have been either prejudiced or insensible to have beheld with indifference. She has been, and still is, what often pleases and always attaches more than beauty. She is extremely well made, the neck and hands remarkably beautiful, and the limbs so elegantly turned as equally to become the dress of either sex. Her eyes are blue, their vivacity tempered by a languor in which there is much sensibility and no insipidity. She has the air of paying no attention to what she wears, yet she is always too well drest for a woman who is entirely indifferent to her appearance. A man's dress is what suits her best; she wears it always when she rides on horseback. It is scarce credible what she does in that way, managing horses, even fiery horses, with all the skill and courage of a groom. She excels, too, in the serious as well as livelier dances. She expresses herself with elegance in French, and I am assured that she speaks Russian with as much precision as German, which is her native language, and that she has a critical knowledge of both languages. She speaks and reasons with fluency and precision, and some letters which must have been of her own composing have been admired and applauded by the scholars of the nation in whose language they were wrote.

Reading made her amusement in the retirement in which she lived in the days of the late Empress. The history and the interests of the European Powers are familiar to her. When she spoke to me of English history, I perceived that what had struck her the most was the reign of Elizabeth.

Time will show where such an emulation may lead her. Finding herself superior in information and argument to most of those about her, she thinks she is equally so to everybody, and, understanding clearly what she has learnt, she sometimes thinks herself mistress of what she has not. When she was on board the Admiral's ship at Cronstadt, her imperial standard flying, and flattered with the inexperienced grandeur of commanding more than twenty large ships, she disputed with me which end of a man-of-war went first — a circumstance which indeed she was not obliged to know — but the actual situation made the doubt ridiculous.

Much stress is laid upon her resolution, particularly in the instance of dethroning her husband. Desperate situations make cowards valiant. She was compelled either to ruin him or to submit herself to that confinement which she knew had long been in deliberation. Those who know her well say she is rather enterprising than brave, and that her appearance of courage arises sometimes from a conviction of the pusillanimity of her enemies, at others from her not seeing her danger. She certainly is bolder than the generality of her sex, but I have seen her twice very much afraid without reason: once when she was getting out of boat into a ship; the other time, upon hearing a little noise in the ante-chamber at Court. But when the occasion requires it she dares all, and in many critical and dangerous situations her courage has never failed her. Yet she has all the delicacy of her sex. To see her is to know that she could love, and that her love would make the happiness of a lover worthy of her.

Two capital errors, which are equally evident and inexcusable, are the meanness with which she submits to the ill-bred inattention of Orlow, and the little affection she shows to the Grand Duke.

The amusements of her retirement, into which she enters with a youthful spirit, are trifling beyond expression, and much the same which children in other countries leave off at twelve years old.

Those who are most in her society assure me that her application to business is incredible. The welfare and prosperity of her subjects, the glory of her empire, are always present to her; and to all appearance her care will raise the reputation and power of Russia to a point which, at present, they have never reached, if she deos not indulge too much in far-fetched and unpractical theories, which interested or ignorant people are too ready to suggest to her. Her foible is too systematic, and that may be the rock on which she may, perhaps, split. She embraces too many objects at once; she likes to begin, regulate, and correct projects all in a moment. Indefatigable in everything that she undertakes, she obliges her ministers to work incessantly. They argue, make plans, and sketch out a thousand schemes, and decide upon nothing. Among those who hold the first rank in her confidence, some will be found who have experience, but few if any who possess superior talents. There is, however, one of her Majesty's secretaries who has knowledge, wit, and even application, when women and the pleasures of the table — which always demand his first cares — give him any leisure for business.

Unwilling to touch so tender a string, I have deferred till the last speaking of the Revolution and the most melancholy catastrophe which succeeded.

The Empress has frequently talked to me of her husband, and, without exaggerating his indiscretions, pointed out those which principally occasioned his ruin. Once, in her absence, I saw his picture in her cabinet; it was without a frame and stood upon the floor, as if brought in for her to look at. The Vice-Chancellor told me it was a strong likeness. I examined it with attention, and could not help running over in my mind the hard fate of the heir of Russia, Sweden, and Holstein, who, with many defects in his understanding, had none in his heart.

The Vice-Chancellor seemed surprised at my silent attention, and asked me what employed my thoughts. Was it so difficult to guess?

When this is considered as a portrait drawn by one who knew her and who wished with candour to steer the middle course between calumny and adulation, who will not mourn the steps she took to raise herself to Empire, and the fatal measures which the worst of her followers judged necessary to secure her in that throne she fills so well?

Many, and some of the deepest hue, are the blemishes which shade a character otherwise so amiable. Her enemies, and particularly the French and Austrians, have taken every method to place them in the strongest light, and, not contented with those which were known to be true, and others but too probably, they have sought to blacken her still more with fictions which have almost been generally received, even by those from whom her political disposition might claim a fairer hearing. She is accused of dethroning her husband; of usurping that empire of which, even from her own declaration, she could only pretend to be Regent; of causing her husband to be put to death; of changing the whole system of her Empire in order to make one of her former lovers king of Poland; and, lastly, of contriving the murder of the late Prince Ivan. That her present favourite is the fourth person she has distinguished is as certain as that she was persuaded to receive the first by the Empress Elizabeth, who thought her nephew incapable of begetting children; and possibly anyone who is acquainted with the abandoned scenes which passed at that Court will wonder that a young, lively woman, who had long seen debauchery sanctified by usage and the highest example, should want any persuasion at all. When I allow that the seizing the Crown herself does not admit of justification, nor even of palliation, that adopting the most favourable and improbable supposition that her husband was put to death, not only without her order, but contrary to her intention, her not clearing up the fact and punishing the guilty at any risk is unpardonable. Shall I incur a suspicion of partiality when I assert that the folly and imprudence of the ill-fated Emperor, his avowed intention of confining her, his further plan of setting aside the Great Duke, his ill-conceived expedition against the Danes, his mean, subservient adulation of the King of Prussia, which in the end must have been destructive to his country, and lastly, the insults she was hourly exposed to from his abandoned mistress — too powerful an incentive of that feminine resentment which so often decides the fate of empires — may, in a great measure, apologise for her conduct so far as removing him from the throne?

. . .

To assert that some time ago I should have thought it an easy task to draw a full and just character of the Empress, and that now, having frequent opportunities of seeing her in the hours of dissipation when the veil of restraint and ceremony was thrown off, the undertaking puzzles and embarrasses me, has something the air of a paradox, which, however, is easily solved by mentioning that then I knew only the great outlines and was unacquainted with the little weaknesses and inconsistencies which almost efface some and shade many of those eminent qualities which adorn her. It is impossible to consider the general tenour of her conduct, since she placed herself upon the throne, without tracing evident marks of a laudable ambition to distinguish herself; to make her subjects happy at home and respectable abroad; to encourage arts, sciences and commerce; to form by a liberal education the young nobility of both sexes; to extend in a great degree the same advantages to inferior ranks; to improve the public revenue without oppressing individuals; to check the tyranny with which the clergy distressed their vassals; and to introduce that ease of society, that urbanity and general good breeding which prevail in other European nations; in a word, to transmit her name with glory to posterity, and by the use she makes of empire to palliate the means by which she has acquired it.

In the course of two years, though hourly alarmed by the attempts of her enemies, she has exerted her good offices for the general pacification of Europe; she has given a King to Poland, established a sovereign in Courland, and greatly contributed to the overturning of the so long prevailing French system in Sweden. These are facts of which it is as necessary to labour the proof as it would be vain to contest the reality, and surely it is greatly to be lamented that vanity, self-sufficiency, avarice, and a taste for trifling pleasures should cloud so bright a future?

The expenses of the Court are in some instances retrenched to a degree of meanness, and many persons of the first rank seize officiously the first pretence to retire from Petersburg, as, receiving no longer the same presents from the

Sovereign, they cannot affort to pay the daily-increasing price of every article of consumption.

Political intrigue and fruitful imaginations have variously accounted for her most imprudent journey to Riga; in fact, it was determined by the desire of a little mind to make a naval parade, to enjoy the pageantry and adulations with which the provinces received her, and to see a sovereign of her own creating at her feet. Deaf to the friendly advice which combated her inclination, she was obstinate to prove her steadiness.

Her face and figure are greatly altered for the worse since her accession. It is easy to discover the remains of a fine woman, but she is now no longer an object of desire. The many who wish to arraign the conduct and vilify the character of this Princess tax her with the same disposition to debauchery as sullied the reign of her predecessor. This makes it necessary to say something on the subject, and succinctly state such information as upon the strictest inquiry I have obtained, which when candidly considered may palliate though not justify her conduct. She had been married some years to the Grand Duke without being with child, and, as this was supposed to arise from the inability of her husband, distant hints were thrown out by the Empress, which were not taken. At last she sent her confidante, Madame Shouvalow, to inform the Grand Duchess that if she did not soon contrive to produce an heir to the Empire she must expect to be divorced. After some hesitation she yielded. One Soltikow (now abroad) was the man pitched upon, and he is said to be the father of the present Grand Duke. The first scruples being got over, the rest followed but too naturally. Soltikow having left the country, the solitude in which she generally lived made every possible amusement necessary, and General Chernichow and, soon after, Poniatowski enjoyed her favour. Orlow was one of the young people who entered early into the conspiracy to place her upon the throne. She saw him frequently; the beauty of his person, and his particular affection for her, of which she has since declared she had long been sensible, induced her to yield. Her being with child at the time of the Revolution was a circumstance which, as her husband never approached her, made it necessary to hasten that event. She was brought to bed of a son at Moscow some months after. The child is under the care of Schurin at Petersburg, where her Imperial Majesty has sometimes visited him.

Catherine II: "Enlightened Despot"

Catherine's pride in her "enlightenment" is well known. The two letters which follow are illustrative of this aspect of her character. The first was written to Voltaire in answer to a request for her aid to some victims of persecution; the

*second was written to Vladimir Orlov, Director of the Academy of Science at
St. Petersburg. The source is: Tooke, Life of Catharine II, vol. 1, pp. 425,
556–557.*

Sir, The brightness of the northern star is a mere aurora borealis. It is
nothing more than giving to a neighbour something of our own superfluity.
But to be the advocate of human kind, the defender of oppressed innocence;
by this you will be indeed immortalized. The two causes of Calas and Sirven
have procured you the veneration due to such miracles. You have combated
the united enemies of mankind, superstition, fanaticism, ignorance, chicane,
bad judges, and the power lodged in them, all together. To surmount such
obstacles, required both talents and virtue. You have shown the world that
you possess both. You have carried your point. You desire, sir, some relief
for the Sirven family. Can I possibly refuse it? Or, should you praise me
for the action, would there be the least foundation for it? I own to you, that
I should be much better pleased if my bill of exchange could pass unknown.
Nevertheless, if you think my name, unharmonious as it is, may be of any
service to those victims of the spirit of persecution, I leave it to your discretion; and you may announce me, provided it be no way prejudicial to the
parties.

• • •

Mons. Count Orlov, Having been informed that in the summer of the year
1769, the planet Venus will pass over the sun, I write you this letter, that
you may acquaint the Academy of Sciences on my part, 1. That it is my
pleasure that the academy should procure the observations to be made with
the utmost care; and that I desire, in consequence, to know, 2. which are
the most advantageously situated places of the empire that the academy has
destined for this observation; to the end that, in case it should be necessary
to erect any buildings, workmen, etc. may be sent, and proper measures be
taken. 3. That if there be not a sufficient number of astronomers in the
academy for completing the observations in the places pitched upon by the
academy, I propose, and take upon me to find out, among my marine subjects,
such as, during the interval between the present time and the transit of
Venus, may be perfected in the habit of observing, under the eyes of the
professors, so as to be employed to advantage in this expedition, and to the
satisfaction of the academy. You will, Mr. Count, transmit me the answer of
the academy, with its full opinion about every thing above, that I may give
orders for the whole without loss of time. Moscow, 3d March, 1767. Catharine.

Catherine and the French Revolution

*The French Revolution had an immediate and profound effect on Catherine's
"liberalism" and "enlightenment." The process and nature of the change*

produced in her ideas and policies was brilliantly summarized mostly from Catherine's own writings, by M. Kasimerz Waliszewski. The source is: Waliszewski, K., The Romance of an Empress: Catherine II of Russia. New York: D. Appleton and Co., 1894. Pp. 246–261.

In 1769 the cause of liberty has no more enthusiastic defender in Europe than the Empress of Russia.

"To the brave Corsicans, defenders of liberty and of their country, and, in particular, to General Paoli: Gentlemen! All Europe has for many years seen you oppose oppression, defend and redeem the country from an unjust usurpation, and fight for liberty. It is the duty of every human creature to aid and support all who manifest sentiments so nobel, so great, and so natural."

The letter is from the hand of Catherine, and is signed "Your sincere friends, the inhabitants of the North Pole (*sic*)." A sum of money is added, which passes in the eyes of the brave Corsicans as the result of a subscription. This, doubtless, is in order to spare them the humiliation of being subventioned by an absolute monarch, and also to make them believe that there is, in the neighborhood of the "North Pole," a respectable number of people capable of sympathising with the cause they defend.

In 1781 Catherine comes forward on behalf of Necker. His famous *Compte rendu*, which is practically an act of accusation against the administration of royal finances, that is to say against royalty itself, enchants and delights her. She does not doubt that heaven has destined the able Genevese for the salvation of France.

Certainly she has not much love, just then, either for France or for the turn that things are taking there; but in her hostile feelings the court holds as large, if not larger, a place than the people, and the old *regime* foundering under the rising flood of social claims has no part in her favor. This is the impression we receive from her correspondence with her son and her daughter-in-law, during the visit of their Imperial Highnesses, in 1782, to Paris. Here is a specimen. It is Catherine who writes:—

"May God bless her most Christian Majesty, her shows, her balls and her plays, her rouge and her beards, well or ill adjusted. I am not sorry that this annoys you and makes you anxious to return. But, how is it that, with its passion for the play, Paris is no better off than we? I know the reason; it is because every one leaves the good show for the bad; that in tragedy they have nothing but what is atrocious; that plays are written by those who know neither how to make comedies for laughter nor tragedies for tears; that comedy, instead of bringing laughter, brings tears; that nothing is in its proper place; that colors even have only abject and indecent names. All that encourages no sort of talent, but spoils it."

A frivolous and corrupt court, in the midst of a society which its evil example has brought to the verge of a fatal precipice, that is the idea Catherine seems to hold, at this time, in regard to the country of her "dear master," who himself has given color to her opinions, in denying at every opportunity his kinship with the pitiable "Vandals." Her dominant idea, however, is a feeling of indifference in regard to men and things there. For a long time, up to the very verge of the revolutionary crisis, the events and agitations, in this far country, seem to her without any general importance; she does not perceive their bearing. Nor, whatever may have been said to the contrary, does she see the approach of the tempest. On April 19, 1788, she writes to Grimm: "I do not share the belief of those who imagine that we are on the eve of a great revolution." Hearing, in the course of her tour through the Crimea, of the resolution of Louis XVI: to convoke an "Assembly of Notables," she sees in it only an imitation of her own legislative commissions. She invites Lafayette to visit her at Kief. To open her eyes on what is being prepared by the Lafayettes, it needs the thunderclap of the taking of the Bastille. Then she begins to understand what is in the air, and the *Gazette de St.-Petersbourg*, which had been silent on the Assembly of the States and the Tennis-court Oath, breaks out in indignant protestations: "Our hand shakes with horror," etc. The rest of the article may be imagined. Soon the constituents are compared by the officious journal to "a drunken mob," as their successors are to be compared to "canibals."

From this moment Catherine's ideas underwent a rapid change, and it is curious to follow, in her correspondence and her confidential conversation, the progress of this evolution. In June 1790 Grimm, who has not yet had time to perceive the change which is coming over the Empress's mind, asks for her portrait on behalf of Bailly, offering in exchange that of the revolutionary hero of the day. Catherine replies—

"Listen; I cannot accede to your request, and it is as little suitable for the mayor who has dismonarchised France to have the portrait of the most aristocratic Empress in Europe, as it would be for her to send it to the dismonarchising mayor; it would be to place both the dismonarchising mayor and the *aristocrasissime* Empress in contradiction with themselves and their functions, past, present, and future."

And two days after—

"I repeat that you are not to give to the dismonarchising mayor the portrait of the greatest aristocrat in Europe; I would have nothing to do with Jean Marcel, who will be strung up *a la lanterne* some day soon."

Here is a complete throwing overboard of republicanism. It is not so with regard to philosophy, to which the Empress still clings. She endeavors to find out how far it is responsible for the present events—

June 25, 1790.

To GRIMM.

"The National Assembly should burn all the best French authors, and all that has carried their language over Europe, for all that declares against the abominable mess that they have made. . . . As for the people and its opinion, that is of no great consequence!"

It is this last phrase especially which shows the antagonism, now only capable of increase, between the spirit of Catherine and of the Revolution. It is the part, more and more prominent, played by the people in the events of which Paris has become the theatre that shocks and offends the sovereign. There was a time when, in this respect also, she had other ideas. At the outset of her reign, in gathering together her legislative commission, she did nothing less, in reality, than summon it from the mass of her subjects. But it is then, too, that, coming for the first time in contact with the popular element, she began little by little to change her mind in regard to it. Perhaps she was unwise in generalising from her impressions, but she had no other points of comparison. She could but form her opinion on what was before her eyes, and this opinion became profound contempt. In 1787, as her secretary, Chrapowicki, points out to her the enormous number of peasants who crowd to see her and pay homage to her in a certain country town, she replies with a shrug of the shoulders: "They would come just the same to see a bear." It is the same spirit to which she gives utterance two years after, when, referring to the composition of the political clubs in France, she says: "How can shoemakers have anything to do with affairs? A shoemaker only knows how to make shoes."

Soon philosophy in turn is abandoned. Catherine still speaks with respect of "good French authors," but she makes her choice, and, Voltaire excepted, she throws overboard all those of the eighteenth century. Diderot d'Alembert, and Montesquieu himself, are sacrificed at one blow—

Sept. 12, 1790.

To GRIMM.

"I must tell you the truth, the tone with you now is that of mere intemperance; this is not the time to make France illustrious. . . . What will the French do with their best writers, *who almost all lived under Louis XIV.?* All—Voltaire himself—are royalists; they preach order and tranquillity, and all that is opposed to the system of this hydra with twelve hundred heads."

The National Assembly is referred to more and more bitterly. On August 7th, 1790, Chrapowick notes in his journal: "Said in presence of her Majesty, speaking of France: 'It is a metaphysical country; every member of the assembly is a king, and every citizen is an animal.' Received with approbation." At the same time Catherine writes to Grimm—

"In bed I reflected over things, and, among others, I thought that one reason why the Mathieu de Montmorencys, the Noailles, etc., are so illtaught and so base in spirit that they are among the first promoters of the decree abolishing the nobility . . . is that the schools of the Jesuits have been abolished among you: whatever you may say, those scamps looked well after the morals and tastes of the young people, and whatever is best in France came out of their schools."

Jan. 13, 1791.

"One never knows if you are living in the midst of the murders, carnage, and uproar of the den of thieves who have seized upon the government of France, and who will soon turn it into Gaul as it was in the time of Caesar. But put them down! When will this Caesar come? Oh, come he will, you need not doubt."

May 23, 1791.

"The best of possible constitutions is worth nothing when it makes more people unhappy than happy, when brave and honest folk have to drudge, and only the rogues are in clover, because their pockets are filled, and nobody punishes them."

Observe, however, with what moderation Catherine is still capable, at this period, of discussing one of the revolutionary principles most repugnant to her. Her letter of June 30th, 1791, to the Prince de Ligne may be given in evidence—

"I think that the Academies ought to offer a first prize for the question: What do honor and worth, synonyms dear to heroic ears, become in the mind of an active citizen under a jealous and suspicious government, which proscribes all distinction, while nature itself has given to the intelligent man a pre-eminence over the fool, and courage is founded on the sentiment of the force of the body or of the head? Second prize for the question: Are honor and worth really needful? And if so, surely one should not restrain the desire of emulation, and clog it with an insupportable enemy, equality."

But soon she is carried away by more violent feelings—

Sept. 1, 1791.

"If the French Revolution takes in Europe, there will come another Gengis or Tamerlane to restore it to reason: that is what I prophesy, and be sure it will come time, but it will not be in my time, nor, I hope, in that of M. Alexandre."

When the news of the death of Louis XVI. reaches her, Catherine, as we have mentioned, is out to the heart; she betakes herself to bed, in a sort of fever, and she cries to her confidant—

Feb. 1, 1793.

"The very name of France should be exterminated! Equality is a monster. It would be fain be king!"

This time the holocaust is complete. Voltaire is sacrificed with the rest. And in the words and writing of the Empress there are almost savage calls to vengeance, the most extravagant projects of repression—

Feb. 15, 1794.

"I propose that all the Protestant powers should embrace the Greek religion, to save themselves from the irreligious, immoral, anarchical, abominable, and diabolical plague, enemy of God and of thrones; it is the sole apostolic and truly Christian religion—an oak with wide-spreading roots."

Thus, after Caesar, she calls for Tamerlane and his exterminating sword; after the Jesuits, a long-bearded pope, who will bring the lost peoples into the safe fold of the Orthodox Church. Is the Caesar for whom she calls, he whom France and Europe have indeed felt? Yes and no. This Caesar she did not at first perceive. In 1791 she is evidently dreaming of some officer of justice coming from without—some Brunswick. It is only later on that her point of view changes, becomes clearer, and then it must be admitted, she comes very near the truth—touches it almost. Catherine sees Napoleon before he has appeared; she points to him, describes his characteristics—

"If France is to come out of this alive," she writes, February 11, 1794, "she will be more vigorous then ever; she will be meek and obedient as a lamb; but it will need a man both great and bold, a man above his contemporaries, and perhaps above the age. Is he born? Is he not? Will he come? All depends on that. If he is found, he will arrest the last downfall, and that will be arrested whenever he is found, in France or elsewhere."

The men of the Revolution who preceded Napoleon all shared in the imagination of the Empress, and in the severity of her judgments. Lafayette is now called "the big booby." Mirabeau is at first better treated. The praises showered on his tardy loyalism in the *Gazette de St.-Petersbourg* show that the relations of the tribune with the Russian Legation at Paris were not unknown, nor yet the services that were looked for from him. But, after his death, Catherine's personal opinion is emphatically expressed in her letters to Grimm—

"Mirabeau was the colossus or monster of our time; in any other he would have been avoided, detected, imprisoned, hanged, or broken on the wheel."

And three days afterwards—

"I do not like the honors paid to Mirabeau, and I do not understand the why or wherefore, unless it be to encourage wickedness and all the vices. Mirabeau merits the esteem of Sodom and Gomorrha."

She retracts, too, her admiration for Necker—

"I agree with the views of M. F. on Malet du Pan and on that bad and foolish Necker: to me they are not merely hateful, but mere bores and chatterboxes."

She is not more tender towards the Duke of Orleans—

"I hope that no Bourbon will ever again bear the name of Orleans, after the horror that I feel towards the last who bore it."

As for the Abbe Sieyes, she settles his account at once: "I subscribe to the hanging of the Abbe Sieyes."

It is but just to say that the Revolutionaries give her back her own. Volney returns the gold medal which the Empress has formerly bestowed on him. Sylvain Marechal, in his *Jugement Dernier des Rois*, depicts the Empress in grotesque hand-to-hand conflict with the Pope, who throws his tiara at her head, after which she is swallowed up with all her accomplices by a volcano that opens under her feet. The *Moniteur* is not always amiable towards her.

Nevertheless, it must be noted that, for a long time, Catherine, while severely condemning the revolutionary movement, does not, in Russia or elsewhere, set on foot against it any act of direct repression. She remains a passive, and in some sort disinterested, spectator of passing events. Her whole attitude seems to say that all these things have no concern for her; that, whatever may happen, she has nothing to fear for herself or for the empire. At bottom, she is probably convinced of it to the last. Only it happens that the combinations, or we might better say the improvisations, of her policy come to impose upon her convictions. The precise epoch when she decides to abandon her inaction sufficiently indicates her reasons for doing so: it is the moment when, having settled affairs with Turkey and Sweden, she judges the hour come to interfere in Poland, and to put her hand to the masterwork of her reign. The French Revolution then appears in her eyes as one of those propitious "conjunctions" which, with conjectures and circumstances, make up, for her, the whole of politics. A dialogue with her secretary Chrapowicki, December 14, 1791, gives clear utterance of her view in this respect—

"I am doing all I can to get the courts of Berlin and Vienna to concern themselves with French affairs."

"They are not very active."

"No. The court of Berlin goes forward, but that of Vienna remains behind. They do not see my point. Am I wrong? There are reasons that one cannot say openly. I wish them to become concerned in the French affairs in order to leave me elbow-room. I have many undertakings to be achieved. I would have them occupied so that they may leave my way clear."

And immediately Catherine sets the tocsin ringing. Up to the present she has been content to publish in Paris, through her minister Simoline (in August 1790) a ukase commanding all her subjects to quit France, in order that more of them should not think to imitate the example of the young Count Alexander Strogonof, who, with his tutor, had joined a revolutionary club. But it had not occurred to her to interdict in her empire the incendiary publications coming from the banks of the Seine. Russia remained the sole country in Europe open to the circulation of the papers printed at Paris. One number of the *Moniteur* had been confiscated, because it enlarged somewhat too explicitly on the score of the Grand Duke and different personages of the court. From that day Catherine examined every number before authorising the distribution. She soon came across one where she herself, in her turn, was very hardly treated: she was described as "the Messalina of the North." "That concerns no one but myself," she said proudly, and ordered its distribution. She tolerated the presence in St. Petersburg of the brother of Marat, who, while condemning the sanguinary furies of the other, did not conceal his republican views. Tutor in the house of Count Saltykof, he often comes to court with his pupil. It is only in 1792 that he changes his name, and takes that of Boudri. Then, in truth, all around him changes: the Empress embarks in the anti-revolutionary campaign, at first without much enthusiasm, purely as a political maneuver, but more and more sincerely, and more and more passionately too, entering little by little into the part she has wished to play, and adopting as her own these ideas, sentiments, and instincts. Not content with attacking the revolutionary spirit in France and among the French, she pursues it in Russia, among the Russians themselves, which is really doing it more honor than it deserves. In regard to France she draws up, in 1792, a memorandum on the means of restoring the monarchy. It must be said that she does not manifest much common-sense in the project. She imagines that a force of ten thousand men, marching from end to end of the country, would suffice to the task. The cost would only be 500,000, which could be borrowed at Genoa. France, once handed back to its king, would return the amount. In regard to the Frenchmen imbued with the revolutionary spirit, who might be found in her dominions, she concocts the famous ukase of February 3, 1793, which constrains them under threat of immediate ex-pulsion, to take an oath, of which the terms could not have been better imagined by a tribunal of inquisitors. Nor does she treat her subjects with more indulgence. To ward them off from the contagion of Jacobinism, she has recourse to means which she could not have sufficiently scorned at the commencement of her reign. Learning the choice that had been made of Prozorofski for the post of Governor of Moscow, Patiomkine writes to his imperial friend—

"You have taken out of your arsenal the most ancient piece of artillery, which will certainly shoot in the direction in which you set it, for it has no motion of its own; but beware lest it covers with blood for ever the name of your Majesty."

Prozorofski and his collaborators of Moscow and St. Petersburg, Arharof, Chechkofski, and Pestel, seemed, in the vigorous phrase of a Russian writer, "to have risen into the light of day out of the torture-chambers of the *Preobrajenski Prikas,* already lost in the night of oblivion." The trial of the Muscovite publicist, Novikof, condemned to fifteen years' imprisonment for carrying on certain publications to which the Empress herself had formerly contributed, inaugurates a *regime* which justifies only too well the appre-hensions of Patiomkine. Catherine bears a grudge even against the high French cravats, covering the chin, which the dandies of St. Petersburg, Prince Borys Galitzine at their head, persist in wearing.

We have endeavored to present the notions inspired in Catherine by the great political and social upheaval of the end of the eighteenth century. These notions, it is evident, were narrow. Catherine could not see that, under all its deplorable errors, its culpable mistakes, the movement that she sought to repress contained something noble, lofty, and generous. Perhaps mere intelligence could not suffice for the comprehension of these things. What was wanted was a certain personal elevation of sentiment, which Catherine never possessed. In trying to fight with the Revolution, she seized her chance of stifling the last vestiges of national independence on the banks of the Vistula: that was a matter of policy, and we may waive our judgment respecting it. But, the fight once at end in Poland, she was neither touched as a woman, nor impressed as a sovereign, by what made the glory of the expiring republic and its rehabilitation before posterity, by the last resistance of the vanquished, by the hero who personified all its useless effort and its tragic destiny. Having summoned to St. Petersburg as a common malefactor the vanquished soldier whom Michelet named "the last Knight of the West and the first Citizen of the East," whom Napoleon afterwards, at the height of his power, would have called to his aid, and who, in his Swiss shelter, was not to be dazzled by Napoleon, Catherine was not even curious to see him. She was content to abuse him. "Kostiouchko"—she did not even know how to spell his name— "has been brought here; he is seen to be in every way a mere fool, quite beneath contempt." That is how she judges the man. "Ma pauvre bete de Dostiouchka," we read in another letter. That is all the pity she can spare to the soldier who had fallen on the field of Macieiowice, the soldier in whose wounds the very soul of a great and noble people seemed to pass in one last cry of agony.

Paul I., on reaching the throne, is said to have visited the ex-dictator in his prison, and, bending low before him, desired his pardon for his mother. Perhaps it is only a legend, and if so, so much worse for the son of Catherine. At all events he set the prisoner free. Catherine had never thought of doing it.

We once heard a German, who today occupies a high position at Vienna, declare that, being cosmopolitan in his tastes, he liked every nationality equally, except one, and that his own; for, said he, along with many good qualities, it had one defect which he disliked above all others, it did not know how to be generous.

In one sense, and from this point of view, just or not, Catherine remained German. She knew how to give, sometimes even how to pardon, but she was utterly inaccessible to certain sentiments that awaken naturally in all true hearts at the sight of weakness, suffering, and misfortune. Her ideas, as we know them, did not allow her to appreciate a certain type of simple grandeur. Her own simplicity was all made of show and convention. She was always playing a part when she showed herself under this aspect. She was willing to come down from Olympus, and all its train must be not far off. This is why, in 1782, she refused the honor of receiving Franklin. "I do not care for him," she said. She did not understand him. In 1795 she did not understand Kosciuszko.

Is it true that she ever echoed the one among all the kings her contemporaries for whom she professed the most scorn, Louis XV., by repeating in her way the famous saying "After me the deluge"? *"Doslie mienia hot trava nie rosti* (After me the grass may cease to grow)" she is said to have said at the end of her life. It may well be. But to arrive at that point, she had need to abjure all that made the true glory of her reign, all to which she owes today that immortality of which she had the sublime thirst.

Catherine and Pugachev

Catherine, in 1773, faced a full-scale revolt of malcontents under the leader-ship of Emelian Pugachev, a Cossack of the Don. A capable and inspiring leader, Pugachev welded many discontented groups into a large army. Mastering the Ural and Volga areas, the rebels moved westward toward Moscow, gathering strong peasant support on the way. Catherine's generals, aided not a little by a famine in the Volga region, gradually destroyed the rebel forces. Pugachev was captured and executed in 1775. Catherine issued the following manifesto at the beginning of the revolt. The source is: Tooke, Life of Catharine, vol. 2, pp. 425–427.

By the grace of God, we Catharine II, empress and autocratrix of all the Russias, &c. make known to all our faithful subjects, that we have learnt, with the utmost indignation and extreme affliction, that a certain Kozak, a deserter and fugitive from the Don, named Ikhelman Pugatshef, after having traversed Poland, has been collecting, for some time past, in the districts that border on the river Irghis, in the government of Orenburg, a troop of vaga-bonds like himself; that he continues to commit in those parts all kinds of excesses, by inhumanly depriving the inhabitants of their possessions, and even of their lives; and that in order to draw over to his party, hitherto composed of robbers, such persons as he meets, and specially the unhappy patriots, on whose credulity he imposes, he has had the insolence to arrogate to himself the name of the late emperor Peter III. It would be superfluous here to prove the absurdity of such an imposture, which cannot even put on a shadow of probability in the eyes of sensible persons: for, thanks to the divine goodness, those ages are past, in which the Russian empire was plunged in ignorance and barbarism; when a Griska, an Outreper, with their adherents, and several other traitors to their country, made use of impostures as gross and detestable, to arm brother against brother, and citizen against citizen.

Since those eras, which it is grievous to recollect, all true patriots have enjoyed the fruits of public tranquillity, and shudder with horror at the very remembrance of former troubles. In a word, there is not a man deserving of the Russian name, who does not hold in abomination the odious and insolent lie by which Pugatshef fancies himself able to seduce and to deceive persons of a simple and credulous disposition, by promising to free them from the bonds of submission, and obedience to their sovereign, as if the Creator of the universe had established human societies in such a manner as that they can subsist without an intermediate authority between the sovereign and the people.

Nevertheless, as the insolence of this vile refuse of the human race is attended with consequences pernicious to the provinces adjacent to that district; as the report of the flagrant enormities which he has committed, may affright those persons who are accustomed to imagine the misfortunes of others as ready to fall upon them, and as we watch with indefatigable care over the tranquillity of our faithful subjects, we inform them by the present manifesto, that we have taken, without delay, such measures as are the best adapted to stifle the sedition: and in order to annihilate totally the ambitious designs of Pugatshef, and to exterminate a band of robbers, who have been audacious enough to attack the small military detachments dispersed about those countries, and to massacre the officers who were taken prisoners, we have dispatched thither, with a competent number of troops, general Alexander Bibikof, general in chief of our armies, and major of our regiment of life guards.

Accordingly we have no doubt of the happy success of these measures, and we cherish the hope that the public tranquillity will soon be restored, and that the profligates who are spreading devastation over a part of the government of Orenburg, will shortly be dispersed. We are moreover persuaded, that our faithful subjects will justly abhor the the imposture of the rebel Pugatshef, as destitute of all probability, and will repel the artifices of the ill-disposed, who seek and find their advantage in the seduction of the weak and credulous, and who cannot assuage their avidity but by ravaging their country, and by shedding of innocent blood.

We trust, with equal confidence, that every true son of the country will unremittedly fulfil his duty, of the contributing to the maintenance of good order and of public tranquillity, by preserving himself from the snares of seduction, and by duly discharging his obedience to his lawful sovereign. All our faithful subjects, therefore, may dispel their alarms and live in perfect security, since we employ our utmost care, and make it our peculiar glory, to preserve their property, and to extend the general felicity.

Given at St. Petersburg, Dec. 23, 1773, O.S.

Life in Eighteenth Century Russia

William Tooke, a distinguished English observer and student of Russia, spent several years in Russia during the latter part of Catherine's reign making a careful study of the land, the peoples, the government and of Russian society in general. The Russians honored him by election to memberships in the Imperial Academy of Sciences and in The Free Economical Society of St. Petersburg. The published report of his studies is a store house of information about many aspects of Russian life under Catherine. The following selections deal with the people, living conditions and agriculture. The source is: Tooke, W., View of the Russian Empire During the Reign of Catharine the Second, and to the Close of the Present Century, *Three volumes. London, 1799, Vol. 1, pp. 332–334, 341–352, 355–368, 371–372, 372–373, 374–376, 379–381; vol. 2, pp. 128–133, 252–256.*

THE PEOPLE. The Russians are a moderate-sized, vigorous, and durable race of men. The growth and longevity of this people are very different in different districts; but in general rather large than small, and they are commonly well-built. It is very rare to see a person naturally deformed; which doubtless is chiefly owing to their loose garments and the great variety of bodily exercises. All the sports and pastimes of the youth have a tendency to expand the body and give flexibility to the muscles.

Easy as it is occasionally by comparison to discriminate the Russian by his outward make from other Europeans, it will, however, be found very difficult to point out the principal lineaments of the national physiognomy, as speaking features are in general extremely rare. The following may be deemed common and characteristical: A small mouth, thin lips, white teeth, little eyes, a low forehead; the nose has a great variety of forms; it is most frequently seen to be small and turned upwards. The beard is almost always very bushy; the colour of the hair varies through all the shades from dark brown to red, but it is seldom quite black. The expression of the countenance is gravity and good-nature or sagacity.—Hearing and sight are usually very acute; but the other senses more or less obtuse by manner of living and climate. The gait and gestures of the body have a peculiar and often impassioned vivacity, partaking, even with the mere rustics, of a certain complaisance and an engaging manner.

The same features, on the whole, are conspicuous in the female sex, but in general improved, and here and there actually dignified. A delicate skin and a ruddy complexion are in the vulgar idea the first requisites of beauty; in fact fine rosy cheeks are perceived more commonly among the Russian women than in other countries, but no where is paint so essential an article of the toilet as here, even among the lowest classes of the people. As the growth of the Russian ladies is not confined by any bandages, stays, or other compresses, the proportions of the parts usually far exceed the line which the general taste of Europe has prescribed for the contour of a fine shape.—The early maturity of girls, at which they generally arrive in the twelfth or thirteenth year, is only to be accounted for, in so cold a climate, by the frequent use of hot baths, which, while it accelerates this expansion, also brings on an early decay of beauty and solidity of bodily frame. Married women seldom retain the fresh complexion and the peculiar charms of youth beyond the first lying-in. By their baths, their paint, and the great submission in which they live with their husbands, the moderate share of beauty with which nature has endowed these daughters of the northern earth is generally faded at an age when the husband is just entering his prime.

The bodily frame of the Russians is excellent. Their happy organization, their cheerful and blithe temper, that hardness which they oppose to every inconveniency, the natural simplicity of their manner of living, and their rude, but dry and wholesome climate, procure to the great mass of the people a degree of physical complacency of which few other nations can boast.—The Russians are endowed with a vitality, of which an instance has scarcely ever yet been found in any other country, as we have seen in the foregoing section. If the Englishman or the Spaniard excels the Russian in bodily strength, the latter is superior to them by far in the endurance, or in the patient suffering of severer hardships. Hunger and thirst, want of accommodation and repose the Russian can bear longer than any other nation.—In all the lower classes, the soldiery excepted, a healthy old age is very common; lively old men of a hundred years are in all parts of Russia no unusual appearance, but probably the number of them would be far greater if the propensity to dram-drinking were not the occasion of so great a mortality in the middle periods of life.

The general disposition of the people is gay, careless even to levity, much addicted to sensuality, quick in comprehending whatever is proposed, and not less prompt in its execution; ingenious in finding out means of abridging their work; in all their occupations ready, alert, and dexterous. Violent in their passions, they easily mistake the golden mean, and not infrequently rush into the contrary extreme. They are attentive, resolute, bold, and enterprising. To trade and barter they have an irresistible impulse. They are hospitable and liberal, frequently to their own impoverishment. Anxious sollicitudes about the future here cause but a few grey pates. In their intercourse with others, they are friendly, jovial, complaisant, very ready to oblige, not envious, slanderous, or censorious, and much given to secrecy. From their natural and simple way of life, their wants are few, and those easily satisfied, leaving them leisure for recreations and repose; and the constant cheerfulness of their temper frees them from troublesome projects, procures them satisfaction in all situations, keeps them healthy and strong, and brings them to an undisquieted, contented, brisk, sometimes a very advanced old age.

* * *

Thus far we are enabled to ground the calculation of the number of the people on actual enumerations; but for the state of the unnumbered classes, and for the increase of the population, as well by the great acquisitions since the year 1783, as by the very considerable surplus of the births, and the numerous accessions of foreign colonists, we have only probable and partly-authenticated data to proceed upon, as the result of the fifth revision, in 1796, if it be published, is not yet come to hand. In the meantime, the following calculations, made with the greatest nicety of examination, may well be admitted to supply that defect.

By the revision of 1783, there were in the said 41 governments, computing the female sex as equal to the male, of registered persons 25,677,000

The amount of the Kozaks of the Don and the Euxine, according to the most authentic private accounts, at least 220,000

For the unnumbered tribes and classes at the time of the fourth revision, we cannot, without the highest improbability, allow less than 1,500,000

Consequently, the Russian Empire, in the year 1783, might have inhabitants amounting all together to 27,397,000

According to the results deduced from experiments and observations on the fruitfulness and mortality in Russia, this mass must of itself have increased annually more than half a million. If, in order to keep as far as possible from all exaggeration, we deduct the half of this surplus of births, to allow for the diminution it may have suffered by an extraordinary mortality, as by war; there remains for every year an increase of 25,000 new citizens, which, exclusively of all ascending proportion, in 12 years makes a sum total of 3,000,000

The new acquisitions since the year 1783, or the present nine viceroyalties of Taurida, Minsk, Bratzlau, Vosnesensk, Podolia, Volhynia, Courland, Vilna, and Slonim, contain, according to a legitimated statement already mentioned 5,755,000

Consequently, we may admit, by the most moderate estimate, the population of the Russian Empire at present to be 36,152,000

or in a round sum thirty-six millions of persons.

Of this prodigious mass the greater part by far belongs to European Russia. The five governments of Perm, Ufa, Kolhyvan, Tobolsk, and Irkutsk, comprehended under the general name of Siberia, contain all together, according to the revision-lists, only 2,215,000, or, with the unnumbered classes and tribes, perhaps above three millions and a half of inhabitants. The population of the European part is therefore about fourteen times greater; and the Russian Empire, which in regard to its superficial contents mostly belongs to Asia, must in regard to its population be reckoned as belonging to Europe.

On the scale of the population of the European states, Russia holds the second place, having in this respect only the Ottoman Empire above it, which is usually admitted to have 49 millions of inhabitants, whereof 8 millions are stated to be in Europe, 36 in Asia, and 5 in Africa. Excluding the parts of both these countries which lie out of Europe from this comparison, it will follow that Russia has the largest population of all the states of Europe.—The countries which come nearest to the Russian Empire in this regard, are the Germanic States, which may be admitted at 26 millions; France, to which we may still notwithstanding the havoc brought on by various means since the Revolution, allow 25 millions; and the states of Austria, which may be taken at about an equal number. Of the neighbouring states whose relative interests are of importance to Russia, Prussia and Sweden are the most remarkable. The former, with its lately acquired possessions in Poland and the circle of Franconia, has about the fourth; the latter the eleventh part of the population of the Russian Empire.

. . .

LIVING CONDITIONS. The employments of the female sex, both in town and country, vary but little from those in the neighbouring countries. They see to the cleanliness of the house, spin, weave linen and coarse cloth on frames, in quality but little inferior to what is brought from Germany; they bleach, full, and colour, knot the ends of the threads for a span long, for table-cloths, neck-cloths, &c. make felt, bake bread every day &c. In general they are kept closer to work, and fare harder than is customary among their European neighbours.

The country market-towns and hamlets are commonly open; are mostly built in irregular streets, with little kitchen-gardens and large yards to the houses. They are situated on the banks of the rivers, as the digging of wells is not in practice: as in most parts pebbles are not to be had in any considerable quantity, the roads and streets are frequently made of timbers, or bauks laid close together having the upper-part made flat with the hatchet. They contain many, not large, but good-looking churches, mostly of brick and plaister. The monasteries in and near the towns, from their strong walls, massy gates, and numerous church-towers, have the appearance of castles. The fortresses dispersed about the country, have seldom earth-ramparts, mostly batteries of bauks laid one on the other, in the same manner as they build their houses; and about these a low palisade. The canons stand on the gates, and upon the angles of the ramparts or batteries on wooden carriages. Their design is to keep the tributary tribes in awe, and the neighbouring nomades from the borders. Ostrogs, or houses surrounded with a palisade of upright pointed bauks, are either in towns, where they serve as prisons for criminals, or stand solitary in various parts of the country, for the same purpose as the fortresses.

Villages of very various dimensions, and parishes are situated on the margin of rivers, brooks, lakes, and sometimes on mere morasses and springs. The parishes, or church-villages, are sometimes very extensive; and contain, it may be 500 or even 1000 and more farms, from 3 to 7 churches, many of brick, markets, and trafficking places. Large villages are frequently called slobodes; but many slobodes are less than church-villages: the houses are ranged in straight streets, and the streets mostly laid with timbers.

The proper Russian architecture is alike in towns and villages. A messuage consists of a dwelling-house, a few little store-rooms, stables, and a stew, or hot-bath, by which the yard is inclosed. All these structures are built of bauks, unhewn, placed on one another, and notched into each other at the four corners; sometimes, though but rarely, on a brick foundation; these houses are covered with boards, and when the owner can afford it, with oak shingles. The meanest dwelling-houses consist solely of one little room, which therefore has the door to the street. In it is an oven, taking up almost one fourth part of the whole space; adjoining to it, of equal height with the oven, is a broad shelf of board. The top of the oven and this shelf are the sleeping places of the family. The light is admitted into these houses through two or three holes in the walls furnished with shutters, or through a little window of muscovy-glass, or only of bladder, oiled linen or paper. The smoke finds its way out as well as it can through these apertures in the wall. These rooms, as may well be supposed, are as black as a chimney; and, as all the household functions are performed in them, such as baking, cooking, washing, &c. it is hardly possible to keep them clean. They are called, with the utmost propriety of speech, black-rooms. Under the floor of the room is a cellar.

A complete town or country-house, for the sake of having a cellar, stands raised a fathom above the ground, and has a black-room and a white-room, and between the two, a small passage. The black-room has frequently a chimney to the oven, and a window of glass or marienglas; but the white-room has the oven of tiles, or bricks covered with plaster. The entrance, by a covered flight of wooden steps to the aforementioned passage, is from the back-yard, not from the street.

The magazines or store-rooms are small detached huts, for provisions, corn, in short all the necessary stores. The stables are mere hovels or sheds, open to the yard, or at most fronted with wattles, paid with mortar; in the latter case they are called pokleti. The bathroom resembles a detached black-room. It stands alone; has an oven like the other, smoke-holes, a water-tub, brushes, and benches raised one above another in the form of a scaffold. The corn-kilns are without the towns and villages. Places thus built must be very liable to raging fires; and, when once they break out, they rarely leave anything unconsumed.

The household-furniture, both in town and country, even among people of opulence, is very simple. In the room, which, with very few exceptions, is, at the same time, the kitchen, are a table, benches, the shelf, which serves for the dormitory, and in the corner one or more holy figures. The rich have a great many of them, some with rims of beaten silver. Before these, lamps or wax-candles are kept constantly burning, or at least on all the festivals, which amounts to nearly the same thing; so that many of these summer-rooms have the appearance of little chapels. Culinary utensils, and those for the use of the table, are as few as can well be conceived. As vehicles they make use of quite small open one-horse carts, or somewhat larger, and half covered over like a child's cradle, also with one horse, without shafts, so that a collateral horse can at any time be put to; both kinds of such a simple mechanism, that almost any boor can make a new one or at least repair the defects of the old one even upon the road. They are extremely light and commodious. —— Splinters, like laths, of fir or very dry birch-wood are much more commonly used for giving light in the room, after dark, than tallow-candles.

As the country towns, in general, progressively endeavour to imitate the Residence, one perceives from time to time loftier houses of wood or brick spring up, built in a superior style, with fashionable furniture within, gardens laid out in a regular method, &c.

The inferior houses are much pestered with domestic vermin; besides the common house-rat and mouse, they swarm with water-rats, bats, large beetles very frequent, crickets, bugs, fleas in abundance; various kinds of very troublesome flies, gnats, moths, bullmoths, wood-lice; in southern low places frogs, toads, and tadpoles; in Siberia little beetles; about the Tsheremtshan, lapland beetles.

The preparation of their victuals is so simple, that foreigners do not easily bring themselves to relish it, but adhere to the customary way of dressing their food in their own countries. Fresh meats with watery sauce, or baked pastries of common crust, with minced-meat, or whole fish, fish with water and salt, without other sauce, cabbage and roots chopped to-gether, cabbage-soup, which is never omitted, meagre fish and flesh soups, cool-drinks, quas, with eggs, minced-meat, and leeks, pancakes, soup of ground hemp and linseed, millet-soup and grits, turned milk with meal and sour milk, &c. almost all seasoned with onions, leeks, garlic, and sometimes pimento, are their ordinary dishes. Where Tartars dwell, they use likewise a few wild roots, especially dog-tooth, lily-roots, and others. For the evening repast are served up nuts, orchard-fruits, and the several wild fruits pro-duced by the country round; blackberries, strawberries, sloes, &c. At an entertainment of their friends and acquaintance they provide a surprising variety of these kinds of dishes. The lower sort feed very poorly at all times, but particularly in the fasts. In large towns, the table in good houses is becoming more luxurious and fashionable from day to day.

The most common domestic drink is quas, a liquor prepared from pol-lard, meal, and bread, or from meal and malt, by an acid fermentation. It is cooling and well-tasted. Corn-spirits, and rectified corn-spirits, supply the place of wine. In good houses, fruit-wines, rasberry-wine, cherry-wine, bilberrywine, &c. from the juices of those fruits, mead and brandy made by fermentation, which are pleasant enough to the palate. Brown beer and metheglin are more in use than braga or white cloudy beer brewed from malted millet or wheat, with hops, and busa or white unhopped wheat-beer. Tea is in very general use. The true russian tea is a concoction of honey, water, and spanish pepper, and drank warm. It tastes well and cheers the stomach. Many even of the common people drink chinese tea, sweetened with honey or sugar. Persons of distinction keep their tables supplied with meats and drinks entirely in the foreign taste, hire french cooks, &c. as in other countries. Tobacco is but little used.

In the article of dress they adhere as faithfully, in the country towns and villages, to the manners of their fathers, as they do in food and lodging. The noblesse, all the officers in the civil department; and, besides the light troops, the soldiery all over the empire, the merchants of the chief towns and those who trade with them, the mine-owners, and almost all the people of quality throughout the empire, dress after the german fashion; and the ladies, even in the remotest and most retired parts of the country, appear more modishly attired than would easily be imagined. The burghers and mercantile class, however, generally speaking, stick close to the national dress, no less than the peasantry. Of this I shall speak a little more particularly.

The men let their beards grow, which are commonly long and bushy: the hair is cut and combed: their shirt is short, without any sort of collar, and made of white, blue, or red linen. Their trousers are loose, and tied below the knees. The shirt usually hangs over the trousers, and is girt round the waist with a string. Stockings are not so commonly worn by the lower class of people, as leg-wrappers, which they tie about their feet and legs with pack-thread, so as to make them look very thick. Shoes are worn by the better sort, and mat-slippers by the common people; but half-boots are in very general use. Over the shirt they wear a short breast-cloth, or a vest furnished with buttons. The coat is made so big as to allow of one side lapping over the other before, with little buttons, close sleeves, and a collar. The skirt is made with gathers at the hips, and reaches below the calves of the legs, and the garment is girt round with a sash that passes twice round the body. At the sash commonly hangs a long-bladed knife, in a sheath. The covering for the head is either a flat fur-cap, with a narrow brim; or, in other places, a cap which forms a bag of a span in depth, in which they keep their handkerchief on their head. In summer they go with flapped high-crowned dutch hats, ornamented with a narrow ribband of some gaudy colour. The materials of the dress vary according to the rank and circumstances of the wearer; the rich wear fine broad cloth, sometimes decorating the edges with gold cording, and little silver buttons for fastenings; common people clothe themselves in homespun cloth, and the summer in linen, made likewise at home. A well-dressed Russian makes a very good figure. In winter the common people wear sheep-skins, with the woolly side turned inwards; the better sort put on furs of a higher price.

The habits of the clergy, as well in their everyday wear, as when offici-ating at the altar, are in the oriental style; the latter of different colours, often in brocade, mostly very rich. The monks are always clad in black, and are also distinguishable by their high pasteboard caps, wound about with crape.

The women wear stockings or leg-wrappers, and shoes like the men, some-times likewise picked-pointed slippers. The lower class frequently go bare-foot, or simply in slippers on their naked feet: their shifts are white; but in Dauria the female peasants put on silk-coloured shifts of gauze or cot-ton; they fasten about the neck with a collar, and are decorated with fancied ornaments of needle-work: the vest is close about the neck without sleeves, and fits tight to the body down to the hips; from the hips it spreads without gathers and reaches down to the shoes; on the facing it is garnished with a thick row of little buttons from the top to the very bottom; it is however girt with a sash, to which the bunch of keys is suspended. The quality of the saraphan is various according to circumstances: of glazed linen, kaitaka, silks, frequently edged with fur, or lined with it throughout. The dress of the lower sort of females in winter is more complete, consisting of coarse cloth, or sheep skin, with sleeves. Another dress is the usual woman's gown, and a contushe without sleeves. The dushagrek is also worn on the saraphan, without a gown. In the winter they wear furs made after the manner used in Poland, with pointed sleeves. As this is usually a present made by the bridegroom, and the best piece of dress, the common people, in order to make a show of it, go, the whole summer through, to church, to make visits, &c. in the pelice. They also wear necklaces of corals, pearls, or golden chains, ear-rings of precious stones, and decorate their fingers and wrists with rings and bracelets.

The head-dress is somewhat different in different districts. The girls in general wear their hair uncovered more than the women; the former plait it in three plaits, with ribbands and beads tied to the point of them. In Tver, Novgorod, &c. they wear a band across the forehead, bedizoned with pearls and beads of various colours, which gives the appearance of a tiara or open coronet. At Voronets and the parts adjacent, both women and girls wear coifs made to fit the head, with cheek-pieces and tresses. About the Oka, at Murom, and the country round, the caps are in the form of an up-right crescent. In the governments of Mosco, Yaroslaf, Kaluga, and the circumjacent parts, the coif has a stiff flap before, like a jockey-cap, which is decorated with tresses, pearls, and various-coloured stones. On this they hang in the tartarian fashion, a veil; but which they usually keep thrown back. The veil is generally of silk, set off with gold or silver lace. In their ordinary dress, they tie on the veil over the hair, without any cap. In western Russia caps are in use that are a kind of fillet, with tresses, pearls, and stones. Numbers wear caps having a stiff rim one or two inches broad, like a small skreen or a flapped hat. Persons of consequence, in towns, wind pieces of silk about their heads in such manner to let the hair hang down in ringlets from under it; and these head-dresses have very much the resemblance of a high turban. A complete woman's attire is very dear, but remarkably handsome.

Paint is as necessary an article in the dress of a Russian lady, as linen. The freshest and ruddiest young woman of the place puts on both white and red; and, as this practice is prejudicial to natural beauty, therefore such antiquated dames as would not appear hideous are forced to continue it. Fine white paint is made of pulverized marcasite; more commonly whitelead. The rouge in the shops seems to be compounded of florentine-lake and talc, with powder of marcasite; red tiffany is also very much worn. The village-toasts gather the roots of onosma echioides Linn. or of lithospermum arvense, which, after being dried, they moisten with their tongue, and then rub their cheeks with it; or they extract the colour with boiling water and alum from the rind of these roots. Some rub their cheeks with river-spunge, till the skin is sufficiently thinned or inflamed for being transparent to the blood. From the toilet, however, we will now retire with awe, and presume no farther to pry into its mysteries.

They have usually two meals in the day; in the forenoon about nine o'clock, and in the afternoon at three. The family at these times eat all together; and, when it is numerous, first the males and afterwards those of the other sex. They allow themselves but a short time at table, and are easy and cheerful. Even among the inferior people the table-linen, platters, and vessels are kept in great cleanliness. If strangers sit down with them there are very copious potations. Intoxication is not disgraceful, and even among people of good condition, if a lady be overtaken in liquor, it is no subject of reproach. They are never quarrelsome or scurrilous in their cups, but friendly, jovial, courteous, speak in praise of the absent, and boast of their friendship, and those that are not able to stand, find ready assistance from those that can. On journies, merchants and others take their food with remarkably few formalities. In towns and great village-stations, women sit in the street, near public-houses, with tables having roast and boiled meat, fish, piroggees, cabbage-soup, cucumbers, bread, and quas, consequently a superb and every where a cheap repast, which is taken standing, and always accompanied with a glass or two of brandy.

To hot and cold bathing they are so habituated from their earliest infancy that the practice is indispensable. They usually go into the hot-bath once a week, besides other frequent occasions, such as, after a slight indisposition, hard work, on returning from a journey, and the like. They use the bath very hot, heating the room with large stones made glowing red, and raising a vapour by repeatedly throwing water upon them; the room all the while being so tight that no particles of heat or vapour can transpire. The bather lies extended naked upon a mat thrown on one of the shelves of the scaffold already described, which the higher he ascends the greater the heat he feels. When he has thus lain perspiring for some time, the waiter of the bath, generally a female, comes and washes his body all over with hot water, scourges and rubs him with bunches of leafy birch, wipes him with cloths, and then leaves him to lie and sweat as long as he chooses. Numbers of them run from the hot bath into the cold water flowing by, and in winter roll themselves in the snow, without deriving any bad consequences from it.

The intercourse between the sexes is more free than elsewhere, particularly in the country, on account of the contracted space of their habitations and sleeping room, their baths, the simplicity of their conversation, and their artless songs. The behaviour of husbands toward their wives is, in general, comparatively with european manners, rough and austere. The wives must work hard, and are often obliged to be the tame spectators of their husband's intemperance and irregularities without daring to complain; but to this they are so early accustomed that they are seldom heard to vent a murmur even while smarting under very tyrannical treatment. In larger towns, however, and even among people of condition, the lady is in a quite contrary predicament; and they are either very much slandered or many a kind husband sometimes gets a rap of the slipper. It is a maxim with parents of the common class, never to become dependent on their children; and therefore keep the management of the house in their own hands, till they die. Indeed the laws of the land are more favourable to widows and mothers than they are in other countries.

With substantial people the marriage-contract is made with mercantile punctuality; the common sort enter into the nuptial state, for its peculiar purposes, as young as they can; and, as housekeeping is not expensive, and as education is neither attended with cost nor trouble, they live as much at their ease as before. The betrothing is performed with ecclesiastical rites, generally eight days previous to the marriage, and is indissoluble. During this interval, the bride is only visited by the bridegroom, and the girls of her acquaintance, who amuse her with singing. On the last evening the young women bring the bride into the hot-bath, where they plait and tie up her hair, all the while singing ballads descriptive of her future happiness.

The marriage is solemnized in the church, before the altar, whither they proceed, with the figure of some saint carried before them. During the ceremony a crown is put on each of their heads. The priest, with due forms, changes their rings, reads to them an admonition of their reciprocal duties, gives them to drink of a cup in token of the present union of their fortunes, and dismisses them with his blessing.

At their return from church the father of the bride presents the young couple with a loaf of bread and some salt, accompanied with a wish that they may never know the want of either, for which they thank him on their knees. They then sit down to supper, and when the shift that the bride is to put on has been inspected, the new-married pair are put to bed. This shift is produced the next day to the guests, who, upon seeing the tokens of virginity upon it, felicitate the mother of the bride on that fortunate event. All things considered, it need not be mentioned that these tokens never fail to appear. This day passes with far more jollity than the former, as the young woman, being now freed from all restraint, can bear a part in the sports and entertainments of the company.

Dancing is a diversion every where followed. Even the common people, who here are not apt to become stiff with work, dance to admiration. They generally dance to the voice. The universal dance of the country consists in frequent genuflexions of the man, and a gentle step in proper cadence of the woman. It is pantomimic and very engaging. The woman lays her arms on her breast crosswise, beckons to the man with her fingers, shrugs her shoulders, and glides by him hanging down her head, with some side-glances, without giving of hands. In another dance, the man and woman shew a repugnance to each other; they reciprocally pass by with averted and disdainful looks; make faces of derision at one another as their backs are towards them; turn about and shew by their looks and gestures an ambiguous aversion. The dove-dance exhibits an imitation of the coaxing airs of turtle-doves or lovers. Generally one stands still to the other; presently the man dances about with vehement motion, while the woman proceeds in gentle and delicate movements. Polish dances are also much in use, not only in the Ukraine, but in most other parts of the country, likewise during the winter evening-companies are very common. They consist in absurd and ridiculous masquerades by young people. They sometimes, though but rarely, put on disguises, humorously represent grotesque and romantic stories, imitate particular persons and animals, and usually indulge themselves in coarse and licentious buffooneries. After these comedies, or masquerades, which are sometimes omitted, the party amuse themselves with singing, dancing, playing for stakes, and always with eating and drinking.

They are very much attached to gymnastic diversions. In severe winter-nights the ladies make sledge-parties, in which there is always much vehement singing. The swing and round-abouts are diversions of the easter holidays. The former is carried to great perfection; five or six people stand or sit, one behind another on a plank, which is swung to a great height. Instead of a plank, some of these swings have wooden lions, swans, bears, coaches, chairs, sofas, &c. The girls divert themselves in summer in jumping on a board, resting in the middle on a block of wood as a fulcrum; one standing on each end of this board, they alternately bound one another up to a surprising height. The diversion of the ice-hills has been described in a former section of this work. Wrestling and boxing are another diversion, though very awkwardly performed. Ringing the bells, on church and court holidays, is a species of exercise of which they are remarkably fond; but they produce nothing like harmony from them. The sole excellency consists in striking the clappers the oftenest.

. . .

AGRICULTURE. Agriculture, therefore, is not so generally the business of the peasantry in Russia as in other countries. However, on the whole it is carried on to so great an extent, as not only to furnish the nations of the empire that eat bread with that article, and the prodigious quantities of corn, at a very moderate price, consumed by the brandy-distilleries; but also can export a great superfluity to foreign countries. Even from the 55th to the 60th deg. of north lat. in Siberia, are large tracts of arable land, mostly fertile, good crops of hay, and spacious forests. More to the north, cultivation is less to be depended on, and the whole system of rural economy is very liable to failures, and attended with great difficulties. Throughout Russia every village has its proper territory, and every estate its allotted inclosures and commons. In the less cultivated plains of Siberia, every man takes as much ground from the open steppes as he can manage. When such a portion of ground is exhausted, the countryman lets it lie fallow for a year or two, goes and turns up another piece, and so proceeds. Frequently these little strips of ground lie scattered at 20, 50, and even 80 versts distance from the village. The size of these fields is measured eastwards, each of which being 60 fathom long and 40 wide; but in some parts, and all over the Ukraine, they are 80 fathom in length and 40 in breadth.

In Russia and Siberia they cultivate winter rye and summer rye, winter-wheat only in Russia as far as the Kama, summer-wheat both in Russia and Siberia; barley, spelt-barley, or. bear-barley, plentifully in Russia; oats, in Russia and Siberia; few pease, still fewer vetches and beans; a great deal of buck-wheat; in Siberia tartarian buck-wheat, millet, and the grain called panicum germanicum, only in Russia.

The manure depends much on the quality of the soil, climate, and greater or inferior population. In well peopled regions the fields are dunged, because the husbandman can afford them but little respite; in fertile districts, however, of less numerous habitations, the good arable land endures no dung, requiring only after every 5 or 10 years use, 3, 4, or 5 years rest. Such powerful soil is found in different parts of the governments of Simbirsk and Penza, and about Ufa and Orenburg, as also in the southern steppes of Siberia, in the steppes of the Iset, the Ishim, the Baraba, about Irkutsk and in southern Dauria. The corn, after dunging, shoots up into high straw, and bears no solid ears. The most ungrateful soils are in Finnland, Archangel, and the north of Russia, also the north and north-eastern parts of Siberia, in Kamtshatka, &c. They rarely yield an increase above threefold, and often entirely fail by the intenseness of the frost. The common land brings an increase of from 5 to 8 fold, and the fresh broke pieces in the above-mentioned steppes for some years successively will give an increase of 10 up to 15 fold.

The country people generally make use of the little Russian or Livonian one-horse plough. For winter corn they plough twice, for summer corn only once, and always quite flat. On some lands the corn is first strewn, then ploughed in, and harrowed smooth with an additional horse by the side of the other; by which method one man, with two poor feeble horses, can rid a good bit of ground. In woody districts the boors make new land in the swedish manner, by burning the forests, which if they let alone for three or four years will all be covered over again with young trees and saplings.

The corn is cut with sickles, in which employment the women and children assist. They bind it in little sheaves, set it up on the fields in shocks, and carry it home in winter on sledges. They then dry it in small wooden kilns, with a smouldering fire, which they keep burning in a hole near the kiln, and the smoke whereof rushes into it. The corn thus dried, is spread upon the ice of a river, or a floor wetted with water, where it is threshed with light flails, then stored in little barns; and, what remains over from domestic uses, is conveyed to town, which is sometimes a hundred, nay two hundred, or even four hundred versts distant; where it is sold, not by measure, but by weight; rye and wheat as well as meal, in mat-sacks of 8 pood, and, especially in Siberia, at an inconceivably low price. In Krasnoyarsk, for example, where it is particularly cheap, a pood of rye meal will sell for 2 to 3 kopeeks; or about a penny. Wheat flour 5 kopeeks, and so of the rest. In Irkutsk they are about three times dearer. — In many parts of the country every boor has his own water-mill built by himself, with a horizontal water-wheel. In cold regions the straw is given to the cattle; but in the southern parts, where the cattle remain out all the winter, it is left to rot.

The villagers, with whom winter provender is a requisite, have hay-fields, bordering on the banks of lakes and rivers, in brakes and fens of the forests. In order to get rid of the old withered grass, the dry weeds, twigs, and light stuff, for warming the ground, and for manuring it with wood-ash, they set it on fire, as they are apt to do with the meadow-lands of the steppe in spring; though, on account of the great mischief occasioned by this practice to the forests, whole versts of them being frequently burnt at once, it is strictly prohibited. When the steppes and meadow-lands are thus on fire, the appearance they make, especially at night, is truly tremendous; the fire works its way in all directions, frequently in lines that extend farther than the eye can reach, and fill the horizon in such manner with smoke, that one may look steadfastly at the sun the whole day through. The grass is mowed with very small scythes, and not before the month of July, that it may have time to reach its full growth and scatter its feed.

Besides corn, they grow flax, in large quantities, chiefly on the shores of the Volga; but most of all in the government of Yaroslaf, where one sees flax-fields, as elsewhere corn-fields; the next in the produce of flax are the governments of Mosco and Kazan. It is thought that the common flax would not prosper in Siberia; nevertheless some Poles, settled about the Irtish and in Dauria upon the Selenga, cultivate valakhian flax with good success. The perennial flax, frequent in the south of Siberia, is entirely unheeded, though it might be propagated to great advantage.

Hemp is indigenous in all the south and middle of Russia and Siberia, and in all these parts is propagated in great abundance, both on account of its material, for linens, sail-cloth, &c. and of the oil expressed from its feed, of which an amazing quantity is consumed for food during the fasts, and, as well as the hemp itself, exported annually to a great amount.

Woad likewise grows wild in southern Russia and Siberia; it is gathered in the Ukraine and employed in staining and dying. It is also cultivated, but only in the government of Penza, and about the Don.

Tobacco is planted almost only in the Ukraine; but there in great abundance.

Hops are propagated by the villagers only in small quantities, in the governments of Kazan, Nishney-Novgorod, &c. and in Siberia in the province of Irkutsk. They are plentifully supplied with the wild sort, which thrives almost every where, among the bushes that grow about the banks of rivers, in brakes and low forests.

But little account is made of orchards except in the chief towns: however they are seen about the towns and villages, on the Volga from the region round Mosco down the river to Astrakhan, along the Oka, and the other rivers on the right of the Volga and the inferior parts of the river Ural, and all over the Ukraine, where orchard fruits are cultivated with great diligence and success. After all the attempts that have been made, no fruit-trees will thrive in Siberia. Something of a country wine is made about the Don, in Little Russia, on the Terek, and on the Volga, near Saratof, and especially about Astrakhan. Every villager has a little kitchen-garden adjoining to his cottage, particularly for the growth of cabbages, turnips, bete, carrots, cucumbers, radishes, onions, and leeks, a few potatoes, some dill, gourds, and melons, indispensable to him on account of the numerous fast-days. Water-melons are cultivated in surprising numbers in the south-eastern parts of Russia, from the Don to the Ural, especially on the Volga, in open fields got from the steppes, and are eaten raw, or salted like cucumbers.

The forests, which are scattered sparingly about the southernmost parts of Russia, in the northern extremities above the 60th degree, are not seen. They are very common in the middle regions of Russia and in Siberia, and consist alternately of the fir, the pine, the white fir, the white and black poplar, the aspin, the ash, the alder, the birch, the beech, the oak, the linden, the mountain-ash, the elm, the willow, the palm-willow, and several others: also in the caucasean mountains a great variety of fruit-trees, walnuts, and a kind of red wood; in Siberia and in lofty mountains the larch, the siberian cedar, and balsam-poplar, every where employing a great number of hands. Almost every villager is a carpenter, who builds his own house of balku or trunks of trees, makes wharfs on the navigable rivers, and whatever else belongs to the carpenter's trade. In the upper parts of the Oka and its superior rivers, and on the rivers to the left of the Volga, from the Unsha as far as the Kama, their chief employment is to strip the linden of its bark; the inner rind whereof, they work up into baskets for sledges and carts, or make a light covering to their houses of it, to the sheds where the salt is kept in heaps; little huts for sleeping in upon the floats and vessels that go down the rivers, &c. All sorts of household cups, baskets, and the like, are made of it, in common use throughout the whole empire; and the making of what we call russia-mats, trays, troughs, ladles, skimmers, spoons, &c. of the linden wood, is a great part of their business. A no less number gain their livelihood merely by preparing the birch-tar, not to mention the occupation of so many in stripping all kind of trees of their bark for the several uses of the tanneries, particularly the youft-manufactories, and the burning of wood for charcoal, which is sent to the mines, and the different storehouses belonging to government.

In the breeding of cattle, the countryman is directed by climate and pasturage. In regions where the cattle must be stalled and foddered during the winter, the boor has at most but a scanty herd; where they can stay out in the open steppe all the winter, or the greater part of it; as in the south of Siberia, a man is often master of 300 horses, not fewer sheep, somewhere about half the number of horned cattle, always a few swine, and a great deal of poultry; sometimes geese and ducks.

The russian horses are of a middling size, with large heads, long flabby ears, not very handsome, but spirited, strong, and hardy. The horned cattle are little and brisk. The cows give but little milk, and that is poor and thin. In little Russia the oxen are used for draught. Every where about Archangel there is a fine breed of large cows, brought originally from Holland, and are not found to degenerate in the least. The true russian sheep are distinguishable from the common sort by their short tail, not above the length of three inches. Their wool is coarse, but better than that of the broad-tailed kirghistzian sheep, and would probably improve in some of the dry steppes. There are nowhere any particular sheep-folds; that is, there are no people who make it their sole business to breed and fatten them. It is never the practice to milk the ewes. Hogs, dogs, and cats, are of the ordinary kinds.

The poultry are housed all the winter in the cottage, under the hearth and the sleeping-benches, for the sake of having Easter-eggs. The goose is not in all places the common domestic species; many keep wild geese. They catch the young before they can fly, fatten them, and kill them in autumn. On the approach of spring, they catch others, and thus save themselves the winter's feed. In Siberia at times one sees the white-headed little goose tamed. Besides, and instead of the domstic duck, some cottagers keep the wood-duck, the red duck, the muscovy duck, and several other species. Doves and pigeons nestle about the villages, without owners. Turkey-fowl are very common among the poultry in the southern parts of Russia, and wherever there is a good market for them in the large towns.

Additional Readings

Pares, *History*. Pp. 147-274.

Tompkins, *Russia*. Pp. 146-290.

Vernadsky, *History*. Pp. 67-127.

Martin, *Picture History*. Pp. 64-107.

Nowak, *Medieval*. Pp. 62-113.

Rambaud, *Russia*. Vol. 1, Chaps. 19-22; vol. 2, chaps. 1-10.

Leroy-Beaulieu, A., *The Empire of the Tsars and Russians*. New York, 1898. Vol. 3, Book 3, *passim et seriatim*.

Goodall, *Soviet Russia*. Pp. 4-6.

Allen, *Ukraine*. Chap. 4.

Elnett, *Historic Origins*. Pp. 46-89.

Hrushchevsky, *History*. Chaps. 14 and 16.

Miliukov (Karpovich, ed.), *Outlines*. Vol. 1, chaps. 3-6; vol. 3, chaps. 1-2.

Waliszewski, K., *Peter the Great*. Two volumes. New York: D. Appleton, 1897.

Lobanov-Rostovsky, A., *Russia and Asia*. New York: Macmillan, 1933. Chaps. 1-4.

Bain, R. N., *The First Romanovs, 1613-1725*. London: A. Constable, 1905
The Pupils of Peter the Great. London: A. Constable, 1897
Peter III. London: A. Constable, 1902
"Peter the Great and His Pupils, 1689-1730," *Cambridge Modern History*, Vol. 5, chap. 17
"Russia under Anne and Elizabeth," *Cambridge Modern History*, Vol. 6, chap. 10.

Hoetzsch, O., "Catherine II," *Cambridge Modern History*. Vol. 6, chap. 19.

Anthony, K., *Catharine the Great*. New York: Garden City Publishing Co., 1925.

Kaus, G., *Catherine: the Portrait of an Empress*. New York: The Viking Press, 1935.

Lord, R. H., *The Second Partition of Poland*. Cambridge: Harvard University Press, 1915.

Platonov, *History*. Pp. 205-303.

Kluchevsky, *History*. Vols. 4 and 5.

Pokrovsky, M. M. (J. D. Clarkson & M. R. M. Griffiths, trs. & eds.), *History of Russia*. New York: International Publishers, 1931. Chaps. 11-13.

Tolstoy, A., *Peter the Great*. New York: Covici Friede, 1932.

Gogol, N., *Taras Bulba*. Everyman's Library Edition. (E. P. Dutton & Co.)

Curtiss, *Church and State*. Pp. 15-32.

Lobanov-Rostovsky, A., *Russia and Europe, 1789-1825*. Durham: Duke University Press, 1947. Pp. 3-67.

Part IV. THE REIGNS OF ALEXANDER I AND NICHOLAS I

The Murder of Paul

Alexander I, like his grandmother, Catherine II, was elevated to the throne as the result of a palace revolution which involved the murder of his predecessor. The predecessor in Alexander's case was his father, Paul, and throughout his life, Alexander was haunted by a sense of guilt over his complicity in the murder. The following version of the murder is Alexander's own, as he told it to his friend and confidant, Prince Czartoryski. The source is: Gielgud, Adam (Editor), Memoirs of Prince Adam Czartoryski and his Correspondence with Alexander I. *Second edition. Two volumes. London, 1888. Vol. 1, pp. 227 ff. (abridged).*

Then he spoke to me of his father's death with inexpressible grief and remorse. We often returned to this subject, and Alexander gave me full details of it which I shall repeat below, together with information communicated to me by other actors in the tragedy.

Alexander told me that the first man who spoke to him about the plans of the conspirators was Count Panin, and he never forgave him. Panin was one of the chief leaders of the conspiracy which brought about Paul's death, though he did not actually take part in it. During my previous stay in the Russian capital I had never met him. When I returned to St. Petersburg, I first made his acquaintance. Apart from other reasons, the Count's exterior, would I think, almost have alone been sufficient to make friendship impossible. I have often been struck by his icey expression; his impassive countenance, on a body as straight as a spike, did not induce one to address him. I saw him but little, however, and my judgment of his character might have been erroneous and even unjust.

The two Counts Panin and Pahlen were at that time the strongest heads of the Empire. They saw further and more clearly than the other members of Paul's Council, to which both of them belonged; and they agreed to initiate Alexander into their plans. It would not have been prudent to attempt anything without being assured of the consent of the heir to the throne. Devoted fanatics or enthusiasts might no doubt have acted otherwise. By not implicating the son in the dethronement of his father, by exposing themselves to a certain death, they would have better served both

Russia and the prince who was to be called upon to govern her; but such a course would have been almost impracticable, and it would have demanded an audacity and antique virtue which in these days very few men possess. Pahlen obtained a secret audience for Panin with the Grand-Duke. Panin represented to Alexander the evils from which Russia was suffering and would continue to suffer if Paul continued to reign. He said that Alexander's most sacred duty was to his country, and that he must not sacrifice millions of people to the extravagant caprices and follies of a single man, even if that man was his father; that the life, or at least the liberty, of his mother, of himself, and of the whole of the Imperial family was threatened by Paul's inconceivable aversion for his wife, from whom he was entirely separated; that this aversion increased from day to day, and might prompt him to the most outrageous acts; and that it was therefore necessary to save Russia, whose fate was in Alexander's hands, by deposing Paul, which would be the only means of preventing him from inflicting greater calamities on his country and his family, and securing to him a quieter and more happy life. This speech produced a great impression on Alexander, but it did not convince him. It required more than six months to enable his tempters to obtain his consent to their plans.

It was a thousand pities that a prince so anxious and so well qualified to be a benefactor to his country did not hold entirely aloof from a conspiracy which resulted almost inevitably in his father's assassination. Russia certainly suffered much under the almost maniacal Government of Paul, and there are no means in that country of restraining or confining a mad sovereign; but Alexander felt and exaggerated in his own mind all his life the sombre reflection of the crime committed on his father, which had fallen on himself, and which he thought he could never wipe out. This ineffaceable stain, although it was brought about solely by his inexperience and his total and innocent ignorance of Russian affairs and the Russian people, settled like a vulture on his conscience, paralysed his best faculties at the commencement of his reign, and plunged him into a mysticism sometimes degenerating into superstition at its close.

It must be admitted that the Emperor Paul was precipitating his country into incalculable disorders and into a complete deterioration of the Government machine. The principal officials and other officers of rank were more or less convinced that the Emperor had fits of mental alienation. His rule became a reign of terror. He was hated even for his good qualities, for at bottom he desired justice, and this impulse sometimes led him to do a just thing in his outburst of rage; but his feeling of justice was blind and struck at all without discrimination; always passionate, often capricious and cruel, his decrees were constantly suspended over the heads of officers, and made them detest the man who filled their lives with uncertainty and terror. The conspiracy had the sympathy of all, for it promised to put an end to a regime which had become intolerable. The deposition, if not the murder, of Paul had become inevitable in the natural course of events. Although everybody sympathized with the conspiracy, nothing was done until Alexander had given his consent to his father's deposition.

Those who approached Alexander after the murder often feared that his mind would be affected. I think I was of some use in preventing him from succumbing to the weight of the terrible thought that pursued him. Temporarily he found some consolation in the absorption of all his faculties, but I am certain that toward the end of his life it was the same terrible thought that so depressed him, filling him with a disgust of life and a piety which was perhaps exaggerated, but which is the sole possible and real support in the most poignant grief. When we return to this sad topic in our conversation, Alexander often repeated to me the details of the plans he had formed to establish his father in the palace of St. Michael, and afterwards to enable him as much as possible to reside in the imperial palaces in the country. . . . He judged of his father by himself. There was always in his noble character, a feminine element, with its strength and weaknesses. He often used to make plans which could not be realized, and on this idealistic foundation he raised complete structures which he made as perfect as possible. Nothing was more impracticable — especially in Russia — than the romantic means which Alexander has devised of rendering his father happy, while depriving him of his crown and of the possibility of tormenting and ruining the country. Alexander was not only young and inexperienced; he had almost the blind and confiding inexperience of childhood, and this characteristic remained with him for some years until it was destroyed by the realities of life.

A Friendly Description of Alexander I

The author of the following flattering descriptions of Alexander I was his intimate and devoted friend, the Countess de Choiseul-Gouffier. The Countess who was born at Vilna in Russian Poland, was the daughter of a wealthy land-owner. She first met the Tsar in 1812 and their friendship lasted until his death. The source is: Mme. la Comtesse de Choiseul-Gouffier (M. B. Patterson, Translator), Historical Memoirs of the Emperor Alexander I and The Court of Russia. 2d edition. Chicago: A. C. McClurg & Co., 1901. Pp. 82-83, 25.

Notwithstanding the regularity and delicacy of his features, the brightness and freshness of his complexion, his beauty was less striking at first sight, than that air of benevolence and kindness which captivated all hearts and instantly inspired confidence. His tall, noble, and majestic form, which often stooped a little with grace, like the pose of an antique statue, already threatened to become stout, but he was perfectly formed. His eyes were blue, bright and expressive; he was a little short-sighted. His nose was straight and well shaped, his mouth small and agreeable. The rounded contour of his face, as well as his profile, resembled that of his august mother. His forehead was somewhat bald, but this gave to his whole countenance an open and serene expression, and his hair, of a golden blond, carefully arranged as in the heads on antique cameos or medallions, seemed made to receive the triple crown of laurel, myrtle, and olive. He had an infinity of shades of tone and manner. When he addressed men of distinguished rank, it was with dignity and affability at the same time; to persons of his retinue, with an air of kindness almost familiar; to women of a certain age, with deference; and to young people, with an infinite grace, a refined and attractive manner, and a countenance full of expression.

This prince in his early youth had had his hearing seriously impaired by the report of a discharge of artillery, in consequence of which his left ear was somewhat deaf, and he usually turned the right toward the speaker to hear better.

.   .   .

Alexander loved to learn. He had a remarkable memory and quick, penetrating, and refined perceptions. In his early years he showed a taste for military science, occupying himself zealously with what he was pleased to call his service, following exactly and observing punctiliously the strictest discipline and subordination. He possessed in a high degree the love of order and work. That which one could not help most admiring in him was the perfect evenness of his temper, a quality very rare and very valuable in a sovereign, which had for its source the goodness of his heart. Nothing could change the sweet benevolence which showed itself in his face as well as in his actions.

Alexander spoke several languages, especially French, with elegance and fluency. His manners were charming. A certain timidity was noticeable in his early youth. No one ever possessed to a greater degree the happy gift of gaining all hearts; and no one, I am sure, could have seen Alexander and heard him speak without saying to himself, "How happy I should be to call this man my friend!"

Alexander's Character

Prince Adam Czartoryski, author of the following sketch of Alexander, was a brilliant Polish statesman who was drafted into the service of Paul in 1796. He served Paul well and was on intimate terms with him. Later he was intimately associated with Alexander whom he served in various official and unofficial capacities. Their close friendship continued throughout the Tsar's lifetime although Czartoryski did not hold office throughout the period. His comments upon Alexander are of especial interest due to the closeness of the two men. The source is: Gielgud, Memoirs, etc., vol. 1, pp. 118-120.

His opinions were those of one brought up in the ideas of 1789, who wishes to see republics everywhere, and looks upon that form of government as the only one in conformity with the wishes and the rights of humanity. Although I was myself at that time very enthusiastic — although born and brought up in a Republic where the principles of the French Revolution had been accepted with ardour — yet I had constantly to moderate the extreme opinions expressed by Alexander. He held, among other things, that hereditary monarchy was an unjust and absurd institution, and that the supreme authority should be granted not through the accident of birth but by the votes of the nation, which would best know who is most capable of governing it. I represented to him the arguments against this view, the difficulty and the risks of an election, what Poland had suffered from such an institution, and how little Russia was adapted to or prepared for it. I added that now at any rate Russia would not gain anything by the change, as she would lose the man who by his benevolent and pure intentions was most worthy of acceding to the throne. We had incessant discussions on this point. Sometimes during our long walks we talked of other matters. We turned from politics to nature, of whose beauties the young Grand-Duke was an enthusiastic admirer. One had to be a great lover of nature to discover its beauties in the country we walked in; but everything is relative in this world, and the Grand-Duke flew into ecstasies about a flower, the greenness of a tree, or the view over an undulating plain. There is nothing uglier or less picturesque than the neighbourhood of St. Petersburg. Alexander loved gardens and fields, and was fond of agriculture and the rustic beauty of village girls; the occupations and labours of the country, a simple, quiet, and retired life in some pretty farm, in a wide and smiling landscape — such was the dream he would have liked to realise, and to which he was always returning with a sigh.

I knew well that this was not the thing best suited to him; that for so high a destiny more elevation, force, ardour, and self-confidence were necessary than Alexander seemed to possess; that it was not right for a man in his position to wish to rid himself of the enormous burthen which was reserved for him, and to yearn for the pleasures of a quiet life. It was not enough to perceive and feel the difficulties of his position; he should have been filled with a passionate desire to surmount them. These reflections occasionally presented themselves to my mind, and even when I felt their truth, they did not diminish my feelings of admiration and devotion for Alexander. His sincerity, his frankness, his self-abandonment to the beautiful illusions that fascinated him, had a charm which it was impossible to resist. Moreover, he was still so young that his character might yet gain the qualities in which it was defective; circumstances and necessities might develop faculties which had not the time or the means of showing themselves; and although he was afterwards much changed, he retained to the last a portion of the tastes and opinions of his youth.

Many people — my countrymen especially — in later years reproached me for having placed too much confidence in Alexander's assurances. I have often maintained against his detractors that his opinions were sincere. The impression produced by the first years of our relations could not be effaced. Assuredly, when Alexander, at the age of eighteen, spoke to me with an effusiveness which relieved his mind, about opinions and sentiments which he concealed from everybody else, it was because he really felt them, and wished to confide them to someone. What other motive could he have had? Whom could he have wished to deceive? He certainly followed the inclination of his heart and expressed his real thoughts.

Besides our political discussions, and the ever-welcome topic of the beauties of nature, and the dream of a quiet country life after the destinies of free Russia should have been secured, Alexander had also a third object to which he ardently devoted himself, and which was not at all in accordance with the others, namely, the army, which was his hobby, as it was that of his father, the Grand-Duke Paul.

The Education of Alexander

The source is: Gielgud, Memoirs, etc., vol. 1, pp. 127-132.

It is certainly astonishing that Catherine, who took pleasure in the thought that Alexander would continue her reign and her glory, did not think of preparing him for this task by familiarising him in his early youth with the various branches of government. Nothing of the sort was attempted. Perhaps he would not have acquired very correct information on many things, but he would have been saved from the want of occupation. Yet it would seem that either the Empress and her council had no such idea, or that the former did not at least insist upon its being carried out. Alexander's education remained incomplete at the time of his marriage, in consequence of the departure of M. de la Harpe. He was then eighteen years old; he had no regular occupation, he was not even advised to work, and in the absence of any more practical task he was not given any plan of reading which might have helped him in the difficult career for which he was destined. I often spoke to him on this subject, both then and later. I proposed that he should read various books on history, legislation, and politics. He saw that they would do him good, and really wished to read them; but a Court life makes any continued occupation impossible. While he was Grand-Duke, Alexander did not read to the end a single serious book. I do not think he could have done so when he became Emperor, and the whole burthen of a despotic government was cast upon him. The life of a Court is fatiguing and yet idle. It furnishes a thousand excuses for indolence, and one is constantly busy in doing nothing. When Alexander came to his rooms it was to take rest and not to work. He read by fits and starts, without ardour or zeal. The passion of acquiring knowledge was not sufficiently strong in him; he was married too young, and he did not perceive that he still knew very little. Yet he felt the importance of useful study, and wished to enter upon it; but his will was not sufficiently strong to overcome the daily obstacles presented by the duties and unpleasantnesses of life. The few years of his early youth thus passed away, and he lost precious opportunities which he had in abundance so long as Catherine was alive, and of which he might have recovered a part even under the Emperor Paul.

While he was Grand-Duke, and even during the first years of his reign, Alexander remained what his education had made him, and was very different from what he became later on when he followed his natural propensities. It must be concluded that nature had endowed him with rare qualities, as notwithstanding the education he had received he became the most amiable sovereign of his age and the cause of Napoleon's fall. After having reigned for some years, and acquired the experience entailed by the necessity of at once taking the management of important affairs of State and by constant intercourse with men in office, people were surprised to find him not only an accomplished man of the world, but an able politician, with a penetrating and subtle mind, writing without assistance excellent letters on complicated and difficult subjects, and always amiable, even in the most serious conversations. What would he have become had his education been less neglected and more adapted to the duties which were to occupy his life? M. de la Harpe was the only man that can be mentioned with praise among those to whom the education of the two Grand-Dukes was entrusted. I do not know exactly who were the persons directed by Catherine to select their tutors; probably they were some encyclopædists of the clique of Grimm or the Baron d'Holbach.

M. de la Harpe does not seem to have directed Alexander into any serious course of study, though he had acquired so much influence over the Grand-Duke's mind and heart that I believe he could have made him do anything. Alexander derived from his teaching only some superficial knowledge; his information was neither positive nor complete. M. de la Harpe inspired him with the love of humanity, of justice, and even of equality and liberty for all; he prevented the prejudices and flatteries which surrounded him from stifling his noble instincts. It was a great merit in M. de la Harpe to have inspired and developed these generous sentiments in a Russian Grand-Duke, but Alexander's mind was not penetrated by them; it was filled with vague phrases, and M. de la Harpe did not sufficiently make him reflect on the immense difficulty of realising these ideas — on the thorny task of finding means to obtain possible results. He was, however, merely charged with Alexander's literary education; the choice which was made of those who were to look after his moral training was extraordinary. Count Nicholas Soltykoff, who was a subaltern during the Seven Years' War and had not since seen any active service (which did not prevent him from attaining the highest rank in the army), was the superintendent of the education of the two Grand-Dukes. Short, with a large head, affected, nervous, and of health so delicate that it required constant attention (he could not wear braces, and constantly hitched up his breeches like a sailor) he had the reputation of being the most astute courtier in Russia. When Catherine discovered that her favourite Momonoff had formed intimate relations with one of her maids of honour, she ordered the culprits to come before her, had them married, and then expelled them from her Court; after which Soltykoff at once introduced to her Plato Zuboff, who speedily became Momonoff's successor. The elevation of Zuboff so angered Prince Potemkin that he declared he would go to St. Petersburg to extract this tooth (*zub* means tooth in Russian); but he died before he could carry out his intention, and Soltykoff remained in high favour with the Empress. He was not only the channel by which her messages and admonitions were conveyed to the young princes; he also acted as intermediary whenever Catherine had anything to communicate to the Grand-Duke Paul. Soltykoff used to omit or soften any words which seemed too disagreeable or severe in the orders or the reproaches of his Imperial mistress, and he did the same with regard to the replies he had to convey to her. This gave satisfaction to both sides; he alone knew the truth, and took good care not to tell it. There was perhaps some merit in doing this successfully, but Count Soltykoff was certainly not the man to direct the education of the young heir to the throne, or to make a salutary impression on his character.

Besides Count Soltykoff, each of the two princes had a special director of studies with assistants. The selection of the two directors was even more extraordinary than that of the chief superintendent. The one attached to Alexander was Count Protasoff, whose only merit was to be the brother of the *demoiselle à portrait,* an old favourite of the Empress as to whose functions, though she was a good woman at heart, there were all sorts of extraordinary anecdotes. Constantine's special director was Count Sacken, a weak-minded man who was the object of incessant ridicule on the part of his pupil. Count Protasoff may justly be said to have been a complete imbecile; Alexander did not laugh at him, but he had never the smallest esteem for him. The assistant directors were selected solely by favour, with the exception of Mouravieff, whom Alexander when he ascended the throne made his secretary for petitions, and afterwards appointed curator of the schools of the Moscow district. He was a worthy man and was said to be well informed, but he was so timid as to be almost incapable of transacting business. I should also not omit Baron Budberg, who some years later succeeded me as Minister of Foreign Affairs.

Such surroundings could only produce a bad effect on the young princes, and the qualities displayed by Alexander are the more astonishing and praiseworthy, as he developed them notwithstanding the education he had received and the examples which were before his eyes.

A Feminine View of Alexander's Russia

During the Napoleonic Wars two young ladies of a distinguished Anglo-Irish family, Catherine and Martha Wilmot, paid an extended visit to Russia as guests of the famous Princess Dashkov. Their hostess was a most remarkable woman, an intimate of Catherine II, a gifted writer, the founder and the first president of the Russian Academy. Exiled by Paul to one of her distant estates, she was allowed to return to the vicinity of Moscow by Alexander I. With such a hostess, the Wilmot sisters had a most unusual opportunity to observe Russian life at first-hand. The source is: The Marchioness of Londonderry and M. M. Hyde (Editors), The Russian Journals of Martha and Catherine Wilmot, 1803-1808. London: Macmillan and Co., Ltd., 1934. Pp. 146-147, 199-201.

. . . There is a Small Meadow opposite to my Windows in which 150 Mowers are mowing this moment, Men & Women. All the Men are clothed in white linnen Jacket & trowsers (no that's a fib, white trowsers & a Shirt border'd at bottom with the scarlet work of the Peasants & likewise on the Shoulders, girdled round the waist with a guady girdle). The effect is excessively picturesque, and those who imagine the Russ peasantry sunk in sloth & misery imagine a strange falsehood. Wou'd to God our Paddys (dear Spalpines & Broaganeers that they are, for on my *oath* I doat down upon them) were half as well clothed or fed the year round as are the Russians. There is *for & against* in every state, but take the two Nations to Rob''s touchstones, "Have they eneough to eat, to drink?" "Have they Houses, firing & a bed to lie on?" and trust me the *Bears* would triumph, oh beyond comparison. If they are *Slaves* 'tis likewise the Master's interest to treat them kindly. His population constitutes his riches, & he who neglects or oppresses his subjects becomes their victim & sinks himself. Those indeed who class with Servants are different there. A Master's caprice comes in contact with every act of his Domestics, and as they *cannot be dischar'd* corporal punishment must be sometimes inflicted. Oh Zandy, there's what we Islanders cannot even bear to think of. Yet to sum up all in one word, the greatest punishment that can be inflicted is to be "given for a Soldier." 'Tis probably therefore that the former situations could not be *very* miserable, & *on ne peut desirer ce qu'on ne cannoit pas. . . .*

I believe I never mention'd Troitska. It is a fine place, the Princess has made it herself, and situated in the midst of 16 Villages belonging to her. Three thousand Peasants, "my subjects" (as she calls them) live most happily under her absolute power; and of all the blessed hearted beings that ever existed on that subject she is the most blessed (excepting your Mother). There are two hundred servants, taking in all denominations inside and outside, in this establishment, more than a hundred horses, two hundred stock of cows, and everything else in proportion. The Church establishment too belongs to her, and is built at the back of the House. A lovely wood belonging to the estate 9 miles long and 4 broad is within a few yards of the place inhabited by Wolves, and in it the Princess and I lost our way yesterday evening for an hour and half. A beautiful river winds all through the grounds and serpentines amidst the entire estate. However Troitska is a dead flat almost, and to the cultivation alone its beauty is attributable. An immense quantity of ground is laid out under shrubberies and all sorts of pleasure grounds completely in the English stile. The House is enormous with wings on either side which are only connected by balconies raised on iron railings up to the 2nd Story. Matty and I inhabit one of these wings and Anna Petrovna the other. 20 bearded Men are now busily employ'd in making a temporary wooden passage from the hall door to the door of our Castle, as in winter (strange to say) they had provided for no internal communication so much was sacrificed to the appearance of the outside.

There are a hundred whimsical and most ridiculous peculiarities of custom, such as letting you provide your own bed cloaths, in a Palace even! We have our own sheets, blankets and Quilts which we give to the washerwoman with our wearing apparel, and they would look upon one as extraordinary to expect the House was to provide for these things, as you would if I laid myself up at Glanmire and sent for your gown to wear as a matter of right. (Black eneough you'd look at me and soon eneough you'd shew me the door in case of such an outrage!) In fact this system of each person having a seperate little establishment is observ'd in more ways than that, for saucepans, candles, candlesticks, tea and coffee equipage and a hundred &c. &c. are regularly found in the care of the *Femmes de Chambre;* and I might lock my Castle door, or Anna Petrovna or Matty, and we have provisions to keep the Citadel a week in flourishing health. The system of hoards is without bounds, and presents appropriate to this comical system are perfectly the fashion. The Princess sent up a pair of silver candlesticks on our arrival here and a store of wax candles! I expected a spit or gridiron next, but tho' not exactly so we all got presents! When I left London I laid in as many beads, necklaces, and trinkets as if I was going to trade with Otahiete, and they are almost exhausted already amongst the band of Damsels who attend the Chambers fair. To be sure Eleanor comes in for costly offerings in return, but it is a torment and horrid waste of money, for bawbles accumulate without mercy; and besides one scarcely has the liberty of choice as on certain days they must be given and receiv'd or else outrage the customs of the Country and give universal offence. Matty has already provided 14 volumes beautifully bound in green and gold for Anna Petrovna's Easter gift; she has seen them and look'd them over, but till the day comes she is not to receive or acknowledge them.

In the midst of this immense Establishment and in the center of riches and honours I wish you were to see the Princess go out to take a walk, or rather to look over her subjects! An old brown great coat and a silk handkerchief about her neck worn to rags is her dress, & well may it be worn to rags for she has worn it 18 years and will continue to do so as long as she lives because it belong'd to Mrs. Hamilton. Her originality, her appearance, her manner of speaking, her doing every description of thing, (for she helps the masons to build walls, she assists with her own hands in making the roads, she feeds the cows, she composes music, she sings & plays, she writes for the press, she shells the corn, she talks out loud in Church and corrects the Priest if he is not devout, she talks out loud in her little Theatre and puts in the Performers when they are out in their parts, she is a Doctor, an Apothecary, a Surgeon, a Farrier, a Carpenter, a Magistrate, a Lawyer; in short she hourly practices every species of incongruity, corresponds with her brother, who holds the first post in the Empire, on his trade, with Authors, with Philosophers, with Jews, with Poets, with her Son, with all her Relations, and yet appears as if she had her time a burthen on her hands) altogether gives me eternally the idea of her being a Fairy! And I protest it is not jokingly I say so, for the impression never quits me for a moment. The marvellous contradiction too of her speaking like an Infant in her broken English and with her unaccountable expressions! She is unconscious whether she speaks French, English or Russian, and mingles these in every sentence. She speaks German and Italien equally well, but her pronunciation is not clear which takes from the pleasure I shou'd otherwise receive from her conversation. I have just finish'd reading Voltaire's, Diderot's, Garrick's & the Abbe Raynall's letters to her. She has promised me the Empress Catherine's, and I have also read a good part of her life written by herself. Indeed it is necessary to qualify oneself with the knowledge of public things and characters in Russia since the time of Catherine, since the Princess alludes to them perpetually and her mind wanders so naturally back to the Court & Study & Toilet & Boudoir of Catherine that I am beginning to fancy I recollect her habits of life & conversation & that I was a party concern'd in the revolution. By the by, the principal reception room at Troitska is ornamented with an immense picture of Catherine on Horseback in uniform taken the very day of her husband's destruction, & the P^ss says a perfect resemblance. Besides this there are Portraits of her in every room.

The Unofficial Committee

For a period of eight months during 1801 and 1802, Alexander associated himself with a group of young men of liberal reputation. This group, known as the Unofficial Committee was largely responsible for the reform of the Senate and the replacement of the colleges by ministries on the western model. Prince Czartoryski who wrote these accounts of the Committee and of the reforms was an active participant in the affairs which are here described. The source is: Gielgud (editor), Memoirs, etc., vol. 1, pp. 257–258, 260–263, 267, 279–280, 291–306, 322–325, 306–310. (Somewhat adapted.)

In order to remedy the discrepancy between Alexander's opinions and his acts, he established a Secret Council composed of persons whom he regarded as his friends and believed to be animated by sentiments and opinions in conformity with his own. The first nucleus of this Council was formed by the young Count Paul Strogonoff, M. de Novosiltzoff, and myself. We had long been in near relations with each other, and these now became more serious. The necessity of rallying round the Emperor and not leaving him alone in his desire of reform drew us more closely together. We were regarded for some years as models of intimate and unshakeable friendship. To be superior to every personal interest, and not to accept either presents or distinctions, was the principle of our alliance. Such a principle could not take root in Russia, but it was in accordance with the ideas of Alexander's youth and inspired him with special esteem for his friends. I was the sole author of the principle, which indeed was specially suited to my peculiar position. It was not always liked by my companions, and the Emperor himself afterwards grew tired of servants who wished to distinguish themselves by refusing to accept rewards which were so eagerly sought by everyone else.

The understanding between us had, as I have shown, begun at the coronation of the Emperor Paul at Moscow, and we had for a long time been on intimate terms, as we met daily at Count Strogonoff's. The fourth member admitted by the Emperor to the Secret Council was Count Kotchoubey.

.   .   .

We were priveleged to dine with the Emperor without a previous invitation and we used to meet two or three times a week. After coffee and a little conversation, the Emperor used to retire, and while the other guests left the palace, the four members of the Secret Council entered through a corridor into a little dressing-room, which was in direct communication with the private rooms of their Majesties, and there met the Emperor. Various plans of reforms were debated; each member brought his ideas, and sometimes his work, and information which he had obtained as to what was passing in the existing administration and the abuses which he had observed. The Emperor freely expressed his thoughts and sentiments, and although the discussions at these meetings for a long time had no practical result, no useful reform was tried or carried out during Alexander's reign which did not originate in them. Meanwhile the Official Council, namely, the Senate and the Ministers, governed the country in the old way. Directly the Emperor left his dressing-room he came under the influence of the old Ministers, and could do nothing of what had been decided upon in the Secret Council; it was like a masonic lodge from which one entered the practical world.

This mysterious Council, which was not long concealed from the suspicions, or ultimately from the knowledge, of the Court, and was designated "the young men's party," grew impatient at not obtaining any result whatever from its deliberations; it pressed the Emperor to carry out the views he had expressed to us and the proposals he considered desirable and necessary. Once or twice an attempt was made to induce him to adopt energetic resolutions, to give orders and make himself obeyed, to dismiss certain superannuated officials who were a constant obstacle to every reform and to put young men in their place. But the Emperor's character inclined him to attain his end by compromises and concessions, and moreover he did not yet feel sufficiently master of the position to risk measures which he thought too violent. In our Council, Strogonoff was the most ardent, Novosiltzoff the most prudent, Kotchoubey the most time-serving, and I the most disinterested, always striving to curb undue impatience. Those who urged the Emperor to take immediate and severe measures did not know him. Such a proposal always made him draw back, and was of a nature to diminish his confidence. But as he complained of his Ministers and did not like any of them, an attempt was made in the Council, before inducing him to change them, to discuss abstract considerations of reform which had previously occupied us. Strogonoff accepted the post of Procurator of the First Department of the Senate; and Novosiltzoff was appointed one of the Emperor's secretaries, a place which gave him many advantages, as every letter addressed to the Emperor passed through his hands, and he had a right to publish the Emperor's ukases. His special department, however, was at first to deal with promotors of public undertakings, who are sometimes men of talent, but more often adventurers of very doubtful honesty who flock to Russia from abroad at the beginning of each new reign. This was a duty for which he was qualified by his varied knowledge in matters of finance and industry, and it was at the same time a school which did much to form his character. I must not here forget the fifth member of the Secret Council, M. de la Harpe, Alexander's tutor, who had come on a visit to his former pupil. He did not take part in the after dinner meetings, but he used to have private conversations with the Emperor, and frequently handed to him memoranda reviewing all the branches of the administration. These memoranda were first read at the secret sittings, and afterwards passed on from one member of the Council to the other to be considered at leisure, as they were interminable long. M. de la Harpe was at that time about forty-four years of age; he had been a member of the Swiss Directory, and always wore the uniform of that appointment, with a large sword fastened to an embroidered belt outside his coat. We were all of opinion that he did not merit his high reputation and the esteem in which Alexander held him. He belonged to the generation of men nourished with the illusions of the last part of the eighteenth century, who thought their doctrine a sort of philosopher's stone, or universal remedy which removed all difficulties to the regeneration of society. M. de la Harpe had his own particular panacea for Russia, and he explained it in such diffuse papers that Alexander himself had not the courage to read them. One of his favourite phrases was *organisation réglementairs;* an important idea no doubt, but he used to repeat it so often and with such emphasis that it was at last attached to him as a sort of nickname.

. . .

During the summer of 1801 the Secret Council continued to meet. The only measure it decided upon before the coronation was the dismissal of Count Panin, whose participation in the conspiracy which brought about the death of Paul filled Alexander with dislike and suspicion. After much discussion it was resolved that Panin should be succeeded as Minister of Foreign Affairs by Count Kotchoubey, but should be allowed to remain at St. Petersburg. The Emperor, wishing to avoid disagreeable scenes, treated Panin as a Minister up to the last moment, and this again was interpreted as a sign of duplicity. The Emperor's will was notified as to Panin by letter, the Kotchoubey entered upon his duties to the great satisfaction of Alexander and of our council.

. . .

The Emperor was at that time beginning to pay special attention to foreign affairs. Kotchoubey, the Foreign Minister, had adopted a system which he believed to be in entire conformity with the Emperor's opinions and views, and at the same time with his own. This was to hold Russia aloof from European affairs, and to keep on good terms with all foreign Powers, so as to devote all her time and attention to internal reforms. Such was indeed the Emperor's wish and that of his intimate advisers, but none of them had adopted it with more conviction, or maintained it with more persistence, than Kotchoubey. Russia, he used to say, is great and powerful enough both as regards population and extent of territory, and geographical position; she has nothing to fear from any one so long as she leaves other Powers in peace; and she has too often mixed herself up with matters which did not directly affect her. Nothing had happened in Europe but she claimed to have a part in it; she had made costly and useless wars. The Emperor Alexander was now in such a fortunate position that he could remain at peace with all the world and devote himself to internal reforms. It was at home, not abroad, that Russia could make immense conquests, by establishing order, economy, and justice in all parts of her vast empire, and by making agriculture, commerce, and industry flourish. European affairs and European wars were of no advantage whatever to the numerous inhabitants of the Russian Empire; they only lost their lives through them or had to furnish new recruits and taxes. What was necessary to their prosperity was a long peace and the incessant care of a wise and pacific administration—a task eminently suited to the Emperor, with his ideas of reform and liberal government.

This system was somewhat similar to that advocated by the English radicals. The idea is plausible and not without a basis of truth, but it has the disadvantage of reducing to insignificance and humiliation the State which follows it too literally, as by so doing it incurs the risk of becoming the vassal and tool of more enterprising and active States. Moreover, a consistent adherence to such a system would require much tact and firmness to avoid damaging compromises, which, in the then existing state of European relations, would have become almost inevitable.

Alexander's Dream of Reforms

At length the Emperor's vague and floating ideas were consolidated into a practical shape. All the eccentric views which were mere fireworks were abandoned, and Alexander had to restrict his wishes to the realities and possibilities of the moment. He consoled himself by indulging in his hours of leisure, which were daily becoming more rare, in hopes of progress which enabled him not to give up entirely the dreams of his youth. These dreams seemed to me like a tree transplanted into a dry and arid soil and deprived of its exuberant vegetation, whose despoiled trunk puts forth a few weak branches and then perishes. The Emperor's first step was to issue an ukase or manifesto to restore the authority and dignity of the Senate; this was a prudent course, calculated to predispose the public for the changes which were to follow. In speaking of the Senate he spoke a language which the Russians understood and which flattered the nobility; it was already the Supreme Court of Justice and Administration, for although every order of the Emperor, whether written or spoken, had the force of law, they had (especially those relating to general administration and the civil and criminal law) all to be addressed to the Senate, which was entrusted with the task of publishing them and seeing to their due execution. The various departments of the Senate were charged not only with trying on final appeal the civil and criminal cases of the empire, but also with punishing contraventions of the administrative regulations. It had the right of issuing ukases of its own founded on those of the Emperor, and, when necessary, explaining and developing them; and it presented him with reports for his approval. The governors and financial authorities of the provinces were under its direct supervision, and it was their duty to send to the Senate regular and formal reports upon which the sovereign gave such orders as he pleased. It was accordingly called "The Senate administering the Empire." Its vague functions, partly judicial and partly executive, were not in accordance with modern ideas, being so cumbrous in form that they retarded and might even embarrass the course of government; but there was no way of touching this ancient organisation without exposing internal affairs to even greater confusion, as the institution of the Senate had become part of the routine and the habits of the government machine. The Senate was consequently allowed to retain its administrative functions, though it was intended to let them fall by degrees into desuetude. All its powers were confirmed in pompous terms of which the author was Vorontzoff, and to them was added the right of making representations on the Emperor's ukases. It was at the same time laid down that all the Ministers should make detailed reports of their functions which the Emperor would send to the Senate for its opinion.

This, it was hoped, would be a first step in the direction of national and representative government. The idea was to deprive the Senate of its executive powers, to leave it those of a Supreme Court of Justice, and gradually to convert it into a sort of upper chamber to which would afterwards be attached deputies of the nobility who, either as part of the chamber or as a separate body, would, for the Emperor's information, state their views on the management of affairs by the Ministers and on the laws which were in existence or in preparation. This plan was never carried out, and what really happened was very different.

Those who think that the Senate of St. Petersburg can ever be of any importance for the destinies of Russia are entirely mistaken, and only show that they do not know Russia. The Russian Senate in its present form is less able than any political body in the world to make itself respected or to act on its own initiative. It can neither give an impulse nor even receive one, it is a marionette which one can move about as one pleases, but which has no motive power of its own.

Those who are tired of official life and wish to retire and live quietly in idleness are the sort of people who seek the appointment of Senator. The Senate thus becomes a receptacle for the indolent and the superannuated; all its work is done by the procurators and the secretaries, who decide questions at their pleasure and then take the decisions to the Senators, who as a rule sign them without reading them. These decrees are drawn up in a more diffuse and tedious style even than the official documents of other countries; the minutes in each case fill an immense volume, and it would require some courage to read them. One or two Senators who do read the decrees that are submitted to them for signature are spoken of with admiration as heroes. It is evident that such a political body is incapable of undertaking or following up any reform.

After laying the first stone of the edifice of a regulated legislative power, and devising a limit to the autocratic power, the Emperor turned his attention to the organisation of his government, so as to make its action more enlightened, more just, and more methodical. The government machine was irregular and intermittent in its action, and the administration was a chaos in which nothing was regulated or clearly defined. The only administrative authorities that were recognised were the Senate and the Committees of War, of the Navy, and of Foreign Affairs. These were not deliberative or consultative bodies; one of the members of each committee, usually the president, brought the reports of the committee to the sovereign and then informed it of his decisions. The Procurator-General united in his person the offices of Minister of the Interior, of Police, of Finance, and of Justice; but sometimes the sovereign created separate departments, and the Empress Catherine placed the conquered provinces under the direction of one of her favourites, such as Potemkin or Zuboff, who were independent of the Senate and reported direct to the sovereign. Moreover, when the reports of the Senate and the various committees were handed to the sovereign by the Ministers or other high functionaries of State, they were often put away in a drawer, and after some time had elapsed a decision totally opposed to the one suggested was issued. Thus there was practically no bar to the caprice of the sovereign. Paul, who thought he was a great general, and was especially jealous of any control over the army apart from his own, appointed one of his aides-de-camp in whom he had confidence to examine and submit to him all the proposals of the War Committee, and all promotions and appointments. The direction of Foreign Affairs was nominally entrusted to a committee of three members, each of whom worked with the sovereign separately, and had the management of some particular question which was kept a secret from his colleagues. This post was much sought after, and Catherine's favourites obtained some magnificent presents from foreign powers in employing for a negotiation with which they had been charged by the Empress one of the members of the Foreign Affairs Committee on whose complaisance they could rely. This was the case with Prince Zuboff and Count Markoff, who were handsomely rewarded for advocating the two last partitions of Poland.

In the time of the Emperor Paul foreign affairs were often directed by his favourite aides-de-camp. The Vice-Chancellor or the eldest of the members of the committee only had the direction of the administrative and financial branch, and of the current correspondence. This system suited an able sovereign like the Empress Catherine, who, notwithstanding its disadvantages and a complete absence of unity, still ultimately carried out a consistent policy. Paul, with his incessant caprices and changes of mind, yet had a most decided, almost furious, will which all the wheels of the government machine had at once to obey. But with a sovereign of vacillating character it is evident that the system of administration above described must lead to serious evils. The Emperor was continually exposed to making mistakes, to seeing only one side of a question; he was liable to be confused by a mass of opinions from persons many of whom had an interest in not letting him know the whole truth; and he could never advance towards a definite object. Russia therefore had reason to be grateful to the Emperor Alexander and those whose advice he then followed for having sought to introduce more order and method in the Imperial administration.

The object of the reform was to establish a system somewhat similar to those adopted in most other European States by separating the departments, defining their limits, assembling in each department matters of the same kind, centralising their management, and thereby augmenting the responsibility of the principal functionaries of State. It was hoped among other things that this would be an efficacious means of checking the numberless abuses and frauds which are the curse of Russia. The Emperor accordingly created for the first time Ministries of the Interior and of Police, of Finance, of Justice, of Public Instruction, of Commerce, of Foreign Affairs, of War, and of the Navy. As to the War Department, Alexander continued the system adopted by his father, insisting that everything relating to the army, down to the smallest appointment, should emanate direct from the sovereign, and that the army should know it. The post of aide-de-camp charged with the management of the *personnel* of the army became gradually converted, in imitation of Napoleon, into that of Major-General, so as to show that Russia always considers herself in a state of war, and wishes to be in position to make war at any moment. In the manifesto establishing the changes above referred to, it was stated that all the Emperor's ukases were in future to be countersigned by one of the Ministers—an attempt to introduce the principle of responsibility—and the Ministers were directed to meet in a council, in which they were to discuss the most important questions of State. This was a new administrative machine superior to the Senate, which retained all its functions and was invested with new ones; but those which related to administration properly so called, became in its case almost purely formal. By the creation of the new Ministers the administrative authority of the Government was concentrated, while hitherto it had not had any legal or definite status except in the person of the sovereign. The Council of State also was not changed, although some of its most eminent members became Ministers. The Emperor continued occasionally to refer to this Council various disagreeable or complicated questions, in order to give it something to do, and not let it die too soon; but it speedily perished through its insignificance, and Alexander afterwards created another Imperial Council on quite a different and much more extensive plan.

These changes, which elsewhere would seem the very A B C of politics, seemed at that time to the Russians novel and immense. The manifesto made much noise in the whole Empire and especially in the salons of St. Petersburg and Moscow; each man had his own opinion of it, and the majority judged it not by its intrinsic merits or the benefits it might confer on the State, but by the effect it would be likely to have on their own advancement. Those who obtained places approved it, while those who remained in the cold criticised the juvenile infatuation that wished to change the old and venerable institutions under which Russia had become great. The personages high in office who had not been consulted, and did not expect so considerable a change, were taken by surprise, finding themselves eclipsed by those who during the reign of Paul and the beginning of that of Alexander had held aloof. They strove to vent their disappointment by smiling with pity at the young men who were trying to reform the Empire, and at the foolishness of some older men who consented to be the instruments of a servile and awkward imitation of foreign institutions. The easy good-nature of the Emperor encouraged these criticisms, so far as they were possible in Russia, and they found a certain amount of support in the Empress Dowager, who was annoyed; without admitting it, at not having been more consulted by her son and at not being able to influence his decisions. She perceived in all these novelties a germ of liberalism whose development she feared, and her salon became a centre of opposition where people came to express their discontent.

The head of the new administration was Count Alexander Vorontzoff, who was made Foreign Minister, and also Chancellor—a title which had not been given to any one for years. Kotchoubey had entirely to reorganise an administration which had been long neglected, and which in the more distant provinces was without any direction or supervision, and given up to all the abuses arising from the ignorance and cupidity of subordinate officials. It was a noble and arduous task, and if he did not succeed as well as he had wished, it was not for want of zeal or good will. He began by organising his office, dividing it into several sections, each of which had to deal with a distinct branch of the vast department. He invited the assistance of all the able and experienced officials he could find, and endeavoured to raise in general estimation the post of Governor of a province by appointing in that capacity men whose character and position afforded guarantees of integrity, and who, though inexperienced in official work, were likely soon to obtain the necessary knowledge. It seemed as if order was going to break through the chaos, and the immediate effects of the change were soon felt by the people.

One of the reforms he introduced was in the supply of salt, which in Russia is a matter of great importance. This was not nominally a Government monopoly, but the Government alone was able to supply salt to all parts of the Empire by obtaining it from the salt marshes or distilling it from sea-water. Kotchoubey took steps to reduce the cost of production and of conveyance to the lowest posible point, so as to enable the people to buy salt more cheaply, and the Government to be repaid its expenses.

The new Finance Minister was Count Vasilieff, a capable and honest official who had in financial matters been the right hand of Prince Viaziemskoy, the only Procurator-General who had been mentioned with praise at the time of the Empress Catherine. In the various changes which had taken place since the Prince's death in 1794, M. Vasilieff, as treasurer of the Empire, had been indispensable; he was a steady worker, appreciated new ideas, and adopted them when he thought they were opportune. All the branches of the public revenue, the brandy traffic, the Imperial Bank, etc., were comprised in this department, to which was added the mines department, which had been reorganised on a larger scale.

The functions of Minister of Justice were united to those of Procurator-General of the Senate. General Beklescheff did not wish to stop in this department, as it had been deprived of the greater part of its functions by the creation of the Ministers of the Interior and of Finance; and he was succeeded by the Senator Dzierzanin. He was the personal choice of the Emperor, without comunication with the Secret Council. A worthy man, and the writer of some much admired lyrics which were full of swing and passion, he was imperfectly educated and knew no language but Russian. The Emperor had been attracted to him by his ardent sentiments and poetic dreams, not being able to resist fine phrases; the vaguer they were the better they pleased him, as he could then easily assimilate them to his hopes, which also were not very clear. He liked expressions of energetic liberalism, and was especially attracted by admiration of himself when it was couched in the language of devotion to the cause of humanity.

The Emperor had direct and special relations with certain persons whom he himself introduced at our meetings; he liked to patronise them and defend them against objections raised sometimes by people who knew them more intimately. It gave him pleasure to have these relations without the knowledge of his friends, who already at that time had begun to displease him because they were so united among themselves. Yet it was absolutely necessary to introduce members of "the young men's party" into the administration, for all Alexander's hopes rested upon them for the zealous continuation and accomplishment of the reforms he had at heart. Kotchoubey was provided for, but what was to be done with the others? It would be too much to make them Ministers, and it was accordingly decided that assistants to the Ministers should be appointed; in this way the Emperor's friends would be able to direct their chiefs in accordance with the Emperor's views, and to keep him fully acquainted with what was going on.

Count Paul Strogonoff was at his request appointed assistant to the Minister of the Interior, and Novosiltzoff obtained the post of assistant to the Minister of Justice, retaining his former appointment of Secretary of the Emperor. This gave Novosiltzoff the most important place in the administration, as it was through him that the Emperor was to begin the work of reforming jurisprudence and the existing laws. He was well qualified for the task, as he had studied jurisprudence and political economy in England, and had more good use of the opportunities thereby afforded him of becoming conversant with those subjects. No one in Russia was at that time his superior in that administrative knowledge which was then only to be obtained by reading French and English works. His practical mind rejected all vain theories; he possessed skill and tact in dealing not only with individuals, but with the Russian public, which he knew thoroughly. He had bad qualities also; but these had not yet developed themselves. One of his greatest merits was that he seconded Alexander's wishes as to the improvement of the condition of the peasants, and he drew up the first ukase on this subject. He also reconstituted the commission for the revision of the law. This commission had been formed by the Empress Catherine, who thereby gained the flattering appreciation of Voltaire and the Diderots; but the only result was the publication of the philanthropic and philosophical instructions addressed by Catherine to the commission. It was dissolved soon after, and its proceedings were never made public. The new commission was organised by Novosiltzoff with the assistance of a German jurist, Baron Rosenkampf, on a vast and well-conceived plan. It was directed to codify all the existing Russian laws, which were very numerous and often contradicted each other, classifying them according to subjects, omitting such as were obsolete, and adding new ones when necessary, but taking care to retain in the new codes all that had entered for many years into the life of the Russian people, even if not quite reconcilable with the ideas of modern jurisprudence. The system adopted was somewhat similar to that of Justinian; but the task of the Russian codifiers was far more difficult than that of the Roman ones. The latter merely had to select and classify out of a somewhat confused mass of laws, most of which were admirable examples of wisdom and legislative science, while in Russia the laws were not only confused, but in many respects defective and insufficient. For such a work not only jurists, but real legislators were wanted. A similar code was to be prepared for the outlying provinces of the Empire, such as Livonia, Esthonia, Courland, and the Polish provinces of Little Russia, each of which had its own particular language, laws, and customs.

This great undertaking was begun methodically and pursued for some time with activity; Novosiltzoff was allowed by the Minister of Justice to make it his exclusive occupation. The classifications were prepared by Baron Rosenkampf, and so long as they were adhered to the work progressed; but it did not produce the results which were expected of it. This is usually the case in Russia; if there is no immediate result, the persons entrusted with the execution of the work are changed, and it has to be begun over again.

I was the only member of the Secret Council who remained without employment. Alexander offered me, with Count Vorontzoff's concurrence, the post of assistant to the Minister of Foreign Affairs, and all my friends, the Emperor especially, pressed me to accept the offer. I hesitated for a long time, feeling how much surprise and dissatisfaction such an appointment would cause in Russia. The Emperor observed that during my mission to the King of Sardinia I had made myself favourably known by my despatches, and that my nomination to the Foreign Office ought not therefore to be a matter of astonishment, besides which Count Vorontzoff, who alone had a right to be consulted on the subject, had consented to my becoming his assistant. I replied that he (the Emperor) knew more than anyone my feelings with regard to my country; that they could never change, and that I had some reason to fear that they might be incompatible with the duties of the appointment he wished to give me; the safest and most proper course, therefore, would be for me not to accept it. To this Alexander rejoined that he did not at present anticipate any such contradiction as that which I feared; that I should always be at liberty to give up my post if such a contradiction were to arise; and that, on the contrary, he thought that events would occur which would be favourable to my views. He added some very flattering expressions with regard to my qualifications for the post. It is every man's duty, he said, to pay his debt to humanity; when one has talents one must not refuse to employ them in the most useful way. I still declined, but Alexander was bent 'on my taking the appointment; this was one of his irresistible fancies which nothing could induce him to abandon until they were satisfied. His persistence and kindness to me were such that at length I yielded, on the express condition that I should be allowed to resign the appointment directly its functions should become incompatible with my feelings as a Pole. My chief object in this was, by spending some years in the Emperor's service, to prove to him my sincere attachment and my gratitude for his friendship and confidence. I accepted with some sadness, as by so doing I was entering on a new career full of pitfalls which would retain me at St. Petersburg.

Reforms in Practice: the Senate

The progress of internal reform in Russia was abruptly stopped by an unexpected incident. Count Severin Potocki, who, as I said above, was a great admirer of the Emperor, often addressed memoranda to him on various subjects. The Senate had received from the Emperor, among other important prerogatives, the right of making representations to him, but it had hitherto not made any use of this right. Count Severin naturally thought the Emperor was sincere in his liberal opinions; the Emperor himself thought so; and the Count therefore imagined it would be a good thing, and would please his Imperial master, if the Senate were prompted to exercise its prerogatives. For this an opportunity soon presented itself. Although almost every noble in Russia entered the army, he was not obliged to do so, and could leave it when he thought proper. This double privilege was granted by Peter III in an ukase for which many blessed his memory. Alexander, however, restricted the privilege to nobles who held the rank of officers, those below that rank were obliged to serve for twelve years. This was looked upon as an attack on the guaranteed rights of the nobility, and produced a deep and painful sensation. The Minister of War, an old military bureaucrat of low origin, was said to be the author of the new ukase, and Count Severin Potocki proposed to the Senate that it should address representations to the Emperor on this violation of the nobles' charter. His proposal was read to the general assembly of all the departments, and the senators, seeing that one of the confidential advisers of the Court was taking the initiative in the matter, and that his opinion was warmly supported by Count Strogonoff, thought they could safely vote in its favour. They gladly did this, under the impression that by so doing they could without danger assume an air of independence in a matter to which it was believed the Emperor did not attach any serious importance. Count Severin's proposal was adopted, notwithstanding the opposition of the Procurator-General (Minister of Justice), which was supposed to be feigned in order to give more appearance of reality to the little scene which it was believed had been got up for the occasion. Count Strogonoff, who was deputed with two other senators to take the representations of the Senate to the Emperor, readily set out on his mission; but the deputation was received by Alexander very coldly, and Strogonoff, disconcerted and not knowing what to say, withdrew. The Emperor sharply reprimanded the Senate, ordered it not to meddle with things which did not concern it, and directed it by a new decree to carry out the very ukase against which it had appealed. To my great astonishment that it was Novosiltzoff who was the agent of the Emperor's move of the Senate in the direction of liberalism sufficed to discourage people whose generous aspirations were not, it must be admitted, very strong. The Senate did not again attempt any independent action, and its rights became a dead letter. At my first interview with the Emperor after this incident, I could not help smiling at his extreme alarm in presence of the new attitude of the Senate. My jocular remarks on this point were ill received by Alexander, and I believe they left in his mind a certain anxiety as to my liberal tendencies which afterwards came back to him. This was an indication of Alexander's true character, which then appeared to me in a novel and unfortunately too real light. Grand ideas of the general good, generous sentiments, and the desire to sacrifice to them part of the Imperial authority, and resign an immense and arbitrary power in order the better to secure the future happiness of the people, had really occupied the Emperor's mind and did so still, but they were rather a young man's fancies than a grown man's decided will. The Emperor liked forms of liberty as he liked the theatre; it gave him pleasure and flattered his vanity to see the appearances of free government in his Empire; but all he wanted in this respect was forms and appearances; he did not expect them to become realities. In a word, he would willingly have agreed that every man should be free, on the condition that he should voluntarily do only what the Emperor wished.

Reforms in Practice: Education

The creation of a Ministry of Public Instruction was a remarkable innovation in Russia which was fruitful of great and salutary results, and posterity will owe gratitude both to Alexander and to the young men, then so much criticised, who supported him in his plans and gave them practical shape by dividing into special branches the confused organisation which was then in existence. Nothing could be more wretched or insufficient than public instruction in Russia up to the reign of Alexander. There was an Academy of Science at St. Petersburg which owed its only celebrity to the presence of some learned men whom the Government had brought to the Russian capital from abroad. Euler came when he was already an old man, and died there soon after. The transactions of this Academy were for the most part written in the French and German languages; it had no relations whatever with the country, and exercised no influence on its progress. At Moscow there was a university which was equally isolated, and was attended by not more than a hundred students maintained at the expense of the Government. The only other educational establishments in Russia proper were the so-called "National Schools." The teaching in these schools was bad and extremely meagre; the teachers were poor wretches whom idleness and *ennui* had rendered drunkards, and no respectable person sent his children to them. The establishment of the Ministry of Public Instruction completely changed all this. The existing universities of Moscow, Wilna, and Dorpat were better endowed, and three new ones were created—those of St. Petersburg, Kharkoff, and Kazan,—each forming an educational centre for a prescribed district, in which it directed all the educational arrangements. The University of Wilna was exclusively Polish, and during the next few years the whole of Russian Poland was covered with schools in which Polish feeling freely developed itself. This University, to which I appointed the most distinguished literary and scientific men of the country, and some eminent professors from abroad, directed the movement with admirable zeal and intelligence, and its consequences, which the Russians afterwards deeply regretted, seemed at that time to flow naturally from the Emperor's generous intentions with regard to the Poles. The University of Kazan was to look after the instruction of the Tartars and of Siberia generally. Each university had its curator, and the curators formed a council of public instruction, the President of which was the Minister. The persons appointed to these posts by the Emperor were such as to give a hope that the work of public instruction would be pushed forward with zeal and success. General Klinger, commandant of one of the cadet corps, was appointed curator of Dorpat. He was a distinguished German author, with liberal opinions which might almost be called utopian, although he had been in the service of the greatest despots; his intentions, however, were good, and he was full of zeal for the advancement of science and instruction. His eccentric and dreamy views were expressed with a German bluntness which gave him an appearance of frankness and energy, and all this had gained him Alexander's favour. Count Severin Potocki was appointed Curator of the University of Kharkoff, which was the centre of a district the inhabitants of which were strongly desirous of obtaining the means of instruction. Count Severin, as a Pole, had been treated with great consideration by Alexander when he was Grand-Duke; he had been admitted, like my brother and myself, into his familiar circle, and was one of his most enthusiastic admirers. The Emperor appointed him not only curator of Kharkoff, but also senator of the third department of the Senate, which issued decisions on appeals against measures taken by the administrations of the Polish provinces. Count Severin obtained some celebrity in Russia as a senator and in his capacity of curator he showed zeal and perseverance.

The universities which were most progressive were Wilna, Dorpat, and Kharkoff. The nobility of Livonia, Esthonia, and Courland did not look with favour upon the University of Dorpat, which had declared itself the protector of the peasants and the bourgeoisie. One of the professors of this university was named Parot; he was a worthy man who expressed boundless attachment to the Emperor Alexander, and was very anxious about his health. Once Madame Parot sent a waistcoat, woven by herself, which she said would preserve the Emperor's life. Parot begged him to wear it, and by such manifestations of affection he gained Alexander's favour, and had private conferences with him during his frequent journeys to St. Petersburg. The Curator of Moscow was M. de Mouravieff, one of the gentlemen formerly attached to Alexander's service when he was Grand-Duke, and also his former secretary. He was a worthy man, but excessively timid and quite devoid of energy. The Emperor appointed him assistant to the Minister of Instruction in order that it should not be said that young men only performed the duties of assistant, and that these posts were created only for the members of the

Secret Council. Novosiltzoff was appointed Curator of St. Petersburg. As there was already in that capital a faculty of medicine dependent on the Ministry of the Interior, and a faculty of law could not be established before the commission for the revision of the laws had terminated its labours, Novosiltzoff for the present confined himself to establishing a faculty of philosophy, with the special object of training professors of the exact sciences, of administration, and of literature. This faculty began brilliantly by turning out some distinguished pupils, but they did not afterwards realize the hopes that had been formed of them, and the institution perished without leaving any durable results. A university with privileges and endowments would have better maintained itself, as was shown by the universities of Moscow and Kharkoff, which, though they declined, were still active in the midst of the indifference and oblivion by which they were long surrounded.

The Napoleonic Invasion

Alexander I bought time by the Treaties of Tilsit of 1807. That time ran out when on the 23d of June, 1812, Napoleon led his army of 600,000 troops across the River Nieman into Russia. Two days later, Alexander issued to his army the propaganda appeal which is printed below. The source is: Wilson, General Sir Robert (H. Randolph, editor) Narrative of Events during The Invasion of Russia by Napoleon Bonaparte, and the Retreat of the French Army. 1812. *London, 1860. Pp. 23–24. Sir Robert was the official British military observer attached to the Russian armies at the time of the invasion.*

PROCLAMATION TO THE ARMY. Wilna, the 25th of June, 1812. We had long observed on the part of the Emperor of the French the most hostile proceedings towards Russia, but we had always hoped to avert them by conciliatory and pacific measures. At length, experiencing a continued renewal of direct and evident aggression, notwithstanding our earnest desire to maintain tranquillity, we were compelled to complete and assemble our armies. But even then we flattered ourselves that a reconciliation might be effected while we remained on the frontiers of our empire and, without violating one principle of peace, were prepared only to act in our own defence: all these conciliatory and pacific measures could not preserve the tranquillity which we desired. The Emperor of the French, by suddenly attacking our army at Kowno, has been the first to declare war. As nothing, therefore, could inspire him with those friendly sentiments which possessed our bosoms, we have no choice but to oppose our forces to those of the enemy, invoking the aid of the Almighty, the witness and the defender of the truth. It is unnecessary for me to recall to the minds of the generals, the officers, or the soldiers, their duty and their bravery. The blood of the valiant Slavonians flows in their veins. Warriors! you defend your religion, your country, and your liberty! I am with you. God is against the aggressor.

Within a month after the start of the Napoleonic invasion, Alexander found it necessary to issue a general appeal to his subjects and a special call to the City of Moscow. These examples of early nineteenth century war propaganda are from: Wilson, op. cit., pp. 46–50.

First Proclamation. To the Nation. The enemy has passed the frontiers, and carried his arms into the interior of Russia. Since perfidy cannot destroy an empire which has existed with a dignity always increasing for so many generations, he has determined to attack it by violence, and to assault the empire of the Czars with the forces of the continent of Europe.

With treason in the heart and loyalty on the lips, he flatters the ears of the credulous and enchains their arms; and if the captive perceives fetters under the flowers, the spirit of domination discovers itself; and he calls forth war to assure the work of treason! But Russia has penetrated his views. The path of loyalty is open to her: she has invoked the protection of God; she opposes to the plots of her enemy an army strong in courage, and eager to drive from her territory this race of locusts who consume the earth, and whom the earth will reject, finding them too heavy a burden to sustain.

We call our sufficient armies to annihilate the enemy. Our soldiers who are under arms are like lions who dart on their prey; but we do not disguise from our faithful subjects that the intrepid courage of our warriors actually under arms needs to be supported by an interior line of troops. The means ought to be proportioned to the object; and the object placed before you is to overthrow the tyrant who wishes to overthrow all the earth.

We have called on our ancient city of Moscow, the first capital of our empire, to make final efforts, and she is accustomed to make them, by sending her sons to the succour of the empire. After her, we call on all our subjects of Europe and Asia to unite themselves for the cause of humanity! We call on all our civil and religious communities to co-operate with us by a general rising against the universal tyrant.

Wherever in this empire he turns his steps he will be assured of finding our native subjects laughing at his frauds, scorning his flattery and his falsehoods, trampling on his gold with the indignation of offended virtue, and paralyzing, by the feeling of true honour, his legions of slaves. In every noble Russian he will find a Pojarskoi, in every ecclesiastic a Palistyn, in every peasant a Minin.

Nobles! you have been in all ages the defenders of our country! Holy Synod! and you members of your Church! you have in all circumstances by your intercession called down upon our empire the Divine protection! Russian people! intrepid posterity of Slavonians! it is not the first time that you have plucked out the teeth from the head of the lion, who sprung on you as upon a prey, and met his own destruction! Unite yourselves! carry the cross in your hearts and the sword in your hands, and human force never can prevail against you.

I have delegated the organization of the new levies to the nobles of every province; and I have charged with the care of assembling the brave patriots who will present themselves of their own accord for the defence of the country the gentlemen amongst whom the officers will be chosen. The number of those who will be assembled ought to be sent to Moscow, where they will be made acquainted with the commander-in-chief.

Given at our camp of Polo⁺zk, the 18th of July, 1812.

(Signed) ALEXANDER.

SECOND PROCLAMATION. To our ancient City and Capital of Moscow. The enemy, with a perfidy without parallel, and with forces. equal to his immeasurable ambition, has passed the frontiers of Russia. His design is to ruin our country. The Russian armies burn with desire to throw themselves upon his battalions and to punish by their destruction this perfidious invasion; but our paternal regard for our faithful subjects will not permit us to allow so desperate a sacrifice. We cannot suffer that our brave soldiers should immolate themselves thus upon the altar of this Moloch! We are ready to contend with him in the open field, man against man in equal combat, he for his ambition, we for our country.

Fully informed of the bad intentions of our enemy and of the great means he has prepared for the execution of his projects, we do not hesitate to declare to our people the danger of the empire; and to call on them to destroy, by their patriotic efforts, the advantages that the aggressor hopes to draw from our present inferiority in number.

Necessity commands the gathering of new forces in the interior, to support those which are in the presence of the enemy, determined to perish or to form a barrier between him and the liberty of our country. To assemble these new armies, we address ourselves to the ancient capital of our ancestors—to the city of Moscow! She was always the sovereign seat of all the Russias, and the first in every moment of public danger to send forth from her bosom her courageous children to defend the honour of the empire. As the blood flows invariably towards the heart of heroes to recall valour to their energetic souls, the children of our country also from the surrounding provinces spring towards her, seeking in her breast the lessons of courage, with which they ought to defend their children on the material bosom and save the tombs of their fathers from a sacrilegious violation!

The existence of your name in the list of nations is threatened—the enemy announces the destruction of Russia!

The safety of our holy Church and the throne of the Czars, the independence of the ancient Muscovite empire, all loudly proclaim that the object of the appeal will be received by our faithful subjects as a sacred law.

We will not delay to appear in the midst of our faithful people of Moscow, and from this centre we will visit the other portions of our empire to advise upon and direct the armaments.

May the hearts of our nobles and of the other orders of the state, propagate the spirit of this holy war that is blessed by God, and fight under the banners of this holy Church! may the filial zeal extend from Moscow to the extremities of our dominions! The nation then, assembled round its monarch, may defy the thousand legions of the perfidious aggressor; then the evils which he has prepared for you will recoil on his own head; and Europe, delivered from slavery, will hail the name of Russia.

Camp of Polotzk, the 18th of July, 1812.

(Signed) ALEXANDER.

Despite Alexander's exhortations, things did not go well with the Russian armies which proved themselves unable to beat back the Napoleonic drive. The Russian army was all but broken at Borodino and shortly thereafter Napoleon entered Moscow. Here is Alexander's proclamation after that event. The source is: Wilson, op. cit., pp. 191–194.

PROCLAMATION. The enemy entered Moscow the 15th of September.

It might be expected that consternation should be general at this news, but let us disdain a pusillanimous despondency. Let us swear rather to redouble our perseverance and our courage; let us hope that, whilst combating in a cause so just as ours, we may direct upon the heads of our enemy the calamities he is heaping up for our destruction. Moscow, it is true, is in their hands, but our army is not disgraced or dispersed. The General-in-chief has yielded to a necessity, but only to reunite with advancing forces, and then to snatch from the enemy his ephemeral triumph.

We know and feel how grieved all the hearts of the faithful Russians will be at the desolation of our provinces and the ancient capital of the empire, but the enemy occupies only its ramparts. Deserted by its inhabitants— stripped of its treasures—it resembles no more a peopled city, but a vast tomb, in which the merciless invader may erect his throne.

This haughty destroyer of kingdoms on entering Moscow flattered himself that he was the arbiter of our destinies, and might dictate peace at his will; but his presumption is already foiled: he has found in Moscow not only no aid for his domination, but not even the means of subsistence.

Our forces augment every day. They occupy all the roads, and destroy all the detachments of the enemy in search of food:

He will soon be convinced of the fatal error which led him to consider the possession of Moscow as the subjection of the empire; and famine will compel him to attempt an escape through a country of which our intrepid warriors with closed roads will bar the passage.

Look at the condition of this enemy: he entered Russia at the head of more than three hundred thousand men, but how is that force composed?

Is there any national unity in this multitude?

No! the different nations who march under his standards do not serve him from attachment or patriotism, but servile fear.

Already the disorganising effect of his principle of fusion is apparent.

Half the army is destroyed by Russian valour, by desertion, by want of discipline, by sickness and hunger!

The pride of the conqueror is doubtless increased by the apparent success of his enterprise, but the "end crowns the work."

Through the whole course of his invasion he has not found a spot where a Russian from terror has fallen at his feet.

Russia is attached to the paternal throne of her Sovereign, who extends over her the guardian arm of his affection.

She is not accustomed to the yoke of oppression. She will not endure a foreign domination. She will not surrender the treasurers of her laws, her religion, and independence. She is ready to shed the last drop of her blood in their defence. This sentiment is ardent and universal.

It has manifested itself by the prompt and voluntary organisation of the people under the banner of patriotism! Under such an ægis, where can there be any ground for a disgraceful fear? Can there be a man in the empire so base as to despair, when vengeance is the rallying word of the state?—when the enemy, deprived of all resources, sees his numbers daily diminishing, and a powerful nation environing him, with an army in his front and rear intercepting his supplies and retreat?

Can a true Russian feel alarm? Has Spain not broken her chains, and menaced the integrity of the French empire? Does not the greatest portion of Europe, degraded and plundered by the ruler of France, serve him with a reluctant heart, and turn an impatient regard on us for the signal of general deliverance?

Does not France herself sigh for the termination of a sanguinary war, in which she has been involved by a boundless ambition?

Does not an oppressed world look to us for example and encouragement, and can we shrink from such an honourable mission as is confided to us? No; let us rather kiss the hand that has selected us to act as the leaders of nations in the struggle for independence and virtue.

Too long has humanity been afflicted by the calamities of war, and the cruelties of this horrible ambition; but we will brave it, for our freedom and the interests of mankind.

We will enjoy the noble sentiment of a good action; immortal honour shall be the recompense of a nation enduring all the ills of a savage war, and contending with courage and constancy to obtain a durable peace, not only for herself, but for those unhappy countries which the tyrant is now forcing to fight in his quarrel.

It is glorious—it is worthy a great people to render good for ill.

Almighty God! is the cause for which we are battling not just? Cast an eye of compassion on our holy church. Preserve to this people its courage and constancy. Suffer it to triumph over its adversary and Thine. May it be in Thy hand the instrument of his destruction—and in delivering itself, redeem the freedom and independence of nations and kings.

(Signed) ALEXANDER.

General Sir Robert Wilson did not fall into the error, which entrapped many western military experts in 1940–41, of underestimating the Russian army. Here is a portion of one of his confidential reports to Earl Cathcart, written late in August, 1812, when everything seemed to be going against the Russians. The source is: Wilson, op. cit., pp. 385–386 (abridged).

THE RUSSIAN ARMY. I have had occasion to ascertain that great improvements have been made in the Russian commissariat department, and that the medical department is also in rapid progress to a respectable system; but I have seen with regret that the interior economy of this army is still very distant from necessary method and order.

The columns of march, notwithstanding General Barclay's commands and, I may add, example—considering his station, are still encumbered with immense numbers of private carriages: and I verily believe several thousand Cossacks are employed in the service of officers.

The duties of our divisionary assistant Quartermasters-general are not known, or never performed.

No ground is ever previously reconnoitered by the junior staff, no roads examined, no reports made of the local conveniences or inconveniences of the proposed post, camp, or quarters.

The pioneers' duty is equally neglected. No bridges are ever repaired to anticipate the necessity; no additional passages are made over the numerous little marshy rivulets that intersect the road, so that the line of march unnecessarily extends for miles, is frequently interrupted for hours, confusion daily prevails, and ruin would ensue if the enemy were enterprising.

I have seen moments when one thousand five hundred daring men would have accomplished that which Buonaparte, with one hundred and fifty thousand, will not achieve when the Russian army is arrayed in order of battle.

I have mentioned to your Lordship that the Russian ammunition-waggons were not calculated to descend hilly ground without great delay and much risk.

General Kutaisow, who commands the artillery, has now, however, accepted my suggestion, and I am to order, at the St. Petersburg arsenal, staples to fix on the shafts, and straps to connect the breechings with that support.

Without this arrangement, the top of the collar affords the only resistance, for there is no breast-strap to connect the lower part of the collar with the belly-bands; consequently, as the horse leans back, the collar flies forward and upward to the end of the shafts.

It is true that iron shoes, to lock or fix the wheels, ought to have been with each waggon, but these have been long broken away; and if they remained, the driver must always have dismounted to set and to unloosen them.

I have also General Kutaisow's request to procure dragropes, after the English fashion, for the guns. At the present the Russians use cords that wound the hands and afford no purchase.

I have been thus particular in making your Lordship acquainted with the result of my observations and my impressions, that your Lordship may be enabled to form an opinon of the character and temper of the force which is engaged in this awful contest. Its excellences are manifold, and its means are equal to final success. Its defects and imperfections are of a nature to be corrected as soon as qualified persons are charged with the superintendence of its interior arrangements.

It is fitting that this series should end on a note of triumph. By January, 1813, Napoleon had been routed; his troops driven from Russian soil. Two days before he led his victorious army across the western frontier to pursue the French across Europe, Alexander issued the following order to his soldiers. The source is: Wilson, op. cit., pp. 368–369.

VICTORY PROCLAMATION. Merecz, 13th Jan., 1813. Soldiers, The year has ended—a year for ever memorable and glorious—one in which you have trampled in the dust the pride of the insolent aggressor.

The year has passed, but your heroic deeds survive.

Time will not efface their trace. They are present to your contemporaries —they will live with their posterity.

You have purchased at the price of your blood the deliverance of your country from the hostile powers leagued against its independence.

You have acquired rights to the gratitude of Russia, and to the admiration of mankind. You have proved by your fidelity, your valour, and your perseverance, that when hearts are filled with the love of God, and devotion to their Sovereign, the efforts of the most formidable enemies resemble the furious waves of the ocean, which break in impotent lashings against indestructible rocks, and leave behind only confused sounds.

Soldiers! desirous of distinguishing all those who have participated in these immortal exploits, I have ordered medals of silver to be struck, which have been blessed by our holy Church. They bear the date of the memorable year 1812: suspended to a blue ribbon, they will decorate the warrior breasts which have served as bucklers of the country.

Each individual of the Russian army is worthy to bear this honourable recompense of valour and constancy.

You have all shared the same fatigues and dangers; you have had but one heart, one mind; you will all be proud to wear the same distinction; it will proclaim every where that you are the faithful children of Russia,—children on whom God the Father will pour his benedictions.

Your enemies will tremble on seeing these decorations: They will know that under these medals hearts are beating, animated with unconquerable valour, and imperishable, because it is not based upon ambition or impiety, but on the immutable foundation of patriotism and religion.

(Signed) ALEXANDER.

Alexander's Mysticism

During the latter part of his reign, Alexander I was much attracted to and influenced by religious mysticism. The following brief quotation from the Manifesto which he issued on the conclusion of the Peace of Paris in 1814 is illustrative of this aspect of the man. The source is: LaCroix, Paul, Histoire de la vie et du regne de Nicolas Iᵉʳ Empereur de Russia. *Three volumes. Paris, 1864–66. Vol. 1, pp. 82–83.*

Thus the All Powerful has put an end to our unhappiness, has illuminated our country in the eyes of future generations, and has granted the wishes of our heart. In addressing to heaven fervent and respectful prayers of thanks to the Author of all good, we order that solemn thanksgiving shall be returned throughout the length and breadth of our empire. We are convinced that Russia, on her knees before the throne of the Eternal One, will pour out tears of joy.

The Problem of Succession

Tsarevich and heir-presumptive to Alexander I was his brother Constantine Pavlovich. But Constantine who long served as governor of Warsaw, divorced his wife and married a woman not of royal blood. The divorce and re-marriage were with the consent of Alexander, but imperial law prohibited children of this second union from inheriting the throne. At least partly because of this, Constantine determined to renounce the throne for himself. Alexander agreed to the renunciation and in a secret manifesto named his brother Nicholas Pavlovich as his successor. Because this arrangement was not published, considerable confusion arose when Alexander I died in 1825. It was precisely this situation which made possible the Decembrist Rising.

The following selections set forth the pertinent letters and other documents in the case. They are arranged in chronological order. The source is: LaCroix, op. cit., vol. 1, pp. 238–239, 239–240, 244–247, 326–327, 328–329, 346, 363, 395–399, 401–402.

CONSTANTINE TO ALEXANDER. Encouraged by all the proofs of the infinitely sympathetic disposition of your Imperial Majesty toward me I dare once more lay at your feet, Sire, a most humble prayer.

Not finding in myself the genius, the talents, nor the force necessary to be elevated to the Sovereign dignity to which I would have the right by my birth, I beg your Imperial Majesty to transfer this right to whom it would come after me, and thus to assure forever, the security of the empire. As to me, I will add by this renunciation a new guarantee and a new force to the engagement which I have voluntarily and solemnly contracted on the occasion of my divorce from my first wife.

All the circumstances of my own situation, bearing more and more upon this measure, prove to the Empire and to the entire world the sincerity of my sentiments.

Deign, Sire, to accept with good will my prayer; help me secure the consent of our Imperial Mother to this plan and sanction it with your Imperial assent.

In the sphere of private life, I shall pledge myself always to serve as an example to your faithful subjects, and to all those who are animated by a love for our dear country.

I am with a profound respect for your Majesty.

> Your most faithful subject and brother
> Constantine Tsarevich

> St. Petersburg,
> 14/26 January, 1822.

ALEXANDER'S REPLY. Very dear brother: I have read your letter with all the attention that it merited. Having always fully appreciated the high sentiments of your heart, I found nothing in your letter to make me change my judgment. It has given me a new proof of your sincere attachment to the Empire, and of your solicitude for its continued tranquillity.

In accordance with your desire I presented your letter to our beloved Mother; she has read it with the same recognition of the noble motives which guided you. Having taken into considerations the reason which you set forth, we both agree that you should be given full liberty to follow your immutable resolution, and we pray the All Powerful to bless the consequence of a purpose so pure.

I am ever your affectionate brother,

Alexander
St. Petersburg,
2/14 February, 1822.

MANIFESTO OF ALEXANDER I ON THE SUCCESSION. By the grace of God, we, Alexander I, Emperor and Autocrat of all The Russias, etc., etc., etc., make it known to our faithful subjects:

From the moment of our coming to the throne of all the Russias, we have constantly realized that it was our duty toward all powerful God not only to guarantee and increase during our life, the happiness of our country and our people, but also to prepare for and to assure their security and their good fortune after us by a clear and precise designation of our successor according to the laws of our Imperial House and the interests of the Empire. We could not name him immediately as our predecessors had done, but waited in the hope that it would perhaps please Providence to give to us an heir to the throne in a direct line. But as the years have gone on, it has more and more seemed to us our duty to place our throne in such a position that it will not remain vacant even momentarily.

While we bear this solitude in our heart, our well beloved brother, the Tsarevich and Grand Duke Constantine, obeying only the impulse of his own free will, has addressed to us the demand that we transfer his right to the sovereign dignity, a position to which he would one day be elevated by his birth, to the head of some person who might possess this right after him. He showed at the same time his intentions to give a new force to the additional act relative to the succession of the throne which was promulgated by us in 1820, an act voluntarily and solemnly recognized by him insofar as that act was of concern to him.

We are profoundly touched by the sacrifice which our well beloved brother has believed that he ought to make in his own interests for the consolidation of the fundamental laws of our Imperial House, and the ineffable tranquility of the Empire of all the Russias. Having invoked the aid of God, having seriously reflected upon a subject as dear to our heart as it is important for the Empire, and finding that the statutes which exist on the order of the succession to the throne do not deprive those who have the right, of the power to renounce it, since in this special circumstance it does not present any difficulty in the order of hereditary succession to the throne, we have with the consent of our distinguished Mother, in turn the supreme head of the Imperial family to which we belong, and by the absolute power which we hold from God Himself, have ordered and shall order:

First, the voluntary act by which our brother, the tsarevich and Grand Duke Constantine, renounces his rights to the throne of all the Russias shall be irrevocable. The said act of renunciation shall be, in order to insure its being known, preserved in the Cathedral of the Assumption in Moscow and in the three high Courts of our empire, in the Holy Synod, in the Council of the Empire, and in the Directing Senate. Secondly, following the strict provision of the statute on the succession to the throne, be it known that our successor shall be our second brother, the Grand Duke Nicholas.

In consequence, we have the well founded hope that on the day when it shall please the King of Kings to recall us, following the common law of all mortals, from our temporal reign to eternity, the properly constituted authorities of the Empire to whom we have made known our irrevocable wish in this matter will hasten to swear submission and fidelity to the emperor whom we have just designated as heir to the invisible crown of the Empire of all the Russias, of the Kingdom of Poland, and of the Grand Duchy of Finland. As to us, we ask all our faithful subjects, that, with the same sentiment of affection with which we have considered our first responsibility on earth to be the care given to their constant prosperity, they address fervent prayers to our Lord Jesus Christ that He might deign, in His infinite sympathy, to receive our soul in His eternal kingdom.

Given a Tsarskoe-selo, the sixteenth of August [O.S.] year of Grace 1823 and of our reign the 23rd.

Alexander.

CONSTANTINE TO THE EMPRESS MOTHER. Very gracious Sovereign and Beloved Mother; It is with the deepest affliction of the heart that I have received at 7 o'clock in the evening . . . the news of the decease of our beloved Sovereign and my benefactor the Emperor Alexander. . . .

The position in which this unhappiness places me imposes upon me the duty of spreading before your Imperial Majesty with complete frankness my true sentiments on this essential point.

Your Imperial Majesty is not unaware that following only my own impulse I asked the Emperor Alexander of glorious memory, for the authority to renounce my right to the succession to the throne, and that I received in consequence an Imperial autograph rescript, dated the second/fourteenth of February, 1822, and of which I send here a copy, by which the Emperor gave his absolute assent to this demand, adding that your Imperial Majesty would be also advised, and that he himself would confirm it in conversation.

The absolute orders of the Emperor were that the supreme rescript mentioned above would stay in my hands under a secret seal until the death of his Majesty.

. . . I consider it an obligation to cede my right to the throne, in accordance with the dispositions of the Act of the Empire on the order of succession in the Imperial family, to his Imperial Highness, the Grand Duke Nicholas and to his heirs.

It is with the same frankness that I feel it my duty to declare that, not having changed my mind, I should esteem myself very happy if, after more than thirty years of service consecrated to the Emperors, my brother and my father of glorious memory, it should be permitted to me to continue these services to his Majesty, the Emperor Nicholas, with the same deep veneration, with the same burning zeal which has animated me on all occasions, and which shall move me until the end of my days.

After having expressed my sentiments which are as true as they are irrevocable, I place myself at the feet of your Imperial Majesty, and very humbly beg the honor of a gracious acceptance of the present letter, and ask that you will notify him [Nicholas] of that part of it which pertains to him in order that it may be placed into execution with all the force and all the will of his Imperial Majesty, my deceased Sovereign and benefactor, as well as with the assent of your Imperial Majesty. I am taking the liberty of submitting herewith a copy of the letter which I have addressed simultaneously with this to his Majesty, the Emperor Nicholas.

I am with the deepest veneration, very gracious Sovereign and very much beloved Mother,

> Your humble and most submissive son
> Constantine,
> Warsaw, 25 November/7 December, 1825.

CONSTANTINE TO NICHOLAS. Very dear brother: It is with an inexpressible affliction that I received at 7 o'clock in the evening the unhappy news of the death of our beloved Sovereign, of my benefactor, the Emperor Alexander.

. . . I ought to inform you that with this present letter I have addressed to her Imperial Majesty, our well beloved mother, a letter which announces to her, in virtue of an autograph receipt which I have received from the Emperor, on the second [fourteenth] of February, 1822, in response to a letter which I have written him renouncing succession to the Imperial throne, Mother, and honored by her assent which she has deigned to confirm to me, my irrevocable resolution to cede to you my rights to the succession to the Imperial throne of all the Russias.

After this declaration, I regard as a sacred duty to beg very humbly of your Imperial Majesty, that you would deign to accept from me first, my oath of royalty and fidelity, and permit me to expose to you that I have not raised my wishes to any new dignity or any new title—that I desire only to save that of tsarevich with which I have been honored for my services to our father.

My unique good fortune will always be that your Imperial Majesty deigns to accept the assurancies of my most profound veneration and of my devotion without limit, sentiments of which I offer as a pledge more than 30 years in the faithful and zealous service, to their Majesties the Emperors, my brother and my father, of glorious memory. It is with the same sentiments that I shall not cease to the end of my days, to serve your Imperial Majesty and his descendants in my function and my proper place.

I am with the most profound veneration, Sire, of your Imperial Majesty, the most faithful subject,

Constantine

Warsaw, 25 November/7 December 1825

NICHOLAS TO CONSTANTINE. My Dear Constantine: I bow before my sovereign, after having pronounced together with those persons who found themselves before me, the oath which is due him. . . . In the name of heaven do not abandon us, and do not desert us!

Your brother and your faithful subject in life and in death,

Nicholas

27 November/9 December 1825

CONSTANTINE TO NICHOLAS. Your Aid de camp, my dear Nicholas, has just given me your letter. I have read it with the most vivid chagrin. My decision sanctified by him who was my benefactor and my Sovereign, is irrevocable. I am not able to accept your proposal to hasten my departure for St. Petersburg, and I warn you that I shall leave Warsaw only to retire to some greater distance, if everything is not arranged following the will of our deceased Emperor.

Your faithful brother and sincere friend,

Constantine

Warsaw, 6/18 December

EDICT OF NICHOLAS. By the grace of God, we, Nicholas, Emperor and Autocrat of all the Russias, etc. make known to all our faithful subjects:

In the affliction of our heart, in the middle of the general sadness which surrounds us, we, our Imperial house and our dear country, humiliate ourselves before the impenetrable decrees of the Most High, it is from Him alone that we seek our strength and our consolations. He has just called to Him the Emperor Alexander I, of glorious memory, and we have all lost a father and a sovereign, who for twenty-five years has worked for the well-being of Russia and us.

On the 27th of the month of November [O. S.] we learned the news of this deplorable event. We have taken pains even in this moment of sadness and tears to perform a sacred duty and follow only the impulse of our heart. We have already taken the oath of fidelity to our beloved brother the Tsarevitch, Grand Duke Constantine as the legitimate heir of the throne of Russia by the right of primogeniture.

We had just discharged this holy obligation when we were notified by the Council of Empire that on the fifteenth of October, 1823, there had been placed in their hands a packet, sealed with the sign of the Emperor, on which there had been written in the hand of his Majesty himself "to hold in the Council of Empire until I order otherwise, but in the case of my death to be opened at an extraordinary sitting, before proceeding to any other act." This sovereign order had been executed by the Council and the following pieces had been found in the said packet:

1. A letter of the Tsarevich, Grand Duke Constantine, dated 14th of January, 1822 [O. S.], addressed to the Emperor by which his Imperial Highness renounced his succession to the throne which belonged to him by the law of primogeniture.

2. A manifesto of the 16th of August, 1823 [O. S.] signed by his Imperial Majesty's own hand by which, after having expressed his assent to the renunciation of the Tsarevich and Grand Duke Constantine, it is stated that being the next in age after him, We are, following the fundamental law, the proper heir of the throne. We were informed at the outset that identical documents had been deposited with the Holy Synod and in the Cathedral of Assumption at Moscow.

The above mentioned facts could in no way change the determination which We had taken. We recognize the acts of renunciation made by his Imperial Highness during the life of the Emperor and confirmed by the assent of his Imperial Majesty; but We have neither the wish nor the right to consider this renunciation as irrevocable since it has not been published and has not been converted into law. We wish thus to show our respect for the first fundamental law of our country on the invariable order of succession to the throne; and faithful to the oath which we have taken, We insist that the entire Empire follow our example. In this grave circumstance our need is not to contest the validity of the resolutions expressed by his Imperial Highness. He has again besought us not to oppose the wishes of the Emperor, our father and common benefactor, wishes which we shall hold sacred. We seek only to guarantee the letter of the law which rules the order of succession to the throne . . . and to preserve our dear country in a moment of uncertainty over the person of the legitimate sovereign. This determination taken in the purity of our conscience before God who reads the depths of our hearts, was blessed by her Imperial Majesty Marie, our beloved Mother.

However, the unhappy news of the decease of his Majesty, the Emperor was taken directly from Taganrog to Warsaw the 25th of November, two days sooner than it was received here. Immovable in his resolution, the Tsarevich and Grand Duke Constantine confirmed it on the following day by two acts, dated the 26th of November [O. S.] which he charged our well beloved brother the Grand Duke Michael to send to us. These acts consist: first of a letter addressed to her Imperial Majesty, our beloved mother, a letter in which renewing his earlier decision and resting upon a rescript of the Emperor of the date of the second of February 1822 [O. S.] which served as a response to his act of renunciation of which there was a copy attached, his Imperial Highness renounced definitively and solemnly all his rights to the throne, and after the order established by fundamental law, made them known to us as well as to our heirs; second a letter addressed to us in which his Imperial Highness reiterates the first expression of his determination, gives to us the title of Imperial Majesty reserving only for himself that of Tsarevich which he bore formerly, and calling himself the most faithful of our subjects.

. . .

In consequence of all these acts, and after the fundamental law of the Empire on the order of succession, with a heart full of respect for the impenetrable decrees of Providence who leads us, We ascended the throne of our ancestors, the throne of the empire of all the Russians, and those of the kingdom of Poland and the Grand Duchy of Finland which are inseparable, and we order:

1. That the oath of fidelity be taken to us and to our heir, His Imperial Highness Alexander, our well beloved son;

2. That the epoch of our accession to the throne shall be dated from the 19th November 1825. [O. S.]

Finally we ask all our faithful subjects to raise with us their fervent prayers toward the All-High that He will give us the power of His support for the burden which Holy Providence has imposed upon us, that He will sustain us in our firm intentions to live only for our beloved country . . . and to follow in the footsteps of the monarch who preceded us. Then our reign will be only a continuation of his, and we shall be able to accomplish all the wishes which he formed for the good of Russia, he whose sacred memory nourished in us the desire and hope to merit the benedictions of heaven and the love of our people!

Given in our imperial residence of St. Petersburg, the 12th/24th of December in the years of grace, 1825 and of our reign the first.

Nicholas

TSAR NICHOLAS TO THE GRAND DUKE CONSTANTINE—*written immediately after Nicholas assumed the throne.* Dear Brother: Sharing from the bottom of my soul the cruel sorrow over the irreparable loss which we have both just suffered, I had hoped to find some consolation in you, my beloved brother, whom I have learned to venerate and love from the time of our babyhood, to find, I say, in you a father and a sovereign.

Your letter dated November 25 deprived me of this consolation. You have stopped me from following the impulse of my heart, and you have not been willing to accept the oath of allegiance to you which I pronounced not only from duty but also from deepest conviction.

. . . The wishes of your Highness have been carried out. I have occupied the elevated post which you have designated for me, and which you have not wished to occupy although it belonged to you by right. Your will is done!

But permit me to hope that He who, against my will and intention, placed me in this troublous and difficult position, let me believe, I say, that He will be my guide and my support. Before God, you must not repulse this duty, and you must not renounce the moral power which has been accorded to you by Providence itself, in your position as a beloved brother, a power sacred for me and one which I will obey with good will all my life, as your faithful subject of the heart.

It is by the expression of these sentiments that I end my letter, in begging the Most-High that He will mercifully preserve your days for a long time so precious are they to me.

From your Imperial Highness, the faithful subject of heart and soul,

Nicholas

St. Petersburg, 12/24 December 1825

Economic Development during the Two Reigns

The attention of historians has been so arrested by the dramatic happenings in the reigns of Alexander I and Nicholas I that the economic developments of Russia during those years have been somewhat neglected. The following selection, not hitherto available in English, may serve as an introductory sketch of this phase of Russian History. The source is: N. A. Rozhkov, "Ekonomicheskoe Razbitie Rossii v Pervoi Polovin XIX veka," Istoriia Rossii v XIX vek. Nine volumes. St. Petersburg, n. d. Vol. 1, pp. 138–142, slightly abridged.

The outstanding feature of the economic history of Russia in the first part of the 19th century or, more correctly, until the fall of landlordism, was undoubtedly the much greater speed and breadth, than previously, of the development of trade and money economy. There had been a marked development of money economy in 16th century Russia, but at the beginning this process took place very slowly and affected comparatively small groups. Only with the 19th century began the transfer from agrarian economy to the second stage, when the majority of the people became accustomed to trading, to producing for market and to satisfy the owners' desires to purchase products of foreign labor, and also learned to carry their goods to market with a view to trade.

The outstanding characteristic economic feature of this epoch was first of all the change in trade statistics. The value of Russian exports increased from 75 million rubles at the beginning of the 19th century to 230 million rubles on the eve of the peasant reform; at the same time, imports of foreign goods reached 200 million rubles whereas at the opening of the century such imports had not exceeded 52 million rubles. The most important of the Russian exports were grain and, in general, the products of the land, livestock and the products of livestock, lumber, etc. The importance of the grain exports is apparent from the following figures: Between 1800 and 1845, grain exports comprised 15 to 16% of the value of all Russian exports; between 1846 and 1860, 30 to 35%. The average exports of grain in the decade preceding 1846 did not exceed 454 thousands of tons, but in the next ten years it was 918 thousand tons a year, so that there is noted a huge increase — amounting to 88% — as compared to the preceding decade. It is wholly clear that the development and improvement of their industries by the advanced Western European countries toward the middle of the 19th century, were sharply felt in their demand for Russian grain, chiefly wheat.

So much wheat was exported, mostly from the South Russian ports, that the Black Sea ports — Odessa and Taganrog — attained first place in the export of farm products, surpassing the Baltic ports. The export of linseed and hops also increased. In 30 to 40 years even the Caucasus (i.e., the northern part, which belonged to Russia) exported significant quantities of linseed through the port of Taganrog. The value of lumber exports in 1815 amounted to 1,320,000 silver rubles; in 1850, it reached 2,745,000 silver rubles (increasing over 100%). Livestock and the products of livestock (tallow, bristles and hides) were exported in 1825 to the value of 15,885,000 rubles; by 1850, this had increased to 17 million silver rubles.

Corresponding developments are observable in the case of foreign imports. It is impossible to find a better illustration of the movement toward money economy than this: in 1820, the total import of machines into Russia was 10 thousand silver rubles; in 1850, 2,221,000. The value of imports of foreign woolen goods into the country rose from 1,500 silver rubles in 1815 to 39,000 in 1850.

Side by side with this, and, it is even possible to say, of more rapid growth than this, was the domestic trade. Previously it had been the custom not only among the peasants, but also among the land and serf owners, to satisfy their needs by products entirely of home manufacture — not buying but making such goods at home as coarse homespun cloth and home-made linen. Little by little, these primitive textiles were replaced by purchasing finer fabrics. As late as 1804, several landowners in the Moscow province had factories whose products were intended only "for domestic consumption" or for "our own use," but gradually the largest landowners increased their estate factories and mills to produce for market. There were, for example, in the same province of Moscow: the cloth factories of Prince Khovanski and Princess Golitsin; the silk and paper factories of Belavin; and the linen mills of Prince Dolgoruki and Count Protasov. The value of domestic trade had already increased to 260 million silver rubles by 1812. At the Nizhni-Novgorod Fair in 1824 there had been offered for sale, goods valued at 40,500,000 rubles. By 1838, this had increased to 129,200,000 rubles. There was also a rapid increase in mercantile capital: in the province of Moscow in 1822, the total of this capital approached 27 million rubles, but eleven years later (in 1833) it reached 39 million — an increase of 45% in the short space of one decade. Improvements were made in the ways of communication. A beginning was made in railway construction and in steam navigation of the Volga, the Dnieper, and other rivers. But chiefly what strikes one as the most outstanding characteristic of this development of money economy was the division of labor among the various territorial divisions of the state — a division which inevitably led to the exchange of goods and the revival of trade.

The comparatively less fertile northern and central sections of Russia greatly needed quantities of foodstuffs which they could not raise for themselves. According to the evidence of Baron Haxthausen, who travelled through Russia in the 1840's, some provinces such as Iaroslavl did not produce half enough food for its people. Furthermore, Kaluzhskaia Province in 1822 was already buying foodstuffs from Orel and Tula Provinces. On the other hand, southern Russia traded much foodstuff to the East. Thus, the regions of what was then Orienburg Province, which now belongs in the enlarged Province of Ufa, during the 1820's and thereafter, sent much grain by boat on the Kama and the Volga. Livestock was also sold from there to the Kazak and Simbirsk lands along the Volga. Moreover, this trade involved not only the land and serf owners, but also all the people. . . .

This trade took place even among distant parts of the country. Kharkhov, Poltava, Ekaterinoslav, and Kherson Provinces provided timber for the rest of Russia. Little Russia and New Russia in 1854 consumed Great Russian goods to the value of about 80 million silver rubles. These imports went to the numerous fairs of Little Russia, of which there were 425 a year in Kharkhov, and 372 a year in Poltava. Goods were sent to Little Russia from Moscow, Vladimir, Kostroma, Iaroslavl, Riazin, Tula, Nizhni-Novgorod, Orel, Kalzhska, and even from the West — from the provinces of

Smolensk, Grodnensk, and Lifland; from the South — Bessarabia, Crimea, Ekaterinoslav; and East from the Don and Voronezh Provinces. In the mid-nineteenth century, Pavlov and Worms purchased the iron which they needed for their metal industries from the Urals through the medium of the Nizhni-Novgorod fairs. In the town of Pestiaki, Vladimir Province, the women knit stockings and sold them in Siberia and elsewhere to the value of 120 thousand rubles a year. The materials for the stockings — wool to the amount of 225 tons — were purchased in the provinces of Astrakhan, Orienburg, Saratov, and in the military colonies of the Don.

In short, the division of Russia into the central and northern non-agrarian regions, and the southern agrarian and livestock areas was clearly marked. Each helped the other in economic relations and neither could live without the other. They formed a unit, a coherent economic whole, an indispensable pillar for the development of money economy.

. . .

The publisher of the journal "The Russian Farmer," in 1838, printed the statement that: as to agriculture in Russia, "it stands almost motionless," while manufacturing "attained an amazing development." Without doubt this phrase satisfactorily echoes the impressions of the contemporaries who observed the economic development of Russia in the first half of the 19th century. But it is also, without doubt, contrary to fact in two respects. First, to avow that the development of Russian manufacturing at that time was "amazing" is an obvious exaggeration. Second, it is a pretense that agrarian economy was "motionless." As a matter of fact, while manufacturing developed rather quickly, it did not develop amazingly or even astonishingly fast. Its growth came as a necessary prerequisite to money economy. In an important branch of manufacturing — the cotton industry — the amount of cotton manufactured increased sixteen times during the first fifty years of the nineteenth century. Smelting of iron in the same period increased from 144 thousand tons to 288 thousand tons a year. Rapid progress in the textile industry also bears witness to this fact. There were in Russia in 1850, 492 textile factories. Between 1820 and 1830 the number of factories in Russia had increased from three to four thousand, and the number of workers in these plants rose from 170 thousand to 240 thousand. During the 1840's, one such village as Ivanov in the Shuiski district provided work for 42 thousand people and produced cotton goods to the value of 23,400,000 paper rubles. The first Russian sugar beet refinery was built in 1802. By 1845 there were 206 sugar refineries with a production of 8,712 tons. Three years later, in 1848, the number of refineries had increased to 340, and the amount produced to 16,200 tons. . . .

Thus in 1812, agricultural products were valued at 23,400,000 silver rubles; livestock and its products at 17,800,000; the products of extractive industries at 7,200,000 and manufactured goods at 10,800,000. The corresponding figures for 1850 were: agriculture — 44,700,000 silver rubles; livestock and its products — 23,500,000 rubles; the extractive industries — 7,300,000; and manufactured goods — 11,300,000 rubles.

Nicholas and Repression

Liberal historians have often referred to the reign of Nicholas I as "the period of outward repression and inner liberation." The repression was exemplified by the notorious Third Section of His Majesty's Own Chancery and by the censorship. This description of the repression under Nicholas was written by the great Czech scholar and statesman, Thomas G. Masaryk. The source is: Masaryk, T. G., The Spirit of Russia. Two volumes. New York: Macmillan and Co., 1919. Vol. 1, pp. 106–109, 111–113.

In this sketch it would be difficult to give an adequate idea of the abominable stupidity and provocative brutality that characterised reaction under Nicholas. For the utterance of liberal ideas conflicting with the official program, leading men were simply declared insane. This happened to Čaadaev (Chadayev) and to a number of officers inclined towards revolutionary notions. In one case Nicholas had the death announced of a certain Engelhardt whose sentence had in reality been commuted to imprisonment for life; his wife was compelled to wear mourning; and the very number of his grave in the churchyard was entered in the records. When the poet Ševčenko (Tsevchenko) and his associates were sentenced in 1847 as members of the slavophil Cyrillo-Methodian Union, the tsar aggravated the punishment in the case of Ševčenko, to whom the use of writing materials was denied. In his diary the poet complains that while the pagan Augustus permitted Ovid to write, this indulgence was forbidden to himself by the Christian ruler. Not merely was the tsar chief officer of police, but in his own exalted person he revised the sentences of the courts. In the year 1837 two Jews were condemned to death in Odessa because, from fear of the plague, they had attempted to escape across the frontier. Nicholas commuted the death penalty as follows: "The convicts are to run the gauntlet — a thousand men — twelve times. God be thanked, with us the death penalty has abolished, and I will not reintroduce it." This is but one among numerous instances of the theocratic sovereign's power of self-deception and of his cruelty — for who had proposed that the decabrists (Men of December or Dekabristi) should be quartered and who had commuted their punishment to hanging? In the year 1838 a student gave the director of the surgical academy a box on the ear. He was sentenced to run the gauntlet — five hundred men — three times. Nicholas revised the sentence thus: "To be carried out in the presence of all the students of the academy. Subsequently the offender, instead of being sent to Siberia, is to spend ten years, wearing fetters, in the disciplinary battalion at Kronstadt." It is hardly necessary to add that though there was no capital punishment, the men thus sentenced died under the blows of the soldiers.

The severities of Nicholas were hardly credible. The wives of the decabrists who followed their husbands to Siberia were not permitted to return to Russia after the death of these; those among the decabrists who lived on into the reign of Alexander II received amnesty from that ruler. Only to one like Nicholas was it possible to have sane men declared insane, or to inflict upon Dostoevskii the tortures of a death sentence.

Here is an additional contribution to the psychology, perhaps it would be better to say the psychopathology, of Tsar Nicholas. A young man wrote a satire upon contemporary student life. The work was circulated in manuscript, and a copy fell into the hands of the emperor, who was especially incensed at the strictures upon the church and political institutions. He sent for the author and compelled him to read the composition aloud to himself and the minister for education. After a severe reprimand, wherein the writing was stigmatised as a product of decabrist sentiment, Nicholas kissed his victim upon the forehead and dismissed him with the sentence that he was to serve at the front, the minister's advocacy averting a worse issue. The tsar granted the offender the privilege of writing to his sovereign in order to recount progress on the right path. He availed himself of this privilege to beg for pardon, or at least for a mitigation of punishment, but his petitions were disregarded, and his biographers tell us how the unhappy man was tantalized, how in his despair he took to drink, and how finally he died of consumption, at the age of two and thirty years. We learn from Poležaev's verses what the age of Nicholas seemed to reflective minds.

Reforms, properly speaking, were unknown in the reign of Nicholas. Much was done to safeguard order, and especial attention was devoted to the army. Under the guidance of Speranskii, legislation was codified in 1833, a new criminal code was issued (1845), and the ministry of the state domains was founded (1837). In 1839, in order to promote the efficiency of centralisation, the village replaced the volost as the administrative unit.

I must not omit to mention that under Nicholas the use of the rod in punishment was abolished, the lash taking its place (1845). Humanitarian considerations, however, were not solely determinative, for those chastised with the rod were no longer fit for military service.

Some of the changes introduced in this reign were beneficial. For example, educational reform was forced upon the Jews, and thereby some of the Jews had opened to them the path to general culture.

Naturally, the reaction under Nicholas was based upon the state church, just as happened in Austria and Prussia, and quite in accordance with the teachings of de Maistre, de Bonald, Görres, Gentz, and the various other theorists of the antirevolutionary restoration and reaction.

All independent thought was to be inexorably suppressed; higher education was to be reduced to the minimum of essential knowledge; philosophy and literature, attempts at general culture and at the attainment of a philosophic outlook upon the universe, were to be stifled in the germ. Count Uvarov, minister for education from 1833 to 1849, addressing the governing committees of the schools, announced his advent to office in the following terms: "It is our joint task to secure that the culture of the nation shall be carried on in the unified spirit of Orthodoxy, autocracy and patriotism." Yet more thoroughly did Uvarov, in the course of the same year, formulate this trinitarian doctrine as "the main principle of the social system of education," writing as follows: "Amid the rapid decay of religious and civil institutions in Europe, amid the widespread diffusion of revolutionary ideas, it becomes our duty to establish the foundations of the fatherland so firmly that they cannot be shaken. We must find a basis from which right conduct can spring; we must discover energies which will develop the distinctive characteristics of Russia, and will ultimately enable our country to assemble the sacred heritage of nationality into a compact whole, to which we must anchor our salvation. How fortunate is it that Russia has preserved ardent faith in those saving principles in default of which right conduct is impossible, without which an energetic and worthy life is unknown. A Russian devoted to his fatherland is as little willing to permit the subtraction of a single dogma from our Orthodox faith as he would be to allow the theft of a pearl from the crown of Monomachus. Autocracy is the main condition of Russia's political existence. In conformity with these two national bases is the third basis, equally important and equally strong — patriotism." . . .

Hardly had Nicholas become tsar when he abolished the chair of philosophy at Moscow university. Driving past the university on one occasion, looking very serious, he pointed to the building and said, "There is the wolf's den." The less developed universities were dealt with in accordance with this estimate. A fuller activity had begun at the universities during the liberal epoch of Alexander I, with the issue of the studies' ordinance of 1804, although even then the police outlook towards these institutions was not abandoned. In 1835 Uvarov reorganised the universities in conformity with his general program, making the study of theology and ecclesiastical history obligatory in all faculties. In 1850, owing to the alarm inspired by the revolution of 1848, certain disciplines, and notably the study of European constitutional law, were banished from the university as deleterious; whilst philosophy was reduced to courses upon logic and psychology which had in future to be delivered by theologians, the pretext given for the change being "the blameworthy development of this science by German professors." The historian Granovskii was not permitted to lecture on the Reformation. The number of students was restricted to three hundred. The object of universities was announced to be, "the education of loyal sons for the Orthodox church, of loyal subjects for the tsar, and of good and useful citizens for the fatherland." Not until the days of Alexander II. were these and other reactionary measures abrogated. Nevertheless, even during the reign of Nicholas one new university was founded, at Kiev in 1833, for these "wolves' dens" were indispensable to the civil administration and the army.

Reform of the higher schools (1847) was effected in conformity with the restrictions imposed on the universities. The study of classical tongues was discontinued lest youth should be corrupted by the reading of Greek authors who had written in republics. In this connection we may refer to a European example of the same way of thinking. Napoleon III held the like view of Greek authors, and Nicholas might have appealed to the French emperor for support. But reaction in Russia works and thinks from day to day only. In 1854 classical studies were partially reintroduced, the idea being that Greek and Latin fathers of the church would inspire refractory youths with due veneration for the official program.

The history of recent Russian literature is filled with stories of the oppression which great writers had to suffer under Alexander and still more under Nicholas. The work of Griboedov, Puškin, Lermontov, and Gogol was hindered in every possible way. Banishment was a frequent penalty. Books were mutilated by the censorship. Newspapers were suppressed, among them an opposition journal edited by Rylěev and Marlinskii, and entitled "Poljarnaja Zvězda" (Polar Star, a name chosen later by Herzen for his organ). In the "Moskovskii Telegraf," Polevoi adopted an opposition standpoint from 1825 onwards, and was able to continue his journalistic advocacy of liberal ideas down to 1834, but this "Revue des décabristes" was in the end suppressed by Uvarov. I record, not in jest but in earnest, that this minister for education and president of the Academy of Sciences expressed a strong desire that Russian literature should cease to exist. Almost all notable authors suffered during the reign of Nicholas. I have previously referred to Čaadaev and Ševčenko. Bělinskii was unable to print his first drama. Puškin was informed of the tsar's exalted disapproval.

Puškin's aristocratic inclinations led him astray not infrequently, and he experienced a shortsighted pleasure when Polevoi's newspaper was suppressed, for he regarded the Moscow journalist as "unduly jacobin." Polevoi was one of the non-aristocratic *raznocinčy* (unclassed, plebeian). In 1845 the tsar seriously thought of having obstacles imposed to the entry of the *raznocinčy* into the higher schools.

The events of 1848 caused intense anxiety to Nicholas, and a regular

witches' sabbath of reaction was inaugurated. The members of the Petra-
ševcy group (the two Dostoevskiis, Pleščeev, Durov, etc.) were all prosecuted; measures were taken against Saltykov; Ostrovskii, Turgenev, Kirěev-
skii, Homjakov, and Herzen, successively fell into disfavour — Turgenev's
offence being an obituary notice of Gogol! It was forbidden to mention the
very name of Bělinskii, and those who wished to refer to him had to employ
circumlocutions!

Censorship was developed to an almost incredible extent. There were
twenty-two distinct censorships. Criticism of the government and of official
proceedings was absolutely prohibited. Even those who at a later date were
considered pillars of reaction, even such men as Bulgarin, were now suspect as revolutionaries; Pogodin suffered the same fate; to the ultra-reaction-
aries, Uvarov actually seemed insufficiently reactionary, and he had to resign
his position as minister for education. Upon a ministerial report which con-
included the word "progress," Nicholas wrote the comment, "Progress?
What progress? This word must be deleted from official terminology." . . .

Nicholas' Codification of Law

*The "inner liberation" of Nicholas' reign refers in general to the literary and
artistic advances which took place in that period. It could also be stretched
to cover his efforts toward reform, among which the codification of law was
perhaps the most progressive. This task was carried out by the Second
Section of His Majesty's Own Chancery, headed by Mikhail Speransky. The
published codification filled forty-five volumes. A condensation and digest
was also published. Here are Nicholas' instructions to Speransky concerning the bases for the codification. The source is: LaCroix, op. cit., vol. 3, pp.
38–39.*

1. To exclude from the body of law all those which are obsolete.
2. To exclude also those which are only identical repetitions of previous
laws, always giving preference to the most complete text.
3. To conserve scrupulously the letter of the law and reproduce in a
single text the sense of all the laws which treat of the same matter.
4. To indicate exactly the ukases from which each particular law is
composed.
5. Of two laws in contradiction, to give the preference to the most recent,
following the principle which establishes that all new law virtually abrogates
the law which preceded it.
6. Each part of the work of the Commission ought to be submitted for
revision to the ministers and the administrations in their respective special-
ties, committees established for that purpose being charged with this revi-

sion. A superior committee composed of senators and high functionaries under the presidency of the Minister of Justice will be set up to examine the civil and criminal laws.

7. Russia having laws of two kinds, those which act throughout the empire and those essentially local whose action is circumscribed in some provinces, there should be besides the body of general law, two bodies of provincial law, one for the government of the West, and one for that of the Baltic.

8. The codification of the laws in fixing legislation for its passage should leave a considerable latitude for the future when new needs will bring forth new laws.

A Contemporary Report on Russia in the 1840s

Among the first foreign observers to call special attention to that important and peculiar Russian institution, the Mir, was Baron von Haxthausen. The Baron made an extensive tour through European Russia in 1843, carefully observing and studying all aspects of Russian life which came under his view. He published his findings in three long volumes. His style is somewhat pompous and repetitious, but the report is valuable because he was a trained and experienced observer, keen in curiosity, searching in his inquiries and meticulous in recording his findings.

The series which follow are from his work, considerably abridged. The source is: Baron von Haxthausen (Robert Farie, translator), The Russian Empire, its people, institutions and resources. Two volumes. London, 1856. Vol. 2, pp. 229 ff.

THE MIR. The Russian word *Mir* has a different signification in the language of business, the law, and of the educated classes, from what it has in that of the people. In the first place it is identical with the French word *Commune,* being the aggregate of persons living together in the same place, the police jurisdiction of a city, town, or village; but the meaning is quite different in the common conception of the people. Even the literal signification of the word *Mir* indicates the sacredness of the idea, denoting both Commune and World: the Greek *Cosmos* is the only equivalent to the Russian word. I can recollect no German or Romanic proverb in which the power, right, and sacredness of the Commune are recognized; the Russian language has a great number: —

God alone direct the Mir.

The Mir is great.

The Mir is the surging billow.

The neck and shoulders of the Mir are broad.

Throw everything upon the Mir, it will carry it all.

The Mir sighs, and the rock is rent asunder.
The Mir sobs, and it re-echoes in the forest.
A thread of the Mir becomes a shirt for the naked.
No one in the world can separate from the Mir.
What is decided by the Mir must come to pass.
The Mir is answerable for the country's defence.

The source is: Haxthausen, op. cit.; vol. 1, pp. 119 ff. and 133 ff.

THE MIR AND THE LAND. The Russians say that the earth belongs to the Creator, and has been granted by Him to Adam and his descendants. Successive generations inherited the possession; and as their numbers increased they occupied a greater extent of the earth's surface, which they shared under the Divine guidance in the world's history. The country now called Russia fell to the progenitor of the Russians; and his descendants, remaining united under the head of their race, and thus constituting a people, spread over the territory which has thus by the providence of God become their property. The disposal of it, as in a family, belongs to the father, the head of the race, the Czar; an individual has a right to share in it only so long as he lives in unity with the Czar and his people. The soil is the joint property of the national family, and the father or Czar has the sole disposal of it, and distributes it among the families into which the nation in the course of time has been divided. A joint occupancy of the whole could only exist when the people led a nomadic life: when they became settled, a portion was assigned to each family, which occupied its share under a separate head. The right of the family thus arose in a manner quite analogous to that of the nation. The property is a family property, belonging equally but undivided to all the members of the family, — the father having the disposal and distribution of the produce. If a member insists on a division, he receives his portion, but loses all claim upon the joint possession; he is paid off and excluded, and thenceforth constitutes a new family. The families thus remained for many generations under their respective heads, and became family communes.

The Commune is still considered in law to form a family. If a stranger comes to reside in a village, he is adopted. Every member has an equal claim upon the joint and undivided communal property; the distribution of the produce rests with the fathers, the "White-heads" or Starosta (Elders). A member cannot possess private property in the land and therefore cannot bequeath it; but his sons, by virtue of their birth into the family, have an immediate right to a share in the joint property and its usufruct.

．．．

COMMUNAL LAND DISTRIBUTION. The principle is, that the whole of the land (tillage, meadows, pasture, woods, streams, etc.) belongs to the population regarded as a unity, and every male inhabitant has a right to an equal share. This share is therefore constantly changing; for the birth of every boy creates a new claim, and the shares of those who die revert to the Commune. The woods, pastures, hunting-grounds, and fisheries remain undivided, and free to all the inhabitants; but the arable land and meadows are divided, according to their value, amongst the males. This equal division is of course difficult, as the soil differs in quality, and portions of it may be distant or inconveniently situated. There are however in each Commune skilfull land-surveyors, without any education but what has been acquired from the traditional habits of the place, who execute the work to the satisfaction of all. The land is first divided, according to its quality, position, or general value, into sections, each possessing on the whole equal advantages; the sections are then divided into as many portions, in long strips, as there are shares required, and these are taken by lot. This is the usual plan, but each District, and frequently each Commune, has its local customs. In the Government of Yaroslaf, for instance, many of the Communes have peculiar measuring rods, which are almost regarded as sacred; they correspond with the quality of the soil, the rod for the best land being the shortest, and that for the worst the longest: the shares therefore vary in size, but are equal in value.

The preceding remarks apply to the free Communes, to whom the land belongs as their own property: these are very numerous, all the Cossack Communes for instance being of this class. The principle however is the same whether the peasants are owners of the land, or merely tenants as on the Crown estates, or only attached to the soil, as in the case of the serfs. . . . Equal division prevails in Russia, even among the private serfs, who in Great Russia were formerly always, and still are generally, placed upon obrok. It is however somewhat modified in the case of those who have to perform corvees for the proprietor. The following is the most ancient method of cultivating an estate by the labour of the serfs, and one which is still adopted in Great Russia when they are unable to pay the obrok and the proprietor is consequently obliged to set up a farming establishment of his own. The latter sets apart for himself a portion of the estate, at most onethird or one-fourth; and the remainder is retained by the peasants, who are required to cultivate without payment the part reserved by the proprietor. They manure the land, plough and harrow it, reap the crop and carry it to market, at their own expense. . . .

Where the obrok is paid, every male receives an equal share of the land (the father takes it for his infant son), and each must undertake to pay an equal share of the tax. Where the corvee system prevails, of course the boys and old men cannot work, and have no claim to the land, which is given as an equivalent for labour.

. . .

The following selection is largely interpretive. The reader may wish to take some of Haxthausen's statements cum grano salis. The source is: Haxthausen, op. cit., vol. 2, pp. 230 ff.

THE PEASANT AND THE TSAR. The patriarchal government, feelings, and organization are in full activity in the life, manners, and customs of the Great Russians. The same unlimited authority which the father exercises over all his children is possessed by the mother over her daughters: the same reverence and obedience are shown to the Communal authorities, the Starostas and the White-heads, and to the common father of all, the Czar. The Russian addresses the same word to his real father, io the Starosta, to his proprietor, to the Emperor, and finally to God, viz. Father; in like manner he calls every Russian, whether known to him or not, Brother.

The common Russian entertains no slavish, but simply a childlike, fear and veneration for the Czar; he loves him with devoted tenderness. He becomes a soldier reluctantly, but, once a soldier, he has no feeling of vindictiveness for the coercion exercised upon him, and serves the Czar with utmost fidelity. The celebrated expression "Prikazeno" (It is ordered), has a magical power over him. Whatever the Emperor commands must be done; the Russian cannot conceive the impossibility of its execution; the orders of the Police even are not worded *Zaprestcheno* (It is forbidden), but *Ne prikazeno* (It is not ordered). The profound veneration felt for the Czar is also shown in the care of everything belonging to him; the Russian has the deepest respect for *Kaziomne*, or property of the Czar. "Kaziomne does not die, does not burn in fire, or drown in water," says a Russian proverb.

There is scarcely an instance recorded of any collectors of the Crown taxes, who often traverse the country with considerable sums of money, being attacked and robbed. In the north, in the Government of Vologda, where the morals of the people are still particularly pure and simple, and great confidence and honesty prevail, when a collector enters a village, he taps at each window and calls out, "Kaza!" Then each person brings out his Crown tax for the year and throws it into the open bag: the collector does not count the money, being well assured that he is never cheated. If his visit is in the night, he enters the first substantial house, places the money-bag under the image of the Saint, looks for a place to rest on, and sleeps with perfect assurance of finding his money safe in the morning.

The patriarchal ruler or Czar appears necessary to the very existence of the people; we never find an insurrection against the Government or Czardom, but only against certain persons, and generally upon the grounds of legitimacy, as in the instance of the false Demetrius or Pugatchef, who represented himself as the exiled Peter III, or as in the insurrection of 1825.

The people have shown invariable obedience to every government, even to that of the Mongols; they frequently indeed complain of supposed wrongs, but there the matter ends.

The Czar is the father of his people; but the descent, and even the sex, of the sovereign is indifferent to them. The Empress Catherine II, a foreign princess, experienced the same veneration and attachment as princes born in Russia; she became nationalized on assuming the Czardom. This profound veneration for authority passes to the person of every one who assumes the office of Czar.

• • •

The Baron's report on local government, unlike his comments on the imperial government which were quoted above, was factual rather than interpretive. The source is: Haxthausen, op. cit., vol. 1, pp. 16–18.

LOCAL GOVERNMENT. The communal organizations of the Crown peasants have undergone some alterations in recent times. At the head of each village has always stood, and still stands, the Starosta, chosen by the peasants from among themselves; under him, and as his assistants, are the Tenth-men, each chosen by ten heads of families: these remain usually one year on duty, although by law they ought to be elected every month. In very small villages there is often only a Tenth-man at the head: these have no salary, but the Starostas receive sums varying up to 175 roubles, according to the number of inhabitants. Here and there, even in former times, several villages constituted an Associated Commune; this is now the universal organisation. Formerly the head of the Associated Commune, the Starshina, was the oldest Starosta of the villages; he is now elected by the collective heads of houses of all the villages; every ten houses electing two heads of families, and these appointing the Starshina. The latter receives a salary of 300 to 400 roubles. As many villages as contain together about 500 or 600 heads of families are united into one, and form an Associated Commune, which appoints the recruits for the army, who were formerly taken by general levies, so many from every thousand inhabitants.

The union of several Associated Communes constitutes a district, at the head of which stands the chief; he too is elected, and for three years. The Chief of the Circle must give in writing his opinion upon the choice, and the Governor confirms it. He may be re-elected if no complaints are made against him.

Several Districts form a Circle, which is presided over by an officer of state, the Chief of the Circle, who is named by the Minister. He belongs to the 7th or 8th class of civil servants, and has an assistant, who is of the 9th class. The Chiefs of Circles are under the head of the department of Domains in each Government.

Each village has a tribunal, composed of the Starosta and two assistants, who are likewise elected. It has the right to inflict 25 blows with a stick, and to fine to the amount of 5 roubles; it also decides cases of *meum* and *teum* but not of heritable property. It exercises no criminal jurisdiction, but only presents informations, instructions, issues writs of arrest, etc.

The Chief of the District, and two assistants, who are likewise elected, form the District Tribunal. This constitutes an appeal court from the communal tribunal; but it can only diminish, not augment the punishments inflicted by the latter.

. . .

The two descriptions which follow may be taken as typical not only of the Russian scene but also of Haxthausen's reporting. He made searching and detailed inquiries wherever he went, and recorded his findings at length. The description of Veliko Selo is much abridged. The source is: Haxthausen, op. cit., vol. 1, pp. 101 ff. and 106 ff.

A FARM. From hence we went to a small village in the neighbourhood, and examined the farm of one of the peasants. The gable-end of the house faced the street. Next to it was a long narrow courtyard with a gate. This house had also an entrance from the street, which is not very usual; the door was situated on the left, with another small one on the right, for the lower story of the house in which are the smaller animals. We ascended a staircase, to the dwelling room, which had no other furniture than a bench running round it. Opposite the door in the corner stood the image of the saint, with a lamp burning under it; and on the walls were some shelves, upon which were placed all kinds of vessels and utensils. Spinning-wheels and hand-looms testified to the widely disseminated linen manufacture in this district. An enormous stove, built up with bricks, filled one third of the room; this in winter is a sleeping-place; beside it a small staircase led down to the lower part of the house, which serves as a store, and where the smaller animals, fowls and swine, take up their abode in the night; in winter also the cows are milked here. On the other side of the staircase are some closets, with very small windows, receptacles for all sorts of things, such as boxes — one for each member of the family, containing clothes. In summer the family generally sleep here. The stove of the dwelling-room serves for cooking, and is always heated, even in summer. Immediately adjoining the house is the stable for the cattle, into which is an entrance from the house: it is covered with two roofs, so that the house and the stable had three roofs, one lower than the other. Here stand the horses and cows, separated by partitions, but not by walls; in the winter it is very cold, but to this they are accustomed.

Behind the stable stands a building in which the carts and agricultural implements are kept. Here the supply of salt and meal is also stored, and a strong padlock is put upon the door. Some paces distant, but in a line with it, is a covered cellar, containing cabbages, fruits, etc., then a small cabbage-garden, with the granary at the end, then the spot where the peasant places his grain before putting it in the granary and dries the hay; the last of this row of buildings is always the bath-house.

It might be imagined that the dwelling would be very dirty, the atmosphere mephitic, — with so many animals and a low, heated room, — but it was not so; the air was purer than I could have expected, to which the constantly burning fire and open windows contributed; moreover the room was kept so clean and neat that it was a pleasure to see.

* * *

THE VILLAGE OF VELIKO. The land and its inhabitants had been the property of seven sisters, three of whom were already dead; the rest did not live here, and having no agricultural establishment, had placed the peasants upon obrok; not however laying the tax upon the separate families, but upon the township at large as a tribute, proportioned to its population, the extent and quality of arable land conceded, together with the meadows, woods, and manufacture (an extensive one of linen is carried on), in the township. The amount of this tribute was calculated, first, from the rent derivable from the land; secondly, from the number of individuals to whom it was granted; thirdly, from the peculiar resources of skill and industry with which the inhabitants carry on certain branches of manufacture.

* * *

The buildings are such as are usual in small towns; there is also a bazaar, some good modern houses, which testify to the well-being of the inhabitants, and a considerable manufactory of linen. The inhabitants do not themselves spin, but buy the yarn. The weaving of fine linen is paid for at the rate of 7d. per arshine (28 inches); and even a woman, if a good weaver, can with ease earn 11d. to 1s. 4d. a day. These are high wages, and quite disproportionate to the price of agricultural produce; for, in good years, the price of 5¾ bushels of rye falls generally as low as 4s. 6d.

* * *

This place possesses a well-arranged school which the priest had undertaken to conduct.

* * *

A considerable horse-fair is held here annually, although there are not 50 horses in the place. Veliko Selo is a peasant village, but has no agriculture; its inhabitants manufacture linen, but grow no flax; there is a horse-fair, but they have no horses.

* * *

In one of the peasant houses we found a tailor working at a kaftan; and we were told that in some villages in this government the entire population are tailors. At certain times, generally in the winter, they travel about for work; and on arriving at a village they work from house to house, until all the inhabitants appear in new trim: then they go to another village. They are paid by piece-work, not by day wages: for making a grey coat they receive from 5½d. to 8d., and for a blue kaftan from 1s. 10d. to 3s. 9d., in addition to their board.

• • •

Haxthausen was especially interested in the economy of Russia, and perhaps the most valuable parts of his study are those which deal with agriculture, trade and industry. His observations in these matters have long been regarded as first class sources. The notes which follow have been culled from scattered sections of his book. They have been greatly abridged and slightly adapted. The source is: Haxthausen, op. cit., vol. 1, pp. 127, 136 ff., 142 ff., 147, 148 ff., 162 ff., 164 ff., 183 ff., 215 ff., and 236 ff.

NOTES ON RUSSIAN ECONOMY. In the central parts of the empire, in the country of the "black soil," the fertility is so great that manure is not required; the land is ploughed only once, often indeed the surface is scarcely disturbed: thus but little capital is required for tillage and manure, and in abundant years, seed-corn costs only about tenpence a bushel. Meadow improvements are rare, and fruit-trees are hardly anywhere to be seen. Sheep are seldom reared among the peasantry, cattle only to a limited extent, and horses are cheap. In the Government of Yaroslaf the usual price of a good farm horse is about £ 2. A Russian peasant builds his house entirely without assistance, and obtains the timber gratis from the woods of his Commune; the whole cost is scarcely fifteen shillings. Thus in the greater part of Russia the capital invested in agriculture is hardly worth taking into account; permanency of occupation is therefore by no means of the same importance as in the rest of Europe. Generally speaking, in the greater part of the empire the soil has very little value of itself. Here it is valued only as a basis for human industry. Until the last few years it was customary to make contracts, sales, donations, and bequests, with reference merely to the number of peasant families, — in such or such a village so many peasants were sold, bequeathed, etc.; the land was regarded only as an appendage to the human beings upon it.

• • •

The peasants in this part of the Government of Yaroslaf practise the simple three-course husbandry. From the end of June to the beginning of August the winter-field is supplied with manure, which frequently lies four to six weeks before it is plowed in. The land is then broken up with the heavy plow, and harrowed; the winter corn is sown, and the soil afterwards turned over with the light fork-plough. The summer-field is not ploughed again in the autumn by the peasants, but this occurs sometimes on estates where a better system of cultivation has been introduced. The summer seed-time is over by the middle of May. In the field-labour an almost military order prevails. On the same day, at the same hour, the peasants all proceed to their ploughing etc., and return home in the same manner: this regularity is not compulsory, but arises spontaneously from their social and imitative disposition: the influence of communal life is everywhere manifest.

In the township of Veliko Selo the wealthiest of the inhabitants are linen-manufacturers; agriculture is left to the poor, and is in a very rude state. In order to retain the stubble-fields for pasturage as long as possible, as well as on account of the short summer and the inferior breed of horses, the land is ploughed only once, — immediately after manuring and before sowing. Complaints are made that the meadows are either too dry, or marshy and sour; but neither drainage nor irrigation has been attempted, although the soil presents no difficulties. . . . The rearing of cattle and sheep is but little attended to, and the horned cattle are inferior. The horses of the peasants are small, but the landowners and richer class of peasants possess a larger and stronger breed. . . . A considerable quantity of hemp and flax is grown in these districts. . . . Potatoes have only been introduced about five years among the peasants, as they considered the cultivation of them sinful; these people are now however becoming accustomed to them, and on the nobles' estates they are even used as food for cattle.

The forests are not under any regular management; those belonging to proprietors who live upon their estates are, to some extent, protected; but in the villages which pay obrok they are given up to the unrestrained use of the peasants, who cut down the trees recklessly, and a scarcity of wood begins already to be felt.

• • •

Ribinsk is 54 miles from Yaroslaf, and is the centre of the internal trade of Russia. All the various products brought by the Volga and its tributary streams, and destined for St. Petersburg have here to be re-embarked in smaller vessels to be sent on the canals. These commodities arrive here in 1700 or 1800 large vessels, and are re-laden upon 6000 barges and boats, and thus sent on to St. Petersburg; the value of the commodities is said to amount to forty or fifty million roubles. Before the formation of the canals which unite St. Petersburg with the Volga, Ribinsk was an insignificant township, whose inhabitants paid an obrok either in fish or money. When it rose to the rank of a city the obrok was remitted, and the inhabitants now pay only the usual poll-tax to the Crown, in addition to the town rates, which amount to 50,000 or 60,000 roubles. At the present time, it contains more than 600 merchants of the three guilds. The retail trade is carried on by the small burghers and by the Raznotchinstzi, a class between the burghers and the peasants. . . . Among the labourers here is a class called Burlaki, whose occupation is to tow the vessels on the river. They are a robust and active race of men, and have formed themselves into communes and artels, with leaders, Starostas, and masters, whom they elect. For the journey from Samara to Ribinsk (a distance of 650 miles, but not less than 1000 by the river) a Burlak receives 70 roubles; for the journey from Nizhni Novgorod (perhaps 460 miles), 50 roubles. A Burlak, when fortunate, can perform the journey between Samara and Ribinsk three times in the course of the summer; he has then perhaps 70 roubles left; but if, through adverse circumstances, he only makes the trip twice, he generally consumes all he earns.

• • •

At Yaroslaf we visited some of the manufactories. The work-people are paid by the piece: for weaving shirt linen, they receive 6 copecks per arshine, and a woman can with ease weave from ten to 12 arshines a day. For weaving table-linen a man is paid one rouble ten copecks per arshine, and can earn two roubles a day. A man who was weaving towelling told us he could produce from 40 to 50 arshines, and was paid 34 copecks per arshine. I believe that compared with the price of food, the wages of labour are no where so high as in Russia.

• • •

In the Government of Yaroslaf (one of the most interesting provinces of the empire from the point of view of my study), the soil is not fertile and the climate is severe, but the situation along the Volga is favorable. Trade and commerce of all kinds pay well while agriculture yields no profits. Labour which in the countries on the Danube is spread over seven months, here, on account of the short summer has to be concluded in four months. Work which could be done in the former area with four men and four horses, here would require seven men and seven horses. The net return on labour and capital for an estate north of the Volga would be about half that for an estate of equal size and fertility in Mainz. Actually, the land at Mainz will return six to seven times the seed; that along the Volga at Yaroslaf, hardly three times the seed.

Agricultural operations can be carried on only in the four summer months: during this period, all the labour is employed, but in the remaining eight months, as far as agriculture is concerned, it is completely at rest. The consequence has been, from the earliest times, a remarkable development of manufacturing industry, as well in the country as in the towns. This industry was originally applied only to the raw produce of the district, which was converted into manufactures and carried to market by the inhabitants and producers in the eight winter months, during which agriculture left them at leisure. The majority of serfs in this Government have always been obrok peasants. This gave an extraordinary stimulus to manufacturing. Agriculture yielded only a bare subsistence, but no profit, and money had to be procured for the payment of the obrok. The raw products fetched low prices, but all the manufactured articles high ones. Thus these raw products were converted into commodities; and carpenters, wheel-wrights, makers of wooden shoes, bast-weavers, tar-boilers, boat builders, spinners and weavers of linen and sailcloth, ropemakers, saddlers, curriers, and shoe makers, brought to market their various articles in wood, hemp, flax and leather. These artisans however did not live scattered amongst the population, working only for the supply of the immediate wants of a neighbourhood; they worked together as in a factory, and produced articles for the markets; and in this way the remarkable spirit of association was developed, grounded upon the organization of the Russian Communes.

The various trades have mostly formed themselves into separate Communes: for instance, all the inhabitants of one village are shoemakers, those of another are smiths, etc. The members of the artisan communes also constantly assist each other with their capital and labour; purchases and sales are transacted in common, and they send their commodities together to the markets and towns, where they have shops for the sale of them.

. . .

I will give here some statistical tables of the year 1841, of the five Circles of the Government of Yaroslaf.

Circle	No. of villages in 21 sq. miles	Av. No. of houses in each village	Av. No. of inhabitants in each village	Av. No. of acres to each village
Poshekhon	9	13	83	1417
Mologa	8	16	124	1803
Ribinsk	21	11	63	634
Mishkin	16	15	114	840
Uglitch	15	13	99	940

Circle	Average No. of Acres to Each Male Inhabitant			
	Arable	Meadow	Good Wood	Bad Wood
Poshekhon	9.31	2.03	9.72	12.62
Mologa	6.07	1.35	9.31	11.14
Ribinsk	6.75	.90	6.75	1.42
Mishkin	8.10	.81	.25	4.86
Uglitch	6.30	.90	2.16	9.45

It is manifest from this that agriculture cannot maintain the inhabitants in these districts. In the Circle of Uglitch there are about six acres of arable land to each male inhabitant; 2½ being here reckoned the average grain producers, the calculation stands as follows:

2 acres sown with rye (after deducting the seed) ..... 7 bushels
1 acre sown with barley (after deducting the seed) ..... 3½ bushels
―――――
·10½ bushels

The remaining acre is sown with oats for the cattle. 7 bushels of rye give 387 pounds of bread; 3½ bushels of barley give 169 pounds of bread:—total 556 pounds.

The principal food of the Russian people consists of bread; potatoes are unknown in most districts; cabbage is the only vegetable which is much used. Animal food, milk, and butter are little eaten. In the army, each soldier receives 2½ pounds of bread a day. A healthy Russian peasant cannot subsist without three pounds; in the harvest he eats five pounds; and in White Russia even as much as seven pounds. If women, old people, and children are counted, one pound and a half must be reckoned for each individual of the population. A man and woman, according to this calculation, require on an average 1094 pounds of bread in the year. There is always a deficit therefore of 538 pounds of bread for each couple, or of 22,855,000 pounds of bread for the whole population of the Circle, which can only be supplied by importations from other districts, and therefore only with the aid of auxiliary occupations and manufacturing profits, to enable the people to purchase these supplies.

In the northern districts, Olonetz, Vologda, Archangel, there is a tolerably dense population and little agriculture. The most important sources of production and employment are furnished by the forests: wood for ship-building, logs, planks, pitch, tar and turpentine. These employments occupy the population during the winter and the short season of spring floods, but the people have little to do in the summer. They therefore proceed in large numbers to the regions further south and assist the inhabitants in field labour and the harvest for wages. Such migratory workers earn from sixty to eighty roubles for the four summer months.

The number of these migratory workers cannot be ascertained with certainty, but they are many. Some go away for short periods, some for longer, and some permanently. All of them customarily retain their communal rights and continue to be inscribed in the Revision lists of their homes. In one unusual instance, of the 9500 male souls inscribed in the Commune; 7000 are go-aways.

. . . . These traveling artisans remain together, according to their respective trades, in the large towns, and form artisan communes. When any work is to be done, the cleverest among them assume the office of contractors. If a house is to be built, a contractor is sought. He makes the bargain and concludes the contract. Then he collects his comrades, and agrees with them as to their assistance and share of the profits. If the project is expensive, he goes to his native village and begs the money necessary for the undertaking. The people of the village, who share in the profit, collect the money and hand it to the contractor. They merely pledge their word, and all depends upon their mutual truth and fidelity; cases seldom or never occur of their defrauding one another. These are ordinary, uneducated people, who can often neither read nor write, but possess a remarkable technical genius. . . .

A large number of these young travelers are pedlars. Perhaps the greater number are carriers. A considerable number, particularly those from the neighbourhood of Rostof, are gardeners. A large number of persons go to Moscow and St. Petersburg as bakers. Others become drivers, joiners, carpenters, etc. . . .

Fairs in Russia are numerous and important. There are 37 large fairs in the Government of Yaroslaf. In 1842 goods to the value of six million silver roubles were exposed for sale in these fairs, and about two-thirds of them were sold. . . .

In the year 1839, there were 105 modern factories in Yaroslaf; in the year 1842, 158 factories with an annual production valued at 2,430,000 silver roubles. . . . There is also considerable trade. Corn, flour and iron are brought from the south and east, and sent to the north and west; on the other hand wine and colonial products come from St. Petersburg, and are sent to western Siberia. The great water and land highways cross each other here. The value of the whole trade is estimated at four million silver roubles. . . .

The people of Kubensk are unable to supply the labour necessary in summer, and procure assistants from the districts further north; one of these servants receives for the summer months his board and sixty roubles; a day-labourer with his horse is paid in seed-time 2s. 3d., in the hay-harvest 1s. 10 d., and without a horse 11d. to 2s. 3d.; the day-labour of a woman during harvest is paid 7d. to 9d.

In winter, as soon as the snow has become hard, the men employ themselves in trade, and the transport of mercantile commodities. But in the spring and harvest also, when there is sufficient water, they carry on some trade upon the lake, which is connected with navigable rivers. They likewise convey from their own farms grain, vegetable, hides, tallow, and fish (from the lake). The vegetables they dispose of mostly in Vologda, but the other articles they convey to the Volga, and even to St. Petersburg, whence they bring back other commodities as return cargo, for their own trade and that of others. The gardens alone are said, by the sale of vegetables, to yield on an average a surplus of £3 13s. to each household. The villagers therefore are generally in easy circumstances, and often very rich, a fortune of 40,000 to 50,000 roubles being not at all infrequent. . . .

In driving through the fields of some of the small villages (never of the larger ones), I observed that after every five to eight strips of arable land there was always a ridge of turf; this is from a foot to 18 inches broad, and forms the boundary of the two pieces of land. On inquiry I found that in these very small villages the yearly division of land did not exist, or had been given up, but that the ground was allotted once for all, a part to each house. Each portion is divided into as many strips as there are houses in the village, and then the whole portion is parted from the next by the green ridge. This is the only exception to the popular mode of dividing the land I have found.

. . .

The Polovnik system may be briefly explained as follows. The land is let to a free tenant farmer for a term of years on condition of his delivering yearly to the landlord half the produce. The word *Polovnik* is derived from *polovinia,* half. In certain areas of North Russia, there have been of old some families belonging to the nobles, but they possess no land with serfs living upon it: they however, as well as a number of citizens in the towns, own large districts and entire villages as their own property, without the right of cultivating them by serfs but only according to the Polovnik law—by letting them to peasant farmers for the half or a certain part of the produce. The contracts are from 6 to 20 years. Each party is free at the conclusion of the contract or a year's notice, to dissolve the relation. The contract is extremely simple in form: the parties appear before the Circle Court, and cause to be inscribed in the Polovnik books, which are kept there, this declaration:—"Mr. W........ has granted to the peasants N. N. N. the village of A. and the land annexed to it, according to Polovnik law, for 6, 10, or 20 years." . . .

The village of Vizena is well built, and contains several stone houses. At the last Revision there were 1820 souls in the village Commune. I have remarked that the majority of the inhabitants form an association of boot and shoe-makers. There are also six glue and two wax-light manufactories, and 8 large ones in which carpets and felt boots are prepared from horse and cow hair, a branch of industry carried on in many of the houses as a sub-sidiary occupation. At the Fair of Nizhni Novgorod a quantity of these, valued at 50,000 roubles are sold, and in smaller fairs in the vicinity an additional quantity amounting to 10,000 or 20,000 roubles. About 500 members of the Commune are always absent with passports; they wander about in search of work as far as Saratof, Astrakhan, Uralsk, and even into the interior of Siberia. Some remain away ten or fifteen years, others establish themselves permanently in various towns, never returning to their homes; they do not however cease to belong to the Commune, but pay their taxes here, and retain their houses, gardens, and communal rights, which they let out or deliver over to some other person.

Two hundred of the inhabitants proceed every year to the Fair at Nizhni Novgorod, and remain there two months, working and selling the goods belonging to the villagers. There is a great disparity of wealth among the inhabitants. Formerly there was more wealth than at present, two peasants possessing each above 500,000 roubles; but there are even still 15 houses whose trade receipts amount to between 20,000 and 50,000 roubles.

The Prince has imposed a certain tax upon the inhabitants and leaves it to the Commune to divide this among them. They have elected one White-head for every 100 souls, who taxes the members of the Commune according to their means, the richer ones paying for so many souls.

Additional Readings

Pares, *History.* Pp. 277–340

Tompkins, *Russia.* Pp. 291–444

Vernadsky, *History.* Pp. 128–150

Martin, *Picture History.* Pp. 108–143

Goodall, *Soviet Russia.* Pp. 7–8

Karpovich, M. M., *Imperial Russia, 1801–1917.* New York: Henry Holt & Co., 1932. Pp. 1–34

Rambaud, *Russia.* Vol. 2, chaps. 11–14

Miliukov (Karpovich, ed.) *Outlines.* Vol. 2, chap. 2

Lobanov-Rostovsky, *Russia and Asia.* Chaps. 5 and 6

Kornilov, A. (A. S. Kaun, tr.) *Modern Russian History from the Age of Catherine the Great to the End of the Nineteenth Century.* Two volumes in one. New York: A. A. Knopf, 1943. Vol. 1

Scott, J. F. & Baltzly, A., *Readings in European History since 1814.* New York: F. S. Crofts & Co., 1934. Pp. 15–16, 31–43, 268–282

Stschepkin, E., Russia Under Alexander I and the Invasion of 1812," *Cambridge Modern History.* Vol. 9, chap. 16

Askenazy, S., "Russia," *Cambridge Modern History.* Vol. 10, chap. 13

Drage, G., "Russia and the Levant," *Cambridge Modern History.* Vol. 11, chap. 9, part 1

Tarle, E., *Napoleon's Invasion of Russia, 1812.* New York: Oxford University Press, 1942.

Libaire, G. & Hanoteau, J. (eds.) *With Napoleon in Russia. The Memoirs of General de Caulaincourt, Duke of Vicenza.* New York: William Morrow & Co., 1935.

Mazour, A. G., *The First Russian Revolution, 1825; the Decembrist Movement, Its Origins, Development and Significance.* Berkeley: U. of California Press, 1937.

Waliszewski, K., *Paul the First of Russia, the Son of Catherine II.* Philadelphia: J. B. Lippincott, 1913.

Blease, W. L. *Suvorof.* London: A. Constable, 1920.

Paleologue, M. (E. & W. Muir, trs.), *The Enigmatic Czar. The Life of Alexander I of Russia.* London: Hamish-Hamilton, 1938.

Strakhovsky, L. I., *Alexander I of Russia: The Man Who Defeated Napoleon.* New York: Norton, 1947.

Kulomzin, A., "The Siberian Hermit, Theodore Kuzmich," *Slavonic & East European Review.* (London) Vol. 2, pp. 381–387

Schmitt, B. E., "The Diplomatic Preliminaries of the Crimean War," *American Historical Review.* October, 1919. Pp. 36–67

Bancroft, H. H., *History of Alaska, 1730–1885. San Francisco: Bancroft & Co., 1886.*

Cresson, W. P., *The Holy Alliance.* New York: Oxford University Press, 1922.

Herzen, A., *The Memoirs of Alexander Herzen.* New Haven: Yale University Press, 1923.

Chevigny, H., *Lord of Alaska; Baranov and the Russian Adventure.* New York: The Viking Press, 1943.

Turgenev, I., *A Sportsman's Sketches.* New York: E. P. Dutton & Co., 1932

Tolstoy, L., *War and Peace.* Three volumes. Everyman's Library Edition, (E. P. Dutton & Co.)

Tolstoy, L., *The Cossacks.* World's Classic Series.

Gogol, N., *Dead Souls.* Everyman's Library Edition.

Aksakov, S., *A Russian Gentleman.* New York: The Readers Club, 1943.

Lobanov-Rostovsky, *Russia and Europe.* Chaps. 3–13.

Part V. THE REIGNS OF ALEXANDER II AND ALEXANDER III

Wallace on Russia

When Sir Donald Mackenzie Wallace first sought a publisher for his careful and scholarly study of Russia he met only rebuffs. No one, they told him, would be interested in such a work; and the fact that it was the product of years of first-hand investigation seemed almost to count against it. Sir Donald perforce bowed to their judgments and rewrote the entire study in a more popular manner, sugar-coating facts with anecdotes. The new version was accepted and first published in 1877. Revised editions were published in 1905 and 1912. The selections which follow were taken from the first edition in order to show how Russia of the 1870s looked to a very talented and careful observer at that time. Some of the judgments and conclusions set forth in this edition were revised and modified in the subsequent editions. The source is: Wallace, D. M., Russia. London, 1877. Pp. 2, 57–58, 78–80, 88–97, 105–110, 120–137, 165–168, 172–174, 195–208, 213–218, 229–240, 250–256, 282–284, 286–288, 424–431, 443–448, 472–484, 500–509.

AN AUTOCRAT IN ACTION. From St. Petersburg to Moscow the locomotive runs for a distance of 400 miles, almost as "the crow" is supposed to fly, turning neither to the right hand nor to the left. For fifteen weary hours the passenger in the express train looks out on forest and morass, and rarely catches sight of human habitation. Only once he perceives in the distance what may be called a town; it is Tver which has been thus favored, not because it is a place of importance, but simply because it happened to be near the straight line. And why was the railway constructed in this extraordinary fashion? For the best of all reasons—because the Tsar so ordered it. When the preliminary survey was being made, Nicholas learned that the officers intrusted with the task—and the Minister of Ways and Roads in the number—were being influenced more by personal than technical considerations, and he determined to cut the Gordian knot in true Imperial style. When the Minister laid before him the map with the intention of explaining the proposed route, he took a ruler, drew a straight line from the one terminus to the other, and remarked in a tone that precluded all discussion,

"You will construct the line so!" And the line was so constructed—remaining to all future ages, like St. Petersburg and the Pyramids, a magnificent monument of autocratic power.

PRIESTS AND THE PEOPLE. Since that time I have frequently spoken on this subject with competent authorities, and nearly all have admitted that the present condition of the clergy is highly unsatisfactory, and that the parish priest rarely enjoys the respect of his parishioners. In a semi-official report, which I once accidentally stumbled upon when searching for material of a different kind, the facts are stated in the following plain language: "The people"—I seek to translate as literally as possible—"do not respect the clergy, but persecute them with derision and reproaches, and feel them to be a burden. In nearly all the popular comic stories, the priest, his wife, or his laborer is held up to ridicule, and in all the proverbs and popular sayings where the clergy are mentioned it is always with derision. The people shun the clergy, and have recourse to them not from the inner impulse of conscience, but from necessity. . . . And why do the people not respect the clergy? Because it forms a class apart; because, having received a false kind of education, it does not introduce into the life of the people the teaching of the Spirit, but remains in the mere dead forms of outward ceremonial, at the same time despising these forms even to blasphemy; because the clergy itself continually presents examples of want of respect to religion, and transforms the service of God into a profitable trade. Can the people respect the clergy when they hear how one priest stole money from below the pillow of a dying man at the moment of confession, how another was publicly dragged out of a house of ill fame, how a third christened a dog, how a fourth whilst officiating at the Easter service was dragged by the hair from the altar by the deacon? Is it possible for the people to respect priests who spend their time in the gin-shop, write fraudulent petitions, fight with the cross in their hands, and abuse each other in bad language at the altar? One might fill several pages with examples of this kind—in each instance naming the time and place—without over-stepping the boundaries of the province of Nizhni-Novgorod. Is it possible for the people to respect the clergy when they see that truth has disappeared from it, and that the consistories, guided in their decisions not by rules, but by personal friendship and bribery, destroy in it the last remains of truthfulness? If we add to all this the false certificates which the clergy give to those who do not wish to partake of the Eucharist, the dues illegally extracted from the Old Ritualists, the conversion of the altar into a source of revenue, the giving of churches to priests' daughters as a dowry, and similar phenomena, the question as to whether the people can respect the clergy requires no answer."

As these words were written by an orthodox Russian, celebrated for his extensive and intimate knowledge of Russian provincial life, and were addressed in all seriousness to a member of the Imperial family, we may safely assume that they contain a considerable amount of truth. The reader must not, however, imagine that all Russian priests are of the kind abo˙ referred to. Many of them are honest, respectable, well-intentioned men, who conscientiously fulfill their humble duties, and strive hard to procure a good education for their children.

PEASANT CREDULITY. Of the ignorant credulity of the Russian peasantry I might relate many curious illustrations. The most absurd rumors sometimes awaken consternation throughout a whole district. One of the most common reports of this kind is that a female conscription is about to take place. About the time of the Duke of Edinburgh's marriage this report was specially frequent. A large number of young girls were to be sent, it was said, to England in a red ship. Why the ship was to be painted red, and what was to be done with the Russian maidens when they should arrive at their destination, I never succeeded in discovering. Perhaps it was that the people confounded Queen Victoria with the King of Dahomey, or imagined that we were about to adopt that potentate's peculiar military organization; or perhaps it was, as one peasant explained, simply because it was supposed that there were very few women in England. This false conception might have been corrected by a landed proprietor whom I once met, and from whom I learned that about one-third of the entire population of the British Isles was composed of unfortunate spinsters condemned to celibacy by the paucity of the male population.

The most amusing instance of credulity which I can recall was the following, related to me by a peasant-woman who came from the village in question. One day in winter, about the time of sunset, a peasant-family was startled by the entrance of a strange visitor—a female figure, dressed as St. Barbara is commonly represented in the religious pictures. All present were very much astonished by this apparition; but the figure told them, in a low, soft voice, to be of good cheer, for she was St. Barbara, and had come to honor them with a visit as a reward for their piety. The peasant thus favored was not remarkable for his piety, but he did not consider it necessary to correct the mistake of his saintly visitor, and requested her to be seated. With perfect readiness she accepted the invitation, and began at once to discourse in an edifying way. Meanwhile the news of this wonderful apparition spread like wildfire, and all the inhabitants of the village, as well as those of a neighboring village about a mile distant, collected in and around the house of the favored family. Whether the priest was among those who came my informant did not know. Many of those who had come could not get within hearing, but those at the outskirts of the crowd hoped that the saint might come out before disappearing. Their hopes were gratified. About midnight the mysterious visitor announced that she would go and bring St. Nicholas, the miracle-worker, and requested all to remain perfectly still during her absence. The crowd respectfully made way for her, and she passed out into the darkness. With breathless expectation all awaited the arrival of St. Nicholas, who is the favorite saint of the Russian peasantry; but hours passed, and he did not appear. At last, towards sunrise, some of the less zealous spectators began to return home, and those of them who had come from the neighboring village discovered to their horror that during their absence their horses had been stolen! At once they raised the hue-and-cry; and the peasants scoured the country in all directions in search of the *soi-disant* St. Barbara and her accomplices, but they never recovered the stolen property. "And serve them right, the blockheads!" added my informant, who had herself escaped falling into the trap by being absent from the village at the time.

AN OLD-FASHIONED PEASANT FAMILY. Ivan's household was a good specimen of the Russian peasant family of the old type. Previous to the Emancipation in 1861, there were many households of this kind, containing the representatives of three generations. All the members, young and old, lived together in patriarchal fashion under the direction and authority of the Head of the House, called usually *Khozaïn,* that is to say, the Administrator; or, in some districts, Bolshák, which means literally "the Big One." Generally speaking, this important position was occupied by the grandfather, or, if he was dead, by the eldest brother, but this rule was not very strictly observed. If, for instance, the grandfather became infirm, or if the eldest brother was incapacitated by disorderly habits or other cause, the place of authority was taken by some other member—it might be by a woman—who was a good manager, and possessed the greatest moral influence. The relations between the Head of the Household and the other members depended on custom and personal character, and they consequently varied greatly in different families. If the Big One was an intelligent man, of decided, energetic character, like my friend Ivan, there was probably perfect discipline in the house, except perhaps in the matter of female tongues, which do not readily submit to the authority even of their owners; but very often it happened that the Big One was not thoroughly well fitted for his post, and in that case endless quarrels and bickerings inevitably took place. Those quarrels were generally caused and fomented by the female members of the household—a fact which will not seem strange if we try to realize how difficult it must be for several sisters-in-law to live together, with their children and a mother-in-law, within the narrow limits of a peasant's house. The complaints of the young bride, who finds that her mother-in-law puts all the hard work on her shoulders, form a favorite motive in the popular poetry.

The house, with its appurtenances, the cattle, the agricultural implements, the grain and other products, the money gained from the sale of these products —in a word, the house and nearly everything it contained—was the joint-property of the family. Hence, nothing was bought or sold by any member— not even by the Big One himself, unless he possessed an unusual amount of authority—without the express or tacit consent of the other grown-up males, and all the money that was earned was put into the common purse. When one of the sons left home to work elsewhere, he was expected to bring or send home all his earnings, except what he required for food, lodgings, and other *necessary* expenses; and if he understood the word "necessary" in too lax a sense, he had to listen to very plain-spoken reproaches when he returned. During his absence, which might last for a whole year or several years, his wife and children remained in the house as before, and the money which he earned was probably devoted to the payment of the family taxes.

The peasant household of the old type is thus a primitive labor association, of which the members have all things in common, and it is not a little remarkable that the peasant conceives it as such rather than as a family. This is shown by the customary terminology and by the law of inheritance. The Head of the Household is not called by any word corresponding to Paterfamilias, but is termed, as I have said, Khozaïn, or Administrator—a word that is applied equally to a farmer, a shopkeeper, or the head of an industrial under-taking, and does not at all convey the idea of blood-relationship.

The law of inheritance is likewise based on this conception. When a house-hold is broken up, the degree of blood-relationship is not taken into considera-tion in the distribution of the property. All the adult male members share equally. Illegitimate and adopted sons, if they have contributed their share of labor, have the same rights as the sons born in lawful wedlock. The married daughter, on the contrary—being regarded as belonging to her husband's family—and the son who has previously separated himself from the house-hold, are excluded from the succession. Strictly speaking, there is no suc-cession or inheritance whatever, except as regards the wearing apparel and any little personal effects of a similar kind. The house and all that it contains belong not to the Khozaïn, but to the little household community; and, consequently, when the Khozaïn dies and the community is broken up, the members do not inherit, but merely appropriate individually what they had hitherto possessed collectively. Thus there is properly no inheritance or suc-cession, but simply liquidation and distribution of the property among the members. The written law of inheritance, founded on the conception of personal property, is quite unknown to the peasantry, and quite inapplicable to their mode of life. In this way a large and most important section of the Code remains a dead letter for about four-fifths of the population!

This predominance of practical economic consideration is likewise exempli-fied by the way in which marriages are arranged in these large families.

In all respects the Russian peasantry are, as a class, extremely practical and matter-of-fact in their conceptions and habits, and are not at all prone to indulge in sublime, ethereal sentiments of any kind. They have little or nothing of what may be roughly termed the Hermann-and-Dorothea element in their composition, and consequently they know very little about those sentimental, romantic ideas which we habitually associate with the preliminary steps to matrimony. This fact is so patent to all who have studied the Russian peasantry, that even those who have endeavored to idealize peasant life have rarely ventured to make their story turn on a sentimental love affair. These general remarks I insert here parenthetically, in order that the reader may more clearly understand what I have to say regarding peasant marriages.

In the primitive system of agriculture usually practiced in Russia, the natural labor-unit—if it be allowed to use such a term—comprises a man, a woman, and a horse. As soon, therefore, as a boy becomes an able-bodied laborer he ought to be provided with the two accessories necessary for the completion of the labor-unit. To procure a horse, either by purchase or by rearing a foal, is the duty of the Head of the House; to procure a wife for the youth is the duty of "the female Big One" (bolshúkha). And the chief consideration in determining the choice is in both cases the same. Prudent domestic administrators are not to be tempted by showy horses or beautiful brides; what they seek is not beauty, but physical strength and capacity for work. When the youth reaches the age of eighteen he is informed that he ought to marry at once, and as soon as he gives his consent negotiations are opened with the parents of some eligible young person. In the larger villages the negotiations are sometimes facilitated by certain old women called *svakhi*, who occupy themselves specially with this kind of mediation; but very often the affair is arranged directly by, or through the agency of, some common friend of the two houses. Care must of course be taken that there is no legal obstacle to the marriage, and these obstacles are not always easily avoided in a small village, the inhabitants of which have been long in the habit of intermarrying. According to Russian ecclesiastical law, not only is marriage between first-cousins illegal, but affinity is considered as equivalent to consanguinity—that is to say, a mother-in-law and a sister-in-law are regarded as a mother and a sister—and even the fictitious relationship created by standing together at the baptismal font as godfather and godmother is legally recognized. If all the preliminary negotiations are successful, the marriage takes place, and the bridegroom brings his bride home to the house of which he is a member. She brings nothing with her as a dowry except her trousseau, but she brings a pair of good strong arms, and thereby enriches her adopted family. Of course it happens occasionally for human nature is everywhere essentially the same—that a young peasant falls in love with one of his former playmates, and brings his little romance to a happy conclusion at the altar; but such cases are very rare, and as a rule it may be said that the marriages of the Russian peasantry are arranged under the influence of economic rather than sentimental considerations.

The custom of living in large families has many decided economic advantages. We all know the edifying fable of the dying man who showed to his sons by means of a piece of wicker-work the advantages of living together and mutually assisting each other. In ordinary times the necessary expenses of a large household of ten members are considerably less than the combined expenses of two households comprising five members each, and when a "black day" comes, a large family can bear temporary adversity much more successfully than a small one. These are principles of world-wide application, and in the life of the Russian peasantry they have a peculiar force. Each adult peasant possesses, as I shall hereafter explain, a share of the Communal land, but this share is not sufficient to occupy all his time and working power. One married pair can easily cultivate two shares—at least in all provinces where land is not very abundant. Now if a family is composed of two married couples, one of the men can go elsewhere and earn money, whilst the other, with his wife and sister-in-law, can cultivate the two combined shares of land. If, on the contrary, a family consists merely of one pair with their children, the man must either remain at home, in which case he may have difficulty in finding work for the whole of his time, or he must leave home, and intrust the cultivation of his share of the land to his wife, whose time must be in great part devoted to domestic affairs.

In the time of serfage the proprietors clearly perceived these and similar advantages, and compelled their serfs to live together in large families. No family could be broken up without the proprietor's consent, and this consent was not easily obtained unless the family had assumed quite abnormal proportions, and was permanently disturbed by domestic dissension. In the matrimonial affairs of the serfs, too, the majority of the proprietors systematically exercised a certain supervision, not necessarily from any paltry, meddling spirit, but because their material interests were thereby affected. A proprietor would not, for instance, allow the daughter of one of his serfs to marry a serf belonging to another proprietor—because he would thereby lose a female laborer—unless some compensation were offered. The compensation might be a sum of money, or the affair might be arranged on the principle of reciprocity, by the master of the bridegroom allowing one of his female serfs to marry a serf belonging to the master of the bride.

However advantageous the custom of living in large families may appear when regarded from the economic point of view, it has very serious defects, both theoretical and practical.

That families connected by the ties of blood-relationship and marriage can easily live together in harmony is one of those social axioms which are accepted universally and believed by nobody. We all know by our own experience, or by that of others, that the friendly relations of two such families are greatly endangered by proximity of habitation. To live in the same street is not advisable; to occupy adjoining houses is positively dangerous; and to live under the same roof is certainly fatal to prolonged amity. There may be the very best intentions on both sides, and the arrangement may be inaugurated by the most gushing expressions of undying affection and by the discovery of innumerable secret affinities, but neither affinities, affection, nor good intentions can withstand the constant friction and occasional jerks which inevitably ensue. Now the reader must endeavor to realize that Russian peasants, even when clad in sheep-skins, are human beings like ourselves. Though they are often represented as abstract entities—as figures in a table of statistics or dots on a diagram—they have in reality "organs, dimensions, senses, affections, passions." If not exactly "fed with the same food," they are at least "hurt with the same weapons, subject to the same diseases, healed by the same means," and liable to be irritated by the same annoyances as we are. And those of them who live in large families are subjected to a kind of probation that most of us have never dreamed of. The families comprising a large household not only live together, but have nearly all things in common. Each member works not for himself, but for the household, and all that he earns is expected to go into the family treasury. The arrangement almost inevitably leads to one of two results—either there are continual dissensions or order is preserved by a powerful domestic tyranny infinitely worse than serfage.

It was quite natural, therefore, that when the authority of the landed proprietors was abolished in 1861, the large peasant families almost all fell to pieces. The arbitrary rule of the Khozaïn was based on, and maintained by, the arbitrary rule of the proprietor, and both naturally fell together. Households like that of our friend Ivan have been preserved only in exceptional cases, where the Head of the House happened to possess an unusual amount of moral influence over the other members. This change has unquestionably had a prejudicial influence on the material welfare of the peasantry, but it must have added considerably to their domestic comfort, and can scarcely fail to produce good moral results. For the present, however, the evil consequences are by far the most prominent. Every married peasant strives to have a house of his own, and many of them, in order to defray the necessary expenses, have been obliged to contract debts. This is a very serious matter. Even if the peasants could obtain money at five or six per cent, the position of the debtors would be bad enough, but it is in reality much worse, for the village usurers consider twenty or twenty-five per cent. a by no means exorbitant rate of interest. Thus the peasant who contracts debts has a hard struggle to pay the interest in ordinary times, and when some misfortune overtakes him—when, for instance, the harvest is bad or his horse is stolen—he probably falls hopelessly into pecuniary embarrassments. I have seen peasants not specially addicted to drunkenness or other ruinous habits sink to a helpless state of insolvency. Fortunately for such insolvent debtors, they are treated by the law with extreme leniency. Their house, their share of the common land, their agricultural implements, their horse—in a word, all that is necessary for their subsistence, is exempt from sequestration. The Commune may, however, subject them to corporal punishment if they do not pay their taxes, and in many other respects the position of a peasant who is protected against utter destitution merely by the law is very far from being enviable.

COMMUNAL AGRICULTURE. Ivánofka may be taken as a fair specimen of the villages in the northern half of the country, and a brief description of its inhabitants will convey a tolerably correct notion of the northern peasantry in general.

Nearly the whole of the female population, and about one-half of the male inhabitants, are habitually engaged in cultivating the Communal land, which comprises about two thousand acres of a light sandy soil. The arable part of this land is divided into three large fields, each of which is cut up into long narrow strips. The first field is reserved for the winter grain—that is to say, rye, which forms, in the shape of black bread, the principal food of the peasantry. In the second are raised oats for the horses, and buckwheat, which is largely used for food. The third lies fallow, and is used in the summer as pasturage for the cattle.

All the villagers in this part of the country divide the arable land in this way, in order to suit the triennial rotation of crops. This triennial system is extremely simple. The field which is used this year for raising winter grain will be used next year for raising summer grain, and in the following year will lie fallow. Before being sown with winter grain it ought to receive a certain amount of manure. Every family possesses in each of the two fields under cultivation one or more of the long, narrow strips or belts into which they are divided.

The annual life of the peasantry is that of simple husbandmen, inhabiting a country where the winter is long and severe. The agricultural year begins in April with the melting of the snow. Nature has been lying dormant for some months. Awaking now from her long sleep, and throwing off her white mantle, she strives to make up for lost time. No sooner has the snow disappeared than the fresh young grass begins to shoot up, and very soon afterwards the shrubs and trees begin to bud. The rapidity of this transition from winter to spring astonishes the inhabitants of more temperate climes.

On St. George's Day (April 23rd), the cattle are brought out for the first time and sprinkled with holy water by the priest. The cattle of the Russian peasantry are never very fat, but at this period of the year their appearance is truly lamentable. During the winter they have been cooped up in small unventilated cow-houses, and fed almost exclusively on straw; now, when they are released from their imprisonment, they look like the ghosts of their former emaciated selves. All are lean and weak, many are lame, and some cannot rise to their feet without assistance.

Meanwhile the peasants are impatient to begin the field labor. An old proverb which they all know says: "Sow in mud and you will be a prince;" and they always act in accordance with this dictate of traditional wisdom. As soon as it is possible to plow they begin to prepare the land for the summer grain, and this labor occupies them probably till the end of May. Then comes the work of carting out manure and preparing the fallow field for the winter grain, which will last probably till about St. Peter's Day (June 29th), when the hay-making generally begins. After the hay-making comes the harvest, by far the busiest time of the year. From the middle of July—especially from St. Elijah's Day (July 20th), when the saint is usually heard rumbling along the heavens in his chariot of fire—until the end of August, the peasant may work day and night, and yet he will find that he has barely time to get all his work done. In little more than a month he has to reap and stack his grain—rye, oats, and whatever else he may have sown either in spring or in the preceding autumn—and to sow the winter grain for next year. To add to his troubles, it sometimes happens that the rye and the oats ripen almost simultaneously, and his position is then still more difficult than usual.

Whether the seasons favor him or not, the peasant has at this time a hard task, for he can rarely afford to hire the requisite number of laborers, and has generally the assistance merely of his wife and family; but he can at this season work for a short time at high pressure, for he has the prospect of soon obtaining a good rest and an abundance of food. About the end of September the field labor is finished, and on the 1st day of October the harvest festival begins—a joyous season, during which the parish fêtes are commonly celebrated.

SERFS AND PEASANTS. During all my travels in Russia, one of the objects which I constantly kept in view was the collection of materials for a History of the Emancipation of the Serfs—a great reform, which has always seemed to me one of the most interesting events of modern history. It was natural, therefore, that I should gather in this northern region as much information as possible regarding the life of the peasantry and their relation to the landed proprietors during the time of serfage; and I think that a little of this information will be not unacceptable to the reader.

In this, as in other parts of Russia, a very large portion of the land— perhaps as much as one-half—belonged to the State. The peasants living on this land had no masters, and were governed by a special branch of the Imperial Administration. In a certain sense they were serfs, for they were not allowed to change their official domicile, but practically they enjoyed a very large amount of liberty. By paying a small sum for a passport they could leave their villages for an indefinite length of time, and so long as they paid regularly their taxes and dues they were in little danger of being molested. Many of them, though officially inscribed in their native villages, lived permanently in the towns, and not a few of them succeeded in amassing large fortunes.

Of the remaining land, a considerable portion belonged to rich nobles, who rarely or never visited their estates, and left the management of them either to the serfs themselves or to a steward, who acted according to a code of instructions. On these estates the position of the serfs was very similar to that of the State peasants. They had their Communal land, which they distributed among themselves as they thought fit, and enjoyed the remainder of the arable land in return for a fixed yearly rent.

Some proprietors, however, lived on their estates and farmed on their own account, and here the condition of the serfs was somewhat different. A considerable number of these, perhaps as many as ten per cent. were, properly speaking, not serfs at all, but rather domestic slaves, who fulfilled the functions of coachmen, grooms, gardeners, gamekeepers, cooks, lackeys, and the like. Their wives and daughters acted as nurses, domestic servants, ladies' maids, and seamstresses. If the master organized a private theater or orchestra, the actors or musicians were drawn from this class. These serfs lived in the mansion or the immediate vicinity, possessed no land, except perhaps a little plot for a kitchen-garden, and were fed and clothed by the master. Their number was generally out of all proportion to the amount of work they had to perform, and consequently they were always imbued with an hereditary spirit of indolence, and performed lazily and carelessly what they had to do. On the other hand, they were often sincerely attached to the family they served, and occasionally proved by acts their fidelity and attachment. Here is an instance out of the many for which I can vouch. An old nurse, whose mistress was dangerously ill, vowed that, in the event of the patient's recovery, she would make a pilgrimage first to Kief, the Holy City on the Dnieper, and afterwards to Solovetsk, a much-revered monastery on an island in the White Sea. The patient recovered, and the old woman walked in fulfillment of her vow more than two thousand miles!

I have called this class of serfs "domestic slaves," because I cannot find any more appropriate term, but I must warn the reader that he ought not to use this phrase in presence of a Russian. On this point Russians are extremely sensitive. Serfage, they say indignantly, was something quite different from slavery; and slavery never existed in Russia!

This assertion, which I have heard scores of times from educated Russians, cannot be accepted unreservedly. The first part of it is perfectly true; the second, perfectly false. In old times slavery was a recognized institution in Russia, as in other countries. It is almost impossible to read a few pages of the old native chronicles without stumbling on references to slaves; and I distinctly remember—though I cannot at this moment give chapter and verse —that there was one Russian Prince who was so valiant and so successful in his wars, that during his reign a slave might be bought for a few coppers.

How the distinction between serfs and slaves gradually disappeared, and how the latter term fell into disuse, I need not here relate; but I must assert, in the interests of truth, that the class of serfs above mentioned, though they were officially and popularly called *dvorovuiye lyudi*—that is to say, court-yard people—were to all intents and purposes domestic slaves. Down to the commencement of the present century the Russian newspapers contained advertisments of this kind—I take the examples almost at random from the *Moscow Gazette* of 1801: "TO BE SOLD, three coachmen, well-trained and handsome; and two girls, the one eighteen and the other fifteen years of age, both of them good-looking and well acquainted with various kinds of handi-work. In the same house there are for sale two hair-dressers: the one twenty-one years of age can read, write, play on a musical instrument, and act as huntsman; the other can dress ladies' and gentlemen's hair. In the same house are sold pianos and organs." A little further on, a first-rate clerk, a carver, and a lackey are offered for sale, and the reason assigned is super-abundance of the articles in question (*za izlisheston*). In some instances it seems as if the serfs and the cattle were intentionally put in the same category, as in the following: "In this house one can buy a coachman, and a Dutch cow about to calve." The style of these advertisements and the frequent recur-rence of the same address show plainly that there was at that time a regular class of slave-dealers.

The humane Alexander I. prohibited public advertisements of this kind, but he did not put down the custom which they represented; and his successor, Nicholas, took no active measures for its repression. Thus until the com-mencement of the present reign—that is to say, until about twenty years ago —the practice was continued under a more or less disguised form. Middle-aged people have often told me that in their youth they knew proprietors who habitually caused young domestic serfs to be taught trades, in order afterwards to sell them or let them out for hire. It was from such proprietors that the theaters obtained a large number of their best actors.

Very different was the position of the serfs properly so-called. They lived in villages, possessed houses and gardens of their own, tilled the Communal land for their own benefit, enjoyed a certain amount of self-government, of which I shall speak presently, and were rarely sold except as part of the estate. They might, indeed, be sold to a landed proprietor, and transferred to his estates; but such transactions rarely took place. The ordinary relations which existed between serfs and the proprietor may be best explained by one or two examples. Let us take first Ivánofka.

Though the proprietor's house was situated, as I have said, close to the village, the manor land and the Communal land had always been kept clearly separate, and might almost be said to form two independent estates. The proprietor who reigned in Ivánofka during the last years of serfage was keenly alive to his own interests, and always desirous of increasing his revenue; but he was, at the same time, a just and intelligent man, who was never guilty of extortion or cruelty. Though he had the welfare of his serfs really at heart, he rarely interfered in their domestic or Communal arrangements, because he believed that men in general, and Russian peasants in particular, are the best administrators of their own affairs. He did not, indeed, always carry out this principle to its logical consequences, for he was not by any means a thorough doctrinaire. Thus, for example, he insisted on being consulted when a Village Elder was to be elected, or any important matter decided; and when circumstances seemed to demand his interference, he usually showed the peasants that he could be dictator if he chose. These were, however, exceptional incidents. In the ordinary course of affairs he treated the Commune almost as a respected farmer or trusted steward. In return for the land which he ceded to it, and which it was free to distribute among its members as it thought fit, he demanded a certain amount of labor and dues; but he never determined what particular laborers should be sent to him, or in what way the dues should be levied.

The amount of the labor-dues was determined in this way. The tyagló, or labor-unit, was composed of a man, a woman, and a horse; and each tyagló owed to the proprietor three days' labor every week. If a household contained two tyágla, one of them might work for the proprietor six days in the week, and thereby liberate the other from its obligation. In this way one-half of a large family could labor constantly for the household, whilst the other half fulfilled all the obligations towards the proprietor. The other dues consisted of lambs, chickens, eggs, and linen-cloth, together with a certain sum of money, which was contributed by those peasants who were allowed to go away and work in the towns.

At a short distance from Ivánofka was an estate, which had been managed in the time of serfage on entirely different principles. The proprietor was a man who had likewise the welfare of his serfs at heart, because he knew that on their welfare depended his own revenues, but he did not believe in the principle of allowing them to manage their own affairs. The Russian peasant, he was wont to say, is a child—a foolish, imprudent, indolent child, who inevitably ruins himself when not properly looked after. In accordance with this principle the proprietor sought to regulate not merely the Communal, but also the domestic concerns of his serfs. Not only did he always nominate the Village Elder and decide all matters touching the communal welfare, but he at the same time arranged the marriages, decided who was to seek work in the towns and who was to stay at home, paid frequent visits of inspection to the peasants' houses, prohibited the heads of families from selling their grain without his permission, and exercised in various other ways a system of minute supervision. In return for all this paternal solicitude he was able to extract a wonderfully large revenue from his estate, though his fields were by no means more fertile or better cultivated than those of his neighbors. The additional revenue was derived not from the land, but from the serfs. Knowing intimately the domestic affairs of each family, he could lay on them the heaviest possible burdens without adding that last hair which is said to break the camel's back. And many of the expedients he employed did more credit to his ingenuity than to his moral character. Thus, for instance, if he discovered that a family had saved a little money, he would propose that one of the daughters should marry some one of whom, he knew, her father would certainly disapprove, or he would express his intention of giving one of the sons as a recruit. In either case a ransom was pretty sure to be paid in order to ward off the threatened danger.

All the proprietors who lived on their estates approached more or less nearly to one of these two types; but here in the northern regions the latter type was not very often met with. Partly from the prevailing absenteeism among the landlords, and partly from the peasants' old-established habit of wandering about the country and going to the towns in search of work, these peasants of the north are more energetic, more intelligent, more independent, and consequently less docile and pliable than those of the fertile central provinces. They have, too, more education. A large proportion of them can read and write, and occasionally one meets among them men who have a keen desire for knowledge. Several times I encountered peasants in this region who had a small collection of books, and twice I found in such collections, much to my astonishment, a Russian translation of Buckle's "History of Civilization"!

THE MIR. On my arrival at Ivánofka, my knowledge of the institution was of that vague, superficial kind which is commonly derived from men who are fonder of sweeping generalizations and rhetorical declamation than of serious, patient study of phenomena. I knew that the chief personage in a Russian village is the *Selski starosta*, or the Village Elder, and that all important communal affairs are regulated by the *Selski Skhod*, or Village Assembly. Further, I was aware that the land in the vicinity of the village belongs to the Commune, and is distributed periodically among the members in such a way that every able-bodied peasant possesses a share sufficient, or nearly sufficient, for his maintenance. Beyond this elementary information I knew little or nothing.

My first attempt at extending my knowledge was not very successful. Hoping that my friend Ivan might be able to assist me, and knowing that the popular name for the Commune is *Mir*, which means also "the world," I put to him the direct, simple question, "What is the Mir?"

Ivan was not easily disconcerted, but for once he looked puzzled, and stared at me vacantly. When I endeavored to explain to him my question, he simply knitted his brows and scratched the back of his head. This latter movement is the Russian peasant's method of accelerating cerebral action; but in the present instance it had no practical result. In spite of his efforts, Ivan could not get much further than the "Kak vam skatzat'?" that is to say, "How am I to tell you?"

It was not difficult to perceive that I had adopted an utterly false method of investigation, and a moment's reflection sufficed to show me the absurdity of my question. I had asked from an uneducated man a philosophical definition, instead of extracting from him material in the form of concrete facts, and constructing therefrom a definition for myself. These concrete facts, Ivan was both able and willing to supply; and as soon as I adopted a rational mode of questioning, I received an abundant supply of most interesting information. This information, together with the results of much subsequent conversation and reading, I now propose to present to the reader in my own words.

The peasant family of the old type is, as we have just seen, a kind of primitive association, in which the members have nearly all things in common. The village may be roughly described as a primitive association on a larger scale.

Between these two social units there are many points of analogy. In both there are common interests and common responsibilities. In both there is a principal personage, who is in a certain sense ruler within, and representative as regards the outside world: in the one case called Khozaïn, or Head of the Household, and in the other Starosta, or Village Elder. In both the authority of the ruler is limited; in the one case by the adult members of the family, and in the other by the heads of households. In both there is a certain amount of common property: in the one case the house and nearly all that it contains, and in the other the arable land and pasturage. In both cases there is a certain amount of common responsibility: in the one case for all of the debts, and in the other for all the taxes and Communal obligations. And both are protected to a certain extent against the ordinary legal consequences of insolvency, for the family cannot be deprived of its house or necessary agricultural implements, and the Commune cannot be deprived of its land, by importunate creditors.

On the other hand, there are many important points of contrast. The Commune is, of course, much larger than the family, and the mutual relations of its members are by no means so closely interwoven. The members of a family all farm together, and those of them who earn money from other sources are expected to put their savings into the common purse; whilst the households composing a Commune farm independently, and pay into the common treasury only a certain fixed sum.

From these brief remarks the reader will at once perceive that a Russian village is something very different from a village in our sense of the term, and that the villagers are bound together by ties quite unknown to the English rural population. A family living in an English village has little reason to take an interest in the affairs of its neighbors. The isolation of the individual families may not be quite perfect, for man, being a social animal, takes, and ought to take, a certain interest in the affairs of those around him, and this social duty is sometimes fulfilled by the weaker sex with more zeal than is absolutely indispensable for the public welfare; but families may live for many years in the same village without ever becoming conscious of common interests. So long as the Jones family do not commit any culpable breach of public order, such as putting obstructions on the highway or habitually setting their house on fire, their neighbor Brown takes probably no interest in their affairs, and has no ground for interfering with their perfect liberty of action. Jones may be a drunkard and hopelessly insolvent, and he may some night decamp clandestinely with his whole family and never more be heard of; but all these things do not affect the interests of Brown, unless he has been imprudent enough to entertain with the delinquent more than simply neighborly relations. Now, amongst the families composing a Russian village, such a state of isolation is impossible. The Heads of Households must often meet together and consult in the Village Assembly, and their daily occupations must be influenced by the Communal decrees. They cannot begin to mow the hay or plow the fallow field until the Village Assembly has passed a resolution on the subject. If a peasant becomes a drunkard, or takes some equally efficient means to become insolvent, every family in the village has a right to complain, not merely in the interests of public morality, but from selfish motives, because all the families are collectively responsible for his taxes. For the same reason no peasant can permanently leave the village without the consent of the Commune, and this consent will not be granted if all his actual and future liabilities are not met. If a peasant wishes to go away for a short time, in order to work elsewhere, he must obtain a written permission, which serves him as a passport during his absence; and he may be recalled at any moment by a Communal decree. In reality he is rarely recalled so long as he sends home regularly the full amount of his taxes — including the dues which he has to pay for the temporary passport — but sometimes the Commune uses the power of recall for the purpose of extorting money from the absent member. If it becomes known, for instance, that an absent member receives a good salary in one of the towns, he may one day receive a formal order to return at once to his native village, and be informed at the same time, unofficially, that his presence will be dispensed with if he will send to the commune a certain amount of money. The money thus sent is generally used by the commune for convivial purposes. Whether this method of extortion is frequently used by the Communes, I cannot confidently say, but I suspect that it is by no means rare, for one or two cases have accidentally come under my own observation, and I know that the police of St. Petersburg have been recently ordered not to send back any peasants to their native villages until some proof is given that the ground of recall is not a mere pretext.

In order to understand the Russian village system, the reader must bear in mind these two important facts: the arable land and the pasturage belong not to the individual houses, but to the Commune, and all the households are collectively and individually responsible for the entire sum which the Commune has to pay annually into the Imperial Treasury.

In all countries the theory of government and administration differs considerably from the actual practice. Nowhere is this difference greater than in Russia, and in no Russian institution is it greater than in the Village Commune. It is necessary, therefore, to know both theory and practice; and it is well to begin with the former, because it is the simpler of the two. When we have once thoroughly mastered the theory, it is easy to understand the deviations that are made to suit peculiar local conditions.

According, then, to theory, all male peasants in every part of the Empire are inscribed in census lists, which form the basis of the direct taxation. These lists are revised at irregular intervals, and all males alive at the time of the "revision," from the newborn babe to the centenarian, are duly inscribed. Each Commune has a list of this kind, and pays to the Government an annual sum proportionate to the number of names which the list contains, or, in popular language, according to the number of "revision souls." During the intervals between the revisions the financial authorities take no notice of the births and deaths. A Commune which has a hundred male members at the time of the revision may have in a few years considerably more or considerably less than that number, but it has to pay taxes for a hundred members all the same until a new revision is made for the whole Empire.

Now in Russia, so far at least as the rural population is concerned, the payment of taxes is inseparably connected with the possession of land. Every peasant who pays taxes is supposed to have a share of the arable land and pasturage belonging to the Commune. If the Communal revision lists contain a hundred names, the Communal land ought to be divided into a hundred shares, and each "revision soul" should enjoy his share in return for the taxes which he pays.

The reader who has followed my explanations up to this point may naturally conclude that the taxes paid by the peasants are in reality a species of rent for the land which they enjoy. So it seems, and so it is sometimes represented, but so in reality it is not. When a man rents a bit of land he acts according to his own judgment, and makes a voluntary contract with the proprietor; but the Russian peasant is obliged to pay his taxes whether he desires to enjoy land or not. The theory, therefore, that the taxes are simply the rent of the land, will not bear even superficial examination. Equally untenable is the theory that they are a species of land-tax. In any reasonable system of land-dues the yearly sum imposed bears some kind of proportion to the quantity and quality of the land enjoyed; but in Russia it may be that the members of one Commune possess six acres, and the members of the neighboring Commune seven acres, and yet the taxes in both cases are the same. The truth is that the taxes are personal, and are calculated according to the number of male "souls," and the Government does not take the trouble to inquire how the Communal land is distributed. The Commune has to pay into the Imperial Treasury a fixed yearly sum, according to the number of its "revision souls," and distributes the land among its members as it thinks fit.

How, then, does the Commune distribute the land? To this question it is impossible to give a definite general reply, because each Commune acts as it pleases. Some act strictly according to the theory. These divide their land at the time of the revision into a number of portions or shares corresponding to the number of revision souls, and give to each family a number of shares corresponding to the number of revision souls which it contains. This is from the administrative point of view by far the simplest system. The census list determines how much land each family will enjoy, and the existing tenures are disturbed only by the revisions which take place at irregular intervals. Since 1719 only ten revisions have been made, so that the average length of these intervals has been about fifteen years — a term which may be regarded as a tolerably long lease. But, on the other hand, this system has serious defects. The revision list represents merely the numerical strength of the families, and the numerical strength is often not at all in proportion to the working power. Let us suppose, for example, two families, each containing at the time of the revision five male members. According to the census list these two families are equal, and ought to receive equal shares of the land; but in reality it may happen that the one contains a father in the prime of life and four able-bodied sons, whilst the other contains a widow and five little boys. The wants and working power of these two families are of course very different; and if the above system of distribution be applied, the man with four sons and a goodly supply of grandchildren will probably find that he has too little land, whilst the widow with her five little boys will find it difficult to cultivate the five shares allotted to her, and utterly impossible to pay the corresponding amount of taxation — for in all cases, it must be remembered, the Communal burdens are distributed in the same proportion as the land.

But why, it may be said, should the widow not accept provisionally the five shares, and let to others the part which she does not require? The balance of rent after payment of the taxes might help her to bring up her young family.

So it seems to one acquainted only with the rural economy of England, where land is scarce, and always gives a revenue more than sufficient to defray the taxes. But in Russia the possession of a share of Communal land if often not a privilege, but a burden. In come Communes the land is so poor and abundant that it cannot be let at any price. Witness, for instance, many villages in the province of Smolensk, where the traveler may see numerous uncultivated strips in the communal fields. In others the soil will repay cultivation, but a fair rent will not suffice to pay the taxes and dues.

To obviate these inconvenient results of the simpler system, some communes have adopted the expedient of allotting the land, not according to the number of revision souls, but according to the working power of the families. Thus, in the instance above supposed, the widow would receive perhaps two shares, and the large household, containing five workers, would receive perhaps seven or eight. Since the breaking-up of the large families, such inequality as I have supposed is, of course, rare; but inequality of a less extreme kind does still occur, and justifies a departure from the system of allotment according to the revision lists.

Even if the allotment be fair and equitable at the time of the revision, it may soon become unfair and burdensome by the natural fluctuations of the population. Births and deaths may in the course of a very few years entirely alter the relative working power of the various families. The sons of the widow may grow up to manhood, whilst two or three able-bodied members of the other family may be cut off by an epidemic. Thus, long before a new revision takes place, the distribution of the land may be no longer in accordance with the wants and capacities of the various families composing the Commune. To correct this, various expedients are employed. Some Communes transfer particular lots from one family to another, as circumstances demand; whilst others make from time to time, during the intervals between the revisions, a complete re-distribution and re-allotment of the land.

The system of allotment adopted depends entirely on the will of the particular Commune. In this respect the Communes enjoy the most complete autonomy, and no peasant ever dreams of appealing against a Communal decree. The higher authorities not only abstain from all interference in the allotment of the Communal lands, but remain in profound ignorance as to which system the Communes habitually adopt. Though the Imperial Adminstration has a most voracious appetite for symmetrically-constructed statistical tables — many of them formed chiefly out of materials supplied by the mysterious inner consciousness of the subordinate officials — no attempt has yet been made to collect statistical data which might throw light on this important subject. In spite of the systematic and persistent efforts of the centralized bureaucracy to regulate minutely all departments of the national life, the rural Communes, which contain about five-sixths of the population, remain in many respects entirely beyond its influence, and even beyond its sphere of vision! But let not the reader be astonished overmuch. He will learn in time that Russia is the land of paradoxes; and meanwhile he is about to receive a still more startling bit of information — a statement that should be heralded in by a flourish of trumpets. In "the great stronghold of Cæsarian despotism and centralized bureaucracy," these Village Communes, containing about five-sixths of the population, are capital specimens of representative Constitutional government of the extreme democratic type!

When I say that the rural Commune is a good specimen of Constitutional government, I use the phrase in the English, and not in the continental sense. In the continental languages a Constitutional government means a government which possesses a long, formal document, composed of many successive paragraphs, in which the functions of the various institutions, the powers of the various authorities, and all the possible methods of procedure are carefully defined. Such a document was never heard of in Russian Village Communes. Their Constitution is of the English type — a body of unwritten, traditional conceptions, which have grown up and modified themselves under the influence of ever-changing practical necessity. If the functions and mutual relations of the Village Elder and the Village Assembly have ever been defined, neither the Elders nor the members of the Assembly know anything of such definitions; and yet every peasant knows, as if by instinct, what each of these authorities can do and cannot do. The Commune is, in fact, a living institution, whose spontaneous vitality enables it to dispense with the assistance and guidance of the written law.

As to its thoroughly democratic character there can be no possible doubt. The Elder represents merely the executive power. All the real authority resides in the Assembly, of which all Heads of Households are members.

The simple procedure, or rather the absence of all formal procedure, at the Assemblies, illustrates admirably the essentially practical character of the institution. The meetings are held in the open air, because in the village there is no building—except the church, which can be used only for religious purposes — large enough to contain all the members; and they almost always take place on Sundays or holidays, when the peasants have plenty of leisure. Any open space, where there is sufficient room and little mud, serves as a Forum. The discussions are occasionally very animated, but there is rarely any attempt at speech-making. If any young member should show an inclination to indulge in oratory, he is sure to be unceremoniously interrupted by some of the older members, who have never any sympathy with fine talking. The whole assemblage has the appearance of a crowd of people who have accidentally come together, and are discussing in little groups subjects of local interest. Gradually some one group, containing two or three peasants who have more moral influence than their fellows, attracts the others, and the discussion becomes general. Two or more peasants may speak at a time, and interrupt each other freely — using plain, unvarnished language, not at all parliamentary — and the discussion may become for a few moments a confused, unintelligible noise, "a din to fright a monster's ear"; but at the moment when the spectator imagines that the consultation is about to be transformed into a promiscuous fight, the tumult spontaneously subsides, or perhaps a general roar of laughter announces that some one has been successfully hit by a strong *argumentum ad hominem,* or biting personal remark. In any case there is no danger of the disputants coming to blows. No class of men in the world is more good-natured and pacific than the Russian peasantry. When sober they never fight, and even when under the influence of alcohol they are more likely to be violently affectionate than disagreeably quarrelsome. If two of them take to drinking together, the probability is that in a few minutes, though they may never have seen each other before, they will be expressing in very strong terms their mutual regard and affection, confirming their words with an occasional friendly embrace.

Theoretically speaking, the Village Parliament has a Speaker, in the person of the Village Elder. The word Speaker is etymologically less objectionable than the term President, for the personage in question never sits down, but mingles in the crowd like the ordinary members. Objection may be taken to the word on the ground that the Elder speaks much less than many other members, but this may likewise be said of the Speaker of the House of Commons. Whatever we may call him, the Elder is officially the principal personage in the crowd, and wears the insignia of office in the form of a small medal suspended from his neck by a thin brass chain. His duties, however, are extremely light. To call to order those who interrupt the discussion is no part of his functions. If he calls an honorable member Durák (blockhead), or interrupts an orator with a laconic "Moltchi!" (hold your tongue!), he does so in virtue of no special prerogative, but simply in accordance with a time-honored privilege, which is equally enjoyed by all present, and may be employed with impunity against himself. Indeed, it may be said in general that the phraseology and the procedure are not subjected to any strict rules. The Elder comes prominently forward only when it is necessary to take the sense of the meeting. On such occasions he may stand back a little from the crowd and say, "Well, orthodox, have you decided so?" and the crowd will probably shout, "Ladno! ladno!" that is to say, "Agreed! agreed!"

Communal measures are generally carried in this way by acclamation; but it sometimes happens that there is such a decided diversity of opinion that it is difficult to tell which of the two parties has a majority. In this case the Elder requests the one part to stand to the right and the other to the left. The two groups are then counted, and the minority submits, for no one ever dreams of opposing openly the will of the "Mir."

Nearly half a century ago an attempt was made to regulate by the written law the procedure of Village Assemblies amongst the peasantry of the State Demesnes, and among other reforms voting by ballot was introduced; but the new custom never struck root. The peasants did not regard with favor the new method, and persisted in calling it, contemptuously, "playing at marbles." Here, again, we have one of these wonderful and apparently anomalous facts which frequently meet the student of Russian affairs: the

Emperor Nicholas, the Incarnation of Autocracy and the Champion of the Reactionary Party throughout Europe, forces the ballot-box, the ingenious invention of extreme radicals, on several millions of his subjects!

In the crowd may generally be seen, especially in the northern provinces, where a considerable portion of the male population is always absent from the village, a certain number of female peasants. These are women who, on account of the absence or death of their husbands, happen to be for the moment Heads of Households. As such they are entitled to be present, and their right to take part in the deliberations is never called in question. In matters affecting the general welfare of the Commune they rarely speak, and if they do venture to enounce an opinion on such occasions they have little chance of commanding attention, for the Russian peasantry are as yet little imbued with the modern doctrines of female equality, and express their opinion of female intelligence by the homely adage: "The hair is long, but the mind is short." According to one proverb, seven women have collectively but one soul, and according to a still more ungallant popular saying, women have no souls at all, but only a vapor. Woman, therefore, as woman, is not deserving of much consideration, but a particular woman, as head of a household is entitled to speak on all questions directly affecting the household under her care. If, for instance, it be proposed to increase or diminish her household's share of the land and the burdens, she will be allowed to speak freely on the subject, and even to indulge in a little personal invective against her male opponents. She thereby exposes herself, it is true, to uncomplimentary remarks; but any which she happens to receive she will probably repay with interest — referring, perhaps, with pertinent virulence to the domestic affairs of those who attack her. And when argument and invective fail, she is pretty sure to try the effect of pathetic appeal, supported by copious tears — a method of persuasion to which the Russian peasant is singularly insensible.

As the Village Assembly is really a representative institution, in the full sense of the term, it reflects faithfully the good and the bad qualities of the rural population. Its decisions are therefore usually characterized by plain, practical common sense, but it is subject to occasional unfortunate aberrations in consequence of pernicious influences, chiefly of an alcoholic kind. An instance of this fact occurred during my sojourn at Ivánofka. The question under discussion was whether a *kabák,* or gin-shop, should be established in the village. A trader from the district town desired to establish one, and offered to pay to the Commune a yearly sum for the necessary permission. The more industrious, respectable members of the Commune, backed by the whole female population of the locality, were strongly opposed to the project, knowing full well that a kabák would certainly lead to the ruin of more than one household; but the enterprising trader had strong arguments wherewith to seduce a large number of the members, and succeeded in obtaining a decision in his favor.

The Assembly discusses all matters affecting the Communal welfare, and, as these matters have never been legally defined, and there is no means of appealing against its decisions, its recognized competence is very wide. It fixes the time for making the hay, and the day for commencing the plowing of the fallow field; it decrees what measures shall be employed against those who do not punctually pay their taxes; it decides whether a new member shall be admitted into the Commune, and whether an old member shall be allowed to change his domicile; it gives or withholds permission to erect new buildings on the Communal land; it prepares and signs all contracts which the Commune makes with one of its own members or with a stranger; it interferes, whenever it thinks neecssary, in the domestic affairs of its members; it elects the Elder — as well as the Communal tax-collector, and watchman, where such offices exist — and the Communal herd-boy; above all, it divides and allots the Communal land among the members as it thinks fit.

Of all these various proceedings, the English reader may naturally assume that the elections are the most noisy and exciting. In reality this is a mistake. The elections produce little excitement, for the simple reason that, as a rule, no one desires to be elected. Once, it is said, a peasant who had been guilty of some misdemeanor was informed by an Arbiter of the Peace — a species of official of which I shall have much to say in the sequel — that he would be no longer capable of filling any Communal office; and instead of regretting this diminution of his civil rights, he bowed very low, and respectfully expressed his thanks for the new privilege which he had acquired. This anecdote may not be true, but it illustrates the undoubted fact that the Russian peasant regards office as a burden rather than as an honor. There is no civic ambition in those little rural Commonwealths, whilst the privilege of wearing a bronze medal, which commands no respect, and the reception of a few roubles as salary, afford no adequate compensation for the trouble, annoyance, and responsibility which a Village Elder has to bear. The elections are therefore generally very tame and uninteresting. The following description may serve as an illustration.

It is a Sunday afternoon. The peasants, male and female, have turned out in Sunday attire, and the bright costumes of the women help the sunshine to put a little rich color into the scene, which is at ordinary times monotonously gray. Slowly the crowd collects on the open space at the side of the church. All classes of the population are represented. On the extreme outskirts are a band of fair-haired, merry children — some of them standing or lying on the grass and gazing attentively at the proceedings, and others running about and playing at tag. Close to these stand a group of young girls, convulsed with half-suppressed laughter. The cause of their merriment is a youth of some seventeen summers, evidently the wag of the village, who stands beside them with an accordian in his hand, and relates to them in a half-whisper how he is about to be elected Elder, and what mad pranks he will play in that capacity. When one of the girls happens to laugh outright, the matrons who are standing near turn round and scowl; and one of them, stepping forward, orders the offender, in a tone of authority, to go home at once if she cannot behave herself. Crest-fallen, the culprit retires, and the youth who is the cause of the merriment makes the incident the subject of a new joke. Meanwhile the deliberations have begun. The majority of the members are chatting together, or looking at a little group composed of three peasants and a woman, who are standing a little apart from the others. Here alone the matter in hand is being really discussed. The woman is explaining, with tears in her eyes, and with a vast amount of useless repetition, that her "old man," who is Elder for the time being, is very ill, and cannot fulfill his duties.

"But he has not yet served a year, and he'll get better," remarks one peasant, evidently the youngest of the little group.

"Who knows?" replies the woman, sobbing. "It is the will of God, but I don't believe that he'll ever put his foot to the ground again. The Feldsher has been four times to see him, and the doctor himself came once, and said that he must be brought to the hospital."

"And why has he not been taken there?"

"How could he be taken? Who is to carry him? Do you think he's a baby? The hospital is forty versts off. If you put him in a cart he would die before he had gone a verst. And then, who knows what they do with people in the hospital?" This last question contained probably the true reason why the doctor's orders had been disobeyed.

"Very well; that's enough; hold your tongue," says the gray beard of the little group to the woman; and then, turning to the other peasants, remarks, "There is nothing to be done. The Stanovoi (officer of rural police) will be here one of these days, and will make a row again if we don't elect a new Elder. Whom shall we choose?"

As soon as this question is asked, several peasants look down to the ground, or try in some other way to avoid attracting attention, lest their names should be suggested. When the silence has continued a minute or two, the gray beard says, "There is Alexei Ivánof; he has not served yet!"

"Yes, yes, Alexei Ivánof!" shout half a dozen voices, belonging probably to peasants who fear they may be elected.

Alexei protests in the strongest terms. He cannot say that he is ill, because his big ruddy face would give him the lie direct, but he finds half a dozen other reasons why he should not be chosen, and accordingly requests to be excused. But his protestations are not listened to, and the proceedings terminate. A new Village Elder has been duly elected.

Far more important than the elections, is the redistribution of the Communal land. It can matter but little to the Head of a Household how the elections go, provided he himself is not chosen. He can accept with perfect equanimity Alexei, or Ivan, or Nikolaï, because the office-bearers have very little influence in communal affairs. But he cannot remain a passive, indifferent spectator, when the division and allotment of the land come to be discussed, for the material welfare of every household depends to a great extent on the amount of land and of burdens which it receives.

In the southern provinces, where the soil is fertile, and the taxes do not exceed the normal rent, the process of division and allotment is comparatively simple. Here each peasant desires to get as much land as possible, and consequently each household demands all the land to which it is entitled — that is to say, a number of shares equal to the number of its members inscribed in the last revision list. The Assembly has, therefore, no difficult questions to decide. The Communal revision list determines the number of shares to be allotted to each family. The only difficulty likely to arise is as to which particular shares a particular family shall receive, and this difficulty is commonly obviated by the custom of casting lots. There may be, it is true, some difference of opinion as to when a re-distribution should be made, but this question is easily decided by a simple vote of the Assembly.

Very different is the process of division and allotment in many Communes of the northern provinces. Here the soil is often very unfertile, and the taxes exceed the normal rent, and consequently it may happen that the peasants strive to have as little land as possible. In these cases such scenes as the following may occur.

Ivan is being asked how many shares of the Communal land he will take, and replies in a slow, contemplative way, "I have two sons, and there is myself, so I'll take three shares, or somewhat less if it is your pleasure."

"Less!" exclaims a middle-aged peasant, who is not the Village Elder, but merely an influential member, and takes the leading part in the proceedings. "You talk nonsense. Your two sons are already old enough to help you, and soon they may get married, and so bring you two new female laborers."

"My eldest son," explains Ivan, "always works in Moscow, and the other often leaves me in summer."

"But they both send or bring home money, and when they get married, the wives will remain with you."

"God knows what will be," replies Ivan, passing over in silence the first part of his opponent's remark. "Who knows if they will marry?"

"You can easily arrange that!"

"That I cannot do. The times are changed now. The young people do as they wish, and when they do get married they all wish to have houses of their own. Three shares will be heavy enough for me!"

"No, no. If they wish to separate from you, they will take some land from you. You must take at least four. The old wives there who have little children cannot take shares according to the number of souls."

"He is a rich Muzhík!" (peasant), says a voice in the crowd. "Lay on him five souls!" (that is to say, give him five shares of the land and of the burdens).

"Five souls I cannot! By God, I cannot!"

"Very well, you shall have four," says the leading spirit to Ivan; and then, turning to the crowd, inquires, "Shall it be so?"

"Four! four!" murmurs the crowd; and the question is settled.

Next comes one of the old wives just referred to. Her husband is a permanent invalid, and she has three little boys, only one of whom is old enough for field labor. If the revision list were taken strictly as the basis of distribution, she would receive four shares; but she would never be able to pay four shares of the Communal burdens. She must therefore receive less than that amount. When asked how many she will take, she replies with downcast eyes, "As the Mir decides, so be it!"

"Then you must take three."

"What do you you say, little father?" cries the woman, throwing off suddenly her air of subservient obedience. "Do you hear that, ye orthodox?" They want to lay upon me three souls! Was such a thing ever heard of? Since St. Peter's Day my husband has been bed ridden — bewitched, it seems, for nothing does him good. He cannot put a foot to the ground — all the same as if he were dead; only he eats bread!"

"You talk nonsense," says a neighbor; "he was in the kabák (gin-shop) last week."

"And you!" retorts the woman, wandering from the subject in hand, "what did *you* do last parish fête? Was it not you who got drunk and beat your wife till she roused the whole village with her shrieking? And no further gone than last Sunday — pfu!"

"Listen!" says the old man sternly, cutting short the torrent of invective. "You must take at least two shares and a half. If you cannot manage it yourself, you can get some one to help you."

"How can that be? Where am I to get the money to pay a laborer?" asks the woman, with much wailing and a flood of tears. "Have pity, ye orthodox, on the poor orphans! God will reward you;" and so on, and so on.

I need not weary the reader with a further description of these scenes, which are always very long and sometimes violent. All present are deeply interested, for the allotment of the land is by far the most important event in Russian peasant life, and the arrangement cannot be made without endless talking and discussion. After the number of shares for each family has been decided, the distribution of the lots gives rise to new difficulties. The families who have manured plentifully their land strive to get back their old lots, and the Commune respects their claims so far as these are consistent with the new arrangement; but often it happens that it is impossible to conciliate private rights and Communal interests, and in such cases the former are sacrificed in a way that would not be tolerated by men of Anglo-Saxon race. This leads, however, to no serious consequences. The peasants are accustomed to work together in this way, to make concessions for the Communal welfare, and to bow unreservedly to the will of the Mir. I know of many instances where the peasants have set at defiance the authority of the police, of the provincial governor, and of the central Government itself, but I have never heard of any instance where the will of the Mir was openly opposed by one of its members.

In the preceding pages I have repeatedly spoken about "shares of the Communal land." To prevent misconception, I must explain carefully what this expression means. A share does not mean simply a plot or parcel of land; on the contrary, it always contains at least four, and may contain a large number of distinct plots. We have here a new point of difference between the Russian village and the villages of Western Europe.

Communal land in Russia is of three kinds: the land on which the village is built, the arable land, and the meadow or hay-field. On the first of these each family possesses a house and garden, which are the hereditary property of the family, and are never affected by the periodical re-distributions. The other two kinds are both subject to re-distribution, but on somewhat different principles.

The whole of the Communal arable land is first of all divided into three fields, to suit the triennial rotation of crops already described, and each field is divided into a number of long narrow strips — corresponding to the number of male members in the Commune — as nearly as possible equal to each other in area and quality. Sometimes it is necessary to divide the field into several portions, according to the quality of the soil, and then to subdivide each of these portions into the requisite number of strips. Thus in all cases every household possesses at least one strip in each field; and in those cases where subdivision is necessary, every household possesses a strip in each of the portions into which the field is subdivided. This complicated process of division and subdivision is accomplished by the peasants themselves, with the aid of simple measuring-rods, and the accuracy of the result is truly marvelous.

The meadow, which is reserved for the production of hay, is divided into the same number of shares as the arable land. There, however, the division and distribution take place not at irregular intervals, but annually. Every year, on a day fixed by the Assembly, the villagers proceed in a body to this part of their property, and divide it into the requisite number of portions. Lots are then cast, and each family at once mows the portion allotted to it. In some Communes the meadow is mown by all the peasants in common, and the hay afterwards distributed by lot among the families; but this system is by no means so frequently used.

As the whole of the Communal land thus resembles to some extent a big farm, it is necessary to make certain rules concerning cultivation. A family may sow what it likes in the land allotted to it, but all families must at least conform to the accepted system of rotation. In like manner, a family cannot begin the autumn plowing before the appointed time, because it would thereby interfere with the rights of the other families, who use the fallow field as pasturage.

It is not a little strange that this primitive system of land tenure should have succeeded in living into the nineteenth century, and still more remarkable that the institution of which it forms an essential part should be regarded by many intelligent people as one of the great institutions of the future, and almost as a panacea for social and political evils.

TOWNS AND TOWNSMEN. At about eighty miles from St. Petersburg the Moscow railway crosses the Volkhof, a rapid, muddy river, which connects Lake Ilmen with Lake Ladoga. At the point of intersection I got on board a small steamer, and sailed up the river for about fifty miles. The journey was tedious, for the country is flat and monotonous, and the steamer did not make more than nine knots an hour. Towards sunset Novgorod appeared on the horizon. Seen thus, in the soft twilight, the town appears decidedly picturesque. On the western bank of the river stands the kremlin, a slightly-elevated piece of ground surrounded by high brick walls, over which peep the painted cupolas of the cathedral. On the opposite bank stands the larger part of the town, the sky-line of which is agreeably broken by the green roofs and pear-shaped cupolas of many churches. Here and there a bit of foliage indicates the existence of gardens. Spanning the river between the kremlin and the town on the opposite bank is a long stone bridge, half hidden by a high temporary wooden bridge, which does duty — or at least did duty at that time — for the older structure. Many people asserted then that the temporary structure was destined to become permanent, because it yielded a comfortable revenue to the officials whose duty it was to keep it in repair; but whether this uncharitable prediction has been realized, I know not.

Those who wish to enjoy the illusions produced by scene-painting and stage-decorations should never go behind the scenes. In like manner he who wishes to preserve the delusion that Russian towns are picturesque should never enter them, but content himself with viewing them from a distance. A walk through the streets inevitably dispels the illusion, and proves satisfactorily that irregularity, even when combined with squalor, is not necessarily picturesque.

However imposing Russian towns may look when seen from the outside, they will generally be found on closer inspection to be little more than villages in disguise. If they have not a positively rustic, they have at least a suburban, appearance. The streets are straight and wide, and are either miserably paved or not paved at all. *Trottoirs* are not considered indispensable. The houses are built of wood or stone, generally one-storied, and separated from each other by spacious yards. Many of them do not condescend to turn their façades to the street. The general impression produced is that the majority of the burghers have come from the country, and have brought their country houses with them. There are few or no shops with merchandise tastefully arranged in the window to tempt the passer-by. If you wish to make purchases you must go to the Gostinny Dvor, or Bazaar, which consists of long symmetrical rows of low-roofed, dimly-lighted stores, with a colonnade in front. This is the place where merchants most do congregate, but it presents nothing of that bustle and activity which we are accustomed to associate with commercial life. The shopkeepers stand at their doors or loiter about in the immediate vicinity waiting for customers. From the scarcity of these latter I should say that when sales are effected the profits must be enormous. In the other parts of the town the air of solitude and languor is still more conspicuous. In the great square, or by the side of the promenade — if the town is fortunate enough to have one — cows or horses may be seen grazing tranquilly, without being at all conscious of the incongruity of their position. And, indeed, it would be strange if they had any such consciousness, for it does not exist in the minds either of the police or of the inhabitants. At night the streets are not lighted at all, or are supplied merely with a few oil-lamps, which do little more than render the darkness visible, so that cautious citzens returning home late often arm themselves with lanterns. A few years ago an honorable town-councilor of Moscow opposed a project for lighting the city with gas, and maintained that those who chose to go out at night should carry their lamps with them. The objection was over-ruled, and Moscow was supplied with gas-lamps, but very few of the provincial towns have as yet followed the example of the ancient capital.

This description does not apply to St. Petersburg and Odessa, but these cities may for the present be left out of consideration, for they have a distinctly foreign character. The genuine Russian towns — and Moscow may still almost be included in the number — have a semi-rustic air, or at least the appearance of those retired suburbs of a large city which are still free from the jurisdiction of the municipal authorities.

The scarcity of towns in Russia is not less remarkable than their rustic appearance. I use the word here in the popular and not in the official sense. In official language a town means a collection of houses, containing certain organs of administration, and hence the term is sometimes applied to petty villages. Let us avoid, then, the official list of the towns, and turn to the statistics of population. It may be presumed, I suppose, that no town is worthy of the name unless it contains at least 10,000 inhabitants. Now, if we apply this test, we shall find that in the whole of European Russia in the narrower sense of the term — excluding Finland, the Baltic provinces,

Lithuania, Poland, and the Caucasus, which are politically but not socially parts of Russia — there are only 127 towns. Of these, only twenty-five contain more than 25,000, and only eleven contain more than 50,000 inhabitants.

These facts indicate plainly that in Russia, as compared with Western Europe, the urban element in the population is relatively small; and this conclusion is borne out by statistical data. In Russia the urban element composes only a tenth part of the entire population, whereas in Great Britain more than one-half of the inhabitants are dwellers in towns. A serious effort to discover the causes of this would certainly bring out some striking peculiarities in the past history and present condition of the Russian Empire. I have myself made the attempt, and I propose now to communicate a few results of the investigation.

The chief cause is that Russia is much less densely populated than Western Europe. Towards the East she has never had a natural frontier, but always a wide expanse of fertile, uncultivated land, offering a tempting field for emigration; and the peasantry have ever shown themselves ready to take advantage of their geographical position. Instead of improving their primitive system of agriculture, which requires an enormous area and rapidly exhausts the soil, they have always found it easier and more profitable to emigrate and take possession of the virgin land to the eastward. Thus the territory — sometimes with the aid of, and sometimes in spite of, the Government — has constantly expanded, and has already reached Behring's Straits and the northern offshoots of the Himalayas. The little district around the sources of the Dnieper has grown into a great empire forty times as large as France, and in all this vast area there are only about eighty millions of inhabitants. Prolific as the Russian race is, its powers of reproduction could not keep pace with its power of territorial expansion, and consequently the country is still very thinly peopled. If we take European Russia as a whole, we find that the population is only about fourteen to the square verst, whilst in Great Britain, for a similar area, the average density is about 114. Even the most densely-populated region — the northern part of the Black-earth zone — has only about forty to the square verst. A people that has such an abundance of land, and can support itself by agriculture, is not likely to devote itself to industry, and not likely to congregate in towns.

The second cause which hindered the formation of towns was serfage. Serfage, and the administrative system of which it formed a part, hemmed the natural movements of the population. The nobles habitually lived on their estates, and taught a portion of their serfs to supply them with nearly everything they required; and the peasants who might desire to settle as artisans in the towns were not free to do so, because they were attached to the soil. Thus arose those curious village industries of which I have already spoken.

The insignificance of the Russian towns is in part explained by these two causes. The abundance of land tended to prevent the development of industry, and the little industry which did exist was prevented by serfage from collecting in the towns. But this explanation is evidently incomplete. The same causes existed during the Middle Ages in Central Europe, and yet, in spite of them, flourishing cities grew up and played an important part in the social and political history of Germany. In these cities collected traders and artisans, forming a distinct social class, distinguished from the nobles on the one hand, and the surrounding peasantry on the other, by peculiar occupations, peculiar aims, peculiar intellectual physiognomy, and peculiar moral code.

According to Catherine's legislation, which remained in full force down to the present reign, and still exists in its main features, towns are of three kinds: (1) "Government towns" (gubernskie gorodá) — that is to say, the chief towns of provinces, or "Governments" (gubernii) — in which are concentrated the various organs of provincial administration; (2) District towns (uyezdnie gorodá), in which resides the administration of the districts (uyezdi) into which the provinces are divided; and (3) Supernumerary towns (zashtatnie gorodá), which have no particular significance in the territorial administration.

In all these the municipal organization is the same. Leaving out of consideration those persons who happen to reside in the towns but in reality belong to the noblesse, the clergy, or the lower ranks of officials, we may say that the town population is composed of three groups: the merchants (kuptsi), the burghers in the narrower sense of the term (meshtchanye), and the artisans (tsekhoviye). Those categories are not hereditary castes, like the nobles, the clergy, and the peasantry. A noble may become a merchant, or a man may be one year a burgher, the next year an artisan, and the third year a merchant, if he changes his occupation and pays the necessary dues. But the categories form, for the time being, distinct corporations, each possessing a peculiar organization and peculiar privileges and obligations.

Of these three groups the first in the scale of dignity is that of the merchants. It is chiefly recruited from the burghers and the peasantry. Any one who wishes to engage in commerce inscribes himself in one of the three guilds, according to the amount of his capital and the nature of the operations in which he wishes to embark, and as soon as he has paid the required dues, he becomes officially a merchant. As soon as he ceases to pay these dues he ceases to be a merchant in the legal sense of the term, and returns to the class to which he formerly belonged. There are some families whose members have belonged to the merchant class for several generations, and the law speaks about a certain "velvet-book" (barkhatnaya kniga) in which their names should be inscribed, but in reality they do not form a distinct category, and they descend at once from their privileged position as soon as they cease to pay the annual guild dues.

The artisans form the connecting link between the town population and the peasantry, for peasants often enroll themselves in the trades corporations, or Tsekhi, without severing their connection with the rural communes to which they belong. Each trade or handicraft constitutes a Tsekh, at the head of which stands an elder and two assistants, elected by the members; and all the Tsekhi together form a corporation under an elected head (Remeslenny Golová), assisted by a council composed of the elders of the various Tsekhi. It is the duty of this council and its president to regulate all matters connected with the Tsekhi, and to see that the multifarious regulations regarding masters, journeymen, and apprentices are duly observed.

The nondescript class, composed of those who are inscribed as permanent inhabitants of the towns but who do not belong to any guild or Tsekh, constitutes what is called the burghers in the narrower sense of the term. Like the other two categories, they form a separate corporation with an elder and an administrative bureau.

Some idea of the relative numerical strength of these three categories may be obtained from the following figures. In European Russia the merchant class (including wives and children) numbers about 466,000, the burghers about 4,033,000, and the artisans about 260,000.

The link of connection between these three categories is the Town Council (Gorodskaya Dûma), the central and highest organ of the municipal administration, with its president the Mayor (Gorodskoi Golová). A few years ago this body was thoroughly re-organized according to the most recent theories of municipal administration; and now all house-proprietors, to whatever class they belong, may take part in its proceedings, and serve as its office-bearers. The consequence of this has been that many towns have now a noble as mayor, but it cannot be said that the spirit of the institution has radically changed. Very few seek election, and those who are elected display very little zeal in the discharge of their duties. Not long ago it was proposed, in the Town Council of St. Petersburg, to insure the presence of a quorum by imposing fines for non-attendance! This fact speaks volumes for the low vitality of these institutions. When such an incident occurs in the capital, we can readily imagine what takes place in the provincial towns.

THE IMPERIAL ADMINISTRATION. The gigantic administrative machine which holds together all the various parts of the vast Empire, and secures for all of them a certain amount of public order and tranquillity, has been gradually created by successive generations, but we may say roughly that it was first designed and constructed by Peter the Great. Before his time the country was governed in a rude, primitive fashion. The Grand Princes of Moscow, in subduing their rivals and annexing the surrounding principalities, merely cleared the ground for a great homogeneous State, and made no attempt to build a symmetrical political edifice. Wily, practical politicians, rather than statesmen of the doctrinaire type, they never dreamed of introducing uniformity and symmetry into the administration. They spared and developed the ancient institutions, so far as these were useful and consistent with the exercise of autocratic power, and made only such alterations as practical necessity demanded. And these necessary alterations were more frequently local than general. Special decisions, instruction to particular officials, and charters for particular communes or proprietors, were much more common than general legislative measures. In short, the old Muscovite Tsars practiced a tentative, hand-to-mouth policy, ruthlessly destroying whatever caused temporary inconvenience, and giving little heed to what did not force itself upon their attention. Hence, under their rule the administration presented not only territorial peculiarities, but also an ill-assorted combination of different systems in the same district — a conglomeration of institutions belonging to different epochs, like a fleet composed of triremes, three-deckers, and ironclads.

This irregular system, or rather want of system, seemed highly unsatisfactory to the logical mind of Peter the Great, who was all his life a thorough doctrinaire. He conceived the grand design of sweeping it away, and putting in its place a symmetrical bureaucratic machine, constructed according to the newest principles of political science. It is scarcely necessary to say that this magnificent project, so foreign to the traditional ideas and customs of the people, was not easily realized. Imagine a man, without technical knowledge, without skilled workmen, without good tools, and with no better material than soft, crumbling sandstone, endeavoring to build a palace on a marsh! The undertaking would seem to reasonable minds utterly absurd, and yet it must be admitted that Peter's project was scarcely more feasible. He had neither technical knowledge, nor the requisite materials, nor a firm foundation to build on. With his usual Titanic energy he demolished the old structure, but his attempts to construct were little more than a series of failures. In his numerous ukazes he has left us a graphic description of his efforts, and it is at once instructive and saddening to watch the great worker toiling indefatigably at his self-imposed task. His instruments are constantly breaking in his hands. The foundations of the building are continually giving way, and the lower tiers crumbling under the superincumbent weight. A whole section is found to be unsuitable, and is ruthlessly pulled down, or falls of its own accord. And yet the builder toils on, with a perseverance and energy of purpose that compel admiration, frankly confessing his mistakes and failures, and patiently seeking the means of remedying them, never allowing a word of despondency to escape him, and never despairing of ultimate success. And at length death comes, and the mighty builder is snatched away suddenly in the midst of his unfinished labors, bequeathing to his successors the task of carrying on the great work.

None of these successors possessed Peter's genius and energy, but they were all compelled by the force of circumstances to adopt his plans. A return to the old rough and ready rule of the Voyevods was impossible. As the autocratic power became more and more imbued with Western ideas, it felt more and more the need of a thoroughly good instrument for the realization of its policy, and accordingly strove to systematize and centralize the administration.

In this change we may perceive a certain analogy with the history of the French administration from the time of Philippe le Bel to that of Louis XIV. In both countries we see the central power bringing the local administrative organs more and more under its control, till at last it succeeds in creating a thoroughly centralized bureaucratic organization. But under this superficial resemblance lie profound differences. The French kings had to struggle with provincial sovereignties and feudal rights, and when they had annihilated this opposition, they easily found materials with which to build up the bureaucratic structure. The Russian sovereigns, on the contrary, met with no such opposition, but they had great difficulty in finding bureaucratic material amongst their uneducated, undisciplined subjects. For many generations schools and colleges in Russia were founded and maintained simply for the purpose of preparing men for the public service.

The administration was thus brought much nearer to the West-European ideal, but some people have grave doubts as to whether it became thereby better adapted to the practical wants of the people for whom it was created. On this point, a well-known Slavophil once made to me some remarks which are worthy of being recorded. "You have observed," he said, "that till very recently there was in Russia an enormous amount of official peculation, extortion, and misgovernment of every kind, that the courts of law were dens of iniquity, that the people often committed perjury, and much more of the same sort, and it must be admitted that all this has not yet entirely disappeared. But what does it prove? That the Russian people are morally inferior to the German? Not at all. It simply proves that the German system of administration, which was forced upon them without their consent, was utterly unsuited to their nature. If a young growing boy be compelled to wear very tight boots, he will probably burst them, and the ugly rents will doubtless produce an unfavorable impression on the passers-by; but surely it is better that the boots should burst than that the feet should be deformed. Now the Russian people was compelled to put on not only tight boots, but also a tight jacket, and, being young and vigorous, it burst them. Narrowminded, pedantic Germans can neither understand nor provide for the wants of the broad Slavonic nature."

In its present form the Russian administration seems at first sight a very imposing edifice. At the top of the pyramid stands the Emperor, "the autocratic monarch," as Peter the Great described him, "who has to give an account of his acts to no one on earth, but has a power and authority to rule his states and lands as a Christian sovereign according to his own will and judgment." Immediately below the Emperor we see the Council of State, the Committee of Ministers, and the Senate, which represent respectively the legislative, the administrative, and the judicial power. An Englishman glancing over the first volume of the Code might imagine that the Council of State is a kind of parliament, and the Committee of Ministers a ministry in our sense of the term, but in reality both institutions are simply incarnations of the autocratic power. Though the Council is intrusted by law with many important functions — such as examining and criticising the annual budget, declaring war, concluding peace, and performing other important duties — it has merely a consultative character, and the Emperor is not in any way bound by its decisions. The Committee is not at all a ministry as we understand the word. The ministers are all directly and individually responsible to the Emperor, and therefore the Committee has no common responsibility or other cohesive force. As to the Senate, it has descended from its high estate. It was originally intrusted with the supreme power during the absence or minority of the monarch, and was intended to exercise a controlling influence in all sections of the administration, but now its activity is restricted to judicial matters, and it is little more than a supreme court of appeal.

Immediately below these three institutions stand the Ministries, ten in number. They are the central points, in which converge the various kinds of territorial administration, and from which radiates the Imperial will all over the Empire.

For the purposes of territorial administration Russia Proper — that is to say, European Russia, exclusive of Poland, the Baltic Provinces, Finland, and the Caucasus, each of which has a peculiar administration of its own — is divided into forty-six provinces, or "Governments" *(gubernii)* and each Government is subdivided into districts *(uyezdi)*. The average area of a province is about the size of Portugal, but some are as small as Belgium, whilst one at least is twenty-five times as big. The population, however, does not correspond to the amount of territory. In the largest province, that of Archangel, there are less than 300,000 inhabitants, whilst in some of the smaller ones there are over two millions. The districts likewise vary greatly in size. Some are smaller than Oxfordshire or Buckingham, and others are much bigger than the whole of the United Kingdom.

Over each province is placed a Governor, who is assisted in his duties by a Vice-Governor and a small council. According to the legislation of Catherine II., which still appears in the Code and has only been partially repealed, the Governor is termed "the steward of the province," and is intrusted with so many and such delicate duties, that in order to obtain men qualified for the post, it would be necessary to realize the great Empress's design of creating, by education, "a new race of people." Down to very recent times the Governors understood the term "stewards" in a very literal sense, and ruled in a most arbitrary, high-handed style, often exercising an important influence on the civil and criminal tribunals. These extensive and vaguely-defined powers have now been very much curtailed, partly by positive legislation, and partly by increased publicity and improved means of communication. All judicial matters have been placed completely beyond the Governor's control, and many of his former functions are now fulfilled by the Zemstvo — the new organ of local self-government, of which I shall have more to say presently. Besides this, all ordinary current affairs are regulated by an already big and ever-growing body of instructions, in the form of Imperial orders and ministerial circulars, and as soon as anything not provided for by the instructions happens to occur, the minister is consulted through the post-office or by telegraph. Even within the sphere of their lawful authority the Governors have now a certain respect for public opinion, and occasionally a very wholesome dread of casual newspaper correspondents. Thus the men who were formerly described by the satirists as "little satraps," have sunk to the level of very subordinate officials. I can confidently say that many (I believe the majority) of them are honest, upright men, who are perhaps not endowed with any unusual administrative capacities, but who perform their duties faithfully according to their lights. Certainly, M. Lerche, who was Governor of Novgorod during my sojourn there, was a most honorable, conscientious, and intelligent man, who had gained golden opinions from all classes of the people. If any representatives of the old "satraps" still exist, they must be sought for in the outlying Asiatic provinces.

Independent of the Governor, who is the local representative of the Ministry of the Interior, are a number of resident officials, who represent the other ministries, and each of them has a bureau, with the requisite number of assistants, secretaries, and scribes.

To keep this vast and complex bureaucratic machine in motion it is necessary to have a large and well-drilled army of officials. These are drawn chiefly from the ranks of the noblesse and the clergy, and form a peculiar social class called Tchinovniks, or men with "Tchins." As the Tchin plays an important part in Russia not only in the official world, but also to some extent in social life, it may be well to explain its significance.

All offices, civil and military, are, according to a scheme invented by Peter the Great, arranged in fourteen classes or ranks, and to each class or rank a particular name is attached. As promotion is supposed to be given according to personal merit, a man who enters the public service for the first time must, whatever be his social position, begin in the lower ranks, and work his way upwards. Educational certificates may exempt him from the necessity of passing through the lowest classes, and the Imperial will may disregard the restrictions laid down by law, but as a general rule a man must begin at or near the bottom of the official ladder, and he must remain on each step a certain specified time. The step on which he is for the moment standing, or, in other words, the official rank or Tchin which he possesses, determines what offices he is competent to hold. Thus rank or Tchin is a necessary condition for receiving an appointment, but it does not designate any actual office, and the names of the different ranks are extremely apt to mislead a foreigner.

We must always bear this in mind when we meet with those imposing titles which Russian tourists sometimes put on the visiting-cards, such as "Conseiller de Cour," "Conseiller d'État," "Conseiller privé de S. M. l'Empereur de toutes les Russies." It would be uncharitable to suppose that these titles are used with the intention of misleading, but that they do sometimes mislead there cannot be the least doubt. I shall never forget the look of intense disgust which I once saw on the face of an American who had invited to dinner a "Conseiller de Cour," on the assumption that he would have a court dignitary as his guest, and who casually discovered that the personage in question was simply an insignificant official in one of the public offices. No doubt other people have had similar experiences. The unwary foreigner who has heard that there is in Russia a very important institution called the "Conseil d'État," naturally supposes that a "Conseiller d'État" is a member of that venerable body; and if he meets "Son Excellence le Conseiller privé," he is pretty sure to assume—especially if the word "actuel" has been affixed—that he sees a real living member of the Russian Privy Council. When to the title is added, "de S. M. l'Empereur de toutes les Russies," a boundless field is opened up to the non-Russian imagination. In reality these titles are not nearly so important as they seem. The *soi-disant* "Conseiller de Cour" has probably nothing to do with the court. The Conseiller d'État is so far from being a member of the Conseil d'État that he cannot possibly become a member till he receives a higher Tchin. As to the Privy Counsellor, it is sufficient to say that the Privy Council, which had a very odious reputation in its lifetime, died more than a century ago, and has not since been resuscitated. The explanation of these anomalies is to be found in the fact that the Russian Tchins, like the German honorary titles—Hofrath, Staatsrath, Geheimrath—of which they are a literal translation, indicate not actual office, but simply official rank. Formerly the appointment to an office generally depended on the Tchin; now there is a tendency to reverse the old order of things and make the Tchin depend upon the office actually held.

The reader of practical mind who is in the habit of considering results rather than forms and formalities desires probably no further description of the Russian bureaucracy, but wishes to know simply how it works in practice. What has it done for Russia in the past, and what is it doing in the present?

At the present day, when faith in despotic civilizers and paternal government has been rudely shaken, and the advantages of a free, spontaneous national development are fully recognized, centralized bureaucracies have everywhere fallen into bad odor. In Russia the dislike to them is particularly strong, because it has there something more than a purely theoretical basis. The recollection of the reign of Nicholas, with its stern military régime, and minute, pedantic formalism, makes many Russians condemn in no measured terms the administration under which they live, and most Englishmen will feel inclined to indorse this condemnation. Before passing sentence, however, we ought to know that the system has at least an historical justification, and we must not allow our love of constitutional liberty and local self-government to bind us to the distinction between theoretical and historical possibility. What seems to political philosophers abstractly the best possible government may be utterly inapplicable in certain concrete cases. We need not attempt to decide whether it is better for humanity that Russia should exist as a nation, but we may boldly assert that without a strongly centralized administration Russia would never have become one of the great European powers. Until comparatively recent times the part of the world which is known as the Russian Empire was a conglomeration of independent or semi-independent political units, animated with centrifugal as well as centripetal forces; and even at the present day it is far from being a compact homogeneous State. In many respects it resembles our Indian Empire more closely than a European country, and we all know what India would become if the strong cohesive power of the administration were withdrawn. It was the autocratic power, with the centralized administration as its necessary complement, that first created Russia, then saved her from dismemberment and political annihilation, and ultimately secured for her a place among European nations by introducing Western civilization. Theoretically it would have been better that the various units should have united spontaneously, and the European civilization should have been voluntarily adopted by all classes of the inhabitants, but historically such a phenomenon was impossible.

Whilst thus recognizing clearly that autocracy and a strongly centralized administration were necessary first for the creation and afterwards for the preservation of national independence, we must not shut our eyes to the evil consequences which resulted from this unfortunate necessity. It was in the nature of things that the Government, aiming at the realization of designs which its subjects neither sympathized with nor clearly understood, should have become separated from the nation; and the reckless haste and violence with which it attempted to carry out its schemes aroused a spirit of positive opposition among the people. A considerable section of the people long looked on the reforming Tsars as incarnations of the spirit of evil, and the Tsars in their turn looked upon the people as a passive instrument for the carrying out of their political designs. This peculiar relation between the nation and the Government has given the key-note to the whole system of administration. The Government has always treated the people as minors, utterly incapable of understanding its political designs, and only very partially competent to look after their own local affairs. The officials have naturally acted in the same spirit. Looking for direction and approbation merely to their superiors, they have systematically treated those over whom they were placed, as a conquered or inferior race. The State has thus come to be regarded as an abstract entity, with interests entirely different from those of the human beings composing it; and in all matters in which State interests are supposed to be involved, the rights of individuals are ruthlessly sacrificed.

If we remember that the difficulties of centralized administrations are always in direct proportion to the extent and territorial variety of the country to be governed, we may readily understand how slowly and imperfectly the administrative machine necessarily works in Russia. The whole of the vast region stretching from the Polar Ocean to the Caspian, and from the shores of the Baltic to the confines of the Celestial Empire, is administered from St. Petersburg. The genuine bureaucrat has a wholesome dread of formal responsibility, and generally tries to avoid it by taking all matters out of the hands of his subordinates, and passing them on to the higher authorities. As soon, therefore, as affairs are caught up by the administrative machine they begin to ascend, and probably arrive some day at the cabinet of the minister. Thus the ministries are flooded with papers—many of the most trivial import—from all parts of the Empire; and the higher officials, even if they had the eyes of an Argus and the heads of a Briareus, could not possibly fulfill conscientiously the duties imposed on them. In reality the Russian administrators of the higher ranks recall neither Argus nor Briareus. They commonly show neither an extensive nor a profound knowledge of the country which they are supposed to govern, and seem always to have a fair amount of leisure time at their disposal.

Besides the unavoidable evils of excessive centralization, Russia has had to suffer much from the jobbery, venality, and extortion of the officials. When Peter the Great one day prepared to hang every man who should steal as much as would buy a rope, his Procurator-General frankly replied that if his Majesty put his project into execution there would be no officials left. "We all steal," added the worthy official; "the only difference is that some of us steal larger amounts and more openly than others." Since these words were spoken more than a century and a half has passed, and during all that time Russia has steadily made progress in many respects, but until the commencement of the present reign little change took place in the moral character of the administration. The elder half of the present generation can still remember the time when they could have repeated, without much exaggeration, the confession of Peter's Procurator-General.

To appreciate aright this ugly phenomenon we must distinguish two kinds of venality. On the one hand there was the habit of exacting what are vulgarly termed "tips" for services performed, and on the other there were the various kinds of positive dishonesty. Though it might not be always easy to draw a clear line between the two categories, the distinction was fully recognized in the moral consciousness of the time, and many an official who received regularly "sinless revenues" (*bezgreshniye dokhodi*), as the tips were sometimes called, would have been very indignant had he been stigmatized as a dishonest man. The practice was, in fact, universal, and could be, to a certain extent, justified by the smallness of the official salaries. In some departments there was a recognized tariff. The "brandy farmers," for example, paid regularly, a fixed sum to every official, from the governor to the policeman, according to his rank. I know of one case where an official, on receiving a larger sum than was customary, conscientiously handed back the change! The other and more heinous offences were by no means so common, but were still fearfully frequent. Many high officials and important dignitaries were known to receive large revenues, to which the term "sinless" could not by any means be applied, and yet they retained their position, and were received in society with respectful deference. That undeniable fact speaks volumes for the moral atmposhere of the official world at that time.

The sovereigns were always perfectly aware of the abuses, and all strove more or less to root them out, but the success which attended their efforts does not give us a very exalted idea of the practical omnipotence of autocracy. In a centralized bureaucratic administration, in which each official is to a certain extent responsible for the sins of his subordinates, it is always extremely difficult to bring an official culprit to justice, for he is sure to be protected by his superiors; and when the superiors are themselves habitually guilty of malpractices, the culprit is quite safe from exposure and punishment. The Tsar, indeed, might do much towards exposing and punishing offenders, if he could venture to call in public opinion to his assistance, but in reality he is very apt to become a party to the system of hushing up official delinquencies. He is himself the first official in the realm, and he knows that the abuse of power by a subordinate has a tendency to produce hostility towards the fountain of all official power. Frequent punishment of officials might, it is thought, diminish public respect for the Government, and undermine that social discipline which is necessary for the public tranquility. It is therefore considered expedient to give to official delinquencies as little publicity as possible. Besides this, strange as it may seem, a Government which rests on the arbitrary will of a single individual is, notwithstanding occasional outbursts of severity, much less systematically and invariably severe than authority founded on free public opinion. When delinquencies occur in very high places the Tsar is almost sure to display a leniency approaching to tenderness. If it be necessary to make a sacrifice to justice, the sacrificial operation is likely to be made as painless as may be, and illustrious scape-goats are not allowed to die of starvation in the wilderness—the wilderness being generally Paris or Baden-Baden. This fact may seem strange to those who are in the habit of associating autocracy with Neapolitan dungeons and the mines of Siberia, but it is not difficult to explain. No individual, even though he should be the Autocrat of all the Russias, can so case himself in the armor of official dignity as to be completely proof against personal influences. The severity of autocrats is reserved for political offenders, against whom they naturally harbor a feeling of personal resentment. It is so much easier for us to be lenient and charitable towards a man who sins against public morality, than towards one who sins against our own interests!

In justice to the bureaucratic reformers in Russia, it must be said that they have preferred prevention to cure. Refraining from all Draconian legislation, they have put their faith in a system of ingenious checks and a complicated formal procedure. When we examine the complicated formalities and labryrinthine procedure by which the administration is controlled, our first impression is that administrative abuses must be almost impossible. Every possible act of every official seems to have been foreseen, and every possible outlet from the narrow path of honesty seems to have been carefully walled up. As the English reader has probably no conception of formal procedure in a highly centralized bureaucracy, let me give an instance by way of illustration.

In the residence of a Governor-General one of the stoves is in need of repairs. An ordinary mortal may assume that a man with the rank of Governor-General may be trusted to expend a few shillings conscientiously, and that consequently his Excellency will at once order the repairs to be made and the payment to be put down among the petty expenses. To the bureaucratic mind the case appears in a very different light. All possible contingencies must be carefully provided for. As a Governor-General may possibly be possessed with a mania for making useless alterations, the necessity of the repairs ought to be verified; and as wisdom and honesty are more likely to reside in an assembly than in an individual, it is well to intrust the verification to a council. A council of three or four members accordingly certifies that the repairs are necessary. This is pretty strong authority, but it is not enough. Councils are composed of mere human beings, liable to error and subject to be intimidated by the Governor-General. It is prudent, therefore, to demand that the decision of the council be confirmed by the Procureur, who is directly subordinated to the Minister of Justice. When this double confirmation has been obtained, an architect examines the stove, and makes an estimate. But it would be dangerous to give *carte blanche* to an architect, and therefore the estimate has to be confirmed, first by the aforesaid council and afterwards by the Procureur. When all these formalities—which require sixteen days and ten sheets of paper—have been duly observed, his Excellency is informed that the contemplated repairs will cost two roubles and forty kopeks, or about five shillings of our money. Even here the formalities do not stop, for the Government must have the assurance that the architect who made the estimate and superintended the repairs has not been guilty of negligence. A second architect is therefore sent to examine the work, and his report, like the estimate, requires to be confirmed by the council and the Procureur. The whole correspondence lasts thirty days, and requires no less than thirty sheets of paper! Had the person who desired the repairs been not a Governor-General but an ordinary mortal, it is impossible to say how long the procedure might have lasted.

It might naturally be supposed that this circuitous and complicated method, with its registers, ledgers, and minutes of proceeding, must at least prevent pilfering; but this *á priori* conclusion has been emphatically belied by experience. Every new ingenious device had merely the effect of producing a still more ingenious means of avoiding it. The system did not restrain those who wished to pilfer, and it had a deleterious effect on honest officials, by making them feel that the Government reposed no confidence in them. Besides this, it produced among all officials, honest and dishonest alike, the habit of systematic falsification. As it was imposible for even the most pedantic of men—and pedantry, be it remarked, is a rare quality among Russians—to fulfill conscientiously all the prescribed formalities, it became customary to observe the forms merely on paper. Officials certified facts which they never dreamed of examining, and secretaries gravely wrote the minutes of meetings that had never been held! Thus, in the case above cited, the repairs were in reality begun and ended long before the architect was officially authorized to begin the work. The comedy was nevertheless gravely played out to the end, so that any one afterwards revising the documents would have found that everything had been done in perfect order.

Perhaps the most ingenious means for preventing administrative abuses was devised by the Emperor Nicholas. Fully aware that he was regularly and systematically deceived by the ordinary officials, he formed a body of well-paid officers, called the "Gendarmerie," who were scattered over the country, and ordered to report directly to his Majesty whatever seemed to them worthy of attention. Bureaucratic minds considered this an admirable expedient; and the Tsar confidently expected that he would, by means of these official observers who had no interest in concealing the truth, be able to know everything, and to correct all official abuses. In reality the institution produced a few good results, and in some respects had a very pernicious influence. Though picked men and provided with good salaries, these officers were all more or less permeated with the prevailing spirit. They could not but feel that they were regarded as spies and informers—a humiliating conviction, little calculated to develop that feeling of self-respect which is the main foundation of uprightness—and that all their efforts could do but little good. They were, in fact, in pretty much the same position as Peter's Procurator-

General, and with that *bonhomie* which is a prominent trait of the Russian character, they disliked ruining individuals who were no worse than the majority of their fellows. Besides this, according to the received code of official morality, insubordination was a more heinous sin than dishonesty, and political offenses were regarded as the blackest of all. The Gendarmerie shut their eyes, therefore, to the prevailing abuses, which were believed to be incurable, and directed their attention to real or imaginary political delin-quencies. Oppression and extortion remained unnoticed, whilst an incautious word or a foolish joke at the expense of the Government was too often magnified into an act of high treason.

This force still exists, and has at least one representative in every im-portant town. It serves as a kind of supplement to the ordinary police, and is generally employed in all matters in which secrecy is required. Unfor-tunately it is not bound by those legal restrictions which protect the public against the arbitrary will of the ordinary authorities. It has a vaguely-defined roving commission, to watch and arrest all persons who seem to it in any way dangerous or *suspects,* and it may keep such in confinement for an indefinite time, or remove them to some distant and inhospitable part of the Empire, without making them undergo a regular trial. It is, in short, the ordinary instrument for punishing political dreamers, suppressing secret societies, counteracting political agitations, and in general executing the extra-legal orders of the Government.

THE ZEMSTVO. Very soon after my arrival in Novgorod I made the acquaint-ance of a gentleman, who was described to me as "the president of the provincial Zemstvo-bureau," and finding him amiable and communicative I suggested that he might give me some information regarding the institution of which he was the chief representative. With the utmost readiness he pre-pared to be my Mentor with regard to the Zemstvo, at once introduced me to his colleagues, and invited me to come and see him at his office as often as I felt inclined. Of this invitation I made abundant use. At first my visits were discreetly few and short, but when I found that my friend and his colleagues really wished to instruct me in all the details of Zemstvo admin-istration, and had arranged a special table for my convenience, I became a regular attendant, and spent daily several hours in the bureau, studying the current affairs, and noting down the interesting bits of statistical and other information which came before the members, as if I had been one of their number. When they went to inspect the hospital, the lunatic asylum, the seminary for the preparation of village schoolmasters, or any other Zemstvo institution, they invariably invited me to accompany them, and made no attempt to conceal from me the defects which they happened to discover.

I mention these facts because they illustrate well the extreme readiness of the Russians to afford every possible facility to a foreigner who wishes seriously to study their country. They believe that they have long been misunderstood and systematically calumniated by foreigners, and they are extremely desirous that all misconceptions regarding their country should be removed. It must be said to their honor that they have little or none of that false patriotism which seeks to conceal national defects; and in judging themselves and their institutions they are inclined to be over-severe rather than unduly lenient. In the time of Nicholas those who desired to stand well with the Government proclaimed loudly that they lived in the happiest and best governed country of the world, but this shallow official optimism has long since gone out of fashion. During the six years which I spent in Russia I found everywhere the utmost readiness to assist me in my investigations, and very rarely noticed that habit of "throwing dust in the eyes of foreigners," of which some writers have spoken so much.

The Zemstvo is a kind of local administration which supplements the action of the rural communes, and takes cognizance of those higher public wants which individual communes cannot possibly satisfy. Its principal duties are to keep the roads and bridges in proper repair, to provide means of conveyance for the rural police and other officials, to elect the justices of peace, to look after primary education and sanitary affairs, to watch the state of the crops and take measures against approaching famine, and in short to undertake, within certain clearly-defined limits, whatever seems likely to increase the material and moral well-being of the population. In form the institution is parliamentary—that is to say, it consists of an assembly of deputies which meets at least once a year, and of a permanent executive bureau elected by the assembly from among its members. If the assembly be regarded as a local parliament, the bureau corresponds to the ministry. In accordance with this analogy my friend the president was sometimes jocularly termed the prime minister. Once every three years the deputies are elected in certain fixed proportions by the landed proprietors, the rural communes, and the municipal corporations. Every province (*guberniya*) and each of the districts (*uyezdi*) into which the province is subdivided has such an assembly and such a bureau.

Not long after my arrival in Novgorod I had the opportunity of being present at a District Assembly. In the ball-room of the "Club de la Noblesse" I found thirty or forty men seated round a long table covered with green cloth. Before each member lay sheets of paper for the purpose of taking notes, and before the president—the Marshal of Noblesse for the district—stood a small hand-bell, which he rang vigorously at the commencement of the proceedings and on all occasions when he wished to obtain silence. To the right and left of the president sat the members of the executive bureau (uprava), armed with piles of written and printed documents, from which they read long and tedious extracts, till the majority of the audience took to yawning and one or two of the members positively went to sleep. At the close of each of these reports the president rang his bell—presumably for the purpose of awakening the sleepers—and inquired whether any one had remarks to make on what had just been read. Generally some one had remarks to make, and not unfrequently a discussion ensued. When any decided difference of opinion appeared, a vote was taken by handing round a sheet of paper, or by the simpler method of requesting the Ayes to stand up and the Noes to sit still.

What surprised me most in this assembly was that it was composed partly of nobles and partly of peasants—the latter being decidedly in the majority —and that no trace of antagonism seemed to exist between the two classes. Landed proprietors and their *ci-devant* serfs evidently met for the moment on a footing of equality. The discussions were always carried on by the nobles, but on more than one occasion peasant members rose to speak, and their remarks, always dear, practical, and to the point, were invariably listened to with respectful attention by all present. Instead of that violent antagonism which might have been expected considering the constitution of the assembly, there was a great deal too much unanimity—a fact indicating plainly that the majority of the members did not take a very deep interest in the matters presented to them.

This assembly was held in the month of September. At the beginning of December the Assembly for the Province met, and during nearly three weeks I was daily present at its deliberations. In general character and mode of procedure it resembled closely the District Assembly. Its chief peculiarities were that its members were chosen, not by the primary electors, but by the assemblies of the ten Districts which compose the Province, and that it took cognizance merely of those matters which concerned more than one District. Besides this, the peasant deputies were very few in number—a fact which somewhat surprised me, because I was aware that, according to the law, the peasant members of the District Assemblies were eligible, like those of the other classes. The explanation is that the District Assemblies choose their most active members to represent them in the Provincial Assemblies, and consequently the choice generally falls on landed proprietors. To this arrangement the peasants make no objection, for attendance at the Provincial Assemblies demands a considerable pecuniary outlay, and payment to the deputies is expressly prohibited by law.

To give the reader an idea of the elements composing this assembly, let me introduce him to a few of the members. A considerable section of them may be described in a single sentence. They are commonplace men, who have spent part of their youth in the public service as officers in the army, or officials in the civil administration, and have since retired to their estates, where they gain a modest competence by farming. Some of them add to their agricultural revenues by acting as justices of the peace. A few may be described more particularly.

You see there, for instance, that fine-looking old general in uniform, with the St. George's Cross at his button-hole—an order given only for bravery in the field. That is Prince S......, a grandson of one of Russia's greatest men. He has filled high posts in the administration without ever tarnishing his name by a dishonest or dishonorable action, and has spent a great part of his life at Court without ceasing to be frank, generous, and truthful. Though he has no intimate knowledge of current affairs, and sometimes gives way a little to drowsiness, his sympathies in disputed points are always on the right side, and when he gets to his feet he speaks in a clear soldier-like fashion.

The tall gaunt man, somewhat over middle age, who sits a little to the left is Prince W....... He, too, has an historical name, but he cherishes above all things personal independence, and has consequently always kept aloof from the Administration and the Court. The leisure thus acquired he has devoted to study, and he has produced several very valuable works on political and social science. An enthusiastic but at the same time cool-headed abolitionist at the time of the Emancipation, he has since constantly striven to ameliorate the condition of the peasantry by advocating the spread of primary education, the establishment of rural credit associations in the villages, the preservation of the communal institutions, and numerous important reforms in the financial system. Both of these gentlemen, it is said, generously gave to their peasants more land than they were obliged to give by the Emancipation law. In the Assembly Prince W.... speaks frequently, and always commands attention; and in all important committees he is a leading member. Though a warm defender of the Zemstvo institutions, he thinks that their activity ought to be confined to a comparatively narrow field, and thereby he differs from some of his colleagues, who are ready to embark in hazardous, not to say fanciful, schemes for developing the natural resources of the province. His neighbor, Mr. P...., is one of the most able and energetic members of the assembly. He is president of the executive bureau in one of the Districts, where he has founded many primary schools, and created several rural credit associations on the model of those which bear the name of Schultze-Delitsch in Germany. Mr. S...., who sits besides him, was for some years an arbitrator between the proprietors and emancipated serfs, then a member of the Provincial Executive Bureau, and is now director of a bank in St. Petersburg.

To the right and left of the president—who is Marshal of Noblesse for the province—sit the members of the bureau. The gentleman who reads the long reports is my friend "the prime minister," who began life as a cavalry officer, and after a few years of military service retired to his estate; he is an intelligent, able administrator, and a man of considerable literary culture. His colleague, who assists him in reading the reports, is a merchant, and director of the municipal bank. His neighbor is also a merchant, and in some respects the most remarkable man in the room. Though born a serf, he is already, at middle age, an important personage in the Russian commercial world. Rumor says that he laid the foundation of his fortune by one day purchasing a copper caldron in a village through which he was passing on his way to St. Petersburg, where he hoped to gain a little money by the sale of some calves. In the course of a few years he amassed an enormous fortune; but the cautious people think that he is too fond of hazardous speculations, and prophesy that he will end life as poor as he began it.

All these men belong to what may be called the party of progress, which anxiously supports all proposals recognized as "liberal," and especially all measures likely to improve the condition of the peasantry. Their chief opponent is that little man with close-cropped, bullet-shaped head and small piercing eyes, who may be called the leader of the opposition. That gentleman opposes many of the proposed schemes, on the ground that the province is already overtaxed, and that the expenditure ought therefore to be reduced to the smallest possible figure. In the District Assembly he preaches this doctrine with considerable success, for there the peasantry form the majority, and he knows how to use that terse, homely language, interspersed with proverbs, which has far more influence on the rustic mind than scientific principles and logical reasoning; but here, in the Provincial Assembly, his following composes only a respectable minority, and he confines himself to a policy of obstruction.

The Zemstvo of Novgorod has—or at least had at that time—the reputation of being one of the most enlightened and energetic, and I must say that in the assembly of 1870 the proceedings were conducted in a business-like, satisfactory way. The reports were carefully considered, and each article of the annual budget was submitted to minute scrutiny and criticism. In several of the provinces which I afterwards visited I found that affairs were conducted in a very different fashion: quorums were formed with extreme difficulty, and the proceedings, when they at last commenced, were treated as mere formalities and dispatched as speedily as possible. The character of the assembly depends of course on the amount of interest taken in local public affairs. In some districts this interest is considerable; in others it is very near zero.

PROPRIETORS OF THE OLD SCHOOL. Of all the foreign countries in which I have traveled Russia certainly bears off the palm in all that regards hospitality. Every spring I found myself in possession of a large number of invitations from landed proprietors in different parts of the country—far more than I could possibly accept—and a great part of the summer was generally spent in wandering about from one country-house to another. I have no intention of asking the reader to accompany me in these expeditions—for, though pleasant in reality, they might be tedious in description—but I wish to convey to him some idea of the Russian landed proprietors, and shall therefore single out for description a few typical specimens of the class.

Among the Russian landed proprietors are to be found nearly all ranks and conditions of men, from the rich magnate, surrounded with all the refined luxury of West-European civilization, to the poor, ill-clad, ignorant owner of a few acres which barely supply him with the necessaries of life. Let us take, first of all, a few specimens from the middle ranks.

In one of the central provinces, near the bank of a sluggish, meandering stream, stands an irregular group of wooden constructions—old, unpainted, blackened by time, and surmounted by high, sloping roofs of moss-covered planks. The principal building is a long, one-storied dwelling-house, constructed at right angles to the road. At the front of the house is a spacious, ill-kept yard, and at the back an equally spacious shady garden, in which art carries on a feeble conflict with encroaching nature. At the other side of the yard, and facing the front door—or rather the front doors, for there are two—stand the stables, hay-shed, and granary, and near to that end of the house which is furthest from the road are two smaller houses, one of which is the kitchen, and the other the Lyudskáya, or servants' apartments. Beyond these we can perceive, through a single row of lime-trees, another group of time-blackened wooden constructions in a still more dilapidated condition. That is the farm-yard.

There is certainly not much symmetry in the disposition of these buildings, but there is nevertheless a certain order and meaning in the apparent chaos. All the buildings which do not require stoves are built at a considerable distance from the dwelling-house and kitchen, which are more liable to take fire; and the kitchen stands by itself, because the odor of cookery where oil is used is by no means agreeable, even for those whose olfactory nerves are not very sensitive. The plan of the house is likewise not without a certain meaning. The rigorous separation of the sexes, which formed a characteristic trait of old Russian society, has long since disappeared, but its influence may still be traced in houses built on the old model. The house in question is one of these, and consequently it is composed of three sections —at the one end the male apartments, at the other the female apartments, and in the middle the neutral territory, comprising the dining-room and the salon. This arrangement has its conveniences, and explains the fact that the house has two front doors. At the back is a third door, which opens from the neutral territory into a spacious veranda overlooking the garden.

Here lives and has lived for many years Ivan Ivanovitch K......, a gentleman of the old school, and a very worthy man of his kind. If we look at him as he sits in his comfortable arm-chair, with his capacious dressing-gown hanging loosely about him, and his long Turkish pipe in his hand, we shall be able to read at a glance something of his character. Nature endowed him with large bones and broad shoulders, and evidently intended him to be a man of great muscular power, but he has contrived to frustrate this benevolent intention, and has now more fat than muscle. His close-cropped head is round as a bullet, and his features are massive and heavy, but the heaviness is relieved by an expression of calm contentment and imperturbable good-nature, which occasionally blossoms into a broad grin. His face is one of those on which no amount of histrionic talent could produce a look of care and anxiety, and for this it is not to blame, for such an expression has never been demanded of it. Like other mortals he experiences sometimes little annoyances, and on such occasions his small gray eyes sparkle and his face becomes suffused with a crimson glow that suggests apoplexy; but ill-fortune has never been able to get sufficiently firm hold of him to make him understand what such words as care and anxiety mean. Of struggle, disappointment, hope, and all the other feelings which give to human life a dramatic interest, he knows little by hearsay and nothing by experience. He has, in fact, always lived outside of that struggle for existence which modern philosophers declare to be the law of Nature.

Somewhere about sixty years ago Ivan Ivan'itch was born in the house where he still lives. His first lessons he received from the parish priest, and afterward he was taught by a deacon's son, who had studied in the ecclesiastical seminary to so little purpose that he was unable to pass the final examination. By both of these teachers he was treated with extreme leniency, and was allowed to learn as little as he chose. His father wished him to study hard, but his mother was afraid that study might injure his health, and accordingly gave him several holidays every week. Under these circumstances his progress was naturally not very rapid, and he was still very slightly acquainted with the elementary rules of arithmetic, when his father one day declared that he was already eighteen years of age, and must at once enter the service. But what kind of service? Ivan had no natural inclination for any kind of activity. The project of entering him as a "Junker" in a cavalry regiment, the colonel of which was an old friend of his father's, did not at all please him. He had no love for military service, and positively disliked the prospect of an examination. Whilst seeming, therefore, to bow implicitly to the paternal authority, he induced his mother to oppose the scheme.

The dilemma in which Ivan found himself was this: in deference to his father he wished to be in the service and gain that official rank which every Russian noble desires to possess, and at the same time, in deference to his mother and his own tastes, he wished to remain at home and continue his indolent mode of life. The Marshall of Noblesse, who happened to call one day, helped him out of the difficulty by offering to inscribe him as secretary in the *Dvoryánskaya Opéka,* a bureau which acts as curator for the estates of minors. All the duties of this office could be fulfilled by a paid secretary, and the nominal occupant would be periodically promoted as if he were an active official. This was precisely what Ivan required. He accepted eagerly the proposal, and obtained, in the course of seven years, without any effort on his part, the rank of "collegiate secretary," corresponding to the "capitaine-en-second" of the military hierarchy. To mount higher he would have had to seek some place where he could not have fulfilled his duty by proxy, so he determined to rest on his easily-won laurels, and sent in his resignation.

Immediately after the termination of his official life his married life began. Before his resignation had been accepted he suddenly found himself one morning on the high road to matrimony. Here again there was no effort on his part. The course of true love, which is said never to run smooth for ordinary mortals, ran smooth for him. He never had even the trouble of proposing. The whole affair was arranged by his parents, who chose as bride for their son the only daughter of their nearest neighbor. The young lady was only about sixteen years of age, and was not remarkable for beauty, talent, or any other peculiarity, but she had one very important qualification —she was the daughter of a man who had an estate contiguous to their own, and who might give as a dowry a certain bit of land which they had long desired to add to their own property. The negotiations, being of a delicate nature, were intrusted to an old lady who had a great reputation for diplomatic skill in such matters, and she accomplished her mission with such success, that in the course of a few weeks the preliminaries were arranged and the day fixed for the wedding. Thus Ivan Ivan'itch won his bride as easily as he had won his Tchin of "collegiate secretary."

Though the bridegroom had received rather than taken to himself a wife and did not imagine for a moment that he was in love, he had no reason to regret the choice that was made for him. Maria Petrovna was exactly suited by character and education to be the wife of a man like Ivan Ivan'itch. She had grown up at home in the society of nurses and servant-maids, and had never learned anything more than could be obtained from the parish priest and from "Ma'mselle," a personage occupying a position midway between a servant-maid and a governess. The first events of her life were the announcement that she was to be married and the preparations for the wedding. All her life afterwards she remembered the delight which the purchase of her trousseau afforded her, and kept in her memory a full catalogue of the articles bought. The first years of her married life were not very happy, for she was treated by her mother-in-law as a naughty child who required to be frequently snubbed and lectured; but she bore the discipline with exemplary patience, and in due time became her own mistress and autocratic ruler in all domestic affairs. From that time she lived an active, uneventful life. Between her and her husband there is as much mutual attachment as can reasonably be expected in phlegmatic natures after thirty years of matrimony. She devotes all her energies to satisfying his simple material wants—of intellectual wants he has none—and securing his comfort in every possible way. Under this fostering care he has, as he is wont to say, "effeminated himself" (obábilsya).

His love of hunting and shooting has died out, he cares less and less to visit his neighbors, and each successive year he spends more and more time in his comfortable arm-chair.

The daily life of this worthy couple is singularly regular and monotonous, varying only with the changing seasons. In summer Ivan Ivan'itch gets up about seven o'clock, and puts on, with the assistance of his *valet de chambre,* a simple costume, consisting chiefly of a faded, plentifully-stained dressing-gown. Having nothing particular to do, he sits down at the open window and looks into the yard. As the servants pass he stops and questions them, and then gives them orders, or scolds them, as circumstances demand. Toward nine o'clock tea is announced, and he goes into the dining-room—a long, narrow apartment with bare wooden floor and no furniture but a table and chairs, all in a more or less rickety condition. Here he finds his wife with the tea-urn before her. In a few minutes the younger children come in, kiss their papa's hand, and take their places round the table. As this morning meal consists merely of bread and tea, it does not last long; and all disperse to their several occupations. The head of the house begins the labors of the day by resuming his seat at the open window and having his Turkish pipe filled and lighted by a boy whose special function is to keep his master's pipes in order. When he has smoked two or three pipes and indulged in a proportionate amount of silent contemplation, he goes out with the intention of visiting the stables and farmyard, but generally before he has crossed the court he finds the heat unbearable, and returns to his former position by the open window. Here he sits tranquilly till the sun has so far moved round that the veranda at the back of the house is completely in the shade, when he has his arm-chair removed thither, and sits there till dinner-time.

Maria Petrovna spends her morning in a more active way. As soon as the breakfast-table has been cleared, she goes to the larder, takes stock of the provisions, arranges the *menu du jour,* and gives to the cook the necessary materials, with detailed instructions as to how they are to be prepared. The rest of the morning she devotes to her other household duties.

Towards one o'clock dinner is announced, and Ivan Ivan'itch prepares his appetite by swallowing at a gulp a wine-glassful of home-made bitters. Dinner is the great event of the day. The food is abundant and of good quality, but mushrooms, onions, and fat play a rather too important part in the repast, and the whole is prepared with very little attention to the recognized principles of culinary hygiene. Many of the dishes, indeed, would make a British valetudinarian stand aghast, but they seem to produce no bad effect on those Russian organisms which have never been weakened by town life, nervous excitement, or intellectual exertion.

No sooner has the last dish been removed than a deathlike stillness falls upon the house; it is the time of the after-dinner siesta. The young folks go into the garden, and all the other members of the household give way to the drowsiness naturally engendered by a heavy meal on a hot summer day. Ivan Ivan'itch retires to his own room, from which the flies have been carefully expelled by his pipe-bearer. Maria Petrovna dozes in an arm-chair in the sitting-room, with a pocket-handkerchief spread over her face. The servants snore in the corridors, the garret, or the hayshed; and even the old watch-dog in the corner of the yard stretches himself out at full length on the shady side of his kennel.

In about two hours the house gradually re-awakens. Doors begin to creak; the names of various servants are bawled out in all tones, from base to falsetto; and footsteps are heard in the yard. Soon a man-servant issues from the kitchen, bearing an enormous tea-urn, which puffs like a little steam-engine. The family assemble for tea. In Russia, as elsewhere, sleep after a heavy meal produces thirst, so that the tea and other beverages are very acceptable. Then some little delicacies are served—such as fruit and wild berries, or cucumbers with honey, or something else of the kind, and the family again disperses. Ivan Ivan'itch takes a turn in the fields on his *begovuiya droshki*—an extremely light vehicle, composed of two pairs of wheels joined together by a single board, on which the driver sits stride-legged; and Maria Petrovna probably receives a visit from the Popadyá (the priest's wife), who is the chief gossipmonger of the neighborhood. There is not much scandal in the district, but what little there is the Popadyá carefully collects, and distributes among her acquaintances with undiscriminating generosity.

In the evening it often happens that a little group of peasants come into the court, and ask to see the "master." The master goes to the door, and generally finds that they have some favor to request. In reply to his question, "Well, children, what do you want?" they tell their story in a confused, rambling way, several of them speaking at a time, and he has to question and cross-question them before he comes to understand clearly what they desire. If he tells them he cannot grant it, they probably do not accept a first refusal, but endeavor by means of supplication to make him reconsider his decision. Stepping forward a little, and bowing low, one of the group begins in a half-respectful, half-familiar, caressing tone—"Little father, Ivan Ivan'-itch, be gracious; you are our father, and we are your children"—and so on. Ivin Ivan'itch good-naturedly listens, and again explains that he cannot grant what they ask, but they have still hopes of gaining their point by entreaty, and continue their supplications till at last his patience is exhausted and he says to them in a paternal tone, "Now, enough! enough! you are block-heads—blockheads all round! there's no use talking, it can't be done." And with these words he enters the house, so as to prevent all further discussion.

A regular part of the evening's occupation is the interview with the steward. The work that has just been done, and the programme for the morrow, are always discussed at great length; and much time is spent in speculating as to the weather during the next few days. On this latter point the calendar is always carefully consulted, and great confidence is placed in its predictions, though past experience has often shown that they are not to be implicitly trusted. The conversation drags on till supper is announced, and immediately after that meal, which is an abridged repetition of dinner, all retire for the night.

Thus pass the days, and weeks, and months, in the house of Ivan Ivan'itch, and rarely is there any deviation from the ordinary programme. The climate necessitates, of course, some slight modifications. When it is cold, the doors and windows have to be kept shut, and after heavy rains, those who do not like to wade in mud have to remain in the house or garden. In the long winter evenings the family assemble in the sitting-room, and all kill time as they best can. Ivan Ivan'itch smokes his long pipe, and meditates, or listens to the barrel-organ played by one of the children. Maria Petrovna knits a stocking. The old aunt, who commonly spends the winter with them, plays Patience, and sometimes draws from the game conclusions as to the future. Her favorite predictions are that a stranger will arrive, or that a marriage will take place, and she can determine the sex of the stranger and the color of the bridegroom's hair; but beyond this her art does not go, and she cannot satisfy the young ladies' curiosity as to further details.

Books and newspapers are rarely seen in the sitting-room, but for those who wish to read, there is a book-case full of miscellaneous literature, which gives some idea of the literary tastes of the family during several generations. The oldest volumes were bought by Ivan Ivan'itch's grandfather—a man who, according to the family traditions, enjoyed the confidence of the great Catherine. Though wholly overlooked by recent historians, he was evidently a man who had some pretensions to culture. He had his portrait painted by a foreign artist of considerable talent—it still hangs in the sitting-room— and he bought several pieces of Sévres ware, the last of which stands on a commode in the corner and contrasts strangely with the rude home-made furniture and squalid appearance of the apartment. Among the books which bear his name are the tragedies of Sumarókof, who imagined himself to be "the Russian Voltaire;" the amusing comedies of Von-Wisin, some of which still keep the stage; the loud-sounding odes of the courtly Derzhávin; two or three books containing the mystic wisdom of Freemasonry as interpreted by Schwarz and Novikoff; Russian translations of Richardson's "Pamela," "Sir Charles Grandison" and "Clarissa Harlowe;" Rousseau's "Nouvelle Héloise," in Russian garb; and three or four volumes of Voltaire in the original. Among the works collected at a somewhat later period are translations of Ann Radcliffe, of Scott's early novels, and of Ducray Duménil, whose stories, "Lolotte et Fanfan" and "Victor" once enjoyed a great reputation. At this point the literary tastes of the family appear to have died out, for the succeeding literature is represented exclusively by Kryloff's Fables, a farmer's manual, a hand-book of family medicine, and a series of calendars. There are, however, some signs of a revival, for on the lowest shelf stand recent editions of Pushkin, Lérmontof, and Gógol, and a few works by living authors.

Sometimes the monotony of the winter is broken by visiting neighbors and receiving visitors in return, or in a more decided way by a visit of a few days to the capital of the province. In the latter case Maria Petrovna spends nearly all her time in shopping, and brings home a large collection of miscellaneous articles. The inspection of these by the assembled family forms an important domestic event, which completely throws into the shade the occasional visits of peddlers and colporteurs. Then there are the festivities at Christmas and Easter, and occasionally little incidents of a less agreeable kind. It may be that there is a heavy fall of snow, so that it is necessary to cut roads to the kitchen and stables; or wolves enter the courtyard at night and have a fight with the watch-dogs; or the news is brought that a peasant who had been drinking in a neighboring village has been found frozen to death on the road.

Altogether the family live a very isolated life, but they have one bond of connection with the great outer world. Two of the sons are officers in the army, and both of them write home occasionally to their mother and sisters. To these two youths is devoted all the little stock of sentimentality which Maria Petrovna possesses. She can talk of them by the hour to any one who will listen to her, and has related to the Popadyá a hundred times every trivial incident of their lives. Though they have never given her much cause for anxiety, she lives in constant fear that some evil may befall them. What she most fears is that they may be sent on a campaign or may fall in love with actresses. War and actresses are in fact the two bugbears of her èxistence, and whenever she has a disquieting dream she asks the priest to offer up a *molében* for the safety of her absent ones. Sometimes she ventures to express her anxiety to her husband, and recommends him to write to them; but he considers writing a letter a very serious bit of work, and always replies evasively, "Well, well, we must think about it."

During the Crimean War—though the two sons were not yet in the army —Ivan Ivan'itch half awoke from his habitual lethargy, and read occasionally the meagre official reports published by the Government. He was a little surprised that no great victories were reported, and that the army did not at once advance on Constantinopole. As to causes he never speculated. Some of his neighbors told him that the army was disorganized, and the whole system of Nicholas had been proved to be utterly worthless. That might all be very true, but le did not understand military and political matters. No doubt it would all come right in the end. All did come right, after a fashion, and he again gave up reading newspapers; but ere long he was startled by reports much more alarming than any rumors of war. People began to talk about the peasant question, and to say openly that the serfs must soon be emancipated. For once in his life Ivan Ivan'itch asked explanations. Finding one of his neighbors, who had always been a respectable, sensible man, and a severe disciplinarian, talking in this way, he took him aside and asked what it all meant. The neighbor explained that the old order of things had shown itself bankrupt, and was doomed, that a new epoch was opening, that everything was to be reformed, and that the Emperor, in accordance with a secret clause of the Treaty with the Allies, was about to grant a Constitution! Ivan Ivan'itch listened for a little in silence, and then, with a gesture of impatience, interrupted the speaker: "Polno durátchitsya! enough of fun and tomfoolery. Vassili Petrovitch, tell me seriously what you mean."

When Vassili Petrovitch vowed that he spoke in all seriousness, his friend gazed at him with a look of intense compassion, and remarked, as he turned away, "So you, too, have gone out of your mind!"

The utterances of Vassili Petrovitch, which his lethargic, soberminded friend regarded as indicating temporary insanity in the speaker, represented fairly the mental condition of very many Russian nobles at that time, and were not without a certain foundation. The idea about a secret clause in the Treaty of Paris was purely imaginary, but it was quite true that the country was entering on an epoch of great reforms, among which the Emancipation question occupied the chief place. Of this even the skeptical Ivan Ivan'itch was soon convinced. The Emperor formally declared to the noblesse of the province of Moscow that the actual state of things could not continue for ever, and called on the landed proprietors to consider by what means the condition of their serfs might be ameliorated. Provincial committees were formed for the purpose of preparing definite projects, and gradually it became apparent that the Emancipation of the serfs was really at hand.

Ivan Ivan'itch was somewhat alarmed at the prospect of losing his authority over his serfs. Though he had never been a cruel task-master, he had not spared the rod when he considered it necessary, and he believed birch-twigs to be a necessary instrument in the Russian system of agriculture. For some time he drew consolation from the thought that peasants were not birds of the air, that they must under all circumstances require food and clothing, and that they would be ready to serve him as agricultural laborers; but when he learned that they were to receive a large part of the estate for their own use, his hopes fell, and he greatly feared that he would be inevitably ruined.

These dark forebodings have not been by any means realized. His serfs have been emancipated and have received about a half of the estate, but in return for the land ceded they pay him annually a considerable sum, and they are always ready to cultivate his fields for a fair remuneration. The yearly outlay is now considerably greater, but the price of grain has risen, and this quite counterbalances the additional yearly expenditure. The administration of the estate is much less patriarchal; much that was formerly left to custom and tacit understanding is now regulated by express agreement on purely commercial principles; a great deal more money is paid out and a great deal more received; there is much less authority in the hands of the master, and his responsibilities are proportionately diminished; but in spite of all these changes, Ivan Ivan'itch would have great difficulty in deciding whether he is a richer or a poorer man. He has fewer horses and fewer servants, but he has still more than he requires, and his mode of life has undergone no perceptible alteration. Maria Petrovna complains that she is no longer supplied with eggs, chickens, and home-spun linen by the peasants, and everything is three times as dear as it used to be; but somehow the larder is still full, and abundance reigns in the house as of old.

PROPRIETORS OF THE MODERN SCHOOL. In the district in which Nikolai Petróvitch lives the resident landed-proprietors are, for the most part, as I have said, men of the old school, decidedly rustic in their manners and conceptions. But there are a few exceptions, and among the most conspicuous of these is Victor Alexandr'itch L....... As we approach his house we can at once perceive that he differs from the majority of his neighbors. The gate is painted and moves easily on its hinges, the fence is in good repair, the short avenue leading up to the front door is well kept, and in the garden we can perceive at a glance that more attention is paid to flowers than to vegetables. The house is of wood, and not large, but it has some architectural pretensions in the form of a great, pseudo-Doric wooden portico that covers three-fourths of the façade. In the interior we remark everywhere the influence of Western civilization. Victor Alexandr'itch is by no means richer than Ivan Ivan'itch, but his rooms are much more luxuriously furnished. The furniture is of a lighter model, more comfortable, and in a much better state of preservation. Instead of the bare, scantily furnished sitting-room, with the old-fashioned barrel-organ which played only six airs, we find an elegant drawing-room, with a piano by one of the most approved makers, and numerous articles of foreign manufacture, comprising a small buhl table and two bits of genuine old wedgewood. The servants are clean, and dressed in European costume. The master, too, is very different in appearance. He pays great attention to his toilet, wearing a dressing-gown only in the early morning, and a fashionable lounging coat during the rest of the day. The Turkish pipes which his grandfather loved he holds in abhorence, and habitually smokes cigarettes. With his wife and daughters he always speaks French, and calls them by French or English names. But the part of the house which most strikingly illustrates the difference between the old and new styles is "le cabinet de monsieur." In the cabinet of Ivan Ivan'itch the furniture consists of a broad sofa which serves as a bed, a few deal chairs, a long range of pipes, and a clumsy deal table, on which are generally to be found a bundle of greasy papers, an old chipped ink-bottle, a pen, and a calendar. The cabinet of Victor Alexandr'itch has an entirely different appearance. It is small, but at once comfortable and elegant. The principal objects which it contains are a library-table, with ink-stand, presse-papier, paper-cutters, and other articles in keeping, and in the opposite corner a large bookcase. The collection of books is remarkable, not from the number of volumes or the presence of rare editions, but from the variety of the subjects. History, art, fiction, the drama, political economy, and agriculture are represented in about equal proportions. Some of the works are in Russian, others in German, a large number in French, and a few in Italian. The collection illustrates the former life and present occupations of the owner.

The father of Victor Alexandr'itch was a landed proprietor, who had made a successful career in the civil service, and desired that his son should follow the same profession. For this purpose Victor was first carefully trained at home, and then sent to the University of Moscow, where he spent four years as a student of law. From the University he passed to the Ministry of the Interior in St. Petersburg, but he found the monotonous routine of official life not at all suited to his taste, and very soon sent in his resignation. The death of his father had made him proprietor of an estate, and thither he retired, hoping to find there plenty of occupation more congenial than the writing of official papers.

At the University of Moscow he had attended the lectures of the famous Granófski, and had got through a large amount of desultory reading. The chief result of his studies was the acquisition of many ill-digested general principles, and certain vague, generous, humanitarian aspirations. With this intellectual capital he hoped to lead a useful life in the country. When he had repaired and furnished the house he set himself to improve the estate. In the course of his promiscuous reading he had stumbled on some descriptions of English and Tuscan agriculture, and had there learned what wonders might be effected by a rational system of farming. Why should not Russia follow the example of England and Tuscany? By proper drainage, plentiful manure, good plows, and the cultivation of artificial grasses, the production might be multiplied tenfold; and by the introduction of agricultural machines the manual labor might be greatly diminished. All this seemed simple as a sum in arithmetic, and Victor Alexandr'itch, "more scholarium rei familiaris ignarus," without a moment's hesitation expended his ready money in procuring from England a threshing-machine, plows, harrows, and other implements of the newest model.

The arrival of these was an event that was long remembered. The peasants examined them with attention, not unmixed with wonder, but said nothing. When the master explained to them the advantages of the new instruments, they still remained silent. Only one old man, gazing at the threshing-machine, remarked, in an audible "aside," "A cunning people these Germans!" On being asked for their opinion, they replied vaguely, "How should we know? It *ought* to be so." But when their master had retired, and was explaining to his wife and the French governess that the chief obstacle to progress in Russia was the apathetic indolence and conservative spirit of the peasantry, they expressed their opinions more freely. "These may be all very well for the Germans, but they won't do for us. How are our little horses to drag these big plows and harrows? And as for that" — the threshing-machine — "it's of no use." Further examination and reflection confirmed this first impression, and it was unanimously decided that no good would come of the new-fangled inventions.

These apprehensions proved to be only too well-founded. The plows and harrows were much too heavy for the peasants' small horses, and the threshing-machine broke down at the first attempt to use it. For the purchase of lighter implements or stronger horses there was no ready money, and for the repairing of the threshing-machine there was not an engineer within a radius of a hundred and fifty miles. The experiment was, in short, a complete failure, and the new purchases were put away out of sight.

For some weeks after this incident Victor Alexandr'itch felt very despondent, and spoke more than usual about the apathy and stupidity of the peasantry. His faith in infallible science was somewhat shaken, and his benevolent aspirations were for a time laid aside. But this eclipse of faith was not of long duration. Gradually he recovered his normal condition, and began to form new schemes. From the study of certain works on political economy he learned that the system of communal property was ruinous to the fertility of the soil, and that free labor was always more productive than serfage. By the light of these principles he discovered why the peasantry in Russia were so poor, and by what means their condition could be ameliorated. The communal land should be divided into family lots, and the serfs, instead of being forced to work for the proprietor, should pay a yearly sum as rent. The advantages of this change he perceived clearly — as clearly as he had formerly perceived the advantages of English agricultural implements — and he determined to make the experiment on his own estate.

His first step was to call together the more intelligent and influential of his serfs, and to explain to them his project; but his efforts at explanation were eminently unsuccessful. Even with regard to ordinary current affairs he could not express himself in that simple, homely language with which alone the peasants are familiar, and when he spoke on abstract subjects he naturally became quite unintelligible to his uneducated audience. The serfs listened attentively, but understood nothing. He might as well have spoken to them, as he often did in another kind of society, about the comparative excellence of Italian and German music. At a second attempt he was rather more successful. The peasants came to understand that what he wished was to break up the "Mir," or rural commune, and to put them all "on Obrok" — that is to say, make them pay a yearly sum instead of giving him a certain amount of agricultural labor. Much to his astonishment, his scheme did not meet with any sympathy. As to being put "on Obrok," the serfs did not much object, though they preferred to remain as they were; but his proposal to break up the "Mir" fairly astonished and bewildered them. They regarded it as a sea-captain might regard the proposal of a scientific wise-acre to knock a hole in the ship's bottom in order to make her sail faster. Though they did not say much, he was intelligent enough to see that they would offer a strenuous, passive opposition, and as he did not wish to act tyrannically, he let the matter drop. Thus a second benevolent scheme was shipwrecked. Many other schemes had a similar fate, and Victor Alexandr'itch began to perceive that it was very difficult to do good in this world, especially when the persons to be benefited were the Russian peasants.

In reality the fault lay less with the serfs than with their master. Victor Alexandr'itch was by no means a stupid man. On the contrary, he had more than average talents. Few men were more capable of grasping a new idea and forming a scheme for its realization, and few men could play more dexterously with abstract principles. What he wanted was the power of dealing with concrete facts. The principles which he had acquired from University lectures and desultory reading were far too vague and abstract for practical use. He had studied abstract science without gaining any technical knowledge of details, and consequently when he stood face to face with real life he was like a student who, having studied mechanics in text-books, is suddenly placed in a workshop and ordered to construct a machine. Only there was one difference: Victor Alexandr'itch was not ordered to do anything. Voluntarily, without any apparent necessity, he set himself to work with tools which he could not handle. It was this that chiefly puzzled the peasants. Why should he trouble himself with these new schemes, when he might live comfortably as he was? In some of his projects they could detect a desire to increase the revenue, but in others they could discover no such motive. In these latter they attributed his conduct to pure caprice, and put it into the same category as those mad pranks in which proprietors of jovial humor sometimes indulged.

In the last years of serfage there were a good many landed proprietors like Victor Alexandr'itch — men who wished to do something beneficent, and did not know how to do it. When serfage was being abolished the majority of these men took an active part in the great work and rendered valuable service to their country. Victor Alexandr'itch acted otherwise. At first he sympathized warmly with the proposed emancipation and wrote several articles on the advantages of free labor, but when the Government took the matter into its own hands he declared that the officials had deceived and slighted the noblesse, and he went over to the opposition. Before the Imperial Edict was signed he went abroad, and traveled for three years in Germany, France, and Italy. Shortly after his return he married a pretty, accomplished young lady, the daughter of an eminent official in St. Petersburg, and since that time he has lived in his country-house.

Though a man of education and culture, Victor Alexandr'itch spends his time in almost as indolent a way as the men of the old school. He rises somewhat later, and instead of sitting by the open window and gazing into the courtyard, he turns over the pages of a book or periodical. Instead of dining at mid-day and supping at nine o'clock, he takes déjeûner at twelve and dines at five. He spends less time in sitting in the veranda and pacing up and down with his hands behind his back, for he can vary the operation of time-killing by occasionally writing a letter, or by standing behind his wife at the piano while she plays selections from Mozart and Beethoven. But these peculiarities are merely variations in detail. If there is any essential difference between the lives of Victor Alexandr'itch and of Ivan Ivan'itch, it is in the fact that the former never goes into the fields to see how the work is done, and never troubles himself with the state of the weather, the condition of the crops, and cognate subjects. He leaves the management of his estate entirely to his steward, and refers to that personage all peasants who come to him with complaints or petitions. Though he takes a deep interest in the peasant as an impersonal, abstract entity, and loves to contemplate concrete examples of the genus in the works of certain popular authors, he does not like to have any direct relations with peasants in the flesh. If he has to speak with them he always feels awkward, and suffers from the odor of their sheepskins. Ivan Ivan'itch is ever ready to talk with the peasants, and give them sound, practical advice, or severe admonitions; and in the old times he was apt, in moments of irritation, to supplement his admonitions by a free use of his fists. Victor Alexandr'itch, on the contrary, never could give any advice except vague common-place, and as to using his fist, he would have shrunk from that, not only from respect to humanitarian principles, but also from motives which belong to the region of esthetic sensitiveness.

This difference between the two men has an important influence on their pecuniary affairs. The stewards of both steal from their masters, but that of Ivan Ivan'itch steals with difficulty, and to a very limited extent, whereas that of Victor Alexandr'itch steals regularly and methodically, and counts his gains, not by kopeks, but by roubles. Though the two estates are of about the same size and value, they give a very different revenue. The rough, practical man has a much larger income than his elegant, well-educated neighbor, and at the same time spends very much less. The consequences of this, if not at present visible, must soon become painfully apparent. Ivan Ivan'itch will doubtless leave to his children an unencumbered estate and a certain amount of capital. The children of Victor Alexandr'itch have a different prospect. He has already begun to mortgage his property and to cut down timber, and he always finds a deficit at the end of the year. What will become of his wife and children when the estate comes to be sold for payment of the mortgage, it is difficult to predict. He thinks very little of that eventuality, and when his thoughts happen to wander in that direction, he consoles himself with the thought that before the crash comes he will have inherited a fortune from a rich uncle who has no children. He knows very well — or at least might know, if he took the trouble to think — that this calculation is founded on mere possibilities. The uncle may still marry, and have children, or he may choose some other nephew as his heir, or he may simply live on and enjoy his fortune for thirty years to come. The chances, therefore, are very uncertain; but Victor Alexandr'itch, like other improvident people, likes to think that there must be somewhere behind the scenes a beneficent *Deus ex machina*, that will doubtless appear at the proper moment, and miraculously rescue him from the natural consequences of his folly.

The proprietors of the old school lead the same uniform, monotonous life year after year, with very little variation. Victor Alexandr'itch, on the contrary, feels the need of a periodical return to "civilized society," and accordingly spends a few weeks every winter in St. Petersburg. During the summer months he has the society of his brother — *un homme tout-à-fait civilisé* — who possesses an estate a few miles off.

THE NOBILITY. Certainly the Noblesse as a whole cannot be called an aristocracy. If the term is to be used at all, it must be applied to a group of families which cluster around the Court and form the highest ranks of the Noblesse. This social aristocracy contains many old families, but its real basis is official rank and general culture rather than pedigree or blood. The feudal conceptions of noble birth, good family, and the like have been adopted by some of its members, but do not form one of its conspicuous features. Though habitually practicing a certain exclusiveness, it has none of those characteristics of a caste which we find in the German *Adel,* and is utterly unable to understand such institutions as *Tafelfähigkeit,* by which a man who has not a pedigree of a certain length is considered unworthy to sit down at a royal table. It takes rather the English aristocracy as its model, and harbors the secret hope of one day obtaining a social and political position similar to that of the nobility and gentry of England. Though it has no peculiar legal privileges, its actual position in the Administration and at Court gives its members great facilities for advancement in the public service. On the other hand, its semi-bureaucratic character, together with the law and custom of dividing landed property among the children at the death of their parents, deprives it of stability. New men force their way into it by official distinction, whilst many of the old families are compelled by poverty to retire from its ranks. The son of a small proprietor or even of a parish priest may rise to the highest offices of State, whilst the descendants of the half-mythical Rurik may descend to the rank of peasants. It is said that not long ago a certain Prince Krapotkin gained his living as a cabman in St. Petersburg!

It is evident then, that this social aristocracy must not be confounded with the titled families. Titles do not possess the same value in Russia as in Western Europe. They are very common — because the titled families are numerous, and all the children bear the titles of the parents even while the parents are still alive — and they are by no means always associated with official rank, wealth, social position, or distinction of any kind. There are hundreds of princes and princesses who have not the right to appear at Court, and who would not be admitted into what is called in St. Petersburg "la société," or indeed into refined society in any country.

The only genuine Russian title is Knyaz, commonly translated "Prince." It is borne by the descendants of Rurik, of the Lithuanian Prince Ghedimin, and of the Tartar Khans and Murzi officially recognized by the Tsars. Besides these, there are fourteen families who have adopted it by Imperial command during the last two centuries. The titles of count and baron are modern importations, beginning with the time of Peter the Great. From Peter and his successors sixty-seven families have received the title of count and ten that of baron. The latter are all, with two exceptions, of foreign extraction, and are mostly descended from Court Bankers.

There is a very common idea that Russian nobles are as a rule enormously rich. This is a mistake. The majority of them are poor. At the time of the Emancipation, in 1861, there were 100,247 landed proprietors, and of these, more than 41,000 were possessors of less than twenty-one male serfs — that is to say, were in a condition of poverty. A proprietor who was owner of 500 serfs was not considered as by any means very rich, and yet there were only 3,803 proprietors belonging to that category. There were a few, indeed, whose possessions were enormous. Count Sheremetief, for instance, possessed more than 150,000 male serfs, or in other words more than 300,000 souls; and at the present day Count Orloff-Davydof owns considerably more than half a million of acres. The Demídof family derive colossal revenues from their mines, and the Strógonofs have estates which, if put together, would be sufficient in extent to form a good-sized independent state in Western Europe. The very rich families, however, are not numerous. The lavish expenditure in which Russian nobles often indulge indicates too frequently not large fortune, but simply foolish ostentation and reckless improvidence. Of the present economic position of the proprietors I shall have more to say when I come to speak of serf-emancipation and its consequences.

Social Classes. What are social classes in the Russian sense of the term? It may be well, therefore, before going further, to answer this question.

If the question were put to a Russian it is not at all unlikely that he would reply somewhat in this fashion: "In Russia there are no social classes, and there never have been any. That fact constitutes one of the most striking peculiarities of her historical development, and one of the surest foundations of her future greatness. We know nothing, and have never known anything, of those class-distinctions and class-enmities which in Western Europe have often shaken society to its basis, and imperil its existence in the future."

This statement will not be readily accepted by the traveler who visits Russia with no preconceived ideas and forms his opinions from his own observations. To him it seems that class distinctions form one of the most prominent characteristics of Russian society. In a few days he learns to distinguish the various classes by their outward appearance. He easily recognizes the French-speaking nobles in West-European costume; the burly, bearded merchant in black cloth cap and long, shiny, double-breasted coat; the priest with his uncut hair and flowing robes; the peasant with his full, fair beard and unsavory, greasy sheep-skin. Meeting everywhere those well-marked types, he naturally assumes that Russian society is composed of exclusive castes; and this first impression will be fully confirmed by a glance at the Code. Of the fifteen volumes which form the codified legislation, he finds that an entire volume — and by no means the smallest — is devoted to the rights and obligations of the various classes. From this he concludes that the classes have a legal as well as an actual existence. To make assurance doubly sure he turns to official statistics, and there he finds the following table: —

Hereditary nobles	652,887
Personal nobles	374,367
Clerical classes	695,905
Town classes	7,196,005
Rural classes	63,840,291
Military classes	4,767,703
Foreigners	153,135
	77,680,293

Armed with these materials, the traveler goes to his Russian friends who have assured him that their country knows nothing of social classes. He is confident of being able to convince them that they have been laboring under a strange delusion, but he will be disappointed. They will tell him that these laws and statistics prove nothing, and that the classes therein mentioned are mere administrative fictions.

This apparent contradiction is to be explained by the equivocal meaning of the Russian terms Sosloviya and Sostoyaniya, which are commonly translated "social classes." If by these terms are meant "castes" in the Oriental sense, then it may be confidently asserted that such do not exist in Russia. Between the nobles, the clergy, the burghers, and the peasants there is no distinction of race and no impassable barriers. The peasant often becomes a merchant, and there are many cases on record of peasants and sons of parish priests becoming nobles. Until very recently the parish clergy composed, as we have seen, a peculiar and exclusive class, with many of the characteristics of a caste; but this has been changed, and it may now be said that in Russia there are no castes in the Oriental sense.

If the word Soslovié be taken to mean an organized political unit with an *esprit de corps* and a clearly-conceived political aim, it may likewise be admitted that there are none in Russia. As there has been for centuries no political life among the subjects of the Tsars, there have been no political parties.

On the other hand, however, it is a piece of exaggeration to say that social classes have never existed in Russia, and that the categories which appear in the legislation and in the official statistics are mere administrative fictions.

CHURCH AND STATE. The Russian Patriarchate came to an end in the time of Peter the Great. Peter wished among other things to reform the ecclesiastical administration, and to introduce into his country many novelties which the majority of the clergy and of the people regarded as heretical; and he clearly perceived that a bigoted, energetic Patriarch might throw considerable obstacles in his way, and cause him infinite annoyance. Though such a Patriarch might be deposed without any flagrant violation of the canonical formalities, the operation would necessarily be attended with great trouble and loss of time. Peter was no friend of roundabout tortuous methods, and preferred to remove the difficulty in his usual thorough violent fashion. When the Patriarch Adrian died, the customary short interregnum was prolonged for twenty years, and when the people had thus become accustomed to having no Patriarch, it was anounced that no more Patriarchs would be elected. Their place was supplied by an ecclesiastical council or Synod, in which, as a contemporary explained, "the mainspring was Peter's power, and the pendulum his understanding." The great autocrat justly considered that such a council could be much more easily managed than a stubborn Patriarch, and the wisdom of the measure has been duly appreciated by succeeding sovereigns. Though the idea of re-establishing the Patriarchate has more than once been raised, it has never been carried into execution. The Holy Synod remains, and is likely to remain, the highest ecclesiastical authority.

But the Emperor? What is his relation to the Synod and to the Church in general?

This is a question about which zealous Orthodox Russians are extremely sensitive. If a foreigner ventures to hint in their presence that the Emperor seems to have a considerable influence in the Church, he may inadvertently produce a little outburst of patriotic warmth and virtuous indignation. The truth is that many Russians have a pet theory on this subject, and have at the same time a dim consciousness that the theory is not quite in accordance with reality. They hold theoretically that the Orthodox Church has no "Head" but Christ, and is in some peculiar, undefined sense entirely independent of all terrestrial authority. In this respect it is often compared with the Anglican Church, and the comparison is made a theme for semi-religious, semi-patriotic exultation, which finds expression not only in conversation, but also in the literature. Khomiakóf, for instance, in one of his most vigorous poems, predicts that God will one day take the destiny of the world out of the hands of England in order to give it to Russia, and he adduces as one of the reasons for this transfer the fact that England "has chained, with sacrilegious hand, the Church of God to the pedestal of the vain earthly power." So far the theory. As to the facts, it is unquestionable that the Church enjoys much more liberty in England than in Russia, and that the Tsar exercises a much greater influence in ecclesiastical affairs than the Queen and Parliament. All who know the internal history of Russia are aware that the Government does not draw a clear line of distinction between the temporal and the spiritual, and that it occasionally uses the ecclesiastical organization for political purposes.

What then are the relations between Church and State?

To avoid confusion, we must carefully distinguish between the Eastern Orthodox Church as a whole and that section of it which is known as the Russian Church.

The Eastern Orthodox Church is, properly speaking, a confederation of independent churches without any central authority — a unity founded on the possession of a common dogma and on the theoretical but now unrealizable possibility of holding Ecumenical Councils. The Russian National Church is one of the members of this ecclesiastical confederation. In matters of faith, it is bound by the decisions of the ancient Ecumenical Councils, but in all other respects it enjoys complete independence and autonomy.

In relation to the Orthodox Church as a whole, the Emperor of Russia is nothing more than a simple member, and can no more interfere with its dogmas or ceremonial than a King of Italy or an Emperor of the French could modify Roman Catholic theology; but in relation to the Russian National Church his position is peculiar. He is described in one of the fundamental laws as "the supreme defender and preserver of the dogmas of the dominant faith," and immediately afterwards it is said, "the autocratic power acts in the ecclesiastical administration by means of the most Holy Governing Synod, created by it." This describes very fairly the relations between the Emperor and the Church. He is merely the defender of the dogmas, and cannot in the least modify them; but he is at the same time the chief administrator, and uses the Synod as an instrument.

Some ingenious people who wish to prove that the creation of the Synod was not an innovation, represent the institution as a resuscitation of the ancient Local Council; but this view is utterly untenable. The Synod is not a council of deputies from various sections of the Church, but a permanent college, or ecclesiastical senate, the members of which are appointed and dismissed by the Emperor as he thinks fit. It has no independent legislative authority, for its legislative projects do not become law till they have received the Imperial sanction; and they are always published, not in the name of the Church, but in the name of the Supreme Power. Even in matters of simple administration it is not independent, for all its resolutions require the consent of the Procureur, a layman nominated by his Majesty. In theory this functionary protests only against those resolutions which are not in accordance with the civil law of the country; but as he alone has the right to address the Emperor directly on ecclesiastical concerns, and as all communications between the Emperor and the Synod must pass through his hands, he possesses in reality considerable power. Besides this, he can always influence the individual members by holding out prospects of advancement and decorations, and if this device fails, he can make the refractory members retire, and fill up their places with men of more pliable disposition. A council constituted in this way cannot, of course, display much independence of thought or action, especially in a country like Russia, where no one ventures to oppose openly the Imperial will.

It must not, however, be supposed that the Russian ecclesiastics regard the Imperial authority with jealousy or dislike. They are all most loyal subjects, and warm adherents of autocracy. Those ideas of ecclesiastical independence which are so common in Western Europe, and that spirit of opposition to the civil power which animates the Roman Catholic clergy, are entirely foreign to their minds. If a bishop sometimes complains to an intimate friend that he has been brought to St. Petersburg and made a member of the Synod, merely to append his signature to official papers and to give his consent to foregone conclusions, his displeasure is directed, not against the Emperor, but against the Procureur. He is full of loyalty and devotion to the Tsar, and has no desire to see his Majesty excluded from all influence in ecclesiastical affairs; but he feels saddened and humiliated when he finds that the whole government of the Church is in the hands of a lay functionary, who may be a military man, and who certainly looks at all matters from a layman's point of view.

A foreigner who hears ecclesiastics grumble or laymen express dissatisfaction with the existing state of things is apt to imagine that a secret struggle is going on between Church and State, and that a party favorable to

Disestablishment is at present being formed. In reality there is no such struggle and no such party. I have heard Russians propose and discuss every conceivable kind of political and social reforms, but I have never heard any of them speak about disestablishing the Church. Indeed, I do not know how the idea could be expressed in Russian, except by a lengthy circumlocution. So long as the autocratic power exists, no kind of administration can be exempted from Imperial control.

This close connection between Church and State and the thoroughly national character of the Russian Church is well illustrated by the history of the local ecclesiastical administration. The civil and the ecclesiastical administration have always had the same character and have always been modified by the same influences. The terrorism which was largely used by the Muscovite Tsars and brought to a climax by Peter the Great appeared equally in both. In the episcopal circulars, as in the Imperial ukazes, we find frequent mention of "most cruel corporal punishment," "cruel punishment with whips, so that the delinquent and others may not acquire the habit of practicing such insolence," and much more of the same kind. And these terribly severe measures were sometimes directed against very venial offenses. The Bishop of Vologda, for instance, in 1748 decrees "cruel corporal punishment" against priests who wear coarse and ragged clothes, and the records of the Consistorial courts contain abundant proof that such decrees were rigorously executed. When Catherine II. introduced a more humane spirit into the civil administration, corporal punishment was at once abolished in the Consistorial courts, and the procedure was modified according to the accepted maxims of civil jurisprudence. But I must not weary the reader with tiresome historical details. Suffice it to say that, from the time of Peter the Great downwards, the character of all the more energetic sovereigns is reflected in the history of the ecclesiastical administration.

Each province, or "government," forms a diocese, and the bishop, like the civil governor, has a council which theoretically controls his power, but practically has no controlling influence whatever. The Consistorial council, which has in the theory of ecclesiastical procedure a very imposing appearance, is in reality the bishop's *chancellerie,* and its members are little more than secretaries, whose chief object is to make themselves agreeable to their superior. And it must be confessed that so long as they remain what they are, the less power they possess, the better it will be for those who have the misfortune to be under their jurisdiction. The higher dignitaries have at least larger aims and a certain consciousness of the dignity of their position, but the lower officials, who have no such healthy restraints and receive ridiculously small salaries, grossly misuse the little authority which they possess, and habitually pilfer and extort in the most shameless manner. The Consistories are in fact what the public offices were in the time of Nicholas.

The ecclesiastical administration is entirely in the hands of the monks, or "Black Clergy," as they are commonly termed, who form a large and influential class.

The monks who first settled in Russia were, like those who first visited North-Western Europe, men of the earnest, ascetic, missionary type. Filled with zeal for the glory of God and the salvation of souls, they took little or no thought for the morrow, and devoutly believed that their Heavenly Father, without whose knowledge no sparrow falls to the ground, would provide for their humble wants. Poor, clad in rags, eating the most simple fare, and ever ready to share what they had with any one poorer than themselves, they performed faithfully and earnestly the work which their Master had given them to do. But this ideal of monastic life soon gave way in Russia, as in the West, to practices less simple and severe. By the liberal donations and bequests of the faithful the monasteries became rich in gold, in silver, in precious stones, and above all in land and serfs. Troitsa, for instance, possessed at one time 120,000 serfs and a proportionate amount of land, and it is said that at the beginning of last century more than a fourth of the entire population had fallen under the jurisdiction of the Church. Many of the monasteries engaged in commerce, and the monks were, if we may credit Fletcher, who visited Russia in 1588, the most intelligent merchants of the country.

During last century the Church lands were secularized, and the serfs of the Church became serfs of the State. This was a severe blow for the monasteries, but it did not prove fatal, as many people predicted. Some monasteries were abolished and others were reduced to extreme poverty, but many survived and prospered. These could no longer possess serfs, but they had still three sources of revenue: a limited amount of real property, Government subsidies, and the voluntary offerings of the faithful. At present there are about 500 monastic establishments, and the great majority of them, though not wealthy, have revenues more than sufficient to satisfy all the requirements of an ascetic life.

Thus in Russia, as in Western Europe, the history of monastic institutions is composed of three chapters, which may be briefly entitled: asceticism and missionary enterprise; wealth, luxury, and corruption; secularization of property and decline. But between Eastern and Western monasticism there is at least one marked difference. The monasticism of the West made at various epochs of its history a vigorous, spontaneous effort at self-regeneration, which found expression in the foundation of separate Orders, each of which proposed to itself some special aim — some special sphere of usefulness. In Russia we find no similar phenomenon. Here the monasteries never deviated from the rules of St. Basil, which restrict the members to religious ceremonies, prayer, and contemplation. From time to time a solitary individual raised his voice against the prevailing abuses, or retired from his monastery to spend the remainder of his days in ascetic solitude; but neither in the monastic population as a whole, nor in any particular monastery, do we find at any time a spontaneous, vigorous movement toward reform. During the last two hundred years reforms have certainly been effected, but they have all been the work of the civil power, and in the realization of them the monks have shown little more than the virtue of resignation. Here, as elsewhere, we have evidence of that inertness, apathy, and want of spontaneous vigor which form one of the most characteristic traits of Russian national life. In this, as in other departments of national activity, the spring of action has lain not in the people but in the Government.

My personal acquaintance with the Russian monasteries is too slight to enable me to speak with authority regarding their actual condition, but I may say that during casual visits to some of them I have always been disagreeably impressed by the vulgar, commercial spirit which seemed to reign in the place. Several of them have appeared to me little better than houses of refuge for the indolent, and I have had on more than one occasion good grounds for concluding that among monks, as among ordinary mortals, indolence leads to drunkenness and other vices.

THE CRIMEAN DEFEAT AND REFORM. Under the sting of the great national humiliation the upper classes awoke from their optimistic resignation. They had borne patiently the oppression of a semi-military administration, and for this! The system of Nicholas had been put to a crucial test, and found wanting. The policy which had sacrificed all to increase the military power of the Empire was seen to be a fatal error, and the worthlessness of the drill-sergeant régime was proved by bitter experience. Those administrative fetters which for more than a quarter of a century cramped every spontaneous movement had failed to fulfill even the narrow purpose for which they had been forged. They had, indeed, secured a certain external tranquility during those troublous times when Europe was convulsed by revolutionary agitation; but this tranquility was not that of healthy normal action, but of death — and underneath the surface lay secret and rapidly-spreading corruption. The army still possessed that dashing gallantry which it had displayed in the campaigns of Suvórof, that dogged, stoical bravery which had checked the advance of Napoleon on the field of Borodino, and that wondrous power of endurance which had often redeemed the negligence of generals and the defects of the commissariat; but the result was now not victory, but defeat. How could this be explained except by the radical defects of that system which had been long practiced with such inflexible perseverance? The Government had imagined that it could do everything by its own wisdom and energy, and in reality it had done nothing, or worse than nothing. The higher officers had learned only too well to be mere automatons; the ameliorations in the military organization, on which Nicholas had always bestowed special attention, were found to exist for the most part only in the official reports:

the shameful exploits of the commissariat department were such as to excite the indignation of those who had long lived in an atmosphere of official jobbery and peculation; and the finances, which people had generally supposed to be in a highly-satisfactory condition, had become seriously crippled by the first great effort.

This deep and wide-spread dissatisfaction was not allowed to appear in the press, but it found very free expression in the manuscript literature and in conversation. In almost every house — I mean, of course, among the educated classes — words were spoken which a few months before would have seemed treasonable, if not blasphemous. Philippics and satires in prose and verse were written by the dozen, and circulated in hundreds of copies. A pasquil on the Commander-in-chief, or a tirade against the Government, was sure to be eagerly read and warmly approved of. As a specimen of this kind of literature, and an illustration of the public opinion of the time, I may translate here one of these metrical tirades. Though it was never printed, it obtained a wide circulation: —

" 'God has placed me over Russia,' said the Tsar to us, 'and you must bow down before me, for my throne is His altar. Trouble not yourselves with public affairs, for I think for you and watch over you every hour. My watchful eye detects internal evils and the machination of foreign enemies; and I have no need of counsel, for God inspires me with wisdom. Be proud, therefore, of being my slaves, O Russians, and regard my will as your law.'

"We listened to these words with deep reverence, and gave a tacit consent; and what was the result? Under mountains of official papers real interests were forgotten. The letter of the law was observed, but negligence and crime were allowed to go unpunished. While groveling in the dust before ministers and directors of departments, in the hope of receiving *Tchins* and decorations, the officials stole unblushingly; and theft became so common that he who stole the most was the most respected. The merits of officers were decided at reviews; and he who obtained the rank of General was supposed capable of becoming at once an able governor, an excellent engineer, or a most wise senator. Those who were appointed governors were for the most part genuine satraps, the scourges of the provinces intrusted to their care. The other offices were filled up with as little attention to the merits of the candidates. A stable-boy became Press-censor! an Imperial fool became admiral!! Kleinmichel became a count!!! In a word, the country was handed over to the tender mercies of a band of robbers.

"And what did we Russians do all this time?

"We Russians slept! With groans the peasant paid his yearly dues; with groans the proprietor mortgaged the second half of his estate; groaning, we all paid our heavy tribute to the officials. Occasionally, with a grave shaking of the head, we remarked in a whisper that it was a shame and a disgrace — that there was no justice in the courts — that millions were squandered on

Imperial tours, kiosks, and pavilions — that everything was wrong; and then, with an easy conscience, we sat down to our rubber, praised Rachel, criticised the singing of Frezzolini, bowed low to venal magnates, and squabbled with each other for advancement in the very service which we so severely condemned. If we did not obtain the place we wished we retired to our ancestral estates, where we talked of the crops, fattened in indolence and gluttony, and lived a genuine animal life. If any one, amidst the general lethargy, suddenly called upon us to rise and fight for the truth and for Russia, how ridiculous did he appear! How cleverly the Pharisaical official ridiculed him, and how quickly the friends of yesterday showed him the cold shoulder! Under the anathema of public opinion, in some distant Siberian mine he recognized what a heinous sin it was to disturb the heavy sleep of apathetic slaves. Soon he was forgotten, or remembered as an unfortunate madman; and the few who said, 'Perhaps after all he was right,' hastened to add, 'but that is none of our business.'

"But amidst all this we had at least one consolation, one thing to be proud of — the might of Russia in the assembly of kings. 'What need we care,' we said, 'for the reproaches of foreign nations? We are stronger than those who reproach us.' And when at great reviews the stately regiments marched past with waving standards, glittering helmets, and sparkling bayonets, when we heard the loud hurrah with which the troops greeted the Emperor, then our hearts swelled with patriotic pride, and we were ready to repeat the words of the poet —

'Strong is our native country, and great the Russian Tsar.'

Then British statesmen, in company with the crowned conspirator of France, and with treacherous Austria, raised Western Europe against us, but we laughed scornfully at the coming storm. 'Let the nations rave,' we said; 'we have no cause to be afraid. The Tsar doubtless foresaw all, and has long since made the necessary preparations.' Boldly we went forth to fight, and confidently awaited the moment of the struggle.

"And lo! after all our boasting we were taken by surprise, and caught unawares, as by a robber in the dark. The sleep of innate stupidity blinded our Ambassadors, and our Foreign Minister sold us to our enemies. Where were our millions of soldiers? Where was the well-considered plan of defense? One courier brought the order to advance; another brought the order to retreat; and the army wandered about without definite aim or purpose. With loss and shame we retreated from the forts of Silistria, and the pride of Russia was humbled before the Hapsburg eagle. The soldiers fought well, but the parade-admiral (Menshikof) — the amphibious hero of lost battles — did not know the geography of his own country, and sent his troops to certain destruction.

"Awake, O Russia! Devoured by foreign enemies, crushed by slavery, shamefully oppressed by stupid authorities and spies, awaken from your long sleep of ignorance and apathy! You have been long enough held in bondage by the successors of the Tartar Khan. Stand forward calmly before the throne of the despot, and demand from him an account of the national disaster. Say to him boldly that his throne is not the altar of God, and that God did not condemn us to be slaves. Russia intrusted to you, O Tsar, the supreme power, and you were as a God upon earth. And what have you done? Blinded by ignorance and passion you have lusted after power and have forgotten Russia. You have spent your life in reviewing troops, in modifying uniforms, and in appending your signature to the legislative projects of ignorant charlatans. You created the despicable race of Press-censors, in order to sleep in peace — in order not to know the wants and not to hear the groans of the people — in order not to listen to Truth. You buried Truth, rolled a great stone to the door of the sepulcher, placed a strong guard over it, and said in the pride of your heart: For her there is no resurrection! But the third day has dawned, and Truth has arisen from the dead.

"Stand forward, O Tsar, before the judgment-seat of history and of God! You have mercilessly trampled Truth under foot, you have denied Freedom, you have been the slave of your own passions. By your pride and obstinacy you have exhausted Russia and raised the world in arms against us. Bow down before your brethren and humble yourself in the dust! Crave pardon and ask advice! Throw yourself into the arms of the people! There is now no other salvation!"

The innumerable tirades of which the above is a fair specimen were not very remarkable for literary merit or political wisdom. For the most part they were simply bits of bombastic rhetoric couched in doggerel rhyme, and they have consequently been long since consigned to well-merited oblivion — so completely that it is now difficult to obtain copies of them. They have, however, an historical interest, because they express in a more or less exaggerated form the public opinion and prevalent ideas of the educated classes at that moment. In order to comprehend their real significance, we must remember that the writers and readers were not a band of conspirators, but ordinary, respectable, well-intentioned people, who never for a moment dreamed of embarking in revolutionary designs. It was the same society that had been a few months before so indifferent to all political questions, and even now there was no intention of putting the loud-sounding phrases into action. We can imagine the comical discomfiture of those who read and listened to these appeals, if the "despot" had obeyed their summons, and suddenly appeared before them. How they would have instantly changed their tone, and assured the august accused that they had no intention of curbing his power, that they had merely given way to a momentary impulse of patriotic indignation, that they were perfectly loyal subjects, and that they did not really intend to do anything contrary to his will!

Was the movement, then, merely an outburst of childish petulance? Certainly not. The public were really and seriously convinced that things were all wrong, and they were seriously and enthusiastically desirous that a new and better order of things should be introduced. It must be said to their honor that they did not content themselves with accusing and lampooning the individuals who were supposed to be the chief culprits. On the contrary, they looked reality boldly in the face, made a public confession of their past sins, sought conscientiously the causes which had produced the recent disasters, and endeavored to find means by which such calamities might be prevented in the future. The public feeling and aspirations were not strong enough to conquer the traditional respect for the Imperial will and create an open opposition to the autocratic power, but they were strong enough to do great things by aiding the Government, if the Emperor voluntarily undertook a series of radical reforms.

THE SERFS. If we compare the development of serfage in Russia and in Western Europe, we find very many points in common, but in Russia the movement had certain peculiarities. One of the most important of these was caused by the rapid development of the autocratic power. In feudal Europe, where there was no strong central authority to control the noblesse, the free Communes entirely, or almost entirely, disappeared. They were either appropriated by the nobles or voluntarily submitted to powerful landed proprietors or to monasteries, and in this way the whole of the reclaimed land, with a few rare exceptions, became the property of the nobles or of the church. In Russia we find the same movement, but it was arrested by the Imperial power before all the land had been appropriated. The nobles could reduce to serfage the peasants settled on their estates, but they could not take possession of the free Communes, because such an appropriation would have infringed the rights and diminished the revenues of the Tsar. Down to the commencement of the present century, it is true, large grants of land with serfs were made to favored individuals among the noblesse, and in the reign of Paul (1796-1801), a considerable number of estates were affected to the use of the Imperial family under the name of appanages *(Udyélniya iméniya)*; but, on the other hand, the extensive church-lands, when secularized by Catherine II., were not distributed among the nobles, as in many other countries, but were transformed into State Demesnes. Thus, at the date of the Emancipation (1861), by far the greater part of the territory belonged to the State, and one-half of the rural population were so-called State Peasants *(Gosudárstvennie krestyané)*.

Regarding the condition of these State Peasants, or Peasants of the Demesnes, as they are sometimes called, I may say briefly that they were, in a certain sense, serfs, being attached to the soil like the others; but their condition was, as a rule, somewhat better than the serfs in the narrower acceptation of the term. They had to suffer much from the tyranny and extortion of the special administration under which they lived, but they had more land and more liberty than was commonly enjoyed on the estates of resident proprietors, and their position was much less precarious. It is often asserted that the officials of the Demesnes were worse than the serf-owners, because they had not the same interest in the prosperity of the peasantry; but this *à priori* reasoning does not stand the test of experience.

It is not a little interesting to observe the numerical proportion and geographical distribution of these two rural classes. In European Russia, as a whole, about three-eighths of the population were composed of serfs belonging to the nobles; but if we take the provinces separately we find great variations from this average. In five provinces the serfs were less than three per cent., whilst in others they formed more than seventy per cent. of the population! This is not an accidental phenomenon. In the geographical distribution of serfage we can see reflected the origin and history of the institution.

If we were to construct a map showing the geographical distribution of the serf population, we should at once perceive that serfage radiated from Moscow. Starting from that city as a center and traveling in any direction towards the confines of the Empire, we find that, after making allowance for a few disturbing local influences, the proportion of serfs regularly declines in the successive provinces traversed. In the region representing the old Muscovite Tsardom they form considerably more than a half of the peasantry. Immediately to the south and east of this, in the territory that was gradually annexed during the seventeenth and first half of the eighteenth century, the proportion varies from twenty-five to fifty per cent., and in the more recently annexed provinces it steadily decreases till it almost reaches zero.

We may perceive, too, that the percentage of serfs decreases toward the north much more rapidly than toward the east and south. This points to the essentially agricultural nature of serfage in its infancy. In the south and east there was abundance of rich "black earth" celebrated for its fertility, and the nobles in quest of estates naturally preferred this region to the inhospitable north, with its poor soil and severe climate.

A more careful examination of the supposed map would bring out other interesting facts. Let me notice one by way of illustration. Had serfage been the result of conquest we should have found the Slavonic race settled on the State Demesnes, and the Finnish and Tartar tribes supplying the serfs of the nobles. In reality we find quite the reverse; the Finns and Tartars were nearly all State Peasants, and the serfs of the proprietors were nearly all of Slavonic race. This is to be accounted for by the fact that the Finnish and Tartar tribes inhabit chiefly the outlying regions, in which serfage never attained such dimensions as in the center of the Empire.

The dues paid by the serfs were of three kinds: labor, money, and farm produce. The last-named is so unimportant that it may be dismissed in a few words. It consisted chiefly of eggs, chickens, lambs, mushrooms, wild berries, and linen cloth. The amount of these various products depended entirely on the will of the master. The other two kinds of dues, as more important, we must examine more closely.

When a proprietor had abundance of fertile land and wished to farm on his own account, he commonly demanded from his serfs as much labor as possible. Under such a master the serfs were probably entirely free from money dues, and fulfilled their obligations to him by laboring in his fields in summer and transporting his grain to market in winter. When, on the contrary, a land-owner had more serf labor at his disposal than he required for the cultivation of his fields, he put the superfluous serfs "on *obrók*" — that is to say, he allowed them to go and work where they pleased on condition of paying him a fixed yearly sum. Sometimes the proprietor did not farm at all on his own account, in which case he put all the serfs "on *obrók*," and generally gave to the Commune in usufruct the whole of the arable land and pasturage. In this way the *Mir* played the part of a tenant.

We have here the basis for a simple and important classification of estates in the time of serfage: (1) Estates on which the dues were exclusively in labor; (2) Estates on which the dues were partly in labor and partly in money; and (3) Estates on which the dues were exclusively in money.

In the manner of exacting the labor dues there was considerable variety. According to the famous manifesto of Paul I., the peasant could not be compelled to work more than three days in the week; but this law was by no means universally observed, and those who did observe it had various methods of applying it. A few took it literally, and laid down a rule that the serfs should work for them three definite days in the week — for example, every Monday, Tuesday, and Wednesday — but this was an extremely inconvenient method, for it prevented the field labor from being carried on regularly. A much more rational system was that according to which one-half of the serfs worked the first three days of the week, and the other half the remaining three. In this way there was, without any contravention of the law, a regular and constant supply of labor. It seems, however, that the great majority of the proprietors followed no strict method, and paid no attention whatever to Paul's manifesto, which gave to the peasant no legal means of making formal complaints. They simply summoned daily as many laborers as they required. The evil consequences of this for the peasants' crops were in part counteracted by making the peasants sow their own grain a little later than that of the proprietor, so that the master's harvest-work was finished, or nearly finished, before their grain was ripe. This combination did not, however, always succeed, and in cases where there was a conflict of interests, the serf was, of course, the losing party. All that remained for him to do in such cases was to work a little in his own fields before six o'clock in the morning and after nine o'clock at night, and in order to render this possible, he economized his strength, and worked as little as possible in his master's fields during the day.

It has frequently been remarked, and with much truth — though the indiscriminate application of the principle has often led to unjustifiable legislative inactivity — that the practical result of institutions depends less on the intrinsic abstract nature of the institutions themselves than on the character of those who work them. So it was with serfage. When a proprietor habitually acted towards his serfs in an enlightened, rational, humane way, they had little reason to complain of their position, and their life was much easier than that of many men who live in a state of complete individual freedom and unlimited, unrestricted competition. When I say that the condition of many free men is worse than was the condition of many Russian serfs, the reader must not imagine that I am thinking of some barbarous tribe among whom freedom means an utter absence of law and an unrestricted right of pillage. On the contrary, I am thinking of a class of men who have the good fortune to live under the beneficent protection of British law, not in some distant, inhospitable colony, but between St. George's Channel and the North Sea. However paradoxical the statement may seem to those who are in the habit of regarding all forms of slavery from the sentimental point of view, it is unquestionable that the condition of serfs under such a proprietor as I have supposed was much more enviable than that of the majority of English agricultural laborers. Each family had a house of its own, with a cabbage-garden, one or more horses, one or two cows, several sheep, poultry, agricultural implements, a share of the Communal land, and everything else necessary for carrying on its small farming operations; and in return for this it had to supply the proprietor with an amount of labor which was by no means oppressive. If, for instance, a serf had three adult sons — and the households, as I have said, were at that time generally numerous — two of them might work for the proprietor, whilst he himself and the remaining son could attend exclusively to the family affairs. From those events which used to be called "the visitations of God" he had no fear of being permanently ruined. If his house was burnt, or his cattle died from the plague, or a series of "bad years" left him without seed for his fields, he could always count upon temporary assistance from his master. He was protected, too, against all oppression and exactions on the part of the officials; for the police, when there was any cause for its interference, applied to the proprietor, who was to a certain extent responsible for his serfs. Thus the serf might live a tranquil, contented life, and die at a ripe old age, without ever having been conscious that serfage was a burden.

If all the serfs had lived in this way we might, perhaps, regret that the Emancipation was ever undertaken. In reality there was, as the French say, *le revers de la médaille,* and serfage generally appeared under a form very different from that which I have just depicted. The proprietors were, unfortunately, not all of the enlightened, humane type. Amongst them were many who demanded from their serfs a most inordinate amount of labor, and treated them in a most inhuman fashion.

These oppressors of their serfs may be divided into four categories. First, there were the proprietors who managed their own estates, and oppressed simply for the purpose of increasing their revenues. Secondly, there were a number of retired officers, who wished to establish a certain order and discipline on their estates, and who employed for this purpose the barbarous measures which were until lately used in the army, believing that merciless corporal punishment was the only means of curing laziness, disorderliness, and other vices. Thirdly, there were the absentees who lived beyond their means, and demanded from their steward, under pain of giving him or his son as a recruit, a much greater yearly sum than the estate could be reasonably expected to yield. Lastly, in the latter years of serfage, there were a number of men who bought estates as a mercantile speculation, and endeavored to make as much money out of them as possible in the shortest possible space of time.

Of all hard masters, the last-named were the most terrible. Utterly indifferent to the welfare of the serfs and the ultimate fate of the property, they cut down the timber, sold the cattle, exacted heavy money dues under threats of giving the serfs or their children as recruits, presented to the military authorities a number of conscripts greater than was required by law — selling the conscription receipts *(zatchétniya kvitántsii)* to the merchants and burghers who were liable to the conscription but did not wish to serve — compelled some of the richer serfs to buy their liberty at an enormous price, and, in a word, used every means, legal and illegal, for extracting money. By this system of management they ruined the estate completely in the course of a few years; but by that time they had realized probably the whole sum paid, with a very fair profit from the operation; and this profit could be considerably augmented by selling a number of peasant families for transportation to another estate *(na svoz),* or by mortgaging the property in the Opekúnski Sovêt—a Government institution which lent money on landed property without examining carefully the nature of the security.

As to the means which the proprietors possessed of oppressing their peasants, we must distinguish between the legal and the actual. The legal were almost as complete as any one could desire. "The proprietor," it is said in the Laws (Vol. IX., 1045, ed. an. 1857), "may impose on his serfs every kind of labor, may take from them money dues (obrok) and demand from them personal service, with this one restriction, that they should not be thereby ruined, and that the number of days fixed by law should be left to them for their own work." Besides this, he had the right to transform peasants into domestic servants, and might, instead of employing them in his own service, hire them out to others who had the rights and privileges of noblesse (1047–48). For all offenses committed against himself or against any one under his jurisdiction he could subject the guilty ones to corporal punishment not exceeding forty lashes with the birch or fifteen blows with the stick (1052); and if he considered any of his serfs as incorrigible he could present them to the authorities to be drafted into the army or transported to Siberia as he might desire (1053–55). In cases of insubordination, where the ordinary domestic means of discipline did not suffice, he could call in the police and the military to support his authority.

Such were the legal means by which the proprietor might oppress his peasants, and it will be readily understood that they were very considerable and very elastic. By law he had the power to impose any dues in labor or money which he might think fit, and in all cases the serfs were ordered to be docile and obedient (1027). Corporal punishment, though restricted by law, he could in reality apply to any extent. Certainly none of the serfs, and very few of the proprietors, were aware that the law placed any restriction on this right. All the proprietors were in the habit of using corporal punishment as they thought proper, and unless a proprietor became notorious for inhuman cruelty, the authorities never thought of interfering. But in the eyes of the peasants corporal punishment was not the worst. What they feared infinitely more than the birch or the stick was the proprietor's power of giving them or their sons as recruits. The law assumed that this extreme means would be employed only against those serfs who showed themselves incorrigibly vicious or insubordinate; but the authorities accepted those presented without making any investigations, and consequently the proprietor might use this power as an effective means of extortion.

Against these means of extortion and oppression the serfs had no legal protection. The law provided them with no means of resisting any injustice to which they might be subjected, or of bringing to punishment the master who oppressed and ruined them. The Government, notwithstanding its sincere desire to protect them from inordinate burdens and cruel treatment, rarely interfered between the master and his serfs, being afraid of thereby undermining the authority of the proprietors, and awakening among the peasantry a spirit of insubordination. The serfs were left, therefore, to their own resources, and had to defend themselves as they best could. The simplest way was open mutiny; but this was rarely employed, for they knew by experience that any attempt of the kind would be at once put down by the military and mercilessly punished. Much more favorite and efficient methods were passive resistance, flight, and fire-raising or murder.

We might naturally suppose that an unscrupulous proprietor, armed with the enormous legal and actual power which I have just described, could very easily extort from his peasants anything he desired. In reality, however, the process of extortion, when it exceeded a certain measure, was a very difficult operation. The Russian peasant has a capacity of patient endurance that would do honor to a martyr, and a power of continued, dogged, passive resistance such as is possessed, I believe, by no other class of men in Europe; and these qualities formed a very powerful barrier against the rapacity of unconscientious proprietors. As soon as the serfs remarked in their master a tendency to rapacity and extortion, they at once took measures to defend themselves. Their first step was to sell secretly all the cattle which they did not actually require, and all the movable property which they possessed, except the few articles necessary for everyday use; and the little capital that they thus realized was carefully hidden somewhere in or near the house. When this had been effected, the proprietor might threaten and punish as he liked, but he rarely succeeded in unearthing the hidden treasure. Many a peasant, under such circumstances, bore patiently the most cruel punishment, and saw his sons taken away as recruits, and yet he persisted in declaring that he had no money to ransom himself and his children. A spectator in such a case would probably have advised him to give up his little store of money, and thereby liberate himself from persecution; but the peasants reasoned otherwise. They were convinced, and not without reason, that the sacrifice of their little capital would merely put off the evil day, and that the persecution would very soon recommence. In this way they would have to suffer as before, and have the additional mortification of feeling that they had spent to no purpose the little that they possessed. Their fatalistic belief in the "perhaps" (*avos'*) came here to their aid. Perhaps the proprietor might become weary of his efforts when he saw that they led to no result, or perhaps something might happen which would remove the persecutor.

It always happened, however, that when a proprietor treated his serfs with extreme injustice and cruelty, some of them lost patience, and sought refuge in flight. As the estates lay perfectly open on all sides, and it was utterly impossible to exercise a strict supervision, nothing was easier than to run away, and the fugitive might be a hundred miles off before his absence was noticed. Why then did not all run away as soon as the master began to oppress them? There were several reasons which made the peasant bear much, rather than adopt this resource. In the first place, he had almost always a wife and family, and he could not possibly take them with him; flight, therefore, was expatriation for life in its most terrible form. Besides this, the life of a fugitive serf was by no means enviable. He was liable at any moment to fall into the hands of the police, and to be put in prison or sent back to his master. So little charm indeed did this life present that not unfrequently after a few months or a few years the fugitive returned of his own accord to his former domicile.

Regarding fugitives or passportless wanderers in general, I may here remark parenthetically that there were two kinds. In the first place, there was the young, able-bodied peasant, who fled from the oppression of his master or from the conscription. Such a fugitive almost always sought out for himself a new domicile—generally in the southern provinces, where there was a great scarcity of laborers, and where many proprietors habitually welcomed all peasants who presented themselves, without making any inquiries as to passports. In the second place, there were those who chose fugitivism as a permanent mode of life. These were, for the most part, men or women of a certain age—widowers or widows—who had no close family ties, and who were too infirm or too lazy to work. The majority of these assumed the character of pilgrims. As such they could always find enough to eat, and could generally collect a few roubles with which to grease the palm of any zealous police-officer who should arrest them. For a life of this kind Russia presented, and still presents, peculiar facilities. There are abundance of monasteries, where all comers may live for three days without any questions being asked, and where those who are willing to do a little work for the patron saint may live for a much longer period. Then there are the towns, where the rich merchants consider almsgiving as very profitable for salvation. And, lastly, there are the villages, where a professing pilgrim is sure to be hospitably received and entertained so long as he refrains from stealing and other acts too grossly inconsistent with his assumed character. For those who contented themselves with simple fare, and did not seek to avoid the usual privations of a wanderer's life, these ordinary means of subsistence were amply sufficient. Those who were more ambitious and more cunning often employed their talents with great success in the world of the Old Ritualists and Sectarians.

The last and most desperate means of defense which the serfs possessed were fire-raising and murder. With regard to the amount of fire-raising there are no trustworthy statistics. With regard to the number of agrarian murders I possessed some interesting statistical data, but have, unfortunately, lost them. I may say, however, that these cases were not very numerous. This is to be explained in part by the patient, long-suffering character of the peasantry, and in part by the fact that the great majority of the proprietors were by no means such inhuman taskmasters as is sometimes supposed. When a case did occur, the Administration always made a strict investigation—punishing the guilty with exemplary severity, and taking no account of the provocation to which they had been subjected. The peasantry, on the contrary—at least, when the act was not the result of mere personal vengeance—secretly sympathized with "the unfortunates," and long cherished their memory as that of men who had suffered for the Mir.

In speaking of the serfs I have hitherto confined my attention to the members of the Mir, or rural Commune—that is to say, the peasants in the narrower sense of the terms; but besides these there were the Dvoróvuié, or domestic servants, and of these I must add a word or two.

The Dvoróvuié were domestic slaves rather than serfs in the proper sense of the word. Let us, however, avoid wounding unnecessarily Russian sensibilities by the use of the ill-sounding word. We may call the class in question "domestics"—remembering, of course, that they were not quite domestic servants in the ordinary sense. They received no wages, were not at liberty to change masters, possessed almost no legal rights, and might be punished, hired out, or sold by their owners without any infraction of the written law.

These "domestics" were very numerous—out of all proportion to the work to be performed—and could consequently lead a very lazy life; but the peasant considered it a great misfortune to be transferred to their ranks, for he thereby lost his share of the Communal land and the little independence which he enjoyed. It very rarely happened, however, that the proprietor took an able-bodied peasant as domestic. The class generally kept up its numbers by the legitimate and illegitimate method of natural increase; and involuntary additions were occasionally made when orphans were left without near relative, and no other family wished to adopt them. To this class belonged the lackeys, servant-girls, cooks, coachmen, stable-boys, gardeners, and a large number of nondescript old men and women who had no very clearly-defined functions. Those of them who were married and had children occupied a position intermediate between the ordinary domestic servant and the peasant. On the one hand they received from the master a monthly allowance of food and a yearly allowance of clothes, and they were obliged to live in the immediate vicinity of the mansion-house, but on the other hand they had each a separate house or apartment, with a little cabbage-garden, and commonly a small plot of flax. The unmarried ones lived in all respects like ordinary domestic servants.

Of the whole number of serfs belonging to the proprietors, the domestics formed, according to the last census, no less than 6¾ per cent. (6.79), and their numbers were evidently rapidly increasing, for in the preceding census they represented only 4.79 per cent. of the whole. This fact seems all the more remarkable when we observe that during this period the number of peasant serfs had diminished from 20,576,229 to 20,158,231.

I must now bring this long chapter to an end, though I feel that I have been able to do little more than sketch roughly in outline the subject which I desired to describe. I have endeavored to represent serfage in its normal, ordinary forms rather than in its occasional monstrous manifestations. Of these latter I have a collection containing ample materials for a whole series of sensational novels, but I refrain from quoting them, because I do not believe that the criminal annals of a country give a fair representation of its real condition. Imagine an author describing family life in England by the chronicles of the Divorce Court! The method would, of course, seem to all men incredibly absurd, and yet it would not be much more unjust than that of an author who should describe serfage in Russia by those cases of reckless oppression and inhuman cruelty which certainly did sometimes occur, but which as certainly were exceptional. Most foreigners are already, I believe, only too disposed to exaggerate the oppression and cruelty to which serfage gave rise, so that in quoting a number of striking examples I should simply be pandering to that taste for the horrible and the sensational which is for the present in need of no stimulus.

It must not, however, be supposed that in refraining from all description of those abuses of authority which the proprietors sometimes practiced I am actuated by any desire to whitewash serfage or attenuate its evil consequences. No great body of men could long wield such enormous uncontrolled power without abusing it, and no great body of men could long live under such power without suffering morally and materially from its pernicious influence. And it must be remembered that this pernicious influence affected not only the serfs, but also the proprietors. If serfage did not create that moral apathy and intellectual lethargy which formed, as it were, the atmosphere of Russian provincial life, it did much at least to preserve it. In short, serfage was the chief barrier to all material and moral progress, and it was, therefore, natural that in a time of moral awakening such as that which I have described in the preceding chapter the question of Serf Emancipation at once came to the front.

PEASANT OPINIONS ON EMANCIPATION. It might be reasonably supposed that the serfs received with boundless gratitude and delight the Manifesto proclaiming these principles. Here at last was the realization of their long-cherished hopes. Liberty was accorded to them, and not only liberty, but a goodly portion of the soil—more than a half of all the arable land possessed by the proprietors.

In reality the Manifesto created among the peasantry a feeling of disappointment rather than delight. To understand this strange fact we must endeavor to place ourselves at the peasant's point of view.

In the first place it must be remarked that all vague, rhetorical phrases about free labor, human dignity, national progress, and the like, which may readily produce among educated men a certain amount of temporary enthusiasm, fall on the ears of the Russian peasant like drops of rain on a granite rock. The fashionable rhetoric of philosophical liberalism is as incomprehensible to him as the flowery circumlocutionary style of an Oriental scribe would be to a keen city merchant. The idea of liberty in the abstract and the mention of rights which lie beyond the sphere of his ordinary everyday life awaken no enthusiasm in his breast. And for mere names he has a profound indifference. What matters it to him that he is officially called, not a "serf," but a "free village inhabitant," if the change in official terminology is not accompanied by some immediate material advantage? What he wants is a house to live in, food to eat, and raiment wherewithal to be clothed, and to gain these first necesaries of life with as little labor as possible. If, therefore, the Government would make a law by which his share of the Communal land would be increased, or his share of the Communal burdens diminished, he would in return willingly consent to be therein designated by the most ugly name that learned ingenuity could devise. Thus the sentimental considerations which had such an important influence on the educated classes had no hold whatever on the mind of the peasants. They looked at the question exclusively from two points of view—that of historical right and that of material advantage—and from both of these the Emancipation Law seemed to offer no satisfactory solution of the question.

On the subject of historical right the peasantry had their own traditional conceptions, which were completely at variance with the written law. According to the positive legislation the Communal land formed part of the estate, and consequently belonged to the proprietor; but according to the conceptions of the peasantry it belonged to the Commune, and the right of the proprietor consisted merely in that personal authority over the serfs which had been conferred on him by the Tsar. The peasants could not, of course, put these conceptions into a strict legal form, but they often expressed them in their own homely laconic way of saying to their master. "Mui vashi no zemlyá nasha"—that is to say, "We are yours, but the land is ours." And it must be admitted that this view, though legally untenable, had a certain historical justification. In old times the nobles had held their land by feudal tenure, and were liable to be ejected as soon as they did not fulfill their obligations to the State. These obligations had been long since abolished, and the feudal tenure transformed into an unconditional right of property, but the peasants clung to the old ideas in a way that strikingly illustrates the vitality of deep-rooted popular conceptions. In their minds the proprietors were merely temporary occupants, who were allowed by the Tsar to exact labor and dues from the serfs. What then was Emancipation? Certainly the abolition of all obligatory labor and money dues, and perhaps the complete ejectment of the proprietors. On this latter point there was a difference of opinon. All assumed, as a matter of course, that the Communal land would remain the property of the Commune, but it was not so clear what would be done with the rest of the estate. Some thought that it would be retained by the proprietor, but very many believed that the nobles would receive salaries from the Tsar, and that *all* the land would be given to the Communes. In this way the Emancipation would be in accordance with historical right and with the material advantage of the peasantry, for whose exclusive benefit, it was assumed, the reform had been undertaken.

Instead of this the peasants found that they were still to pay dues, even for the Communal land which they regarded as unquestionably their own! So at least said the expounders of the law. But the thing was incredible. Either the proprietors must be concealing or misinterpreting the law, or this was merely a preparatory measure, which would be followed by the real Emancipation. Thus were awakened among the peasantry a spirit of mistrust and suspicion and a widespread belief that there would be a second Emancipation, by which all the land would be divided and all the dues abolished.

On the nobles the Manifesto made a very different impression. The fact that they were to be intrusted with the putting of the law into execution, and the flattering allusions made to the spirit of generous self-sacrifice which they had exhibited, kindled amongst them enthusiasm enough to make them forget for a time their just grievances and their hostility towards the bureaucracy. They found that the conditions on which the Emancipation was effected were by no means so ruinous as they had anticipated; and the Emperor's appeal to their generosity and patriotism made many of them throw themselves with ardor into the important task confided to them.

Unfortunately they could not at once begin the work. The law had been so hurried through the last stages that the preparations for putting it into execution were by no means complete when the Manifesto was published. The task of regulating the future relations between the proprietors and the peasantry was intrusted to local proprietors in each dictrict, who were to be called Arbiters of the Peace (*Mirovuié Posrédniki*); but three months elapsed before these Arbiters could be appointed. During that time there was no one to explain the law to the peasants and settle the disputes between them and the proprietors; and the consequence of this was that many cases of insubordination and disorder occurred. The peasants naturally imagined that, as soon as the Tsar said they were free, they were no longer obliged to work for their old masters—that all obligatory labor ceased as soon as the Manifesto was read. In vain the proprietors endeavored to convince them that, in regard to labor, the old relations must continue, as the law enjoined, until a new arrangement had been made. To all explanations and exhortations the peasants turned a deaf ear, and to the efforts of the rural police they too often opposed a dogged, passive resistance. In many cases the simple appearance of the authorities sufficed to restore order, for the presence of one of the Tsar's servants convinced many that the order to work for the present as formerly was not a mere invention of the proprietors. But not unfrequently the birch had to be applied. Indeed, I am inclined to believe, from the numerous descriptions of this time which I have received from eye-witnesses, that rarely, if ever, had the serfs seen and experienced so much flogging as during these first three months after their liberation. Sometimes even the troops had to be called out, and on three occasions they fired on the peasants with ball cartridge. In the most serious case, where a young peasant had set up for a prophet and declared that the Emancipation Law was a forgery, fifty-one peasants were killed and seventy-seven were more or less seriously wounded. But in spite of these lamentable incidents, there was nothing which even the most violent alarmist could dignify with the name of an insurrection. Nowhere was there anything that could be called organized resistance. Even in the case above alluded to, the 3,000 peasants on whom the troops fired were entirely unarmed, made no attempt to resist, and dispersed in the utmost haste as soon as they discovered that they were being shot down. Had the military authorities shown a little more judgment, tact, and patience, the history of the Emancipation would not have been stained even with those three solitary cases of unnecessary bloodshed.

This interregnum between the reigns of serfage and liberty was brought to an end by the appointment of the Arbiters of the Peace. Their first duty was to explain the law, and to organize the new self-government of the peasantry. The lowest instance or primary organ of this self-government, the rural Commune, already existed, and at once recovered much of its ancient vitality as soon as the authority and interference of the proprietors were removed. The second instance, the Vólost—a territorial administrative unit comprising several contiguous Communes—had to be created, for nothing of the kind had previously existed on the estates of the nobles. It had existed, however, for nearly a quarter of a century among the peasants of the Demesnes, and it was therefore necessary merely to copy an already existing model.

As soon as all the Vólosts in his district had been thus organized, the Arbiter had to undertake the much more arduous task of regulating the agrarian relations between the proprietors and the Communes—with the individual peasants, be it remembered, the proprietors had no direct relations whatever. It had been enacted by the law that the future agrarian relations between the two parties should be left, as far as possible, to voluntary contract; and accordingly each proprietor was invited to come to an agreement with the Commune or Communes on his estate. On the ground of this agreement a statute-charter (*ustávnaya grámota*) was prepared, specifying the number of male serfs, the quantity of land actually enjoyed by them, any proposed changes in this amount, the dues proposed to be levied, and other details. If the Arbiter found that the conditions were in accordance with the law and clearly understood by the peasants, he confirmed the charter, and the arrangement was complete. When the two parties could not come to an agreement within a year, he prepared a charter according to his own judgment, and presented it for confirmation to the higher authorities.

The dissolution of partnership, if it be allowed to use such a term, between the proprietor and his serfs was sometimes very easy and sometimes very difficult. On many estates the charter did little more than legalize the existing arrangements, but in many instances it was necessary to add to, or subtract from, the amount of Communal land, and sometimes it was even necessary to remove the village to another part of the estate. In all cases there were, of course, conflicting interests and complicated questions, so that the Arbiter had always abundance of difficult work. Besides this, he had to act as mediator in those differences which naturally arose during the transition period, when the authority of the proprietor had been abolished but the separation of the two classes had not yet been effected. The unlimited patriarchial authority which had been formerly wielded by the proprietor or his steward now passed with certain restrictions into the hands of the Arbiters, and these peacemakers had to spend a great part of their time in driving about from one estate to another to put an end to alleged cases of insubordination—some of which, it must be admitted, existed only in the imagination of the proprietors.

At first the work of amicable settlement proceeded slowly. The proprietors generally showed a spirit of concession, and some of them generously proposed conditions much more favorable to the peasants than the law demanded; but the peasants were filled with vague suspicions, and feared to commit themselves by "putting pen to paper." Even the highly-respected proprietors, who imagined that they possessed the unbounded confidence of the peasantry, were suspected like the others, and their generous offers were regarded as well-baited traps. Often I have heard old men, sometimes with tears in their eyes, describe the distrust and ingratitude of the peasantry at this time. Many peasants believed that the proprietors were hiding the real Emancipation Law, and imaginative or ill-intentioned persons fostered this belief by professing to know what the real law contained. The most absurd rumors were afloat, and whole villages sometimes acted upon them. In the province of Moscow, for instance, one Commune sent a deputation to the proprietor to inform him that, as he had always been a good master, the *Mir* would allow him to retain his house and garden during his lifetime. In another locality it was rumored that the Tsar sat daily on a golden throne in the Crimea, receiving all peasants who came to him, and giving them as much land as they desired; and in order to take advantage of the Imperial liberality a large body of peasants set out for the place indicated, and advanced quickly till they were stopped by the military!

As an illustration of the illusions in which the peasantry indulged at this time, I may introduce here one of the many characteristic incidents related to me by gentlemen who had served as Arbiters of the Peace.

In the province of Riazán there was one Commune which had acquired a certain local notoriety for the obstinacy with which it refused all arrangements with the proprietor. My informant, who was Arbiter for the locality, was at last obliged to make a statute-charter for it without its consent. He wished, however, that the peasants should voluntarily accept the arrangement he proposed, and accordingly called them together to talk with them on the subject. After explaining fully the part of the law which related to their case, he asked them what objection they had to make a fair contract with their old master. For some time he received no answer, but gradually by questioning individuals he discovered the cause of their obstinacy: they were firmly convinced that not only the Communal land, but also the rest of the estate, belonged to them. To eradicate this false idea he set himself to reason with them, and the following characteristic dialogue ensued:—

Arbiter. "If the Tsar gave all the land to the pesantry, what compensation could he give to the proprietors to whom the land belongs?"

Peasant. "The Tsar will give them salaries according to their service."

Arbiter. "In order to pay these salaries he would require a great deal more money. Where could he get that money? He would have to increase the taxes, and in that way you would have to pay all the same."

Peasant. "The Tsar can make as much money as he likes."

Arbiter. "If the Tsar can make as much money as he likes, why does he make you pay the poll-tax every year?"

Peasant. "It is not the Tsar that receives the taxes we ·pay."

Arbiter. "Who then receives them?"

Peasant (after a little hesitation, and with a knowing smile). "The officials, of course!"

Gradually, through the efforts of the Arbiters, the peasants came to know better their real position, and the work began to advance more rapidly. But soon it was checked by another influence. By the end of the first year the "liberal," patriotic enthusiasm of the nobles had cooled. All the sentimental idyllic tendencies had melted away at the first touch of reality, and those who had imagined that liberty would have an immediately salutary effect on the moral character of the serfs confessed thmselves disappointed. Many complained that the peasants showed themselves greedy and obstinate, stole wood from the forest, allowed their cattle to wander on the proprietor's fields, failed to fulfill their legal obligations, and broke their voluntary engagements. At the same time the fears of an agrarian rising subsided, so that even the timid were tranquilized. From these causes the conciliatory spirit of the proprietors decreased.

The work of conciliating and regulating was thus extremely difficult, but the great majority of the Arbiters showed themselves equal to the task, and displayed an impartiality, tact, and patience beyond all praise. To them Russia is in great part indebted for the peaceful character of the Emancipation. Had they sacrificed the general good to the interests of their class, or had they habitually acted in that stern, administrative, military spirit which caused the instances of bloodshed above referred to, the prophecies of the alarmists would, in all probability, have been realized, and the historian of Emancipation would have had a terrible list of judicial massacres to record. Fortunately they played the part of mediators, as their name signified, rather than that of administrators in the bureaucratic sense of the term, and they were animated with a just and humane rather than a merely legal spirit. Instead of simply laying down the law, and ordering their decisions to be immediately executed, they were ever ready to spend hours in trying to conquer, by patient and laborious reasoning, the unjust claims of proprietors or the false conceptions and ignorant obstinacy of the peasants. It was a new spectacle for Russia to see a public function filled by conscientious men who had their heart in their work, who sought neither promotion nor decorations, and who paid less attention to the punctilious observance of prescribed formalities than to the real objects in view.

There were, it is true, a few men to whom this description does not apply. Some of these were unduly under the influence of the feelings and conceptions created by serfage. Some, on the contrary, erred on the other side. Desirous of securing the future welfare of the peasantry and of gaining for themselves a certain kind of popularity, and at the same time animated with a violent spirit of pseudo-liberalism, these latter occasionally forgot that their duty was to be, not generous, but just, and that they had no right to practice generosity at other people's expense. All this I am quite aware of—I could even name one or two Arbiters who were guilty of positive dishonesty—but I hold that these were rare exceptions. The great majority did their duty faithfully and well.

The work of concluding contracts for the redemption of the dues, or, in other words, for the purchase of the land ceded in perpetual usufruct, proceeded slowly, and is, in fact, still going on. The arrangement was as follows: The dues were capitalized at six per cent., and the Government paid at once to the proprietors four-fifths of the whole sum. The peasants were to pay to the proprietor the remaining fifth, either at once or in installments, and to the Government six per cent. for forty-nine years on the sum advanced. The proprietors willingly adopted this arrangement, for it provided them with a sum of ready money, and freed them from the difficult task of collecting the dues. But the peasants did not show much desire to undertake the operation. Some of them expected a second emancipation, and those who did not take this possibility into their calculations were little disposed to make present sacrifices for distant prospective advantages which would not be realized for half a century. In most cases the proprietor was obliged to remit, in whole or in part, the fifth which was to be paid by the peasants. Many Communes refused to undertake the operation on any conditions, and in consequence of this not a few proprietors demanded the so-called obligatory redemption, according to which they accepted the four-fifths from the Government as full payment, and the operation was thus effected without the peasants being consulted. The total number of *male* serfs emancipated was about nine millions and three-quarters, and of these, only about seven millions and a quarter had already, at the beginning of 1875, made redemption contracts. Of the contracts signed at that time, about sixty-three per cent. were "obligatory."

The serfs were thus not only liberated, but also made possessors of land and put on the road to becoming Communal proprietors, and the old Communal institutions were preserved and developed. In answer to the question, Who effected this gigantic reform? we may say that the chief merit undoubtedly belongs to the Emperor. Had he not possessed a very great amount of energy he would neither have raised the question nor allowed it to be raised by others, and had he not shown a decision and energy of which no one suspected him to be capable, the solution would have been indefinitely postponed. Among the members of his own family he found an able and energetic assistant in his brother, the Grand Duke Constantine—a man who would be remarkable in any sphere of life—and a warm sympathizer with the cause in the Grand Duchess Helena, a German Princess, thoroughly devoted to the welfare of her adopted country. But we must not overlook the important part played by the nobles. Their conduct was very characteristic. As soon as the question was raised, a large number of proprietors threw themselves enthusiastically into the work, and as soon as it became evident that emancipation was inevitable, all made a holocaust of their ancient rights, and demanded to be liberated at once from all relations with the serfs. And when the law was passed it was the proprietors who faithfully put it into execution. Lastly, we should remember that considerable merit is due to the peasantry for the patience and long-suffering which they displayed, as soon as they understood the law. Thus it may justly be said that the Emancipation was not the work of one man, or one party, or one class, but of the nation as a whole.

The "Redistribution" Myth

A most curious peasant reaction to the Emancipation is here described by S. M. Kravchinski, a revolutionary terrorist who wrote under the pseudonym of Stepniak. A colleague of the early socialist, Chaikovski, and a member of the Land and Liberty Party, Kravchinski was forced to flee Russia after having committed a political murder. He continued his fight against the tsardom by numerous books and articles which were published in Great Britain and the United States. The source is: Stepniak, The Russian Peasantry. Their Agrarian Condition, Social Life and Religion. *New Edition. London: George Routledge & Sons, 1905. Pp. 626–630.*

To begin with, they declined to believe in the authenticity of the Emancipation Act. To their candid, unsophisticated minds it seemed utterly incredible that their Tzar should have "wronged" them so bitterly as to the land. They obstinately repeated that their "freedom," *i.e.,* the Emancipation Act, had been tampered with by the nobility, who had concealed the Tzar's real "freedom," which had been quite a different thing. The most emphatic declarations made before the peasants' deputies and elders by the Emperor's ministers and by the Emperor in person could not disabuse them. They persisted in believing against belief. There were hundreds of peasants' rebellions in all parts of the empire, owing to this misunderstanding, especially during the first years which followed the Act of Emancipation. They subsided at last. After ten years of incessant persuasion through the medium of speeches, *ukazes,* floggings, and an occasional shooting, this superstition began to give way. It did not disappear, however,—it only changed its shape.

Since 1870 or thereabouts we hear no more of the peasants' doubts as to the authenticity of the agrarian arrangements of 1861. They have ended by admitting that it was really the work of the Tzar's own hands, but the whole of our peasantry have made up their minds, and expect a *new* agrarian arrangement from the Tzar, which will rectify the blunders of the old regulations. Rumours as to the coming agrarian *ravnenie* or "redistribution," which is to take place next spring, next summer, and so forth, now and then spread like wildfire over whole provinces and regions. It is not uncommon for them to give rise to "disorderly" and illegal conduct, such as refusal to pay rent due to the landlords, or the arbitrary appropriation of his fields by the peasants. The authorities of course intervene, and the central Government, which ascribes all things to the Nihilist propaganda, makes strenuous efforts to dissipate these dangerous rumours.

Up to the present time official and Imperial declarations have not opened the peasants' eyes. The *moujiks* see in them either a new trick of the nobles (landlords), or by some strange aberration of intellect understand the plainest statements in an exactly inverse sense to the real one. We know, for instance, cases where peasants' deputies, expressly summoned before a Governor-General to be instructed in the right views on the agrarian question, have on their return to their villages emphatically affirmed that "His Excellency has positively charged them to be reassured, because the Tzar will ere long effect an agrarian 'redistribution.' " They have doubtless been spoken to "about the land," and then probably the General has indulged in some vapouring about the Tzar's solicitude and benevolence. The two things when put together could for them mean nothing but "agrarian redistribution."

In 1878–79, after the enormous strain of the Turkish war, rumours relating to this supposed coming agrarian "redistribution" assumed particular definiteness and enlargement. They penetrated everywhere, and even into the ranks of the army; people openly discussed the coming rearrangements at the village meetings, in the presence of the rural authorities, who, as peasants, fully shared in the common expectations.

General Makov, then Minister of the Interior, issued a circular letter, to be publicly read in all villages, and affixed to the walls in all communal houses. This circular contradicted these rumours, and declared positively that there would be no "redistribution," and that the landlords would retain their own property. It produced no effect. Professor Engelhardt, who wrote one of his Letters from a Village at the time of this fit of popular hopefulness, says that the *moujiks* who heard Makov's circular understood it in the following sense: —"It is requested that people shall, for a time, abstain from gossiping at random about the 'redistribution.'" As to the ministerial warnings against the evil-intentioned disseminators of false reports, and the orders to apprehend them, they produced the most amusing bewilderment. The superior and the inferior agents of the administration could not understand each other's language. The superior officers, the gentlemen, as Engelhardt calls them, by "evil-intentioned people" meant to imply the Nihilists, the advocates and partisans of agrarian "redistribution;" whilst according to the Elders and other village authorities the "evil-intentioned" were those who opposed this movement.

The year 1880, which was almost a year of famine, gave new zest to the popular expectations. "There is no bread in the country," they said, "the *moujiks* are so pressed that they cannot move on their little patches of land, and the landlords have no end of land lying waste." A universal conviction grew up among the peasants that in the course of the next spring (1881) the Tzar's surveyor would come and start upon the work of general readjustment.

Local Government

This description of local government in Russia was written by one of the outstanding Russian scholars of the early twentieth century, Paul Vinogradoff. Deprived of his position as Professor of History in the University of Moscow because of his opposition to tsarist autocracy, Professor Vinogradoff went into voluntary exile in Great Britain where he achieved the distinction of becoming Corpus Professor of Jurisprudence at Oxford. The source is: Vinogradoff, P., Self Government in Russia. London: Constable and Co., Ltd., 1915. Pp. 42–43, 52–56.

Provinces and districts were formed on lines which have more or less endured up to now: the province was assigned a territory with approximately 300–400,000 heads of population, and the district (uyezd) one with 30,000. Governors remained at the heads of provinces and captains (ispravniks) exercised similar functions in a greatly limited manner in the district. Judicial authority was separated from administration and from fiscal affairs. The main point was that in all the tribunals and collegiate institutions assessors elected by the gentry and, in the lower instances, also by merchants or craft guilds and by the free peasantry, were called upon to play a prominent part. The gentry in particular was organised in corporations according to provinces. Its members met once in three years to elect marshals and the assessors of different courts, to audit accounts, to receive reports, to draw up petitions and statements of claims, etc.

.   .   .

In fact, the beginning of local government reform had to be made in connection with the very statute of emancipation, because an administrative machinery had to be set up to replace the authority of the lords abolished by the statute. Certain principles were laid down in this respect in 1861 and developed in detail in 1866. The main point was the organisation of the civil parish (volost) for administrative and judiciary purposes. This unit was not a new one: it had existed all through ancient Russia at a time when the free peasantry had not yet been subjected to secular and ecclesiastical lords. It lingered on in the North and East, where the black, i.e. the free, population had kept its ground. It was resorted to on the domains of the Imperial family and of the State in the reigns of Paul and Nicholas I.

In the 'sixties the civil parish, consisting of several neighbouring villages with a normal area formed by a radius of some 9 miles and a population ranging from some 700 to 5000, was used as the pivot of local administration in rural districts.

1. Its institutions were: (i) an assembly of representatives of the component villages for the principal purpose of electing the officers of the volost; (ii) an executive consisting of a volost elder, assessors and a parish clerk; and (iii) a court with elective judges. These are the three parts of the volost machinery. There was a good deal of election, as you see, and those who framed the arrangement meant it undoubtedly to form the basis of popular self-government. It was, however, vitiated by substantial drawbacks which made themselves felt from the very beginning. The organisation came into being as an institution devised for a particular class and designed to keep up the isolation of the latter from the rest of the people. The civil parish is exclusively composed of members belonging to the peasant order or of persons of other orders who have joined the volost under special conditions: the gentry, the clergy, merchants, members of liberal professions do not participate in its work, although their interests as landowners or occupiers of rural holdings are materially affected by it.

2. As regards the peasant class itself, the unit which displays the greatest vitality is not the volost, but the township or village. Business transactions, questions as to education, etc., are usually settled by the officers and the assembly of the township, especially in districts where the communal system still prevails. Yet the township unit is considered in the light of a private law corporation, and it is the volost which plays the part of the lowest administrative subdivision.

3. While the volost is thus not very active for the promotion of its own interests, it is overburdened with tasks of police and finance imposed on it

by the Government, with the result that it represents everything irksome and onerous in rural practice and that the best men try in every way to avoid it.

4. The judicial activity of the volost court is confused and devoid of authority. The judges are supposed to administer customary law, but in truth they are bewildered by the variety and complexity of relations created by the movement of legislations and of economic practice, and their jurisdiction in civil and petty criminal matters is at best a kind of shifting equity tempered by corruption. The clerk of the parish is too often a crafty promoter of the latter. Lastly, this whole cumbersome system of rural administration is under the meddlesome and by no means disinterested supervision of Government officials and of nominees of the local gentry, who even exercise the power to subject the luckless parish officers to fines and imprisonment. All these features have proved a great handicap in the development of rural self-government.

This short sketch of peasant administration discloses the characteristic and unfortunate dualism of the reform legislation in the 'sixties. It was a compromise between liberal ideals and bureaucratic limitations: sometimes the latter actually succeeded in distorting the progressive intentions of the reformers, in most cases they at least hampered them.

One of the results of the situation was that while the peasants were presented with local self-government of a kind, the gentry and other upper classes of rural districts were left without any. Their affairs and interests were diverted in the direction of *provincial* institutions. A committee for the reorganisation of the counties was created immediately after the completion of the emancipation statute. It was initiated by Nicholas Milutine with a view of endowing Russia with a network of efficient self-governing provinces, but it was intercepted at the start by the reactionaries, smarting from the effects of emancipation and apprehensive of further inroads at the hands of the "revolutionary" Milutine. The great reformer was traduced and ousted in a manner which will be an ever-memorable example of political ingratitude. D. Valuieff, a clever time-server, took his place, and the proceedings were conducted in a spirit of duplicity which deprived the provincial reform of a great deal of its significance. Enough was achieved, however, by the public spirit of the age to make the Zemstvo reform of 1864 a landmark in the history of Russia.

The Zemstva and Their Development

Professor Vinogradoff, writing at a much later date and from quite a different viewpoint, presents a somewhat different description of that the Zemstva than the one given by Wallace. The source is: Vinogradoff, op cit., pp. 57–70.

The "Zemstvo Statute" of January 1, 1864, created two sets of institutions

—assemblies and executive boards. Each district (uyezd) elected representatives for the district assembly, meeting once a year for some ten days, according to a certain system which will be described presently, and an executive board (uprava) transacting business under the direction and the supervision of the assembly and a board acted in the province or government comprising several districts, the members of the assembly in this case being elected at the district meetings. The electoral system in the district, from which all the authorities were derived either directly or indirectly, was characterised by high franchise qualifications and by the splitting up of the electorate into colleges. Of these there were three: the first was composed of landowners possessed of real estate of the value of 15,000 Rb. (about £ 1500 at the rate of exchange before the war), or of owners of factories and other business undertakings of a similar value or of 6000 Rb. yearly turnover. Smaller owners were not disenfranchised, but had to club together and meet previously in order to elect representatives according to the above rates. The second college comprised townspeople with analogous franchise qualifications. The third consisted of representatives of the peasantry by volosts. The economic importance of the gentry in the rural districts assured it of a very great share in the ultimate electoral results: about 43% of the deputies in the early Zemstvos belonged to the gentry class; the peasants sent 38%, while all other professions were represented by about 18%. Another feature designed to secure the predominance of the gentry was the fact that the assemblies were to be presided over by the provincial and district marshals, although the executive boards were granted elective chairmen. It was intended to restrict the Zemstvos to the management of economic interests, while administrative affairs were to be reserved to functionaries appointed by the Government; the class group of the gentry or hereditary *noblesse* retained corporate existence and the right of presenting petitions as to political questions. As a matter of fact it was impossible to draw a definite line between administration and economic functions, as may be gathered even from a simple enumeration of the departments of Zemstvo activity: (1) imposition and collection of provincial and district rates and services in kind; (2) the management of property belonging to the Zemstvos; (3) taking care of a sufficiency of food and other supplies and measures of relief in case of shortage; (4) the construction and keeping in good order of roads, canals, quays and other means of communication; (5) arrangements as to the mutual insurance of local bodies; (6) the rearrangement of hospitals, charity organisations, asylums, relief of the poor and of the sick; (7) measures of public health, of veterinary supervision and treatment; (8) the prevention and suppression of fires; (9) the spread of popular education and participation in the management of schools and other institutions of enlightenment; (10) assistance to industry and commerce, measures for checking the ravages of insects and diseases of plants; (11) the performance of obligations imposed on localities for the benefit of the military and civil administration, e.g. the provision of barracks or the quartering of soldiers.

To mention one example of the inevitable overlapping of attributions—as regards popular education the Zemstvos were invited to open schools, to provide them with equipment, to pay teachers, in fact to maintain the schools in a state of efficiency, and yet the appointment of the teachers and the supervision of the instruction was put in the hands of a school board in which Crown officials and representatives of the *noblesse* and of the clergy were in the majority. However, the saying that he who pays the piper orders the tune' held good in this as in other cases. As the Zemstvos provided the means they acquired the actual management of this important branch of local administration—not without much friction and obstruction. Another point in which the distrust of the Government as regards the newly created bodies found vent was the absence of compulsory power. In all cases when force was required to put by-laws into execution, to collect rates, to seize goods, etc., the Zemstvos could not act by themselves but had to apply for help to the general police, which was often very remiss in assisting the new organisations and in any case regarded their requirements as of secondary importance. Lastly, the acts of the Zemstvos, both as to decrees or by-laws and as to appointments of all kinds, were subjected to constant and suspicious supervision by governors and other agents of the Central Authority; when the trend of general policy pointed towards reaction, as it often did, the Zemstvos were hampered and harassed under the slightest pretexts. This was not a fortunate situation: many strong liberals were driven away from Zemstvo work and did not spare bitter criticism of such incomplete and stunted institutions.

Yet it would be not only wrong, but absurd to disparage the immense work achieved by the Zemstvos in an exceedingly short space of time. The wonder is not that they were hampered and distracted, but that they achieved so much. It is not an exaggeration to say that a new age was initiated by their activity in Russia. Such bodies as, for example, the Moscow provincial Zemstvo, under the leadership of Dmitry Shipoff, would have done honour to any country, and it is not their fault that they were not able to carry out their plans in their entirety. An estimate of the activity of the Zemstvos and of the rate of their progress may be obtained by glancing at the movement of receipts and expenditure in the years 1865–1912. In 1865 the Zemstvo provinces started with a modest income of 5 millions Rb. In 1912 it had reached 220 millions in the original thirty-four Zemstvo provinces and 250 together with the receipts of the western provinces placed under a special régime: in other words, the original figure has been multiplied fifty times. As to expenditure, a considerable share has to be assigned to cover duties imposed by the State, e.g., the construction of barracks or the maintenance of prisons. Productive Zemstvo expenditure develops outside such necessary, imposed payments. Now, in 1871, 43% of the expenditure budget could be devoted to voluntary requirements, while in 1910 80% was allotted to them. The repartition of expenditure under various heads is very characteristic. In 1895 nearly 13½ millions or 20.5% were contributed for the needs of the central government; the service of loans and the formation of reserve capitals swallowed somewhat over 10 millions, or rather more than 15%; the cost of Zemstvo administration amounted to somewhat over 6 millions (9.5%); popular education was represented by 9.3 millions (14%); charitable purposes by 1 million (1.5%); roads about 4 millions (6%); medicine and sanitation 17.8 millions (27%); veterinary department 1 million (1.5%); measures for economic assistance 0.7 (1%); various sundries 1.5 million (3.5%). The same items work out in the following manner in 1912:—

Government requirements	10½ mill.	(5%)
Zemstvo administration	15½ mill.	(7%)
Loans and reserve capitals	27 mill.	(11%)
Roads, etc.	15 mill.	(7%)
Education	66½ mill.	(30%)
Charities and poor relief	3½ mill.	(1.7%)
Medicine and sanitation	57½ mill.	(26%)
Veterinary service	6 mill.	(2.8%)
Economic measures	14 mill.	(6.3%)

In the budget of the six western governments with modified Zemstvo organisation, expenditure on schools and on medical arrangements figured in each case with 7 millions Rb., corresponding to 23% of the whole. We shall have occasion to consider in detail the remarkable progress achieved by the Zemstvos in the field of popular education, and the history of this department may be taken as typical of the aspirations and methods of Russian self-government. A reference to the above tables will show that not less momentous progress was marked by the activity of the Zemstvos in connection with medical help and sanitation. Measures of economic policy have been taken up energetically of late years by the more progressive Zemstvos in other ways: the acquisition of agricultural machinery, the spread of agronomic education, improved methods of cultivation, insurance against fires and bad harvests, etc.

Particularly striking results have been obtained by organising statistical work on an extensive scale. A singular gap is noticeable under the head of poor relief and charities. The explanation of this strange fact is certainly not to be sought in callous indifference for destitution. The charitable disposition and the sensitive pity of the Russians is proverbial. The scanty column of expenditure under this head is explained partly by the lack of a comprehensive poor law and partly by the fact that the burden of supporting the poor falls principally on village communities and on towns, while the Church and private individuals are very lavish of alms—an attitude condemned by political economists but connected with deeply rooted habits of mind. This is in any case a side of Zemstvo activity in which there is evidently most room for improvement.

Taken as a whole, the services rendered to Russia by the Zemstvos have been immense. The new factor of self-government introduced into the life of the country by the reforms of 1864 has brilliantly justified its right to existence and development. And yet its very success has called forth bitter opposition from the forces of the half-defeated old *régime.* It is my painful duty to call attention to the stages of a campaign of persecution which, though it has not achieved its end, has materially curtailed the beneficial effects of the organisation. The honour of carrying on the war against the most promising force of modern Russia appertains to the reaction which set in after the murder of Alexander II, and has been going on with some interruptions until now. It has been engineered and encouraged in the highest spheres of Petersburg bureaucracy, and it is not for lack of official sanction that it has been unable to carry out its main purpose. As the rise of provincial self-government was preceded by tho local reorganisation of the volost, even so the reactionary measures affecting provincial self-government have to be considered in connection with a far-reaching scheme for subjecting the peasantry to the strong government of officials representing the class interests of the gentry, and deriving their power from administrative centralisation. An attempt in this direction was made by the institution of "land-captains" *(Zemskie natchalniki)* under the law of June 12, 1889.

"The new officer was, on the one hand, made the centre of all the administrative affairs of his district—sanitary measures, relief of the poor, relief in cases of agricultural distress, supervision as to all material and moral interests of the population. On the other, he was to be judge in the first instance in minor civil and criminal cases. Thirdly, he was to act more especially as a guardian and controller in all cases which concerned the peasantry. As one of these land-captains pointedly expressed it, they were to act as nurses to the peasantry. The punishing power of these nurses is very extensive. They have the right of sentencing village elders and judges to prison, and are even provided with discretionary power to put a peasant into prison without any form of trial and without any possibility of appeal, simply for supposed disobedience."

" . . . a guarantee seems provided by the right of the inhabitants to appeal from the decision of land-captains to sessions, composed of the same magistrates under the chairmanship of the marshal of the district and with the adjunct of a few trained lawyers. This minority of jurists, exerting some beneficial influence on the lawless practices of the board, are themselves subject to be overruled by the board of the province, in which the legal element is all but absent, and there the procedure stops. The department of this peculiar arbitrary justice is not in direct communication with the Senate, which towers over all other courts of law."

Simultaneously with this measure, designed to revive squirearchy in a new shape, a new statute was enacted for the Zemstvos. The arch-reactionary Minister of the Interior, Count Dmitry Tolstoy, had planned to subordinate the Zemstvos completely to the Crown officials and to turn them into boards for carrying out the orders of centralised bureaucracy. The Count died, however, without having put this delightful scheme into operation. The new statute of 1890 turned out to be only a corrected edition of that of 1864— corrected, to be sure, in a characteristic manner. The gist of the change is disclosed by the altered franchise. Instead of the three colleges of 1864 arranged mainly on property qualifications, the electoral groups were formed frankly on class lines. The first college is composed of members of the gentry (*noblesse*), the second of persons belonging to all other classes except the peasantry and the clergy. A third group is formed by the peasants, who have to elect their representatives not in colleges, but in the volosts, the lists of these representatives being submitted for confirmation to the governor of the province. This is explicit enough, and the character of the change is further emphasised by the proportional distribution of the deputies among the orders; 57% of the seats fall to the gentry, 13% to intermediate classes, about 30% to the peasantry. The clergy do not take part in the representation. This reorganisation undoubtedly poured a good deal of water into the wine of Zemstvo workers. The policy both of the Home Office and of provincial governors kept on a level with the reactionary tendency initiated by the statute of 1890. For instance, after agrarian troubles in the South in 1902, statistical work carried on by the Zemstvos was stopped in twelve provinces because the statisticians were accused of carrying on revolutionary agitation. And yet, strange to say, even these energetic counter-attacks did not succeed in stifling the progressive spirit of the self-governing provinces. The latter could not be prevented from spending money on schools and hospitals, on roads and statistics. In 1900 the magician of the Ministry of Finance, Witte, himself entered the lists against the obnoxious counties. The law of June 12, 1900, enacted that—

"No province is to increase rates by more than three per cent of the previous year."

It has been pointed out that this method of holding expenditure and self-imposition chained to the budget of previous years is entirely lacking in a rational basis. It just falls as a block on schemes of development, and the greatest sufferers are those who for one reason or the other had held back with their imposition and requirements.

Moreover, the late Count Witte presented a secret memoir to the Emperor in which he drew an elaborate comparison between bureaucracy and self-government, and sought to prove that the further progress of the latter would inevitably lead to the downfall of autocratic monarchy. Some of his arguments are so characteristic that I cannot refrain from referring to them at some length.

They amount to this, that self-government, even local or provincial, is in its essence a political arrangement and as such opposed to absolute monarchy. If self-government is to live and to act rationally it has to develop into a constitution. If it cannot be allowed to do so, it has to be replaced by a centralised bureaucracy. After granting that such a bureaucracy leads to arbitrary power and dead formalism, and quoting the contemptuous remarks of Stein as to official writing machines, Count Witte nevertheless assumes that Russian bureaucracy will produce a new political type, unknown to history, that it will in fact turn out to be an aristocracy of work and enlightenment. . . . This government will somehow abstain from arbitrary measures, arrests, exceptional tribunals and other kinds of oppression, it will guarantee freedom of labour, thought and conscience. As for society, it must be left to follow private interests and in them to seek an outlet for its energies. Nothing is more apt to ruin the prestige of authority than a frequent and extensive employment of repression. Measures of repression are dangerous, and when they get to be continuous, they either lead to an explosion or else turn the people into a casual throng, into human dust.

As you see, the most prominent among Russian bureaucrats, Witte, boldly challenged self-government on behalf of an all-powerful bureaucracy. The trial by battle might have been decided in favour of the latter if the opponents had been left to fight out their duel in a "stricken field." But the contest was not waged on these lines: it assumed the shape of a competition for the production of masterpieces. In other words, self-government was able to produce some very creditable results in spite of difficulties. Bureaucracy had also to show what it could do for the people. And its achievements were far from brilliant at the very time when it was especially overbearing and oppressive.

Exile by Administrative Process

The general tone of the following indictment of the Russian police state is such that except for the very much smaller numbers of persons involved, one might imagine that it was a current report. George Kennan, who wrote the material, first visited Russia in connection with the abortive scheme of connecting America with Europe by telegraph via Siberia. Later Mr. Kennan lived for some time in Russia and traveled very extensively throughout the Empire. Siberia and the exile system greatly interested him and in 1885 he went to Russia as a special correspondent of The Century Magazine *to make a study of these things. His published report created a sensation in the West and even forced the Russian government to reform some of the worst abuses of the system. The system itself, however, continued in operation. The source is: Kennan, G., Siberia and the Exile System. Two volumes. New York: The Century Co., 1891. Vol. 1, pp. 242 ff. passim. (Much abridged.)*

Exile by administrative process means the banishment of an obnoxious person from one part of the empire to another without the observance of any of the legal formalities that, in most civilized countries, precede the deprivation of rights and the restriction of personal liberty. The obnoxious person may not be guilty of any crime, and may not have rendered himself amenable in any way to the laws of the state, but if, in the opinion of the local authorities, his presence in a particular place is "prejudicial to public order," or "incompatible with public tranquillity," he may be arrested without a warrant, may be held from two weeks to two years in prison, and may then be removed by force to any other place within the limits of the empire and there be put under police surveillance for a period of from one year to ten years. He may or may not be informed of the reasons for this summary proceeding, but in either case he is perfectly helpless. He cannot examine the witnesses upon whose testimony his presence is declared to be "prejudicial to public order." He cannot summon friends to prove his loyalty and good character, without great risk of bringing upon them the same calamity that has befallen him. He has no right to demand a trial, or even a hearing. He cannot sue out a writ of habeas corpus. He cannot appeal to his fellow-citizens through the press. His communications with the world are so suddenly severed that sometimes even his own relatives do not know what has happened to him. He is literally and absolutely without any means whatever of self-defense. To show the nature of the evidence upon which certain classes of Russians are banished to Siberia, and to illustrate the working of the system generally, I will give a few cases of administrative exile from the large number recorded in my note-books.

. . . .

In the year 1880 the well-known and gifted Russian novelist Vladimir Korolenko, two of whose books have recently been translated into English, was exiled to Eastern Siberia as a result of what the Government itself finally admitted to be an official mistake. Through the influence of Prince Imeretinski, Mr. Korolenko succeeded in getting this mistake corrected before he reached his ultimate destination and was released in the West Siberian city of Tomsk. Hardly had he returned, however, to European Russia, when he was called upon to take the oath of allegiance to Alexander III, and to swear that he would betray every one of his friends or acquaintances whom he knew to be engaged in revolutionary or anti-Government work. No honorable and self-respecting man could take such an oath as that, and of course Mr. Korolenko declined to do so. He was thereupon exiled by administrative process to the East Siberian territory of Yakutsk, where, in a wretched native *ulus,* he lived for about three years.

. . .

Mr. Borodin, another Russian author, was banished to the territory of Yakutsk on account of the alleged "dangerous" and "pernicious" character of a certain manuscript found in his house by the police during a search. This manuscript was the spare copy of an article upon the economic condition of the province of Viatka, which Mr. Borodin had written but which had not been published. The author went to Eastern Siberia in a convict's grey overcoat with a yellow ace of diamonds on his back, and three or four months after his arrival in Yakutsk he had the pleasure of reading in a magazine the very same article for which he had been exiled. The Minister of the Interior had sent him to Siberia merely for having in his possession what the police called a "dangerous" and "pernicious" manuscript, and then the St. Petersburg committee of censorship had certified that another copy of the same manuscript was perfectly harmless, and had allowed it to be published, without the change of a line, in one of the most popular and widely circulated magazines of the empire.

A gentleman named Achkin, in Moscow, was exiled to Siberia by administrative process in 1885 merely because, to adopt the language of the order that was issued for his arrest, he was "suspected of the intention to put himself into an illegal situation." The high crime which Mr. Achkin was "suspected of an intention" to commit was the taking of a fictitious name in the place of his own. Upon what ground he was "suspected of an intention" to do this terrible thing he never knew.

Another exile of my acquaintance, Mr. Y, was banished merely because he was a friend of Mr. Z., who was awaiting trial on the charge of political conspiracy. When Mr. Z's case came to a judicial investigation he was found to be innocent and was acquitted; but in the meantime Mr. Y., merely for being a friend of this innocent man, had gone to Siberia by administrative process. . . .

Exile by administrative process is not a new thing in Russia, nor was it first resorted to by the Russian Government as an extraordinary or exceptional measure of self-defense in the struggle with the revolutionists. It is older than nihilism, it is older than the modern revolutionary movement, it is older than the imperial house of Romanof. It has been practiced for centuries as a short and easy method of dealing with people who happen to be obnoxious or in the way, but who cannot conveniently be tried or convicted in a court of justice. Administrative exile has been not only a recognized but a well established method of dealing with certain classes of offenders ever since the seventeenth century. In the reign of the Emperor Nicholas, for example, nihilism had not been so much as heard of — the very word was unknown — and yet men and women were being exiled to Siberia by administrative process, not in hundreds merely, but in thousands, and not only by the order of the Tsar, but by order of the administrative authorities, by order of the ecclesiastical authorities, by order of the village communes, and even by the order of private landowners. Most of them, it is true, were not political offenders; but they were nonetheless entitled to a trial, and they were all victims of the system. . . .

Between 1827 and 1846 there was not a year in which the number of persons sent to Siberia by administrative process fell below three thousand, and it reached a maximum, for a single year, of more than six thousand. The aggregate number for the twenty year period is 79,909. . . .

In the latter part of the reign of Alexander II, and particularly between the years 1870 and 1880, administrative exile was resorted to, in political cases, upon a scale never before known, and with a recklessness and cynical indifference to personal rights that were almost unparalleled. In Odessa, General Todleben, by virtue of the unlimited discretionary power given him in the Imperial ukaz of April 17, 1879, proceeded to banish, without inquiry or discrimination, the whole "politically untrustworthy" class — that is, to exile every person whose loyalty to the existing Government was even doubtful. The mere fact that a man had been registered as a suspect in the books of the secret police, or had been accused, even anonymously, of polical disaffection, was a sufficient reason for his deportation to the remotest part of the empire. Parents who had never had a disloyal thought were exiled because their children had become revolutionists; school-boys who happened to be acquainted with political offenders were exiled because they had betrayed the latter to the police; members of the provincial assemblies were exiled because they insisted upon their right to petition the crown for the redress of grievances; and university students who had been tried for political crime and duly acquitted by the courts were immediately rearrested and exiled by administrative process. . . .

The grotesque injustice, the heedless cruelty, and the preposterous "mistakes" and "misunderstandings" that make the history of administrative exile in Russia seem to an American like the recital of a wild nightmare are due to the complete absence, in the Russian form of government, of checks upon the executive power, and the almost equally complete absence of official responsibility for unjust or illegal action. The Minister of the Interior, in dealing with politicals, is almost wholly unrestrained by law; and as it is utterly impossible for him personally to examine all of the immense number of political cases that come to him for final decision, he is virtually forced to delegate a part of his irresponsible power to chiefs of police, chiefs of gendarmes, governors of provinces, and subordinates in his own administration. They in turn are compelled, for similar reasons, to intrust a part of their authority and discretion to officers of still lower grade; and the latter, who often are stupid, ignorant, or unscrupulous men, are the persons who really make the investigations, the searches, and the examinations upon which the life or liberty of an accused citizen may depend. Theoretically the Minister of the Interior, aided by a council composed of three of his own subordinates and two officers from the Ministry of Justice, reviews and re-examines the cases of all political offenders who are dealt with by administrative process; but practically he does nothing of the kind, and it is impossible that he should do anything of the kind for the very simple reason that he has not the time.

The Character of Political Exiles

There was a quite general impression that all Russian revolutionaries were dangerous desperadoes of the toughest sort. Some of them were dangerous and fanatically ruthless, but most of them did not resemble the stereotype of the bomb-throwing radical. Mr. Kennan's account of them was based upon interviews with many of them as well as upon his study of the general problem. The source is: Kennan, op. cit., vol. 2, pp. 436–440, 448–456. (Slightly abridged.)

For the purposes of this chapter I shall divide Russian political exiles into three classes as follows.

1. THE LIBERALS. In this class are included the cool-headed men of moderate opinions, who believe in the gradual extension of the principles of popular self-government; who favor greater freedom of speech and of the press; who strive to restrict the power of bureaucracy; who deprecate the persecution of religious dissenters and of the Jews; who promote in every possible way the education and the moral up-lifting of the peasants; who struggle constantly gainst official indifference and caprice; who insist pertinaciously upon "due process of law"; who are prominent in all good works; but who regard a complete overthrow of the existing form of government as impracticable at present even if desirable.

2. THE REVOLUTIONISTS. In this class are comprised the Russian socialists, the so-called "peasantists" *(naródniki)*, "people's-willists" *(narodovóltsi)*, and all reformers who regard the overthrow of the autocracy as a matter of such immediate and vital importance as to justify conspiracy and armed rebellion. They differ from the terrorists chiefly in their unwillingness to adopt the methods of the highwayman and the blood-avenger. If they can see a

prospect of organizing a formidable insurrection, and of crushing the autocracy by a series of open blows, fairly delivered, they are ready to attempt it, even at the peril of death on the scaffold; but they do not regard it as wise or honorable to shoot a chief of police from ambush; to wreck an Imperial railroad train; to rob a Government sub-treasury; or to incite peasants to revolt by means of a forged manifesto in the name of the Tsar. The objects which they seek to attain are the same that the liberals have in view, but they would attain them by quicker and more direct methods, and they would carry the work of reform to greater extremes. The socialistic revolutionists for example, would attempt to bring about a redistribution of the land and a more equitable division of the results of labor, and would probably encourage a further development of the principle of association, as distinguished from competition, which is so marked a feature of Russian economic life.

3. THE TERRORISTS. The only difference between the terrorists and the revolutionists is a difference in methods. So far as principles and aims are concerned the two classes are identical; but the revolutionists recognize and obey the rules of civilized warfare, while the terrorists resort to any and every measure that they think likely to injure or intimidate their adversaries. A terrorist, in fact, is nothing more than an embittered revolutionist, who has found it impossible to unite and organize the disaffected elements of society in the face of a cloud of spies, an immense body of police, and a standing army; who has been exasperated to the last degree by cruel, unjust, and lawless treatment of himself, his family, or his friends; who has been smitten in the face every time he has opened his lips to explain or expostulate, and who, at last, has been seized with the Berserker madness, and has become, in the words of the St. Petersburg *Gólos*, "a wild beast capable of anything."

In point of numerical strength these three classes follow one another in the order in which I have placed them. The liberals, who are the most numerous, probably comprise three-fourths of all the university graduates in the Empire outside of the bureaucracy. The revolutionists, who come next, undoubtedly number tens of thousands, but, under existing circumstances, it is impossible to make a trustworthy estimate of their strength, and all that I feel safe in saying is that, numerically, they fall far short of the liberals. The terrorists never were more than a meager handful in comparison with the population of the country, and they constituted only a fraction even of the anti-Government party; but they were resolute and daring men and women, and they attracted more attention abroad, of course, than a thousand times as many liberals, simply on account of the tragic nature of the roles that they played on the stage of Russian public life. The liberals, who were limited by the censorship and the police on one side, and by their own renunciation of violence on the other, could do very little to attract the attention of foreign observers;

but the terrorists, who defied all restrictions, who carried their lives constantly in their hands, and who waged war with dagger, pistol, and pyroxylin bomb, acquired a notoriety that was out of all proportion to their numerical strength.

I met among the political exiles in Siberia representatives of all the classes above described, and I have tried, in the earlier chapters of this work, to convey to the reader the impressions that they made upon me in personal intercourse. I desire now to state, as briefly as I can, my conclusions with regard to their character.

1. THE LIBERALS. So far as I know, it is not pretended by anybody that the Russian liberals are bad men or bad citizens. The Government, it is true, keeps them under strict restraint, prohibits them from making public speeches, drives them out of the universities, forbids them to sit as delegates in provincial assemblies, expels them from St. Petersburg, suppresses the periodicals that they edit, puts them under police surveillance and sends them to Siberia; but, notwithstanding all this, it does not accuse them of criminality, nor even of criminal intent. It merely asserts that they are "politically untrustworthy"; that the "tendency" of their social activity is "pernicious"; or that, from an official point of view, their presence in a particular place is "prejudicial to public tranquillity." These vague assertions mean, simply, that the liberals are in the way of the officials, and prevent the latter, to some extent, from doing what they want to do with the bodies, the souls, or the property of the Russian people. . . .

It seems to me foolish and impolitic for Russian Government officials to try to make it appear that the revolutionists, as a class, are despicable in point of intellectual ability, or morally depraved. They are neither the one nor the other. So far as education is concerned they are far superior to any equal number of Russian officials with whom, in the course of five years' residence in the Russian Empire, I have been brought in contact. In the face of difficulties and discouragements that would crush most men — in financial distress, in terrible anxiety, in prison, in exile, and in the straitjacket of the press censorship — they not only "keep their grip," but they fairly distinguish themselves in literature, in science, and in every field of activity that is open to them. Much of the best scientific work that has been done in Siberia has been done by political exiles. Mikhaiélis in Semipalátinsk was an accomplished naturalist; Andréief in Minusínsk was a skilled botanist and made an exhaustive study of the flora of central Siberia and the Altái; Kléments in Minusínsk was a geologist and an archæologist of whom his country ought to have been proud; Alexander Kropótkin, who committed suicide in Tomsk, was an astronomer and meteorologist who made and recorded scientific observations for the Russian Meteorological Bureau almost up to the time of his death; Belokónski, in Minusinsk, continued these observations, and was a frequent contributor, moreover, to the best Russian magazines and reviews; Chudnófski, in Tomsk, was engaged for many years in active work for the West-Siberian section of the Imperial Russian Geographical Society, and is the author of a dozen or more books and monographs; Leóntief and Dr. Dolgopólof, in Semipalátinsk, made valuable anthropological researches among the Kírghis, and the work of the former has recently been published by the Semipalátinsk Statistical Committee under the title "Materials for the Study of the Legal Customs of the Kírghis"; Lesévich, who was in exile in Yeniséisk, is one of the best-known writers in Russia upon philosophy, morals, and the history and influence of Buddhism; Hoúrwitch, who was in exile in Tiukalínsk, but who is now in New York City, is the author of a monograph on "Emigration to Siberia" which was published in the "Proceedings of the Imperial Geographical Society," and is also the author of the excellent article upon the treatment of the Jews in Russia which was published in the *Forum* for August, 1891; and, finally, the novels, stories, and sketches of the political exiles Korolénko, Máchtet, Staniukóvich, Mámin (Sibiriák), and Petropávlovski are known to every cultivated Russian from the White Sea to the Caspian and from Poland to the Pacific.

Morally, the Russian revolutionists whom I met in Siberia would compare favorably with any body of men and women of equal numerical strength that I could collect from the circle of my own acquaintances. I do not share the opinions of all of them; some of them seem to me to entertain visionary and over-sanguine hopes and plans for the future of their country; some of them have made terrible and fatal mistakes of judgment; and some of them have proved weak or unworthy in the hour of trial; but it is my deliberate conviction, nevertheless, that, tested by any moral standard of which I have knowledge, such political exiles as Volkhófski, Chudnófski, Blok, Leontief, Lobonófski, Kropotkin, Kohan-Bérnstein, Belokónski, Prisédski, Lázaref, Charúshin, Kléments, Shishkó, Nathalie Armfeldt, Heléne Máchtet, Sophie Bárdina, Anna Pávlovna Korbá, and many others whom I have not space to name, represent the flower of Russian young manhood and young womanhood. General Strélnikof may call them "fanatics" and "robbers," and Mr. Gálkine Wrásskoy may describe them as "wretched men and women . . . whose social depravity is so great that it would shock the English people if translated into proper English equivalents," but among these men and women, nevertheless, are some of the best, bravest, and most generous types of manhood and womanhood that I have ever known. I am linked to them only by the ties of sympathy, humanity, or friendship; but I wish that I were bound to them by the tie of kindred blood. I should be proud of them if they were my brothers and sisters, and so long as any of them live they may count upon me for any service that a brother can render.

The last of the three classes into which I have divided the anti-Government party in Russia comprises the terrorists. A recent writer in the Russian historical magazine *Rússkaya Stariná,* in a very instructive paragraph, describes them, and the attitude of the Russian people towards them, as follows:

We have been present at a strange spectacle. Before our eyes there has taken place something like a duel between the mightiest Power on earth armed with all the attributes of authority on one side, and an insignificant gang of discharged telegraph operators, half-educated seminarists, high-school boys and university students, miserable little Jews and loose women on the other; and in this apparently unequal contest success was far from being on the side of strength. Meanwhile the immense mass of the people who without doubt spontaneously loved the serene *(svétloi)* personality of the Tsar, and were sincerely devoted to law and order, and to the embodiment of law and order in the form of monarchical institutions, stood aside and watched this duel in the capacity of uninterested, if not indifferent, observers. We have called this a "strange spectacle," but it ought, with more justice, to be characterized as a shameful spectacle. It was only necessary for the great mass of the Russian people to move — to "shake its shoulders," as the saying is — and the ulcer that had appeared on the body of the social organism would have vanished as completely as if it never had existed. Why this saving movement was not made we shall not attempt to ascertain, since the inquiry would carry us too far from the modest task that we have set for ourselves. We merely state the fact, without explanation, and, in the interest of historical truth, refer, in passing, to one extremely distressing phase of it. The repetition, one after another, of terrible crimes, each of which deeply shocked the social organism, inevitably led, by virtue of the natural law of reaction, to exhaustion. There was danger, therefore, that a continuance of persistent activity in this direction would fatally weaken the organism and extinguish all of its self-preservative energies. . . . Ominous forewarnings of such symptoms had begun already to make their appearance. . . .

According to the statements of this writer the terrorists of 1879-81 were nothing but "an insignificant gang of discharged telegraph-operators, half-educated school-boys, miserable little Jews, and loose women"; but this heterogeneous organization, notwithstanding its insignificance, almost succeeded in overthrowing "the mightiest power on earth, armed with all the attributes of authority." To a simple-minded reader there seems to be an extraordinary disproportion here between cause and effect. So far as I know there is not another instance in history where a gang of telegraph-operators, school-boys, Jews, and loose women have been able to paralyze the energies of a great empire, and almost to overthrow long-established "monarchical institutions" to which a hundred millions of people were "sincerely devoted." If the statements of Count Lóris-Mélikof's biographer are to be accepted as true, Russian telegraph-operators, Russian school-boys, Russian Jews, and Russian loose women must be regarded as new and extraordinary types of the well-known classes to which they nominally belong. There are no telegraph-operators and loose women, I believe, outside of Russia, who are capable of engaging in a "duel" with the "mightiest power on earth" and of "extinguishing all the self-preservative energies" of so tough an "organism" as the Russian bureaucracy. It would be interesting to know how this combative — not to say heroic — strain of telegraphers, school-boys and loose women was produced, and why they should have directed their tremendous energies against the "serene personality" that was so universally and so "spontaneously" beloved, and against the "monarchical institutions" to which all Russians, except telegraphers, school-boys, Jews, and loose women, were so "sincerely devoted." But it is unnecessary to press the inquiry. Every thoughtful student of human affairs must see the absurdity of the supposition that a few telegraph-operators, school-boys, Jews, and loose women could seriously imperil the existence of a Government like that of Russia.

As a matter of fact the Russian terrorists were men and women of extraordinary ability, courage, and fortitude; of essentially noble nature; and of limitless capacity for heroic self-sacrifice.

Most of the Russian terrorists were nothing more, at first, than moderate liberals, or, at worst, peaceful socialistic propagandists; and they were gradually transformed into revolutionists, and then into terrorists, by injustice, cruelty, illegality, and contemptuous disregard, by the Government, of all their rights and feelings. I have not a word to say in defense of their crimes. I do not believe in such methods of warfare as assassination, the wrecking of railway trains on which one's enemies are riding, the robbing of Government sub-treasuries, and the blowing up of palaces; but I can fully understand, nevertheless, how an essentially good and noble-natured man may become a terrorist when, as in Russia, he is subjected to absolutely intolerable outrages and indignities and has no peaceful or legal means of redress. It is true, as the Russian Government contends, that after 1878 the terrorists acted in defiance of all the generally accepted principles of civilized combat; but it must not be forgotten that in life and in warfare, as in chess, you cannot disregard all the rules of the game yourself and then expect your adversary to observe them. The Government first set the example of lawlessness in Russia by arresting without warrant; by punishing without trial; by cynically disregarding the judgments of its own courts when such judgments were in favor of politicals; by confiscating the money and property of private citizens whom it merely suspected of sympathy with the revolutionary movement; by sending fourteen-year-old boys and girls to Siberia; by kidnapping the children of "politically untrustworthy" people and exiles and putting them into state asylums; by driving men and women to insanity and suicide in rigorous solitary confinement without giving them a trial; by burying secretly at night the bodies of the people whom it had thus done to death in its dungeons; and by treating as a criminal, *in posse* if not *in esse*, every citizen who dared to ask why or wherefore. A man is not necessarily a ferocious, blood-thirsty fanatic, if, under such provocation, and in the absence of all means of redress, he strikes back with the weapons that lie nearest his hand. It is not my purpose to justify the policy of the terrorists, nor to approve, even by implication, the resort to murder as a means of tempering despotism; but it is my purpose to explain, so far as I can, certain morbid social phenomena; and in making such explanation circumstances seem to lay upon me the duty of saying to the world for the Russian revolutionists and terrorists all that they might fairly say for themselves if the lips of the dead had not already moldered into dust, and if the voices of the living were not lost in the distance or stifled by prison walls. The Russian Government has its own press and its own representatives abroad; it can explain, if it chooses, its methods and measures. The Russian revolutionists, buried alive in remote Siberian solitudes, can only tell their story to an occasional traveler from a freer country, and ask him to lay it before the world for judgment.

Press Censorship

Mr. Kennan's record of censorship, from which these excerpts were taken, fills ten pages of his book. These are random samples. The source is: Kennan, op. cit., vol. 2, pp. 484, 485, 491.

Below will be found a list of cases in which Russian periodicals have been punished, or wholly suppressed, for giving voice to ideas and sentiments regarded as objectionable by the ruling class. I have made this list from my own reading of Russian newspapers and magazines, and I am well aware that it probably does not comprise more than a fractional part — perhaps not more than one-tenth — of all the "warnings," "suspensions," and "suppressions" that have been dealt out to the Russian press in the course of the last decade.

1881. July 7.　　The *Odéssa Listók* is suspended for four months.

1882. Jan. 17.　　The *Moscow Telegraph* receives a first warning.

　　　Jan. 19.　　The St. Petersburg *Gólos* reappears, after a suspension of six months.

　　　Jan. 22.　　The newspaper *Poriádok* is suspended for six weeks.

　　　Jan. 31.　　The *Moscow Telegraph* receives a second warning.

　　　Feb. 11.　　The St. Petersburg *Gólos* receives a first warning, with the prohibition of its street sales.

　　　March 26.　The *Moscow Telegraph* is suspended for four months.

　　　April 8.　　Application for permission to publish a new newspaper in St. Petersburg is denied.

April 15. The *Poriádok* gives up the struggle with the censorship and goes into liquidation.

April 15. The April number of the magazine *Russian Thought* is seized and suppressed.

May 27. Application for permission to publish a new newspaper in Ekaterínburg is denied.

June 17. The *Riga Véstnik* publishes the following in lieu of a leading editorial: "In to-day's issue it was our intention to have had a leading editorial, urging the Esthonians to unite more closely among themselves, and with the Russians, and to work with manly energy for the Fatherland; but we have not been allowed to print it."

July 1. The humorous illustrated newspaper *Guslá* is seized by order of the censor, and its 24th number is suppressed, for making fun of an irrigation scheme in which the censor is interested.

July 1. Application for permission to publish a new newspaper, to be called the *Donskói Pchéla,* on the Don is denied.

July 15. The *Zémstvo,* the organ of the provincial assemblies, gives up the struggle with the censorship and goes into liquidation, after an existence of a year and a half.

Aug. 19. The *Vostók* receives a first warning for criticism of the higher clergy.

1886. Feb. 19. The Moscow *Rússkia Védomosti,* having been forbidden to refer editorially to the emancipation of the serfs on the twenty-fifth anniversary of that event, does not appear on that day at all, and thus commemorates it by voluntary silence.

April 3. An application for leave to publish a newspaper in the East-Siberian town of Nérchinsk is denied.

April 3. Street sales of the Moscow *Rússkia Védomosti* are forbidden.

April 10. Street sales of the *Sovrémmenia Izvéstia* are forbidden.

April 24. A correspondent of the Irkútsk newspaper *Sibír* is arrested by order of a Siberian *isprávnik,* kept two days in prison without food, flogged, put into leg-fetters, and sent back to his place of residence by étape in a temperature of thirty-five degrees below zero (Réaum.). He is not charged with any other crime than furnishing his paper with news.

May 6. The editor of the St. Petersburg *Police Gazctte,* a purely official Government organ, is arrested and imprisoned because, in an article in his paper referring to a "requiem for Alexander II.," there was a typographical error which made it read "a requiem for Alexander III."

A Revolutionary Manifesto

The use of terrorism as a regular weapon of the revolutionaries dates from 1878, when Vera Zasulich sought to murder Trepov, Chief of Police in St. Petersburg. During the following summer the revolutionaries split into a right wing which sought to continue the old "V Narod" program and a left wing which took the name "Narodnaya Volya" (The People's Will). The latter was avowedly terroristic. Its formal program was set forth in the manifesto printed below. The source is: Kennan, op. cit., vol. 2, pp. 495–499. (Slightly adapted.)

By fundamental conviction we are socialists and men of the people. We are sure that only through socialistic principles can the human race acquire liberty, equality, and fraternity; secure the full and harmonious development of the individual as well as the material prosperity of all; and thus make progress. We are convinced that all social forms must rest upon the sanction of the people themselves, and that popular development is permanent only when it proceeds freely and independently, and when every idea that is to be embodied in the people's life has first passed through the people's consciousness and has been acted upon by the people's will. The welfare of the people and the will of the people are our two most sacred and most inseparable principles.

A

1. If we look at the environment in which the Russian people are forced to live and act, we see that they are, economically and politically, in a state of absolute slavery. As laborers they work only to feed and support the parasitic classes; and as citizens they are deprived of all rights. Not only does the actual state of things fail to answer to their will, but they dare not even express and formulate their will; they cannot even think what is good and what is bad for them; the very thought that they can have a will is regarded as a crime against the State. Enmeshed on all sides, they are being reduced to a state of physical degeneration, intellectual stolidity, and general inferiority.

2. Around the enchained people we see a class of exploiters whom the state creates and protects. The state itself is the greatest capitalistic power in the land, it constitutes the sole oppressor of the people, and only through its aid and support can the lesser robbers exist. This bourgeois excrescence in the form of a government sustains itself by mere brute force — by means of its

military, police, and bureaucratic organization — in precisely the same way that the Mongols of Genghis Khan sustained themselves in Russia. It is not sanctioned by the people, it rules by arbitrary violence, and it adopts and enforces governmental and economical forms and principles that have nothing whatever in common with the people's wishes and ideals.

3. In the nation we can see, crushed but still living, its old traditional principles, such as the right of the people to the land, communal and local self-government, freedom of speech and of conscience, and the rudiments of federal organization. These principles would develop broadly, and would give an entirely different and a more popular direction to our whole history, if the nation could live and organize itself in accordance with its own wishes and its own tendencies.

B

1. We are of opinion, therefore, that it is our first duty, as socialists and men of the people, to free the people from the oppression of the present Government, and bring about a political revolution, in order to transfer the supreme power to the nation. By means of this revolution we shall afford the people an opportunity to develop, henceforth, independently, and shall cause to be recognized and supported, in Russian life, many purely socialistic principles that are common to us and to the Russian people.

2. We think that the will of the people would be sufficiently well expressed and executed by a national Organizing Assembly, elected freely by a general vote, and acting under the instructions of the voters. This, of course, would fall far short of an ideal manifestation of the people's will; but is the only one that is practicable at present, and we therefore think best to adopt it. Our plan is to take away the power from the existing Government, and give it to an Organizing Assembly, elected in the manner above described, whose duty it will be to make an examination of all our social and governmental institutions, and remodel them in accordance with instructions from the electors.

C

Although we are ready to submit wholly to the popular will, we regard it as none the less our duty, as a party, to appear before the people with our program. This program we shall use as a means of propaganda until the revolution comes, we shall advocate it during the election campaign, and we shall support it before the Organizing Assembly. It is as follows:

1. Perpetual popular representation, constituted as above described and having full power to act in all national questions.

2. General local self-government, secured by the election of all officers, and the economic independence of the people.

3. The self-controlled village commune as the economic and administrative unit.

4. Ownership of the land by the people.

5. A system of measures having for their object the turning over to the laborers of all mining works and factories.

6. Complete freedom of conscience, speech, association, public meeting, and electioneering activity.

7. Universal right of franchise, without any class or property limitation.

8. The substitution of a territorial militia for the army.

We shall follow this program, and we believe that all of its parts are so interdependent as to be impracticable one without the other, and that only as a whole will the program insure political and economic freedom and the harmonious development of the people.

D

In view of the stated aim of the party its operations may be classified as follows:

1. *Propaganda and agitation.* Our propaganda has for its object the popularization, in all social classes, of the idea of a political and popular revolution as a means of social reform, as well as popularization of the party's own program. Its essential features are criticism of the existing order of things, and a statement and explanation of revolutionary methods. The aim of agitation should be to incite the people to protest, as generally as possible against the the present state of affairs, to demand such reforms as are in harmony with the party's purposes, and, especially, to demand the summoning of an Organizing Assembly. The popular protest may take the form of meetings, demonstrations, petitions, leading addresses, refusals to pay taxes, etc.

2. *Destructive and terroristic activity.* Terroristic activity consists in the destruction of the most harmful persons in the Government, the protection of the party from spies, and the punishment of official lawlessless and violence in all the more prominent and important cases in which such lawlessness and violence are manifested. The aim of such activity is to break down the prestige of Governmental power, to furnish continuous proof of the possibility of carrying on a contest with the Government, to raise in that way the revolutionary spirit of the people and inspire belief in the practicability of revolution, and, finally, to form a body suited and accustomed to warfare.

3. *The organization of secret societies and the arrangement of them in connected groups around a single center.* The organization of small secret societies with all sorts of revolutionary aims is indispensable, both as a means of executing the numerous functions of the party and of finishing the political training of its members. In order, however, that the work may be carried on harmoniously, it is necessary that these small bodies should be grouped about one common center, upon the principle either of complete identification or of federal union.

4. *The acquirement of ties, and an influential position in the administration, in the army, in society, and among the people.* The administration and

the army are particularly important in connection with a revolution, and serious attention should also be devoted to the people. The principal object of the party, so far as the people are concerned, is to prepare them to coöperate with the revolution, and to carry on a successful electioneering contest after the revolution — a contest that shall have for its object the election of popularly chosen delegates to the Organizing Assembly. The party should enlist acknowledged partizans among the more prominent classes of the peasantry and should prearrange for the active coöperation of the masses at the more important points and among the more sympathetic portions of the population. In view of this, every member of the party who is in contact with the people must strive to take a position that will enable him to defend the interests of the peasants, give them aid when they need it, and acquire celebrity among them as an honest man and a man who wishes them well. In this way he must keep up the reputation of the party and support its ideas and aims.

5. *The organization and consummation of the revolution.* In view of the oppressed and cowed condition of the people, and of the fact that the Government, by means of partial concessions and pacifications, may retard for a long time a general revolutionary movement, the party should take the initiative, and not wait until the people are able to do the work without its aid.

6. *The electioneering canvass before the summoning of the Organizing Assembly.* However the revolution may be brought about — as the result of an open revolution, or with the aid of a conspiracy — the duty of the party will be to aid in the immediate summoning of an Organizing Assembly, to which shall be transferred the powers of the Provisional Government created by the revolution or the conspiracy. During the election canvass the party should oppose, in every way, the candidacy of *kuláks* of all sorts, and strive to promote the candidacy of purely communal people.

The Law on Political Offenses

The terroristic actions of Narodnaya Volya culminated in the murder of Alexander II. Naturally enough the government of his son and successor, Alexander III, vigorously prosecuted and persecuted all suspects, and took stringent measures to prevent the recurrence of such acts. The following selections from the "Rules relating to measures for the preservation of national order and public tranquility" will show the nature of the government's reaction. The source is: Kennan, op. cit., vol. 2, pp. 507–509.

Section 5. (a) When public tranquility in any locality shall be disturbed by criminal attempts against the existing imperial form of government, or against the security of private persons and their property, or by preparations for such attempts, so that, for the preservation of order, a resort to the existing permanent laws seems to be insufficient, then that locality may be declared in a state of reinforced safeguard.

(b) When by reason of such attempts the population of a certain place shall be thrown into a state of alarm which creates a necessity for the adoption of exceptional measures to immediately reëstablish order, then the said place may be declared in a state of extraordinary safeguard.

Section 15. Within the limits of such places (places declared to be in a state of reinforced safeguard) governors-general, governors, and municipal chiefs of police may (a) issue obligatory ordinances relating to matters connected with the preservation of public tranquillity and the security of the Empire, and (b) punish by fine and imprisonment violations of such ordinances.

Section 16. Governors-general, governors, and municipal chiefs of police are authorized also (a) to settle by administrative process cases involving violation of the obligatory ordinances issued by them; (b) to prohibit all popular, social, and even private meetings; (c) to close temporarily, or for the whole term of reinforced safeguard, all commercial and industrial establishments; and (d) to prohibit particular persons from residing in places declared to be in a state of reinforced safeguard. (Remark. — Banishment to a specified place, even to one's native place, with obligatory residence there, will be allowed only after communication with the Minister of the Interior. Rules for such banishment are set forth in Sections 32-36.)

Section 32. The banishment of a private person by administrative process to any particular locality in European or Asiatic Russia, with obligatory residence there for a specified time, may not take place otherwise than with an observance of the following rules:

Section 33. The proper authority, upon becoming convinced of the necessity for the banishment of a private person, shall make a statement to that effect to the Minister of the Interior, with a detailed explanation of the reasons for the adoption of this measure, and also a proposition with regard to the period of banishment. (Remark. — The preliminary imprisonment of a person thus presented for exile to a specified place may be extended, by authority of the Minister of the Interior, until such time as a decision shall be reached in his case.)

Section 34. Presentations of this kind will be considered by a special council in the Ministry of the Interior, under the presidency of one of the Minister's associates, such council to consist of two members from the Ministry of the Interior and two members from the Ministry of Justice. The decisions of this council shall be submitted to the Minister of the Interior for confirmation.

Section 35. While considering presentations for exile the above-mentioned council may call for supplemental information or explanations, and, in case of necessity, may summon for personal examination the individual nominated for banishment.

Section 36. A period of from one to five years shall be designated as the term for continuous residence in the assigned place of exile. (Remark. — The term of banishment may be shortened or lengthened, in the manner prescribed in Section 34, within the limits set by section 36.)

The following are the sections of the Russian penal code under which political offenders are prosecuted when brought before the courts:

Section 245. All persons found guilty of composing and circulating written or printed documents, books, or representations calculated to create disrespect for the Supreme Authority, or for the personal character of the Gossudar (the Tsar), or for the Government of his Empire, shall be condemned, as insulters of Majesty, to deprivation of all civil rights, and to from ten to twelve years of penal servitude. (This punishment carries with it exile in Siberia for what remains of life after the expiration of the hard-labor sentence.)

Section 249. All persons who shall engage in rebellion against the Supreme Authority — that is, who shall take part in collective and conspirative insurrection against the Gossudar and the Empire; and also all persons who shall plan the overthrow of the Government in the Empire as a whole, or in any part thereof; or who shall intend to change the existing form of government, or the order of succession to the throne established by law; all persons who, for the attainment of these ends, shall organize or take part in a conspiracy, either actively and with knowledge of its object, or by participation in a conspirative meeting, or by storing or distributing weapons, or by other preparations for insurrection — all such persons, including not only those most guilty, but their associates, instigators, prompters, helpers, and concealers, shall be deprived of all civil rights and be put to death. Those who have knowledge of such evil intentions, and of preparations to carry them into execution, and who, having power to inform the Government thereof, do not fulfill that duty, shall be subjected to the same punishment.

Section 250. If the guilty persons have not manifested an intention to resort to violence, but have organized a society or association intended to attain, at a more or less remote time in the future, the objects set forth in Section 249, or have joined such an association, they shall be sentenced, according to the degree of their criminality, either to from four to six years of penal servitude, with deprivation of all civil rights (including exile to Siberia for life) . . . or to colonization in Siberia (without penal servitude), or to imprisonment in a fortress from one year and four months to four years.

Russian Imperialism in Central Asia

The Russian counterpart of overseas expansion was overland expansion into adjacent territories. The second half of the nineteenth century saw a consistent and vigorous Russian drive in the general direction of Persia, India and China. This expansion was of some concern to all Europe but especially so to Great Britain. The constant hostility between Russia and Britain was in considerable measure due to the Russian imperial advance which is summarized in the following selection. The source is: Harris, Norman D., Europe and the East. Boston: Houghton Mifflin Co., 1926. Pp. 129–131, 134–149.

One of the most remarkable movements of modern times has been the expansion of Russia from the small duchy of Moscovy with an area of 748,000 square miles — approximately the size of Mexico — to a great empire of over 8,300,000 square miles of territory and a population exceeding 170,000,000. After Peter the Great had wrested the supremacy of the Baltic from Charles XII of Sweden, and secured an opening for Russia on the seas of the north, and Catherine II had obtained a large portion of Poland and a foothold upon the Black Sea, Russia found herself precluded from further expansion on the west and southwest by reason of the established European states there and the jealous opposition of those same states to her designs on Turkey and Constantinople.

Accordingly the Muscovite rulers early transferred their activities to Asia. There they met with little opposition, for no established states of any importance were encountered till the borders of the Chinese Empire were reached. The Russian advance, however, was slow and not always the product of deliberate design. Sometimes the gains were accidental or the result of propitious circumstances; but ultimately some 6,000,000 square miles of territory were acquired. This expansion took place in three regions: northern Asia — through Siberia to the Pacific Ocean; the "Heart of Asia" — through Turkestan to China, Afghanistan, and India; and the Caucasus — through Georgia and Daghestan to Persia. The chief motives for increased territory were economic, commercial, political, and philanthropic. The economic were based upon the natural desire of a typically agricultural nation for more territory and outlets for the development of its economic life. The commercial centered in an ambition for increased trade connections with the great trade centers of the East. The political was a combination of a need for defensible frontiers on the east and southeast (against the pillaging, wild, nomadic tribes of the Steppes and northern Asia), of a national necessity for ice-free seaports and of a natural craving for empire. And the philanthropic was a dual force composed of a desire to bring order, good government, and civilization to Asia, and a racial longing to give assistance and protection to all the brother Slavic nations and followers of Greek Christianity, which should ultimately lead to a triumph of Pan-Slavism, and which embraced other Christian and even Mohammedan tribal states as well, — such as the native communities of Khiva, Bokhara, and of the Caucasus.

The success of the Russian expansion was due primarily to four things: a favorable geographical location, it being the only European state whose borders touched the continent of Asia; an absolute monarchical form of government which was especially adapted to continuous and effective diplomacy, and which was understood by, and appealed to, Asiatics; the absence of powerful and determined competitors, there being fifty-nine different nationalities in Siberia, thirty-four in the Caucasus, and forty-two in Central Asia; and skillful method of dealing with Orientals. The Russians were adept in the use of bribery, of intrigue, and of force when necessary. As General Skobelev remarked, when referring to the Turkomans, "The harder you hit them, the longer they will be quiet afterwards." Moreover, the Russians were among the earliest Europeans to study the customs and languages of the East. And in asserting their supremacy they demanded of the subject peoples only recognition of the Czar, annual tribute, trade privileges, and cessation of pillagings, without insisting on any extreme or vexatious social or political changes. . . .

In 1554, Ivan the Terrible subdued Kazan and Astrakazan, extending the Russian territory to the Caspian Sea. The outpost of Orenburg on the Ural River was established; and a series of forts and trading posts created eastward, gradually, via Omsk to Semipalatinsk on the Irtish River. In 1732 and 1790, the Little and Middle Hordes of Kirghiz tribes submitted finally to Russia. And, by the beginning of the nineteenth century, the Russians had formed an irregular frontier — for approximately twelve hundred miles — across the Kirghiz Steppes, maintained by a series of fortified posts which were centers for military operations and commercial activities, and by a small force of twenty thousand Cossacks. This desert borderland remained, however, a constant source of trouble and annoyance to the Empire. The guard was never sufficient to prevent violations of the line; and marauding bands were frequently crossing into Russian territory to loot and destroy villages and property. Conditions of life and of trade were hard and uncertain. Communication with the outside world was difficult and infrequent. The attempts of the Russians to open trade routes to the chief marts of Central Asia were constantly thwarted, and their caravans pillaged by the roving, robber tribes of the steppes. Accordingly, the Russian statesmen determined to seek a defensible frontier and to take what steps they could to stabilize conditions in Turkestan. This movement, inaugurated in the early thirties and covering fifty years of activity, did not attain its full fruition till the Russians took Merv and reached the great Persian-Afghan-Hindu Kush mountain borderland in 1884.

Their progress for the first thirty years was very slow, for the difficulties of the undertaking were enormous, their officers and men inexperienced, and their resources limited. In the last twenty years, however, the Russian Government possessed much greater resources for its adventures in foreign expansion; and its forces were much better officered, manned, and equipped than in the earlier period. Consequently, their progress — directed by a superior group of able diplomats — was much more rapid. They had, fortunately, comparatively few setbacks; and their success was secured through a combination of exploration, intrigue, economic infiltration, and military force.

These Russian activities began at three points: Semipalatinsk on the Irtish River, Orenburg on the Ural River, and Krasnovodsk on the Caspian Sea — the movement from the last-named town did not take place, however, until nearly ten years after the Russians had occupied Krasnovodsk in 1869, and after the advance from the other points had been successfully accomplished. After Humboldt had explored successfully the region south of Semipalatinsk, the Russians established their first fort at Sergiopol — two hundred miles south of their outpost on the Irtish River just mentioned. Then followed another period of exploration to the south and southwest, in which Federov Karelin and Schrenk distinguished themselves. In 1884 the Great Horde of the South Steppes and Lake Balkash — the last of the Kirghiz national groups — submitted to Russia; and Prince Gortchakov advanced the Russian forces two hundred miles to Kopal at the foot of the Ala Tau Mountains, and built a fort there in 1846-47. By 1855, another two hundred miles had been traversed and Verni (Vernoe) and the valley of the Ili River occupied, where great numbers of peasants and settlers followed the military forces, seeking new homes. Once more the explorers pressed on: Semenov up the Ili River, Valekinov to Kashgar and south as far as the Pamirs, and Goluber and Matkov to Issik Kul Lake in 1858-59. Meanwhile, the Russian forces followed slowly. They seized and fortified Tokmak in 1860; and in the same year China transferred to them the Issik Kul region and the valley of the Naryn River to the south of this lake. Finally they pushed on some forty to fifty miles and in 1862 occupied Pishpek — two hundred and sixty miles from Kikand to which they were already advancing from another direction. And in 1867, the whole of this great region was organized into the Russian province of Semipalatinsk with Verni as a capital, which was later divided into the two provinces of Semipalatinsk and Semirechinsk having a combined area of over 322,000 square miles and a population of over 2,000,-000.

Meanwhile, the second movement, inaugurated from Orenburg, had made equally good progress to the south and southeast via the Aral Sea. By 1834, the Russians, going via the Ural River, had reached Dead Bay — an arm of the Caspian Sea — and established a fort there. In 1847, we find them holding outposts on the Irgiz and Turgai Rivers, known as Forts Uralsk and Orenburg. The following year they reached Karabutak and set up another fortified post at Aralsk, near the northeastern extremity of the Aral Sea, called Fort Number One. From there the Russian outposts were gradually pushed southeastward along the Syr Daria (river) for one hundred and fifty miles to their next important station — Fort Perovsk — built in 1853. Their progress was expedited by a steamer brought from Sweden in parts and put together on the river. But, ere long, the Khivans and Tartars of Turkestan fortified the Syr Daria and effectively barred their advance for nine years.

Finally, General Chernaiev, with a large and well-equipped army and in accordance with a carefully planned program, forced his way rapidly one hundred and fifty miles to Djulek and the town of Turkestan, and then to Chimkent — a hundred miles farther — in 1864. When the news of this expedition reached Europe, it aroused considerable excitement in the capitals of the leading powers whose statesmen began at length to grasp the proportions of the Russian advance — although comparatively little was known of Turkestan in those days — and to begrudge her any considerable increase of territory or of trade. Great Britain, fearing chiefly for her Indian possessions, led the chorus of protests that ensued. But Prince Gortchakov — then Minister of Foreign Affairs — in a skillfully worded circular letter to the powers, dated November 21, 1864, succeeded in allaying all fears. He assured them that the chief motive of Russia in this advance was simply to secure an effective boundary in Central Asia — one that could be defended from border raids. It was highly desirable that the robberies and feuds of the Steppes should cease, but there was no chance of securing this while Russia merely bordered on the lands of a number of irresponsible tribes. It was therefore imperative: that the Russian Empire should advance her line till it touched the boundaries of the organized agricultural states of Khiva and Bokhara, and reached the mountains extending from Kikand to China; that a line of forts should be established to hold this line and to maintain peace; and that the "western civilization" should be given to the natives, who must be taught that trade is better than pillage. Accordingly, the Russians were permitted to pursue their advance unhampered; and General Chernaiev took Fort Niazbek and the populous and important city of Tashkent — sixteen miles northeast of it and commanding its water supply — in 1865, while General Romanovski occupied Khojent, a strong military town covering the roads to Kokland, Tashkent, Bokhara, and Balkh, in the following year.

By this time the khanates and tribal chieftains of the interior of Turkestan had become suspicious of the motives of the Russians; and, in 1866, they all united, under the leadership of the Khan of Bokhara, in a "Holy League" against Russia. The Russian generals thereupon deliberately provoked a conflict with the ruler of the Khanate of Bokhara whose intentions were peaceful, by seizing the property of Bokharan merchants in Khojent and Tashkent, and by arresting some Bokharan envoys who had been sent on a mission of protest to St. Petersburg. The Amir retaliated indiscreetly by imprisoning the members of a Russian mission sent to his capital to re-establish friendly relations and to secure trade concessions; and General Chernaiev led an army across the Syr Daria at Chinaz against him — only to be defeated. The Russians succeeded, however, in capturing and holding the two forts of Jizak and Ura Tube within the Amir's domains before the year closed.

The next year the Russian Government organized the whole region already occupied southeast of the Aral Sea into the province of Turkestan, containing a population of about 1,500,000 people, with the town of Turkestan as its capital, and on November 17, 1867, appointed General Kaufmann commander-in-chief of its forces in Central Asia. Kaufmann proceeded promptly to organize an efficient expedition against Bokhara; and in 1868 he thoroughly defeated the Khan's forces on the Zerafshan River, took the important city of Samarkand — noted as the burial place of Tamerlane and as the religious capital of Turkestan with its marvelous Arab edifices — and compelled the Khan to sign a treaty of peace dated the 18th of June. By the terms of this agreement, the city of Bokhara was not to be molested; but the khanate was to be opened to the free trade and free passage of Russians. A small indemnity amounting to 125,000 gold tilla was to be paid Russia, to whom was to be transferred the valley of the Zerafshan and the cities of Smarkand and Katta Kurgan, which gave them control of the waters of the Zerfshan and the crops of the Khanate of Bokhara.

These successes again aroused Great Britain, whose statesmen viewed with apprehension every step taken by the Russians that brought their boundary nearer to the frontier of India. During the years 1869 and 1870, an attempt was made by the British Government to secure an agreement with Russia that should govern the future policy and protect the interests of both states in Central Asia. It resulted in what was afterwards known as the "St. Petersburg Correspondence" in the course of which the idea of a system of "buffer states" was evolved. Lord Mayo, who was Viceroy of India from 1869 to 1872, suggested that the British and Russian possessions should be kept safely aloof from one another by the maintenance of two series of independent buffer states. The three northern ones — Khiva, Bokhara, and Kokland — were to enjoy the protection of Russia, while the three southern — Kelat, Afghanistan, and Harkand — should have the support of Great Britain or India. In this way definite limits would be set to the territorial expansion of both powers, and each state would have its share in the trade and commercial development of Central Asia. Russian gave the scheme her tacit approval, but did not consent to any definite arrangement in the matter.

Meanwhile, difficulties were arising between Russians and Khivans. The latter resented the presence of the former in Central Asia and their inter- ference in the affairs of Bokhara and neighboring states. Moreover, the Khivans were suspicious of the Russians and embittered because of the way the latter were obtaining the control of the trade of Central Asia. The presence of the Russians was as obnoxious to them as it was to the Boxharans and the other peoples of that region; while the intriguing, pushing manners of the western traders and settlers was equally irritating. There is little doubt that the Khivan chieftains were secretly taking what steps they could to retard the Russian advance and to keep them away from Khivan territory; for fear of annexation was ever hanging over their heads. In 1870, the Khan of Khiva forbade the exportation of grain or food into regions held by Russian forces; an an attempt was made to prevent all commerce between Russian forces and Khivans. And, in the next two years every effort was made diplomatically and commercially to hold up Russian progress; but all in vain.

The Russian Government, which considered a protectorate over the Khivans as an essential stepping-stone to the commercial and political domination of Central Asia, viewed these hasty, fruitless activities in defense of national independence as the unfriendly acts of a defiant competitor and enemy. And she began to look about for excuses to start a movement that not only would remove an irritating opponent, but also would furnish a pretext for the establishment of a protectorate over the khanates. It was not necessary to wait long. By the end of 1872, Russia was able to report to the powers that another military expedition into Central Asia would soon be necessary, owing to the unsettled conditions and raids upon trade along the Khivan border.

Khiva, to which Russia held a legitimate claim since certain Kirghiz chiefs had transferred to the Russian czars their family rights to Khiva, was reported as sheltering rebellious Kirghiz tribes, defying Russian power by the practice of brigandage, and conspiring with Bokhara, Kokand, and Kashgar to over- throw Russian control in Central Asia. In a well-authenticated interview in London in January, 1873, Count Schouvalov — then Russian Minister of Foreign Affairs — gave positive assurance to Lord Granville, at that time holding the portfolio of Foreign Affairs in the British Cabinet, that this would be merely a punitive expedition. Four and one half battalions only — about 4200 men — were to be sent. And there was no intention of taking possession since positive orders had been given that nothing should be done which would lead to a prolonged occupancy. What actually occurred was something quite different. General Kaufmann crossed the Krivan boundary with three columns composed of fifty-three companies of infantry and twenty-five Cossacks — about 14,000 men all told — and secured the submission of Khiva without difficulty, even though Bokhara, aroused at the invasion of territory belonging to her friend and ally, came rather tardily to the rescue. She, too, was forced to submit to the Russian army and to sign a treaty at General Kaufmann's dictation on September 28th, similar to that signed by Khiva on August 25th. These agreements provided for the opening of the khanates and the Oxus River to the trade of Russia with but a two and one half per cent import duty on goods going into Bokhara or Russian territory. No person should be admitted into the khanates without a Russian passport; and the Russians admitted were to enjoy the right of holding property and carrying on business. And, while Bokhara the noble, with its four hundred mosques, its baths, its gardens, its great caravansaries, and its flourishing trade, was required only to receive a Russian agent and to send a representative to the Russian Government at Tashkent, its political status, as well as that of Khiva, became a dependent one. The direction of their foreign affairs passed into the hands of Russia, for they were forbidden to make any commercial or other treaty without the consent of the Russian Government; and they became subject protectorates of the Russian Empire, retaining, however, in other respects their local autonomy.

In this way were acquired two rich and fertile oasis communities, one (Khiva) having 24,000 square miles of territory and 800,000 population and the other (Bokhara) 83,000 square miles of territory and 1,250,000 population. And last, but not least, the slave-trade in Central Asia was abolished, commerce with the interior communities and peoples was unfettered, and protection afforded to life and property. For in the same year — 1873 — the Russian province of Samarkand, comprising some 26,000 square miles of territory and a population approximately 700,000, was established with the city of Samarkand as its capital; and three years later, General Kaufmann, taking advantage of an uprising started by the Khan of Kokand — now a metropolis of Central Asia with 112,000 people — assisted by the leading chiefs of Khojent, divided and defeated these leaders, and added a large district to the east and southeast of Smarlkand. The local chieftans all submitted and the whole region was organized the same year into the Russian province of Ferghana, which embraced 55,483 square miles of territory with a population of over 1,200,000.

Within a short time, a connection was established between the province of Ferghana and that of Semipalatinsk where we have seen the Russians advancing from Semipalatinsk to Pishpek. This completed the main Russian forward movement into Central Asia. Three things remained to be done, however, before the Russians could reap the full reward of their efforts and feel secure in their control of the region and its trade. The district between the Caspian Sea and the Khivan territory — known as Tukomania — had to be occupied; the Russian outposts had to be pushed forward till they controlled the northern outlets of the great passes through the mountain barriers of Persia, Afghanistan, and India; and all the centers of Terkestan had to be connected by rail with the Russian system.

The Russians had early sought to obtain a foothold on the inhospitable eastern coast of the Caspian Sea. They made three attempts to establish a base of operations of the Caspian Sea. They made three attempts to establish of Astrabad in 1837–38 in the face of vain protests by Persia and England; a second at Krasnovodsk — south of Kara Bugaz Bay — in 1869; and a third at Chikishliar — above the Atrek River — in 1871. After the failure of General Lomakin's first attempt in 1877 to penetrate Transcaspia from Chikishliar, Kransnovodsk became the base of all the future Russian activities in that region as well as the starting-point of its Transcaspian railway in later years. It was a difficult region for military operations under the most favorable conditions, for it is a country of deserts and arid plateaus extending southward to the rugged, wild foothills of the Kopat Dagh (mountain range), then forming the northern border of Persia. And in these foothills dwelt the powerful Turkoman tribes — the most warlike people in all Turkestan.

The dangers and difficulties having been fully demonstrated by the crushing defeat of General Lomakin's second expedition at Geok Teppe on September 9, 1879, the St. Petersburg statesmen selected their ablest warrior — General Michael Dmitriavitch Skobelev — as the commander-in-chief of their next army of invasion. He was assisted by General Kuropatkin — then a young man — who, after a distinguished career, became commander-in-chief of the Russian armies in the Russo-Japanese War. After careful preparations, Skobelev's army left Krasnovodsk in July, 1880, 18,000 strong, and proceeded to occupy the inland territory by a series of marches toward the southeast. The brave Turkoman forces were defeated and driven back to their famous stronghold at Deok Teppe. Here the last remnant of their troops surrendered after a three weeks' siege on January 24, 1881, and 8000 of the garrison were deliberately slain as a warning to the other peoples of the region.

Thereafter, Skobelev's progress was steady and without serious opposition. On February 9, 1881, he took Ashkabad, and then moved his advance posts south-eastward toward the oases of Tejend and Merv, and the commercial centers of Kaaka-Kalch and Sarkhs. And the success of his operations enabled the Russians to conclude with Persia the Akhak-Khorassan Boundary Convention on December 21, 1881, which assigned to Russia all of the north-east rim of the plateau of Iran, north of the river Atrek, and confirmed her possession of the Merv and Sarakhs districts. This gave Russia access to the great mountain frontier of Persia and gave her a direct connection with the trade of Khorassan. Alexander III, who had no wish to draw the attention of Europe to these successes or arouse the suspicions of Great Britain, recalled Skobelev, after the receipt of a protest from the British Foreign Office, and appointed General Komarov in his place.

M. Alikhanov was sent on a special mission to Merv in 1882–83, where he secured a preferential commercial treaty by winning over the leading merchants to the Russian cause. And the Russian control became so extensive and effective throughout the whole region that, within a year, they were able to organize the vast area of 200,000 square miles lying between Persia, Afghanistan, the Khanates of Khiva and Bokhara and the Caspian and Aral Seas, into the Russian province of Transcaspia. General Komarov became its governor-general in the spring of 1883. On February 18, 1884, Komarov secured at Ashkabad the allegiance of four leading chiefs and twenty-four notables of the Merv Tekkes, and was then able to penetrate without serious resistance the remarkable Tejend Oasis in the Kara Kum Desert, where for centuries the famous town of Merv — the "Queen of the World" — had flourished amid cultivated fields and orchards. He occupied the place and its noted fortress — the Koushid — on March 16, 1884, and, pushing on steadily southward, took the fortress of Sarakhs in May of the same year. Thus the occupation of all the strategic centers of the region was completed and the Russian forces brought within striking distance of the Afghan frontier.

Meanwhile, in 1873, England and Russia had reached an agreement concerning frontiers in Central Asia. This Anglo-Russian understanding was the result of a correspondence between the Earl of Granville and Prince Gortchakov during the period from October 17, 1872, to January 31, 1873. At that time the Russian advance having reached the Khanate of Bokhara, the British were anxious to see limited the unmarked frontier between that state and Afghanistan. The agreement then reached provided that the boundary line of Afghanistan should run from Siri Kul, or Lake Victoria, to the junction of the Oxus and Kokcha Rivers, and follow the Oxus (Amu-Daria) and the district of Andkjui on the north and northwest to pillar number 79 on the Oxus, set at about the sixty-sixth degree of east longitude. In this way, Badakshan, Wakshan, Afghan Turkestan (including the districts of Kunduz, Khulm, Balkh, Andkhui), and Herat were retained by Afghanistan. The desert to the north and northwest of the Afghan boundary was referred to as "belonging to independent tribes of Turkoman" which included the Tekkes of Merv.

Therefore, when the Russian forces seized Ashkabad, Merv, Sarakhs, the British Government felt that this agreement of 1873 had been deliberately violated; and they entered a vigorous protest at St. Petersburg, which led to a spirited diplomatic controversy lasting nearly three years. The British statesmen were fully awake to the significance of the Russian advance in Turkestan, which now threatened to absorb Herat and push through Afghanistan to the border of India. But their hands had been tied by troubles in the Sudan where General Gordon was besieged in Khartoum, and by the reluctance of some of their leaders, such as Gladstone, to use force in the protection of the British interests abroad.

However, while the diplomats wrote dispatches, the soldiers of Komarov were gaining possession of the Zulfikar Pass on the road to Herat early in 1885; and in March they engaged with the Afghans in battle on the Kushk.

The Government of India hastened to the aid of the Afghans; and there ensued the famous "race for Herat," as it was termed by the writers of that day. Before any serious conflict took place, however, the diplomats of the two empires had secured the appointment of a joint commission to settle this vexatious frontier question. It met in St. Petersburg, and its findings were embodied in the Russo-Afghan Boundary Convention in 1887, which determined the northwest frontier line of Afghanistan from the Persian border on the Hari-rud River to the Bokhara line on the Oxus (pillar number 79). Later this was surveyed and marked for one hundred and fifty miles with pillars. In the main, this was a favorable decision for Russia, since it gave her access to the chief passes and trade routes into northern Afghanistan. Yet it was a great advantage to Afghanistan and India to have this vexatious frontier problem settled, to have Herat retained by Afghanistan, and to have adequate protection provided for the caravans and trace of this region through the control exercised by Russia over the restless Turkomans and desert peoples to the north of the line.

This Russo-Afghan Agreement marks the third step in the final erection of the southern mountain frontier of Russia Turkestan (the first two being the Russo-Persian Convention in 1881 and the Russo-British understanding in 1873). The fourth and last step in this work was the determination of the boundaries of the Pamir plateau. This famous highland barrier is a tremendous plateau and mountain region with an altitude of from 14,000 to 25,000 feet, situated north of the Hindu Kush and opposite to Chitral in northern India. It is known locally as the "Roof of the World"; but little information existed in Europe concerning this region till the exploration of the eighties and nineties. Russian explorers appeared there from the north, while. British travelers worked their way through from the south — notably the mission of Colonel Gromtchevski in 1889 and that of Colonel Younghusband and Davidson about a year later, both of which were forced to retire by the hostility of the Afghan natives. In 1891 Colonel Yonov attempted to occupy the plateau with a strong force. The Afghans resisted his advance stoutly, and England ordered several regiments of Goorkhas to their assistance. So Yonov was compelled to withdraw. But Russia apologized for the invasion of Afghan territory and agreed to a partition of the Pamir, after a long and heated correspondence. Finally, the matter was amicably adjusted in the Anglo-Russian Convention of March, 1895; and by the appointment of a commission in the following September to survey the region and mark the boundary line. By this convention it was agreed that this line should run from the eastern end of Lake Victoria (Siri Kul) to the Chinese frontier, and that it should mark, not only the boundary line between Afghan and Russian territory, but also the line of division between the Russian and British spheres of influence. The long strip of land, now stretching like a finger between Turkestan and India, was to be retained by Afghanistan, this preventing the possessions of the two empires from coming into direct contact. China was to be urged to mark her boundary, so that all cause for further disputes would be removed. And the whole region was carefully explored and studied by two Danish expeditions so that the world might have definite information concerning this heretofore inaccessible country.

Meanwhile, the work of railway construction had been begun, at the suggestion of General Annenkov, at Krasnovodsk, and a line built via Ashkabad and Merv to Bokhara and Samarkand, to which last-mentioned place the road was opened in 1888. Later, this was connected with a line from Orenburg coming by way of Kazalinsk, Turkestan, and Tashkent, and the railway extended to Khojent, Kokand, and Andiijan in Ferghanna, with a branch from Merv to Kushlk on the border of Afghanistan. In this way the Russian Government completed its expansion in Central Asia, rounded out its frontiers, and consolidated its possessions by railways and trade routes. And altogether the Russian acquisition in the Steppes, Turkestan, and Transcaspia amounted to 1,366,833 miles bearing a population of over 9,000,000 in 1910. Included in their new territory was a large district received from China when the Kuldkja affair was settled at the Treaty of Peking in 1881. This region, reaching from the Ala Tau range to the Tienshan Mountains, rounded out the Russian holdings along the great Chinese mountain barriers, including the Issik Kul district, and gave her an additional share of Turkestan which she added to the province of Semirechensk.

Alexander III as Seen by Witte

The outstanding Russian statesman of the late nineteenth and early twentieth centuries was Count Sergius Witte who served both Tsar Alexander III and Tsar Nicholas II. Nicholas did not like Witte whom he considered to be an unscrupulous and ambitious trouble-maker. Witte, on his part, held an exceedingly poor opinion of Nicholas and compared him most unfavorably with Alexander III whom he admired enormously. Here is Witte's description of his tsar-hero. The source is: Yarmolinsky, Avrahm (Translator and editor), Memoirs of Count Witte. *Garden City, New York: Doubleday, Page and Co., 1921. (This is a one volume abridgement of the original three volume Russian version.)*

The unfortunate brevity of Alexander III's reign, thirteen years in all, did not prevent the full growth and display of his noble, outstanding personality, to which the whole world paid homage on the day of his death. His Russian contemporaries and the succeeding generation did not highly esteem him, however, and many looked upon his reign with a scorn altogether unjustifiable, especially in view of the unhappy conditions of his youth and the deplorable circumstances under which he ascended the throne.

To begin with, his education and training were largely neglected, since the older brother, Nicholas, was the heir apparent during that period of Alexander's life. In addition, the family environment was unfavourable. The future emperor's sensitive moral feelings were grievously hurt by his father's late re-marriage at the age of sixty, when he already had numerous grown-up children and even grand-children. Then his uncompromising honesty was outraged by the prevalence in higher Government circles of a traffic in privileges and concessions to mercantile associations and particularly by the implication of Alexander II's morganatic wife, Princess Yuryevski, in this barter.

Consider, too, the unpropitious national situation. Having turned his back upon reform during the latter part of his reign, the Great Liberator (Alexander II) drove the liberals into the ranks of the revolutionists, so that when the heir apparent began to take an interest in politics, he was confronted with the existence of an extremely radical party and strongly impressed, therefore, with the necessity of stern measures to suppress subversive movements. The Heir was encouraged in this attitude by his preceptor, Pobiedonostzev.

Alexander III was undeniably a man of limited education. I cannot agree, however, with those who would class him as unintelligent. Though lacking perhaps in mental keenness, he was undoubtedly gifted with the broad sympathetic understanding which in a ruler is often far more important than rational brilliancy.

Neither in the Imperial family nor among the nobility was there anyone who better appreciated the value of a ruble or a kopeck than Emperor Alexander III. He made an ideal treasurer for the Russian people, and his economical temperament was of incalculable assistance in the solution of Russia's financial problems. Had not the Emperor doggedly warded off the incessant raids upon the Russian treasury and checked the ever-present impulse to squander the public funds accumulated by the sweat and blood of the people, Vyshnegradski and myself could never have succeeded in putting the nation back upon its feet financially.

Alexander III's prudence in government expenditures was matched by his personal thrift. Abhorring luxury and lavish spending, he led an extremely simple life. When he grew tired of his own table, he would ask for a common soldier's or a hunter's meal. This economy was sometimes carried too far. The Imperial table was always relatively poor, and the food served at the Court Marshal's board was sometimes such as to endanger the health. Alexander III was extremely economical with his wearing apparel. I had a curious proof of this when I accompanied the Emperor on one of his railway trips. Since I found it impossible, on account of my responsibility, to sleep of nights, I would often catch glimpses of His Majesty's valet mending the Emperor's trousers. On one occasion I asked him why he didn't give his master a new pair instead of mending the old so often. "Well, I would rather have it that way," he answered, "but His Majesty won't let me. He insists on wearing his garments until they are threadbare. It is the same with his boots. Not only does he wear them as long as possible, but he refuses to put on expensive ones. If I should bring him patent leather boots, he would angrily throw them out of the window." The Emperor's dislike of the expensive included gorgeous rooms. For this reason he never stayed at the Winter Palace, but always occupied the unpretentious quarters of Anichkov or Gatchina. There he took small rooms and lived frugally. He tolerated the Court's luxury as an unavoidable formality, but he always longed for a different mode of existence and created it for himself in his private life.

The entire Imperial family respected and feared Alexander III, who wielded the influence of a veritable patriarch. He believed that the royal family must set a moral example for the whole nation both in their private and social life. In his time dissolute conduct by Russian Grand Dukes in foreign countries, so common now, was very rare. Transgressing members of the Imperial family were sure to incur the Emperor's heavy displeasure. Remarriage was severely frowned upon in the case of anybody connected with the Government.

Alexander III himself led an unimpeachable life and his family was a splendid example of the old-fashioned, godfearing Russian type. He was a stern father and while the children did not fear him, they were uneasy and constrained in his presence with the single exception of Mikhail, the favourite son, who was not only unrestrained, but even inclined to take liberties, as the following amusing anecdote, related to me by his valet, will indicate. Becoming impatient at the boy's impertinence and inattention during a stroll in the gardens early one Summer morning, Alexander III snatched up a watering hose and gave Mikhail a good dousing. Without further ado they went in to breakfast, the youth changing his drenched clothing. After that the Emperor retired to work in his study and as usual indulged in his habit of occasionally leaning out of the window, but was met with an altogether unusual deluge from the upper window, where Misha had stationed himself with a pailful of water in anticipation of the Imperial appearance fenestral. There is very little doubt that none but Mikhail would have dared to think of such a stratagem, and there is no doubt whatsoever that nobody else could have executed it with impunity.

As a ruler, Alexander III made important contribution to the welfare and prosperity of his subjects and the international prestige of the empire. In the first place, he practically reconstructed the army, which had been thrown into a state of serious disorganization by the war with Turkey in the seventies. During the time that I was Director of Railways and later Minister of that department under Alexander III, railroad building, which had practically ceased some years before, was resumed with excellent results and plans were laid for future devlopment. Alexander III also made possible the financial rehabilitation of Russia, in which I had the honor of participation as Minister of Finances. His salutary influence in this matter extended beyond his reign.

In fact, it was only due to this that I was able to retain my position eight years after his death and thus complete the work, for Nicholas II was incapable of appreciating my endeavours and simply relied upon his deceased father's confidence in me.

The Trans-Siberian Railway

WITTE'S ACCOUNT

Sergius Witte served his country well. Among other things, he stabilized the currency, introduced the gold standard, induced foreign investors to lend huge sums of money to Russia and was, in a manner of speaking, the father of the Russian industrial revolution. One of his most spectacular accomplishments was the Trans-Siberian Railroad. In the following excerpts from his Memoirs *Witte tells of the beginnings of the undertaking and describes the moves which preceded the building of Chinese Eastern cut-off. It may be remarked that Witte was shrewd as well as able; scheming and tricky, as well as vigorous; and, as these excerpts show, not at all lacking in vanity. The source is: Yarmolinsky, op. cit., pp. 52–54, 86–87, 89–90, 94–95.*

It will not be an exaggeration to say that the vast enterprise of constructing the great Siberian Railway was carried out owing to my efforts, supported, of course first by Emperor Alexander III, and then by Emperor Nicholas II. The idea of connecting European Russia with Vladivostok by rail was one of the most cherished dreams of Alexander III. He spoke to me about it in the course of one of my first conferences with him following my appointment as Minister of Ways of Communication. As is known, Czarevitch Nicholas, the present Emperor, during his trip through the Far East, inaugurated, on May 19, 1891, the construction of the Ussurian Railroad, connecting Vladivostok with Khabarovsk. The Emperor complained that in spite of his efforts, which extended over ten years, his dream had failed to materialize owing to the opposition of the Committee of Ministers and the Imperial Council. He took my promise that I would bend my energies to the accomplishment of his desire.

In my capacity of Minister of Ways of Communication and later as Minister of Finances, both during the reign of Alexander III and afterwards, I persistently advocated the idea of the necessity of constructing the great Siberian Railway. As much as the former Ministers thwarted the plan, so I, remembering my promise to the Emperor, sought to advance it. As Minister of Finances, I was in a peculiarly favourable position with regard to furthering the project, for what was most needed for the construction of the railway was money. Had I remained Minister of Ways of Communication, I would have had to face the opposition of the Minister of Finances.

I devoted myself body and soul to the task, yet Emperor Alexander III did not live to see the realization of his dream, and it was only under Nicholas II that the immense railroad was completed. I was aided by the circumstance that the young Emperor took a personal interest in the matter. At my instance, while his father was still alive, he was appointed head of the Siberian Railroad Committee, which I had formed to promote the construction of the railroad. This committee was empowered to eliminate all manner of unnecessary delay and had the authority over both the administrative and the legislative matters involved in the construction. For the young heir-apparent this task was something in the nature of a preparatory school of statesmanship. He worked under the guidance of the vice president of the committee, Bunge, who was also his tutor. This was a very happy arrangement. The future ruler took his appointment in earnest and worked with enthusiasm. When he became Emperor, he retained the title of President of the Siberian Committee and did not lose his interest in the matter. This enabled me to complete the work within a few years.

. . .

In the meantime the great Trans-Siberian Railway, which was under construction, had reached Transbaikalia and the question arose as to the further direction which the railroad should follow. I conceived the idea of building the road straight across Chinese territory, principally Mongolia and northern Manchuria, on toward Vladivostok. This direction, I calculated, would considerably shorten the line and facilitate its construction. Considering the enormous mileage of the Trans-Siberian, it was natural to seek to shorten the route. Technically the Amur section presented great difficulties. Besides, the road would run along the Amur River and would thus compete with the Amur steamship companies. The Manchurian route would save 514 versts. In comparison to the Amur region this section also possessed the advantage of a more productive soil and a more favourable climate. The problem was how to get China's permission for this plan, by peaceful means based on mutual commercial interests. The idea appealed to me strongly and I found occasion to draw His Majesty's attention to it. The court physician, Badmayev, a Buriat by birth, who wielded a considerable influence over the Emperor, on the contrary, stood for the Kyakhta-Peking direction. I could not sympathize with his project, first, because I considered Vladivostok as the most desirable terminus for the Trans-Siberian, and, second, because I believed that a railroad to Peking would arouse the whole of Europe against us. It must be borne in mind that the great originator of the Trans-Siberian had no political or military designs in connection with the road. It was an enterprise of a purely economic nature. Alexander III wished to establish communication by the shortest possible route between the distant Maritime Province and Central Russia. Strategically, both Alexander III and his successor attributed a strictly defensive importance to the road. Under no circumstance was the Trans-Siberian to serve as a means for territorial expansion.

. . .

In my conferences with Li Hung Chang I dwelt on the services which we had recently done to his country. I assured him that, having proclaimed the principle of China's territorial integrity, we intended to adhere to it in the future; but, to be able to uphold this principle, I argued, we must be in a position, in case of emergency, to render China armed assistance. Such aid we would not be able to render her until both European Russia and Vladivostok were connected with China by rail, our armed forces being concentrated in European Russia. I called to his attention the fact that although during China's war with Japan we did dispatch some detachments from Vladivostok, they moved so slowly, because of the absence of railroad communication, that when they reached Kirin the war was over. Thus I argued that to uphold the territorial integrity of the Chinese Empire, it was necessary for us to have a railroad running along the shortest possible route to Vladivostok, across the northern part of Mongolia and Manchuria. I also pointed out to Li Hung Chang that the projected railway would raise the productivity of our possessions and the Chinese territories it would cross. Finally I declared, Japan was likely to assume a favourable attitude toward the road, for it would link her with Western Europe, whose civilization she had lately adopted.

Naturally enough, Li Hung Chang raised objections. Nevertheless, I gathered from my talks with him that he would agree to my proposal if he were certain that our Emperor wished it. Therefore, I asked His Majesty to receive Li Hung Chang, which the Emperor did. It was practically a private audience and it passed unnoticed by the press. As a result of my negotiations with the Chinese statesman, we agreed on the following three provisions of a secret pact to be concluded between Russia and China:

(1) The Chinese Empire grants us permission to build a railroad within its territory along a straight line between Chita and Vladivostok, but the road must be in the hands of a private corporation. Li Hung Chang absolutely refused to accept my proposal that the road should be either constructed or owned by the Treasury. For that reason we were forced to form a private corporation, the so-called Eastern Chinese Railroad Corporation. This body is, of course, completely in the hands of the Government, but since nominally it is a private corporation, it is within the jurisdiction of the Ministry of Finances.

(2) China agrees to cede us a strip of land sufficient for the construction and operation of the railway. Within that territory the corporation is permitted to have its own police and to exercise full and untrammelled authority. China takes upon herself no responsibilities with regard to the construction or operation of the road.

(3) The two countries obligate themselves to defend each other in case Japan attacks the territory of China or our Far-Eastern maritime possessions.

I reported the results of my negotiations to His Majesty and he instructed me to take up the matter with the Foreign Minister. I explained to Prince Lobanov-Rostovski that I had come to an oral agreement with Li Hung Chang regarding the provisions of a secret Russo-Chinese pact, and that the only thing left now was to embody the agreement in a formal written instrument. After listening to my statement of the terms of the agreement, the prince took a pen and wrote the text of the treaty. The document was drafted so skilfully that I approved it without the slightest reservation. The prince told me that the following day he would submit the document to His Majesty and return it to me if it was approved by the Emperor.

. . .

Not the slightest information penetrated into the press regarding our secret agreement with China. The only thing Europe learned was the bare fact that China had agreed to grant the Russo-Chinese Bank a concession for the construction of the Eastern Chinese Railway, a continuation of the Trans-Siberian. The concession was drawn up under my instructions by the Assistant Minister of Finances, Piotr Mikhailovich Romanov, in consultation with the Chinese Minister in St. Petersburg, who was also China's envoy to Berlin. Winter and spring he usually spent in St. Petersburg, while the rest of the year he stayed in Berlin. Since it was then summer-time, Romanov went to Berlin and it was there that the terms of the concessions were drafted. The project was subsequently ratified by the two contracting Governments. At the time it was rumoured in Europe, I remember, that Li Hung Chang had been bribed by the Russian Government. I must say that there is not a particle of truth in this rumour.

The terms of the railroad concession granted by China were very favourable for Russia. The agreement provided for China's right to redeem the road at the expiration of 36 years, but the terms of the redemption were so burdensome that it was highly improbable that the Chinese Government would ever attempt to effect the redemption. It was calculated that should the Chinese Government wish to redeem the road at the beginning of the 37th year, it would have to pay the corporation, according to the terms of the concession, a sum not less than 700 million rubles.

AN AMERICAN'S DESCRIPTION

Mr. John W. Bookwalter, an American, traveled over the newly constructed Trans-Siberian from Moscow to Tomsk, which at that time (1898) was the eastern terminus although the railhead had already been pushed as far east as the Yenisei River. His report of this journey was privately published. The following excerpt is much condensed. The source is: Bookwalter, J. W., Siberia and Central Asia. Springfield, Ohio, 1899. Pp. 6–8, 43–46, 49–67, 87–94.

I set out to simply write you of my Siberian trip. The line of the Trans-Siberian railway runs in a general way through middle European Russia, the centre of the southern part of Western Siberia, and along the southern border of Eastern Siberia. Its western terminus is Moscow, and in the east, Vladivostok on the Pacific Ocean. It is difficult to determine its exact length, as the recent Russian-Chinese relations that have sprung up have caused Russia to change the original route down the Amur River in East Siberia. A commission has recently left here to make a new survey from a point about 1,200 miles west of Vladivostok, with the intention of radiating from that point several lines through Manchuria eastward, as China has recently given Russia extensive concessions in that province. One of these lines will run direct to Vladivostok through Manchuria, and, joining with the main line from Moscow, will thus make a much shorter route than the one originally designed to run down the Amur River, of which nearly 1,000 miles is now completed. Even under the new survey the line will not be less than 6,100 miles long.

. . .

There is now completed about 4,000 miles of road from Moscow east, on which trains are running. On the last 1,000 miles, however, only construction trains are running, with an occasional mixed passenger train at intervals of about a fortnight. In the last six weeks they have put on a through train that runs from Moscow to Tomsk, on the Tom River. This train leaves once in ten days and furnishes fairly comfortable facilities. Ordinary trains that break the journey at many points run also, at irregular intervals, as far as Omsk. The distance from Moscow to Tomsk is about 3,000 miles. It is the through train that I am taking. Whatever expeditions I make east of Tomsk will have to be done on construction trains, or over the old Siberian post-route by troikas or droshkies — curious vehicles drawn by three or five horses.

. . .

The Siberian railway, like all railways in Russia, is well constructed, the road-bed firm, track well ballasted, generally with stone, at least as far as Tscheljabinsk, and easy gradients. The road has a five-foot gauge, uniform with all the roads in European Russia. This gives an ample breadth to the cars, which, with their unusual height, imparts an air of comfort not possessed by roads of narrower gauge and less height of ceiling in the car. The stations, without exception, are clean and handsome, constructed often of wood, but frequently of brick or stone. It is a perfect delight to take a meal in the restaurants. They have a most agreeable custom of furnishing meals. On entering the dining-room, you will find at one end an immense sideboard literally groaning under a load of newly prepared Russian dishes, always piping hot, and of such a bewildering variety as to range through the whole gamut of human fancy and tastes.

You are given a plate, with a knife and fork. Making your own selection, you retire to any of the neatly-spread tables to enjoy your meal at your leisure, and, I might add, with infinite zest, for travel in this country, besides pleasing the eye, quickens the palate. The price, too, is a surprise to one accustomed to metropolitan charges. You can get soup, as fine a beefsteak as you ever ate, a splendid roast chicken, whole, done in Russian style, most toothsome and juicy; potatoes and other vegetables, a bottle of beer, splendid and brewed in this country, for one ruble — about fifty cents.

Safety seems to be the one idea uppermost in the minds of the railway ministry. Beside the electrical and other appliances used in the best railway practice they have an immense army of guards both for the train and the track. The road is divided into sections of one verst each — about two-thirds of a mile. For each section there is built a neat little cottage in which the guard and his family live. It is the duty of this guard or one of his family to patrol a section night and day. As soon as a train passes, the guard steps into the middle of the track, holds a flag, at night a lantern, aloft and watches the retreating train until it passes into the next verst or section. Where there is a heavy curve that prevents the view of the road for the distance of a verst, several guards are employed on a section. A train is, therefore, never out of sight of a guard.

I might add that women often perform this service, which is quite apart from that of the section gang, whose duty is to repair the road. On the Siberian railway, as far as Tomsk, there are to be nearly 4,000 of these cottages for the use of the guards; a very costly precaution, but one that gives a pleasing sense of security to the traveller. With the exception of the great post routes to Siberia, the Caucasus, and main highways in European Russia, which are first class and compare well with other countries, the common roads of Russia are indifferent, scarcely equal to those of our own country.

• • •

At Batraki, another important grain port, and celebrated for the fine quality of caviare, the railroad crosses the Volga. The bridge here, owing to its immense size and the difficulties encountered in its construction, deserves well to be classed among the world's great structures of this kind. It is only a little short of a mile in length, being built of fourteen sections, 360 feet span each. The bridge is 135 feet above the river at low water. There were consumed nearly 7,000 tons of iron in its building, and it was designed and executed by a Russian engineer.

The Volga, where we crossed it, very much resembles the Mississippi River, as well in size as in other points. To form some notion of the size and volume of water in this mighty river, I would say, at the point where the railroad crosses the river it is just a mile wide at low water. At times of high water it is from four to eight miles wide. The channel near the bridge at low water has a depth of twenty feet, and at high water of 100 feet.

The velocity of the current when the river is at its flood is said to be thirty feet per second, and in its low stage, fifteen or twenty feet per second.

. . .

From Batraki to Wajsaowaja, a distance of 500 miles, there are the same fertile, treeless plains and prairies as from Moscow to the former place, a distance of 600 miles. At Wasjaowaja we encounter the foot-hills and get our first view of the Ural Mountains. We here also meet the Ufa River, whose sinuous course the road follows until the summit of the mountains is reached. ·Those who from its great length — being over 1,700 miles from north to south — have been led to expect an imposing range of mountains, will be doomed to disappointment. The height is only moderate, being a little over 6,000 feet at the highest, in this respect scarcely equal to the Apennines. The summit is reached a little beyond Zlatoust, at an elevation of 3,000 feet. It is an easy grade and requires no special effort to surmount.

On reaching the summit, if one did not know it was the Ural Mountains, he might well believe he was on the railway summit of the Alleghanies near Altoona, so similar to it are the surroundings. Zlatoust, a large town, is most important in several particulars. It was until recently the "Botany Bay" of Russia. Here one occasionally sees prisoners chained in gangs destined to work in the mines or perhaps, doomed to the solitude of farther Siberia.

Zlatoust is in the centre of the iron regions of Russia. A very fine quality is produced here in great quantities, and being free from both sulphur and phosphorus, it is consumed principally in making sheets and bars for those purposes where the highest quality is required.

The region to the northward, extending to Perm and Ekaterinburg, abounds in gold, copper, malachite, lapis-lazuli, and other precious metals and minerals, all of which are being extensively mined and worked. At the former place, which is located on the Kama River, there are immense government works, employing over 2,000 men. It has one of the largest steam hammers in the world, and the foundry turns out steel cannon of unusual size and quality. They also manufacture firearms here, said to equal anything manufactured in Europe or America, and sidearms of unsurpassed excellence. It is from these localities in the Ural Mountains that what is known in America as "Russian iron" comes.

In Zlatoust, also, there are great government works for the manufacture of steel cannon and other arms. Cutlery of various kinds is made in large quantities, and it is said the swords are of exceptional quality. There are also produced marvellous castings from pig-iron. The statuettes cast out of this metal are marvels of artistic beauty and technical skill. Their quality, it is said, is due largely to the superior moulding sand produced in this region, but I am of the impression that it is more properly attributable to the rare qualities of the iron, which seems to flow with unusual fluidity, producing castings so delicate in detail as to be scarcely distinguishable from bronze. These art products are rapidly finding their way into European markets.

Shortly after leaving Zlatoust we pass a large stone monument erected at some distance from the railway. On one side is, in Russian, the word "Europe," and on the opposite side "Asia." It marks the boundary between Europe and Asia. One, however, does not need a monumental token to learn that he is passing from one great geographical division to another, for the sparce population, uncultivated lands, and general wild aspect only too clearly indicate that he has suddenly entered Siberia.

The eastern slope of the Ural Mountains is, for a space, more abrupt than the western, but it soon enters upon a gentle slope that continues until it touches the western edge of that great level plain which seems to stretch indefinitely to the east. On leaving the summit we joint the Isset, a small river, whose course we closely follow until it deflects to the northeast, becoming a tributary to the Irtish, itself one of the main branches of the great Obi River. Fifty miles farther on in the plains we come to Tscheljabinsk, where ends the first section of this great railway.

It may not be amiss to give the results of my observations respecting this year's crop conditions in the country through which I have passed, constituting as it does the finest cereal region in all European Russia. From a deficiency in rainfall, extending continuously over a period of almost four months, an alarming shortage of all crops, even grass, is certain to exist throughout an immense area, reaching through several hundred miles east and west, and perhaps five hundred miles north and south — an area about equally bisected by the Volga River and the railway line throughout this vast tract. This includes five of the largest and agriculturally the most important governments of Russia, containing from ten to twelve million people, and it is almost certain that enough cannot be raised this year to meet the wants of more than one-fourth of its population.

. . .

The government of Samara (said to be twice as large as Belgium) lies in the centre of the stricken region, and here already much distress has developed. I learn, on passing through, that the Czar has just given 500,000 rubles for the relief of the sufferers. The region over which the drought extends is the finest wheat region in Eastern Russia, and in ordinary seasons supplies a large surplus for export to foreign countries. I was informed by a Russian officially connected with the ministry of railways, that they would probably have to bring into this region where the shortage has occurred, from other sections of Russia, from fifty to eighty million bushels of grain, to supply the necessary food to the inhabitants and seed to the farmers. The self-sustaining power of this great empire is fully made manifest by the fact that while so serious a shortage has occurred in one great section, in many others, such as the

Crimea, the Caucasus, and the newly settled lands in Siberia, abundant and even excessive crops are reported, so that not only can the deficiency be fully supplied from her own home resources, but there will be left over a fair surplus for export.

* * *

The railway on leaving Tscheljabinsk takes an almost due easterly course, which it varies by a few points only until beyond the Yenisei River, a distance of about 2,000 miles, when it deflects to the southeast for nearly 800 miles, until it reaches Lake Baikal, only a short distance from the China border. It follows somewhat closely the old post route from Moscow to Irkutsk, running via Zlatoust, where at Tomsk it joins the more northern post route down the Tobol and Irtish rivers to Tiumen, and thence over the Ural Mountains to Perm and Nijni Novgorod to Moscow.

Curiously enough, the railway follows much the same course as that by which in ancient times the Huns, Tartars, and Moguls made through Southern Russia their numerous and dreaded incursions into Europe.

* * *

A sufficiently accurate general description of the Siberian railroad and its various appointments would, I think, be covered by the statement that it is fully equal to either the Union or Northern Pacific Railway, although the oldest portion east of Tscheljabinsk has been in operation scarcely two years, and the newer portions a few months only. The track is well laid, the grading firm and thorough, and the bridges almost wholly of iron, save a few of the original and temporary ones, which are rapidly being replaced by those of stone and iron. Those over the Irtish, Ishim, Obi, Tobol, Omsk, and Tom rivers I found to be well constructed, of the best materials and most approved modern pattern.

The stations, always artistic and picturesque, and never the same style, are neat, comfortable, of good size, and substantial, fully equal to the average depot on the New York Central or Pennsylvania. I noticed that recent surveys have been made along the line, and on inquiry was informed that they are preparing to build one or more additional tracks. This is a very timely provision as the road is already taxed far beyond its capacity.

A Russian Village in the 1890s

The following description of a peasant village in northern Russia was written after a residence of several years in Russia. Interesting rather than especially significant, it will help to build up a mental image of the Russian people as they were at the end of the Nineteenth century. The source is: Wishaw, F. J., Out of Doors in Tsarland. A Record of the Scenes and Doings of a Wanderer in Russia. London: Longmans, Green and Co., 1893. Pp. 1–19.

Any one journeying through Russia must be struck by the exact similarity of each village to its fellows. He will see the same tumble-down wooden huts extending for a quarter of a mile on each side of the road, with the same solitary two-storied edifice in the centre of the village — the abode of the tradesman of the place, the same lean dogs will come out of the houses as he passes, to contest his right of way; the same herd of cows, at the same hour of the afternoon, will crowd down the street, monopolising every inch of the muddy road (there is no footpath), to his extreme discomfort and no slight alarm; and the same cowherd will wait until the stranger's ear is exactly opposite the end of his long pipe, and will then emit a nondescript sound which will make that stranger wish he had never been born, or at all events that he had been born deaf. It is this sound which brings the cows out of he wonders what hiding-places behind the huts. As the herd moves, wading slowly through the deep mud along the road, each house or yard seems to shoot out its contribution of one cow, or two cows, or six, according to the wealth of the owner, until the last hut is passed, when the whole herd turns abruptly to the side, gets over the ditch as best it can, and distributes itself over the communal pasture-land.

The casual passer-by will not see much of the inhabitants of the village unless he happens to wander through it late in the evening of a summer's day. Then indeed he will find it full of life and sound. A band of girls, all dressed in picturesque colours, are to be seen sitting upon a bench outside one of the houses, singing at the top of their voices, not in unison, but taking at least two and sometimes three parts, the first voice singing about an octave higher than ordinary sopranos can conveniently manage. Further on a band of men will be found standing or lounging about and enjoying similar vocal exercise, their higher tones being exceedingly nasal, but the basses excellent. All these good people are endowed by nature with the gift of harmony. A man with a bass voice can always improvise a bass or sing a second to a higher voice. As for the children of the village, they will have been hounded away to bed at this time of night; but earlier in the day they may be seen playing out in the road, generally with a species of knucklebones, or with a kind of ninepins or skittles played with clubs, which are thrown at the uprights, instead of a ball. The boys make marvellously good shots with these clubs, knocking over a small ninepin with certainty at a distance of twenty or thirty yards. The rival singing bands occasionally leave their seats and parade the village street, never mixing with one another, but occasionally indulging in loud personalities of a humorous but somewhat unrefined nature as they meet or pass.

Let us pay a visit, reader, you and I, to a typical village: let us choose Ruchee, which is not far from St. Petersburg. I shall prove an excellent guide here, for I have visited this hamlet many and many a time, and know it well. In one of yonder huts dwells a gamekeeper, one Ivan, who looks after the shooting interests of the district. Ivan is a great friend of mine, and is employed by an English gentleman, therefore you must not be surprised to find one *moujik* dressed differently from his fellows in this village of Ruchee. He will turn out when we reach his hut, for one of the children whose noses are for ever glued to the window-pane will cry out "Get up, father, here are the English *Barins!*" and when he appears you will see something like a costume!

But we have not reached the village yet. Yonder it lies; a long straight road, you see, as usual, with the houses built at uneven distances along each side. In the middle of the village the road takes a dip, down and up again, the lowest point being an extremely rickety bridge, consisting of wooden planks insecurely nailed to piles driven into the bed of the tiny stream which it spans. Beyond this village we can just see the first houses of another, Mourino. Mourino possesses a church, and is a *selo*, or chief of a group of villages. About Mourino I shall have more to say by-and-by.

Here is Ruchee. A few yards before we reach the first hut is a post with a notice-board upon it. Let us read the legend if we can; it is rather indistinct:

RUCHEE,
46 souls.

That is all. We knew it was Ruchee; but what does 46 *souls* mean? A soul is a man, not a woman. Women have no souls, according to the code of the Russian official district tax-collectors, for whose benefit the post and its information exist. I hope my reader, if I have one, is not a lady; for I feel that I shall incur her odium as the purveyor of this shocking evidence of the ungallant quality of the official Russian mind. But alas! it is too true. In Russia, so the proverb says, there is but one soul to seven women. The taxgatherer, however, does not credit the ladies with even one seventh of a soul apiece, he ignores their claims altogether; in his eyes they do not exist, they are nonentities. The men have all the souls, for they pay all the taxes. Those who pay no taxes have no souls. But whether they have no souls because they pay no taxes, or whether they pay no taxes because they have no souls, I have not yet found a tax-gatherer sufficiently well-informed to tell me.

Well, then, Ruchee claims to contain 46 souls within its limits. A manchild, so soon as born, is a soul; so that some of these 46 souls may be infants. On the other hand, Ruchee may be teeming with a population of hundreds of girls and women, but it can only boast of 46 souls, for the poor girls do not count. I ought to explain, however, that the above estimate of the population of Ruchee dates from the last Government revision, perhaps ten years since. Therefore other souls may have been born to the village, which may of course contain more or less souls by this time, according to the balance of male births and deaths for the period. It is necessary to set up these official statistical posts because the total amount of tax imposed upon the village, as its payment for the use of the communal land, depends upon the number of "souls" alive in the village at the date of revision. The distribution of the land among the souls is looked after within the village itself, as I shall presently explain, without official interference from outside, and is guided by considerations of equity rather than by strict rule. For it is evident that to saddle a family of small male babies with the actual share of land and concomitant taxes for which as "souls" they are responsible, would be as unfair as to expect a widow with one son and five strapping daughters to live on the single share of land to which alone, as possessing but one soul among them, they are entitled.

But let us enter the village. What a barking of dogs greets us as we do so! Every hut seems to have contributed a cur, and every cur looks as if he would eat us up if he had time for anything besides barking. A stone deftly aimed produces a wonderful effect upon these Russian village dogs. They are not brave. Only one is struck, but his sorrow is pitiful to witness as he disappears full gallop down the street, going very much faster and farther than the occasion demands — the sight, and the pathetic sound of his yelps, quickly discouraging the rest, who accept the inevitable and trot home again with a mourning aspect about the tail. Three small children rush shrieking and shouting from the first hut as we pass it, but stop dead on seeing us. They stare in silence until we have proceeded ten yards or so, when they set up a chorus of "Barin, dai kopaykoo" (Give us a kopeck, Mister).

Between the houses we can catch glimpses of the fields, which seem to be divided with mathematical accuracy into long strips. Upon these strips of land red-shirted peasants and women are hard at work, for, strange to say, it is not a holiday, and the villagers are actually up and about. At least half the week in Russia is "holiday" of so pronounced a kind that it is considered wicked to do work of any sort. As it generally takes a day or so to recover from a Russian holiday, which is spent brawling over vodka, in the village *traktir*, little time remains for work. The hay is just ready for cutting, and we may observe that out of yonder huge field of waving grasses an occasional strip is already cut, one patch here and another there. For this is one of the communal fields, and is divided in strips among the "souls" of the village, each soul possessing one, which he may generally cultivate how he pleases. The village owns three or four of these large fields, each subdivided as this one; but one is probably devoted to the growing of oats, another to a crop of rye, this one, as we have seen, is hay, and the fourth is probably lying fallow. The peasants will generally prefer to grow one crop over the entire field, each cutting his own portion when he thinks fit, or when he is not drunk, if he can find a day under the latter category. But if he prefers it he may grow a patch of oats in the middle of the hay-field, or a patch of potatoes amid the rye strips of his neighbours. Shall we enter one of these houses in order to see what ideas the moujiks and their families have as to making themselves comfortable at home? Very well, let us choose my friend Ivan's then. Here it is, no better than its neighbours, though Ivan receives his wages of ten roubles per month regularly, and is therefore richer than his fellows by about £12 a year. This consideration has not apparently induced him to mend his broken window, however, for the hole is stopped up with a piece of one of his wife's old dresses (I remember seeing her dressed in that very print a year or two ago). One of the children is of course staring out of the window — there! she has seen us. Now Ivan will appear. Here he is, rubbing his eyes with the back of his hand, and yawning cavernously. (Ivan! you have been drinking, little father! I shall think twice about presenting you with a rouble "for tea" next time you carry my game-bag after the ptarmigan.)

What an object the man is! On his shaggy head, which is covered with long yellow hair, he wears a soft English hat, the gift of his British employer. Over his broad shoulders is a Norfolk jacket, derived from the same source. So far he is an Englishman, though a disreputable one! From the coat downwards he is a moujik. His feet are encased in a pair of long boots, into which are tucked the ends of a pair of baggy cotton trousers. From beneath the Norfolk jacket protrude the tails of a red shirt, which tails are not tucked into the trousers, but are worn outside. There is a saying in Russia that so long as a Russian wears his shirt outside he remains honest; but when he begins to tuck it in, like a civilised Christian, he is no longer to be trusted. There may be some truth in this. The *chinovniks* and their tribe, being higher up the social ladder, have learned, among other arts, that of dressing themselves according to the usages of modern society. Whether the ancestors of these gentlemen ever were honest in their red-shirted days I am not in a position to state; but this I know, that their descendants are very far from it now. On the other hand, Ivan, who wears his red shirt in a manner which should have ensured his strict adherence to the paths of truth and righteousness, is a very considerable liar. I may say that I have known other moujiks not altogether immaculate. What then becomes of the proverb?

Ivan graciously permits us to enter and explore his domain. In the porch, reached by falling over three decayed steps into a pit, and then getting out of it and climbing, by a gymnastic effort, upon the platform which the steps originally led to — in this porch, hanging from a hook at the top, is a kind of earthen vessel something like a teapot, with two handles and a short spout. This is the family lavatory. When a member of the family desires to wash — which happens on very rare occasions — he stands underneath the water-vessel and tilts a very small quantity of the liquid into one hand. He then divides the water impartially between his two hands and applies both to his face. Part of his countenance thus receives a little attention from one or other of the damp hands, and lo! he is clean — a misleading expression signifying that his ablutions are over for several days. There is another method of washing, but my pen revolts from a description of it. Enough to mention that the mouth is applied to the spout of the teapot, and all further washing is done with the water thus procured. In a word, the Russian moujik considers his weekly or fortnightly steam-bath quite as much in the way of personal cleansing as is good for him. I shall describe the village bath in its proper place, but meanwhile we are keeping Ivan standing outside his door, ready to show us in. As we enter the house three dogs rush out and nearly knock us over, whining and jumping on us with every demonstration of delight. You may see at once that these are English dogs. They belong to Ivan's employer, my old friend A., and are under the impression that we have come to take them out shooting. They know at a glance — perhaps I should say at a sniff — that we are Britons, and are looking about for our guns. Lie down, Bruce and York! we have come to see your house, there is no shooting to be done to-day. These dogs live with Ivan on terms of equality, and feed rather better than he does; but then Ivan gets plenty of vodka, and they do not. Ivan's is a one-roomed house — that is, there is but one room for general use. There is indeed a sort of black hole, opposite, quite dark and very small, where Ivan keeps his poultry, snowshoes, and other articles out of place in a drawing-room. The living room is a good size, perhaps fifteen feet by thirteen. It has two small windows, with four panes in each. Of these eight panes six are intact or nearly so, the seventh is half gone, the eighth entirely so — the latter being stopped up with a portion of Mrs. Ivan's old print skirt, as I have already mentioned. Round two sides of the rooms runs a narrow bench, about a foot in width. In front of this, at the corner, is the table. In another corner of the room is the stove, a huge brick structure reaching almost to the ceiling, five feet in breadth and four feet deep, and having a lower portion jutting out from the side to a length of six feet or so. This branch establishment is used by the family to sleep upon, and a nice warm bed it makes. As for the stove itself, a description of its working may be of interest to the reader. The door of the stove is a foot or so from the ground, and opens into a huge empty cavern formed by the whole of the inside of the stove. Into this logs of wood are thrust, in quantities, and ignited. This is only the beginning, and the heat of the wood while burning is a mere trifle. When the logs are reduced to red embers the door of the stove is shut up tight and the chimney securely closed. By this means all the heat is kept in the stove, which soon becomes a veritable "scorcher," and retains its heat for nearly twenty-four hours. But woe to the inhabitants of the house if the chimney be closed before the wood shall have been properly consumed, for speedy suffocation is their certain fate — death if they happen to be asleep, terrible nausea and sickness if awake and able to whisk off the iron covering which closes the chimney, in time to save their lives. I have spoken to an English gentleman who once nearly fell a victim to suffocation through the carelessness of a Russian servant. He was passing the night at a shooting-box near St. Petersburg, and, the cold being intense, had instructed the keeper, on retiring, to enter his room at six in the morning and relight the stove, in case it should have cooled down by that time. The keeper obeyed these instructions to the letter, but closed the chimney before the wood had been sufficiently reduced. At half-past seven my friend was awakened by the most violent headache he had ever experienced, accompanied by terrible sickness. He barely had strength to crawl out of bed and stagger into the fresh air — thus saving his life — when he fell insensible in the snow. There he was found shortly afterwards half-frozen and very ill, but alive enough to address remarks to that offending keeper which were almost sufficiently strong to thaw the snow in which he found himself outstretched.

Three small children climb down from the top of the stove as we enter Ivan's room, and stand staring up at us. On the table there is a *samovar* hissing comfortably, and Mrs. Ivan smiles and bows over it. She has been cutting hunks from a large round loaf of black bread, for this is dinner-time. There is also a smoked herring lying on the table, half wrapped in a truly horrible scrap of newspaper. Probably Ivan will get the whole of this dainty morsel, for he is a "soul" and must be fed up; black bread will do excellently well for the women, who have no souls to support. No, thank you, Mrs. Ivan, we won't take any tea, though it is very kind of you to offer it. As far as I can see, you only possess one tumbler, and that a remarkably unclean one. What would the Soul do, if we used his only tumbler? You suggest, reader, that Ivan would go to the *kabak* and drink vodka, and so he would; but he will do this anyhow, for we shall probably give him twenty kopecks for his services in showing us over his establishment, and Ivan's money all goes one way. There are small lumps of sugar lying promiscuously about the table. These are not placed in the tea, but are nibbled at before drinking in order to sweeten each mouthful as taken.

A few coppers will make those small children very happy; the money will be spent upon biscuits, and will go a long way.

Ivan's room is not too clean, and as for the scent thereof, well, if it were not for the half-broken pane of glass it would be still worse, and that is all we can say for it.

There is no second story, but there is a garret, under the roof. This is reached by a ladder from outside, and is used by Ivan for drying his clothes, on the rare occasion of a wash; for hiding away a store of grain, if he has managed to accumulate such; and for putting away sundry household rubbish. Behind the house is a yard, knee-deep in mud, and at the end of the yard a shed. Half of this shed is used as a receptacle for Ivan's cart, plough, and sledge; the other half is the dwelling-place of the cows and horses, when these are at home; but the cows are out most of the day and night in the summer-time, on the pasture-lands, while the horses, at work during the day, herd with the cows at night.

So much for Ivan's establishment, which is the facsimile of every other moujik-home in the village, with the exception of that of the trader, whose house is much larger, and is built in two stories, towering thus over its poorer neighbours like a big policeman among a crowd of urchins. It will repay us to look in for a moment upon Abram Timofeyevitch Kapustyin, the powerful and wealthy individual who dispenses bread, vodka, herrings, calico prints, red shirts, and biscuits to the peasant folk of Ruchee. This gentleman is seated at a small table in his shop; he is drinking tea with lemon in it, and is engaged in conversation with a moujik, who turns out to be *Starost*, or elder, of the village. Of the latter, and of his office, I shall speak presently. As for the trader, he is a sleek, well-to-do, comfortable-looking personage. His power in the place is enormous, for every moujik owes him money, and depends upon him, not only for his daily supply of black bread (when the home-grown stock of rye comes to an end), but for his vodka, his clothes, everything he needs. This individual is often a large landholder, though a stranger to the place; for peasants who have fallen heavily into his debt, thanks, generally, to the national partiality for vodka, are glad to wipe off a portion of their indebtedness, and by so doing become qualified to consume further *vedra* of vodka on "tick," by letting their allotments of land.

We will take a cup of tea at Abram Timofeyevitch's invitation, and buy a red shirt and a startingly coloured handkerchief or two to show our friends at home. The tea is good tea before it is drowned by Abram Timofeyevitch. How long he has been drinking from this one decoction in the small teapot I know not; but this I know, that his tea is the colour of the very palest sherry. We drink it out of tumblers and bite our sugar dry. The tea, or rather the very slightly bewitched water, is frightfully hot, and the bit of lemon floating in it gets terribly in the way as we try to dodge it in order to drink the scorching fluid. Abram will continue to replenish your tumbler until you sigh, turn the tumbler upside down, rise from your place, and shake hands with him as a sign that you have had enough. You must also shake hands with every other individual who has assisted in emptying Abram's huge *samovar*, thanking them "for their company."

There are several groups of peasants drinking tea at other tables; some are taking vodka and are rather noisy, but there is not much consumption of strong liquor at this time of day. At night the apartment will present a very different aspect. There will be such a babel of sound — singing and dancing and general uproar on the part of the Souls of the place — that were we to pass the house at a distance of half a mile we should conclude that this village must be the veritable home of Bacchus and his satellites. The shop itself is filthy, the counter being covered with a disorderly array of small bottles containing vodka, piles of black bread, many of the loaves being half cut, a keg of herrings whose odour is making a good fight for supremacy with that of the all-pervading vodka, some dishes of black-looking biscuits, which were once white but have lost their youth and good looks waiting for a purchaser among the children, who have evidently had no harvest of coppers lately, and a tub of Finnish butter. The handkerchiefs and calico prints are not displayed for sale in this room, but are sold in a similar shop adjoining; if you peep in, reader, you will see several women handling these articles and haggling over the price. Nothing, no article of commerce, ever changes hands in Russia without a bargain.

Pobiedonostsev's Philosophy of Reaction

Konstantine Petrovich Pobiedonostsev, tutor and adviser to the last two Romanov tsars, affiliate of the Pan-Slavs and Procurator-General of the Holy Synod, possessed considerable power and great influence upon the Russian government of his day. The outstanding Russian protagonist of the theory and the practice of extreme conservatism, Pobiedonostsev was cordially detested by all Russian liberals as a black reactionary. Certainly his influence on both Alexander III and Nicholas II was staunchly anti-liberal and anti-democratic. An able scholar, he was the leading philosopher of reaction. The following passages are typical of his views and his teachings. The source is: Pobyedonostseff, K. P. (R. Ç. Long, Translator), Reflections of a Russian Statesman. *London: Grant Richards, 1898. Passim et seriatim. (The original Russian edition was titled,* Moscow Conversations.*)*

For, however powerful the State may be, its power is based alone upon identity of religious profession with the people; the faith of the people sustains it; when discord once appears to weaken this identity, its foundations are sapped, its power dissolves away. In spiritual sympathy with its rulers a people may bear many heavy burdens, may concede much, and surrender many of its privileges and rights. In one domain alone the State must not demand concession, or the people concede, and that is the domain where every believer, and all *together, sink the foundations* of their spiritual existence and bind themselves with eternity. There are depths in this domain to which the secular power dare not, and must not, descend, lest it strike at the roots of faith in each and all.

. . .

The oldest and most familiar system of relationship of Church to State is the system of Established or State Churches. Out of the multitude of religions, the State adopts and recognizes as the true faith one, which it maintains and protects exclusively, to the prejudice of all remaining Churches and religions. This prejudice in general means that the remaining Churches are not recognised as true, or entirely true, but practically it is expressed in many forms, with innumerable shadows, from non-recognition and alienation to persecution. In all cases where this system is in force the estranged faiths submit to more or less diminution in honour and prerogative as compared with the established faith. The State must not be the representative of the material interests of society alone; were it so, it would deprive itself of religious forces and would abandon its spiritual community with the people. The stronger will the State be, the more important in the eyes of the masses, the more firmly it stands as their spiritual representative.

Under these conditions alone will the sentiment of respect for the law, and of confidence in the power of the State, be maintained and strengthened among the people. No considerations for the safety of the State, for its prosperity and advantage, no moral principle even, is itself sufficient to strengthen the bonds between the people and its rulers; for the moral principle is never steadfast, and it loses its fundamental base when it is bereft of the sanction of religion. This force of cohesion will, without doubt, be lost to the State which, in the name of impartial relationship to every religious belief, cuts itself loose from all. The confidence of the people in its rulers is founded on faith — that is, not only on identity of religious profession, but on the simple conviction that its rulers have faith themselves and rule according to it. Even the heathen and Mahometan peoples have more confidence and respect for a Government which stands on the firm principles of faith — whatever that faith may be — than for a Government which acknowledges no faith, and is indifferent to all.

. . . The system of a "Free Church in a Free State" is founded on abstract principles and hypotheses. It embodies not the principle of belief, but the principle of religious indifferentism, and it is associated with doctrines which inculcate, not tolerance and respect, but a manifest or tacit contempt for religion, as an outworn factor of the psychical development of individual and national life. In the abstract conception of this system, which is the product of the latest rationalism, the Church appears as a political institution of abstract construction, with a definite aim; or as a private corporation established likewise with a definite aim, as other corporations recognised by the State. The conception of this aim is abstract also, for on it are reflected the diverse shades associated with one or the other conception of religion, from abstract respect for religion, as the highest element of psychical life, to fanatical contempt for it as the basest factor, and as an element of danger and disintegration. Thus, in the construction of this system we see at the first balance the ambiguity and indistinctness of its fundamental principles and propositions.

. . . Thus the free State may decree that the free Church concerns it not; but the free Church, if it be truly founded on faith, will not accept this proposition, and will not endure indifferent relations to the free State. The Church cannot abdicate its influence on civil and social life, and the greater its activity — the stronger its consciousness of internal working forces, the less is it possible for it to tolerate indifferent relations to the State; nor can such relations be tolerated if the Church is not to abjure its duties and abandon its divine mission. On the Church lies the duty of teaching and direction. To the Church pertains the administration of the sacraments, and the performance of ceremonies associated with the gravest acts of civil life. In this activity the Church of necessity is brought into constant contact with public and civil life: of this, marriage and education are sufficient instances. Thus, as the State, denying the Church, assumes control exclusively of the civil part of such affairs and renounces all authority in the spiritual-religious part, the Church assumes the functions surrendered by the State, and, in separation from it, takes possession, little by little but fully and exclusively, of those moral and religious influences which constitute for the State an indispensable element of strength. The State remains master alone of material and, it may be, of intellectual forces, but both one and the other are vain when unsupported by the forces of faith. Little by little, therefore, instead of the imagined equality of influence of the State and Church in a political alliance, inequality and antagonism appear. The position in any case is an abnormal one, which must lead either to the predominance of the Church over the apparently dominant State, or to revolution.

Such are the hidden dangers of the system, so lauded by Liberal theorists, of severance of Church and State. The system of State or Established Churches has many defects, many inconveniences, and many difficulties; it does not preclude the possibility of antagonism or conflict. But it is absurd to suppose that it has outlived its time, and that the formula of Cavour is the only key to the solution of all the difficulties of the most difficult of questions. The formula of Cavour is the fruit of that political doctrinarianism which regards all questions of faith merely as political questions of the equalisation of rights. It lacks spiritual insight, as lacked it another famous political formula, Liberty, Equality, and Fraternity, which to the present day weighs upon superficial minds with a fatal burden. In both cases the passionate apostles of freedom mistake in assuming freedom in equality. Bitter experience has proven a hundred times that freedom does not depend from equality, and that equality is in no wise freedom. It is equally absurd to believe that the equalisation of Churches and religions before the State must result in freedom on belief. The history of modern times demonstrates that freedom and equality are not identical, and that freedom in no way depends from equality.

What is this freedom by which so many minds are agitated, which inspires so many insensate actions, so many wild speeches, which leads the people so often to misfortune? In the democratic sense of the word, freedom is the right of political power, or, to express it otherwise, the right to participate in the government of the State. This universal aspiration for a share in government has no constant limitations, and seeks no definite issue, but incessantly extends, so that we might apply to it the words of the ancient poet about dropsy: *crescit indulgens sibi*. For ever extending its base, the new Democracy now aspires to universal suffrage — a fatal error, and one of the most remarkable in the history of mankind. By this means, the political power so passionately demanded by Democracy would be shattered into a number of infinitesimal bits, of which each citizen acquires a single one. What will he do with it, then? how will he employ it? In the result it has undoubtedly been shown that in the attainment of this aim Democracy violates its sacred formula of "Freedom indissolubly joined with Equality." It is shown that this apparently equal distribution of "freedom" among all involves the total destruction of equality. Each vote, representing an inconsiderable fragment of power, by itself signifies nothing; an aggregation of votes alone has a relative value. The result may be likened to the general meetings of shareholders in public companies. By themselves individuals are ineffective, but he who controls a number of these fragmentary forces is master of all power, and directs all decisions and dispositions. We may well ask in what consists the superiority of Democracy. Everywhere the strongest man becomes master of the State; sometimes a fortunate and resolute general, sometimes a monarch or administrator with knowledge, dexterity, a clear plan of action, and a determined will. In a Democracy, the real rulers are the dexterous manipulators of votes, with their placemen, the mechanics who so skilfully operate the hidden springs which move the puppets in the arena of democratic elections. Men of this kind are ever ready with loud speeches lauding equality; in reality, they rule the people as any despot or military dictator might rule it. The extension of the right to participate in elections is regarded as progress and as the conquest of freedom by democratic theorists, who hold that the more numerous the participants in political rights, the greater is the probability that all will employ this right in the interests of the public welfare, and for the increase of the freedom of the people. Experience proves a very different thing. The history of mankind bears witness that the most necessary and fruitful reforms — the most durable measures — emanated from the supreme will of statesmen, or from a minority enlightened by lofty ideas and deep knowledge, and that, on the contrary, the extension of the representative principle is accompanied by an abasement of political ideas and the vulgarisation of opinions in the mass of the electors. It shows also that this extension — in great States — was inspired by secret aims to the centralization of power, or led directly to dictatorship. In France, universal suffrage was suppressed with the end of the Terror, and was re-established twice merely to affirm the autocracy of the two Napoleons. In Germany, the establishment of universal suffrage served merely to strengthen the high authority of a famous statesman who had acquired popularity by the success of his policy. What its ultimate consequences will be, Heaven only knows!

.   .   .

Among the falsest of political principles is the principle of the sovereignty of the people, the principle that all power issues from the people, and is based upon the national will — a principle which has unhappily become more firmly established since the time of the French Revolution. Thence proceeds the theory of Parliamentarism, which, up to the present day, has deluded much of the so-called "intelligence," and unhappily infatuated certain foolish Russians. It continues to maintain its hold on many minds with the obstinacy of a narrow fanaticism, although every day its falsehood is exposed more clearly to the world.

In what does the theory of Parliamentarism consist? It is supposed that the people in its assemblies makes its own laws, and elects responsible officers to execute its will. Such is the ideal conception. Its immediate realisation is impossible. The historical development of society necessitates that local communities increase in numbers and complexity; that separate races be assimilated, or, retaining their polities and languages, unite under a single flag, that territory extend indefinitely: under such conditions direct government by the people is impracticable. The people must, therefore, delegate its right of power to its representatives, and invest them with administrative autonomy. These representatives in turn cannot govern immediately, but are compelled to elect a still smaller number of trustworthy persons — ministers — to whom they entrust the preparation and execution of the laws, the apportionment and collection of taxes, the appointment of subordinate officials, and the disposition of the militant forces.

In the abstract this mechanism is quite symmetrical: for its proper operation many conditions are essential. The working of the political machine is based on impersonal forces constantly acting and completely balanced. It may act successfully only when the delegates of the people abdicate their personalities; when on the benches of Parliament sit mechanical fulfillers of the people's behests; when the ministers of State remain impersonal, absolute executors of the will of the majority; when the elected representatives of the people are capable of understanding precisely, and executing conscientiously, the programme of activity, mathematically expressed, which has been delivered to them. Given such conditions the machine would work exactly, and would accomplish its purpose. The law would actually embody the will of the people! administrative measures would actually emanate from Parliament; the pillars of the State would rest actually on the elective assemblies, and each citizen would directly and consciously participate in the management of public affairs.

Such is the theory. Let us look at the practice. Even in the classic countries of Parliamentarism it would satisfy not one of the conditions enumerated. The elections in no way express the will of the electors. The popular representatives are in no way restricted by the opinions of their constituents, but are guided by their own views and considerations, modified by the tactics of their opponents. In reality, ministers are autocratic, and they rule, rather than are ruled by, Parliament. They attain power, and lose power, not by virtue of the will of the people, but through immense personal influence, or the influence of a strong party which places them in power, or drives them from it. They dispose of the force and resources of the nation at will, they grant immunities and favours, they maintain a multitude of idlers at the expense of the people, and they fear no censure while they enjoy the support in Parliament of a majority which they maintain by the distribution of bounties from the rich tables which the State has put at their disposal. In reality, the ministers are as irresponsible as the representatives of the people. Mistakes, abuse of power, and arbitrary acts, are of daily occurrence, yet how often do we hear of the grave responsibility of a minister? It may be once in fifty years a minister is tried for his crimes, with a result contemptible when compared with the celebrity gained by the solemn procedure. . . .

Thus the representative principle works in practice. The ambitious man comes before his fellow-citizens, and strives by every means to convince them that he more than any other is worthy of their confidence. What motives impel him to this quest? It is hard to believe that he is impelled by disinterested zeal for the public good. . . .

On the day of polling few give their votes intelligently; these are the individuals, influential electors whom it has been worth while to convince in private. The mass of electors, after the practice of the herd, votes for one of the candidates nominated by the committees. Not one exactly knows the man, or considers his character, his capacity, his convictions; all vote merely because they have heard his name so often. It would be vain to struggle against this herd. If a level-headed elector wished to act intelligently in such a grave affair, and not to give way to the violence of the committee, he would have to abstain altogether, or to give his vote for his candidate according to his conviction. However he might act, he could not prevent the election of the candidate favoured by the mass of frivolous, indifferent, and prejudiced electors.

In theory, the elected candidate must be the favourite of the majority; in fact, he is the favourite of a minority, sometimes very small, but representing an organised force, while the majority, like sand, has no coherence, and is therefore incapable of resisting the clique and the faction. In theory, the election favours the intelligent and capable; in reality, it favours the pushing and impudent. It might be thought that education, experience, conscientiousness in work, and wisdom in affairs, would be essential requirements in the candidate; in reality, whether these qualities exist or not, they are in no way needed in the struggle of the election, where the essential qualities are audacity, a combination of impudence and oratory, and even some vulgarity, which invariably acts on the masses; modesty, in union with delicacy of feeling and thought, is worth nothing. . . .

. . . What is a Parliamentary party? In theory, it is an alliance of men with common convictions, joining forces for the realisation of their views in legislation and administration. But this description applies only to small parties; the large party, which alone is an effective force in Parliament, is formed under the influence only of personal ambition, and centres itself around one commanding personality. By nature, men are divided into two classes — those who tolerate no power above them, and therefore of necessity strive to rule others; and those who by their nature dread the responsibility inseparable from independent action, and who shrink from any resolute exercise of will. These were born for submission, and together constitute a herd, which follows the men of will and resolution, who form the minority. Thus the most talented persons submit willingly, and gladly entrust to stronger hands the control of affairs and the moral responsibility for their direction. Instinctively they seek a leader, and become his obedient instruments, inspired by the conviction that he will lead them to victory — and, often, to spoil. Thus all the important actions of Parliament are controlled by the leaders of the party, who inspire all decision, who lead in combat, and profit by victory. The public sessions are no more than a spectacle for the mass. Speeches are delivered to sustain the fiction of Parliamentarism, but seldom a speech by itself affects the decision of Parliament in a grave affair. Speechmaking serves for the glory of orators, for the increase of their popularity, and the making of their careers; only on rare occasions does it affect the distribution of votes. Majorities and minorities are usually decided before the session begins. Such is the complicated mechanism of the Parliamentary farce; such is the great political lie which dominates our age. . . .

Such is the Parliamentary institution, exalted as the summit and crown of the edifice of State. It is sad to think that even in Russia there are men who aspire to the establishment of this falsehood among us; that our professors glorify to their young pupils representative government as the ideal of political science; that our newspapers pursue it in their articles and feuilletons, under the name of justice and order, without troubling to examine without prejudice the working of the parliamentary machine. Yet even where centuries have sanctified its existence, faith already decays; the Liberal intelligence exalts it, but the people groans under its despotism, and recognizes its falsehood. We may not see, but our children and grandchildren assuredly will see, the overthrow of this idol, which contemporary thought in its vanity continues still to worship. . . .

' . . . In our age the judgment of others has assumed an organised form, and calls itself Public Opinion. Its organ and representative is the Press. In truth, the importance of the Press is immense, and may be regarded as the most characteristic fact of our time — more characteristic even than our remarkable discoveries and inventions in the realm of technical science. No government, no law, no custom can withstand its destructive activity when, from day to day, through the course of years, the Press repeats and disseminates among the people its condemnations of institutions or of men.

What is the secret of this strength? Certainly not the novelties and sensations with which the newspaper is filled, but its declared policy — the political and philosophical ideas propagated in its articles, selection and classification of its news and rumours, and the peculiar illumination which it casts upon them. The newspaper has usurped the position of judicial observer of the events of the day; it judges not only the actions and words of men, but affects a knowledge of their unexpressed opinions, their intentions, and their enterprises; it praises and condemns at discretion; it incites some, threatens others; drags to the pillory one, and others exalts as idols to be adored and examples worthy of the emulation of all. In the name of Public Opinion it bestows rewards on some, and punishes others with the severity of excommunication. The question naturally occurs: Who are these representatives of this terrible power, Public Opinion? Whence is derived their right and authority to rule in the name of the community, to demolish existing institutions, and to proclaim new ideals of ethics and legislation?

But no one attempts to answer this question; all talk loudly of the liberty of the Press as the first and essential element of social well-being. Even in Russia, so libelled by the lying Press of Europe, such words are heard. Our so-called Slavophiles, with amazing inconsistency, share the same delusion, although their avowed object is to reform and renovate the institutions of their country upon a historic basis. Having joined the chorus of Liberals, in alliance with the propagandists of revolution, they proclaim exactly in the manner of the West: "Public Opinion — that is, the collective thought, guided by the natural love of right in all — is the final judge in all matters of public interest; therefore no restriction upon freedom of speech can be allowed, for such restriction can only express the tyranny of the minority over the will of the mass."

Such is a current proposition of the newest Liberalism. It is accepted by many in good faith, and there are few who, having troubled to analyse it, have discerned how it is based upon falsehood and self-deception.

It conflicts with the first principles of logic, for it is based on the fallacious premise that the opinions of the public and of the Press are identical.

To test the validity of this claim, it is only needful to consider the origin of newspapers, and the characters of their makers.

Any vagabond babbler or unacknowledged genius, any enterprising tradesman, with his own money or with the money of others, may found a newspaper, even a great newspaper. He may attract a host of writers and feuilletonists, ready to deliver judgment on any subject at a moment's notice; he may hire illiterate reporters to keep him supplied with rumours and scandals. His staff is then complete. From that day he sits in judgment on all the world, on ministers and administrators, on literature and art, on finance and industry. . . .

This phenomenon is worthy of close inspection, for we find in it the most incongruous product of modern culture, the more incongruous where the principles of the new Liberalism have taken root, where the sanction of election, the authority of the popular will, is needed for every institution, where the ruling power is vested in the hands of individuals, and derived from the suffrages of the majority in the representative assemblies. For the journalist with a power comprehending all things, requires no sanction. He derives his authority from no election, he receives support from no one. His newspaper becomes an authority in the State, and for this authority no endorsement is required. The man in the street may establish such an organ and exercise the concomitant authority with an irresponsibility enjoyed by no other power in the world. That this is in no way exaggeration there are innumerable proofs. How often have superficial and unscrupulous journalists paved the way for revolution, fomented irritation into enmity, and brought about desolating wars! For conduct such as this a monarch would lose his throne, a minister would be disgraced, impeached, and punished; but the journalist stands dry above the waters he has disturbed, from the ruin he has caused he rises triumphant, and briskly continues his destructive work.

This is by no means the worst. When a judge has power to dishonour us, to deprive us of our property and of our freedom, he receives his power from the hands of the State only after such prolonged labour and experience as qualify him for his calling. His power is restricted by rigourous laws, his judgments are subject to revision by higher powers, and his sentence may be altered or commuted. The journalist has the fullest power to defame and dishonour me, to injure my material interests, even to restrict my liberty by attacks which force me to leave my place of abode. These judicial powers he has usurped; no higher authority has conferred them upon him; he has never proven by examination his fitness to exercise them; he has in no way shown his trustworthiness or his impartiality; his court is ruled by no formal procedure; and from his judgment there lies no appeal.

. . . In human souls there exists a force of moral gravity which draws them one to another; and which, made manifest in the spiritual interaction of souls, answers an organic need. Without this force mankind would be as a heap of sand, without any bond, dispersed by every wind on every side. By this inherent force, without preparatory accord, are men united in society. It impels them out of the crowd of men to seek for leaders with whom to commune, whom to obey, and whose direction to seek. Inspired by a moral principle, this instinct acquires the value of a creative force, uniting and elevating the people to worthy deeds and to great endurance.

But for the purposes of civil society this free and accidental interaction is not enough. The natural instinct of man seeks for power in unbroken activity, to which the mass, with its varied needs, aspirations, and passions may submit; through which it may acquire the impulse of activity, and the principles of order; in which it may find amid all the subversions of wilfulness a standard of truth. Thus, by its nature, power is founded on truth, and inasmuch as truth has as its source the All-High God and His commandments written indelibly in the consciences of all, we find a justification in their deeper meaning of the words, "there is no power but of God."

These words are addressed to subjects, but they apply with equal force to power itself, and O, that all power might recognise their import! Power is great and terrible, because it is a sacred thing. This word *sacred (svyastchennui)* in its primitive signification means *elect (otdyelennui)*, dedicated to the service of God. Thus, power exists not for itself alone, but for the love of God; it is a service to which men are dedicated. Thence comes the limitless, terrible strength of power, and its limitless and terrible burden.

Its strength is unlimited, not in the material acceptation of the word, but in its spiritual meaning, because it is the strength of reason and of creation. The first act of creation was the appearance of the light and its separation from darkness. Thus, the first act of power must be the finding of truth and its discrimination from falsehood; on this is founded the faith of the people in power, and the gravitation towards it of all mankind. Many times and everywhere this faith has been deceived, but its fount remains intact, and cannot dry up, because without truth no man can live. From this also springs the creative force of power, the strength to attract just and rational men, to animate them and to inspire them to work and to great deeds. To power belongs the first and last word — it is the alpha and omega of human activity.

While humanity exists it will not cease to suffer, sometimes from power, sometimes from impotence. The violence, the abuse, the folly and selfishness of power raise rebellion. Deceived by their ideals of power, men seek to dispense with it, and to replace it by the authority of the law. This is a vain fancy. In the name of the law arise a multitude of unauthorised factions, which struggle for power, and the distribution of power leads to violence worse than that which went before. Thus poor humanity, searching for an ideal organisation, is borne on the waves of an infinite sea, without a guide, without a harbour in sight.

To live without power is impossible. After the need of communion the need of power is of all feelings most deeply rooted in the spiritual nature of man. Since the day duality entered into his soul, since the day the knowledge of good and evil was vouchsafed to him, and the love of good and justice rose in his soul in eternal conflict with evil and injustice, for him there has been no salvation save to seek sustenance and reconciliation in a high judge of this conflict; in a living incarnation of the principle of order and of truth. And, whatever may be the disenchantment, the betrayal, the afflictions which humanity has suffered from power, while men shall yearn for good and truth, and remember their helplessness and duality, they can never cease to believe in the ideal of power, and to repeat their efforts for its realisation. Today, as in ancient times, the foolish say in their hearts: There is no God, no truth, no good, no evil; and gather around them pupils equally foolish, proclaiming atheism and anarchy. But the great mass of mankind stands firm in its faith in the supreme principle of life, and, through tears and bloodshed, as the blind seeking a guide, seeks for power with imperishable hope, notwithstanding eternal betrayal and disillusion.

Thus the work of power is a work of uninterrupted usefulness, and in reality a work of renunciation. How strange these words must seem beside the current conception of power! It is natural, it would seem, for men to flee and to avoid renunciation. Yet all seek power, all aspire to it; for power men strive together, they resort to crime, they destroy one another, and when they attain power they rejoice and triumph. Power seeks to exalt itself, and words pass through our heads as something in no way concerning us, as Yet the immutable, only true ideal of power is embodied in the words of Christ: "Whosoever of you will be the chiefest shall be servant of all." These words pass through our heads as something in no way concerning us, as especially addressed to a vanished community in Palestine. In reality, they apply to all power, however great, which, in the depth of conscience, does not recognise that the higher its throne, the wider the sphere of its activity, the heavier must become its fetters, the more widely must open before it the roll of social evils, stained by the weeping of pity and woe, and the louder must sound the crying and sobbing of injustice which demands redress. The first necessity of power is faith in itself and in its mission. Happy is power when this faith is combined with a recognition of duty and of moral responsibility! Unhappy is it when it lacks this consciousness and leans upon itself alone! Then begins the decay which leads to loss of faith, and in the end to disintegration and destruction.

Power is the depository of truth, and needs, above all things, men of truth, of clear intellects, of strong understandings, and of sincere speech, who know the limits of yes and no, and never transcend them, whose thoughts develop clearly in their minds, and are clearly expressed by their words. Men of this nature only are the firm support of power, and its faithful delegates. Happy is the power which can distinguish such men, appreciate their merit, and firmly sustain them! Unhappy is the power which wearies of such natures, promoting men of complaisant character, flexible opinions, and flattering tongues!

. . .

Men in authority must always remember the dignity of power. Dignity once forgotten, power decays, and relations to subordinates are falsified.

With dignity is coincident, and should be inseparable, that simplicity which is necessary to impel subordinates to work, to inspire them with interest in their duties, and to maintain with them sincerity of relations. The consciousness of dignity engenders also freedom in relations to men. Power must be free within the limits of the law; being conscious of its worth, it need not consider the appearance it makes, the impressions it creates, or the conduct it should observe in its relations to men. But the consciousness of merit must be inseparable from the recognition of duty; as the recognition of duty is enfeebled, the consciousness of merit swells, till, swollen beyond measure, it degenerates to a disease which may be called the hypertrophy of power. As this disease advances on its course, power may fall into a moral obscurity, in which it considers itself as independent and as existing for itself alone. Then begins the disintegration of power.

While preserving the dignity of power, authority must not forget that it serves as a mirror and example for all its subordinates. As the man in authority conducts himself, so those who will succeed him are preparing to conduct themselves in their relations to others, in their methods of work, in their regard for their work, in their tastes, in their standards of propriety and impropriety. It would be wrong to imagine that power, when it takes off its robe of authority, may without danger mingle in the daily life of the crowd in the fair of human vanity.

Nevertheless, while cherishing his dignity, the leader must as steadfastly guard the dignity of his subordinates. His relations to them must be founded on trustfulness, for, in the absence of trustfulness, there can be no moral bond between him and them. He is a foolish man who fancies that he can know and judge all things without intermediaries and independently of the knowledge and experience of his subordinates; who wishes to decide all questions by his word and command, without recourse to the thoughts and opinions of those who stand directly beneath him. Such men, recognising their helplessness without the knowledge and experience of their subordinates, often end by becoming altogether dependent upon them. Still worse is the case of the leader who falls into the fatal habit of tolerating no objections or contradictions; and this is the attribute not only of narrow minds, but often of able and energetic, but vain and over-confident men. A conscientious worker must avoid everything absolute and arbitrary in his decision, the fruit of these is indifference — the poison of democracy. Power must never forget that papers and reports represent living men and living works, and that life itself demands and expects decisions and directions which conform with its nature. Truth must be in the leader himself, in his sincere, conscientious and practical views of work, and truth also corresponding to the social, moral, and economic conditions of the national life and the national history. Such truth is absent where the ruling principle of power is abstract theory, detached from life with its manifold conditions and needs.

The wider the field of the activity of the leader, the more complex the mechanism of government, the more he needs subordinates capable of work, and able to combine in single directions to a common end. Men are needed in all times and by all governments, but perhaps more than ever today. In our time governments must consider a multitude of forces now rising and affirming themselves — in science, in literature, in the criticism of public opinion, in social institutions with their independent interests. Ability to find and to choose men is the first essential attribute to power; the second is ability to direct them and to establish due discipline upon their activity.

The Imperial Bureaucracy

The graded officials of the Russian bureaucracy (chinoviki) were thoroughly hated by all revolutionaries and many liberals. From the time of Gogol's The Revisor, *the bureaucrats were traditionally and often deservedly the targets of many Russian writers. Stepniak (Kravchinski) who wrote this biting description of the chinoviki was an ardent revolutionary and the avowed enemy of the tsarist regime. The source is: Stepniak, op. cit., pp. 155, 158, 159, 163–166.*

What is a *tchinovnik?* It is a man convinced that were it not for his "prescriptions," "instructions," and "enjoinments" the world would go all askew, and the people would suddenly begin to drink ink instead of water, to put their breeches on their heads instead of on their legs, and to commit all sorts of other incongruities. As all his life is passed from his most tender youth upward in offices, amidst heaps of scribbled papers, in complete isolation from any touch with real life, the *tchinovnik* understands nothing, has faith in nothing but these papers. He is as desperately sceptical as regards human nature as a monk, and does not trust one atom to men's virtue, honesty, or truthfulness. There is nothing in the world which can be relied upon but scribbled papers, and he is their votary. . . .

Now, in modifying the system of rural self-government the St. Petersburg *tchinovniks* were inspired to transform this very modest and humble village elder into a diminutive *tchinovnik,* created in their own image and likeness. The task was not without its difficulties. The elder was as a rule deficient in the most essential qualification for his profession — he could not write! It was therefore necessary that he should be provided with a secretary, who could inscribe the paper to which he should affix his seal or his cross. This important person, the clerk, was generally a perfect stranger to the village, a man picked up from the streets. As the law must needs give him extensive powers, it was all the more desirable that he should be easily controlled.

Our legislators proved equal to their task; for they blessed our villagers with a system of lawcourt proceedings which would do honour to much bigger places. To give some idea of their method, suffice it to say that the clerk of the *volost* is bound to supply his office with no less than sixty-five different registers, wherein to keep a record of the sixty-five various papers he has to issue daily, monthly, or quarterly. This was pushing their solicitude for the welfare of the countrymen rather too far, and taxing the clerk's powers rather too highly. In some of the larger *volosts* one man does not suffice for the task, and the peasants are compelled to maintain two, nay, even three· clerks. It is needless to add that such a complication of legal business can in no way keep an adroit clerk in check nor prevent the abuse of his power. The opposite is rather the case. The figure cut by the *pissar* or clerk in the annals of our new rural local government is a most unseemly one indeed. In its earlier period it was decidedly its blackest point.

The Government has undoubtedly had a hand in making the *pissar* such a disreputable character, by expressly prohibiting the engagement for this office of men of good education, — for fear of a revolution. All who have completed their studies at a gymnasium (college), much more those who have attended a high school, are precluded from filling this post. Only the more ignorant, those who have been expelled from college or who have never passed farther than through a primary school, have been trusted to approach the peasantry at such close quarters. Being generally self-seekers, and not particularly high-minded, they easily turned the peculiar position in which they were placed to their own advantage. The *pissar*, the interpreter of the law, and, more often than not, the only literate man in the district, could practically do whatever he chose. The elder, his nominal chief, in whom the word law inspired the same panic that it did in the breast of every peasant, and who was quite bewildered by the bureaucratic complication of his new administrative duties, was absolutely helpless in the *pissar's* hands. . . .

Local village government had as yet to be linked in hierarchial order with the whole of the administrative machine of the State. After having created, in the midst of the once democratic villages, a sort of *tchin*, it was necessary to discover another *tchin* to which to subject the newly-founded one.

The government, in the honeymoon of its liberalism, acted with sense and discretion in entrusting this function to the *mediators*, officers nominated conjointly by the ministry and by the election of the citizens. These *mediators*, elected from among the liberal and really well-intentioned part of the nobility, exercised their authority with moderation and wisdom, not so much as regarded subjection to the control of the *mir*, which was perfectly equal to its task, but to protect it from the abuses and malversations of the local police and its *pissars*.

Since 1863, the year of the Polish Insurrection, which marks the point at which our Government adopted a policy of reaction, the state of things has changed considerably. The Government then threw all the weight of its authority into the scale with the party of the "planters," as the obdurate advocates of serfdom were, in 1861, christened. The whole administration changed sides, and Russia has since seen *mediators* who have used their powers in order to compel the peasants to gratuitously do all sorts of work on their estates; who have publicly flogged the elders — mocking at the law, which exempted them from corporal punishment, by first degrading them from their office, and then restoring to them the attributes of their dignity after they have been flogged.

The regular bondage of the *mir* began, however, a few years later. From 1868 down to 1874, when the office of the *mediators* was entirely suppressed, the mir gradually passed under the supreme command of the *ispravnik, i.e.,* the superintendents of the local police.

The peasants' bitterest enemy could not have made a worse choice.

A police officer — we are speaking now of the common police, charged with the general maintenance of order and the putting down of common offenders — is a *tchin* in the administrative hierarchy like all the others. But between him and a paper-scribbling *tchin* of the innumerable Government offices, there is as wide a difference as between a decent, peaceful Chinese, votary of his ten thousand commandments, and a brutal and fierce Mogul of Jenghiz — though both have beardless faces and oblique eyes. A police *tchin* is our man of action. With him the instrument of command is not the pen, but the fist, the rod, and the stick. He breaks more teeth and flays more backs than he issues papers. As regards other people's property, *tchins* of all denominations hold the same somewhat strange views. But whilst the scribbling *tchin* cheat and swindle, the police *tchin* ransack and extort like Oriental pachas.

In the villages, amongst the *moujiks,* who will suffer to the uttermost before "going to law," the police can afford to go to any extreme short of open homicide and arson. The function of tax collector alone, which, after the Emancipation, was entrusted to the police, offered a vast field for interference, abuse, and oppression, and of these the early *zemstvos* often complain. When the *ispravniks* were charged with the chief control of the rural administration, and could at their pleasure, and by way of disciplinary punishment, indict, fine, and imprison both the district and communal elders, self-government by the peasants, as such, was practically abolished. It could exist only as far and in so much as the police chose to tolerate it. "The *ispravniks,* thanks to the powers they have received, have transformed the elected officers of the rural government, the elders, into their submissive servants, who are more dependent on them than are even the soldiers of the police-stations," — that is the statement made by the most competent authorities on the subject, the members of the *zemstvos. (Russian Courier,* Nov. 8th, 1884.)

The village communes have become for the country police a permanent source of income, often levied in a way which reminds one forcibly of the good old days of serfdom. Thus, in the circular issued by the Minister of the Interior on March 29th, 1880, we find the significant confession that, "according to the reports accumulated in the offices of the ministry," the country police officers, profiting by their right to have *one* orderly to run their errands, were in the habit of taking from forty to fifty such orderlies from the communes under their command, *whom they used as their house and field labourers.* In some cases the communes, instead of this tribute of gratuitous labour, paid a regular tribute of money (called *obrok* by former serfs), amounting in some provinces, according to the same authority, to from forty thousand to sixty thousand roubles a year per province.

Additional Readings

Pares, *History*. Pp. 341-403.

Tompkins, *Russia*. Pp. 445-489.

Vernadsky, *History*. Pp. 151-173, 191-207.

Martin, *Picture History*. Pp. 144-160.

Karpovich, *Imperial Russia*. Pp. 35-55.

Miliukov (Karpovich, ed.), *Outlines*. Vol. 1, chap. 7; vol. 2, chap. 3; vol. 3, chaps. 3 & 5.

Kornilov, *Modern Russian History*. Vol. 2.

Scott & Baltzly, *Readings*. Pp. 282-289, 289-293, 296-297, 297-298, 298-300, 436-439.

Lobanov-Rostovsky, *Russia and Asia*. Chaps. 7 & 8.

Kropotkin, Prince P. A., *Memoirs of a Revolutionist*. Boston: Houghton Mifflin Co., 1899.

Graham, S., *The Tsar of Freedom*. New Haven: Yale University Press, 1935.

Robinson, G. T., *Rural Russia Under the Old Regime*. New York: Longmans, Green & Co., 1932.

Sumner, B. H., *Russia and the Balkans, 1870-1880*. London: Milford, 1937.

Langer, W. L., *The Diplomacy of Imperialism*. Two volumes. New York: A. A. Knopf, 1935. Vol. 1, pp. 3-60.

————, *The Franco-Russian Alliance, 1890-1894*. Cambridge: Harvard University Press, 1929.

Alexander, *Once A Grand Duke*. New York: Farrar & Rinehart, 1932. Chaps. 3-5, 9, 10.

Footman, D., *Red Prelude. The Life of the Russian Terrorist Zhelyabov*. New Haven: Yale University Press, 1945.

Gorky, M., *My University Days*. New York: Boni & Liveright, 1923.

Dostoevsky, F., *The House of the Dead*.

Turgenev, I., *Fathers and Sons*. Everyman's Library Edition.

Goncharov, I. A., *Oblomov*. Everyman's Library Edition.

Lenin, N. (E. Hill & D. Mudie, eds. & trs.), *Letters of Lenin*. New York: Harcourt, Brace, 1937. Pp. 17-98.

Nekrasov, N., *Who Can Be Happy and Free in Russia?* World's Classic Series.

Dostoevsky, F., *The Idiot*. Everyman's Library Edition.

Gankin, O. H. & Fisher, H. H., *The Bolsheviks and the World War*. Stanford: Stanford University Press, 1940. Pp. 3-9.

Part VI. THE ROAD TO REVOLUTION

Economic Developments, 1890–1914

The following description of some of the major economic developments in the late nineteenth and early twentieth centuries is intended only as a brief introduction. It begins with agrarian economy because, although by 1900 the total output of industry exceeded in value the aggregate output of agriculture, the great majority of the Russian people got their living directly from the land. The sketch, written by the editor, is based mostly upon Russian materials.

Between the Emancipation and the 1905 Revolution the peasants as a class acquired approximately fifty-two million acres of land, but the individual holding of the average peasant at the latter date was only about half what it had been in 1860. The figures for 1905 also show that the peasants, who made up at least 85 per cent. of the total population, owned only 37 per cent. of the land. Of the remaining land, the State owned 34 per cent.; private landlords, 26 per cent.; and the Church, 3 per cent. Moreover, land prices had more than doubled during this generation and a half. This meant that the value of the peasant holding remained constant even though the amount of the holding was less. It also meant, of course, that it was twice as hard for the peasant to acquire additional lands. The peasant hunger for land might have been reduced and the situation might have been greatly eased had the production rates increased during these years. The average harvest returns of the Russian peasants, however, remained low as the following tables show.

Average Harvest Returns (Lbs. per acre) Before 1905

Nation	Wheat	Rye	Oats
Germany	1109	812	1064
United States	868	605	909
Russia	406	468	407

A somewhat different view of this same phenomenon at a later date may be gained from an international comparison of the figures for the per capita average production, export and consumption of small grains.

Small Grains (Stated in lbs. per head), 1909-1914.

Nation	Produced	Exported	Consumed
Canada	3730	811	2919
United States	2523	85	2438

Rumania	1925	1000	925
Russia	979	141	838

An arbitrary but typical account of the imaginary "average peasant" in 1905 shows an investment in land and buildings of 490 rubles upon which he paid 60 rubles a year in taxes and interest. Other annual money expenses amounted to 160 rubles. He could expect an annual cash income from the sale of produce and livestock, supplemented by such extra work as he could get, of 134 rubles. His annual deficit would therefore be 86 rubles. Many peasants, as the official figures show, were on relief.

To put it in somewhat over-simplified form, there were too many peasants for the production per acre. As of the years 1903-1905, there were about 139 millions of persons in Russia. Approximately 111 millions of these were classed as peasants; and 100 millions, more or less, were engaged in agriculture. It is a most significant commentary upon the situation that some 66 millions were unable to support themselves on the produce of their land and had to supplement their income by other work. The government relief figures show that many were not able to earn enough for subsistence. Government expenditures for the relief of poverty rose from approximately 12 million rubles for the period 1871-1890 to 268 million rubles for the period 1901-1906.

These mounting relief costs, as well as the rising expenses of a state which was slowly being modernized, had to be met either by some form of taxation or by borrowing. But taxation had its limits. The peasants paid — or at least were responsible for 90 per cent. of the taxes, but tax collectors could not get blood from a turnip nor tax money from an impoverished peasant. The arrears of unpaid peasant taxes steadily increased. During the years 1871-1880, every peasant-owned acre owed tax arrears of eight cents to the state. By the period 1891-1900, every peasant-owned acre owed tax arrears of twenty cents.

The general agricultural situation, so gloomy in 1905, showed marked improvement in the years immediately before the first World War. The period from 1907 to 1914 was one of general prosperity, perhaps the most prosperous in Russian history. This happy condition was due to a combination of circumstances. First, there was a succession of good harvests, thanks to beneficent weather. Second, the breakdown of the commune as a result of the Stolypin Reforms resulted in an increase in the acreage occupied and cultivated by the more vigorous and progressive peasants. Third, the extension of credit by peasant banks and the steady growth of peasant co-operatives provided cheaper and better financing for peasant landowning and cultivation. The growth of the co-operative movement was especially striking. In 1901 there were roughly 2000 peasant co-operatives with a membership of 700,000. At the outbreak of war in 1914, there were 33,000 co-operatives with a total membership of 12 millions. Finally, prosperity fed upon itself to some extent. The improved economic well-being of certain peasant classes provided a better domestic market for manufactured goods. This, in turn, greatly aided by improvements in transportation, was reflected in the increase and improvement of markets for the peasants' products. Industry and commerce shared and participated in this prosperity.

In terms of self-comparisons — i.e., of Russia with Russia — there were spectacular advances in both industry and commerce. The value of the aggregate industrial output of Russia rose from 541 millions of rubles in 1871 to nearly six billions of rubles in 1912. The production of pig iron increased from 1.3 millions of tons in 1894 to 5.1 millions of tons in 1913. Eighteen thousand tons of coal were mined in 1900; 40 million tons in 1913. Other figures bear out these samples as typical and the following table, showing the values of imports and exports in millions of rubles, rounds out the picture of the Russian commercial advance.

Yearly Average	Imports	Exports
1898-1902	617.4	739.6
1903-1907	723.3	1046.6
1908-1912	1047.4	1397.1
1912	1171.8	1518.8
1913	1374.0	1520.1

It is worth noting in passing that the bulk of the imports in 1913 came from Germany, which supplied 652.4 millions of rubles worth. Great Britain was a poor second with a figure of 207.6.

A somewhat false impression may be created however by these self-comparisons. A few international comparisons will balance the account. During the period 1912-1913, Russia mined 0.2 tons of coal per capita. This was much more than a decade before, but the United States in the same period was mining coal at the per capita rate of 5.12 tons. Similarly, in 1912-13, the United States, on a per capita basis, used 0.23 hp for manufacturing. Russia used 0.01 hp.

Finally, neither Russia nor the Russians owned all this new industrial and commercial wealth. The table below shows the amount of foreign capital entering Russia.

1851-1888	1,600,000 rubles
1889-1894	5,300,000 rubles
1895-1899	305,000,000 rubles
1905-1908	370,700,000 rubles

Between 1904 and 1913, more than three billions of rubles worth of Russian bonds were sold abroad. The foreign investment in Russian industries totaled two billion rubles by 1914. Of this, about 33 per cent. was French; 23 per cent., British; 20 per cent., German; and 14 per cent., Belgian. Approximately one-third of the capital in Russian stock companies was foreign owned. Nearly two-thirds of the pig iron and one-half the coal produced were based on French capital. The government was also directly involved with foreign capital. The Russian state debt owed abroad increased from one billion, seven hundred and thirty-three million rubles in 1894 to four billion, two hundred and twenty-nine million rubles in 1914. France was the creditor for about 80 per cent. of this debt; and Great Britain, for most of the remainder. Clearly there was some truth in the charge that Imperial Russia was not far removed in some respects from semi-colonial status.

The Industrial Revolution

The Industrial Revolution came to Russia much later than to western Europe. The following selection gives a brief description and analysis of the movement in Russia. The source is: Mavor, James, An Economic History of Russia. Two volumes. Second edition. New York: E. P. Dutton & Co., 1925. Volume 2, pp. 363–367.

Apart from the question of the supply of labour, the general economical conditions in Russia prior to the Emancipation were not favourable to the growth of industry on any extensive scale. The economic life of the country was highly self-contained. Each estate, and sometimes each village, was a little world practically complete within itself. Even the noble landowners, who spent a portion of the year in the capitals, transported to their town houses from their estates almost the whole of the produce necessary for their support and for the support of their numerous retinue of servants. With the exception of iron, tea, cotton, and a few other staple commodities not at that time produced in Russia in sufficient quantities to satisfy the existing demand, only articles of luxury were imported, or even transferred from place to place. The great commerce which had been characteristic of early Russia, and which had been the basis of its economical and political strength, had disappeared. The "immobilization" of labour had as inevitable concomitant the "immobilization" of goods. There were, moreover, almost no railways. There was no banking system, and as yet there was but a trifling circulation of money in the country. Yet there are those who look back upon the age of bondage as an age of relative abundance — an age in which there was no freedom, but in which there was in general plenty to eat. All the conditions which have been described had to be greatly modified before extensive industry was possible. The changes began immediately after Emancipation. The creation of Land Redemption Banks and the negotiation of foreign loans provided a financial basis; railways were built rapidly in European Russia, and numbers of foreign capitalists — principally English, German, Belgian, and French — established factories for the manufacture of cottons, woolens, etc., in the late sixties and in the seventies. Some of the ancient towns developed into industrial centres. The regions specially affected by the industrial movement at this time were the Moskovskaya gub., St. Petersburg and its neighbourhood, the Baltic Provinces, and parts of Poland.

The growth of the railway system in the seventies and the protective tariff, which reached its fullest development in 1891, stimulated industry enormously. From this time onward the urban proletariat, which, owing to the various causes indicated above, had previously no considerable existence in Russia, began to become numerous and influential. Movement from the villages, ceased to be impeded by the Government, and artisans began to crowd into the towns. The excess of labour at once rendered labour cheap, and rendered the employers indifferent to the comfort of the labourers. The beginning of the process of industrial development on an extensive scale was not accompanied by the ameliorative legislation which, initiated in England, had been carried far in Germany and France — in all countries, in fact, in which the concentration of workmen in industrial towns had been taking place. Ere long the rigorous exploitation of labour brought the grievances of the workmen under the notice of the Government. Long hours, inadequate wages, and still more importantly, the knowledge that workmen in other countries were reputed to be better off than those in Russia, led to demands upon the Government to intervene. In countries where a measure of laisser faire existed, the natural and obvious method of labour association was productive, to a certain extent, of improved conditions. Even in such countries the power of the State was invoked in restricting the hours of labour, in regulating the system of "truck," and in providing for the protection of the working men against exposed machinery and in inevitably dangerous occupations. But in Russia such steps were taken slowly, and they were regarded by the workmen as inadequate, while labour association was practically prohibited.

Side by side with private enterprises, there were established Government factories for the manufacture of cloth, paper, tinned provisions, etc., together with metal refineries, foundries, porcelain works, etc., etc. These activities of the Government were supplemented by the factories belonging to the Udeli (The Imperial Appanage), in which large numbers of men were employed.

The circumstances that many of the private enterprises were brought into existence by the high protective duties, and that these enterprises were encouraged by the Government in its own factories, and in those of the Udeli, pursued methods similar to those of the private firms, made it inevitable that the responsibility for the situation should rest upon the shoulders of the Government. The labour question thus from the middle of the seventies assumed a definite political aspect.

In Russia, labour combination, in the West European sense, was prohibited. "Protection" appeared to exist solely for the manufacturer, whose enterprises received governmental assistance and encouragement. The Government not only facilitated the development of industries by high tariffs, but through the State Bank·it financed industrial enterprises, and through the State domain it gave land, mining, and timber concessions to persons who were willing to undertake the task of industrial organization. Many of these persons were foreigners, or the agents of foreigners, who were specially protected by the Russian Government. In brief, the hand of the Government was everywhere.

The effect of this situation was to direct against the Government a large part of the irritation engendered in the minds of the working men against their employers. If, for example, a foreman in a factory lost his temper and beat a workman, the latter might complain to the Government factory inspector, but if the latter did not take the workman's view of the case, he came to be looked upon as a partner in the offence committed by the foreman. The chinovneke, or official class, came to bear the burden of the faults of its members, and the whole governmental system came to be called in question. Meanwhile the Government neglected to apply the ameliorating legislation which had been applied under similar conditions of protection and encouragement of industry by Germany, and the factory system, inspection notwithstanding, continued to be conducted in what the workmen now recognized fully to be an archaic manner.

The comparatively small number of working men in the cities, which before Emancipation were rather political and trading than manufacturing centres, accounts for the late appearance of labour organizations, excepting some of a rudimentary character.

* * *

While the development of industry on the large scale in Russia has lagged behind that of Western Europe in point of time, the late development, in the technical and commercial senses, has been accompanied by a late development in a social sense. The exploitation of the working men and women has been more severe than for many years it has been in any Western European country. The practice of "search," universal in Russia, the practice of beating workmen and other similar practices, are incidents in a system of oppression which survived the Emancipation, but which recent events have done much to mitigate. Low wages and unfavourable conditions of work have, as will be seen, played a conspicuous part in producing the "state of mind" which made the Revolution.

While the factory system has been developing in Russia with great rapidity, partly under the influence of a high protective tariff, there has been a spontaneous and very widespread development of the so-called kustarny or household industry in villages. In some gubernie, notably in Moskovskaya gub., the Zemstvos have encouraged the kustars or household artisans by organizing for them the direct supply of raw materials and by facilitating the formation of artels, or co-operative groups. It seems that in some industries, small iron ware, cardboard, leather, woodwork, etc., not only do the kustari compete with the large manufacturers, but they have in some cases succeeded in directing the trade wholly into their own hands.

Early Labor Legislation

Despite the lag in industrialization, Russia was early in the field of regulatory labor laws. The following summary of this little known aspect of Russian industrialization is from: Gordon, Manya, Workers Before and After Lenin. New York: E. P. Dutton & Co., 1941. Pp. 17–20.

The early labor laws were the result of the competitive struggle between the old and overpopulated Moscow and the new, sparsely inhabited St. Petersburg. In the Moscow district there was a surplus of labor. Elaborate machinery was unnecessary because human toil was cheap. Factory owners could employ women and children and run their factories day and night without stopping for repairs as they would have had to do had they used machinery. St. Petersburg, on the other hand, suffered from a shortage of labor and as a result was compelled to install the most modern machinery and to pay higher wages. Night work was physically impossible because of the time required to keep the machinery in repair, and economically unprofitable because of the high cost of labor. Consequently St. Petersburg was being undersold by Moscow and in order to overcome this disadvantage her industrialists demanded the prohibition of night work and child labor. Moscow employers fought vehemently against the proposed laws, but the influence of the capital seems to have been more powerful, and officially at least, night work and child labor were abolished.

Strange as it may seem this was not the first effort that Russia made in the protection of labor. Records prove conclusively that Russia was the pioneer in labor legislation and not, as it was generally assumed, England with her laws of 1802 limiting children in the textile factories to a twelve-hour day. As far back as 1741, during the reign of Anna Leopoldovna, a series of regulations dealt with every phase of factory life: hours of work, wages, working conditions such as lighting in the factories, workers' medical aid, housing, the imposition of fines, the maintenance of discipline, and curious as it may seem, the right of women to receive the same wages as men.

Russia, as it is commonly stated, has been a country of industrial and social forward leaps, of sudden changes, but these labor laws of two centuries ago demonstrate that having made the jump she had no difficulty in returning to the starting point. Thirty-five years later, Russia made her second effort in labor legislation. In 1785 [sic] a law was passed establishing a ten-hour day and six-day week in all trades. What proportion, if any, of the workers derived comfort from this law is difficult to establish, but its presence on the statute books is nevertheless quite extraordinary in view of the fact that in western Europe and the United States the ten-hour day appeared about a hundred years later. The law was not enforced but was not forgotten. It was picked up by the workers of Vilna and Odessa in the early years of the present century and cited as a precedent in their fight for shorter hours.

Labor legislation of the early Eighties was in a measure based on information regarding the condition of the workers gathered in 1859 by the commission of the governor-general of St. Petersburg, the Shtakelburg commission of 1860 and the Ignatiev commission of 1870. The first labor ordinance which was actually enforced was that of June 1, 1882. It was concerned with the working hours of minors in factories, and made it a misdemeanor to employ children under twelve years of age. Children between twelve and fifteen were forbidden to work more than eight hours a day, and the day had to be divided into two shifts of four hours each. Night work between nine in the evening and five in the morning was prohibited for children, as well as work on Sundays and all holidays. Profiting by the errors made in England and France in so far as factory supervision was concerned the same ordinance established a system of periodic factory inspection. There was an insufficient number of inspectors, but these few seem to have taken their duties seriously. In 1884 a fine of 100 rubles was imposed for violation of the law, a considerable sum for that period.

Results, though not one hundred percent attained, were quite satisfactory. In 1882 the children in woolen factories in the Moscow district were 10 percent of all workers. Within three years the number was reduced to less than one percent and an approximate change took place in all other industries. The entire industrial area of Moscow in 1882–83 had 9.5 percent child workers. In 1885 the number had dropped to 3.2 percent. Thus backward Russia had again taken a leap in advance of Europe and the United States. At that time in France it was legal for minors to work twelve hours a day and in the United States the age limit varied between twelve years in California and fourteen years in New York State.

The second important legislative measure of the Eighties prohibited night work for boys and girls under seventeen years of age. At first the ordinance of June 15, 1885, was "an experiment for three years only" in the cotton, linen and woolen factories, but later it was extended to all textile factories and all other branches of industry where women were employed. These laws were not popular among the workers who feared that prohibition of night work for women and minors would eventually lead to the abandonment of the night shift and so deprive the adult men of work. The influence behind this legislation came from the side of the employers and the source of inspiration was again St. Petersburg.

One series of reforms seems to have led to another. The very next year, June 1886, witnessed the enactment of a law and a series of instructions designed to protect workers against exploitation. It made it obligatory for the employer to establish an accurate bookkeeping system and to supply the workers with booklets in which their earnings as well as their fines were entered. These booklets were supposed to show the exact amount of the workers' wages, the basis on which they were earned and the times of payment. A worker who was engaged for a short period was paid once a month. If he was hired for an unlimited period he was paid twice a month. This was a great step forward. Prior to this law workers were paid whenever the employer found it convenient to do so — four, or three or even two times a year. As a result wage earners were compelled to buy their supplies on credit at the company stores. The same law tried to curb the practice of exorbitant fines which until then prevailed in all factories. Thereafter, as in Soviet Russia today, the worker might be fined for truancy and non-fulfillment of his prescribed task but the fine could no longer be more than one-third of his earnings for that particular term and every fine had to be entered in a separate book which was examined by the factory inspector. Moneys so derived could be used only for relief purposes among the workers themselves and for those no longer able to work, — maternity assistance, compensation for loss by fire, burial payments, and the like.

This entire series of labor laws was vehemently opposed by the industrialists of Moscow and Vladimir who at that early period employed all the phrases and methods of the present-day capitalist die-hard. They insisted that the laws were socialistic, utopian and injurious to Russian industry — and succeeded in nullifying some of them, but their ambition to kill all the "socialist laws" was not realized. Many factory laws remained, and the most irksome of these, from the employers' viewpoint, was the one dealing with factory inspection. The inspectors were often suppressed, but they came back to life and their reports of conditions in the factories and of life among the workers generally were precise and soul-stirring. The effort embodied in this social legislation had a significance which was theoretical rather than practical. Many of the laws were not enforced. The condition of the workers remained miserable beyond description. Yet the protection of labor was no longer entirely academic.

The Zubatov Plan

Sergei V. Zubatov, a man of somewhat unsavory reputation who was then head of the Political Department of the Moscow police, conceived the idea of controlling the labor movement by means of "police socialism." The essence of the scheme was for the police to sponsor labor unions which should be guided away from political activities. The plan was approved by Minister of Interior von Plehve and put into effect in 1901. It enjoyed a considerable but very temporary success and failed completely when Zubatov sought to extend it from St. Petersburg to Odessa. For this failure, Zubatov was dismissed from office and exiled from the capital by Plehve. The source is: Mavor, op. cit., vol. 2, pp. 199–200.

The principal points in Zubatov's "programme" were as follows:

1. At present the law confides the safeguarding of the legal rights of employers and employees to the factory inspectorship; but this institution, in the opinion of the Political Police Department, has proved to be powerless to discharge this function, having forfeited the confidence of the workers owing to its partiality to the employers. Therefore the Political Police Department, from considerations of State importance, has not only decided to take upon itself that part of factory inspectorship duties which comprises the mutual relations of employers and employed, but even is almost inclined to put an end to the institution as an anachronism. . . .

2. The widening of the rights of factory workers (in spite of the statute law) shall consist in uniting the workers of each factory into separate groups, each having its committee, voluntarily elected by workers of both sexes from among themselves. These committees must point out changes desirable for workers, in the scale of wages, distribution of working time, and general changes in the rules of internal order. The employer must communicate in future not immediately with his workers, but through the committee. The committees of separate factories of a given district are in communication with each other with a view to uniformity of action, the general supervision of the committees being centralized in the Political Police Department. For the purposes of this supervision the department appoints special agents from among the experienced and promising workers who are wise by long experience in the art of ruling the masses of the people.

3. In order to form this institution, mutually useful as it must be for employees and employers alike, the Political Police Department, in order that the coming occurrences should not take it unaware, took care not only to seek workers promising and experienced in strikes, even from among those who had been in administrative banishment, but also of establishing a school for training the future actors, under the management of people experienced in this branch. All these teachers receive decent remuneration.

4. The sums required for the support of this institution are afforded by the "Society of Mutual Assistance of the Workers in Mechanical Industries," the constitution of which was granted on 14th February 1902. In this society there are taking part as members thousands of workers of both sexes, and

even those under age. Besides contributions from these, there are the subscriptions from high exalted personages, educated classes, clergy, and different persons, but as yet no merchants or manufacturers.

5. By the means described the Political Police Department succeeded in a short time in inspiring the most sincere confidence of the working men, because they became convinced that every humbled and insulted person finds in the Political Police Department paternal attention, advice, support, and assistance by word and deed; so that even the Museum of Labour, established by the Imperial Technical Society, began to lose ground.

The Kishinev Pogrom

The Russian word "pogrom" means literally "a little beating" and the classic pogroms always lasted exactly three days. The most notorious of these violent anti-Semitic outbreaks during the reign of the last Romanov took place at Kishinev in 1903. Professor Mavor's account of it makes clear the part played by the Tsar's government. The source is: Mavor, op. cit., vol. 2, pp. 208–210.

In 1882 and later years pogroms were sporadic; but they had practically disappeared for some years when in 1903, once more the control of the police passed into the hands of M. von Plehve, when immediately pogroms began again to occur. They began at Kishenev. Since 1897 the press of Kishenev had been suppressed, with the exception of two newspapers, *Bessarabits* and Znamya *(Banner)*, both edited by a certain Krushevan. The close relation between these newspapers and the local administration is undoubted. In March 1903, *Bessarabits* published an account of an alleged ritual murder by Jews at Dubossari, a small town in the province of which Kishenev is the capital. This account was false, and on its exposure M. von Plehve issued a circular on 22nd March prohibiting further newspaper reference to the subject. Whether under the auspices of M. von Plehve or of Krushevan does not appear, but soon after the Jewish Passover, some persons made their appearance in Kishenev as agitators in favour of a Jewish pogrom. The Jews became alarmed, and sent a deputation to the governor to request protection. The governor promised to take measures for their safety. This he failed to do, and the destruction of Jewish houses began, while the police stood by indifferently, or even attacked those Jews who attempted to defend themselves. According to *Osvobojdnie* the people who took part in the pogroms were, in the first instance, peasants from the neighbouring country districts, who had had no previous relation with the Jews of Kishenev. Later the local inhabitants, who found the Jews keen competitors in their business, joined the anti-Semitic movement and engaged in pogroms. The Kishenev pogrom took place on 6th and 7th April. About a fortnight previously (on 25th March) von

Plehve, then Minister of Interior, had sent a despatch to General von Raben, Governor of Kishenev. This depatch, which was published at the time by *The Times,* was as follows:

"I have been informed that in the locality entrusted to you there are in preparation vast disorders against Jews who are exploiting the local population. Because of the generally unquiet state of mind of the people of the city, a state of mind which is seeking for an outlet, and also because of the undesirability of exciting anti-governmental feelings among the population not yet touched by the propaganda, and of applying too severe measures, your Excellency will not fail to stop immediately by persuasion, not using armed force, the disorders which are about to begin."

This despatch was naturally interpreted at the time as a callous instruction to leave the Jews to the mercy of the rioters in the interests of the Government, which von Plehve seemed to think would be served by the diversion of popular fury from an anti-governmental to an anti-Semitic direction. *Znamya* and *Bessarabits,* Krushevan's newspapers, offer another explanation. The Jews of Kishenev were, he said, "the redeeming sacrifice for the revolutionary propaganda of the fellow-Jews." That the Jewish pogroms were intended as a counter-revolutionary stroke appears also from the circumstance that the dates fixed for revolutionary demonstrations were also the dates fixed beforehand for the Jewish pogroms. The policy, if such it may be called, was to some extent successful. The revolutionary groups, realizing the connection between their proceedings and the pogroms against the Jews, cancelled many of these demonstrations, and thus it may be said that throughout the south of Russia, the revolutionary movement was thrown back for almost two years. In May 1903 a deputation of three influential Jews went from Odessa to St. Petersburg to remonstrate with von Plehve and to endeavour to see the Tsar. The case for the Jews was skillfully put by Köigshatz, a Jewish lawyer. Von Plehve answered that he was considering measures for the improvement of the condition of the Jews; "but," he said (according to the report of the deputation, drawing himself up to his full height and assuming a menacing tone), "tell this to the Jewish youth, your sons and daughters — tell all your intelligentsia. Let them not think that Russia is an old and rotting organism; the new developing Russia will win, and will put down the revolutionary movement. Much is said about the cowardice of Jews. This is not true. The Jews are the boldest of people. In Western Russia about 90 per cent of the revolutionists are Jews, and in Russia as a whole, about 40 per cent. I will not conceal from you that the revolutionary movement in Russia is disturbing us. From time to time when, here and there, demonstrations are arranged, we come even to confusion; but we shall control this. I wish to let you understand that unless you detain your youth from the revolutionary movement, we will make your situation so intolerable that you will have to go away from Russia to the last man."

This was undoubtedly the true explanation of the pogroms; and M. von Plehve must have know that in putting it in set terms, he was pronouncing his own sentence of death.

"The Liberation Movement"

Sir Bernard Pares, long regarded as the outstanding Western authority on Russia, is especially qualified to write of the development of political opposi-, tion which culminated in the establishment of the Duma. Not only was Sir Bernard intimately associated with the First Duma (He was a Gentleman Usher), but he also knew virtually all the political leaders of "The Liberation Movement." His studies on this subject have long been classics. The following excerpts are from his Russia and Reform. *London: Archibald Constable & Co., Ltd., 1907. Pp. 87, 88, 487–490, 501–506.*

THE FIRST ZEMSTVO CONGRESS. The new Minister authorised the holding of a general Zemstvo Congress in St. Petersburg itself. At last the plan of Alexander II. was on the eve of realisation; but Mirsky had to fight with other influences far stronger than his own at the Court, and, if the people had issued from the atmosphere of suspicion which enveloped Russia, the Emperor had not. After some consultations it was decided that the Congress must be held in a private house, and its resolutions were communicated to Prince Mirsky, not officially, but as a piece of news to a personal friend; in this way they came to the ears of the Emperor.

This first Zemstvo Congress was held under the presidency of Mr. Shipoff. It was clear that the great majority of the deputies from the various Zemstva, who came rather by invitation than by any direct election, were ready to go farther than the minimum of Shipoff: in fact, but for his own great moral influence, the president might have found himself almost entirely isolated; but here, as so often afterwards, the difficulty of the whole task acted as a restraining influence, and the majority was wise enough to content itself with a unanimous vote in favour of the minimum. These so-called requests expressed before all things a desire for order, and for the corporate development of the whole country. The Congress states that Government has been separated from Society, and that this gap must be bridged at all costs. In the tenth out of the eleven articles it puts forward two resolutions, one representing the majority and the other the minority; both alike request that a national assembly should be summoned without delay, but the majority claim for the assembly definite legislative functions. Though the peasants were only indirectly represented on the Congress, a special article, which was accepted unanimously, emphasises the need of improving the conditions of peasant life. The eleven points may be summed up in the following requests:—No one without the sentence of an independent court of law ought to be subjected to punishment or limited in his rights. There must be means for bringing officials to account in the civil or criminal courts. There must be guarantees of freedom of conscience and religion, freedom of speech and press, and also freedom of meeting and association. The personal rights of citizens of the Russian Empire, both civil and political, ought to be equal. The peasants must be made equal in personal rights with the members of other classes. The country population must be freed from the wardenship of administrative authorities in all manifestations of its personal and social life. To peasants must be guaranteed a regular form of trial. Representation in the Zemstva must not be organised on class principles, and must include as far as possible all the actual forces of the local population. Small country units (Parish Councils) ought to be created. The sphere of local government should be extended to the whole province of local needs. Local self-government must be extended over all parts of the Russian Empire. The Conference expresses a hope "that the supreme power will summon freely elected representatives of the people in order, with their co-operation, to bring our country out on to a new path of Imperial development in the spirit of the principles of justice and of harmony between the Imperial power and the people." This great document, so vastly superior in spirit and substance to any proposals that had issued from the Government of the Reaction, marks the beginning of the reform movement. It bears at almost every point the personal impress of the mind of Shipoff. The nobility with which he pleads for reform, as essentially necessary to the cause of order and as the natural request of loyal subjects, continues to stamp the movement at many of its further crises. The minimum programme of Shipoff was accepted with enthusiasm by the whole country, and one public body after another ratified it; the volume of the national demand became so great that Russia could be said to possess a real public opinion which was practically unanimous.

• • •

THE DEMAND FOR "FREEDOMS" AND A NATIONAL ASSEMBLY. The Eleven Points adopted by the Zemstvo Congress of November 19 to 21, 1904, mark an epoch in Russian history. The document bore throughout the impress of Mr. Shipoff's loyalty to tradition and respect for the throne. Personal freedom from the arbitrary control of officials and the calling of some kind of national assembly were put forward, not as demands, but as requests, and the Government was left to settle all details. At the same time the principle that the Emperor must be brought into touch with his people was stated with a simple frankness, and it was clear that behind that modest petition stood practically the whole mass of the educated classes.

Soon after the Congress the Emperor called a meeting of his chief counsellors. Of this meeting we as yet have only one account. It represents that, when the question of reform was raised, Mr. Pobyedonostseff told the Emperor that he had not the right to infringe the principle of autocracy, that his position as Head of the Church would not allow it. Mr. Witte is said to have answered that an autocracy which had no power to make changes would not be an autocracy at all. In any case it is clear that the reactionaries won the day. Prince Mirsky asked leave to resign, and though his request was not at once granted, his power was already gone.

When, in the spring, the "Liberators" had attempted to organise a public banquet, they had found the war mood too strong for them. But on December 3 meetings were held in many towns to celebrate the fortieth anniversary of the reform of the Law-Courts. Many of these meetings took the form of public dinners. In St. Petersburg a dinner was arranged for December 2. It was postponed in consequence of a collision between the public and the police, but on the next day 600 guests met in the Pavloff Hall under the presidency of a well-known Liberator, Mr. Korolyenko; a resolution which followed closely on the lines of the Eleven Points was adopted and signed. In Moscow, on the same day, similar dinners ending with similar resolutions were held by the lawyers and by the Justices of the Peace; on December 4 lawyers, professors, and journalists met at a dinner in the Hermitage. On December 4 the lawyers of St. Petersburg organised a demonstration of protest against the postponement of a banquet arranged by them. Banquets were also held in the provinces; at Saratoff the guests numbered 1,500. In Russia members of the professions could under certain conditions meet to discuss professional subjects. The reformers had the tactical instinct to seize upon this means of making themselves heard. Doctors met presumably to discuss medical matters, and one of them would rise to say: "We cannot discharge our duty as doctors in Russia unless we have freedom of person, freedom of conscience, freedom of the Press, freedom of assembly, freedom of association, and a national assembly." In other words, the vast majority of intelligent opinion formed itself into line under the banner of the Eleven Points. The very fact that the professional unit could thus be used, that all doctors or all lawyers could be unanimous on a political question, made it all the more evident that the Government was quite out of touch with the nation. On December 18 there was a banquet of engineers in St. Petersburg, with a resolution on the needs of Russian industry; on December 27 there was a great dinner in honour of the Decembrists of 1825. The Government prevented some of the meetings; more frequently it punished the owners of the restaurants at which they had taken place. This led to important street demonstrations in St. Petersburg on December 11, and in Moscow on December 19. In the latter case the students came into conflict with the police.

On December 13 the Zemstva received the adhesion of another most important ally. The Town Councils, being elected largely from the merchant class, had so far been backward in the cause of reform; but in Moscow, at the last election, many Intelligents had been elected as representing important corporations, such as the University. The new Moscow Town Council, in the presence of a numerous audience, unanimously decided to telegraph to the Minister of the Interior that the "real obstacle to the further development of civic economy was to be found in those conditions which had been imposed by law upon the community"; the Council definitely adopted the principles of the Eleven Points; other Town Councils too followed the example of Moscow. Meanwhile the Zemstvo deputies had returned to their respective Zemstva, which proceeded in some cases to ratify what had been done at the Congress. Even the Marshals of the Gentry, elected as they were only by the large land-owners, had met to make a moderate plea for reform, and one of them, Mr. Mukhanoff, who was also president of the local Zemstvo, carried through the Zemstvo Assembly a bold repetition of the Eleven Points. This address was telegraphed to the Emperor, and reached him in the midst of the congratulations on his name-day. Those who were present say that they never saw him so angry; on the margin of the telegram he wrote the words "Impudent and tactless." But the voice of public opinion was too powerful to be resisted, and on December 25, there was issued an Imperial Edict which spoke of reforms.

In this decree the Emperor desired to distinguish between "what really corresponded to the interests of the people" and the "faulty and temporary accident of a gust of aspirations." He was not unwilling to make material modifications in the laws if it were really necessary; peasant questions would be attended to. For the rest, the officials would be compelled to observe the law; the Local Councils would have their jurisdiction extended as far as possible; the Law-Courts would be unified and made more independent; workmen would be insured by the State; the administrative ordinances would be revised and their sphere of action limited as far as possible; the edict of toleration of March, 1903, would probably be extended; and the law of aliens would be modified. Superfluous restrictions on the Press would be abolished. The Committee of Ministers would be invited to suggest how these principles should be applied; that is to say, the bureaucracy was to undertake the reform of itself. The Official Communication which was issued two days later accused the popular leaders, such as Mr. Shipoff, "of trying to bring confusion into the life of society and of the State. . . . Their efforts had resulted in a series of noisy conventions which put forward various inadmissible demands, and in mob demonstrations on the streets, with open resistance to the appeals of the authorities." Such phenomena were declared to be "alien to the Russian people, which was true to the ancient principles of the existing Imperial order, though an attempt was being made to give to the above-named disturbances the unwarranted significance of a national movement." The leaders, "blinded by delusive fancies, did not realise that they were working not for their country, but for its enemies." Conventions of an anti-governmental character would be stopped by all means that legally pertained to the authorities. The Zemstva and Town Councils were ordered to return within the limits of their jurisdiction, and not to touch those questions which they had no legal right to discuss. Their presidents were threatened with punishment if they permitted such discussion, and the newspapers were ordered "to restore peace in the public mind, which had lately deviated from its proper direction." Clearly this pronouncement was hopelessly below the level of the situation. It is possible to explain the remarkable difference between the two twin documents, the Decree and the Communication; the second was to serve the purpose of a keeper ring; at the moment when the Government found it necessary to make concessions to a united public opinion, it reasserted its own supremacy. But this was not the way to secure the confidence of the people; on the contrary, the gap between it and the Government was now more visible than ever. At the beginning of January the Technical Congress in Moscow and the Natural Science Congress in Tiflis were closed, but these were trifling victories. At the other end of the Empire, General Stoessel surrendered Port Arthur to the Japanese, before the means of resistance were exhausted and against the advice of his council of war. Scarcely less significant of the demoralisation of the army was the shot fired against the Emperor on January 19 from the fortress of Peter and Paul. Nicholas left his capital, not to return for more than a year; and he was from this time onward more than ever cut off from all knowledge of his people.

The Zemstvo Constitutionalists were the natural link between the Zemstva and the professional classes. These last welcomed with special alacrity the invitation to send in their views to the Minister. From January to May they were rapidly organising themselves. Professional conferences of all kinds met in the capitals and in the chief towns, and each profession showed its unanimity on political questions by forming itself into a union. One of the first unions to form itself was that of the Engineers and Technicians. Its foundations were laid at the banquet of December 18, 1904. The Academic Union, consisting both of professors and students, was formed on the lines of a programme drafted by Professor Vernadsky, of Moscow, at the end of December. The Office Clerks and Book-keepers formed their union on March 12, the Teachers and Workers in Primary Education on March 25, the Medicals at the beginning of April, the Lawyers and the champions of Full Rights for Jews at the same time, the Pharmacists on April 15, the Writers on the 18th, the advocates of Full Rights for Women on May 9, and the Secondary School Teachers in the same month. One of the last and most important of the unions was that of the Railway Servants. From this list it will be clear that the unions embraced the mass of professional intelligence; to take an instance, nearly every doctor belonged to the Union of Medicals. Some amongst them, such as the Unions of Lawyers, Writers, and Advocates of Women's Rights, represented the more irresponsible section of the Intelligence, but others, such as the agricultural experts, the doctors, and the primary teachers, had a direct connection with the work of the Zemstva and

Town Councils, which had done so much to put the educated classes in touch with the needs of the peasants and workmen. The engineers, who were always to the fore in the movement for reform, had secured in other ways a practical experience of the national needs. Many of the Russian Intelligents are not far removed by instincts and associations from the labouring classes, and in the Union of Railway Servants we see an instance of how it was possible for both Intelligents and working men to organise themselves on very similar lines. This union was a beginning of more definite organisation amongst the labouring classes. Later there were formed several other unions, including even a Union of Officials for the reform of officialdom and a Liberal Union of Policemen. The programmes of all the unions were practically identical, and were developed from the original minimum requests of the Zemstvo Congress of November: they claimed a National Assembly elected by universal, equal, direct, and secret suffrage, inviolability of person, and freedom of speech, of the Press, of association, and of meeting. The unions met in various buildings, as opportunity offered, and submitted suggestions to the public or to the Minister. Such were, for instance, the note of 198 engineers on the needs of Russian industry (December 18), the note on the needs of education drawn up by the Academic Union, the resolution of the doctors (December 31st), the note on the necessity of abolishing the restrictions on the Jews (March 9), the note of the primary teachers (March 25), and the note on the needs of Secondary Schools. Many of these notes were the orginal programmes of the unions concerned.

Towards the beginning of this movement Professor Milyukoff, a "Liberator" in close touch with the Zemstva, and one of the most acute politicians in Russia, had conceived the idea of massing all the unions into a Union of Unions. The meeting of protest on January 22 furthered the idea. A few persons constituted themselves as a central committee, and invited deputies from each union. So far they acted only as an intelligence department, and Professor Milyukoff never intended to swamp the individuality of each union in any central body. Many of the unions were themselves still in process of formation; but when the Congresses of the unions had enabled men to acquaint themselves more nearly with political questions and with each other, Milyukoff's idea became capable of execution. On May 21, delegates from fourteen unions met in Moscow. Here was established a loose organisation, which left absolutely free the action of each union. All were, however, declared to be conducting a struggle for the political liberation of Russia on the principles of democracy. A second Congress was held on June 4 in Moscow, after the battle of Tsushima. Without committing itself to any definite tactics, the Union of Unions made suggestions founded on the common experience of the several unions, and, by a vaguely worded resolution, recognised all means of combating the bureaucracy. Certainly one of the most effective of these means was suggested by the central committee itself. When, in June, some persons were prosecuted for belonging to the Union of Engineers, their fellow-members filled up and forwarded to the police the following declaration: "In view of the prosecution of some members of the Union, in accordance with article 126 of the Criminal Code, for belonging to the Union, I declare that I belong to the Union, and if belonging to it is a crime within the meaning of article 126, then I am equally guilty with the persons who have been prosecuted, and am under the same responsibility." So many engineers signed this formula that the authorities, overcome by the hopelessness of the task, set free those who had been arrested. The policy of Milyukoff, then, was one of passive resistance; but the resolution which approved of all methods was easily interpreted to cover political assassination. Milyukoff himself was always opposed to such methods; but he had no business to tamper with the question. In presence of the overwhelming material resources of the bureaucracy, he was certainly bound to secure allies amongst the general public; but he ought never to have deferred to the views of the Terrorists. In so doing, he sought his allies in the wrong place; and thus put upon the beginnings of the new Liberal party a taint of opportunism and worse, which was later to weaken the claims of the first Imperial Duma.

The Union of Unions continued its activity throughout the summer; but obviously its value was only temporary. In the country, a doctor might find himself isolated from most other members of his union, and his natural affinity would be with the schoolmaster who was working in the same village. There was no reason why all the doctors in Russia should have one set of political views and all schoolmasters another. As a means of asserting the opinion of the professional classes, the unions had been of immense service; but their members now began to wish for more frankly political organisations. Milyukoff, who had foreseen this, tried to restrain the central committee from compromising itself by too many definitions; but after his imprisonment in the autumn the Union of Unions passed into the hands of irresponsible doctrinaires; and though it continued to exist, its pronouncements were no longer representative. The more moderate section of its members passed into the Cadet party; the more extreme section took some part in the abortive Moscow rising of December. The working men had by that time made themselves independent of the Union of Unions; and, as it now represented only a very small party, it failed to have any very sensible influence on the elections for the Imperial Duma. In the summer was founded the last of the unions and far the most important, that of the peasants. Though in loose connection with the main body, it had its own programme, and must be studied as a separate development.

The work of drawing up schemes of reform was not confined to the Zemstva and the unions. Obedient to the Imperial command, the Committee of Ministers, assisted by the officials of the different Ministries, plunged into the business of lawmaking; and in the course of five months, from January to June, there were published more new Acts than had before been produced in the course of years. The bureaucrats, who were themselves closely akin to the Russian Intelligents, had even more of a liking for report writing; but the very atmosphere of bureaucracy gave a nerveless character to much of this work. Much energy and time was spent on it, but there was a lack of humour which prevented the authors from seeing that their activity was belated, and a lack of seriousness which made the public think, in many cases very unjustly, that the whole work was insincere. Some measure of freedom of religion was given to the Old Believers on April 30, to alien confessions on May 14, and to the Jews on July 8; Edicts of April 13 and May 19 aimed at bettering the conditions of peasant life. The whole Ministry of Agriculture was hastily remodelled; certain vague and inadequate regulations dealt with the publishing of laws and with the modification of some of the Press laws. The one measure which could have quieted the country was the definite summons to a National Assembly. Over and over again the Government has offered concessions which might have given satisfaction three months before. The bureaucracy was now in that disordered state of mind which history has attributed to the Duke of Newcastle: it seemed to have lost half an hour in the morning, and to be hurrying all day in a vain attempt to catch it up. Its activity at least showed that it too was being driven by public opinion and was reluctantly submitting to the necessity of making concessions. But its conversion, if such it could be called, was only the result of the stress of events and lacked all conviction; the bureaucrats were therefore the last people who could be expected to make any practical settlement of the questions which were at issue.

The real leadership of the movement for reform was still in the hands of the Zemstvo men. The two parties which had formed themselves at the November Congress were now more precisely defined; but far the more numerous was that which followed the lead of the Zemstvo Constitutionalists. This party had very much the views of English Liberals, while the minority, under Shipoff, represented the best instincts of English Conservatism. The Liberal leaders, on the initiative of Mr. Golovin, president of the Moscow Zemstvo, had established an Organising Committee. At the beginning of May this committee summoned another Zemstvo Congress. This time some of the delegates sent by the local Zemstva were formally elected; but others still came by invitation of the committee, or represented no more than the progressive groups in their respective Zemstva. The Congress, by an overwhelming majority, decided that the National Assembly must be not merely consultative, but legislative. The formula of universal suffrage adopted by the Zemstvo Constitutionalists and their attitude towards the commission of Bulyghin were ratified by a large majority. The Zemstvo Conservatives held a separate Congress under the presidency of Shipoff; here a greater proportion of the members came simply by invitation. This too was the moment when the Town Councils also entered the political arena as a corporate unit. So far they had been disunited. Some of them had sent respectful addresses which vaguely reflected the general feeling of the people; some had addressed petitions to the Council of Ministers. Some Town Councils, like that of Saratoff, had put forward the most modest requests as to the constitution and functions of the National Assembly, but a large number had accepted the lead of the Town Council of Moscow. Moscow adopted the formula of universal suffrage; Stavropol spoke boldly of a Constituent Assembly; Erivan even raised the questions of Women's suffrage, land nationalisation, and the municipalisation of economic enterprises. Members of Town Councils began to get into touch with the Organising Committee of the Zemstvo Congresses.

Miliukov on the Zemstva Petition

Sir Bernard, in the preceding article, described the part played in the struggle for the Duma by the scholar-turned-politician, Paul Miliukov. Here is Professor Miliukov's own summary of the events of 1903–4. The source is: Milyoukov, P., Russia and Its Crisis. Chicago: University of Chicago Press, 1905. Pp. 528–535.

The members of the Zemstvos, taken as a whole, are not at all identical with the "Emancipation Party." Yet so powerful is the present current of liberal public opinion that their program, recently formulated in the petition presented to the Tsar, is that of the "Emancipation." We have seen that as early as 1902 voices were heard in the local committees advocating the introduction of a constitution. But these voices were indistinct, and such as had a more positive ring were stifled, and their possessors sent into exile. The cry was, however, raised again — this time not by three or four isolated individuals, but by fully a hundred; and it was not in the local assemblies legally summoned in the districts, but in a semi-official meeting of the members of all the Zemstvos, first invited by the minister Svyatopolk-Mirskee, then forbidden, and finally tolerated to meet at St. Petersburg.

This was the first meeting in Russian history which represented the opinion of the Zemstvos, not about local and economic, but about general and political questions. This meeting formulated a demand which was much more positive than that of the few exiled members of 1902. In its petition it enumerated all the fundamental rights of the individual and the citizen: the inviolability of the person and of the private home; no sentence without trial, and no diminution of rights except by judgment of an independent court; liberty of conscience and of belief; liberty of the press and of speech; equal rights — civil and political — for all social orders, and as a consequence, enfranchisement of the peasants; a large measure of local and municipal self-government; and last, as a general condition and a guaranty for all the preceding rights, "a regular representation in a separate elective body, which must participate in legislation, in working out the budget, and in controlling the administration." Of the ninety-eight members present, seventy-one voted for this last clause as a whole, while the minority of twenty-seven was satisfied with its first half; *i.e.*, the most conservative asked for a "regular representation in a separate elective body, which must participate in legislation"; and they found this reform "absolutely necessary for the normal development of the state and of society." In the last paragraph of their petition the members of the Zemstvos requested that the anticipated reform be carried out with the assistance of the "freely elected representatives of the people"; *i.e.*, demanded the convocation of the "constitutional assembly."

This degree of unanimity in the St. Petersburg assembly has surpassed the boldest expectations even of those observers who have closely followed the latest events in the political life of Russia. "The Petition of Rights" of November 19-21, 1904, will remain a beautiful page in our annals; and whatever be its immediate practical consequences, its political program of the Russian Liberal party, openly proclaimed in an assembly which had full moral right to represent liberalism throughout the empire. Moreover, this petition of the Zemstvo men from all Russia was officially handed to the Tsar, and a deputation of the assembly was received by him. The pacification of Russia depended at that moment on the satisfactory answer of the Tsar to the petition. This answer seemed to have been more or less determined upon in advance; otherwise there would have been no political sense in permitting the assembly to gather in St. Petersburg, and in receiving the petitioners in a formal audience. All Russia was in a state of feverish expectation; and meanwhile all social groups — writers and journalists, professors and men of science, lawyers, engineers, individual Zemstvos, provincial circles of intellectuals, workingmen, students, learned societies, the general public in the street, each in his own way, in demonstrations, banquets, resolutions covered with thousands of signatures, etc., etc. — hastened to indorse the petition of the Zemstvos. No more united and "co-ordinated" political action has ever been witnessed in the history of the country. To be sure, socialistic publications drew a sharp line between their own demands and those of the liberals, and tried to introduce workingmen speakers into all the assemblies of the liberals, proposing to include in their resolutions a more positive demand for a "direct, equal, and secret" general vote, freedom of strikes and a constitutional convention, as well as for the immediate cessation of the war. In many cases these demands were agreed to, as practically they did not contradict — and often were even implied in — the demands of the liberals themselves. The freedom of discussion and the boldness of speech in these assemblies surpassed everything that Russia had ever seen before; and the same spirit pervaded the press. Conservative newspapers —

as *Novoya Vraimya* — became liberal; liberal newspapers became radical; and two new daily papers were started in St. Petersburg to advocate the claims of the more advanced public opinion. Though severely censored, they used a bold, open language, which, with perhaps two exceptions — at the beginning of the era of the "Great Reforms" (1859-61), and in 1881 — was unprecedented in the history of our press. Public manifestations in the streets, though peaceful, were treated with relentless cruelty. Policemen and "janitors" in groups of four or five fell upon single unarmed students and girls, beat them with their fists, and struck them with drawn swords, until the poor disabled victims lost consciousness. Some of them died; others were maimed for life. Evidently this was a deliberate and systematized attempt, intended to inspire horror. Instead, it only inspired hatred and a feeling of revenge.

At the same time the question of reform was under discussion in the Tsar's palace, Tsarskoya Selo; and in a cabinet session on December 15, under the presidency of the Tsar, it received a fatal solution which, instead of ending the conflict, hopelessly enlarged the gulf between the Tsar and his people. Mr. Mooravyov, the minister of justice, who was the first to speak, tried to prove that the Tsar had no right to change the existing political order. Mr. Pobedonostsev attempted to prove the same proposition by arguments from religion. He thought — in his own peculiar language — that Russia "would fall into sin and return to a state of barbarism," if the Tsar should renounce his power; religion and morality would suffer, and the law of God would be violated. It was such arguments as these which for a time decided the fate of Russia. Mr. Svyatopolk-Mirskee tried in vain to prove that the minister of justice talked nonsense; and Mr. Witte grimly concluded: "If it should become known that the emperor is forbidden by law and religion to introduce fundamental reforms of his own will — well, then a part of the population will come to the conclusion that these reforms must be achieved by way of violence. It would be equivalent to an actual appeal to revolution!" Mr. Witte played the prophet.

As a result of this discussion, the manifesto of December 26, 1904, was published. It began with the declaration that "when the need for this or that change shall have been proved ripe, then it will be considered necessary to meet it, even though the transformation to which this change may lead should involve the introduction of essentially new departures in legislation." The meaning of that solemn declaration was, however, ludicrously contradicted and narrowed by the opposite affirmation some few lines previously: "the undeviating maintenance of the immutability of the fundamental laws must be considered as an established principle of government." Such innovations as would interfere with that immutability of the fundamental laws were deliberately classified — and in advance — by the manifesto as "tendencies not seldom mistaken, and often influenced by transitory circumstances." These introductory principles were enough to annihilate any further concessions in the manifesto. All the demands of the Zemstvos, except political reform, were mentioned in the manifesto, but the promised changes were stated in such evasive and ambiguous terms and accompanied with so many "limitations," "possibilities," and other restrictions, that the impression produced was just opposite to what had been expected.

The immediate measures of the government still further increased the contrast between promises and good intentions, and the dire reality. While the manifesto promised to reconsider the "temporary" and exceptional regulations taken in its self-defense, as a matter of fact the government found itself obliged to resort to enforced measures of repression, domiciliary searches, arrests, imprisonments, etc. While it was promising to stop arbitrariness and to enforce a regime of "legality," in Nishnee Novgorod a crowd of policemen made a raid on a local club and treated the members of a party which they found in the clubroom just as they did the political demonstrators in the streets: they struck them with drawn swords — the feat remained unpunished. The manifesto promised to free the press from "excessive" repression; and there was a shower of repressive measures against the press: in three weeks of December there were doled out seven warnings, two prohibitions of retail sale, one "severe reproof," and two periodicals were stopped for three months. The manifesto answered, and tried to comply with, a political demand by the men of the Zemstvos; and at the same time an order was issued that no political demands should be permitted to be discussed in the Zemstvos. The Tsar promised to make more effective his promises of religious freedom given in an earlier manifesto of 1903; and at the same time the Holy Synod, led by Mr. Pobedonostsev, made public an address to the clergy which sounded very much like a disavowal of the Tsar and invited the priests to pray God to give the Tsar more power and wisdom.

In short, it was not pacification, but increasing irritation, that ensued from the publication of the manifesto. Its only positive result was to state that there were good reasons for the complaints and demands of public opinion, and at the same time to show that concessions formerly had been withheld by the government, not in consequence of any systematic plan of wise statesmanship, but simply because there was no urgency in the demand for reform. Evidently, the *onus probandi* now rested upon public opinion. Public opinion had to show that the need for this or that change was "ripe," in order that the government should "consider it necessary to meet it." Instead of diminishing, the tension thus further increased.

Father Gapon and Bloody Sunday

January 22, 1905 was a decisive date in Russian revolutionary history. On that day a peaceful procession of workers, led by the police-supported priest,

Father Georg Gapon, advanced upon the Winter Palace to present a petition to the Tsar. Nicholas was not in residence and the crowd was fired upon by troops. About one hundred and fifty were killed and another two hundred were wounded. The shock to public opinion was terrific and significant. The source for the following account of this incident is: Mavor, op. cit., vol. 2, pp. 456, 461–463, 467–468.

There thus came to be four elements in Gapon's movement: (1) the enthusiastic Gapon himself, apparently disinterested in the early stages, afterwards torn by conflicting interests and unable to pursue an independent course; (2) the police, participating partly overtly through the control provided by the constitution of Gapon's society, and partly covertly through spies, and probably, also, consciously or unconsciously on his part, through Gapon; (3) the small group of working men whose influence Gapon had found it necessary to enlist in order to secure adherents to his movement, and who afterwards forced Gapon into a position from which he would gladly have escaped; and (4) the mass of working men and working women members and strikers joining the society at the last moment, who, on the one hand, were depressed by low wages and by conditions of employment which they regarded as oppressive, and, on the other, were inflated with the promises of liberty and of improved conditions of life which were recklessly made to them by the progressive parties, and whose views about Gapon, as well as their adhesion to him, fluctuated from time to time.

. . .

On the 27th December (O.S.) the employees of all the St. Petersburg factories went on strike and decisive meetings were held on the following day, the 28th December, in Vasilyevsky Ostrov and other places.

On 2nd January 1905 (O.S.) there met in Gapon's house a hundred of the most influential of his adherents. Gapon again urgently pleaded for delay, but the working men "in the most categorical manner" insisted "that the fire of the excitement might die out," and that the strike at the Putilovsky Works presented an opportunity such as was not likely soon to occur again. They told Gapon also that if he did not lead them they would leave him. "We have been branded," some of them said, "as Zubatov's men, and as provocators, and here is the chance to wash out this detestable stain." This appeal was received sympathetically, and those present unanimously resolved upon going with the largest possible crowd to the Winter Palace with a petition on the following Sunday.

"So let it be!" Gapon said at last, worn out by the opposition to his appeals for delay.[1] From this time Gapon concealed himself from the police.

---

[1] The subsequent accusations of Petrov suggest that had Gapon not acquiesced in the demands of the majority at that time, he might then have been denounced as a police spy, or at least as a defender of the autocracy rather than of the liberties of the people.

They had been watching the proceedings at the branches, and it was evident that they had realized the change in the tendencies of the movement. . . .

Troops were hurried into the city on the night of the 8th [January, O.S.], and preparations were made to receive the petitioners. The mode of dealing with the crisis which was adopted is said to have been suggested by the late Grand Duke Vladimir [Uncle of Nicholas II], while the military dispositions were placed in the hands of Prince Vasilchikov, Commander-in-Chief of the Corps of the Guard. The Tsar and the Imperial Family had gone to Tsarskow Selo some days earlier.

At the height of the movement of Gapon, the actual number of registered members of the branches did not exceed 9000, but the number of persons who attended the meetings of the branches was much greater — "some scores of thousands." The number of persons who took part in the procession of "Bloody Sunday" is difficult to estimate owing to the fact that many fractions of the procession were dispersed soon after they started. The usual estimate of the total number of those who set out upon the procession is 200,000.

Early in the morning of the 9th January [22 January, N.S.], red-cross arm-bands were distributed to the women and to some men. The object of this is rather difficult to explain, unless we realize that in so great a concourse, consisting of many widely separated groups, there were many different and even conflicting ideas. These red-cross bands may have been assumed to indicate that their wearers were not militant participants in the procession or they may have been assumed for the practical purpose of calling upon their wearers to act as nurses to the wounded in an anticipated sanguinary struggle. While it is not impossible that arms were carried by some, it is also true that in some of the groups, those who came to the rendezvous with arms were deprived of them by their fellow-workers before the procession started on its way. The more "class conscious" working men seem to have marched in front of the different processions with their arms linked, thus forming chains across the line of the processions.

The early morning of Sunday, 9th January was "bitterly cold, with a piercing wind and fine driving snow." People went to church as usual. There were no troops in the great square opposite the Winter Palace. Traffic across the Neva by the bridges was unimpeded. At ten o'clock in the forenoon the movements of troops began. It was the evident intention of the military authorities to deal with the crowd in detachments, and to hold the constituent elements of the procession at or near their respective starting-points. At the same time the bridges were strongly held, and the Palace square was occupied by troops, which early in the forenoon debouched from the courtyards of the Winter Palace.

The attacks by the troops upon the processions took place at many different points, and for that reason a connected statement of the occurrences is difficult. The procedure appears, however, to have been generally the same at all the points where the military came into collision with the crowd — a summons to disperse — followed speedily by a volley of blank cartridge and then a volley of bullets. The official account admits firing in the Schlusselburg Chaussee, at the Narva Gate, where the crowd was led by Gapon, in the Troitsky Square, in Vasilevsky Ostrov, in the Alexander Gardens, near the Winter Palace, and in the Nevsky Prospekt, especially at the Kazan Cathedral.

The First Duma

The source is: Pares, B., Russia and Reform, pp. 546–560.

The Duma met on May 10, 1906. The Emperor, who had not visited his capital since the attempt made upon his life in January, 1905, in a firm and vigorous voice expressed his hope that the labours of the Assembly would be conducive to the welfare of Russia. The Duma, when it had met in the palace prepared for it, elected its President, Vice-Presidents, and Secretaries. There was no contest; nearly all were chosen from the ranks of the Cadets. All the prominent leaders of different parties had at one time or another been under the displeasure of the Government, and Professor Gredyeskul, a man of no particular eminence, was appointed Vice-President simply because he had been one of the last to suffer persecution. The Assembly made an admirable choice of a president: Professor Muromtseff is a trained lawyer of great distinction, whose nice legal sense and keen and conscientious discrimination would do credit to the English bench. His noble presence gave dignity to the Assembly; and his untiring concentration of mind, though it visibly aged him during the sittings, maintained throughout the debates the control of the spirit of law. In his absence, Prince Peter Dolgorukoff was an able and business-like chairman. Prince Shakhovskoy was a capable secretary.

The Emperor's Speech from the Throne had not contained any programme of legislation, nor did the Ministers suggest any. Of this great mistake the Duma took immediate advantage. We might say that the Emperor wanted a German Parliament, and that the Duma intended to be an English one. It decided to take the initiative by putting forward a whole programme in its "Address to the Throne." This was a policy which would help to keep the Assembly united; for the minimum demands of all sections could be expressed together. The Address was very cleverly drafted. The abruptness of some of the demands was masked by the loyal and moderate tone adopted throughout. The needs of the peasants held a prominent place; the more radical demands of the workmen received less recognition, but then the workmen had by their boycott practically excluded themselves from the Duma, and the object of the Cadets was to secure the unanimity of those present. The debates were animated; a leading part was taken by the Labour Group, which was still in process of formation. The Labour leaders adopted the wise policy of leaving their more extreme claims unexpressed, supporting the Cadets in all their disputes with the Moderates, and trying to secure the most decisive wording which could be passed unanimously. The Address was read three times; at the second reading it was debated sentence by sentence. Discussion centered chiefly round the land question, and the demands for an amnesty for political prisoners and for the abolition of the death penalty. Count Heyden, standing for wise moderation, used his excellent debating power to keep the demands within reasonable bounds. On the land question the Moderates, who more than anyone else represented the country gentry, showed their public spirit by accepting the principle of expropriation of land; the measure of compensation was left to be decided later. Realising the numerical weakness of his party, Mr. Stakhovich reserved his effort for the question of the amnesty. In two great speeches, which came straight from his heart and would have carried conviction to any who were not hopelessly prejudiced, he demanded that the amnesty should be two-sided, and that the Duma, while condemning the death penalty as inhuman and demanding the immediate release of political prisoners, should in the name of the country frankly express its opinion that murders of officials should cease from that day. No more just or more eloquent claim was heard during the sittings of the Duma. The country gentry had not pleaded for themselves; they spoke in the cause of the police, with whom they had nothing in common. Mr. Stakhoyich had seized the exact moment when, with only one dissentient, the Assembly had decided on the abolition of the death penalty. But the Cadets, who always kept their eyes fixed on the extremists to the left of them, and, in their tactical manipulation of the votes, failed to appreciate the great mass of opinion outside, now made their first crucial mistake; and Mr. Rodicheff was put up to oppose the amendment of Stakhovich. Turning his back on the Left, and adopting an almost threatening manner towards the Octobrists, he gradually worked himself up into a rhetorical piece of special pleading, in which he maintained "that the time was not yet come for moderation, that it would come only after the victory." The Labour Group applauded, and on a division Mr. Stakhovich found himself in an insignificant minority. But the Duma had lost its best chance; Mr. Lvoff one of the most able and honest of the Cadets, soon afterwards left the party.

The Address was piloted throughout the debate by Mr. Nabokoff. In a voice under whose soft inflection lay the suggestion of a great reserve of strength, he over and over again gave matter-of-fact and convincing answers to the objections of individual members. When he was not speaking, it was often more interesting to watch him than to follow the debates: he would rise in a casual way from his seat, move through the assembly much as an English gentleman might pass through the smoking room of his club, seat himself beside the terrible Aladin of the Labour Group, and work out with him some formula which could be accepted by that party. This, after very outspoken discussion, would at last be achieved, and Nabokoff, with his little slip of paper in his hands, would walk straight across to Count Heyden, the Conservative leader, with whom the same process would be repeated. It was to be noticed that almost anything proposed by Nabakoff was passed unanimously. The time came for the third reading. Heyden, Stakhovich, and a few others, being unable to accept certain phrases, retired to avoid breaking the unanimity of the House. At 3 a.m. the final draft was accepted in a full House by all present.

The Address expressed a number of general principles and suggested legislation on each. It was far more easy for the Government to break up the unity of the Duma than for Milyukóff to maintain it. Formally, the Address was simply an answer to the Emperor's speech; it remained that each demand contained in it should be turned into a separate Bill. If the Government were still so lacking in initiative as not to produce any Bills of its own, it might leave the Duma to go on with this work in the full assurance that there would sooner or later be divisions inside the Assembly. There was one way of keeping the Duma united against the Government, and that way was adopted by the Ministers. An unnecessary fuss was made as to the way in which the Address should be received by the Emperor. The Duma was ordered to send it to him, not directly, but through the Marshal of the Court. This made a very bad impression, as publishing to the nation the fact that the Emperor was isolated from the Duma. But the Ministers did not stop here: they solemnly came down to the Duma to pronounce a kind of judgment on the Address. The Premier, Mr. Goremykin, read out a long statement in which, while suggesting certain mild reforms, he characterised the chief demands of the Duma as "inadmissible." Above all, he strongly repudiated the policy of expropriation, which he declared to be anti-social. His manner was that of a schoolmaster reading a lesson, yet it was well known that he was not the real possessor of power. His remarks were listened to without the slightest interruption and in a painfully breathless silence. When he sat down, Mr. Nabokoff mounted the tribune. Speaking very simply and quietly, like a man who was thoroughly at his ease, he expressed the disappointment of the Assembly, and proceeded in a matter-of-fact way to move a vote of censure on the Government. Thus thrown upon their defence, the bureaucratic Ministers proved utterly incapable of meeting outspoken criticism. In their own Ministries they could order any critic out of the room; but here was a situation which they had never had to face before. They sat there bowing beneath the storm as one speaker after another drew instances from the vast store of official abuses, and catechised them point-blank on questions both of principle and of detail. Kovalyevsky asked whether the Emperor Alexander II. acted anti-socially, when he emancipated the serfs and endowed them with land. Kokoshkin, in defence of certain English principles to which the Duma had appealed, suggested that the maintenance of order was rather more successful in England than in Russia. One Minister, Mr. Shcheglovitoff, rose to almost apologise for the Government, very much to the chagrin of his colleagues. One can imagine how this scene would lower the prestige of the Government in the eyes of the average non-party peasant. After standing the racket for some time as best they might, the Ministers withdrew; and the vote of censure, which had the support of the Moderates, was carried without any opposition.

The Duma now settled down to its work of discussing separate Bills. The family atmosphere, which is so noticeable in Russia, was here peculiarly strong. The Assembly, having complete control of its own house, turned it into something like a vast caravanserai. The beautiful hall soon came to be regarded, even by the peasant members, as a kind of home. The long side lobbies were furnished with great tables covered with green baize, at which peasants and Intelligents sat down indiscriminately to write letters to their families. A constant stream of members was always passing through these rooms; and all congregated from time to time in the great noisy corridor. Here the chief leaders walked up and down arm in arm; and isolated peasants, Russian, Cossack, or Polish, sat about on the different benches and were quite ready to converse with any stranger. Members and correspondents gathered without distinction at the buffet and in the restaurant, and little groups of acquaintances wandered through the pleasant gardens outside. The building contained its own postal and telegraph office. If the Duma did nothing else, it brought together for the first time representatives of every class and of every interest in Russia. It was of course far more Imperial than any other European Parliament. It would be difficult to imagine a more picturesque gathering. Each man wore the costume of his class. The country gentry of the Intelligents dressed very simply, but there were Russian priests with long beards and hair, a Roman Catholic bishop in skull-cap lined with red, finely accoutred Cossacks from the Caucasus, Bashkirs and Buryats in strange and tinselled Asiatic dress, Polish peasants in the brilliant and martial costumes of their people, and a whole mass of staid, bearded, and top-booted Russian peasants. Strangers easily obtained admittance; and amongst the most picturesque visitors were the so-called "walking deputies" who were sent by peasant constituents to look after their members, and others who had tramped for hundreds of miles to ask the Duma to settle their private disputes. Groups of members and non-members formed in the corridor to discuss without reticence any question of the moment. Small party conferences, sitting in the committee-rooms, seemed in no way disturbed by passing strangers. Milyukoff, in the simple dress of an English country gentleman, walked up and down the corridor receiving the suggestions of various party leaders, which seldom induced him to deviate a yard from the tactics upon which he had determined. One noticed that the Cadets as a body quite failed to get hold of the non-party members. These peasants, who would not sink their individuality in any party formula, expressed the most fresh and interesting opinions of all. Count Heyden could often be seen discussing matters with them; he understood them, and they understood him; but Milyukoff was hardly ever to be seen talking to a non-party man. At one time it appeared that Kovalyevsky and Kuzmin-Karavayeff might capture a considerable section of the Cadets; but the Cadets arranged that every member should register his seat in the House, and this made it more difficult to pass from one party to another. The Labour Group, which continued its organisation throughout the sittings, tried in every way to absorb the Non-Party, but without success.

Bills were introduced into the Duma guaranteeing freedom of conscience and the inviolability of the person. The discussions were not very interesting; everyone was agreed as to these main principles, little more than the principles was expressed in the Bills, and almost as much had been said in the Emperor's manifestos. A month's delay had to pass after the notice of introduction, before the Assembly could deal effectively with any proposed measure. The Duma was allowed to discuss the franchise, and it of course declared in favour of the well-known formula "universal, direct, equal, and secret." The debate on woman's suffrage excited a lively interest. On this day the corridor was invaded by an active band of suffragettes, who evidently thought that they could give the necessary lessons to the non-party peasant. It was amusing to watch the peasants dealing with these young ladies. One very typical peasant admitted that it was most unfair that women should receive lower pay than men for similar work. "We will put that right for you," he said; "let us get on our legs first, then we will give you some rights." But the young ladies wanted not to receive, but to take, and claimed that women ought to be sitting in the Duma. "Look here," said he, "I will tell you what: you go and marry! You will have a husband and children, and your husband will look after you altogether." "Look after, indeed!" said the young ladies; but the peasant would not promise anything more. Equally interesting was the attitude of the Non-Party group towards the Jews: they spoke without any ill-will, but remarked: "Even without rights, the Jews are on the top of us." They were therefore almost the only dissentients on both these questions.

All these Bills were not really practical politics, for not a single measure of the Duma became law except a vote of credit to the Government to relieve peasant distress; they were rather appeals for popular support. Realising from the first that the bureaucracy was definitely hostile to it, and that no frank reform could successfully pass through the various stages ordained by the Government, the Duma naturally set itself to secure strength from elsewhere. With this object, it deliberately turned itself into a machine for propaganda. "The tribune," said one Labour member to me, "is the only part of this House that counts." Nearly every newspaper published the fullest reports of the sittings, and these were eagerly devoured in distant villages all over the country. Immobilised in its legislative work, the Duma put a number of carefully but firmly worded interpellations to the various Ministers. The abuses of the administration were thus brandished before the eyes of the country. This was already war, but it would be difficult to say which side had first declared it. Ministers, severally or together, continued to visit the Duma, to make explanations or to answer interpellations. Each such visit naturally led to a scene; when the Duma had, with one dissentient, abolished the death sentence, the Government sent down General Pavloff to explain that it refused this measure. Pavloff was generally believed to have hurried on the execution of certain death sentences contrary to law, and the Labour Group interrupted him with cries of "Murderer!" The President even had to adjourn the sitting. Aladin, who spoke with far more vehemence inside the Duma than amongst his own party, suggested that it was very amiable of the Ministers to continue to come down to the House after they had been told that the country did not want them. The situation was in fact an entirely false one for all concerned. The only Minister who knew how to face it was Mr. Stolypin. He answered interpellations with the utmost moderation, but with the utmost firmness; and once, when the Labour Group tried to shout him down, he turned on them and addressed the rest of his speech to them in a voice which rose loud and strong above all their clamour. He was the one Minister who was ever cheered by any member of the Duma. But Mr. Stolypin, though universally credited with honesty and courage, had to meet the strongest charges of all: he had to answer for the faults or omissions of his predecessors in office. On June 21 he had just replied to an interpellation on the "pogroms," when Prince Urusoff rose to make his memorable speech on the official circulation of appeals to murder, and the malignant activity of Komisaroff. The Prince spoke in so low a voice as to be almost inaudible; many of the peasant members in no way realised the importance of his speech; but it was published in full in most of the newspapers, and dealt to the Government by far the most crushing blow which it had yet received. The speech was exemplary in its moderation and loyalty; Prince Urusoff in no way inculpated the existing Ministry: the only inference which he drew from his disclosures was that the dualism within the Government itself must be abolished without delay, and that the Emperor must be put into real touch with his people. But to make his meaning clear, he had to attack "those obscure forces which," he said, "are arming against us." This was a more open declaration of war between the Duma and the unofficial advisers of the Crown.

Rumors of dissolution had been in the air ever since the passing of the Address. The Cadets desired to use every day to the full, in order to make the position of the Duma so strong in the country that dissolution would become practically impossible. This is why they gave such prominence to the land question, and why their Bill bore so pretentious a character. Mr. Milyukoff might almost be compared to the gambler in the famous opera of Pushkin and Chaikovsky. Three cards will, he believes, give him fortune, and he dreams that the numbers have been revealed to him: he calls the three, (the three autonomies), and wins; he calls the seven, (the seven freedoms), and wins; he calls the ace, and the card produced is the Queen of Spades; pique—mort. The Queen of Spades was the land question.

The Land Bill of the Cadets was in many ways much less objectionable than it seemed. The principle of expropriation is in itself not revolutionary in Russia; it had been accepted by almost every section of public opinion, including the Conservative representatives of the country gentry; indeed, some reactionaries had blamed Mr. Goremykin for publicly opposing it. The Cadets were all in favour of compensation to the landowner, and were only divided on the question as to what would be a fair price; naturally, many objected to the artificial prices produced by the operations of the Peasants' Bank. Though the Cadets accepted the principle of the Labour Group that there should be a legal limit to the extent of estates, they fixed this limit so high as to rob the principle of all its force. The Cadets also agreed with the Labour party in declaring that land should be State property; but the long leases which they proposed knocked the life out of this declaration. Certainly Mr. Hertzenstein, the chief authority of the Cadets on this question, was not so much a land expert as an expert on land values, and his views were chiefly dictated by theories of almost a socialistic kind. Certainly nothing but theory could explain the assumption that Russia would prosper only on the basis of limited holdings. But leading Cadets themselves suggested in conversation that the Bill would come out of committee robbed of all its disagreeable characteristics. This is itself the sum of their condemnation. As it was they who had drafted the Bill, the pretence of Socialism in the original draft can only be looked upon as a hardly ingenuous piece of tactics, designed to preserve the unanimity of the Duma, and to capture the votes of the Labour Group. For all that, the Labour men introduced a separate Bill of their own. Their Bill was really that which the Cadet Bill only pretended to be, but the very similarity between the two justified the general opinion that the Cadets were almost Socialists. Beyond this, the Cadets had altogether misjudged their public. If I may trust the common conclusions of peasant members from almost every part of the Empire, only the least enterprising of the peasants were still in favour of the communal system of land tenure, though all wished to retain the Village Society. The most cherished dream of the intelligent peasant was that of personal property in land. The first land debates were ruled by the tactics of propagandism. Almost every peasant was encouraged to speak. Nearly all read their speeches; the speaker would afterwards proudly despatch the draft to his constituents. Thus the debate was rambling in the extreme. Next an enormous Commission was chosen to represent every section of the Duma; it was hoped that now the peasants would be willing to wait a little longer for the land; the Commission did not propose to hurry itself.

But the Government was getting ready to move. The recent pogrom in Byelostok, though presenting no signs of collusion with St. Petersburg, was undoubtedly in large part due to the neutrality or worse of local officials. The Duma sent its own investigators to the spot, and they accepted without due examination any evidence offered to them so long as it was hostile to the police. It was now proposed, with the hearty concurrence of the Labour Group, to constitute in the country small committees to investigate the land question in each locality; in other words, the Duma was making a bid to gradually become the Government of the country. The tension between the representatives of the people and the Ministers was too severe to last.

More than once voices were raised even at the Court suggesting an accommodation. This could only be obtained by the resignation of the Ministers and the appointment of men who commanded the support of the Duma. Amongst those who were said to advocate this step the public were surprised to see the name of General Trepoff. The Ministers, it may be imagined, were not unwilling to retire from their exceedingly disagreeable position. From the appointment of a Cadet Ministry certain results were practically sure to follow. There would inevitably be an open conflict between the new Ministers and the so-called camarilla, or unofficial Court clique; but at the same time the Cadets would be forced by their new responsibilities to sever their connection with the Labour Group and to move more to the right; there would then be some kind of a split in the Cadet party itself, and thus there would be constituted inside the Duma a real Opposition. The governing Right Wing of the Cadets would be compelled to lean for support on the Moderates, and this new party of the Right would include nearly all those members of the Duma whom the Zemstva had trained in practical work. It could hardly have failed to take a tinge of class interests from the country gentry and the more responsible section of the middle class. The new Ministry, once in power, would be on its defence; every measure which it brought forward would be severely criticised, and men who had shown ability in opposition would now have to prove that they were more capable in administration than the bureaucracy. As the number of able Cadets was limited, and as they had been trained after all only in the sphere of local government, they could not have dispensed with the support of a certain number of the more Liberal bureaucrats. Such men would have to be retained both in the *personnel* of officialdom and in the Ministry itself. Any failure of the Cadets would help to develop in the public mind a natural movement of moral reaction which was already in process. For the Government, one of the strongest arguments in favour of a Cadet Ministry was that for once Russia possessed a Duma in which the strength lay near the centre. This phenomenon is comparatively rare even in constitutional assemblies of long standing; in Russia it was the artificial result of circumstances already explained; but it made for the formation of a great middle term between the sovereign and his people, and it was something to be seized upon and used to the utmost. Anyhow, the Court was half prepared to compromise; twice Mr. Shipoff was summoned to Peterhof, but as one who had failed to enter the Duma, and whose supporters in it were only a small and unorganised group, he once more refused office. There was much talk of a Ministry which should include both Mr. Muromtseff and Count Heyden. It was definitely resolved to invite Mr. Muromtseff to Peterhof that he might suggest the names of possible colleagues; but a small disturbance in the Preobrazhensky regiment of the Guard led to a Court panic, and the step was deferred. Mr. Muromtseff, admirable as the President of the Assembly, would perhaps not have made a strong Prime Minister; and the Cadets seemed inclined to refuse to serve under any but their recognised party leaders. Certainly they represented the spirit of opposition in the country, and had given so many pledges to the public that they could hardly sink the individuality of their party in a coalition. But for these very reasons the personality of Mr. Milyukoff was highly distasteful to the Court. Not once during the session had the President been invited to Peterhof except as one of many guests at a Court banquet. If he had possessed a right of claiming interviews with the sovereign, or if there had been in the Assembly a responsible person in touch with the majority who reported the daily debates to the Emperor, the Court would have possessed more detailed knowledge of the actual political atmosphere. Anyhow all the chances of an accommodation came to nothing.

Meanwhile the Ministers could not but realise that the Duma was undermining their prestige amongst the people. The Land Bill was the most extreme bid of the Assembly for support against the Government; the Ministers drew up their own alternative measure, and, in a circular which they officially published all over the Empire, they condemned the principles of the Cadet Bill, thus making a direct appeal to the country against the Duma.

So far the propagandism of the Duma had been indirect; the Duma was precluded by law from issuing a direct address to the people; but such action had been equally illegal when these same Cadet leaders had carried their appeal through the Moscow Congress of July, 1905; and the fervour of the Labour Group and of the Cadets of the Left was not likely to be daunted by this formality. It was now that patience snapped on both sides. The Land Commission was the body specially attacked by the Government circular. All parties were represented on it; but its office-holders were not the chief leaders of the Cadets, and Milyukoff, as not being in the Duma, was of course excluded from it. At the Congress of July, 1905, a prominent part had been taken by Kuzmin-Karavayeff, who in the name of legality and order had begged the Congress to proceed with the greatest circumspection. This gentleman had played a prominent part in the Duma; he was supposed to be more Conservative than any of the Cadets; a speaker of remarkable grace and fluency, he always commanded attention. He now proposed to the Land Commission that it should send out to the country a weakly worded appeal asking the constituents not to believe in the Government circular, and to trust the Duma to make an effective Land Bill. The Commission, as representing all parties, adopted the address, and presented it for the acceptance of the whole Duma. The debate on this address was very remarkable. Late at night Mr. Lednitsky, sitting amongst the Cadets of the Right and also representing the Autonomist group, in vigorous language denounced the appeal as both feeble and irritating; he was loudly applauded both by the Moderates and by the Labour Group. But party discipline was strong amongst the Cadets; and the Labour Group preferred to compromise their rivals by a weak appeal rather than have no appeal at all. After pleading for the insertion of a stronger wording at certain points, they supported the address, and it was carried at the first reading by an immense majority.

On the next day there was no sitting, but in the evening there was a party meeting of the Cadets. Milyukoff and others of the leaders looked upon the address as a bad tactical mistake; they might be ready to appeal to the country, but this was neither the right time nor the right way. Many of their followers seemed inclined to break loose from them. However, the leaders in the end triumphed, and on the succeeding day Mr. Petrunkyevich rose at the second reading to suggest an entirely different wording of the whole address. This he moved by way of amendments to each paragraph. The Labour Group saw itself defeated on those points which it had most at heart, and the Cadets, in opposing the Labour amendments, had the support of the Moderates; finally the Labour Group left the hall *en masse,* and decided to draw up a more abrupt appeal of its own. After its departure, the Moderates contested the whole measure, and for the first time a proposal of the Cadets was passed only by a small majority. The suggestion that the address should be officially printed in the *Official Messenger* could not be discussed at all, because it was found that at this late hour the House did not possess the necessary quorum.

The wording of Petrunkyevich was far superior to the original draft. But the Duma had definitely decided to disregard the fundamental laws. Far more important was the obvious fact that the Duma and even the Cadet party were no longer unanimous. It seemed strange that a measure adopted almost unanimously by the Duma should be radically altered at the next sitting because a given party had decided to give it a different character; and an appeal to the people was precisely the measure which, of all others, most required firmness and solidarity. Naturally one asks why the Cadet members of the Land Commission originally adopted the first draft without ascertaining the will of their party. There had been similar mistakes before, as when Professor Petrazhitsky had risen apparently to introduce the Land Bill and had proceeded to condemn it. Tactical unity was hardly to be expected in the first Russian Parliament, and it is immensely to the credit of Milyukoff that he was ever able to keep the Duma united for so long. But now the Duma had published its dissensions before the world, and this was the moment which the Government might choose, if it desired a dissolution.

At Peterhof the counsels of General Trepoff were opposed by Mr. Stolypin, the only Minister who had followed the later debates in the Duma. Stolypin's view was clear and consistent; he recognised Russia as having passed into a constitutional régime: that is to say, there would always be a Duma to join in the work of legislation; but he refused to concede the principle that the Ministers should, as a matter of course, be selected from the party prevailing in the Assembly. He was against the formation of a Cadet Ministry, because it would be compelled by its pledges to surrender almost all the power of the administrative system in a single day. The Duma was at war with the Government; if the Government would not make way for a Cadet Ministry, the only step left for it was to dissolve the Duma. The discussion of the two views at Peterhof was long; but by the evening of Saturday, July 21, the view of Mr. Stolypin had prevailed, and the Emperor had signed the decree of dissolution. The decree expressed in no uncertain terms the Emperor's disappointment at what he regarded as the factious spirit of the Duma. It was read out in churches and posted up in public places all over the Empire; Stolypin himself accepted office as the new Prime Minister.

The dissolution of the Duma was the victory of a single strong-minded man. How he understood the difference between Constitutionalism and Parliamentarism was at once apparent; almost every newspaper in St. Petersburg was stopped except the *Official Messenger*. The public was stupefied and bowed beneath the yoke; it again felt the paralysing weight of an overwhelming governmental force hostile to the vast majority of expressed opinions. However, the Cadets and the Labour Group acted with a remarkable unanimity. They at once made their way to a common rendezvous at Vyborg, in Finland. Here a large majority of those members who had still remained in St. Petersburg discussed the drafting of a far more bold address to the people; Heyden, Stakhovich, and Lvoff, came out to confer with the majority, but were not able to join with it. Some forty of the Cadets, led by Hertzenstein, were against any strong expression of policy; but these were persuaded to make common cause with the rest, and a draft was discussed, accepted, and eventually signed by over two hundred members. In forcible language it invited the people to refuse recruits and the payment of taxes until there was a new Duma. The Cadets and the Labour Group could hardly have believed that isolated peasant communities would take the lead in resisting the Government with arms in their hands, and the Labour Group proposed the establishment of a central committee to represent the late Duma and to organise the resistance. This proposal, however, fell through in consequence of the attitude of the more moderate of the Cadets. A more effective article of the Vyborg manifesto was that which, in the name of the nation, refused responsibility for future foreign loans made to the Government; but the programme of a resistance to the Government all over Russia broke down when the Cadets, accepting the dissolution as final, practically retired into private life. Stolypin was expected to arrest all the members returning from Vyborg, but he was too clever to make this mistake. The Cadets continued to hold party meetings, but after making their great appeal for the support of the nation they themselves failed to take any action whatsoever. They were now looked upon as neither one thing nor the other; even the murder of Mr. Hertzenstein, which might have restored to them the sympathies of public opinion, resulted in nothing but a rather fussy expression of irritation. The artificial character of their tactical victory at the elections now became more and more apparent.

The Tsaritsa and the Government

The personalities of the rulers are always a matter of tremendous importance in an autocracy because the wills and whims of autocrats affect the lives of millions of persons. There are few clearer illustrations of the soundness of this generalization than the story of the inter-relationships of Nicholas II, Alexandra and Rasputin. The source is: Pares, Sir Bernard (Editor), The Letters of the Tsaritsa to the Tsar, 1914-1916. New York: Robert M. McBride and Co., 1924. Pp. ix-xii, xiv-xviii, xxviii-xxix, xxxi-xxxiii, xxxiv-xxxviii.

The future Empress of Russia, Princess Alix of Hesse-Darmstadt, was born on June 5, 1872, at Darmstadt. Her mother was the beloved Princess Alice of England, who died while nursing her children in 1878 at the age of thirty-five. Princess Alix was brought up largely in England at the court of her grandmother, Queen Victoria, whose ideas and discipline she fully assimilated. A large portrait of the Queen hung later in one of the chief living-rooms at Tsarkoe Selo; "She was very tiny," said the Empress, "but she was very forceful." The whole *morale* of Princess Alix was English. English was the language which she always spoke and wrote to the Emperor. The housekeeper of Tsarskoe Selo was an Englishwoman. In her family there was hereditary the hæmophilic ailment. One of her uncles had his life cut short by it, and her sister, Princess Irena of Prussia, married to Prince Henry, lost several of her children by it. This malady appears only in males and is transmitted only by females. The Empress herself was therefore immune from it, and though later she suffered very much from her heart, she had health to support a life full of trials and at times full of activities. Her eldest sister, Princess Victoria of Battenberg, was married in England. Another sister, Ella, married the Grand Duke Sergius, younger brother of Alexander III of Russia, and became on her conversion to the Orthodox Church (which was anything but nominal), the Grand Duchess Elizabeth. It was on a journey to this sister that Princess Alix was first contemplated as a possible bride for the heir to the throne. But nothing came of the idea this time. The whole nature of the Princess was deeply religious. Her strong Protestant honesty of conscience did not allow her to change her faith without conviction. An Orthodox Bishop was sent to Darmstadt to explain to her the Orthodox confession, and, as in her sister's case, it proved capable of satisfying the deepest instincts of her nature far more than was possible for Protestantism. There was in her father's family and also, perhaps, in her mother's a tendency towards mysticism. On the sudden illness of the Emperor Alexander III, in his anxiety for his son's marriage, Princess Alix was hastily summoned to Russia, and her first appearance to the Russian people as the future Empress was at Alexander's funeral.

She was, of course, a woman of wonderful beauty, fair and tall, with the dignity of an empress. But she was from the first painfully shy. Though this shyness gave way when she was with her very few intimate friends, it cannot be denied that she not only was thought, but actually was, very awkward, ill at ease, and unsympathetic in her appearances at the court. One does not need to take the description of one who hated her, Count Witte. M. Paléologue also finds that conversation is an effort to her, that she can hardly get out a word of welcome; and others too carried away the impression that her thought throughout court functions was, "When will this be over, and when will all these people be gone?" The life which she and her family led throughout, a life particularly of her choosing, was remote, not only from the culture and intellect of the country, but even from the other members of the Imperial family. The Grand Dukes themselves complained that they had the greatest difficulty in getting to the Emperor. The extraordinary limitedness and isolation of this life gave the whole atmosphere and background to the part which the Empress was to play in politics. And at the same time they solve the riddle of the extraordinary contrast between her private life and her public influence. It is this isolation which makes so intelligible the wonderful resignation and complete absorption in religion which marked the family life during imprisonment. Mr. Gibbs, colleague of M. Gilliard, and English tutor to the Tsarevich, said the Empress was never so worthy of herself as after the abdication. It was as if her nature could only expand in such a hermitage of remoteness and privation. From the outset, the "funeral bride" seemed marked for misfortune. The coronation festivities were completely marred by the terrible catastrophe on the Hodynsky Plain outside Moscow, where thousands were crushed through extraordinarily incapable arrangements for the distribution of presents to the people. The Emperor and Empress were not told of the extent of the disaster, and their decision to carry out their programme left with many the impression of heartlessness. The investigation which followed led to a conflict between the Court Ministry on the one side and the Moscow administration of the Grand Duke Sergius on the other, and this was a signal for one of those wars of court intrigue which were to disfigure the whole reign. The Empress's ardent wish to give an heir to the throne was disappointed time after time by the successive birth of four daughters, and when at last, in the midst of the disasters of the Japanese War, the little heir arrived in 1904, it was found that he was marked by the hereditary ailment of his mother's family. He was hæmophilic; the slightest scratch might lead to internal bleeding which there was no known means of stopping. Full of spirit, he had to be deterred as far as possible from any childish games and sports. The radiant health of his four sisters seemed a mockery of his ailment, and the Empress could not herself forget that the disease was transmitted through her.

In the most striking contrast with this succession of misfortunes stands out the picture of the home life of the Imperial family. While one is reading this story, one seems almost as much cut off from the outside world as were the actors in it; they had no ambitions, their requirements were healthy and of the most modest kind; there was nothing to make them wish to look outside their own life, everything to deter them from doing so. The Emperor, who as an emperor was so conspicuous a failure, was the most tender and devoted of husbands, and in the home circle that strong natural charm which impressed everyone who met him had full, free play. The Empress adored him, as is clear from these letters. There was no feeling of superiority, but a deep pity for the burden which he had to bear and the unsuitability of it to his yielding and lovable character.

* * *

The mystical tinge of the Empress's mind has already been mentioned. She had, we are told, "a very strong inner life" and could remain for hours absorbed in contemplation. She herself strongly disclaimed spiritualism. "It is a great sin," she said. But to everything mystic her miserable surroundings urged her strongly, and one cannot think that she saw any clear frontier between the two. A charlatan doctor of nervous diseases at Lyons, one Philippe, who worked in what he called "astral medicine" was introduced to the Grand Duchess Militsa, the Montenegrin Princess who had married the Grand Duke Peter Nikolayevich, and to her sister Anastasia, the Stana of these letters, married first to the Duke of Leuchtenberg and after her divorce in 1907 to the Grand Duke Nikolay Nikolayevich. Philippe, who was in person insignificant but had a remarkable attraction of manner, was through the Grand Duchesses presented to the imperial couple in 1901 at Compiègne during their visit to France and was later taken by them to Tsarskoe. We read of séances in which Philippe called up the spirit of Alexander III (whose wishes always possessed an immense authority for his son). We read even of a claim of Philippe that he could fix the sex of children, and from Witte's *Memoirs* and elsewhere we understand that the Empress was strongly persuaded that she was enceinte in the autumn of 1902. In 1904, however, Philippe definitely interfered in politics, and as his first steps in this field were very indiscreet — for instance, he promised quick success in the war against Japan — he left Russia in disgrace and died in France in August 1905. Philippe had told the Empress that she would have a second friend who would talk to her of God. He also, as we learn from the letters, gave her a bell as a symbol that she was to warn the Emperor against those who wished to influence him.

Philippe's successor was the famous Rasputin. The name itself is not a surname, but a nickname given him by his fellow-peasants and meaning "the dissolute." Gregory, who was born in 1871, was a simple peasant of the village of Pokrovskoe, not far from Tobolsk in Siberia. After a most disorderly youth he retired to a neighbouring monastery, and on his return obtained among the peasants a reputation for wonderful spiritual powers. The disorders of his life did not cease; they broke out from time to time with extraordinary violence. But this, it was claimed, only gave the more force to his reiterated repentances. Rasputin was not a monk, but one of those "holy" men who wandered about among the people claiming a direct commission from God, a type of extravagant and unlicensed individualism of which there are many instances in the story of the Orthodox Church. Throughout he claimed to be the typical man of the people, and it was as such that he was welcomed in Petrograd by the Rector of the Theological Academy, Bishop Feofan, who was confessor to the Empress. Certified by Feofan, Rasputin entered the circle of the Montenegrin Grand Duchesses and the Grand Duke Nicholas, and it was from them that he was passed on to the Palace at Tsarkoe in the summer of 1907. Rasputin never sought to flatter the sovereigns; he even spoke roughly to them from the first. He was early associated with another charlatan, the Buryat doctor Badmayev, who was guilty of money frauds. Rasputin's visits to the place have been greatly exaggerated. M. Gilliard, who only once set eyes on him, says that Rasputin did not see either of the sovereigns more than once a month and sometimes much less frequently. According to Anna Vyrubova, it was only twice or thrice a year before the war and from four to six times afterwards; she maintains that Rasputin only saw the Emperor once throughout the critical year, 1916. Most of the meetings took place not in the palace but in the little house outside the park tenanted by Vyrubova. Far more often the messages from Rasputin to the Emperor and Empress were, in the language of these letters, "handed over" by Anna and often they were in the form of telegrams to her. We must believe that the Empress never saw anything of the man's vileness, though once she mentions in the letters that "he was not tipsy." Both Madame Dehn and Anna Vyrubova strongly disclaim any knowledge of this side of his character. Madame Dehn is convinced that even for Anna Vyrubova Rasputin was nothing more than a holy man, though her book, like the Empress's letters, represents Anna as a person who would be in love with anyone. It is possible to believe this. But Petrograd itself could be in no doubt about the man's real character. He was a standing outrage on decencies. Even Vyrubova admits that during the war adventurers "took advantage of his simplicity," took him out to dinner and gave him too much drink. As to the sexual exploits there can be no question. They were innumerable, and several of them were openly vaunted by the women who fell victims to him. In March 1911, to counteract these public scandals, Rasputin made a visit to Jerusalem, but was back in Petrograd by November. There followed further orgies, and Rasputin was now openly condemned both by Bishop Feofan and by two others who had formerly been his strong supporters — Bishop Hermogen of Saratov and the monk Heliodore — who spat at him and struck him, and were very shortly afterwards relegated to monasteries. At this time the newspapers printed numberless instances of Rasputin's seductions. By the so-called press-reform made during the Revolution of 1904-7, the preliminary censorship had been abolished, and papers could print what they pleased at the risk of being arbitrarily fined by the local governors after publication. This risk they were glad to take in the case of Rasputin, but the Empress secured from the Emperor an order that there should be nothing printed at all on the subject. Thereby the Emperor broke his own law and the leader of the Duma, Alexander Guchkov, seized the occasion for an interpellation and a public debate on Rasputin. In March 1912 the Prime Minister, Kokovtsev, a strong but enlightened Conservative, urged the Emperor to send Rasputin away from Petrograd. Rasputin departed of himself with an insolent threat to Kokovtsev, and when the Prime Minister visited the sovereigns in Livadia in May the Empress turned her back on him. At the beginning of 1914 Kokovtsev was summarily dismissed without explanation.

It may be true, as is urged, that in the main the Empress confined her interventions in politics up to the war to obtaining the dismissals of those Ministers who were hostile to Rasputin. As to Rasputin himself, the part which he took in politics was soon an active one. The pleas of Vyrubova on this point will not hold good for an instant. There is no need to regard him as a champion of any particular point of view except that of autocratic absolutism, which alone could enable him to penetrate an ignorant palace as the voice of the Russian peasants. But his good offices were constantly sought by political adventurers, and he himself was probably not conscious of the extent to which he was being used as a tool.

The foundation of Rasputin's influence with the Empress is quite clear. Before 1912 he had been called in to help with his counsel, and more than that, even with his prophecies, at moments critical to the health of the Tsarevich. In the summer of this year the Imperial family was at one of the Emperor's shooting-boxes in Poland, when Alexis fell while getting out of a boat so that he bruised his groin against the gunwale. This and a subsequent piece of negligence brought on a most serious crisis, and the parents were half beside themselves with anxiety. The doctors declared themselves helpless. Of course anything like an operation was at all times out of the question, and the internal bleeding could not be stopped. Recourse was made by telegraph to Rasputin, who replied at once: "This illness is not as dangerous as it looks. Let the doctors not torture him." It was from that moment that the danger rapidly passed away. In December 1915, while the Tsarevich was with his father at General Headquarters, there was another serious crisis, and the Emperor was bringing him back to Tsarskoe with little hope that the boy would arrive alive. Medical help was again impotent, and Rasputin intervened with a message which again coincided exactly with the passing of the crisis. Rasputin was certainly believed by most of his admirers to have the gift of prophecy. Anna Vyrubova says he was never wrong and gives several instances, some of them surprising. M. Gilliard thinks that Rasputin, who was certainly very astute, took care to be excellently posted as to all matters in which he ventured to intervene. As his influence increased, this certainly became much easier for him. Some of his messages almost amount to threats that the child is in danger if he, Rasputin, is not listened to. From this it was an easy step to demand, for instance, the dismissal of a minister or the promotion of a protégé. The Empress looked upon everything that he said as coming from a "Man of God."

• • •

Closer union with the Allies inevitably meant the progress of the constitutional cause in Russia. An appeal to the Duma and to the people had inevitably the same bearing. There was no question whatever as to the Empress's loyalty to Russia during the war, nor as to her devotion to the Russian Army; but constitutionalism was to her anathema. It meant the limitation of absolute power for her son. Since October 1905, no one could have stated exactly whether the Emperor had accepted that limitation of his authority which seemed the logical inference of the manifesto of October 30, 1905; nor could one say that the manifesto itself had ever been carried out with any sincerity. In any case this was the moment when the Empress abandoned all restraint and threw herself heart and soul into a battle with Russian constitutionalism. Rasputin had for some time been absent from Petrograd, but after the reverses of May his influence was stronger than ever. He was very fully informed and at first proceeded cautiously. The Empress herself at first, while urging his opinions on the Emperor, still offers excuses for her own interference. Rasputin on July 22 went to his Siberian home. He returned in the middle of August and threw himself more and more into the fight with the Duma. The Duma at this time with practical unanimity declared for a ministry which should have the full confidence of the people. This formula was a concession of the Liberal majority to those Conservatives who were not ready to demand that the Ministers should be chosen by the Duma. The great majority of the Duma, including nearly all the brains in it, formed into a single Progressive Bloc, for which the way had long been prepared, and was even able to propose a detailed unanimous programme of long-deferred reforms.

From July 11 the Emperor spent two months in Tsarskoe. This of course gave the Empress her opportunity, and the crisis of the struggle is not recorded in the letters. For her, even more odious and more dangerous than the Duma was the Grand Duke Nicholas. In her earlier letters we see that she is morbidly fearful that he would acquire a moral authority replacing that of the Emperor. Madame Vyrubova was always ready to repeat malicious gossip from officers at General Headquarters against the Grand Duke. She even at one time bunches together the names of all the foreign military attachés (including General Hanbury Williams, who was devoted to Nicholas II) as conspirators against the Emperor. The Grand Duke may have let fall the suggestion that the Empress should retire to a convent. This and more than this was current gossip at the time. Some even accused him of having allowed himself to be spoken of as Nicholas III. It can only be said that everything in the conduct of the Grand Duke (and there is plenty of light thrown on this question) is a flat contradiction to any possible doubt as to his loyalty. In any case, on August 24, the Ministers were summoned to Tsarskoe and there informed that the Emperor had decided to take over the Command in Chief. They were astounded; and particularly Sazonov used every effort to dissuade him. Vyrubova relates how on his return to his family he says: "I was firm; see how I have been perspiring"; and tells how he held fast in his left hand throughout the interview the little ikon given him before it. The decision was received with consternation on all sides, but there was at least one point which it finally cleared up. By going permanently to the Army, and still more by the remarkably vigorous manifesto which he then issued, the Emperor showed friends and foes alike that he was absolutely committed to war to the end — a decision in which he never for a moment wavered.

With the Emperor at Headquarters, the Empress assumes an altogether new rôle in the Government. She describes herself later as "his wall in the rear." The Ministers, with a growing regularity, come to her with their reports. She herself remarks later that she is the first Russian Empress to have received them regularly since Catherine the Great — hardly a tactful thing to write to the new Catherine's husband. The change did not come all at once; but from the very outset she was in constant communication with Goremykin for the dismissal of the new more Liberal Ministers. The record of her letters here hardly needs any supplement or explanation. In letter after letter she urges the dismissal of Shcherbatov and of Samarin and more than suggests that of Polivanov and Sazonov.

.   .   .

Already in the autumn of 1915 it was clear that Rasputin was the most powerful man in Russia. For instance, General Mishchenko, with whom I was staying at that time, sent an A.D.C. to Petrograd to find out what was going wrong with army supplies, and the officer, who returned during my visit, explained that nothing at all could be done now without Rasputin's support. He did not assume the direction of affairs. He was still careful in his interventions, but that his approval was the first qualification for a ministerial post was already clear. The shame of this domination led to protests from two honest servants of the Emperor, already mentioned, General Dzhunkovsky and Prince Orlov. Rasputin had in the spring visited the tombs of the Metropolitans at Moscow and spent the evening at the most notorious place of entertainment in the town, a kind of Moulin Rouge, called by the name of Yar. Here he was both drunk and disorderly, and on being challenged used words which were deeply insulting to the Empress herself — "as to the old woman, I can do what I like." Dzhunkovsky, we are told, presented the police record of this scene to the Emperor, and he was dismissed from all Court appointments (September 8). Prince Orlov had more than once urged the dismissal of Rasputin. Now, we are told, he did so upon his knees, with the result that he was called upon to resign (September 5). Both these episodes have several echoes in the Empress's letters. One sees that the separation of the Sovereigns from the people is gradually becoming complete. Even the Moscow nobility, even the Imperial family, even the most loyal servants of the Palace are affronted, and from this time onwards we read in these letters, as a kind of running comment on every appointment or dismissal, "he venerates Our Friend" (that is, Rasputin), or, "he does not like Our Friend."

The prorogation of the Duma was from time to time prolonged. Old Goremykin, nearly ninety years of age, frankly feared to face it under the new conditions, and it was definitely his fear of the Duma and the Empress's own feeling of his weakness that led her in the end to recommend his resignation. The new appointment made on February 2, 1916, on the eve of the meeting of the Duma, was more astonishing than any that preceded it. The new Prime Minister, obviously the choice of the Empress, was Stürmer. He had been Governor in Yaroslavl and had conducted a savage repression of the Liberal County Council in Tver. He was also a Master of Ceremonies at the Court. He was simply known to the public for large defalcations, and typical enough was the report current at this time that at the outset of his premiership he informed his colleagues that a large sum was reserved to him for uncontrolled disposition, to which he asked their signatures. He was of course an obsequious follower of Rasputin. Stürmer himself was not really a man of any strength of character or of will. He was a puppet. With the most various of persons he left the impression of weakness and dishonesty. Stürmer was regularly received by the Empress for the conduct of affairs. The Duma was called for February 22, and on the suggestion of no other than Count Fredericks, who certainly wished the Emperor to stand well with his people, Nicholas took the occasion of the opening to pay his first visit to it. He was rapturously received. For the first time he addressed the Dumas as "representatives" of his people, and there was a great and unanimous outburst of patriotism. Rasputin, we are told, greatly deplored this incident. The Emperor the same day left for the front.

• • •

Rasputin's control of Russia was now complete. His reception-room was more than ever the rendezvous of all charlatans and adventurers. Rasputin would give them ill-written notes on slips of paper to the various authorities, who were simply requested to execute his wishes. Rasputin had all along predicted the greatest disasters from the war, so it was not surprising that he became the mouthpiece of a group of persons who wished to put an end to it. He even interfered in military operations, for instance discountenancing an offensive on the side of the Riga or dictating, or trying to dictate, arrangements as to transport of food or even of troops. He imposed on Bark, who had remained at his post, an enormous loan. The Synod, of course, was entirely in his hands, and so were all Church appointments. There were few sides of the administration of the Empire with which he did not deal. His instructions, handed over by "Ania," were sent on by the Empress to the Emperor. She sometimes even wrote them out for him or actually drafted a form of telegram for him to send to her with his signature. She herself complains more than once that her head goes round with the complications of the matters with which she deals. Yet she receives from the ante-room of Rasputin a man whom she had so far detested, Bonch Bruyevich, to hear his complaints against his chief, General Ruzsky, to which she begs the Emperor to listen. She is furious because Guchkov was written a letter to Alexeyev in which were the words "all depends on you," and she successfully urges that Alexeyev should be sent for a holiday.

At the beginning of July a party of members of the Duma, sent to England and France to promote closer contact with the Allies, returned to Russia. Its leader was Protopopov, Vice-President of the Duma, who had been picked by the President Rodzianko for this task. I had known him well in the summer of 1915 as right-hand man of Guchkov in the patriotic work for munitions. In England and France he had still maintained the same rôle, as he told me himself on the way back. Directly afterwards, while passing through Stockholm, he entered into long conversations on the subject of peace with a German diplomatist. In Petrograd he indeed maintained an appearance of loyalty to the Allies; but suddenly, through the agency of Rasputin, whom he had earlier met in connection with his taste for spiritualism, he was appointed Minister of the Interior (October 3). Of course after that, practically no one in the Duma would speak to him. Again the Empress imagined that a member of the Duma would be the best weapon for suppressing the Duma.

Protopopov himself was no strong man, though he posed to the Emperor as such. He was simply a mouthpiece of Rasputin. The direct slap in the face which had been given both to the Russian people and to the Allies was bitterly resented. Public affairs were now managed from some mysterious subterranean chamber and scandals of every kind flourished. There was the scandal of Manussein-Manuilov, a member of the secret police, journalist and speculator, who had actually been nominated by Stürmer as his principal private secretary. There were the financial scandals connected with the names of Manus and Rubenstein, big speculative financiers unquestionably favourable to Germany. Rasputin in a visit to Moscow is reported to even have asked the Lefts why they too did not use his good offices. The case of Sukhomlinov was arbitrarily withdrawn on the repeated instances of the Empress contained in these letters. Sukhomlinov himself was removed from prison to a hospital on what seemed quite an insufficient plea of ill-health. She urges the same favour for Rubenstein. The Empress again demands that her husband shall contravene the ordinary course of law, and demand back all the papers on the case of Manuilov. Lines which were always ringing in one's head at this time of national abasement were those which immediately follow Shakespeare's magnificent description of England in *Richard II*: "Is now leased out Like to a tenement or pelting farm."

It is interesting that the Empress herself recognised the inevitableness of the Duma. She would advise the Emperor to "cleverly shut it"; but it was only tentatively that she hinted at its abolition. Stürmer, even more than Goremykin, was in mortal fear of the Duma. After all he, a weak and obsequious opportunist, would have to go there and answer for all the iniquities of Rasputin. After long delays the Duma met on November 14. Stürmer had arranged that immediately after the opening speech the Ministers followed by the Ambassadors would walk out. The crowded public remained, and the empty benches of the Ministers were assailed by a storm of national indignation. All along, it had been the policy of the Liberals to endeavour in every way to postpone revolution till after the war, and the Duma endeavoured by the vigour of its protests to represent, and thus to keep in hand, the wholesale indignation of the country. The Cadet leader, Milyukov, made use of a remark of the amiable and incompetent Shuvayev, who had said, "I am perhaps a fool, but traitor never." Turning this round, Milyukov exposed all the sins of the Government, concluding each item in his indictment with the question: "Is this folly or treason?" No less vigorous was Shulgin, the Nationalist; and in a later debate even the most brilliant of the Reactionaries, Purishkevich, came out with a terrible comparison between Rasputin and an earlier "Grishka," the monk Otrepyev, a pretender who in the seventeenth century actually ascended the throne of Moscow. Stürmer never dared to go to the Duma again; he asked of the Emperor and was refused leave to dissolve it and arrest Milyukov, and, with the agreement of the Empress and Rasputin, was dismissed.

Stürmer's successor was appointed by the Emperor at Headquarters without the Empress and against her wishes (November 23). He was an honest, capable, plain-spoken Conservative, Trepov, who had done good work in putting some degree of order into the chaotic administration of the railways. Trepov, who was a man, had demanded the dismissal of Protopopov as a condition to his own acceptance of the premiership. There follows the most feverish period in the Empress's correspondence. Letter after letter she writes to save Protopopov, and ultimately goes down with him to Headquarters herself. The Emperor kept Protopopov, and ordered Trepov to continue in office. On the other hand, Trepov, whose position was little understood by the public, had no success in the Duma, where three times he was shouted down. Trepov dragged on as best he could till January. Ultimately his resignation was accepted and with him went the last chance of saving the dynasty.

The administration was already really in the hands of Protopopov and his puppets. It is impossible that the Empress understood or approved of the outrageous swindles which her authority covered. Her letters show her to have been peculiarly ignorant of public affairs. She complained to a friend that honest Ministers could not be found — repeating a constant excuse put forward by the Russian Reactionaries for choosing the most dishonest. Clearly she had only one thing in mind: that no Minister must stand except by the approval of Rasputin. This comes out plainly in all the letters. Evidently she looked upon herself as saving Russia.

Gilliard Describes the Tsar

Pierre Gilliard had almost unparalleled opportunities to observe the Russian Imperial Family. Appointed Tutor in French to the Grand Duchesses Olga and Tatiana in 1905, he became a member of the imperial household in 1911 and a tutor to the Tsarevich in 1913. Gilliard's contacts with the family, to whom he was devoted, grew increasingly close. After the abdication in 1917, he chose to share the Romanov's imprisonment and exile. He lived with them at Tsarskoie-Selo and Tobolsk, and tried to accompany them to Ekaterinburg but this was not permitted. His account of the family and of his life with them is full of interest. Obviously it is not without bias. The source is: Gilliard, P., Thirteen Years at the Russian Court. (A Personal Record of the Last Years and Death of Czar Nicholas II and His Family.) *New York: George H. Doran and Co., n.d. Pp. 205–206.*

Why did Fate decree that Czar Nicholas II should reign at the beginning of the twentieth century and in one of the most troublous periods of history? Endowed with remarkable personal qualities, he was the incarnation of all that was noblest and most chivalrous in the Russian nature. But he was weak. The soul of loyalty, he was the slave of his pledged word. His fidelity to the Allies, which was probably the cause of his death, proves it beyond doubt. He despised the methods of diplomacy and he was not a fighter. He was crushed down by events.

Nicholas II was modest and timid; he had not enough self-confidence: hence all his misfortunes. His first impulse was usually right. The pity was that he seldom acted on it because he could not trust himself. He sought the counsel of those he thought more competent than himself; from that moment he could no longer master the problems that faced him. They escaped him. He hesitated between conflicting causes and often ended by following that to which he was personally least sympathetic.

The Czarina knew the Czar's irresolute character. As I have said, she considered she had a sacred duty to help him in his heavy task. Her influence on the Czar was very great and almost always unfortunate; she made politics a matter of sentiment and personalities, and too often allowed herself to be swayed by her sympathies or antipathies, or by those of her *entourage.* Impulsive by nature, the Czarina was liable to emotional outbursts which made her give her confidence unreservedly to those she believed sincerely devoted to the country and the dynasty. Protopopoff was a case in point.

The Czar was always anxious to be just and to do the right thing. If he sometimes failed, the fault lies at the door of those who did their utmost to hide the truth from him and isolate him from his people. All his generous impulses were broken against the passive resistance of an omnipotent bureaucracy or were wilfully frustrated by those to whom he entrusted their realisation in him which made him follow life rather than try to lead it. It is one of the characteristics of the Russian nature.

An essentially reflective man, he would have been perfectly happy to live as a private individual, but he was resigned to his lot, and humbly accepted the superhuman task which God had given him. He loved his people and his country with all the force of his nature; he had a personal affection for the least of his subjects, those *moujiks* whose lot he earnestly desired to better. What a tragic fate was that of this sovereign whose only desire during his reign was to be close to his people and who never succeeded in realising his wish. The fact is that he was well guarded, and by those whose interest it was that he should not succeed.

Kerensky's Opinion of Nicholas II

Alexander Kerensky, a brilliant and courageous young lawyer under the old regime, was the only socialist member of the Provisional Government. It fell to him as Minister of Justice to place the Imperial Family under arrest, and so long as he was able, he protected them against the vengeance of the extremists. As Minister and later as Premier, Kerensky had several interviews with Nicholas and was therefore able to revise previous general impressions in the light of first-hand, specific experience. The source is: Kerensky, A., The Crucifixion of Liberty. New York: The John Day Co., 1934. Pp. 173–176. (Slightly abridged.)

There was always this mystery about Nicholas II: why, having been born to rule strictly as a constitutional monarch — to reign but not to rule — did he hate the very word "constitution" so much and refuse to let the burden of absolute rule slip out of his wavering hands, for which it was all too heavy? "Be as Peter the Great was" drummed the Empress into him. But to great Peter his autocratic powers were a mighty instrument of statesmanship: he ruled in order to build a great empire. Nicholas II made no attempt to build, he merely defended his powers, burdensome as they were to him, against internal foes. I do not think he knew the reason himself. He merely believed what his father and Pobiedonostsev had instilled into him: there could be no Russia without autocracy; Russia and the autocracy were one; he himself was the impersonation of the autocracy. So the magic circle closed. There was no way out, unless it was one into disaster and void. Perhaps the very reason why he took his enforced abdication so calmly was that he saw in it divine help, a relief from the burden of power which he could not throw off of his own accord because he was bound by his oath as "The Lord's anointed." Living in the twentieth century, he had the mentality of the Muscovite Kings, even though he had no blood connection with the Moscow dynasty. The daily work of a monarch he found intolerably boring. He could not stand listening long or seriously to ministers' reports, or reading them. He liked such ministers as could tell an amusing story and did not weary the monarch's attention with too much business. But I repeat that never — from the very beginning to the very end of his reign — did he willingly yield one inch of his autocracy. When it came to defending his divine right his usual indifference left him; he became cunning, obstinate and cruel, merciless at times.

.   .   .

Many is the time I have had cause to realize — both in my capacity of political lawyer and as a member of the Duma — that it was in the Czar's own study, and nowhere else, that the fiercest cruelty of the over-keen servants of the autocracy was invariably sponsored. When perusing a report concerning the suppression of revolutionary activities he would put a note of approbation opposite the place where a particularly harsh and lawless measure against the "seditionaries" was described. He stopped legal proceedings against officials accused of open, scandalous and quite unbearable abuses of power in the repression of revolutionary activities. He granted honors and official advancement to people known to the whole of Russia as the organizers of the Jewish pogroms. After 1905, when political parties were legalized in Russia, he took one of them openly under his patronage — that is, if one can call an organized bandit gang like the "Union of the Russian People" a party. From that moment he presented the country with the subversive spectacle of a monarch turned party member. . . . The headquarters of the "Union of the Russian People" were in secret communication with Tsarskoe Selo — through the medium of that evil genius of Russia, the Grand Duke Nicholas. Long before Rasputin came, there was already a second government — side by side with the official one — which engineered pogroms of the Jews and the intelligentsia and organized "political" assassinations (including an attempt against Witte himself). The official government — even Stolypin's government — was powerless to put an end to these outrages because at the decisive moment it was confronted by the Czar's personal, though camouflaged, interference. As I have already said, Nicholas II was in constant conspiracy against his own official decrees, laws and proclamations. He intrigued secretly against his own ministers, preferring the advice of the most manifest adventurers. Rasputin was merely the last of these, though admittedly the most powerful.

And another enigma: although he hated popular representation, although he fiercely fought each new Duma as it came, irrespective of whether it was radical or conservative, yet just as fervently did Nicholas II always seek some personal contact with the people, with the genuine, ordinary, uneducated, hard-working peasantry. He even had a kind of aversion for the courtiers and the aristocracy. He did not like people who were very well-born, rich or very cultured. Just as a surfeited epicure may sometimes be tempted away from champagne and oysters to beer and whelks, so the Czar was drawn towards the lowest of the low, towards the vagrant classes. The palace was never rid of a collection of monks, mad saints, pilgrims and holy beggars.

Rasputin himself was a thorough muzhik with a peasant's sleeveless coat, a girdled shirt, greased boots, and an unkempt beard.

Gilliard Describes the Tsaritsa

Compare this description of Alexandra with that given above by Sir Bernard Pares. The source is: Gilliard, op. cit., pp. 47–55.

The Czarina, Alexandra Feodorovna, formerly Alice of Hesse, and fourth child of the Grand Duke Ludwig of Hesse and Alice of England, youngest daughter of Queen Victoria, was born at Darmstadt on June 6th, 1872. She lost her mother early in life, and was largely brought up at the English Court, where she soon became the favourite granddaughter of Queen Victoria, who bestowed on the blonde "Alix" all the tender affection she had had for her mother.

At the age of seventeen the young princess paid a prolonged visit to Russia, staying with her elder sister Elisabeth, who had married the Grand-Duke Sergius Alexandrovitch, a brother of the Czar Alexander III. She took an active part in Court life, appeared at reviews, receptions, and balls, and being very pretty was made a great fuss of.

Everybody regarded her as the prospective mate of the Heir to the Throne, but, contrary to general expectation, Alice of Hesse returned to Darmstadt and nothing had been said. Did she not like the idea? It is certainly a fact that five years later, when the official proposal arrived, she showed signs of hesitation.

However, the betrothal took place at Darmstadt during the summer of 1894, and was followed by a visit to the Court of England. The Russian Heir at once returned to his country. A few months later she was obliged to leave suddenly for Livadia, where Alexander III was dying. She was present when his end came, and with the Imperial family accompanied the coffin in which the mortal remains of the dead Emperor were carried to St. Petersburg.

The body was taken from Nicholas station to the Cathedral of St. Peter and St. Paul on a dull November day. A huge crowd was assembled on the route of the funeral cortege as it moved through the melting snow and mud with which the streets were covered. In the crowd women crossed themselves piously and could be heard murmuring, in allusion to the young Czarina, "She has come to us behind a coffin. She brings misfortune with her."

It certainly seemed as if from the start sorrow was dodging the steps of her whose light heart and beauty had earned her the nickname of "Sunshine" in her girlhood.

On November 26th, thus within a month of Alexander's death, the marriage was celebrated amidst the general mourning. A year later the Czarina gave birth to her first child — a daughter who was named Olga.

The coronation of the young sovereigns took place in Moscow on May 14th, 1896. Fate seemed already to have marked them down. It will be remembered that the celebrations were the occasion of a terrible accident which cost the lives of a large number of people. The peasants, who had come from all parts, had assembled in masses during the night in Hodinskoie meadows, where gifts were to be distributed. As a result of bad organisation there was a panic, and more than two thousand people were trodden to death or suffocated in the mud by the terror-stricken crowd.

When the Czar and Czarina went to Hodinskoie meadows next morning they had heard nothing whatever of the terrible catastrophe. They were not told the truth until they returned to the city subsequently, and they never knew the whole truth. Did not those concerned realise that by acting thus they were depriving the Imperial couple of a chance to show their grief and sympathy and making their behaviour odious because it seemed sheer indifference to public misfortune?

Several years of domestic bliss followed, and Fate seemed to have loosened its grip.

Yet the task of the young Czarina was no easy one. She had to learn all that it meant to be an empress, and that at the most etiquette-ridden Court in Europe and the scene of the worst forms of intrigue and coterie. Accustomed to the simple life of Darmstadt, and having experienced at the strict and formal English Court only such restraint as affected a young and popular princess who was there merely on a visit, she must have felt at sea with her new obligations and dazzled by an existence of which all the proportions had suddenly changed. Her sense of duty and her burning desire to devote herself to the welfare of the millions whose Czarina she had become fired her ambitions, but at the same time checked her natural impulses.

Yet her only thought was to win the hearts of her subjects. Unfortunately she did not know how to show it, and the innate timidity from which she suffered was wont to play the traitor to her kind attentions. She very soon realised how impotent she was to gain sympathy and understanding. Her frank and spontaneous nature was speedily repelled by the icy conventions of her environment. Her impulses came up against the prevalent inertia about her, and when in return for her confidence she asked for intelligent devotion and real good will, those with whom she dealt took refuge in the easy zeal of the polite formalities of Courts.

In spite of all her efforts, she never succeeded in being merely amiable and acquiring the art which consists of flitting gracefully but superficially over all manner of subjects. The fact is that the Czarina was nothing if not sincere. Every word from her lips was the true expression of her real feelings. Finding herself misunderstood, she quickly drew back into her shell. Her natural pride was wounded. She appeared less and less at the ceremonies and receptions she regarded as an intolerable nuisance. She adopted a habit of distant reserve which was taken for haughtiness and contempt. But those who came in contact with her in moments of distress knew what a sensitive spirit, what a longing for affection, was concealed behind that apparent coldness. She had accepted her new religion with entire sincerity, and found it a great source of comfort in hours of trouble and anguish; but above all, it was the affection of her family which nourished her love, and she was never really happy except when she was with them.

The birth of Olga Nicolaievna had been followed by that of three other fine and healthy daughters who were their parents' delight. It was not an unmixed delight, however, for the secret desire of their hearts — to have a son and heir — had not yet been fulfilled. The birth of Anastasie Nicolaievna, the last of the Grand-Duchesses, had at first been a terrible disappointment . . . and the years were slipping by. At last, on August 12th, 1904, when the Russo-Japanese War was at its height, the Czarina gave birth to the son they so ardently desired. Their joy knew no bounds. It seemed as if all the sorrows of the past were forgotten and that an era of happiness was about to open for them.

Alas! it was but a short respite, and was followed by worse misfortunes: first the January massacre in front of the Winter Palace — the memory of which was to haunt them like a horrible nightmare for the rest of their days — and then the lamentable conclusion of the Russo-Japanese War. In those dark days their only consolation was their beloved son, and it had not taken long, alas! to discover that the Czarevitch had hæmophilia. From that moment the mother's life was simply one dreadful agony. She had already made the acquaintance of that terrible disease; she knew that an uncle, one of her brothers, and two of her nephews had died of it. From her childhood she had heard it spoken of as a dreadful and mysterious thing against which men were powerless. And now her only son, the child she loved more than anything else on earth, was affected! Death would watch him, follow him at every step, and carry him off one day like so many boys in his family. She must fight! She must save him at any cost! It was impossible for science to be impotent. The means of saving must exist, and they must be found. Doctors, surgeons, specialists were consulted. But every kind of treatment was tried in vain.

When the mother realised that no human aid could save, her last hope was in God. He alone could perform a miracle. But she must be worthy of His intervention. She was naturally of a pious nature, and she devoted herself wholly to the Orthodox religion with the ardour and determination she brought to everything. Life at Court became strict, if not austere. Festivities were eschewed, and the number of occasions on which the sovereigns had to appear in public was reduced to a minimum. The family gradually became isolated from the Court and lived to itself, so to speak.

Between each of the attacks, however, the boy came back to life, recovered his health, forgot his sufferings, and resumed his fun and his games. At these times it was impossible to credit that he was the victim of an implacable disease which might carry him off at any moment. Every time the Czarina saw him with red cheeks, or heard his merry laugh, or watched his frolics, her heart would fill with an immense hope, and she would say: "God has heard me. He has pitied my sorrow at last." Then the disease would suddenly swoop down on the boy, stretch him once more on his bed of pain and take him to the gates of death.

The months passed, the expected miracle did not happen, and the ruthless attacks followed hard on each other's heels. The most fervent prayers had not brought the divine revelation so passionately implored. The last hope had failed. A sense of endless despair filled the Czarina's soul: it seemed as if the whole world were deserting her.

It was then that Rasputin, a simple Siberian peasant, was brought to her, and he said: "Believe in the power of my prayers; believe in my help and your son will live!"

The mother clung to the hope he gave her as a drowning man seizes an outstretched hand. She believed in him with all the strength that was in her. As a matter of fact, she had been convinced for a long time that the saviour of Russia and the dynasty would come from the people, and she thought that this humble *moujik* had been sent by God to save him who was the hope of the nation. The intensity of her faith did the rest, and by a simple process of auto-suggestion, which was helped by certain perfectly casual coincidences, she persuaded herself that her son's life was in this man's hands.

Rasputin had realised the state of mind of the despairing mother who was broken down by the strain of her struggle and seemed to have touched the limit of human suffering. He knew how to extract the fullest advantage from it, and with a diabolical cunning he succeeded in associating his own life, so to speak, with that of the child.

This moral hold of Rasputin on the Czarina cannot possibly be understood unless one is familiar with the part played in the religious life of the Orthodox world by those men who are neither priests nor monks — though people habitually, and quite inaccurately, speak of the "monk" Rasputin — and are called *stranniki* or *startsi*.

The *strannik* is a pilgrim who wanders from monastery to monastery and church to church, seeking the truth and living on the charity of the faithful. He may thus travel right across the Russian Empire, led by his fancy or attracted by the reputation for holiness enjoyed by particular places or persons.

The *staretz* is an ascetic who usually lives in a monastery, though sometimes in solitude — a kind of guide of souls to whom one has recourse in moments of trouble or suffering. Quite frequently a *staretz* is an ex-*strannik* who has given up his old wandering life and taken up an abode in which to end his days in prayer and meditation.

Dostoievsky gives the following description of him in *The Brothers Kara-mazof*:

"The *staretz* is he who takes your soul and will and makes them his. When you select your *staretz* you surrender your will, you give it him in utter submission, in full renunciation. He who takes this burden upon him, who accepts this terrible school of life, does so of his own free will in the hope that after a long trial he will be able to conquer himself and become his own master sufficiently to attain complete freedom by a life of obedience — that is to say, get rid of self and avoid the fate of those who have lived their lives without succeeding in sufficing unto themselves."

God gives the *staretz* the indications which are requisite for one's welfare and communicates the means by which one must be brought back to safety.

On earth the *staretz* is the guardian of truth and the ideal. He is also the repository of the sacred tradition which must be transmitted from *staretz* to *staretz* until the reign of justice and light shall come.

Several of these *startsi* have risen to remarkable heights of modern grandeur and become saints of the Orthodox Church.

The influence of these men, who live as a kind of unofficial clergy, is still very considerable in Russia. In the provinces and open country it is even greater than that of the priests and monks.

The conversion of the Czarina had been a genuine act of faith. The Ortho-dox religion had fully responded to her mystical aspirations, and her imagina-tion must have been captured by its archaic and naive ritual. She had ac-cepted it with all the ardour of the neophyte. In her eyes Rasputin had all the prestige and sanctity of a *staretz*.

Such was the nature of the feelings the Czarina entertained for Rasputin — feelings ignobly travestied by calumny. They had their source in maternal love, the noblest passion which can fill a mother's heart.

Fate willed that he who wore the halo of a saint should be nothing but a low and perverse creature, and that, as we shall soon see, this man's evil in-fluence was one of the principal causes of which the effect was the death of those who thought they could regard him as their saviour.

The Tsaritsa and the Tsar

A vivid picture and a clear measure of the control which the dominant Alexandra exercised over the weaker Nicholas is given by her letters to him. A correlation of her letters with political events proves that she assumed the responsibility and the power of governing Russia. The letters also prove the influence upon her of Rasputin. The source of the following is: Pares, B. (Ed.), Letters, etc., pp. 113–116.

Tsarskoje Selo, Aug. 22-nd 1915

My very own beloved One,

I cannot find words to express all I want to — my heart is far too full. I only long to hold you tight in my arms & whisper words of intense love, courage, strength & endless blessings. More than hard to let you go alone, so completely alone — but God is very near to you, more than ever. You have fought this great fight for your country & throne — alone & with bravery & decision. Never have they seen such firmness in you before & it cannot remain without good fruit.

Do not fear for what remains behind — one must be severe & stop all at once. Lovy, I am here, dont laugh at silly old wify, but she has [trousers] on unseen, & I can get the old man to come & keep him up to be energetic — whenever I can be of the smallest use, tell me what to do — use me — at such a time God will give me the strength to help you—because our souls are fighting for the right against the evil. It is all much deeper than appears to the eye — we, who have been taught to look at all from another side, see what the struggle here really is & means — you showing your mastery, proving yourself the *Autocrat* without wh. Russia cannot exist. Had you given in now in these different questions, they would have dragged out yet more of you. Being firm is the only saving — I know what it costs you, & have & do suffer hideously for you, forgive me, I beseech you, my angel, for having left you no peace & worried you so much — but I too well know yr. marvelously gentle character — & you had to shake it off this time, had to win your fight alone against all. It will be a glorious page in yr. reign & Russian history the story of these weeks & days — & God, who is just & near you — will save your country & throne through your firmness.

A harder battle has rarely been faught, than yours & it will be crowned with success, only believe this.

Yr. faith has been tried — your trust — & you remained firm as a rock, for that you will be blessed. God anointed you at your coronation, He placed you where you stand & you have done your duty, be sure, quite sure of Him & He forsaketh not His anointed. Our Friend's prayers arise night & day for you to Heaven & God will hear them.

Those who fear & cannot understand your actions, will be brought by events to realise your great wisdom. It is the beginning of the glory of yr. reign, He said so & I absolutely believe it. Your Sun is rising — & to-day it shines so brightly. And so will you charm all those great blunderers, cowards, led astray, noisy, blind, narrowminded & (dishonest false) beings, this morning.

And your Sunbeam will appear to help you, your very own Child — won't that touch those hearts & make them realise what you are doing, & what they dared to wish to do, to shake your throne, to frighten you with internal black forebodings — only a bit of success out there & they will change.

They will (?) disperse home into clean air & their minds will be purified & they carry the picture of you & yr. Son in their hearts with them. —

I do hope *Goremykin* will agree to yr. choice of *Khvostov* — you need an energetic minister of the interior — should he be the wrong man, he can later be changed — no harm in that, at such times — but if energetic he may help splendidly & then the old man does not matter.

If you take him, then only wire to me tail [*Khovostov*] alright & I shall understand. —

Let no talks worry you — am glad Dmitri wont be there now — snap up *Voyeikov* if he is stupid — am sure he is afraid meeting people there who may think he was against *Nikolasha* & *Orlov* & to smoothe things, he begs you for *Nikolasha* — that would be the greatest fault & undo all you have so courageously done & the great internal fight would have been for nothing. Too kind, don't be, I mean not specially, as otherwise it would be dishonest, as still there have been things you were discontented with him about. Remind others about Misha, the Emperor's brother & then there is war there too. —

All is for the good, as our Friend says, the worst is over. — Now you speak to the Minister of war & he will take energetic measures, as soon as needed — but *Khvostov,* will see to that too if you name him. — When you leave, shall wire to Friend to-night through Ania — & He will particularly think of you. Only get *Nikolasha's* nomination quicker done — no dawdling, its bad for the cause & for *Alexejev* too — & a settled thing quieten minds, even if against their wish, sooner than that waiting & uncertainty & trying to influence you — it tires out ones heart.

I feel completely done up & only keep myself going with force — they shall not think that I am downhearted or frightened — but confident & calm. —

Joy we went to those holy places to-gether — for sure yr. dear Father quite particularly prays for you.

Give me some news as soon as you can — now am afraid for the moment N. P. wiring to Ania until am sure nobody watches again.

Tell me the impression, if you can. Be firm to the end, let me be sure of that otherwise shall get quite ill from anxiety.

Bitter pain not to be with you — know what you feel, & the meeting with N. wont be agreeable — you did trust him & now you know, what months ago our Friend said, that he was acting wrongly towards you & your country & wife — its not the people who would do harm to your people, but *Nikolashna* & set *Gutchkov, Rodzianko, Samarin* etc. —

Lovy, if you hear I am not so well, don't be anxious, I have suffered so terribly, & phisically overtired myself these 2 days, & morally worried (& worry still till all is done at the *Headquarters* & *Nikolasha* gone) only then shall I feel calm — near you all is well — when out of sight others at once profit — you see they are affraid of me & so come to you when alone — they know I have a will of my own when I feel I am in the right — & you are now — we know it, so you make them tremble before your courage & will. God is with you & our Friend for you — all is well — & later all will thank you for having saved your country. Don't doubt — believe, & all will be well & the army is everything — a few *strikes* nothing, in comparison, as can & shall be suppressed. The left are furious because all slips through their hands & their cards are clear to us & the game they wished to use *Nikolasha* for — even *Shvedov* knows it fr. there.

Now goodnight lovy, go straight to bed without tea with the rest & their long faces. Sleep long & well, you need rest after this strain & your heart needs calm hours. — God Almighty bless your undertaking, His holy Angels guard & guide you & bless the work of your hands. — Please give this little Image of St. *John the Warrior* to *Alexeiev* with my blessing & fervent wishes. You have my Image I blessed you with last year — I give no other as that carries my blessing & you have *Gregory's* St. Nicolas to guard & guide you. I always place a candle before St. Nicolas at *Znamenje* for you — & shall do, so to-morrow at 3 o'clock & before the Virgin. You will feel my soul near you.

I clasp you tenderly to my heart, kiss and caress you without end — want to show you all the intense love I have for you, warm, cheer, console, strengthen you, & make you sure of yourself. Sleep well my Sunshine, Russia's Saviour. Remember last night, how tenderly we clung to-gether. I shall yearn for yr. caresses — I never can have enough of them. And I still have the children, & you are all alone. Another time I must give you Baby for a bit to cheer you up. —

I kiss you without end & bless you. Holy Angels guard your slumber — I am near & with you for ever & none shall separate us. —

Yr. very own wife
Sunny.

Rasputin and the Imperial Family

M. Gilliard's position at Court enabled him to watch the rise and dominance of Rasputin from a rare vantage point. The following material deals with Rasputin, Anna Viroubouva and the Imperial Family. The source is: Gilliard, op. cit., pp. 59–65, 82–84.

About one hundred and fifty versts south of Tobolsk the little village of Pokrovskoie lies lost in the marshes on the banks of the Tobol. There Grigory Rasputin was born. His father's name was Efim. Like many other Russian peasants at that time, the latter had no family name. The inhabitants of the village, of which he was not a native, had given him on his arrival the name of Novy (the Newcomer).

His son Grigory had the same kind of youth as all the small peasantry of that part of Siberia, where the poor quality of the soil often compels them to live by expedients. Like them, he robbed and stole. . . . He soon made his mark, however, by the audacity he showed in his exploits, and it was not long before his misdoings earned him the reputation of an unbridled libertine. He was now known solely as Rasputin, a corruption of the word *rasputnik* (debauched), which was destined to become, as it were, his family name.

The villagers of Siberia were in the habit of hiring out horses to travellers passing through the country and offering their services as guides and coachmen. One day Rasputin happened to conduct a priest to the monastery of Verkhoturie. The priest entered into conversation with him, was struck by his quick natural gifts, led him by his questions to confess his riotous life, and exhorted him to consecrate to the service of God the vitality he was putting to such bad uses. The exhortation produced so great an impression on Grigory that he seemed willing to give up his life of robbery and license. He stayed for a considerable time at the monastery of Verkhoturie and began to frequent the holy places of the neighbourhood.

When he went back to his village he seemed a changed man, and the inhabitants could hardly recognise the reprobate hero of so many scandalous adventures in this man whose countenance was so grave and whose dress so austere. He was seen going from village to village, spreading the good word and reciting to all and sundry willing to listen long passages from the sacred books, which he knew by heart.

Public credulity, which he already exploited extremely skilfully, was not slow in regarding him as a prophet, a being endowed with supernatural powers, and in particular the power of performing miracles. To understand this rapid transformation one must realise both the strange power of fascination and suggestion which Rasputin possessed, and also the ease with which the popular imagination in Russia is captured by the attraction of the marvellous.

However, the virtue of the new saint does not seem to have been proof against the enticements of the flesh for long, and he relapsed into his debauchery. It is true that he showed the greatest contrition for his wrongdoings, but that did not prevent him from continuing them. Even at that time he displayed that blend of mysticism and erotomania which made him so dangerous a person.

Yet, notwithstanding all this, his reputation spread far and wide. His services were requisitioned, and he was sent for from distant places, not merely in Siberia, but even in Russia.

His wanderings at last brought him to St. Petersburg. There, in 1905, he made the acquaintance of the Archimandrite Theophanes, who thought he could discern in him signs of genuine piety and profound humility as well as the marks of divine inspiration. Rasputin was introduced by him to devout circles in the capital, whither his reputation had preceded him. He had no difficulty in trafficking in the credulity of these devotees, whose very refinement made them superstitious and susceptible to the magnetism of his rustic piety. In his fundamental coarseness they saw nothing but the entertaining candour of a man of the people. They were filled with the greatest admiration for the naivete of this simple soul. . . .

It was not long before Rasputin had immense authority with his new flock. He became a familiar figure in the *salons* of certain members of the high aristocracy of St. Petersburg, and was even received by members of the royal family, who sang his praises to the Czarina. Nothing more was requisite for the last and vital stage. Rasputin was taken to Court by intimate friends of her Majesty, and with a personal recommendation from the Archimandrite Theophanes. This last fact must always be borne in mind. It was to shelter him from the attacks of his enemies for many years.

We have seen how Rasputin traded on the despair which possessed the Czarina and had contrived to link his life with that of the Czarevitch and acquire a growing hold over his mother. Each of his appearances seemed to produce an improvement in the boy's malady, and thus increased his prestige and confirmed confidence in the power of intercession.

After a certain time, however, Rasputin's head was turned by this unexpected rise to fame; he thought his position was sufficiently secure, forgot the caution he had displayed when he first came to St. Petersburg, and returned to his scandalous mode of life. Yet he did so with a skill which for a long time kept his private life quite secret. It was only gradually that the reports of his excesses spread and were credited.

At first only a few voices were faintly raised against the *staretz*, but it was not long before they became loud and numerous. The first at Court to attempt to show up the impostor was Mademoiselle Tioutcheva, the governess of the Grand-Duchesses. Her efforts were broken against the blind faith of the Czarina. Among the charges she made against Rasputin were several which, in her indignation, she had not checked with sufficient care so that their falsity was absolutely patent to her sovereign. Realising her impotence, and with a view to discharging her responsibilities, she asked that in any case Rasputin should not be allowed on the floor occupied by the children.

The Czar then intervened, and Her Majesty yielded, not because her faith was shaken, but merely for the sake of peace and in the interests of a man whom she believed was blinded by his very zeal and devotion.

Although I was then no more than one of the Grand-Duchesses' professors — it was during the winter of 1910 — Mademoiselle Tioutcheva herself told me all about this debate and its vicissitudes. But I confess that at that time I was still far from accepting all the extraordinary stories about Rasputin. In March, 1911, the hostility to Rasputin became more and more formidable, and the *staretz* thought it wise to let the storm blow over and disappear for a time. He therefore started on a pilgrimage to Jerusalem.

On his return to St. Petersburg in the autumn of the same year the tumult had not subsided, and he had to face the attacks of one of his former protectors, Bishop Hermogenes, who employed terrible threats and eventually extracted a promise from Rasputin to keep away from the Court, where his presence compromised his sovereigns.

He had no sooner left the Bishop, who had actually gone so far as to strike him, than he rushed to his powerful protectress, Madame Wyroubova, the Czarina's all but inseparable companion. The Bishop was exiled to a monastery.

Just as futile were the efforts of the Archimandrite Theophanes, who could never forgive himself for having stood sponsor in some degree for the *staretz's* high moral character, and thus reassuring the Czar and Czarina by his personal recommendation. He did his best to show him up, but the only reward for his pains was to find himself transferred to the Government of Tauris.

The fact was that Rasputin managed to make the two Bishops seem low intriguers who had wanted to use him as an instrument, and then, becoming jealous of a favour they could no longer exploit for their own personal benefit, tried to bring about his downfall.

"The lowly Siberian peasant" had become a formidable adversary in whom an utter lack of moral scruple was associated with consummate skill. With a first-class intelligence service, and creatures of his own both at Court and among the men around the ministers, as soon as he saw a new enemy appear on the scene he was always careful to baulk him cleverly by getting in the first blow.

Under the form of prophecies he would announce that he was going to be the object of a new attack, taking good care not to indicate his adversaries too plainly. So when the bolt was shot, the hand that directed it held a crumbling missile. He often actually interceded in favour of those who had attacked him, affirming with mock humility that such trials were necessary for the good of his soul.

Another element which also contributed to keep alive the blind faith in him which lasted until the end was the fact that the Czar and Czarina were accustomed to see those to whom they paid particular attention become objects of intrigue and cabals. They knew that their esteem alone was sufficient to expose them to the attacks of the envious. The result was that they were convinced that the special favour they showed to an obscure *moujik* was bound in any case to raise a storm of hate and jealousy against him and make him the victim of the worst calumnies.

The scandal, however, gradually spread from the purely ecclesiastical world. It was mentioned in whispers in political and diplomatic circles, and was even referred to in speeches in the Duma.

In the spring of 1912, Count Kokovtzof, then President of the Council of Ministers, decided to take the matter up with the Czar. The step was a particularly delicate one, as hitherto Rasputin's influence had been confined to the Church and the Imperial family circle. Those were the very spheres in which the Czar was most intolerant of any interference by his ministers.

The Czar was not convinced by the Count's action, but he realised that some concession to public opinion was necessary. Shortly after Their Majesties went to the Crimea, Rasputin left St. Petersburg and vanished into Siberia.

Yet his influence was of the kind that distance does not diminish. On the contrary, it only idealised him and increased his prestige.

As in his previous absences, there was a lively exchange of telegrams — through the medium of Madame Wyroubova — between Pokrovskoie and the different residences occupied in turn by the Imperial family during the year 1912.

The absent Rasputin was more powerful than Rasputin in the flesh. His psychic empire was based on an act of faith, for there is no limit to the power of self-delusion possessed by those who mean to believe at all cost. The history of mankind is there to prove it!

But how much suffering and what terrible disasters were to result from the tragic aberration! . . .

The children saw Rasputin when he was with their parents, but even at that time his visits were infrequent. Weeks, and sometimes months, passed without his being summoned to Court. It became more and more usual to see him with Madame Wyroubova, who had a little house quite near to the Alexander Palace. The Czar and his heir hardly ever went there, and meetings were always very rare.

As I have already explained, Madame Wyroubova was the intermediary between the Czarina and Rasputin. It was she who sent on to the *staretz* letters addressed to him and brought his replies — usually verbal — to the palace.

Relations between Her Majesty and Madame Wyroubova were very intimate, and hardly a day passed without her visiting her Imperial mistress. The friendship had lasted many years. Madame Wyroubova had married very young. Her husband was a degenerate and an inveterate drunkard, and succeeded in inspiring his young wife with a deep hatred of him. They separated, and Madame Wyroubova endeavoured to find relief and consolation in religion. Her misfortunes were a link with the Czarina, who had suffered so much herself, and yearned to comfort her. The young woman who had had to go through so much won her pity. She became the Czarina's confidante, and the kindness the Czarina showed her made her her lifelong slave.

Madame Wyroubova's temperament was sentimental and mystical, and her boundless affection for the Czarina was a positive danger, because it was uncritical and divorced from all sense of reality.

The Czarina could not resist so fiery and sincere a devotion. Imperious as she was, she wanted her friends to be hers, and hers alone. She only entertained friendships in which she was quite sure of being the dominating partner. Her confidence had to be rewarded by complete self-abandonment. She did not realise that it was rather unwise to encourage demonstrations of that fanatical loyalty.

Madame Wyroubova had the mind of a child, and her unhappy experiences had sharpened her sensibilities without maturing her judgment. Lacking in intellect and discrimination, she was the prey of her impulses. Her opinions on men and affairs were unconsidered but none the less sweeping. A single impression was enough to convince her limited and puerile understanding. She at once classified people, according to the impression they made upon her, as "good" or "bad," — in other words, "friends" or "enemies."

It was with no eye to personal advantage, but out of a pure affection for the Imperial family and her desire to help them, that Madame Wyroubova tried to keep the Czarina posted as to what was going on, to make her share her likes and dislikes, and through her to influence the course of affairs at Court. But in reality she was the docile and unconscious, but none the less mischievous, tool of a group of unscrupulous individuals who used her in their intrigues. She was incapable either of a political policy or considered aims, and could not even guess what was the game of those who used her in their own interests. Without any strength of will, she was absolutely under the influence of Rasputin and had become his most fervent adherent at Court.

I had not seen the *staretz* since I had been at the palace, when one day I met him in the anteroom as I was preparing to go out. I had time to look well at him as he was taking off his cloak. He was very tall, his face was emaciated, and he had piercing grey-blue eyes under thick bushy eyebrows. His hair was long, and he had a long beard like a peasant. He was wearing a Russian smock of blue silk drawn in at the waist, baggy black trousers, and high boots.

This was our one and only meeting, but it left me with a very uncomfortable feeling. During the few moments in which our looks met I had a distinct impression that I was in the presence of a sinister and evil being.

Russia Between Revolutions

Among the foreign observers and students of Russia in the early twentieth century, no one was more highly regarded by his peers than Harold Williams. A scholar, an accomplished linguist, and a penetrating observer, Mr. Williams

*wrote one of the best general descriptions of Russia as it was between the
Revolution of 1905 and the Fall of the Monarchy in 1917. The following
selections are from this book:* Russia of the Russians. *New York: Charles
Scribner's Sons, 1915. Pp. 54–61, 333–350, 363–369.*

THE CIVIL SERVICE. It would be quite wrong to say that the Russian Civil
Service is wholly composed of bureaucrats pure and simple. There are bureaucrats, a great many of them, and there are also a number of Government
employees who to-day are more or less tinged with the bureaucratic spirit, but
to-morrow would do their duty just as well or even better if a Constitutional
regime were in full swing. The Russian Government Service, taken as a
whole, includes a large number of interesting types, from elegant men of
the world to that pettifogging Dryzasdust familiarly known as a "Chancellory
rat," from the rough red-faced police captain to the mild-mannered bespec-
tacled excise clerk, from the dried-up martinet at the head of a St. Petersburg
department to the slow-moving, long-haired country postmaster. Governors,
senators, clerks of court, tax collectors, school-inspectors, telegraph clerks,
customs officials, wardens of the peasantry, heads of consistories, all are
engaged in the business of the Empire, all are formally in the service of the
Tsar. It is a State in uniform. The very schoolboys wear uniform, and
even high-school girls have to wear brown dresses and brown aprons. Ministers wear uniforms, not in the routine of work in St. Petersburg, but on
State occasions and when they travel about the country. Judges wear uniforms, and so do Government engineers and land-surveyors, and a host of
other people whose salary filters down through many channels from the St.
Petersburg Treasury. Brass buttons and peaked caps, peaked caps and brass
buttons, uniforms with blue, red, or white facings meet the eye with wearisome
monotony from end to end of the Empire, from the Pacific to the Danube.
A Russian may wear uniform his whole life long. As a little boy of eight
he goes proudly off to a preparatory school in a long grey overcoat, reaching
almost to the ground, and in a broad-crowned cap with the peak tilted over
his snub nose. When school days are over he dons the uniform of a student,
and after a few years at University or Technical College, enters a Ministry
and puts on one of the many official uniforms. The years pass, he is gradually
promoted, and at fifty he is trudging in uniform with portfolio under his
arm to his Ministry, just as with bag on shoulders he tramped to school when
he was a little boy of eight.

All the Government officials are *Chinovniks*, that is to say, each of them
stands in a definite *chin*, or rank. Peter the Great established an order of
promotion called the *Tabel Rangov*, or Table of Ranks, and this order is in
force to the present day. Once a man is drawn into the subtle mechanism
of the Table of Ranks he may go on from grade to grade with hardly an

effort on his part, by the mere fact of existing and growing wrinkled and grey-haired. When he enters the Government service he receives a paper called the *formuliarny spisok* or Formular List, in which the events of his life are noted down from year to year — his appointment to a particular table in the Ministry of Justice, his marriage, the birth of his children, his leave, his illnesses, his appointment to a commission or committee, his despatch on special service, and then the long series of decorations and promotions, various degrees of the Order of St. Anne, St. Stanislav, St. Vladimir, and it may be high up on the last rungs of the bureaucratic ladder such coveted decorations as the Order of St. Andrew, or even the White Eagle. The orders are a reward for good service. But the *chins*, or grades, need not necessarily be so. A *chinovnik* may be promoted from grade simply for "having served the due term of years," as the phrase is, but his promotion may be hastened through favour in high places or in recognition of special diligence or ability. The names of grades have no meaning except as indicating the grade. They are the same throughout the civil service, and give no suggestion of the office held by the possessor. They were originally adapted from German titles, and look imposing when re-translated into German. Thus the grade of *nadvorny sovietnik* is not a particularly high one, but when it appears in German as Hofrat, or Court Councillor, the impression is given that the possessor is personage of considerable importance. But the really important *chins* are that of *Staatsky Sovietnik,* which is perhaps not so important as it looks in its German guise of Staatsrath, or Councillor of State, but seems to secure a man against undue caprices on the part of Fortune, and to invest him with an air of respectability; and then the grades that make the man who attains to them a noble if he is not one by birth. There is a *chin* that conveys personal nobility, and the *chin* of *dieistvitelny staatsky sovietnik,* or Real State Councillor, conveys hereditary nobility. In this way the ranks of the gentry are constantly recruited from the bureaucracy, and the traditional connection between rank and Government service is maintained in actual practice. The grade of Real State Councillor also conveys the rank of a general in the Civil Service and the title of Excellency. The average *chinovnik* thinks himself happy if he reaches such as an exalted *chin* as this. Most professors become Real State Councillors by virtue of length of service, and it sounds odd to hear a stooping, frock-coated gentleman who is distinguished as an able lecturer on mediæval history, spoken of as a general. The grades of Secret Councillor and Real State Councillor are reserved either for very old or for very distinguished members of the Civil Service, for ministers and ambassadors, and the like.

The system of grades is one of the forces that hold the bureaucracy together. It secures a certain uniformity of temper, tendency and aim. Russians are the most democratic people in the world, but this carefully adjusted system of grades, decorations, money premiums and, to close with, pensions, corresponding to the *chin* attained, appeals to an ineradicable human instinct for outward symbols of position, security and distinction, and makes of the bureaucracy a world apart, a world in which the interests of all the members are interwoven. It is curious how mortified even a Radical magistrate will be if his name fails to appear among the Real State Councillors in the annual promotion list, and, on the other hand, with what unalloyed pleasure he receives congratulations if he has been given the coveted grade after all. But there is another very characteristic feature of the bureaucracy, and that is its extraordinary centralisation. From the big dreary-looking yellow or brown buildings in St. Petersburg, in which the Ministries are housed, currents of authority, or directive energy go forth to all the ends of the great Empire in the form of telegrams or occasional oral messages by special couriers, but above all in the form of endless "papers." Pens scratch, typewriters click, clerks lay blue covers full of papers before the "head of the table"; the "head of the table" sends them to the "head of the department," to the Assistant Minister, if need be, and in the more important cases, the Assistant Minister to the Minister. Then back go the papers again with signatures appended, down through various grades for despatch to a judge, to another department, to a Governor, to a *chinovnik* on special service, or to some petitioner from the world without. Incoming and outgoing papers are the systole and diastole of the Chancelleries. All sorts of documents go under the general name of *bumaga* or "paper," from a warrant for arrest to a report on a projected railway, or a notification of taxes due. There are *doklady* or reports, and *otnoshenia* or communications between officials of equal rank, and *donesenia* or statements made to superiors, *predpisania* instructions or orders, and *proshenia,* applications or petitions. These and a hundred others besides, are all "Papers," and there is a special style for each of them, and a general dry and formal style for all of them known as the "Chancellery Style," which permeates Russian public life, and creeps into private letters and concert programmes, and newspaper articles, and into the very love-making of telegraph clerks waiting for trains on wayside stations. The "papers," their colour, the stamps upon them, their style, create an immense uniformity of mental content, and tend to level down the striking differences that exist between say, the Tartar policemaster in a town on the Caspian Sea, and the son of a Russian priest who serves as a clerk in the financial department in Tver. It is extraordinary discipline. The lack of variety in the system increases its hold on all its members. There are hardly any of the curious divergencies and inconsistencies of which the English administrative system is so full, hardly any quaint anachronisms left to linger on because of some wise use they have for the affections. There are certain inevitable modifications in the Caucasus, in Central Asia, in Bessarabia and in Siberia, Poland and the Baltic Provinces. But, generally speaking, the system as outlined in mathematical order on smooth white paper, is embodied with surprising accuracy in the network of institutions that cover the great plain from limit to limit. Authority is delegated from the big yellow Ministries in St. Petersburg to the dreary white buildings in the head towns of the governments or territories into which the whole Empire is mapped out, and from the government towns to the head towns of the districts into which each government is divided, and then down to the smallest towns and to the Wardens of the Peasantry. The uniformity of it all is both imposing and depressing, and as wearying as the inevitable redcapped stationmaster and brown-coated gendarme on every one of the scores of railway stations between Wirballen and Harbin.

The integrity and uniformity of the bureaucratic system is maintained, the system is held in its framework, so to speak, by means of the army. The army, in its turn, by means of the conscript system, subjects almost the whole male population to a uniform discipline, levels down, for a time at any rate, the distinctions between various regions and various nationalities, and serves as a most potent means of Russification. Russification, indeed, is not the word, though it is the Russian language that is used in the process, for it is not the interests of the Russian people that are primarily in question but the interests of the State. It is a moulding of all the human material of the Empire upon one State pattern, a persistent elimination of divergencies, a grandiose attempt to subordinate all the wayward impulses of 160 millions of human beings to one common aim unintelligible to the mass. The army supplies the clamps by which the vast mechanism of the bureaucracy is held in position.

But it is through the police that the bureaucracy carries out its function of maintaining order. And the police have of late years assumed an overweening importance in the State because the bureaucracy has constantly tended more and more to limit its functions to the maintenance of order. It has subordinated everything to this end. It has become immensely suspicious. The very success, the very efficiency of the bureaucracy has been its ruin. In so far as it governed well, administered justice, prevented crime, promoted education, built roads and railways, and furthered trade, it encouraged individual initiative, fostered the desire for liberty. And at the same time it opened the eyes of many to its own corruption, to the depredations on the national wealth and welfare carried on under the veil of order, strict uniformity and long-armed discipline. On both occasions when the clamps were loosened, when the army was defeated in the Crimea in 1854-5, and in Manchuria fifty years afterwards, the evils of the bureaucracy were vividly revealed, the system almost fell asunder. Almost, but not quite. For after the Crimean War reforms were effected and the system was modernised, and again after the Japanese war reforms were granted and a further attempt was made at modernisation. But on each occasion concessions were followed by a reassertion of bureaucratic authority by means of the police. The nineteenth century was a century of movement, even in Russia. The emancipation of the serfs meant the freeing of an enormous amount of pent-up energy of economic development, it aroused a hum of fresh and vigorous movement all over the Empire. But for that strange complexity of widely extended, exclusive interests for which the bureaucracy stands, and for that rigid external uniformity which is the aim of its efforts, movement was dangerous. The bureaucracy took fright at the new, high-spirited movement of the sixties and, instead of steadily promoting economic and educational development, set to work to devise a system of checks. It tried to render its own reforms innocuous, set bureaucratic safeguards on its own judicial system, and bound and weakened those Zemstvos, or elective County Councils, which impaired the integrity of the bureaucratic system by exerting the functions of local government in thirty-four governments of European Russia. And the maintenance of order interpreted as the prevention of movement became the bureaucracy's prime care.

THE PEASANTRY. It is the peasant who embodies most distinctly the connection with the soil, and the peasant is the most interesting person in Russia. But there are so many types of peasant, there is such a variety of character and custom that it is difficult to make general statements that will be absolutely true of all. "Not a village but has ways of its own," is a Russian saying. A Siberian peasant on the Yenisei is a very different kind of man from the Tula peasants on Leo Tolstoy's estate of Yasnaia Poliana, and the Cossack of the Don is at once distinguishable from the peasants of the northern governments of Olonets and Archangel. Within the limits of a single government very different types may be met with. In the northern districts of the Chernigov government the peasants have thin, sharp features and speak a dialect of Great Russian. In the southern districts of the same government a dark, broad-faced, broad-shouldered type prevails and the language is Little Russian. Even a single district may display considerable variations. In the Nizhnedievitsky district of the Voronezh government there are three distinct groups, known as Shchekuny, Tsukany, and Galmany, and representing clearly-defined varieties of custom, costume, dialect, and character. The Shchekuny are extremely conservative, ignorant, poor, dirty, and have the reputation of being great thieves. Their neighbours, the Tsukany, pronounce many words differently, are a trading folk, busy, open, communicative, eager for novelties; their women often wear silk and satin, whereas those of the Shchekuny wear only picturesque, old-fashioned, homespun costumes. The third group again, the Galmany, speak a slightly different dialect, are not averse from innovations, but are laughed at by their neighbours for their big, many-coloured, baggy trousers. In fact, the variety of types even within the limits of the Russian nationality is inexhaustible. There are many degrees of prosperity. Side by side with well-to-do peasants there are whole villages that live in wretched poverty. Judging by the dull-eyed, bent-shouldered White Russian peasants one sees amongst the Jews on the railway stations in the governments of Vilna and Minsk, one might easily jump to the conclusion that the White Russian peasants generally were a dead and alive, down-trodden people. Their life is certainly not a cheerful one, but that even the White Russians are not the dumb, driven cattle that many of them seem is shown by a little peasant's paper published in Vilna which prints numbers of stories and a good deal of pretty verse written by peasants, as well as reports of co-operative and educational work undertaken in various villages in the Western Governments. There are three main groups of Russians — White Russians, Little Russians, and Great Russians — and the differences between them are frequently greater than those between an educated Russian and an educated Englishman.

It would be absurd, then, to attempt to describe in a chapter the life of the Russian peasantry as a whole. In the present chapter some account may be given of certain villages on the river Volhov in the Novgorod government, not far from St. Petersburg, it being premised only that a great many of the features noted here are characteristic of all the central and northern governments of European Russia.

The village of Vladimirovo stands on the river bank about ten miles from the St. Petersburg-Moscow railway line, and about half a mile away from a large country house to which the inhabitants of the village were a little over half a century ago attached as serfs. The village consists of one street, containing about thirty-five cottages and lined with birch trees. Behind the village stretch open fields with a long line of forest in the background. The broad, swiftly-flowing river is a highway in the summer. Steamers maintain communication between the railway station and Novgorod. Great rafts of timber with red-shirted raftsmen drift from the rivers beyond Lake Ilmen down the Volhov to Lake Ladoga and so out to the Neva and St. Petersburg. Barges are towed up early in the season and come down later with timber cut small or with immense stacks of hay. Sometimes the long, yellow barges spread magnificent sails and fly many-coloured flags, and with a fair wind go floating past bright green fields triumphantly up the stream, the steersman dexterously managing the heavy rudder. Then there are curious bulging craft, painted in stripes, with covered decks and sharp stern, big rudder and coarse sails. Such vessels as these come down by various rivers from the distant Borovichi district bringing crude pottery which the boatmen sell in the villages by the way. There are plenty of fish in the river and the peasants cast their nets and catch enough for food and for sale. All through the summer the river is alive with unceasing traffic, though nowadays the trade is nothing like what it was in the Middle Ages when Novgorod was a great commercial republic, and German and Italian merchants were constantly bringing their ware up the Volkov and carrying away rich stores of furs and skins.

But in November the Volhov freezes hard and remains frozen till April. Then all the steamers and boats and barges lie still, and the river becomes simply a smooth, white road over which sleighs go gliding in a long and silent procession. But the peasants of Vladimirovo are not greatly affected by the change. Unlike the peasants of the opposite bank they do not trade and they fish very little. Considering that they live on a great river and so near the railway they are surprisingly unenterprising.

Their cottages are built of wood and are unpainted, yellow when new and grey within a year or two; with sloping shingle or thatched roofs and with the gable-end and glazed windows facing the street. The entrance is from the side. You mount a wooden staircase or ladder, push open a door, and find yourself in the upper or main floor of the cottage, the ground floor being mostly used for storage purposes. On the upper floor there may be one, two or three rooms, according to the wealth of the owner and the size of his family. A big, white-washed, brick stove occupies a prominent position in the main room, and on this stove the older people and the children sleep in winter. There is a rough table and a few chairs, a bed, and square, wooden trunks adorned with gaudy pictures; on the walls, cuttings from illustrated papers, in the corners ikons or sacred pictures, and in the middle of the room a child's cot suspended from the ceiling. Pots and pans on the shelves; on the landing at the head of the staircase a barrel of water and a dipper for washing — which is effected not by plunging and rinsing, but by getting another person to pour on the head and hands; then behind the landing lies the hay-loft where half the family sleeps in summer, and under the hay-loft is the stable. Living-rooms and stable are practically under one roof, but men and animals are far apart, and they do not herd together as is the case in Western Ireland, and the cottages are, as a rule, remarkably clean. Some of the women pile upon shelves and walls an incongruous variety of ornaments such as may often be seen in English farm-houses. Often there are pot-flowers in the windows. On the floor are mats of rough canvas, and occasionally there are family photographs on the walls. There is only one flower garden in the village and that exists because, in the first place, the owner's wife is cook at the manor-house where there is a pretty garden, and in the second place the owner himself is the strong man of the village, and the boy who pulled up his narcissi would know what to expect. Behind some of the cottages are vegetable gardens with a fruit tree or two.

At the end of the village and behind many of the cottages are *banias* or Russian bath-houses, which are a necessity of life to the Northern Russians. The *bania* is a low, wooden building, containing a large brick stove on which when it is heated cold water is poured so that the room is filled with steam. There are boilers for hot water. On one side of the room there is a tier of benches, and to lie on the highest bench where the air is hottest is the most effective way of taking the bath. The bath is a combination of perspiring and washing in hot and cold water, and the peasants aid the process by beating themselves with birch twigs. In winter the youths sometimes rush out of the *bania* and roll naked in the snow. Every Saturday the villagers take their bath, and this right through the year, so that it is altogether unfair to describe the peasants of Northern and Central Russia as being indifferent to cleanliness. On the contrary, they are exceptionally scrupulous in this respect.

In the centre of the village is a shop kept by a widow-woman, where sugar, tea, sweetmeats, cotton-fabrics, and a score of odds and ends are sold at a high price, often on credit. There is a tiny chapel or rather a shrine in which services are rarely held. The parish church is several miles away, but the church of the neighbouring parish is just across the river and the Vladimirovo peasants as a rule go there when they go to church at all.

Outside the village is a big, two-storied school building where about sixty children from all the villages in the neighbourhood are taught the elements. The girls are taught sewing, and there is a carpentry class for the boys, with a special teacher and a well-furnished shop. This school, which owes its existence to the neighbouring landowner, is unusually large and well equipped. Very often in the villages the school is held in an ordinary peasant's cottage, roughly adapted for the purpose. The Vladimirovo school is now maintained by the Ministry of Education. There are two teachers, a man and a woman, and the priest from over the river gives religious instruction. The only children's festival in the year is the Christmas tree which is usually provided by the landowner's family. Then the little boys and girls march round the fir-tree in a stumbling, hot, disorderly procession and gaze in wonder at all the marvels agleam in the candlelight amongst the dark branches. They sing lustily the songs they have been taught for the occasion and are full of struggling, despairing eagerness when the time for the distribution of presents comes. On the whole, the children live a jolly life. There are so many of them and they are always trooping about the village street together, the little girls arm-in-arm and sometimes singing in imitation of their big sisters, and the little boys striding about barefoot contemptuous of mere girls with hands deep in the pockets of long, baggy, patched trousers, or else racing off at full speed when big people find them robbing birds'-nests or getting within dangerous reach of forbidden fruit trees. In winter the most absorbing care of the mothers is to see that the children are warmly clad, but in the summer the boys go mostly bareheaded and their hair is bleached to a uniform white. There is no end to the children, six, seven, or eight being quite a normal number in a family, and it is a relief to the mother if a girl of eleven or twelve can go out as nurse to a neighbour for her keep, or if one of the small boys is made a shepherd lad. The bigger boys help their fathers, and the bigger girls may go out to service or else find work in the factory down the river. But in any case it is not easy to make ends meet, and the peasants frankly admit that it is not an unmixed evil if one of the children dies.

The problem of "What shall we eat, and what shall we drink, and where-withal shall we be clothed?" is for the peasants a tolerably simple one, especially as far as eating is concerned. The staple food is home-made rye bread, which is called black, but it is not coal-black, as most of us imagined when we read German stories in our childhood, but dark brown. This bread is pleasant to the taste and very nourishing, but to assimilate it a long training is necessary. It seems ill adapted to English digestions, and the older peasants often suffer violent aches and pains as a result of its use. Black bread is the staple, and the peasant can do an enormous amount of field-work on black bread alone. But this fact is not an absolute argument in favour of vege-tarianism, for as soon as a peasant goes to work in a factory he finds that his strength fails him unless he eats meat; and even the workmen in a brick-kiln near the village declare they cannot do without flesh food. The peasant eats meat rarely, as a rule only on festival days. But every day there is a meatless soup of some kind, most frequently *shchi,* in which preserved cab-bage or sauerkraut is the chief ingredient. Potatoes are eaten as a kind of sauce or condiment to bread; altogether the chief art in eating is to find ways of consuming the largest possible quantity of bread. Barley and buckwheat porridge is frequenty eaten. For special occasions the women bake *pirogi* or pasties filled with cabbage, more rarely with rice, and still more rarely with meat. On their simple but monotonous diet the peasants seem to thrive fairly well, although digestive complaints are not infrequent.

To drink there is plain water and tea. Every peasant cottage has its *samovar* or tea-urn, and tea is drunk regularly, very weak and very pale, without milk. In drinking tea a small lump of sugar is made to go a long way; a tiny morsel is bitten off and held between the teeth and gradually melts as the tea is sipped. Peasants eat slowly and with great decorum, cross-ing themselves before and after meals.

But there is another beverage to which the Russian peasant is greatly addicted, and that is *vodka,* a spirituous liquor as innocent-looking as water, but a most potent kind of brandy. On the whole, the peasant does not drink such an enormous amount of *vodka* as is supposed. The average consumption of alcohol per head is less in Russia than in Great Britain. But the peasant drinks at intervals. He remains sober all the week and celebrates Sundays and festival days by consuming enough *vodka* to raise his spirits; a very small quantity of *vodka* suffices to intoxicate him. On special holidays as the festival of the patron saint of the village, there is heavy drinking, often leading to fierce quarrels in which knives are used; and sometimes murders are com-mitted. Vodka-selling is the monopoly of the State. All over the country there are Government brandy-shops, in which the salesman or saleswoman hands out through a hole in a netting like that of a telegraph office bottles from long rows of shelves like those in a dispensary, for consumption off the premises. There is no State brandy-shop in Vladimirovo, but during one year there was a great deal of illicit grog-selling, and that was a bad time for the village, for the men were always drinking and their earnings melted away. Then the women revolted and took matters into their own hands. They went about the village and broke the windows in the cottages of the sly grog-sellers and made them give up the trade. Only one they left in peace. She was a widow, and they gave her permission to sell *vodka* until she could save enough to buy a cow. After this revolt the peasants were compelled to make journeys to other villages when they needed brandy. The women in this district do not drink, but that is not the case everywhere. In some of the districts around Moscow the women drink at least as much as the men and make a boast of doing so. And the nearer peasants are to the cities or to manufacturing districts the more they drink and the more demoralised they become. Sometimes a revulsion of feeling occurs, and in Vladimirovo several of the hardest drinkers occasionally go to the priest and take a vow not to drink, or in other words sign the pledge for six months or more. And although they are by no means pious men they keep their vow.

. . . The question of dress in the country is at once simpler and more difficult than it used to be. In former days all garments were home-made, the fashions remained unchanged for generations and valuable costumes were handed down from mother to daughter and long kept in the family as heirlooms. In the remoter districts, where the influence of the cities is not strongly felt, the older costumes are still worn, and often the women's costumes are complicated and beautiful, with gorgeous headgear and veils and rich adornment or silver coins of various times and peoples. Occasionally, as in some villages on the Gulf of Finland near St. Petersburg, the old costumes are retained in defiance of the factories and proudly worn on Sundays. But in Vladimirovo the modern spirit rules. Of the typical, red, close-fitting woman's dresses known as the *sarafan*, which is eagerly sought after as a curiosity, not a specimen is now to be found in the village; probably all have been cut up or worn to shreds. There are a few spinning-wheels and rough hand-looms, and the women weave a kind of coarse canvas and linen table-cloths and towels from the flax which is one of the staple crops in the district. Some of the women embroider for sale. But most of the clothing material comes from the factories. About once a month a Tartar comes round with a waggon full of cotton fabrics, and of these the peasants buy what they need for their garments. The women make their own and the children's clothing and also the men's shirts or blouses. In the autumn a tailor goes from cottage to cottage and makes rough suits and overcoats for the men. There is a feltmaker, too, who makes the round of the villages and beats out felt for winter boots. Very often nowadays the men buy their clothing ready-made, and the boys have to be content with more or less clumsy adaptations of their father's or elder brother's garments.

In the district here described, and this is true of most districts near the main highways, the women dress in cotton skirts and blouses, and on their heads wear coloured cotton kerchiefs. The men wear a kind of rough European dress — German dress they call it here — with high boots and cotton blouses, known as Russian shirts, and in colder weather double-breasted coats buttoned up to the neck. Their head-gear is usually a soft peaked cap. On Sundays the younger men flaunt shining top-boots and gaudily embroidered shirts. The younger women are quickly adapting town fashions which they probably bring home from the factory down the river where so many of them are employed. The daughter of a comparatively poor peasant will walk on Sundays in elaborate dresses of a town pattern; none of them dare yet do such an unheard-of thing as wear a hat in the village, though probably they have hats stored away. But it is to be feared that some of them have already gone so far as to complete their transformation by wearing false hair. *O tempora, O mores!*

The inhabitants of Vladimirovo are neither well-to-do nor very poor. They are not geniuses and are not enterprising, but they are no fools, and they are not stubbornly conservative. They have no pronounced political opinions of any kind, take things very much as they come, rarely read newspapers, although during the war and the revolutionary years some of them went so far as to subscribe to the cheaper journals. Few of the men read books, but sometimes the younger women and girls read the story-books to be found in the school library. Nearly all the men have served in the army, but it is difficult to see what trace army life has left on them. Several served in the Japanese War and took part in some of the fiercest engagements, but they tell of their experiences in a humdrum way without the slightest display of emotion. One snub-nosed, broad-cheeked peasant, Alexei, received for his services in the war a premium of £50, which he spent on building a new cottage. He was also appointed military instructor in the school under the new boy-scout system, and aroused the merriment of the whole countryside by his attempts to drill rebellious schoolboys into the proper use of wooden guns. There are hardly any among the villagers who remember the days of serfdom. An old forester and his wife can sometimes be induced to recall the time when they were serfs. But they will not admit that there was any profound and essential difference between then and now, except that in the old days a peasant was bound to be more industrious, which they are inclined to consider was rather a good thing. A former blacksmith, Gerasim, now dead, used to tell with pride that he was rarely flogged and enjoyed the favour of his master, who got him a very pretty bride, naturally also a serf, from another estate of his about twenty miles away. Gerasim fell in love with her at first sight, but he seems to have been a dull fellow and by no means handsome, and the girl cried her eyes out at being compelled to marry him. There was no help for it. It was the master's will, and they were the master's property. But for months after the marriage the bride would not look at Gerasim and turned her back on him every time he approached her. Of the stern master who effected this marriage and who lived in the early part of the last century it is related, amongst other things, that during haymaking and harvest he used to stand on a hill and watch the work through a telescope; any peasant who showed sign of slackness he immediately had flogged. But the pre-emancipation period with its three days a week of compulsory labour on the big estate, the constant floggings, the purchase and sale of men and women, is a fading memory now. The younger generation has hardly an idea of what serfdom meant.

The effects of serfdom linger on, however, in Vladimirovo in a very curious way. Most of the peasants are very good fellows, not idle, and some of them witty and original. But, on the whole, they are strangely flaccid and lacking in initiative, and this is characteristic of most of the villages for a considerable distance along the left bank of the river. On the right bank a very different spirit is manifested. Just opposite Vladimirovo is a large village called Vysoko, which the German traveller, Olearius, notes having visited during his journeys up to Novgorod in the seventeenth century. Here the peasants are much more prosperous, are more industrious, better dressed, have better houses, are more wide-awake and alert, more receptive of new ideas, more enterprising in every way. The chief explanation of the difference is a very simple one. Along the left bank the peasants were the serfs of private landowners. On the right bank they were the serfs of the State, which meant that after the payment of a heavy tax a great deal of room was left for individual initiative. Then there is one other important fact that accounts for the difference in character. The villages on the right bank are the remains of the military settlements founded by Count Arakcheiev early in the nineteenth century. Arakcheiev was a fierce disciplinarian, and applied martial law to field-work and to every detail of life in the settlements. With the help of the cat-o'-nine-tails he got a fine highroad lined with birch trees built from Gruzino some distance down the river to Saraia Rusa beyond Lake Ilmen. The discipline was intolerable, and led to a terrible revolt which was ferociously quelled. But the sense of order and duty inculcated in the settlements in Arakcheiev's stern days has left its impress on the character of the inhabitants of the right bank until now. At the present time the difference between the two banks makes itself continually felt, and while the left bank on the whole remains passive and is sunk in routine, the right bank is undergoing some very remarkable changes. But before describing these changes it is necessary to give some account of the prevailing system of peasant land tenure and of the *mir* or village commune.

In Vladimirovo, which is a small village, the commune exists in a simple form. All the peasants of the village hold their land in common, and there is no rented or bought land to complicate ownership rights. Fifty years ago at the time of the emancipation the Vladimirovo peasants received a portion of the land of the estate to which they had been attached. This land was in effect purchased by them, but the purchase was made through the State, the peasants gradually extinguishing their debt in the form of annual redemption payments which constituted an extra tax. The State in its turn compensated the landlord by means of a complex financial operation. The result, as far as the Vladimirovo peasants were concerned, was that they secured in all about 630 acres of land. The way they put it is that they received 5½ desiatins per soul, a "soul" then being a male householder. At the time of the emancipation there were forty-six souls, so that the total amount was 253 desiatins. This land was divided up amongst the members of the community in such a way that each received his share of forest, meadow, and field. But the system of allotment is a very curious one. If each peasant had his lot in one compact area he could deal with it fairly easily. This is not the case. Justice requires that good and bad soil, forest and bog, the far lands and the near lands should be as nearly as possible equally apportioned. So the land is cut up into narrow strips, and these strips cause considerable confusion, especially if they happen to become entangled with Crown lands or with landlords' land or land that has been bought or rented by individual peasants. This overlapping of strips is one of the most perpetually irritating of land problems in Russia.

In Vladimirovo, however, this particular difficulty is felt less acutely than in other villages, because the peasants' land is fairly clearly marked off from that of the estate on one side, and from that of the neighbouring village community on the other. And, indeed, the Vladimirovo peasants got such a small share of land that they have little difficulty in managing it. Every peasant knows his lot though it is not divided from others by fences or ditches, and disputes are rare. The land is owned legally by the whole community, and each member holds his land only in virtue of his membership. This does not mean, however, that all members of the community are equalised in the matter of wealth. Even if they were equalised at the beginning the lapse of years makes them unequal. The growth of population causes changes. Some families increase, others diminish and disappear. One family has many sons, each of whom has a right to land. Anther family has many daughters who are married off and lost to their father's house. Sometimes if there are several males in the family, some go to work in the towns or on distant estates and leave their father or brothers to work the land which in time practically passes into the hands of the workers. Some families are industrious and enterprising, others indolent and ready to forego their rights. In fact, there is no end to the possibilities of inequality. There exists a legal corrective to the growth of irregularities in the form of a repartition which may be undertaken by the community at certain intervals. But the peasants of Vladimirovo have not once effected a repartition since the emancipation. They seem to have thought it hardly worth while. Part of the surplus of population brought by the years has gradually drifted away and left the community very little larger than it was at the time of the emancipation. And there is a natural disinclination to upset established relationships. But a considerable disproportion now exists. Some families are richer and some are poorer. Some hold the share of two souls or more, others have only half a soul, and some have practically nothing more than the tiny plot of land on which their cottage stands.

The communal land was, until a few years ago, inalienable. It could not be sold or leased, and every peasant, so long as he was a member of the commune and had not forfeited his rights, had a certain safe and sure anchorage to which he might return when life in the world outside buffeted him too severely. The commune is a kind of mutual aid society, and the habit of united action ingrained as a result of centuries of communal life is one of the most marked features of the Russian peasants' character. Living together in a village, not scattered about on separate lots of land, possessing strongly developed social instincts, they are communicative, gossipy, given to lending and borrowing, observant of custom, retentive of tradition. And the communal system largely explains the extreme conservatism of the Russian peasant in methods of cultivation. It is not easy to effect innovations when, after all, your land is not your own and the other members of the community resent the implied aspersion on the traditional methods. The peasants of Vergezha and all the other peasants in the neighbourhood, might get very much more out of their land than they do. With intensive culture a good deal might be done even with thirteen acres. There are, in fact, German and Lettish colonists in the district who prosper greatly on land of the same quality, but the Russian peasants have not shown the slightest disposition to adopt their methods.

The affairs of the community are managed by a *skhod,* or mote of which all the adult males are members. The *skhod* annually selects a *starosta* or elder, who on occasion summons the men for the transaction of necessary business by walking through the village, striking each cottage with a rod and crying, *"Na skhod!"* (To the mote!). In the exercise of his duties the elder is assisted by another peasant who acts as policeman, or *desiatnik*. The chief business of the starosta is to collect the taxes, to note their payment in a register and to convey them to the centre of the canton, or volost, a few miles away. The village mote discusses all matters that concern the whole village; the hire of a shepherd for the cattle during the summer months, the amount to be paid to the neighbouring landlord for the right of pasturing the herd on his estate, and many other such details of the communal life. Sometimes bigger questions are discussed. The peasants of the village of Kurino, up the river, decided some years ago after long discussion to acquire, through the Peasant's Bank, a Government institution which facilitates the purchase of land by the peasantry, a considerable portion of a neighbouring estate.

The question of the interest to be paid to the Bank is now one of the many questions discussed by their mote. More general questions are occasionally touched upon. The mote may pass a resolution (called a *prigovor*, or sentence) urging the removal of an unpopular school teacher or priest, or the retention of one whose dismissal is threatened. During 1905 and 1906 many communes discussed political questions, and a large number of peasants' resolutions were sent to the First Duma demanding a great variety of reforms, chiefly concerning land-tenure. Discussions of this kind have, however, now been pretty thoroughly checked by police measures.

For the peasants are not allowed to act independently. They are under constant tutelage. All the villages in a given area called a canton or volost converge on an administrative centre in the chief village of the canton which has a cantonal mote and a cantonal court under the presidency of a *starshina*, or elder. The books of the canton are kept by a *pisar*, or secretary, who is also the mainspring of the activity of the court. In the cantonal court cases are tried by customary law, but these courts are notorious for their corruption, and it is a common saying among the peasantry that a gift of a bottle of beer to the *starshina* and a rouble to the *pisar* is sufficient to secure judgment in the desired direction. The *uriadnik*, the lowest representative of the Government rural police, lives in the cantonal centre.

The canton contains another personage of great importance to the peasantry. It will be noted that the whole organisation of the canton is concerned only with the peasants. The gentry and other inhabitants of the area are not included in the administrative arrangements. The peasants are, indeed, regarded as being, as a class, in the position of minors, and this fact is emphasised by the appointment of special officials, known as *Zemskie Nachalniki*, Rural Overseers or Wardens of the Peasantry, whose duty it is to exercise a general oversight over the peasants in their respective districts each of which may include two or three cantons. Usually a prominent landowner of the neighbourhood is appointed Warden, and care is taken that his views shall be agreeable to the Government. The Warden has judicial rights with power to fine and imprison, and minor criminal cases are tried before him. If he is politically active and heavy-handed he may make things very unpleasant for the peasants, and as an intitution the wardenship is unpopular. But the peasants regard the Warden as the chief authority in the district, and their favourite threat is to appeal to the Zemsky. Thus Anna, the wife of Nikolai the forester's son in Vladimirovo, had endless trouble with her husband who had not only beat her, which would be considered a normal and a natural thing and a sign of affection, but openly insulted her, and although he earned a great deal of money practically starved her and the children. Several times she retired to her father's house to parley from there, but Nikolai never kept his promises, and finally she went off to lay all her troubles before the Warden. Kusha, a widow in a village down the river, had an incorrigible son of sixteen who beat her, turned her out of her own house, and threatened to kill her. She, too, applied to the Warden and had the boy put in prison.

THE LANDOWNERS. But if the peasant is changing so is his neighbour the landed proprietor, or *pomieshchik*. The estates of the country gentry are a characteristic feature of the landscape in Central and Northern Russia. The house stands preferably on a river-bank or on a hill-side. It is half-hidden amidst a grove of trees. Frequently, especially if the house was built, as a great many of the houses of the country gentry were, at the beginning of the nineteenth century, it has a veranda and a balcony supported by massive white columns. Near the house there is almost sure to be a lime-tree avenue, leading to an orchard of apple, pear, and cherry trees. A flower garden, sometimes with artificial ponds, and a variety of outbuildings complete the number of immediate appurtenances to the manor-house. Indoors a wide entrance-hall, a big dining-room, a drawing-room, a kitchen full of busy, chattering life, stairs leading to all sorts of quaint nooks and corners, well-stocked store-rooms, libraries often containing old and valuable books, pretty, old-fashioned mahogany furniture, family portraits on the walls and generally a snug and soothing sense of leisure, security, and remoteness from the bustle of the world. Such is the home of the average *pomieshchik*. The government of Orel, of which Turgeniev was a native, was studded with such homes as these, and no one has described them more vividly than he. "Gentlefolks' Nests," he calls them, and this name with its lulling note of defence and security is still largely applicable, although the gentry no longer wield, as formerly, exclusive authority in the countryside, and the distributing forces of a new time are beating up against the white-columned mansions.

In some of the great estates stand splendid palaces with magnificent grounds as in Arkhangelskaia and Marfino in the Moscow government. And, on the other hand, there are landowners who by rank belong to the gentry, but who possess little land and live in a condition hardly differing from that of the peasantry. The steppe *pomieshchik*, again, is a type apart and so are pomieshchiks from beyond the Volga. In the south-eastern region and Siberia the conception of a *pomieshchik* as understood in the centre and the north of European Russia is simply lost amidst various categories of Cossacks, peasants, colonists, and big and small farmers of a more or less American type.

The typical *pomieshchik* has no exact counterpart in England. He is neither a country squire nor a yeoman farmer, though he may have features characteristic of both. Very often he is in the government service and devotes his chief energies to administrative work, regarding his estate merely as a place of repose and, under favourable conditions, as a source of income. During the winter months he and his family live in the city, and the estate is left in charge of a steward who may possibly be a German or a Lett, but is, as often as not, a shrewd peasant from a neighbouring village. There are honest stewards, but the average steward has an elastic conception of his rights and privileges, and the absenteeism of many proprietors, and the light-hearted indifference they often display to the business of the estate when they do come down to it during the summer months almost irresistibly tempt to speculation. Even if the proprietor is not in the Government service he probably prefers to live in the city or in the government town, and then it may easily happen that the owner of a considerable estate can barely scrape together enough money to pay the rent of his flat, while his steward on the distant estate builds himself a roomy and comfortable mansion. A landowner in the Novgorod government built on his estate a house of stone. One day his steward came to St. Petersburg with a melancholy story of a storm having risen and the house having been swept away by the river Volhov. The landowner shook his head sadly, but it was long before he learned that the steward had simply pulled the house down and sold the materials. This experience must have disheartened the landowner for he sold his estate through the Peasants' Bank, then made unfortunate investments and was finally ruined.

Indeed the habits acquired by the gentry during centuries of serfdom are not to be thrown off in a day. When a man inherited an estate which, having serfs upon it, produced wealth almost mechanically, fed and clothed its proprietor and provided him almost without any exertion on his part with the money he needed for living in the cities and for travelling, he would naturally pay close attention to working of the estate only if he were personally interested in agriculture or were resolutely bent on adding to his wealth. There were, under the old system, many *pomieshchiks* who scraped and saved and sat year in, year out on their estates without ever visiting the city, who flogged the maximum of work out of their peasantry, outwitted their weaker neighbours, and by dint of economy, careful calculation, and endless litigation succeeded in greatly increasing the extent of their property. These were the methods that secured for the Grand Princess of Moscow their supremacy over their neighbours. But the Grand Princess of Moscow also brushed aside the laws which led to an incessant disintegration of big estates by providing that all the sons should inherit equally. The ordinary *pomieshchik* could in no way evade this law, and the consequence was that after a father had spent a lifetime in extending the frontiers of his property farther than the eye could reach, his death would mean the splitting up of the estate into five or six fragments, and it was not to be expected that all the sons would inherit the acquisitive instincts of their parent. Moreover, the habit of recruiting the ranks of the administration and of the army officers from among the country gentry encouraged the growth of the type of *pomieshchik* who drew his income from his estate without ever troubling as to how it was raised.

This passive and receptive attitude to the soil lingers on to a great extent among the country gentry, and its traces are constantly met with even on estates the proprietors of which are enlightened and progressive Zemstvo-workers, are eagerly interested in agriculture, and personally superintend the cultivation of the soil. A subtle fatalism seems to be latent in the homes of the gentry. There are endless difficulties, but it seems to the proprietors incredible that they should be insurmountable. A way out is sure to be found, things cannot be as bad as they appear. Some one is sure to help, either the Government or the elements or some vague, friendly Providence. Indeed, the gentry are just as responsible as the peasantry for the prevalence in Russian conversation of such comfortable optimistic phrases as *Obrazuietsia* ("It will come out all right"), or the expressive interjections, *Avos* and *Kak-nibud* ("May hap!" and "Somehow or other").

The Government does a great deal to justify the confidence of the gentry. There is an institution called the State Land Bank, which was formed twenty-four years after the emancipation when it had become clear that the gentry for all their wealth in land could not cope with the difficulties of this new situation without direct financial aid. The Government needed a class of landed gentry, and since the gentry showed a tendency to let their land slip out of their hands, to turn it into money as soon as possible and then to squander the proceeds, it was the policy of the Government to find means for maintaining the connection between the gentry and the land. The Gentry's Bank accordingly advances sums on mortgage at a low rate of interest, and on such easy conditions that the advance practically amounts to a donation which enables the Government to hold the land in trust for the mortgagee and to prevent its passing too rapidly into the hands of private money-lenders, or members of other classes. Even such paternal action often fails of its effect, however, and a quarter of the estates now mortgaged are registered as having passed from the possession of gentlemen into that of representatives of other classes. The total number of estates mortgaged in the Bank is over 26,000, the amount advanced on which is nearly 660 million roubles, or about 67 million pounds sterling. The greater number of estates mortgaged are in such central governments as Tula, Orel, Kursk, and Riazan. The Bank is a kindly institution, and until recently it was very tolerant of the weaknesses of the gentry, though it is growing stricter now. There is a pleasant ritual when the *pomieshchik* comes to pay interest on the mortgage; complaints on the part of the pomieshchik of hard times and inability to pay the full sum, commiseration on the part of the Bank officials, but insistence on the absolute necessity of paying the entire amount, expostulation from the pomieshchik, further demurring from the official, a little gentle bargaining, the retirement of the official to inner rooms where consultations are held, after which the official with a sigh accepts the smaller amount and remits the remainder until the following term when the scene is re-enacted.

All the benevolence of the Government does not avail, however, to establish any great fixity of tenure for the families of gentry. The inheritance law is responsible for constant perturbations. The right of primogeniture does not exist in respect of purely Russian estates — the eldest son has an advantage only if the family possesses an entailed estate in Polish districts where the right of Primogeniture does prevail — and all the sons inherit equal portions, while a daughter's interest is one-fourteenth. Then the growing economic strength of other classes menaces the gentry. An emancipated serf makes money as a contractor and advances cash to his former master on the security of considerable areas of meadow or forest land; the security is not redeemed, the land falls into the peasant's hands. He becomes a timber merchant, buys or mortgages forests from the neighbouring gentry who are usually glad enough to sacrifice timber to save their estates, to pay for the education of their children or for travelling, or to cover a variety of debts that have been contracted in the cities. The estates of the gentry grow smaller, those of the timber merchant grow larger. The merchant's sons inherit a large property and develop it. The surrounding peasants earn good money in timber-felling and rafting, for the merchant and the gentry find the wages for agricultural labourers rising and the difficulty of securing labour increasing. Some of the gentry shrink back in alarm before the growing difficulties, and after exhausting all possible methods of raising money on their land abandon the task in despair, finally dispose of their estates and become tonwsmen pure and simple. Others devise new methods of production and cultivation, build a starch factory and grow acres of potatoes to keep it going, start a brick-kiln if the soil is suitable, or a flour-mill, a distillery or some similar enterprise, or, if there is access to a good market engage in dairy-farming, or else try to improve the quality of their land by scientific manuring or by draining swamps. Those landowners who take their estates seriously and exploit their resources according to modern methods as a rule succeed in keeping their heads above water, but that section of the gentry which is unable to take a keen interest in agriculture and resigns itself to the will of kindly fates is being gradually elbowed off the land by pushing merchants and well-to-do commission agents and shrewd peasants and various keen-eyed financiers. Often the landowner sells his estate for a song, and has the bitterness of seeing the purchaser make a fortune out of land that he himself had considered valueless.

This flux in land tenure is inevitable under the modernising process through which Russia is now passing. The break-up of the peasant commune and the creation of a class of peasant farmers with private property means that these farmers, in so far as they are successful, will add to their property by purchasing land from the gentry. And so there will be from all sides a steady encroachment which only economically strong proprietors will be able to resist. The result will undobutedly be immensely to increase the productiveness of the soil in European Russia — for it is in European Russia that the change is chiefly felt. It is obvious, even to the inexperienced eye, that far less is made of Russian estates than might be made, not to speak of the land of the peasants. The traveller who makes the railway journey via Berlin to Moscow or St. Petersburg is inevitably struck by the contrast between the level of cultivation in the estates and farms of East Prussia and those in Russia, and the difference between the agriculture of Central Russia and that of the Baltic Provinces is also very marked. A Western farmer habituated to the microscopic niceties of intensive culture on small patches of land is astonished at the waste, at the indifference to rich opportunities so often met with on Russian estates. The final break with the traditions of serfdom, the development of individual initiative and of a determination to exploit the resources of the soil to the utmost, to make money by farming instead of depending on barely aided nature, should mean a startling increase of national wealth.

The March Revolution in Petrograd[1]

The value of the following lies in the fact that Mr. Edward T. Heald, who wrote it, was not seeking to make a case for any side. The letter was written to Mrs. Heald and was not intended for publication. It does not pretend to be an analysis but only an informal description of what Mr. Heald saw, heard and thought during the stirring first week of the first 1917 Revolution. At that time, Mr. Heald had been a Y.M.C.A. secretary in Petrograd for about nine months.

Contrary to the practice throughout the rest of this anthology, this selection is reprinted with footnotes because the notes not only serve to relate Mr. Heald's report to the general story but also contain numerous bibliographical suggestions. All dates are given in New Style.

Vosnesensky Prospect[2]
Petrograd
March 16, 1917
[Friday]

Dear Emily:

I am not sure whether the new regime and the new freedom which have so suddenly come to this land will give the censor the liberty to allow an American citizen to write to his wife in detail about the thrilling experiences of the past few days, but by avoiding military matters that have a bearing upon the Great War, I will take the chance on getting this detailed account through to you.[3]

---

[1] The source is: Walsh, W. B. (Editor), "Petrograd, March-July, 1917. The Letters of Edward T. Heald." *American Slavic and East European Review*. Vol VI, Nos. 16–17, pp. 116–157; pp. 118–133.

[2] My apartment address (ETH).

[3] "Dear Emily" is Mrs. Heald. This letter went through without censorship as did most of those written after the Revolution. (ETH.)

I realize that we are living too near the events to grasp their real significance, but I feel that they transcend in greatness any revolution in the world's history, affecting as they do the lives of 170 million people. And from all that we can now see, the entire change from one end of the Empire to the other has been completely made in a week's time and with an order and absence of violence that is a wonderful revelation of the natural self-restraint and good-nature of the Russian people.

Little did we realize a week ago today that the strike which had started in the shops here had such a tremendous significance.[4]

The government and military officials seemed to have little more realization of it than we, for the Committee of the Empress met on Thursday night with Mr. Harte[5] and laid plans for the war prisoners work as if nothing unusual was in progress. That the strike was far-reaching, however, speedily became apparent. Street car traffic became irregular Friday [the 9th] and practically ceased during the afternoon. The sleighs with their drivers likewise disappeared from the streets, so that when Day and I had to deliver a letter to Premier Golitsyn, on the other side of the city, we had to walk. We were informed at the palace of the Premier that he was not at home, but had gone to the Tsarskoe Selo that day.[6]

---

[4] Strikes which had already been numerous from January on, now increased rapidly both in seriousness and numbers involved. Chamberlain retails an estimate of 197,000 strikers on March 9th. *Vide*, W. H. Chamberlin, *The Russian Revolution*, 2 vols., N. Y., Macmillan, 1935, I, 75.

Government leaders and government critics both realized the increasing gravity of the whole situation and sought to bring an understanding of it to the tsar. Chiefly under the direction of Protopopov, Minister of the Interior, plans were made to quell the uprising expected in the capital. Heavy batteries were emplaced, machine guns were brought in, and Gurko, Chief of Staff, sent three crews of sailors to maintain order. Despite the urgings of Alexandra and of his advisors and ministers, Nicholas left for Headquarters on March 8th. That same day, the Duma castigated the government's policy on food, and street disorders broke out in Petrograd. For a detailed account, *vide* B. Pares, *Fall of the Russian Monarchy*, Knopf, N. Y. 1939. 412 *et sqq.*, esp. 436–471; Chamberlin, *op. cit.* I; 70–98. For the official Bolshevik interpretation, *vide*, M. Gorki *et al.* (eds), *Istoriya grazhdanskoi voinyi v SSSR*, Moscow, 1938, I: 55–75. This source places the number of strikers on that day (March 9th NS) at "about 200,000."

[5] Dr. A. C. Harte was one of two representatives sent to Europe by the Y.M.C.A. to arrange for service to war prisoners. After consultations with the Central Powers, he reached Moscow in May 1915. Partly because the Y was suspected as pro-German, the Russians were not inclined to cooperate and it was only after considerable difficulties that Dr. Harte won the support of the Empress. Dr. Harte continued to serve as the general European agent of the Y's International Committee, with special responsibility for Russia. *Vide* W. H. Taft, *et. al.*, *Service with fighting men*, 2 vols., Association Press, N. Y., 1922, II: 231 *et sqq.*

[6] George M. Day was a Y.M.C.A. secretary with long experience in Russia. Prince N. D. Golitsyn was President of the Council of Ministers from January to March, 1917.

Crowds of unarmed strikers and [their] families gathered on the Nevsky Prospect during the day, and order was preserved by the Cossacks. We anticipated a repetition of former times of disturbances when women and children were ridden down by the Cossacks. This time, however, they used no violence, but merely rode through the open lanes of the people, while the latter shouted at them "You're ours!" and the Cossacks smiled back.[7]

That Friday night, six of us attended the performance of Gogol's *Revisor*, greatest of Russian comedies, at the Alexandrinsky Theatre. The house was filled and everybody [was] in a lively humor at this satire on the political weaknesses of the mid-nineteenth century. Few of them realized that a greater drama was at that moment unfolding in real life throughout the capital. The Tsar's empty box was guarded by two sentries who maintained their inflexible poise and stare during . . . [the performance.]

B. . . . did not go to the show with us, but continued his walk up the Nevsky. He says that while we were at the play there were volleyings up and down the Nevsky several times; the soldiers [were] firing upon the people.

That day, Friday [the 9th], a notice was posted by the Chief of Police[8] warning people to stay indoors for the next three days, as order would be preserved even if it required the use of arms. The order further stated that those who were promoting the trouble were playing the enemy's game.

Saturday [March 10th] things became noticably more unsettled. Streetcar traffic entirely ceased. We learned that the motormen had taken off the grips so that the cars could not be started. We were told that the cordial feeling existing the previous day between the soldiers and the strikers had changing owing to the fact that one of the officers had been killed while protesting the taking of the grips. . . .

. . . One of the office girls was called up at noon by her mother and notified that the police had instructed that she should come home at once as it was getting unsafe to go through the streets in that part of the city (near the American Embassy). [She left and] the other girls were not long in following suit, all except Miss Golubeva who stayed to get out the mail and telegrams. Nevsky Prospect was closed to traffic except two blocks at the end of our street. When we had to cross the Nevsky on our way to lunch at the Malo Yaroslavets, Saturday noon, the bridges were heavily guarded by soldiers. We could see a dense crowd of the strikers a couple of blocks further up the Prospect, in front of Kazan Cathedral, waving a big red flag at their head.

---

[7] This is confirmed by many sources both Bolshevik and Tsarist.

[8] Presumably, the City Prefect, Balk. Actually he was subordinate to General Habalov, Commander of the Petrograd Military Area. Habalov's own testimony concerning the events of these days is to be found in *Padenie tsarskogo rezhima*, 7 vols., Moscow, 1924–27. I: 182–219.

Saturday evening three of us walked down to the Mayak, but the attendance at the gym class was small.[9] Mr. Gaylord was there and I asked him how this compared with the Revolution of 1905 through which he had passed. He said that there had been more excitement on the Nevsky this time, but less in the rest of the city.

But on Saturday the real movement had not yet gotten underway. The police still had control of the situation, at least in the center of the city. There were reports, however, that there were three hundred thousand armed strikers on the outskirts, in the factory districts, and that when they should break through into the center of the city, nothing could stop them. We also heard that the Government had brought in quantities of ammunition, machine guns, armored automobiles and tanks, as well as large numbers of Cossacks.[10]

Sunday was a beautiful sunshiny day. I attended church in the morning and the English pastor was very much perturbed over the conditions in the city. Then I visited the art gallery and the attendance was not a quarter of what it had been the preceding Sunday. Many people were obeying the warnings to stay off the streets. Then George Day and I set out from our apartments for dinner at the Malo Yaroslavets about three o'clock. We started in the direction of the Admiralty Building, but were stopped, along with many others, at the end of our block by mounted police who ordered us back. We went to the Morskaya and succeeded in crossing the Nevsky on that street. I shall never forget the sight looking up the Nevsky that beautiful afternoon. For the whole length of the Prospect not a person was going along the street, either in the roadway or on the sidewalks, but persons were crossing at each cross street.

After dinner we tried to return by the way we came, but the approach to the Nevsky was blocked by a dense crowd of people and by mounted police, who waved us back. So we had to go back through the Arch of the Winter Square and try to reach our apartment by the route that was closed when we started out. As we crossed . . . the Nevsky at the Admiralty corner there rounded the Square more than five hundred Cossacks, armed with lances, who started up the Nevsky. You could not imagine a more brilliant and martial sight than the Cossack cavalrymen glittering in the sunlight.

. . . There had been volleys up the Nevsky as well as on the other two Prospects frequently that day . . . . towards the Siberian Railroad Sta-

---

[9] The Mayak (Lighthouse) was founded in Petrograd in 1900 by Franklin A. Gaylord. Although engaged in work very similar to that of the Y, it did not officially affiliate with the Y until 1917. Taft, *op. cit.* II: 421.

[10] On this evening, Nicholas wired Habalov: "I command that the disorders in the capital shall be stopped tomorrow, as they are inadmissible in this serious time of war with Germany and Austria." *Padenie*, I: 190; *cf. Istoriya*, 56; and Pares, *op. cit.*, 442. Pares comments, "By this message he signed his own dethronement."

tion . . . [B] had seen the soldiers form lines across the street and fire upon the unarmed crowd. He saw two dead and a number injured. . . . He said that the crowd kept crying "Bread! Bread!" as they came with outstretched arms towards the soldiers.[11]

B. . . . and his wife had been on the Nevsky later in the afternoon and had seen one of the workingmen step from the crowd and go up to a policeman and say something that seemed to be insulting. At any rate, the policeman hauled back and struck the man down with the flat of his sword. The workingman jumped up again and began spitting in the face of the policeman. . . .

Monday, March 12th, was the great day that suddenly sounded the knell of the old regime, though we were slow to realize what was taking place.[12] It was quieter on the Nevsky than the day before. I walked up the Prospect to the Sadovaya at noon, and saw nothing exciting though the banks and most of the business places were closed. The center of action Monday was on the other side of the city. . . .

Mr. Harte, who always treated our predictions of a revolution with a smile saying that nothing of the sort would happen, was still planning to go to Sweden the next morning. His secretary, Penn Davis, had to go through the trouble zone this Monday morning to complete passport arrangements and secure documents for Mr. Harte and himself. When he arrived at the Liteiny Prospect he found barricades, and was stopped by the strikers who had some student soldiers with them. After showing his American passport and explaining his business he was allowed to go on, and got back alright.

During the day the sound of firing became louder in our part of the city. Neither Baker nor I understood what was taking place when we started over to the Narodni Dom after tea that evening to hear Shaliapin in *The Rous-salkas*. There was an atmosphere everywhere of excitement, uncertainty, and danger. Volleys and shots started at every crossing and corner. Around the Winter Palace Square people clung to sides of buildings, and if they came to street intersections where they had to cross they darted across. The gloomy sombre red buildings seemed to be sitting in judgment on the country's doom.

---

[11] During the day, the Pavlovsky regiment mutinied and there was much disorder with many casualties. The primary question was still one of food. Pares, *op. cit.*, 442; *cf.* also, Chamberlin, *op. cit.*, I: 77. For a "White" view, *vide* A. I. Denikin. *The Russian Turmoil*, E. P. Dutton & Co., N. Y., n. d., 40–46: and *The Memoirs of Baron N. Wrangel*, J. B. Lippincott Co., Philadelphia, 1927, 254–275. So many memoirs covering these events have appeared that it would extend this beyond all reason to list even part of them. Very useful bibliographies may be found in works of Pares and Chamberlin, already cited, and elsewhere. F. A. Golder, *Documents of Russian History*, The Century Co., N. Y., 1927, contains translations of various important primary materials.

[12] On this day the Duma heard the Tsar's order for its dissolution; the Volynsky regiment mutinied and was followed by many others; the Cabinet, after many sessions, dispersed; and, in the words of Chamberlin (*op. cit.*, I: 80) "So the city passed completely into the hands of the revolutionaries."

When we reached the middle of the New Nicholaievsky Bridge over the Neva we stopped on the high middle and looked back over the city. We saw flames rising over the Liteiny region, which we afterwards learned were burning law courts. Machine guns were keeping up an incessant rat-atat-tat in a dozen different quarters of the city, and particularly loud in the direction of the Narodni Dom. At the further end of the bridge was a squad of soldiers forming a line across. I went up to the officer and asked if there was any objection to our proceeding on to the Narodni Dom. He asked for passports and when I showed them he said "Alright." As we neared the bridge over the Little Neva a little further on, another squad of soldiers stood facing us. When we were about fifty paces off the crowd of women and working people in front of us broke and ran, and looking ahead we saw the guns raised in our direction. We immediately reversed our direction, and while we didn't run, we never walked faster until we put a building between us and the raised guns. We decided to hear Shaliapin some other evening. Later we learned that no performance was held at the Narodni Dom that night.

We saw no policemen during this walk. It was the first time that they had not been on the streets in the center of the city. We haven't seen any since. They disappeared from the streets late that afternoon.

The real surprise awaited Baker and me when we got back to Mr. Harte's room at the Grand Hotel. He had given up his trip to Sweden the next morning. But not until he and Day had taken a trip to the station that had been full of thrillers. They had loaded the trunks and baggage on one of the high Russian sleds known as lamovois, to take to the station for checking purposes the night before the train leaves according to the Russian custom. As their lamovois passed the big square in front of the Winter Palace they were fired upon. As they continued down the narrow Millionaya Ulitza they were fired upon again. They ducked their heads and Mr. Harte prayed while George used his Russian on the driver to speed him up. The driver didn't need any coaxing. They arrived at the Liteiny Bridge only to be surrounded and held up by a crowd of about a hundred and fifty strikers, students and soldiers. The leader was a student. The strikers thought that Harte and Day were trying to take ammunition over the river to the enemy, and demanded that the trunks be opened for search. There were these two Americans standing up on the high sled, with the crowd of revolutionists thronging around them from every side. What Mr. Harte feared most was that some of the Tsar's cavalry or police would suddenly appear on the scene and proceed to fire uopn them, in which case Mr. Harte and George, standing high above the crowd, would be the best targets.

Another thing was troubling Mr. Harte. He had forgotten to bring one of the trunk keys which he had left with Penn Davis at the Hotel. What would the strikers think when he told them that he did not have the key? But he had one of the keys and opened the trunk it fitted. After carefully searching it, the mob was satisfied and did not ask to look in the other trunk. They provided an escort of soldiers to conduct him to the station. As soon as they got their trunks off the lamovois at the station, the driver disappeared with his horses and sled. Then Mr. Harte could find no one to take charge of their baggage. The customary crowd of porters was nowhere in sight. No officials were to be seen. The platform was almost deserted. Finally a lone official appeared who looked at the Americans in wonderment, and told them that there would be no train in the morning; that the officials had been unarmed by the strikers; that no one was in authority; and that there was no one to look after their trunks.

It was in vain that Mr. Harte and Day searched for another vehicle of any kind to take them and their baggage back to the Hotel. They were almost giving up hope of finding a place to store their baggage when a man appeared who showed them a closet where they could lock their things up. It was characteristic of Mr. Harte that the excitement did not keep him from seeing to it carefully that his wardrobe trunk was set up in the right position, doubtful though it was that he would ever see it again. Then he and Day walked the four miles back to the Hotel, arriving there shortly before we returned. Mr. Harte was ready to acknowledge that the situation was serious. Half of the city that he had been through was in the hands of the strikers.

The next big surprise awaited us at ten o'clock when Day and I returned to our apartments. A Russian sailor was there, who was a friend of Madame Stepan. He gave us the astounding news that the old government was overthrown, that a new government had been established with a committee of twelve at its head responsible to the Duma, and that the entire city was in the hands of the revolutionists, excepting the Police Districts which were all under the fire of the revolutionists. He lived in the Morskaya Police District. Most of the soldiers had already gone over to the strikers and the people and the others were rapidly following suit. Not until then did we realize that we were in the midst of a great revolution that so many of our friends had talked about and dreaded.

One of the pieces of information which our marine friend gave us, which was later verified, was that the same Monday morning the Tsar had appointed Minister Protopopov dictator, ordering the dissolution of the Duma. But the Duma ignored the orders of the Tsar and immediately went into executive session thus defying the Tsar and his government. That was the point where the real revolution began.[13]

---

[13] The order proroguing the Duma was signed by Nicholas on the 10th and countersigned by Golitsyn on the 12th. The leaders of the political parties in the Duma resolved that the members should not disperse. *Cf.* Golder, *Documents,* 277–278. According to Chamberlin (*op. cit.,* 80–81) and *Istoriya,* 63, the Duma accepted the order of dissolution but removed as "private citizens" to another room in the Tauride Palace and held an extralegal conference. At any event, the Duma

Our marine friend said that he could not get home on account of the siege against the Police District near his home. He said that most of the firing then going on in the city was at the Police Districts, and also by boys who had secured fire-arms and were shooting them off in the air for sport. Crowds of soldiers and strikers were holding jubilee meetings over the city, as comrades in a common cause, adopting the red flag of the revolution. Officers who stood by their oath of loyalty to the Tsar were being arrested.

One of the first efforts of the revolutionists was to clean out the Police Department, and the lives of the police were unsafe if seen on the streets. The wrath of the movement seemed directed chiefly towards this institition, the records of which were dumped out of the windows on to the streets and sidewalks below and burned. Russians with whom we talked called the police system a treacherous German institution that had been foisted upon the people back in the time of Peter the Great, and that it had been used as an instrument to keep the masses in ignorance and bondage ever since.

The next piece of news came when B.... arrived home at midnight. He and G.... met an officer in the same block that our apartments are located. Across the street is the building of the War Ministry. This officer asked B.... and G.... if they were English. They replied that they were Americans. The officer replied "Good, I also foreigner. I Finnlandsky. To-morrow that building is ours," pointing to the war ministry. He spoke in Russian and B.... and G.... knew just enough of the language to guess that he said that they were going to blow up the building. We accordingly wondered as we turned in that night whether we would be awakened by an explosion. The Finn was as happy as a boy. Immediately after talking with B.... and G.... he went over to the building and passed into the court between lines of soldiers who evidently held the building for the revolutionists.

A half hour after midnight Eric Christensen, our big Dane secretary, came home. Ordinarily he is very calm, but this time he was dancing and shouting with excitement. He had just shaken hands with a couple of men who had been released from the famous Peter and Paul Fortress. Both the prisoners were Finns, and had a thousand rubles each furnished by some Finnish revolutionary committee, to pay their expenses home. The Fortress had been taken by the soldiers that evening, and all the prisoners, who were there for political and religious reasons, were released, including nineteen soldiers who had been imprisoned during the last few days.

It was hard to shake off enough of the excitement that night to get to sleep.

---

organized an Executive Committee and, a few hours later, a Provisional Committee. The latter undertook the tasks of government. Golder, *Documents,* 280–281. Protopopov, on the demand of the ministers expressed by Golitsyn, resigned and went into hiding on the evening of the 12th. *Cf.* Pares, *op. cit.,* 451–452.

Tuesday March 13th dawned a beautiful clear day. We were awakened by volleys and artillery fire at an early hour, which increased in intensity. People hugged the courtways in the street below us, and if they crossed the streets they did so with a dash. If they began to take to the sidewalks a sudden volley would send them scattering for shelter. Our soldat told us that the Dvornik (house-porter) gave orders to stay in that day.

At nine o'clock, however, I started out as usual for the office planning to stop at Mr. Harte's room in the Grand Hotel on the way. As I reached the end of the block, at the corner of Gogol Street and Vosnesensky Prospect, an imposing sight was before me. Directly ahead, a block away, the square opposite the Astoria Hotel (headquarters for the officers) was full of soldiers. Down the Morskaya came column after column of soldiers, in martial order, greeted with the rousing shouts of the people assembled in the square in front of St. Isaac's Cathedral. The sun shining on the masses of soldiers made a brilliant spectacle. The soldiers stopped short when they came even with the statue of Nicholas, where they faced the Astoria Hotel.

Suddenly there was a tremendous volley and the sidewalks and squares were emptied of people in the twinkling of an eye. I was half way across Gogol Street when the volleys came, and I had that naked feeling the soldiers are said to have when they go over the top. I wasted no time covering the remaining half of the street and was soon in Mr. Harte's room. While we stood at his window looking out on the street, soldiers began to come along the middle of the street leading officers to the Duma to swear allegiance to the new government. These were the officers who surrendered and said they were willing to swear allegiance to the new order. Some of them looked downcast and others happy.

During a lull in the fighting I crossed the street to our office building, and with some of the other secretaries looked down from our sixth floor directly on top of the Astoria Hotel roof at the end of the block on the opposite side of the street, and on the fighting in the street and square in front of the hotel. We could see the marines lying on Gogol Street in front of St. Isaac's shooting at the hotel. We saw several men fall, and some of them afterwards crawled off dragging a wounded arm or leg. The Red Cross automobiles came and went rapidly. The famous storming of the officer's headquarters was in full swing. More and more detachments of soldiers came along leading officers to the Duma. Some of the officers offered resistance and were killed on the spot. Others shouted "We're for you" and were allowed to keep their swords and arms and often given commands. At the height of the fighting we noticed a commotion on top of the Astoria Hotel roof. A machine gun had been placed there and the officers had begun firing down on the sidewalk below. It did not take long for the soldiers to spot the mischief and put an end to it with short shrift for the unfortunate officers.

While we were watching this affair from our windows B.... and G.... had an exciting time down on the street. They were on the Morskaya under the Astoria Hotel when the machine gun began its work from the roof. In the rush for shelter, B.... fell and had many a kick and cuff before he regained his feet. He said he got all the excitement he wanted that time.

We saw the soldiers smashing bottles of liquor on the sidewalks, and we saw the contents running down the street. We saw only a few soldiers carrying off or drinking the liquor.

The battle lasted about a half hour, and by that time the soldiers had everything in their own hands, and the officers had flung out the white flag. This was the day of the private soldier. They told their officers to go home and stay out of sight until things were quiet again. The officers, having taken their individual oath of allegiance to the Tsar, considered themselves more bound to it than the soldiers who took allegiance in groups. For the officers it was a great moral struggle, many [?] of them being in sympathy with the revolution. Caught as they were in a situation where they had to make instant decision, there was a variety of reactions on their part, many paying with their lives for their hesitation.

The way the soldiers took things in their own hands was a revelation. They showed perfect confidence, tackled most difficult tasks with a practical efficiency and did all with a buoyant, smiling assurance and mastery that gave everyone confidence that they knew what they were doing. The "children of the Tsar" this day stepped forth as their own men and masters.

Probably the predominant impression that an American received from the events of the day was the self-restraint and order of the soldiers, as well as of the workingmen. There were cases of killing and bloodshed, and during the day many were taken to the hospitals, but considering the size of the revolution, the number of men and soldiers engaged in the struggle, the amount of bloodshed was small. Outside of the destruction of property in the police districts, the officers' quarters, and the homes of the suspected aristocracy, there was little looting. And this order was maintained despite the fact that there was an indiscriminate distributing of firearms to workingmen and boys. This was one time when prohibition was a blessing to Russia. If vodka could have been found in plenty, the revolution could easily have had a terrible ending.

One of the problems of this day was the snipers. The soldiers quickly handled such cases by bringing up an armored car or tank against the building from which the shots came, and playing the machine gun upon it. Many of the police were in hiding, concealed often through the connivance of dvorniks, who formed a part of the old police system. The H....'s had an exciting experience in their apartments. Shots were fired into the court from some upper floors. A group of fifty or sixty soldiers immediately came in and made a thorough search of every room at the point of a gun. The starshy (head) dvornik was almost shot, but was saved at the last moment by one of the captors who had an argument that had an effect upon the other soldiers.

The center of action was transferred from the Liteiny District to the Gogol and Morskaya District. We had the full benefit of it. In the afternoon the magnificent palace of Baron Friederichs, the German sympathizer, who was the Tsar's personal advisor and Chamberlin, was in flames. It was in plain view up the Gogol from our office and was completely burned out.

Towards evening of this day I picked up on the streets a news-sheet entitled *"Izvestiya Petrogradskago Soveta Rabochikh deputatov"*[14] dated 28 February [OS] 1917, and calling upon the workingmen of all lands to unite. It announced that the bourgeois system had been overthrown, the capitalistic class destroyed, and urged the workingmen and soldiers to elect deputies for a central labor council or soviet. This was the first printed matter that had appeared in the capital for several days. It was also the first announcement of or by the Soviet. The newspapers had all been closed since Friday. We didn't know what was going on in the rest of the world or Empire. The wildest rumors were afloat.

One rumor had the Kaiser overthrown and a revolution successful in Germany. Another had the Tsar's army on the way from the front to put down the revolution. The discovery of five hundred machine guns on the roofs of the buildings in Petrograd, carrying an apparent threat of a St. Bartholomew's Eve massacre to put down the revolution if necessary, did not dispel our nervousness. The minister Protopopov, had ordered one thousand machine guns placed, according to report, but had only succeeded in getting five hundred up when the plan was discovered. The plan was for all the machine guns to begin playing upon the multitudes at the same instant, signal for which was to be an airplane that would come over the city from Tsarskoe Selo. Rumor had it that the Tsarina was to give the fatal order that would start the airplane, but that she lost her nerve at the last moment. Well, to pick up this red revolutionary bulletin on top of these rumors did not quiet our nerves. All restaurants and stores were closed, at night the streets were pitch dark, the street lamps not being lighted. It was a disquieting evening.

Wednesday [the 14th] conditions became more normal. At ten-thirty I started afoot for the American Embassy. Cheering on the Morskaya attracted my attention, and when I arrived on the street I found a great parade in progress, all revolutionists carrying the red flag and the bands playing the Marseillaise. I followed the parade along the Nevsky and shall never forget

---

[14] There were no regular newspapers during the first week of the Revolution. The news-sheet to which Mr. Heald refers was the first number of the Soviet *Izvestiya*. Its name was changed several times during the first year of its existence. Golder (*op. cit.*, 277) lists the changes.

the wonderful sight. From the Morskaya to the Liteiny, over a mile and a half, the great Nevsky Prospect was packed with people from the buildings on one side to the buildings on the other side.

The parade itself consisted of soldiers, officers, marines, workingmen all marching in order, and every division hoisting the big red banners. The marching columns stretched from the curb-stone to the middle of the broad Prospect. The spectators packed the rest of the street, a continuous deafening cheer greeting the marching columns along the whole route. Now and then armored cars darted along with soldiers armed to the teeth. I never expect to see a more thrilling sight in my life.

During the whole time I saw only one drunken man, and heard only two shots fired. The order was wonderful. The people were not so much wild with enthusiasm as they were joyously, freely, intensely, spiritually happy. There was an exhilaration to it that was thrilling and indescribable. One felt that it must be a dream; that it was impossible that such things were happening in Russia. Well dressed people were in evidence and apparently as happy as the bent gray-haired working men who looked about with a dazed sort of happiness, while their faces shone with a rapturous glow. There seemed to be the best of feeling between the officers and soldiers.

When I reached the Embassy I learned that the Tsar was expected to be at the Duma that afternoon to proclaim a new constitution. The people at the Embassy thought he could still save his dynasty if he would grant the constitution and appoint new ministers who would represent the people. But the Tsar never appeared. He let this last chance slip by. Sixty thousand soldiers at Peterhof this day gave their allegiance to the Duma. This same day Grand Duke Cyril went out to the Duma and tendered his allegiance and the service of the marines under his command to the new government. We also got our first outside telegraph news this day, to the effect that Moscow was also in the hands of the revolutionists. The struggle there had been brief and an easy victory for the revolutionists. The Mayor of the city was a liberal. The police took refuge in the Kremlin but had to surrender speedily.

While I was at the Embassy word came that Protopopov, the former Minister of the Interior, had surrendered. He had been in hiding with the other ministers of the old regime at the Admiralty since Monday. At eleven-fifteen Wednesday he appeared at the Tauride Palace, where the Duma meets. A student was at the entrance. Protopopov went up to the student and said, "You are a student?" "I am," was the reply. "I have always been interested in the welfare of our country," said Protopopov, "and therefore I come and give myself voluntarily. I am former Minister of the Interior Protopopov. Lead me to whatever person is necessary." The student led him to the Temporary Executive Committee. On the way the soldiers, recognizing him, gave vent to their indignation, and threatened him, and when he arrived at the committee, he was pale and tottering. Kerensky, the new Minister of Justice, pacified the crowd and prevented violence.[15]

At noon this day the Admiralty passed into the hands of the revolutionary soldiers, and the ministers who had been in hiding either fled or gave themselves up.

On my way home from the Embassy I saw armored cars racing through the streets filled with armed soldiers who were scattering bulletins. I picked one up. It was called *Prikaz No. 1*, was dated March 1, and was signed by the Soviet of the Workers' and Soldiers' Deputies, the uniting of these two groups apparently having taken place during the preceding twenty-four hours. This order called upon the soldiers not to salute their officers except when on duty. All titles were to be dropped. Soldiers could no longer be addressed by their officers with the familiar "Thou" but only by "Sir" and the polite "You." The day before (Tuesday) there had been no saluting, but during the big parade Wednesday morning saluting was general. With the appearance of Prikaz No. 1 however, saluting stopped. Trouble brewed in the atmosphere.

Thursday noon Zemmer[16] showed up at the office. All his enthusiasm for the new regime was gone. "Everybody is out for what he can get for his own profit," said Zemmer. "There is no patriotism. Everything was beautiful the first two days, then differences arose and harmony disappeared." Zemmer had been at the Duma the preceding day to swear allegiance to the new government, along with two thousand other officers. He was worried as to the outcome, as out of eight thousand officers in the city only two thousand had shown up at the Duma. It was reported that a large number had gone out to Tsarskoe Selo to the Tsar. Others were in hiding. Moreover there was a serious struggle going on between the radical revolutionists who wanted a social revolution, and the conservative liberals, who wanted a constitutional monarchy. Zemmer was afraid that they might split and give the old regime its opportunity to regain control. It was reported that a large army loyal to the Tsar was on the way from the front to put down the revolution. Regarding Prikaz No. 1, Zemmer said that it had been dispatched with haste by the truck-load to the front, and that it would ruin the discipline of the whole army.

Banks opened up until one o'clock Thursday. Many stores of provisions were brought to light. Butter, which had been selling at three rubles and twenty kopeks (about $1.00) per pound, dropped to eighty kopeks by revolutionary order. Soldiers were on hand to see that no more than that was charged. Sugar, which had been issued only on tickets, could now be secured without tickets. Great stores of meat were brought forth from cold storage

---

[15] *Cf.* the stirring account of this in Shulgin's memoirs, quoted in Pares, *op. cit.*, 454–455.

[16] A Russian officer, transferred from the Russian Red Cross to assist the Y.M.C.A. (ETH.)

and placed on the market. Out at Nevsky Monastery a couple of thousand tons of sugar were seized by the revolutionists and placed at the disposal of the government. There was a rush for provisions from every hand all day.

In the evening we heard that the Tsar's army had arrived from the front and was engaging the revolutionists in a great battle at the edge of the city near the Baltsky Station. We walked over that way, but heard and saw nothing out of the ordinary and concluded that the rumor was false.

Friday morning [the 16th] we were thrilled to see in the windows of the *Novoye Vremya* newspaper a bulletin reading that Nicolai Romanov (all titles removed) had abdicated at three o'clock that morning[17] for himself and his heir, Alexei, in favor of Michael Alexandrovitch, the next in line. Alongside it another bulletin read that Michael Alexandrovitch declined to accept the throne, stating that the people wanted a Republic, and that he wanted to get back to the front where he belonged. The abdication of the Tsar had been written on his special train near Pskov, after it had been shunted back and forth in vain efforts to elude the revolutionists.

The story of the worries and remarks of the Tsar during those last hours, as reported in the newspapers, reads like a chapter from the Middle Ages. When it was all over and he had signed the abdication he sighed, "How I long to be with my roses in the Crimea." Baron Friederichs, whose palace was burned, was with him to the last.

With the appearance of the morning bulletins the new Cabinet was announced. The new Minister of Justice is Kerensky, a Socialist, and his first order was that any important papers or documents which were found in the Police Headquarters and were worthy of saving were to be transferred to the Academy of Science. He seems to know how to attract the attention and seize the imagination of the people. There was also appointed a new Minister, one for Finnish Affairs, to take the place of the old Governor General of Finland, who has been arrested. Also the man who was responsible for the new restrictive and repressive measures in Finland in 1905 is in custody.

In the same bulletins the Cabinet announces that it will be guided by the following principles: (1) Full and immediate amnesty in all political and religious affairs; (2) Liberty of word, press, assembly, unions and strikes with extension of political liberty to those in military service within the confines permissible by military technical conditions; (3) Abolition of all class, religious and national limitations; (4) Immediate preparations to convoke on the basis of universal, equal, direct, and secret suffrage, a Constitutional Assembly, which will establish the form of administration and constitution; (5) Substitution of national militia in the place of police, with elected leaders

---

[17] Actually the document was dated Pskov, 3 P.M., March 15th. The abdication of the Grand Duke Michael was dated the 16th.

and subject to local administration; (6) Elections to local administration on the basis of universal suffrage. On the following day a proclamation was issued removing all restrictions from the Jews.

On Friday [the 16th] the old flag of Russia was replaced by the red flag in all quarters of the city. Soldiers were busy all day pulling down the coats of arms of the old regime, including those on the Winter Palace. The Singer Sewing Machine Building protected the American Eagle on its top by having it wrapped in the American flag, but all other eagles in the city came down.

Little Alexander, our office boy, when asked what he thought of the revolution, said "Tsar ne nado." (No need of a Tsar.)

One of Mr. Harte's friends, Count Stackelburg, was killed Monday. Revolutionists came to his palace on the Millionaya, and when he refused to open the doors, he was shot down. Sturmer is reported dead in prison. Count Pallen has not been heard of since Monday. He went down to one of his estates in the country near Moscow just before the revolution, and his life is feared for. The girls in our office are back at work, and all seem happy at the new day.

We now feel that we can draw a full breadth; that what we see is no longer a dream but a reality; that a new era has opened with consequences beyond imagination. We are thrilled with the new energy, purpose, and enthusiasm that has taken hold everywhere. It has been good to be alive these marvelous days. We can take our hats off to the Russian people; they know how to put great things across. Their good-nature is impressive; even in the course of the fighting they seemed to retain their good-nature. They don't seem to have the natures that would lead to the excesses of the French Revolution. They handle the most exciting emergencies in a cool matter-of-fact way. And I am struck with their continued loyalty to the Allies. I talked with a number of the soldiers during the week. "Give us a week to clean this up," they said, "and then we'll go back and clean up the Germans so quick no one can stop us."

Additional Readings

Pares, *History*. Pp. 403–475

Tompkins, *Russia*. Pp. 490–546

Vernadsky, *History*. Pp. 177–190, 208–246

Martin, *Picture History*. Pp. 161–202

Karpovich, *Imperial Russia*. Pp. 55–96

Lobanov-Rostovsky, *Russia and Asia*. Chaps. 9–11

Scott & Baltzly, *Readings*. Pp. 337–351, 399–406, 436–445, 473–474, 485–486, 503–507

Golder, F. A., *Documents of Russian History, 1914–1917*. New York: The Century Co., 1927. Pp. 3–39, 78–121, 154–177, 188–302

Harper, P. V. (ed), *The Russia I Believe In: Memoirs of Samuel N. Harper, 1902–1941*. Chicago: U. of Chicago Press, 1945. Pp. 1–108

Pares, B., *The Fall of the Russian Monarchy*. New York: A. A. Knopf, 1939. Pp. 76–186, et passim.

Chamberlin, W. H., *The Russian Revolution*. Two volumes. New York: Macmillan, 1935. Vol. 1, pp. 1–117

Rodzianko, M., *Reign of Rasputin: An Empire's Collapse*. London & New York: 1927. Pp. 40–63, 106–127

Gurko, V. I., *Features and Figures of the Past. Government and Opinion in the Reign of Nicholas II*. Stanford: Stanford University Press, 1939. Chaps. 20–24

Gourko, B., *War and Revolution in Russia, 1914–1917*. New York: Macmillan, 1919. Pp. 59–83

Bresko-Breshkovskaia, K. E., *Hidden Springs of the Russian Revolution*. Stanford University Press, 1931. Pp. 263–292

Zabriskie, E. H., *American-Russian Rivalry in the Far East. A Study in Diplomacy and Power Politics, 1895–1914*. Philadelphia: U. of Pennsylvania Press, 1946. Chap. 1

Florinsky, M. T., *The End of the Russian Empire*. New Haven: Yale University Press, 1931

Tolstoy, A., *Road to Calvary*. New York: A. A. Knopf, 1946. Part 1

Gankin & Fisher, *Bolsheviks*. Pp. 9–132

Fülöp-Miller, R., *Rasputin, The Holy Devil*. New York: Viking Press, 1928.

Curtiss, *Church and State*. Chaps. 2 and 9

The Growth of Russian Industry

The following excerpt from the most recent study of Russian economic history to be made by a scholar having full access to Russian materials will supplement the account given on pp. 451–454. Professor Lyashchenko was born and educated under the tsarist regime. He published three major studies before the 1917 Revolution and, despite the fact that he was a "legal Marxist," he held high academic rank at the University of Tomsk. After the Revolution he served as a professor at the First Moscow State University and at the Institute of National Economy.

The first edition of his History of the National Economy of Russia *was published in 1939 by the Soviet Academy of Sciences and was officially designated for use in "schools of economics." This edition is available in English translation. The 1947/48 edition from which the following excerpts were translated was approved by the Soviet Ministry of Education for use in "institutions of higher learning." There are major differences between the two editions.*

The source is: Lyashchenko, P. I., Istoriia narodnogo khoziaistva SSSR. *Two vols. Moscow: State Publishing House, 1947/48. Vol. II (1948), pp. 148–160, 162, 170, 171, 214, 215, 230–242 passim, 283–285, 287–289. Abridged.*

Industrial Progress in the 1890s

Year	No. of enterprises	No. of workers	Total value of production
1887	30,888	1,318,000	1,334.5 million Rs.
1890	32,254	1,424,700	1,502.7 million Rs.
1897	39,029	2,098,300	2,839.1 million Rs.
1900	38,141	2,373,400	3,005.9 million Rs.

During the decade 1887–97, the number of enterprises increased 26.3%; the number of workers, 59.2%; and the total production, 112.8%. But in the decade 1890–1900, the number of enterprises increased 18.3%; the number of workers, 66.6%; and the total production, 100%. There took place not only an absolute increase in the number of enterprises, but also a concentration and rapid increase in productivity. . . . the rate of increase in the total industrial production during the 1890s, according to the official data was: 1878–1887, 26.1 million rubles a year; 1888–1892, 41.6 million rubles a year; 1892–1897, 161.2 million rubles a year.

. . . although the textile industry was foremost in absolute volume of production, the heavy industries (mining and metallurgy) were rapidly catching up with the light industries during these years. From 1887–1897, the total increase in production for industries was: mining, 11.2%; chemical, 10.7%; lumber, 9.3%; metallurgical, 8.4%; ceramics, 8%; textiles, 7.8%; and food, 1.7%.

Production in Major Industries
(Stated in tons)

Year	Total coal mined	Total oil produced	Total iron mined	Pig iron smelted	Steel & iron produced
1860	329,400			352,800	223,200
1870	763,200	32,400	825,750	372,600	261,000
1880	3,610,800	612,200	1,083,600	469,800	635,400
1890	5,049,600	4,348,000	1,913,400	993,600	871,200
1895	9,999,000	6,948,000	3,024,000	1,561,900	1,121,400
1900	17,913,000	11,376,000	6,609,600	3,182,400	2,419,200

Iron and steel production for the whole country increased two times over during the five years, 1895–1900; iron and steel production in the south increased three to four times during the period. . . . The share of the Urals in the total production dropped from 67% in the 1870s to 28% in 1900, but that of the south increased from 0.1% to 51%.

The percentage increases in various phases of the cotton textile industry between 1890 and 1900 were as follows:

Number of spinning mills 65%
Number of weaving mills 42%
Number of spindles 76%
Number of looms 68%
Raw cotton used 94%
Unbleached cloth made 74%
Value of unbleached cloth 65%
Value of cotton 82%
Value of cotton yarn 107%

. . .

During the decade of the 1890s, therefore, Russian industry was rapidly being converted to large-scale capitalist techniques and to large-scale ways of production. . . . In 1879, factories employing less than 500 workers accounted for 79.7% of all factories and 44.2% of all workers. The respective figures for 1890 were almost the same, but by 1902, they stood at 73.8% of all factories, and only 30.7% of all workers. Factories employing more than 1,000 workers amounted to 7% of the total in 1879; 7.6%, in 1890; and 11% in 1902. The percentages of workers employed in these large factories were, respectively: 32.8, 37.7 and 49.8. By the beginning of the 20th century, large-scale enterprises accounted for half of all the workers; twenty years earlier, for only a third. . . .

Typical Figures Showing Increases in Volume and in Concentration of Production in the Metallurgical Industry

	1880	1900	1909
Pig iron smelted per plant (tons)	4,559	12,888	36,900
Number of workers per plant	899	1,325	1,545
Horsepower per plant	255	1,286	1,805
Horsepower per worker	0.28	0.97	1.17
Pig iron smelted per blast furnace (tons)	9,296	22,644	40,968
Pig iron smelted per worker (lbs.)	10,152	18,676	
Open-hearth steel produced per furnace (tons)	7,164	15,804	
Bessemer steel produced per converter (tons)	25,992	41,148	

. . .

RAILROAD CONSTRUCTION. After the railway fever of 1870–75 — a five year period during which railway trackage was increased by 7,500 versts, construction proceeded at a slower pace from 1876 to 1890. But from 1891 to 1895, new railway construction added 6,257 versts of new trackage, while the next five year period (1896–1900) added 15,139 versts, and the total trackage was increased to 56,130 versts in 1901. During the single decade of the 1890s, in other words, 37% of the total trackage (or half as much as had been built during the preceding half century,) was laid down. . . . It should be noted that . . . the European part of Russia had 9.7 kilometers of railway trackage per thousand square kilometers of territory; England had 106 kilometers and Germany had 80 kilometers for the same unit. . . . At the beginning of the 20th century, the total capital invested in railroads throughout the whole country amounted to 4.7 billion rubles, 3.5 billion rubles of which belonged to the government.

. . .

Basic Capital in Major Industries
(in millions of rubles)

Industry	1890	1900	Percentage increase
Mining	85.7	392.2	358%
Metallurgical	27.8	257.3	826%
Chemical	15.6	93.8	501%
Ceramics	6.7	59.0	781%
Textile	197.5	373.7	89%
Food	87.6	153.1	75%
All industries	580.1	1,742.3	200%

Origin of Each 100 Workers

Year	Peasants	Others
1884/5	91.5	8.5
1899	94.2	5.8

Percentage of Workers Whose
Fathers Had Been Factory Workers

Year	Fathers Had	Fathers Had Not
1884/5	55.0	45.0
1899	55.6	44.4

. . .

Average Wages in Late 1890s and Early 1900s
(Stated in rubles per year for all workers in named industry)

Cotton manufacturing	171
Woolen manufacturing	170
Woodworking (mechanized)	215
Food products	182
Manufacture of mineral products	204
Chemicals	260
Metal works, machine work, etc.	341

. . .

Thus, in the course of the years 1890 to 1899, industrial capitalism overcoming low productivity, stereotyped techniques, and backward social conditions rapidly moved Russian industry far ahead. Russian industry, to be sure, still lagged far behind the advanced countries of the period in the volume of production in certain industries. But in those ten years, nonetheless, it had advanced very significantly, achieving a rate of concentration much higher than in the outstanding capitalist countries. Russian industry outstripped that of nearly all other countries in the speed of its development. For example, the smelting of pig iron during this decade increased in England, by 18%; in Germany, by 72%; in the U.S.A., by 50%; and in Russia, by 190%. . . . The production of iron during this time increased in England, by 8%; in Germany, by 78%; in the U.S.A., by 63%; and in Russia, by 116%. The English coal industry expanded by 22%; the German, by 52%; the American, by 61%; and the Russian, by 131%. Finally, in cotton manufacturing, the number of spindles in England increased 3.8%; in the U.S.A., 25.6%; in continental Europe, 33%; and in Russia, 76%.

. . .

The general European financial crisis which began in 1899 soon affected developments in Russia. There was a rapid fall in stocks, in bank capital, and in prices. Not all industries were hit equally hard, but there were many bankruptcies and rather widespread unemployment. The nadir of the crisis was 1902, but the Russo-Japanese War and the 1905 Revolution produced a slowdown if not a temporary recession which lasted until 1908/09. The following data, meant to illustrate the characteristics of the period from 1900 to 1909, have been adapted from the text and tables given by Professor Lyashchenko. The source is: Lyashchenko, op. cit., Vol. 2, pp. 230–242, seriatim; 283, 284.

Stock Prices in Rubles

Company	1899	1900	1901
Petersburg Discount & Loan Bank	809	665	472
Briansk Factory	511.5	475	240
Donets-Urev	680	530	210
Baku Oil	950	830	695

. . .

Donbas Coal Mines

	1900	1901	1902	1903
Mines operating ..	290	246	240	209
Production in tons	12,445,200	12,499,200	11,557,800	13,104,000

. . .

For example, at Moscow the price for iron girders fell from 2 rubles 30 kopecks in the middle of 1899 to 1 ruble 45 kopecks at the end of 1900, to 1 ruble 25 kopecks at the end of 1901, and to 1 ruble ten kopecks at the end of 1902. The price of structural iron fell from 1 ruble 68 kopecks in 1900 to 1 ruble 40 kopecks in 1901. The price of pig iron dropped from 70–80 kopecks at the middle of 1900 to 45–48 kopecks at the end of the year. The price of coal fell from 9–10 kopecks at the beginning of 1900 to 6–7 kopecks by the end of 1902. The price of crude oil went down from 17 or 18 kopecks in 1900 to 4 or 6 kopecks in 1902. The fall of prices began in the first half of 1900 and continued through most of 1902 when the crisis reached its lowest point.

. . .

Pig iron smelted (in tons)

1899	2,946,600
1900	3,195,000
1901	3,110,400
1902	2,817,000
1903	2,683,800
1904	3.250.800

1905 2,984,400
1906 2,952,000
1907 3,097,800
1908 3,079,800

. . .

Industrial Development, 1887–1908

Year	No. of Factories	Total production (in millions of rubles)	No. of workers
1887	30,888	1,334.5	1,318,000
1897	39,029	2,839.1	2,098,200
1908	39,866	4,908.7	2,679,700

Rate of Growth in Percentages

	1887–1897	1897–1908
No. of enterprises increased by	26.3%	2.1%
Total value of production increased by	112.7%	72.9%
No. of workers increased by	59.2%	27.7%

. . .

The General Situation

[*ibid, Vol. 2, pp. 287–289*]

Despite the relative advances and the high degree of concentration in Russian industry, the general economic development undeniably lagged. A whole range of important and key branches were completely or almost completely lacking in Russia. Thus, the making of machine-tools was very backward. The greater part of the manufacturing equipment for factories and mills, especially of the more complicated types such as electrical equipment, turbines, machine-tools, etc. had to be obtained from abroad. There was absolutely no automobile industry. The basic chemical industry was very weak. . . .

How far Russia lagged behind the advanced countries of the west in industrial economics may be seen from the following figures. In 1913, the total volume of industrial production in Russia was 2.5 times less than that of France; 4.6 times less than that of England; 6 times less than the Germans; and 14.3 times smaller than that of the United States. This backwardness was most marked in certain industries, including some of the major ones. For example, in 1913, the Russian coal industry produced 36,000,000 tons; the German, 190,100,000 tons; the British, 292,000,000 tons; and the American, 517,100,000 tons. Russian iron ore production was 9,500,000 tons; French, 43,000,000 tons; and the American, 63,000,000 tons. Russia produced 4,600,000 tons of pig iron; the United States, 31,500,000 tons; Germany, 16,800,000. American copper production was 557,200 tons; the Russian, 31,100. The backwardness of [Russian] industrial production is even more apparent when stated in terms of per capita production. Thus, in 1913, the production of electrical power in Russia was 14 kilowatt hours per capita against an American per capita output of 175.6 kilowatt hours; the smelting of pig iron was at the per capita rate of 30.3 kilograms in Russia compared to 326.5 in the U.S.A. . . . . Per capita consumption of cotton was 19 kilograms in England, 14 kg. in the United States, and 3.1 kg. in Russia. An even more noteworthy fact is that Russia not only failed to overtake the more advanced capitalist countries but also continued to lag farther behind them. Thus, pig iron production on a per capita basis was eight times greater in the United States than in Russia in 1900; eleven times, in 1913.

. . .

A few scattering items computed from data given in the same source will round out this sketch. The production of farm machinery in 1912 was 570% greater than it had been in 1897; 392% greater than in 1900; and 136% greater than in 1908. The number of cotton-spinning spindles was 137% greater in 1913 than in 1900. Yarn production (cotton) increased by about 160% in the same period. Pig iron production increased by 152% between 1910 and 1913; steel production by about the same percentage; coal by 145%; and the production of linen yarn by 149%.

The Kishinev Program

Prince Sergei Dmitrievich Urussov was an outstanding example of that apparent anomaly, an hereditary nobleman who was also a genuine liberal. Appointed Governor of Bessarabia by Plehve, Urussov arrived at Kishinev (the provincial capital) some few months after the notorious pogrom. While on the spot, and subsequently as well, he made a very careful investigation of the Jewish question in general and of the Kishinev pogrom in particular. His conclusions are at variance with the account of the incident given by Professor Mavor and quoted on pages 461–463 of this volume. It therefore seemed desirable to include some excerpts from Urussov's account. It may be added that Urussov served with distinction in the First Duma and won merited renown by a speech castigating the government for its policies toward the Jews. The source is: Urussov, Prince S. D. (H. Rosenthal, tr. and ed.)

Memoirs of a Russian Governor. *New York: Harper & Bros., 1908. Pp. 77–82, passim.*

First, I must say that in examining . . . the secret papers of the Kishinev case in the Central Police Bureau at St. Petersburg, I found not a thing to justify the assumption that the Ministry of the Interior thought it expedient to permit a Jewish massacre or even an anti-Jewish demonstration in Kishinev. Indeed, such a sinister policy on the part of that ministry is inconceivable; for A. A. Lopukhin . . . was at this time head of this department. . . . Whenever he was charged with being a reactionary, Plehve liked to point to . . . [Lopukhin] to show that he, Plehve, was seeking men with broad views and irreproachable names. . . . My intimacy with Lopukhin, based on our relationship and close friendship, enables me to assert that it is entirely inadmissible to suspect his department of engineering pogroms at that time.

I also entertain grave doubts of the authenticity of a letter alleged to have been addressed by the Minister of the Interior to the Governor of Bessarabia, and published in the English papers. [This is the *Times'* despatch quoted by Mavor.] . . . Plehve was incapable of such an unguarded act . . . . Raaben [Urussov's predecessor at Kishinev] was not the proper agent to carry out any such projects. He was a very decent man . . . and, moreover, was quite tolerant towards the Jews. He himself, losing his official position, suffered from the pogrom. . . . Confidential agents carrying out delicate commissions do not get such treatment. . . .

A significant role in preparing for the pogrom was played by the press, this especially by Krushevan's local paper. . . . Krushevan's authority, in the eyes of his readers, was to a certain degree supported by the open patronage of the chief bureau of the press censorship. . . .

. . . The police, therefore, thought that a hostile attitude towards the Jews was a sort of government watchword; . . . . the conviction grew among the ignorant masses that hostile acts against the Jews could be undertaken with impunity. Things went so far that a legend appeared among the people that the Czar had ordered a three days' massacre of the Jews. . . . Thus, in my opinion, the central government cannot shake off its moral responsibility. . . .

But can one fully exonerate the government . . . [of taking] a direct part in the massacres? . . . I do not care to pass my suppositions for facts. I only pointed out the way in which the anti-Semitism of Plehve, possibly voiced by him as a mere matter of conviction . . . . rolling down the hierarchic incline of the gendarmerie corps, reached Lewandal [head of the Kishinev secret police] in the guise of a *wish* on the part of the higher authorities, reached Pronin and Krushevan as a *call* for a patriotic exploit, and reached the Moldavian rioters as an *order* of the Czar.

The Development of Lenin's Program (Part I)

Official Soviet accounts often give the impression that Marxism was introduced into Russia by Lenin, which was not the case. The founder of Marxism in Russia was George Plekhanov who introduced the Russian intellectuals to Marx at a time when the future Lenin was only thirteen years old. Not until several years later (the dates are somewhat uncertain) did young Vladimir Ilyich Ulyanov (Lenin) become acquainted with the Marx-Engels doctrines, and he first learned of them through the writings of Plekhanov. For the next decade or so, Ulyanov regarded himself as the faithful disciple of Plekhanov.

The young convert threw himself into the work with enthusiastic vigor. His first Marxist writing intended for distribution appeared in 1893. It was the first of a long and voluminous series. Two years later, Ulyanov was arrested by the police, convicted of revolutionary activity and sent first to prison and later into exile. The authorities allowed him to have books and journals, to conduct an extensive correspondence, and to continue his writing. One of his articles served as the basis for discussion at the abortive 1898 Congress at Minsk.

Ulyanov himself was still in exile when nine delegates from various revolutionary groups met in three-day session at Minsk for the purpose of organizing a united party. They issued a manifesto calling for such an organization and elected a Central Committee of three to direct their work. Before anything could come of it, two of the Committeemen and eight of the delegates were arrested. This failure made new tactics necessary, and Ulyanov took a leading part in the work, at first through correspondence and articles; later, in person.

Leaving Russia in 1900, Ulyanov sought out Plekhanov at Geneva. Already serious differences had begun to develop between the "old revolutionaries" (Plekhanov, Axelrod, and Zasulich) and the new generation which Ulyanov headed. After bitter quarrels among themselves it was finally agreed that they should seek to organize their movement by means of a revolutionary newspaper. This was Ulyanov's idea. He named the paper Iskra (The Spark) *and chose as its masthead slogan Pushkin's line, "Out of the spark shall spring the flame." It was quite appropriate, therefore, that the leading editorial in the first issue should also be his work. Writing under the title, "The Urgent Tasks of our Movement," Ulyanov set forth the program of his party-to-be. A translation of this editorial, slightly abridged, follows. The source is:* Iskra. Central Organ of the Russian Social Democratic Workers Party. *Vol. I, No. 1. December, 1900. P. 1.*

The First Iskra Program

The Russian Social-Democrats have already declared more than once that the immediate political task of a Russian workers' party should be to overthrow the autocracy and secure political liberty. This was declared more than fifteen years ago by the representatives of Russian Social-Democracy, the members of the group known as "The Emancipation of Labor." It was again stated two and one half years ago by the representatives of the Russian Social-Democratic organizations who formed the Russian Social Democratic Workers Party in the spring of 1898. But the question of what the political tasks of the Russian Social-Democrats should be is again coming to the front despite these repeated declarations. Many members of our movement are expressing doubts as to whether the answer given above is the right one. The economic struggle, it is claimed, is predominantly important; the political tasks of the proletariat are being narrowed, restricted, and pushed into the background. It is even declared that talk about forming an independent workers' party in Russia is merely an imitation of others, and that the workers ought to take part only in the economic struggle, leaving political matters to the alliance of intellectuals and liberals. This latest profession . . . (the notorious *Credo*) amounts . . . to a complete denial of the Social-Democratic program. . . . The Russian Social-Democratic movement is going through a time of vacillation and doubt. . . . The labor movement, on the one hand, is being cut off from Socialism: the workers are being helped to carry on the economic fight but nothing, or not enough, is being done to explain to them the Socialist aims and the political tasks of the movement as a whole. Socialism, on the other hand, is being cut off from the labor movement: Russian Socialists are once more asserting that the struggle against the government should be carried on by the intelligentsia alone and that the workers should confine themselves to the economic struggle.

. . . The "Economist" trend (if it can be called a trend) has given rise to attempts to raise this narrowness to a regular theory, and has tried to use for this purpose the currently fashionable Bernsteinism . . . which advocates the old bourgeois ideas under a new label. These efforts have resulted in the danger of a weakened connection between the Russian labor movement and Russian Social-Democracy, that foremost champion of political liberty. The most urgent task of our movement is to strengthen this link.

Social-Democracy is a union of the labor movement with Socialism. Its task is not passively to serve the labor movement in each of its separate stages, but to represent the interests of the whole movement, to point out to the movement its ultimate goal and its political tasks, and to protect its ideological and political independence. Cut off from Social-Democracy, the labor movement grows petty in character and tends, necessarily, to become

bourgeoisie. By conducting only an economic fight, the working class loses
its political independence, becomes a hanger-on to other parties, and betrays
the great commandment: "The emancipation of the workers must be done
by the workers themselves." There has been a period in every country when
the workers' movement and the Socialist movement existed separately, each
going its own way. And in every country this separation has resulted in the
weakening of both movements. In every country only the union of Socialism and the workers' movement has given both a firm foundation. In Russia,
the need for a union of Socialism and the labor movement was long ago set
forth in theory, but it is only now being achieved in practice. The process is
very difficult and it is not at all surprising that it should be accompanied
by doubts and vacillations. . . .

The whole history of Russian Socialism has brought it about that its most
urgent task is to fight the autocratic government and to win political freedom.
Our Socialist movement has become focussed, as it were, on the struggle
against the autocracy. History has shown, on the other hand, that the gulf
between Socialist thought and the advanced workers is much wider in Russia
than in other countries, and that as long as this persists the revolutionary
movement in Russia is doomed to impotence. It logically follows that the
task which is the mission of the Russian Social-Democrats is to inculcate in
the proletarian masses the idea of Socialism and of a political awareness, and
to organize a revolutionary party which will be inextricably linked with the
spontaneous labor movement. The Russian Social-Democrats have already
done much along this line, but more remains to be done. As the movement
grows, the field for Social-Democratic action widens. As the work becomes
more diversified, an increasing number of the members of the movement
are concentrating their efforts on doing various particular jobs. . . . This is
unavoidable and quite legitimate, but we must be most careful lest these
particular activities and special methods of fighting become ends in themselves. The preparatory work should not be raised to the level of the main
and only work.

Our principal and fundamental task is to assist the political organization
and political development of the working class. Those who shove this task
into the background and do not subordinate all special jobs and particular
methods of fighting to it are straying along the wrong path and are seriously
hurting the movement. And it is being shoved into the background: first, by
those who summon revolutionaries to fight the government with the help of
isolated conspiratorial circles; and, secondly, by those who reduce the scope
of political propaganda, agitation, and organization — those who think it
fitting and proper to treat the workers to "politics" only on solemn occasions
and at exceptional moments in their lives — those who too zealously whittle
down the fight against the autocracy to demands for partial concessions from

the autocracy, and who are not sufficiently concerned with developing these partial demands into a systematic and implacable struggle by the revolutionary workers' party against the autocracy.

. . . organize not only in mutual aid and strike benefit societies and in workers' circles; organize also in a political party; organize for a determined struggle against the autocratic government and against the whole of capitalist society. Unless the proletariat does organize in this way, it will never rise to the level of a conscious class struggle. Unless the workers organize in this way, the labor movement is doomed to impotence. The working class will never succeed in achieving its great mission, which is to free itself and the whole Russian people from political and economic slavery, by strike funds, mutual-aid societies and circles alone. No class in history has ever gotten power without producing as its foremost representatives political leaders capable of organizing and leading the movement. The Russian working class has already shown that it can produce such men. The struggle of the Russian workers, so widely developed in the past five or six years, has shown how great the potential revolutionary energy of the working class is. It has shown that the most ruthless persecution by this government increases rather than decreases the number of workers who are eager for Socialism, political knowledge and the political struggle.

. . . we must set resolutely to work to do these tasks; we must undertake the questions of program, organization, and tactics for the Party. . . . We are way behind the old workers of the Russian revolutionary movement in this regard. We must admit this fault frankly, and devote our efforts to devising more secret methods, to carrying on systematic training in the rules of carrying on the work, in the ways of tricking the secret police and avoiding the traps of the police. We must train people who will devote not only their spare evenings but the whole of their lives to the revolution. We must build up an organization big enough to allow a precise division of labor. Finally, on the question of tactics, we shall speak here only of the following: Social-Democrats should not tie their hands, should not limit their activities to one preconceived plan or method of political struggle; they should accept all methods of fighting so long as these are commensurate with the forces under the Party's disposal and enable it to attain the maximum possible results under the given conditions. With a strongly organized party, one single strike may grow into a political demonstration, into a political victory over the government. With a strongly organized party, a local uprising may develop into a victorious revolution.

We must remember that the struggle with the government for partial demands, that the winning of partial concessions are only petty skirmishes against the enemy, minor engagements against the outposts — the decisive battle is still to come. The enemy's fortress, raining shot and shell upon us

and mowing down our best fighters, stands before us in all its strength. We
must capture that fortress . . . .

The 1902 Program

During the first eight years of writing and other revolutionary work Ulyanov
used numerous pseudonyms, but in 1901 he first used the name which has
become so much more famous than his real one. His choice, of course, was
Lenin. In later years he customarily combined his own name and patronymic
with the pseudonym, thus: Vladimir Ilyich Lenin. But in the earlier period
he signed himself as N. Lenin. (He never used the name Nicolai or Nicholas.
That was invented for him by others after 1917.)

N. Lenin, in March of 1902, published a book which not only was the point
of departure for the debates at the 1903 Congress, but also remains to this
day the basic strategical and tactical handbook of the Communist Parties. The
following excerpts show Lenin's pattern for the organization of a revolutionary
party. He did not use the now familiar phrases: "united front," "transmission
belts," "fellow-travelers," etc., but the ideas are there.

The source is: Lenin, V. I., What Is To Be Done? Burning Questions of
Our Movement. *New York: International Publishers, copyright 1929. Pp. 8,*
28, 41, 56, 57, 65, 76, 77, 79, 82, 83, 84, 90, 105, 106, 107, 108, 109, 112,
116, 117, 118, 121, 123, 124. Greatly abridged.

Without a revolutionary theory there can be no revolutionary movement.

. . .

. . . the role of the vanguard can be filled only by a party that is guided
by an advanced theory.

. . .

Hence, to belittle Socialist ideology in any way, to deviate from it in the
slightest degree means strengthening bourgeois ideology. There is a lot of
talk about spontaneity, but the spontaneous development of the labour
movement leads to its becoming subordinated to bourgeois ideology. . . .
Hence, our task, . . . is to combat spontaneity, to divert the labour movement, with its spontaneous trade-unionist striving, from under the wing of
the bourgeoisie, and to bring it under the wing of revolutionary Social-
Democracy.

. . .

Recently, the overwhelming majority of Russian Social-Democrats were
almost wholly engaged in this work of exposing factory conditions . . . So
much so indeed, that they lost sight of the fact that this, taken by itself, was

not substantially Social-Democratic work, but merely trade-union work. As a matter of fact, these exposures merely dealt with the relations between the workers in a given trade, with their immediate employers, and all that it achieved was that the vendors of labour power learned to sell their "commodity" on better terms, and to fight the purchasers of labour power over a purely commercial deal. . . . Social-Democrats lead the struggle of the working-class not only for better terms for the sale of labour power, but also for the abolition of the social system which compels the propertyless class to sell itself to the rich. Social-Democracy represents the working-class, not in its relation to any given group of employers, but in its relation to all classes in modern society, to the state as an organized political force.

. . .

The question now arises: What does political education mean? Is it sufficient to confine oneself to the propaganda of working-class hostility to autocracy? Of course not. It is not enough to explain to the workers that they are politically oppressed (any more than it was to explain to them that their interests were antagonistic to the interests of the employers.) Advantage must be taken of every concrete example of this oppression for the purpose of agitation (in the same way as we began to use concrete examples of economic oppression for the purpose of agitation.)

. . .

Up till now we thought . . . that a propagandist, dealing with say the question of unemployment, must explain the capitalistic nature of crises, the reasons why crises are inevitable in modern society, must describe how present society must inevitably become transformed into Socialist society, etc. In a word, he must present "many ideas," so many indeed that they will be understood as a whole only by a (comparatively) few persons. An agitator, however, speaking on the same subject will take as an illustration a fact that is most widely known and outstanding among his audience — say the death from starvation of the family of an unemployed worker . . . etc. — and utilising this illustration, will direct all his efforts to present a single idea to the "masses" . . . he will strive to rouse discontent and indignation among the masses against this crying injustice, and leave a more complete explanation . . . to the propagandist.

. . .

The workers can acquire class political consciousness only from without, that is, only outside of the economic struggle, outside of the sphere of relations between workers and employers. . . . To bring political knowledge to the workers, the Social-Democrats must go among all classes of the population, must despatch units of their army in all directions. . . . The Social-Democrat's ideal should not be a trade-union secretary, but a tribune of the people, able to react to every manifestation of tyranny and oppression, no matter where it takes place, no matter what stratum or class of people it affects; he must be able to group all these manifestations into a single picture of police violence and capitalist exploitation; he must be able to take advantage of every petty event in order to explain his Socialistic convictions and his Social-Democratic demands to all. . . .

* * *

. . . for he who forgets that "the Communists support every revolutionary movement," that we are obliged for that reason to emphasize general democratic tasks before the whole people, without for a moment concealing our Socialistic convictions, is not a Social-Democrat.

* * *

But if "we" desire to be advanced democrats, we must make it our business to stimulate in the minds of those who are dissatisfied only with the university or only with the Zemstvo, etc. conditions the idea that the whole political system is worthless. We must take upon ourselves the task of organizing a universal political struggle under the leadership of our party in such a manner as to obtain the support of all opposition strata for the struggle and for our party. We must train our Social-Democratic practical workers to become political leaders, able to guide all the manifestations of this universal struggle, able at the right time "to dictate a positive programme of action" for the discontented students, for the discontented Zemstvo, for the discontented religious sects, for the offended elementary school teachers, etc., etc. . . . We would be . . . Social-Democrats only in name . . . if we failed to realize that our task is to utilise every manifestation of discontent, and to collect and utilise every grain of even rudimentary protest.

* * *

The spontaneous labour movement is able by itself to create (and inevitably will create) only trade-unionism, and working-class trade-union politics. The fact that the working-class participates in the political struggle and even in political revolution does not in itself make its politics Social-Democratic politics.

* * *

The workers' organisations must in the first place be trade organisations; secondly, they must be as wide as possible; and, thirdly, they must be as public as conditions will allow. . . . On the other hand, the organisations of revolutionists must be comprised first and foremost of people whose profession is that of revolutionists (that is why I speak of organisations of revolutionists, meaning revolutionary Social-Democrats.) . . . Such an organisation must of necessity be not too extensive and as secret as possible.

. . . every Social-Democratic worker should, as far as possible, support and actively work inside these [trade-union] organisations. . . . The wider these organisations are, the wider our influence over them will be. They will then be influenced not only by the "spontaneous" development of the economic struggle, but also by the direct and conscious action of the Socialists on their comrades in the unions.

. . .

We must also expose the conciliatory, "harmonious" undertones that will be heard in the speeches delivered by liberal politicians . . . irrespective of whether they proceed from an earnest conviction as to the desirability of peaceful cooperation of the classes, whether they proceed from a desire to curry favor with the employers, or are simply the result of not being able to do otherwise. . . . Trade-union organisations may not only be of tremendous value in developing and consolidating the economic struggle, but may also become a very useful auxiliary to the political, agitational, and revolutionary organisations.

. . .

A small, compact core, consisting of reliable, experienced and hardened workers, with responsible agents in the principal districts and connected by all the rules of strict secrecy with the organisations of revolutionists, can, with the wide support of the masses and without an elaborate set of rules, perform all the functions of a trade-union organisation, and perform them, moreover, in the manner Social-Democrats desire.

. . . I mean *professional revolutionists*, irrespective of whether they are students or working men. I assert: 1. That no movement can be durable without a stable organisation of leaders to maintain continuity; 2. that the more widely the masses are drawn into the struggle and form the basis of the movement, the more necessary is it to have such an organisation and the more stable must it be (for it is much easier then for demagogues to sidetrack the more backward sections of the masses); 3. that the organisation must consist chiefly of persons engaged in revolution as a profession; 4. that in a country with a despotic government, the more we *restrict* the membership of this organisation to persons who are engaged in revolution as a profession, and who have been professionally trained in the art of combating the political police, the more difficult will it be to catch the organisation; and 5. the wider will be the circle of men and women of the working class or of other classes of society able to join the movement and perform active work in it.

We can never give a mass organisation that degree of secrecy which is essential for the persistent and continuous struggle against the government. But to concentrate all secret functions in the hands of as small a number of professional revolutionists as possible, does not mean that the latter will "do the thinking for all" and that the crowd will not take an active part in the movement. . . . The centralisation of the secret functions of the organisation does not mean the concentration of all the functions of the movement. The active participation of the greatest masses in the dissemination of illegal literature will not diminish because a dozen professional revolutionists concentrate in their hands the secret part of the work; on the contrary, it will increase tenfold. Only in this way will the reading of illegal literature . . . and to some extent even the distribution of illegal literature almost cease to be secret work, for the police will soon come to realise the folly and futility of setting the whole judicial and administrative machine in motion to intercept every copy of a publication that is being broadcast in thousands. This applies not only to the press, but to every function of movement, even to demonstrations. . . . organisations intended for wide membership . . . can be as loose and public as possible, for example, trade unions, workers' circles for self-education . . . and Socialist, and also democratic circles for all other sections of the population, etc., etc. We must have as large a number as possible of such organisations having the widest possible variety of functions, but it is absurd and dangerous to confuse these with organisations of revolutionists. . . .

. . .

If we had such an organisation, the more secret it would be, the stronger and more widespread would be the confidence of the masses in the party, and, as we know, in time of war, it is not only of great importance to imbue one's own adherents with confidence in the strength of one's army, but also the enemy and all neutral elements; friendly neutrality may sometimes decide the outcome of the battle.

. . .

. . . our very first and most imperative duty is to help to train working-class revolutionists who will be on the same level in regard to party activity as intellectual revolutionists (we emphasise the words "in regard to party activity," because although it is necessary, it is not so easy and not so imperative to bring the workers up to the level of the intellectuals in other respects.) . . . the working-class revolutionist must also become a professional revolutionist. . . . A workingman who is at all talented and "promising," must not be left to work . . . in a factory. We must arrange that he be maintained by the party, that he may in due time go underground. . . . .
When we shall have detachments of specially trained working-class revolu-

tionists . . . no political police in the world will be able to contend against them, for these detachments will consist of men absolutely loyal and devoted to the revolution, and will themselves enjoy the absolute confidence and devotion of the broad masses of the workers.

. . .

The 1903 Congress

Friction increased among the members of the editorial board of Iskra, *and it was decided to make another attempt to organize the party and to settle its program by means of another congress (or, as we would probably put it, conference). Because of the Russian police and because the most important leaders were in western Europe, the meeting was convened in Brussels. Lenin took great pains (as far as he could) to arrange for the selection of delegates who would support him. He also carefully prepared detailed plans and arguments in support of them, and busily mended his political fences among the delegates as they arrived. The Belgian police soon ordered the delegates out of Brussels and the session was transferred to London. According to Lenin's count, forty-three delegates, representing fifty-one votes, attended the London meetings. Four of the delegates were or had been workers, the rest were intellectuals.*

One of the most bitterly fought battles came on the nature of the party organization and, especially, on the qualifications to be demanded of members. Lenin demanded, as he had in his earlier writings, that membership be restricted to professional revolutionaries. He also wanted a strong centralization of authority and a most rigid discipline and obedience to the party's leaders. The veterans, Axelrod and Zasulich; Lenin's contemporary, Martov; and the neophyte revolutionary, Trotsky, all favored a party open to all who believed in its program and were willing to work under its leadership. This program (usually called Martov's) won on the first voting, 28 to 22. But Lenin was able to get the matter reconsidered after seven or eight delegates had withdrawn or been forced out. This time the victory went to Lenin by a slender majority.

The Congress was, in fact, hopelessly split. Lenin, with great perspicacity, arrogated to his faction the titles of Bolshinstvo (Majority) *and* Bolsheviki (Members of the Majority) *thus forcing upon his opponents the titles of* Menshinstvo (Minority) *and* Mensheviki (Members of the Minority.) *But the actual tabulation of the votes gives a more accurate picture. On the two very important matters of the election of the editorial board of* Iskra *and the election of the Central Committee the score was: delegates withdrawn or expelled — 7; blank ballots — 2; not voting — 20; for Lenin's side — 22.*

The London Congress actually created not one party but two, namely: Lenin's Bolsheviks and Martov's Mensheviks.

Excerpts from Lenin's resolution which precipitated this split are given below. This is an official Soviet translation of a manuscript note in Lenin's handwriting. The original is in the Central Lenin Museum at Moscow.

1. A member of the Russian Social-Democratic Workers' Party is one who accepts its program, belongs to one of its organizations, and supports the Party both financially and by personal participation in its activities.

2. The supreme organ of the Party is the Party Congress. . . .

3. The following shall be entitled to representation at Congresses: (a) Central Committee; (b) Editorial Board of the Central Organ of the Party; (c) all local committees not belonging to special federations; (d) all federations of committees recognized by the Party. . . .

4. The Party Congress elects the Central Committee and the Editorial Board of the Central Organ of the Party. The Central Committee exercises direct leadership of the political struggle, co-ordinates and guides all practical activities of the Party, and administers the central Party funds. To serve the needs of the movement as a whole, the Central Committee may also appoint special agents or special groups under its direct control. The Central Committee shall settle all conflicts arising between various organizations and institutions of the Party, or within them.

5. The Editorial Board of the Central Organ leads the Party ideologically . . . and [makes] the decision of [on] tactical questions. The Central Committee should be located in Russia and the Central Organ abroad. . . . In the event of the arrest of all the members and alternate members of the Central Committee, a new Central Committee shall be appointed by the Editorial Board of the Central Organ. . . .

The Lenin "Line" on the 1905 Revolution

As a result of the split which was so apparent at the London Congress, Lenin eventually lost control of Iskra. He then established a Bolshevik newspaper which he called Vpered (Forward)· and used it as he had previously used Iskra, that is, to indoctrinate, organize, and direct his followers. The paper was published in Geneva. The issue for January 4 (N.S.) 1905 carried a lead editorial by Lenin in which he laid down the line for his followers in regard to events then taking place in Russia. The translation was made from a facsimile copy of the paper.

. . . For the proletariat, the fight for political freedom and a democratic republic in a bourgeois society is just one of the necessary steps in the fight for a social revolution which will overturn the bourgeois system. . . . The movement which is beginning in Russia is a bourgeois revolution. . . . No, the nearer the time of revolution approaches and the stronger the constitutional movement becomes, the more rigorously must the party of the proletariat uphold its class independence and not allow its class demands to be overwhelmed by the general talk of democracy. The more often and the more vigorously the representatives of so-called society bring forward what they claim to be the demands of the whole people, the more relentlessly must the Social-Democrats expose the real nature of this society. Take the notorious resolution of the "secret" Zemstva congress of November 6/8. You will find in it, shoved well to the background, deliberately vague and timid constitutional aspirations. You will find . . . exceedingly detailed suggestions for reforms in Zemstva and in municipal institutions — that is, in institutions which represent the interests of the landlords and capitalists. You will find mention of peasant reforms — freeing the peasants from guardianship and protecting proper court forms. It is wholly clear that here are representatives of the propertied classes who only desire to secure concessions from the autocracy and who have no desire to make changes in the foundations of the economic systems. . . .

Is there anyone who can't see that it is precisely the interests of all levels of landowners, merchant-industrialists, and middle class peasants which form the foundation and basis for the constitutional demands? Will we really be fooled because the democratic intelligentsia — which always and everywhere in all European middle class revolutions has taken on itself the role of publicist, speaker and political leader — represent these interests?

. . . The proletariat must take advantage of the unusually favorable political position. The proletariat must support the middle-class constitutional movement, incite and rally the widest possible segments of the exploited masses of the people, muster all its forces, and start an uprising at the instant when the government's position is most desperate and the popular unrest is highest.

In what way should the proletariat immediately support the constitutionalists? The most important of all is to use the general unrest to agitate and organize among the least influenced and most backward sections of the peasants and workers. Of course, the Social-Democrats, the organized proletariat, ought to send its detachments among all classes, but . . . the more acute the struggle grows . . . the more should our work be concentrated in getting the proletarians and semi-proletarians ready for the direct struggle for freedom. . . . It is incomparably more important now to increase our ranks, organize our forces, and prepare for a more direct and open mass struggle. . . .

. . . A military disaster is inevitable, and it will inevitably be accompanied by the profound exacerbation of discontent, anger, and unrest. With the utmost energy, we must prepare for that moment.

* * * * *

Vpered (Forward) *survived only until May (1905) when it was replaced by* Proletarii (The Proletarian) *with Lenin again as Editor-in-Chief. The first issue of this new "Central Organ of the Russian Social-Democratic Workers' Party" was published at Geneva on May 14/27. Its leading article was a brief report — written by Lenin, but signed by the Central Committee — of some of the decision made at the Third Party Congress (held at London, April-May, 1905). The following excerpt is an official translation of a portion of that report.*

. . . The Congress drew the attention of all Party members to the necessity of taking advantage of the waverings of the government, of every legal or practical extension of freedom for our activities, to strengthen the class organization of the proletariat and to prepare for open action by the proletariat. . . . The making of a victorious revolution and the defense of its conquests impose tremendous tasks on the proletariat. But the proletariat will not be dismayed by great tasks. . . . It will be able to take the lead of [sic] the armed uprising of the people. It will not shirk the difficult task of participating in a provisional revolutionary government, should such a task fall to its share. It will be able to repulse all counter-revolutionary attempts, ruthlessly crush all enemies of freedom, staunchly defend the democratic republic, and secure the fulfillment of our whole minimum program by revolutionary means. . . .

The Genesis of the Soviets

The soviets which played such an important part during and after 1917 were modeled on those first organized during the 1905 Revolution. The man chiefly responsible for the 1905 movement was George Khrustalyev-Nosar who escaped from his guards while being removed from the prison-fortress of SS. Peter and Paul in October 1905. Mr. Khrustalyev-Nosar went first to Moscow, where he organized a workingmen's association, and then to St. Petersburg where he established the first Soviet of Workers' Deputies. The following selections are excerpts from his own account of these events. The source is: Khrustalyev-Nosar, G., "The Council of Workmen Deputies" in The Russian Review (A Quarterly Review of Russian History, Politics, Economics, and Literature). *Published by The School of Russian Studies in the University of Liverpool. Vol. II (1913), No. 1, pp. 89–100, passim.*

Its story is a story of fifty days. It was constituted on October 26, 1905. Its existence was interrupted by the recrudescence of reaction and by the blind force of soldiers on December 16, 1905. In spite of its short existence, the Council of Workmen Deputies played a decisive part . . . , giving to the revolutionary movement an organised and regular character. . . .

Basing ourselves on this experiment [the organisation of the association in Moscow], we began working to create another such autonomous organisation in St. Petersburg. Our appeal met with an enthusiastic reception among the workmen. In spite of all the objectionable efforts of the Social Democrats, the foundation-stone was laid, and in October took place the first sitting of the new working men's organisation in the quarters of the Technological Institute. At the start it did not possess either a precise title or strictly defined functions. The workmen of the factories and works chose one deputy for every 500 workmen. Small enterprises and the lesser workshops met together and sent a common delegate. Neither political nor religious nor national differences played any part in the matter. Thus the whole mass of workmen scattered over St. Petersburg, who had no access to professional unions or to political parties, was cemented and drawn into the common work. Of course, the revolutionary fever and the general strike which had just begun accelerated this process of organisation. All the workmen of St. Petersburg had every day at their meetings to discuss questions raised by the Council of Workmen Deputies. The electorate of the Council retained the right of referendum . . . [but the deputy could make decisions without consulting his electors]. In its external organisation, the Council of Workmen Deputies was a most democratic "working men's parliament," and its discussions and resolutions were the equivalent of the views and feelings of the agitated working classes in Russia during the revolutionary epoch. They were obeyed *imperio rationis sed non ratione imperii* [by order of reason, but not by reason of orders] as the Council of Workmen Deputies had no means of compelling obedience. But at the word of the Council the workmen struck work, and by resolution of the Council they resumed it. . . .

But the work and the political significance of the Council reached far beyond the limits of the working class. The whole democracy of St. Petersburg acknowledged the hegemony of the Council and its political authority. The Union of Unions . . . several times sought the honour of sending its own delegates to the Council. Officials and the employees of banks, offices, railways, post, telegraph, and telephone sent their representatives to the Council, and submitted to its decisions. The influence of the Council extended over the Peasants' Union. In the country, there began to be formed Councils of Peasant Deputies. In the army and navy, there were Councils of military deputies. In the Universities were organised Councils of student deputies, in the secondary schools, Councils of deputies from the secondary schools.

From St. Petersburg to Tiflis, and from Warsaw to Vladivostok, all Russia was covered with a network of various councils. Ordinary citizens came to the Council of Workmen Deputies for information, protection, and help. . . . . The peasants of an out-of-the-way village sent a complaint against Prince Repnin, and asked us to settle it. Lastly, Count Witte himself [then Prime Minister] being unable to send a Government telegram to . . . Kushka, was obliged to ask the help of the Council. . . .

In St. Petersburg there existed side by side, as the *Novoe Vremya* put it, "two Governments, the Government of Count Witte and the Government of Khrustalyev." . . . The former practically retired; the second took on itself the responsibility of securing the inviolability of citizens by forming a working men's militia; regulated railway, postal, and telegraphic communications and industrial life; realised in practice the freedoms promised by the manifesto of October 30; and appealed to the population to defend and maintain them. It goes without saying that the co-existence of these two governments could not long continue. . . .

The Russian Revolution [of 1905] was a *town* revolution. The overwhelming majority of the population . . . remained outside the movement. Certainly, later the town population found an echo in the "jacqueries" of the peasants. . . . [But] In a word, the town revolution did not find the necessary support among the country peasants. The town revolution made a mistake in counting on a country army of soldiers; the town revolution weakened itself by putting forward extreme social demands. The campaign of the Council of Workmen Deputies for an eight hours' day frightened away from the Council and armed against the Council the liberal elements of the industrial middle class. . . .

The Duma and the Budget

The Duma's power over the budget was very severely limited. Its control covered only about half the budget at best and even this was somewhat uncertain since the upper house (the Imperial Council) also had some budgetary powers. If the two houses were unable to agree on a figure, the Government could accept the figure it liked better. If no budget was passed, that of the preceding year remained in effect. The following excerpts are from an informal report given by the Chairman of the Duma's Finance Committee. The reader may wish to compare these items with claims made by speakers in the Supreme Soviet (and elsewhere) on the nature of the tsarist budget. The source is: Lerche, H., "Five Years of Budget Work" in The Russian Review. Vol. I, No. 3 (1912), pp. 14–48.

. . . The Imperial Duma is limited in the exercise of its legislative power, as to construction, technique, and economic administration of these Ministries [army and navy] and also their institutions and officials. Its part is restricted to the expression of wishes and the stating of views when the military and naval estimates and the various Bills are being debated, and to the granting or refusing of *new* credits for the requirements of the army and fleet.

Though it could only have a weak influence on the actual administration, the Imperial Duma was so possessed and penetrated with the dominant idea of the sacred duty of defending the country and restoring its military power, that it did not hesitate to raise the permanent expenditures for the army and voted large sums for special credits. By the estimates of expenditure of 1907, the ordinary expenditures of the Ministries for War were reckoned at 399.6 million roubles; by the Budget of 1912 which passed the Imperial Duma, the ordinary expenditures were estimated at 492.5 million roubles. . . . Besides this, in the course of the five sessions there were required for the payment of extra expenditures of the Ministry of War about 39 million roubles. For the extraordinary expenditures of the Ministry of War for the renewal of stores and material, the Imperial Duma granted . . . in the five years [1908–1912] 285. million roubles. The expenses of liquidating the war were estimated under a separate fund, and . . . amounted to 89.2 million roubles. The Imperial Duma considerably increased the ordinary permanent expenditure of the army . . . and granted 285.5 million roubles for restoring its military efficiency. . . .

In general, the ordinary expenses of the army and navy rose from 464.6 million roubles in 1907 to 651.6 million roubles in 1912, that is by . . . more than 40 per cent. . . .

Among cultural and productive expenditures we must dwell on public instruction, land settlement, agriculture, and public equipment. . . . the Duma aims at completing a system of universal free elementary instruction with a gradual increase in the number of local schools; it accepts, on behalf of the Treasury, the normal payment of teachers' salaries (which in 1912 demands 43 million roubles); it is helping in the construction of schools, and it is making a ten years' plan for financing schools in order to secure their further development. Unfortunately this plan meets with criticism in the Imperial Council.

The credits for schools are increasing. By estimates of 1907, the expenditures on elementary education amounted to 14.3 million roubles. For 1912, they have increased to 64.4 million roubles . . . or more than 4½ times. The total sum of expenditures on public instruction (including secondary and higher education and learned institutions) has risen from 45.9 million roubles in 1907 to 117.5 millions. . . . But these figures do not give all the expenditures of the State on public education, not to speak of the expenses of public bodies [the Zemstva], private persons, and societies. Besides the schools in the jurisdiction of the Ministry of Public Instruction, there are numerous schools of various classes in the jurisdiction of the Orthodox Church, and of the Ministries of Trade and Commerce, Ways of Communication, War, Justice, and others. The statistics of the expenditures of the State on instruction, science and art, enable us to make the following comparison: in 1907, the expenditures of the State under various jurisdictions amounted to 75.4 million roubles; in 1912, it is 156.7 million roubles . . . .

The expenditures on land settlement rose from 11 million roubles in 1907, to 29 million roubles in 1912. Measures for developing agriculture . . . and improvements of the land (principally irrigation and draining works) called in 1907 for an expenditure of only 5.1 million roubles; for 1912, this expenditure amounts to as much aS 31.5 million roubles . . . .

Among public works, the first place belongs to railway construction. . . . Sixty million roubles were voted for the construction of State railways in . . . 1908; . . . and for 1912, 110.5 million roubles — a total, for the five years [1908–1912] of 338.2 million roubles. . . .

. . . ordinary expenditures have risen from 2173.4 million roubles in 1907 to 2668.9 million roubles in 1912, or a rise of . . . nearly 23 per cent. . . . The total of ordinary revenue of the State has risen from 2342.4 million roubles in 1907, to 2951 million roubles in 1911 . . . or a rise of . . . nearly 26 per cent.

The Development of Lenin's Program (Part II)
Lenin and the Duma Elections

A part of Lenin's success was due to his shrewd and totally amoral opportunism. His program was absolutely fixed as to its ultimate goal, but it was extremely flexible as to tactics. He may have despised the day of small things, but he never made the mistake of being too proud to try to turn even small things to his advantage. He was always ready to adopt any means which seemed most promising in a given situation, and equally ready to abandon these for others when the situation changed. The following brief quotation from one of Lenin's editorials not only illustrates this characteristic, but also very concisely explains and justifies the tactic described. The source is: Pravda, 1/14 August, 1912. Only a portion of the editorial is reprinted.

. . . The workers realize fully that they need expect nothing from either the Third or the Fourth Duma. Nevertheless, we must take part in the elections, first, because the unification and political education of the toiling masses are characteristic of election times when party struggles and political life in general acquire a lively aspect and when the masses, in one way or another, learn about politics; second, for the purpose of getting our working class representatives into the Duma. The workers' deputies did a lot of good for the workers' cause even in the completely reactionary, landlord controlled [Third] Duma. They can continue to do so if they are genuine working class democrats, provided that they keep in touch with the masses, and if the masses learn how to supervise and direct them.

The Bolsheviks and the First World War

The First World War divided the socialist groups, both in Russia and else-where, even more than they had been before. Generally the socialists rallied to the support of their respective countries, but Lenin's position permitted no such action. Under his leadership, the Bolshevik Central Committee un-compromisingly stated its position in a manifesto which was issued in the Fall of 1914. The manifesto was signed by the Central Committee. It had been drafted by Lenin, and was published, among other places, in his news-paper, The Social Democrat. *(This paper had replaced* Forward *as the "Central Organ of the Russian Social Democratic Workers' Party.") The following excerpts from the manifesto are reprinted from an official Soviet translation of it.*

The European war, for which the governments and the bourgeois parties of all countries have been preparing for decades, has broken out. . . . The seizure of territory and the conquest of foreign nations; the ruination of a competing nation and the plundering of its wealth; the diversion of the attention of the working classes of Russia, England, Germany, and the other countries from internal political crises; the division of the workers, fooling them by nationalism, and the wiping out of their advance guard with the object of weakening the revolutionary movement of the proletariat — such is the only real meaning, substance and importance of the present war.

The first duty of the Social-Democrats is to reveal the true meaning of the war and ruthlessly to expose the falsehood, sham, and "patriotic" phrase-making spread by the ruling classes . . . in defence of the war.

The German bourgeoisie heads one group of belligerent nations. It is fooling the working class and the laboring masses . . . .

The other group . . . is headed by the French and British bourgeoisie, which is fooling the working class and the toiling masses . . . .

But the more zealously the governments and the bourgeoisie of all coun-tries strive to divide the workers and to set them against each other . . . the more urgent is the duty of the class-conscious proletariat to preserve its class solidarity, its internationalism, its Socialist convictions . . . .

It is with a feeling of deepest chagrin that we have to record that the Socialist parties of the leading European countries have not discharged this duty. . . .

... The Russian proletariat has not shrunk from making any sacrifice to rid humanity of the disgrace of the tsarist monarchy. But we must say that if anything can ... delay the fall of tsardom, if anything can help the tsardom in its struggle against the whole democracy of Russia, it is the present war which has put the wealth of the British, French, and Russian bourgeoisie at the disposal of the tsardom for its reactionary aims. ...

It is impossible to decide, under present conditions from the standpoint of the international proletariat, the defeat of which of the two groups of belligerent nations would be the lesser evil for socialism. But for us, the Russian Social-Democrats, there cannot be the slightest doubt that from the standpoint of the working class and toiling masses of all the nations of Russia, the lesser evil would be the defeat of the tsarist monarchy, the most reactionary and barbarous of governments . . . .

The only correct proletarian slogan is the transformation of the present imperialist war into a civil war . . . .

Lenin's Orders on Tactics

The Bolsheviks in Russia attempted to carry out Lenin's instructions concerning the war. The Russian government, quite naturally, regarded such actions as treasonable. Eleven Bolsheviks were arrested and sentenced to exile in November, 1914. Lenin's editorial comment on the trial contained the following orders as to the proper behavior of Bolsheviks who found themselves in like circumstances. The source is: The Social Democrat. *No. 40. Geneva. 29 March, 1915. Abridged.*

The aim pursued by the defendants was to obstruct the efforts of the prosecutor to discover the identity of the members of the Central Committee in Russia and of the Party agents in its varied relations with workers' organizations. This goal was attained. And for its future attainment, the method long officially recommended by the Party should be adopted, namely: refusal to give evidence. . . . Our comrades should have refused to testify about the illegal organization [the Party underground]; they should [also] . . . have taken advantage of the fact that this was a public trial to make a direct statement of the views of the Social Democrats. . . .

Lenin Comes Home

The Bolsheviks were as surprised and as unprepared for the first (February/March) 1917 Revolution as was the rest of the world. Lenin was in

Switzerland and the lesser leaders were either also in exile or were operating clandestinely and rather ineffectively on a very small scale. The Party membership had dropped to under 24,000. Lenin at first tried to continue his leadership by remote control through his "Letters From Afar," but this proved inadequate and very unsatisfactory from his point of view. The amnesty granted by the Provisional Government permitted the Bolsheviks to return to Russia from abroad or from Siberia. Lenin determined to take advantage of the amnesty if a way could be found by which he could return to Russia. The western Allies correctly regarded him as their enemy and refused to permit him passage across their territories.

According to the official Communist history, Martov, the Menshevik leader, first suggested that Lenin seek permission to travel across Germany. The German High Command, who evidently agreed with their opponents' belief that Lenin would make trouble for Russia, gave the necessary permission. Lenin and his party crossed Germany by train, went then to Sweden, and finally entered Russia through the frontier station at Tornio, Finland. There is a certain irony in the fact that the Russian officials at Tornio treated Lenin just as they did any other Russian who returned from abroad. He had to fill out a standard "Inquiry Form" and to get a standard entry permit. The permit was signed by the head of the Tornio station. A translation of one side of the Inquiry Form is given below. The reverse side bore the notation that: "Vlad. Ulyanov" had been given a travel permit by the Russian Consul-General in Sweden on March 31st (O.S.). The original is in the Central Lenin Museum.

Inquiry Form

For Russian subjects arriving from abroad through the frontier station of Tornio.

2 April [O.S.], 1917.

Name, patronymic, surname, rank: Vladimir Ilyich Ulyanov
Last residence: Stockholm (Sweden) (Hotel Regina, Stockholm)
Age, nationality, religion: Born 10 April [O.S.], 1870 at Simbirsk; Russian; Orthodox
For what purpose did you go abroad?: Political refugee. Left Russia illegally.
Give address and purpose of visit
    if stopping in Finland: No intention of stopping.
To what city are you going? Give address: Petrograd. Sister's address: Mariya Ilyichna Ulyanova, Shirokaya St. 48/9, Apt. 24.
Profession: Journalist
Signature: [s] Vladimir Ulyanov

"The Transition Stage"

Until Lenin's arrival in Petrograd in April, the lesser leaders of the Bolsheviks (including Stalin) had produced no clear-cut program and had not progressed beyond the stage of general obstructionism and trouble-making. Lenin at once set to work to change that situation. The day after his arrival, he presented a specific program of revolution. His proposals evoked a stormy dissent even among the other Bolshevik leaders, but within a month he had won the majority of the Party's Central Executive Committee to his side. It is not too much to say that Lenin here changed the course of history. The Bolshevik leaders (for example, Stalin, Kamenev, and Molotov) who had returned to Petrograd before Lenin had no such plan as his even if they had had the force to carry it through. It was Lenin who took over full control of the Party; trained, disciplined, and prepared it; set the goals; determined the strategy and picked the tactics; and, finally, chose the time for action.

The statement of the program which he presented on April 17th [N.S.] has been widely reprinted. The version given here is translated from the program as it was published in Pravda *on April 20, 1917.*

"The April Theses"

1. In our attitude toward the war, which on the part of Russia still remains, under the new government of Lvov and Co., unquestionably a predatory, imperialist war because of the capitalist nature of that government, not the slightest concession ought to be made to "a revolutionary movement in favor of defending a capitalist fatherland."

The class-conscious proletariat might give their consent to a revolutionary war, truly justifying a revolutionary movement in favor of defense of a capitalist fatherland, only on condition: (a) that power be transferred to the proletariat and to the poor peasantry which is close to the proletariat, (b) that all annexations be renounced in fact and not just in words, (c) that a genuine break be made with all capitalist interests.

In view of the indubitable good faith with which large sections of the masses accept the war as necessary for the defense of the country . . . , in view of the fact that they are being fooled by the bourgeoisie, it is necessary to explain their mistake to them . . . , to explain the indissoluble tie between capitalism and the imperialist war, to prove to them that it is impossible to end the war by a really democratic, free peace without the overthrow of capitalism. Organize the most widespread propaganda for this view among the troops on active duty. [Preach] fraternization.

2. The uniqueness of the current moment in Russia lies in the transition from the first stage of revolution in which, because of the lack of class-consciousness and organization among the proletariat, power fell to the bourgeoisie to the second stage in which power ought to be put in the hands of the proletariat and the poor peasants.

This transition stage is characterized, in the first place by a maximum of legality (Russia is now the freest of all the warring countries in the world); in the second place, by an absence of violence against the masses; and, finally, by a totally unwarranted confidence in the capitalist government which is really the worst enemy of peace and of socialism.

This situation demands of us flexibility in adapting ourselves to the unique requirements for Party work among unprecedently large masses of the proletariat who have been aroused to political awareness.

3. There must be no support given to the Provisional Government. The complete falseness of its promises, particularly those relating to annexations, must be explained. [There must be] an exposure of the unpardonable, illusion-breeding "demand" that this government, a government of capitalists, cease to be imperialistic.

4. We must recognize the fact that in most of the Soviets of Workers' Deputies our Party is a minority and so far a small minority compared to the bloc of all the petty-bourgeois, opportunist elements who have surrendered to bourgeois influences and who transmit those influences to the masses.

It must be explained to the masses that the Soviets are the only possible form for a revolutionary government; and our task, therefore, as long as this government surrenders to bourgeois influences, is patiently, systematically and persistently to expose — in a way especially adapted to the practical needs of the masses — the errors of their tactics.

So long as we remain a minority, we must carry on the work of criticizing and explaining errors so that the masses may overcome their mistakes through experience; and, simultaneously, we must advocate the transfer of the entire power of the state to the Soviets of Workers' Deputies.

5. [There must be] No parliamentary republic — to return to a parliamentary republic from Soviets of Workers' Deputies would be retrogression — but a republic of Soviets of Workers', Farm-hands', and Peasants' Deputies throughout the land, "from top to bottom."

Abolition of the police, the army, and the bureaucracy. (i.e., the standing army to be replaced by the universally armed people [peoples' militia]).

All officials to be elected and subject to recall at any time, and their salaries shall not be greater than those of good workers.

6. In the agrarian program, the emphasis must be on the Soviets of Farmhands' Deputies. All landowners' estates to be confiscated. All land in the

country to be nationalized; the distribution of the land to be in the hands of the Soviets of Farm-hands' and Peasants' Deputies. Separate Soviets of Poor-Peasants' Deputies to be organized. Model farms to be set up on each large estate (from 270 to 810 acres, depending on local conditions and at the discretion of the local bodies) under the direction of the Soviets of Farm-hands' Deputies and for the common good.

7. All banks in the country to be merged at once into a single national bank which shall be controlled by the Soviet of Workers' Deputies.

8. Our immediate job is not to "introduce" Socialism but only to bring the production and distribution of goods under the control of the Soviet of Workers' Deputies at once.

9. Party tasks:

    a) To summon a Party congress at once;

    b) To change the Party program, mainly: 1) on the question of imperialism and the imperialist war; 2) on the question of our attitude toward the state, and our demand for a "Commune state" (i.e., a state of which the prototype was the Paris Commune.); 3) amendment of our antiquated minimum program.

    c) A new name for the Party (instead of "Social Democrats," whose official leaders . . . have betrayed socialism . . . , we must call ourselves a Communist Party.)

10. A new International. We must take the lead in creating a revolutionary International, an International directed against the social-chauvinists and against the "Center" (. . . i.e. [against] Kautsky & Co. in Germany, Longuet & Co. in France, Chkeidze & Co. in Russia, Turati & Co. in Italy, Mac-Donald & Co. in England, etc.)

Lenin Calls the Revolution

The complete breakdown of the July offensive, the breaking away of Ukraine and the consequent resignation of the Kadet ministers from the coalition government brought new turmoil to Petrograd. A group of irresponsible enthusiasts, including some Bolsheviks, promoted an uprising against the government. Lenin, whose preparations were not completed, correctly judged the movement to be premature and sought to restrain it. When he found that he could not stop it, Lenin made a quick tactical change and ordered his followers to join the movement in the hope of thus being able to control it. After three days of disorder, the rising gradually petered out. Lenin and some of his colleagues were forced to go into hiding in nearby Finland in order to escape arrest. However, he continued to keep in constant contact with his group and was able to maintain his control over it.

By October, Lenin judged that the situation had changed completely. His own preparations were completed, and the government was much weaker, largely as a result of the Kornilov affair. On October 7/20, Lenin returned secretly to Petrograd, and at the meeting of the Central Executive Committee of the Bolsheviks on October 10/23, he proposed the resolution which is the first of two following documents. The resolution was vigorously opposed by some of the Committee, but Lenin finally succeeded in getting it adopted.

The second document is Lenin's "Letter to the Members of the Central Committee," written on the literal eve of the Petrograd coup. The originals of both documents are in the Central Lenin Museum. They are here translated in full.

The C[entral] C[ommittee] recognizes that both the international position of the Russian Revolution (revolution in the German Navy which is an extreme manifestation of the world Socialist Revolution, and the threat by the imperialists to make a peace in order to stifle the revolution in Russia) — and the military situation (certain decision of the Russian bourgeoisie and Kerensky and Co. to surrender Petrograd to the Germans)— and also the securing of a majority in the Soviets by the party of the proletariat — all this in conjunction with the peasant uprisings and the increase of public confidence in our Party (Moscow elections), and lastly the obvious preparations for a second Kornilov affair (removal of the soldiers from Petrograd, sending of Cossacks to Petrograd, encirclement of Minsk by Cossacks, etc.)— all this places armed insurrection on the order of the day.

Therefore, recognizing that armed insurrection is inevitable and that the time is completely ripe for it, the C[entral] C[ommittee] calls upon all Party organizations to govern themselves accordingly, and to discuss and settle all practical questions from this standpoint (Congress of Soviets of the Northern Region, troop withdrawal from Petrograd, action in Moscow and Minsk, etc.)

* * * * *

I am writing these lines on the evening of the 24th [Oct. 24/November 6, 1917]. The situation is critical in the extreme. It is absolutely clear that to delay the insurrection now would be truly fatal.

I exhort my comrades with all my strength to realize that everything now hangs by a thread; that we are being confronted by problems which cannot be solved by conferences or congresses (even Congresses of Soviets) but exclusively by peoples, by the masses, by the struggle of the armed masses.

The bourgeois onslaught of the Kornilovites and the removal of Vekhovsky show that we must not wait. We must at all costs, this very evening, this very night, arrest the government, first disarming the Junkers (defeating them if they resist) and so forth.

We must not wait! We may lose everything!

The value of the immediate seizure of power will be the defense of the people (not of the congress, but of the people, the army and the peasants in the first place) from the Kornilovite government, which has driven out Verkhovsky and has hatched a second Kornilov plot.

Who must take power?

That is not important at the moment. Let the Revolutionary Military Committee take it, or "some other institution" which will declare that it will relinquish the power only to the true representatives of the interests of the people, the interests of the army (immediate proposal of peace) the interests of the peasants (land to be taken immediately and private property abolished) the interests of the starving.

All districts, regiments, forces must be mobilized at once and must immediately send their delegations to the Revolutionary Military Committee and to the Central Committee of the Bolsheviks with the insistent demand that under no circumstances must the power be left in the hands of Kerensky and Co. until the 25th — not under any circumstances; the matter must be decided without fail this very evening, or this very night.

History will not forgive revolutionaries for procrastinating when they could be victorious today (will certainly be victorious today) while they risk losing much, in fact, everything, tomorrow.

If we seize power today, we seize it not in opposition to the Soviets, but on their behalf.

The seizure of power is a matter of insurrection; its political purpose will become clear after the seizure.

It would be a disaster, or a sheer formality, to await the wavering vote of October 25. The people have the right and the duty to decide such questions not by a vote, but by force; in critical moments of revolution, the people have the right and the duty to direct their representatives, even their best representatives, and not to wait for them.

This is proved by the history of all revolutions; and it would be an infinite crime on the part of the revolutionaries were they to let the moment slip, knowing that upon them depends the salvation of the revolution, the proposal of peace, the salvation of Petrograd, salvation from famine, the transfer of the land to the peasants.

The government is wavering. It must be given the finishing blow at all costs.

To delay actions will be fatal.

[s] V. I. Lenin

A Revolutionary Proclamation

This is a translation of the proclamation which announced the Bolshevik coup in Petrograd. It was printed as a poster. The original is in the Central Lenin Museum.

FROM THE REVOLUTIONARY MILITARY COMMITTEE OF THE PETROGRAD SOVIET OF WORKERS' AND SOLDIERS' DEPUTIES

TO THE CITIZENS OF RUSSIA

The Provisional Government has been overthrown. Governing power has passed into the hands of the agent of the Petrograd Soviet of Workers' and Soldiers' Deputies, the Revolutionary Military Committee, which stands at the head of the proletariat and garrison of Petrograd.

The cause for which the people fought: the immediate proposal for a democratic peace, the abolition of landlordism, control of production by the workers, the creation of a Soviet government — is secure.

Long live the revolution of the workers, the soldiers, and the peasants!

> The Revolutionary Military Committee
> for the Petrograd Soviet of Workers'
> and Soldiers' Deputies.

25 October, [O.S.] 1917
10 A.M.

His Opponents Talk

The reader may wish to compare Lenin's dramatic call to planned action with the following account of the activities of the Council of the Republic on October 25/November 7. The description was written by Professor Pitirim Sorokin, then a leading member of the Right-Wing Social Revolutionaries and secretary to Kerensky. The dialogue is meant to convey the sense of what was said; it is not a literal record of the remarks. The source is: Sorokin, Pitirim A., Leaves from a Russian Diary — and Thirty Years After. Enlarged edition. Boston: The Beacon Press, 1950. Pp. 98–100.

On October 25, in spite of illness, I set out for the Winter Palace to get news. In the streets I saw the familiar spectacle of speeding automobiles full of sailors and Latvian soldiers, firing recklessly as they passed; no trams, no droshkies. But so accustomed had all of us grown to this condition of things that I went on quite indifferently. Approaching the Winter Palace,

I found it surrounded by Bolshevist troops. It would have been sheer folly to walk into their arms, so I turned around and sought, in the Mariinsky Palace, the Council of the Republic. There I learned that while Kerensky had fled to the front to seek military assistance, Konovaloff and the other Ministers, with the Governor of Petrograd, Rutenberg and Palchinsky, were barricaded in the Winter Palace defended only by a regiment. of women soldiers and three hundred military cadets.

"This is outrageous!" stormed a Social Democrat deputy. "We sháll certainly protest against such violence."

"What! Are we going to pass another resolution?" I asked.

"In the name of the Soviet, the Council of the Republic and the Government we shall appeal to the country and to the world democracy," he replied, offended at my levity.

"And what is that but another resolution?" I asked banteringly.

"We shall appeal to the military forces."

"What military forces?"

"Officers and Cossacks are still faithful."

"The same men whom the revolutionary democracy treated as counter-revolutionaries and reactionaries," I persisted. "Have you forgotten how you insulted them, especially after Korniloff's failure? After that do you imagine they will be willing to defend us? I think, on the contrary, that they will be rather gratified at what has happened."

The Council of the Republic convened, and a proposal to protest against the criminal attack on the rights of the people and of the Government was made and debated. But the discussion did not last very long, for suddenly the Hall was invaded by a troop of soldiers who announced: "According to a decree of the new Government the Council of the Republic is dispersed. Leave here immediately or submit to arrest."

The chairman of the Council said: "The resolution of protest has been heard. All in favor raise their hands." The resolution was carried. Then the chairman said: "Under pressure of violence the Council of the Republic is temporarily interrupted." Such was the end of the first Republic, an end scarcely more heroic than that of the Duma.

Lenin and the Kulaks

The food shortages which had plagued the Provisional Government grew worse after the October/November Revolution. The Provisional Government had had too many scruple and too little power successfully to carry out their attempted levies of grain. The Bolsheviks had more power and no scruples. To supply the city proletariat, chief supporter of the Bolsheviks, with food was an absolute necessity if the Party was to retain power. Food levies were extended and enforced by armed gangs from the cities, operating under Bolshevik leadership and sanction. "Committees of the Poor" were organized among the peasants to co-operate with these "food-requisitioning squads" in a deliberate class war against the middle class and richer peasants (kulaks).

The following telegram, sent by Lenin to the Zadonsk Soviet, is typical of his ruthlessness and of the methods employed. The original copy is in the Central Lenin Museum.

Take most vigorous action against kulaks and their allies, the Left Socialist-Revolutionary swine. Issue an appeal to the poor peasants. Organize them. Request help from Elets. The kulak bloodsuckers must be unmercifully suppressed. Wire reply.

Lenin

Lenin's Report for 1921

Lenin, as Chairman of the Council of People's Commissars, delivered a report on "the state of the nation" to the Ninth Congress of Soviets which met in December 1921. The major points of his report were printed in poster form for wide distribution. An official Soviet translation of this poster is given below. The original poster is in the Central Lenin Museum.

1. THE INTERNATIONAL SITUATION

A certain equilibrium has been achieved, but it is rather unstable.

The first commandment in our policy, the first lesson to be drawn from this year of the work of our government, a lesson which must be mastered by all workers and peasants, is: be vigilant, remember that we are surrounded by people, classes, governments, which openly proclaim their deepest hatred for us. Therefore we shall always be but a hair's breadth from new invasion.

2. ECONOMIC RELATIONS WITH EUROPE

In 1921 (the first year of trade with foreign countries) we made great progress. If we take the three years, 1918, 1919, and 1920, we shall find that our total imports for this period were a little over 17 million poods [612,000,000 tons]; in 1921 we imported 50 million poods [1,800,000,000 tons] or three times as much as in all three preceding years together.

3. OUR INTERNAL SITUATION AND THE NEW ECONOMIC POLICY

The most fundamental and basic question is [sic] the relations between the working class and the peasantry, the alliance between the working class and the peasantry.

No other economic bond is possible between the peasantry and the workers, that is, between agriculture and industry, than exchange, trade. The substitution of the food tax for the surplus-appropriation [food-levies] system is the essence of our economic policy, and that essence is a very simple one. In the absence of a flourishing large-scale industry capable of immediately satisfying the peasants with its products, there is no other way for the alliance of workers and peasants, for the gradual development of a powerful alliance, than the way of trade.

4. THE FAMINE AND AGRICULTURE

About 75% of the winter crop area in the famine-stricken provinces, 102% in the provinces partially affected by the crop failure, 123% in the producing provinces and 126% in the consuming provinces were sown in the autumn. This at any rate shows that, devilishly hard as the conditions were, we did give some assistance to the peasantry in extending the crop area and combating famine. With conditions as they are now, we are entitled to believe, without the least exaggeration and without fear of error, that in the matter of supplying seed for spring sowing, we shall also render appreciable assistance to the peasantry. I repeat, this assistance will by no means be complete. We shall by no means be able to meet all requirements. That must be made clear. All the more, therefore, must we exert every effort to extend this assistance.

5. THE FOOD TAX

Tortured as we were by imperialist war and by civil war, and hounded by the ruling classes of every country, there is and can be no way out of our situation without the greatest hardships. And therefore we must say quite distinctly, without evading the bitter truth, and affirm it in the name of the congress to all our people in the localities, although they realize the hardships: "Comrades, the very existence of the Soviet Republic, our very modest plan of restoring transport and industry, will wholly depend on our fulfilling the general program of food supply. Therefore one hundred per cent collection of the food tax is absolutely essential."

6. FUEL IS THE FOUNDATION OF INDUSTRY

As regards the supply of wood fuel, I must again say: "Comrades, the utmost exertion of effort in your localities in this field must be the slogan!"

The total output of the Donets Basin in 1920 was 272 million poods [9,792,000,000 tons]; in 1921 it was 350 million poods [12,600,000,000 tons].

7. IRON AND STEEL

Difficult as our position is, we can here observe great progress. In the first half of 1921 we produced 70,000 poods [2,520,000 tons] of pig iron, in

October 130,000 poods [4,680,000 tons], and in November 270,000 poods [8,720,000 tons], or nearly four times as much.

8. ELECTRIFICATION

In 1918 and 1919 together, the number of power stations started was 51 with an aggregate capacity of 3,500 kilowatts. In 1920 and 1921, the number of stations started was 221, with an aggregate capacity of 12,000 kilowatts. Our output of peat in 1920 reached 93 million poods [3,348,000,000 tons], in 1921 it reached 139 million [5,004,000,000]— the only sphere, I should say, in which we have left pre-war figures far behind.

9. TRADE IS THE TOUCHSTONE OF THE NEW ECONOMIC LIFE

Productive forces have already begun to develop, thanks to the New Economic Policy. There is one other aspect of the matter — we must learn. And therein lies the significance of the New Economic Policy. Learn! This learning is a very hard matter. It is not at all like hearing lectures at school and passing examinations. Every attempt to evade this task, every attempt to close our eyes, and to pretend that this is not our affair, would be most criminal and most dangerous conceit — Communist and trade union conceit.

10. THE REFORM OF THE VECHEKA [Cheka]

This institution was our avenging sword against the innumerable plots, the innumerable attempts on the existence of Soviet government made by people who are infinitely stronger than we are. That is the merit of the Vecheka. But at the same time we definitely declare that we must reform the Vecheka, define its functions and jurisdiction and limit it to political tasks. The problem which we are tackling this year, and which up to now we have been tackling with such difficulty and so inadequately — the union of the workers and the peasants in a durable economic alliance — even amidst the utmost ruin and want, that problem we have solved correctly, the line we have adopted is correct — about that there can be no doubt.

Lenin's Electrification Scheme

The development and wide distribution of electric power was one of Lenin's pet dreams. Speaking of it at the Eighth Party Congress in 1920 he said: "Communism is the Soviet government plus the electrification of the whole country."— a statement which clearly indicates the importance Lenin attached to this matter. In 1921, Lenin wrote the following letter to G. M. Krzhizhanovsky, an old Bolshevik who was then Chairman of the State Planning Commission and a member of the Party's Central Committee. This is an official Soviet translation of the original letter which is in the Central Lenin Museum.

Gleb Maximilianovich,

The following idea has occurred to me.

We must make propaganda for electricity. How?

Not only by word, but by example.

What does this mean? It means, above all, popularizing it. For this purpose a plan must be worked out at once for the installation of electric light in every house in the RSFSR.

That will be a long business, for it will be a long time before we have enough wire and the rest for 20,000,000 (—40,000,000) lamps.

Nevertheless, we need a plan at once, if only for a few years ahead.

That is the first thing.

The second thing is that an abridged plan must be worked out at once, and then — this is the third thing, and the most important — we must promptly kindle both emulation and initiative among the masses, so that they tackle the matter immediately.

Could not a plan (approximate) be worked out for this purpose at once on the following lines?

1) Electric light to be installed in all rural district centers (10,000–15,000) within one year.

2) In all villages (500,000–1,000,000, probably not more than 750,000) within two years.

3) In the first place — village libraries and Soviets (two lamps each).

4) Secure the poles immediately in such and such a fashion. [sic]

5) Secure the insulators immediately yourselves (the porcelain factories, if I am not mistaken, are local ones and small?) in such and such a fashion. [sic]

6) Copper for the wire? Collect it yourselves in each county and rural district (a subtle hint at church bells and so on).

7) Organize the teaching of electricity on such and such lines. [sic]

Cannot something along these lines be devised, elaborated and decreed?

Yours, Lenin

Lenin's Description of Himself

All the delegates to the Tenth All-Russian Congress of the Russian Communist Party had to fill out a four-page party questionnaire. Lenin answered his questionnaire as follows. Lack of space makes it impossible to reproduce the form of the questionnaire in facsimile, but his answers are reproduced exactly except that where he used abbreviations which might not be familiar the entire words are given. The document is preserved in the Central Lenin Museum.

Name: Ulyanov (Lenin), Vladimir Ilyich

Party organization: Central Committee, Russian Communist Party, Moscow

Number of delegate mandate (voting/advisory): No. 21 advisory

By whom elected: Central Committee

No. of Party members represented at
   meeting at which elected: Central Committee — 19 members

Which All-Russian Party Congresses
   have you attended: All except July (August?) 1917

Date of birth — age: 1870 — 51 years

State of health: Good

Family — no. of members of dependents: Wife and sister

Nationality: Russian

Native tongue: Russian

Knowledge of other languages: English, German, French — poor, Italian —
   very poor

What parts of Russia do you know well,
   and how long have you lived there: Know Volga country where I was
   born best; lived there until age 17

Have you been abroad (when, where,
   how long): In a number of West European countries — 1895, 1900–1905,
   1908–1917

Military training: None

Education: Graduated (passed examination as externe) Petrograd University, Law Faculty, in 1891

Basic occupation before 1917: Writer

Special training: None

Occupation since 1917 besides Party, Soviet,
   trade union, and similar work: Besides those enumerated, only writing

What trade union do you belong to: Union of Journalists

Positions held since 1917: October 1917 to March 1921; Moscow; Council of
   People's Commissars and Council of Labor and Defense; Chairman

Present position: Since October 1917; Moscow; Chairman, Council of People's
   Commissars and Council of Labor and Defense.

How long have you been a member of the R.C.P. (Bolsheviks): Since 1894

Have you ever belonged to any other parties: No

Participation in the revolutionary movement before 1917: Illegal Social-
   Democratic circles; member of the Russian Social-Democratic
   Workers' Party since its foundation. 1892–3, Samarà; 1894–5, St.
   Petersburg; 1895–7, prison; 1898–1900, Siberia; 1900–05, abroad;
   1905–07, St. Petersburg; 1908–1917, abroad.

Penalties incurred for revolutionary
   activities: 1887 prison; 1895–7 prison; 1898–1900 Siberia; 1900 prison

How long in prison: Several days and 14 months
How long at hard labor: None
How long in exile: Three years
How long a political refugee: 9–10 years
Party functions since 1917: October 1917 to March 1921, Moscow, Member
     of the Central Committee
Present Party function: as above
Have you ever been tried by the courts of the RSFSR or of the Party: No
Date: 7 March, 1921
Signature of delegate: V. Ulyanov (Lenin)

"The Carrot and the Stick"

The rulers of the USSR have skillfully and successfully combined coercion and reward to increase industrial and labor productivity. The 1918 Russian Constitution made all citizens between the ages of fifteen and fifty-one years liable to compulsory labor. This legal compulsion was abolished after 1922 (except in cases of emergency), but it was decreed that a worker who had taken a job thereby became subject to the Labor Code which prohibited his leaving that employment without the specific consent of the head of the enterprise. This proved very difficult to enforce. Absenteeism remained a grave problem despite the decree against it issued in 1932 by the Party's Central Executive Committee and the Council of Peoples' Commissars of the USSR.

Excerpts from this decree are given below. According to an interpretation of this law in 1939, a single tardiness of over twenty minutes was equivalent to a day's absence and was therefore punishable by dismissal. The 1932 law was further modified by a decree of June 26, 1940 which provided that absenteeism should be punished by compulsory labor at reduced wages, but without confinement, at the offender's regular place of employment. The maximum sentence was six months.

The 1932 decree was published in Izvestiia *on November 16, 1932. It was signed by: Kalinin, Molotov, and Yenukidze; and was dated November 15th.*

Decree on Absenteeism

. . . the Central Executive Committee [of the Communist Party] and the Council of Peoples' Commissars resolve: . . .

2. To order that even in the case of one day's absence from work without sufficient reasons the worker shall be dismissed from the services of the factory or enterprise, and shall be deprived of the ration cards issued to him as a member of the staff of the factory or enterprise, and shall also be deprived of the use of lodgings which were given him in houses belonging to the factory or enterprise.

3. To instruct the governments of the federated republics to amend their Labor Codes to correspond with this.

* * * * *

Decree on Labor Passports

In an effort to reduce the distressingly high labor turnover, the Presidium of the Supreme Soviet of the USSR ordered the introduction of Labor Passports (or, Labor Workbooks) in 1938. The system was largely in abeyance immediately after the 1941–1945 War, but it was subsequently restored and expanded. The decree, which is self-explanatory, was issued on December 20, 1938, and was signed by Molotov and Bolshakov. It was published in Izvestiia *on December 21, 1938.*

. . . the Council of Peoples' Commissars decrees:

1. The introduction, effective January 15, 1939, of Labor Workbooks for workers and employees in all state and cooperative institutions and enterprises, [the Workbooks] to be issued by the administrative boards of the institutions (enterprises).
2. Labor books are to contain the following information about the owner, of the book: surname, name, and patronymic; age; education; profession; information about his work and about his movement from one institution (enterprise) to another, the causes of such shifts, and also [a record] of encouragements and rewards received.

. . .

6. Workers and employees must produce their Labor books for inspection by the managing board of the institution (enterprise) when signing on [for a job]. Managing boards have the right to employ workers and employees only if the latter present their Labor books. . . .
7. Managing boards . . . must complete the issuance of Labor books to their workers and employees by January 15, 1939. Persons signing on for work for the first time after that date must get a Labor book not later than five days thereafter.
8. Labor books must be kept for all workers and employees, including seasonal and temporary workers, who work . . . for more than five days.
9. The Labor book is to be kept by the management . . . and returned to the worker or employee on his dismissal.

. . . [*The decree also gave detailed instruction to management as to the information required to be shown on the Labor book; the time and manner of*

recording the data ("All entries in Labor books are to be made in ink.");
manner of issuance; manner of replacement if lost; etc.]

Decree Establishing the "Hero of Socialist Labor"

*Inducements designed to increase industrial and other production have in-
cluded: differential wages, bonuses, larger rations, better housing, and the
award of special honors and recognitions. The decree of the Presidium of the
Supreme Soviet of the USSR establishing one of the honors is printed below.
The decree was signed by Kalinin and Gorkin on December 27, 1938 and
was published in* Izvestiia *on the following day.*

1. To establish the supreme grade of distinction in the sphere of economic
   and cultural construction: the rank of Hero of Socialist Labor.
2. Persons promoted to the rank of Hero of Socialist Labor are simultaneously awarded the Order of Lenin.

Forced Labor

*Coercion to a different and much higher degree is manifested in the Soviet
system of forced labor Most impartial observers are now agreed that forced
labor is an integral part of the Soviet economic system. Whether that system
could operate without it is a matter for speculation. The record shows that
it has not so operated. A staggeringly large number of forced laborers have
been and currently are employed on a wide variety of projects including: the
construction and maintenance of roads, railroads, canals, harbor works, and
airfields; lumbering operations; mining; farming; and certain industries.*

*The following document, which reports the completion of a canal and the
preparation for turning the canal over to the government, is conclusive proof
of the use of forced labor on that project. Yagoda who signed the report was
tried and convicted of treason in 1938 (a portion of his testimony at his trial
is reprinted elsewhere in this collection) but at the time of the report, as his
signature indicates, he was second in command of the secret police. The
translation was made from a photograph of Yagoda's typescript letter which
was published in the Soviet magazine,* The USSR in Construction *(Moscow:
State Publishing House of Graphic Arts, 1933. No. 12.)*

To the Secretary of the C[entral] C[ommittee] of the C[ommunist]
P[arty] (B)[olshevik], Comrade Stalin:
To the Secretary of the C. C. of the C. P. (B), Comrade Kaganovich:

To the CHAIRMAN OF THE COUNCIL OF COMMISSARS OF THE USSR, Comrade
Molotov;

By a government decree of November, 1931, the OGPU was charged with
the construction of the White Sea-Baltic Canal, connecting the White Sea
with the Baltic, from Provonets on Lake Onega to Soroka on the White
Sea, a total distance of 227 kilometers. [141.05 miles.]

I now report that the work of construction, begun at the end of November,
1931, was completed on June 20, 1933, i.e., in one year and nine months.

The entire canal and all its equipment appeared, in preliminary tests and
observations, to be in good working order.

A total of 118 structures were built on the White Sea-Baltic Canal, as
follows: 19 locks, 15 dams, 12 spillways, 40 embankments, 32 canals —
length 40 klm.

For these the following amounts of work were required: [There follow
seven items concerning the amount of dirt moved, of concrete poured, etc.]

[?] A technical commission is examining the canal in preparation for its
acceptance by the government.

Asst. Head of the OGPU,

[s] Yagoda

26 June, 1933.

The Treason Trials

*There was a very extensive Party purge in 1933 which resulted in the expul-
sion of about a third of total Party membership. Purgings — equally drastic
or more so but not as extensive numerically — went on continuously through
1938. After the murder in December of 1934 of Stalin's close associate,
Sergius Kirov, there was a virtual reign of terror highlighted for the world
by several spectacular treason trials. Zinoviev, Kamenev, and several of their
colleagues were tried for treason, convicted and sentenced to imprisonment
in January 1935. In August of the next year, Zinoviev, Kamenev, and some
of their followers were again brought to trial on charges of conspiring under
the leadership of Trotsky for the overthrow of the regime with the help of
foreign Powers. The accused confessed to the charges and sixteen of them
were convicted and executed.*

*Radek, Pyatakov, and various other "old Bolsheviks" were tried for treason
and convicted in January of 1937. Thirteen of them were executed. Eight of
the top-ranking army officers, including Marshal Tukhachevski, were executed
as traitors after a secret court-martial in the following June. The sensational
climax came with the trials of Bukharin, Rykov, Yagoda, and eighteen others
in March of 1938. The accused were charged "of having on the instructions
of the intelligence services of foreign states hostile to the Soviet Union formed
a conspiratorial group named the 'bloc of Rights and Trotskyites' with the*

object of espionage . . . wrecking, diversionist and terrorist activities, under-mining the military power of the USSR . . . dismembering the USSR . . . for the benefit of the aforementioned foreign states, and, lastly, with the object of overthrowing the Socialist social and state system existing in the USSR and of restoring capitalism, of restoring the power of the bourgeoisie." The accused confessed their guilt in open court and, since several of them had been among the most prominent leaders of the Party, the event can only be described as sensationally spectacular.

No attempt is made here, explicitly or implicitly, to explain, interpret, or evaluate the purges and the trials. The excerpts by no means give anything like the whole story or even one side of it. They do, however, give some idea of the nature of the trials and of the confessions. The "last plea" of Bukharin is especially revealing. The Court was composed of four "Military Jurists" and the prosecuting attorney was Andrei Vishinsky, then Procurator-General of the USSR. The excerpts are from the authorized English version of the verbatim report of the trial which was published by the People's Commissariat of Justice of the USSR. The title is: Report of the Court Proceedings in the case of the Anti-Soviet "Bloc of Rights and Trotskyites" heard before the Military Collegium of the Supreme Court of the USSR, Moscow, March 2–13, 1938, etc. *Moscow: 1938. Pp. 401–405, 465–466, 476, 575–578, 777–778, 785–787.*

(Testimony of Bukharin.)

BUKHARIN: I cannot say "No" and I cannot deny that it did take place.

VYSHINSKY: So the answer is neither "Yes" nor "No"?

B . . .: Nothing of the kind because facts exist regardless of whether they are in anybody's mind. This is a problem of the reality of the outer world. I am no solipsist.

V . . .: So that regardless of whether this fact entered your mind or not, you as a plotter and a leader were aware of it?

B . . .: I was not aware of it.

V . . .: You were not?

B . . .: But I can say the following in reply to your question: since this thing was included in the general plan, I consider it likely, and since Rykov speaks of it in a positive fashion, I have no grounds for denying it.

V . . .: Consequently, it is a fact?

B . . .: From the point of view of mathematical probability it can be said, with very great probability, that it is a fact.

V . . .: So that you are unable to give a plain answer?

B . . .: Not "unable," but there are some questions that cannot be answered outright "Yes" or "No" as you are perfectly well aware from elementary logic.

V . . . : Allow me to ask Rykov again: was Bukharin aware of this fact?

RYKOV: I did not speak to him about it.

V . . . : Now, did Bukharin know about it or not?

R . . . : I personally think with mathematical probability that he should have known of it.

V . . . : That's clear. Accused Bukharin, were you aware that Karakhan was a participant in the conspiratorial group of Rights and Trotskyites?

BUKHARIN: I was.

V . . . : Were you aware that Karakhan was a German spy?

B . . . : No, I was not aware of that.

V . . . : (to Rykov) Were you aware, accused Rykov, that Karakhan was a German spy?

RYKOV: No, I was not.

V . . . : Were you aware that Karakhan was engaged in negotiations with certain German circles?

R . . . : Negotiations regarding the centre of the Rights?

V . . . : Yes, of course, regarding the centre of the Rights.

R . . . : Yes, yes.

V . . . : Treasonable negotiations?

R . . . : Treasonable.

V . . . : With whom did he conduct these negotiations, and with what institution?

R . . . : (No reply.)

V . . . : Well?

R . . . : I don't know that.

V . . . : In that case, tell the Court: what was the line of negotiations?

R . . . : The line was . . . At that time negotiations were conducted with German government circles.

V . . . : With which circles?

. . .

V . . . : . . . Can the conclusion be drawn from this that Karakhan, with your knowledge, engaged in negotiations with fascist circles regarding support for your treasonable activity on definite conditions? Was that the case?

R . . . : Yes.

V . . . : And what were the conditions?

R . . . : Firstly, a number of economic concessions, and secondly the so-called dismemberment of the USSR.

V . . . : What does that mean?

R . . . : That means the separation of the national republics and placing them under a protectorate, or making them dependent, formally not dependent, but actually dependent on . . .

V...: That is to say, territorial concessions?

R...: Of course.

V...: Did Karakhan propose in the name of your bloc to cede to the Germans some part of the territory of the Soviet Union?

R...: The matter was somewhat different.

V...: I speak of the meaning of these concessions.

R...: I myself did not meet Karakhan. I know this from Tomsky who explained it in my presence and in that of Bukharin.

V...: So that means Bukharin also knew? Allow me to ask Bukharin. Did you know?

BUKHARIN: I did.

RYKOV: He explained it this way: the German fascists accept these conditions, i.e., privileges as regards concessions, trade agreements, etc., but on their part they demand that the national republics be given the right to free separation.

V...: Well, and what does this mean?

R...: It was not what we had proposed. This was a new demand on the part of the Germans. In plain language, this means, of course, the dismemberment of the USSR.

V...: That is to say, handing over part of the USSR to the Germans?

R...: Of course.

V...: That is to say, you were aware that Karakhan, with your knowledge, engaged in negotiations with German circles to hand over part of the USSR. Precisely what part?

R...: There was no talk about that.

V...: Did your plan include a point about severing the Ukraine for the Germans, or did it not?

R...: I personally cannot say about the Ukraine, I repeat, not because we were against the Ukraine being severed.

V...: But were you against or for its being severed?

R...: There was simply no talk among us about the Ukraine being severed, and the question was not decided then.

V...: Did you have in view severing the Ukraine in favour of German fascism?

R...: Such was the formula.

V...: Not a formula — but in practice?

R...: In practice the question at issue could be that of Byelorussia.

V...: And of the Ukraine?

R...: No. We could not decide this question without the consent of the Ukrainian counter-revolutionary organizations.

V...: Then I address myself to the accused Bukharin. Did you in 1934 engage in negotiations with Radek on this subject?

BUKHARIN: Not negotiations, but conversations.

V...: All right, conversations. Did they take place or not?

B...: They did, only not about that.

V...: Then about what?

B...: Radek told me of his negotiations with Trotsky, that Trotsky had engaged in negotiations with the German fascists regarding territorial consessions in return for help to the counter-revolutionary organizations.

V...: That's it, that's it.

B...: I then objected to Radek.

V...: Did Radek tell you that on Trotsky's instructions the Ukraine was to be ceded, yielded to the Germans?

B...: I definitely remember about the Ukraine.

V...: Were there such conversations or not?

B...: Yes.

V...: And about the Far East?

B...: About the Ukraine I definitely remember; there was talk of other regions, but I do not remember which.

V...: You testified as follows: "Trotsky, while urging the intensification of terrorism, yet considers the main chance for the advent of the bloc to power to be the defeat of the USSR in a war against Germany and Japan at the cost of territorial concessions (the Ukraine to the Germans, and the Far East to the Japanese.)" Was that so?

B...: Yes it was.

V...: That is to say, these are the concessions?

B...: I was not in agreement.

V...: Further it states: "I did not object to the idea of an understanding with Germany and Japan, but did not agree with Trotsky on the extent."

B...: Read the next phrase as well, where the extent and character are explained.

V...: I have read and want to speak about this. [sic]

B...: I said I was against territorial concessions.

V...: No. I want to speak about this. And so Radek told you that Trotsky gave instructions to cede the Ukraine to the Germans. Did he say this?

B...: He did, but I did not consider Trotsky's instructions as binding on me.

V...: Was Rykov aware of this conversation with Radek or not?

RYKOV: Whom are you asking?

V...: Bukharin.

BUKHARIN: I don't remember whether I told Rykov.

V...: And Rykov?

RYKOV: He did not tell me.

V...: Consequently you were unaware of Bukharin's conversation with Radek?

RYKOV: (No reply.)

V...: But did he talk privately to Bukharin?

RYKOV: Who?

V...: Radek. Accused Bukharin, how did Radek talk to you? What post did you occupy at that time?

BUKHARIN: It is not a matter of the post.

V...: What post did you occupy?

B...: I was the editor of "Izvestia."

* * * * *

(Examination of Ossinsky.)

THE PRESIDENT: Accused Bukharin, have you any questions to put to witness Ossinsky?

BUKHARIN: I have. In the first place, I should like to ask Ossinsky whether he could tell us something about the central group of "Left Communists" in Petersburg. Whom did it consist of?

THE PRESIDENT: This question has no bearing on the conspiracy.

B...: It has because inasmuch as negotiations were carried on ...

THE PRESIDENT: We are now concerned with the accused Bukharin.

B...: Why I am appearing here as a representative of the group of "Left Communists" and its centre. When we are asked about the Right and Leftist centre, that concerns us, but if it relates to the centre of the group of "Left Communists," we cannot talk. ...

THE PRESIDENT: In any event the case concerns Nikolai Ivanovich Bukharin.

B...: Citizen the Procurator stated that this was not the case because, owing to the lapse of the time limit prescribed by law, there is no case.

THE PRESIDENT: Accused Bukharin, do you want to put questions to witness Ossinsky?

B...: Yes, I do. I want to ask witness Ossinsky whether Ossinsky was a member of the central group of "Left Communists."

OSSINSKY: Of course I was.

B...: I want to find out from witness Ossinsky whether he wrote the general theses which served as the main platform of the "Left Communists" in that period.

O...: Quite right.

B...: Together with whom did you write those theses?

O...: Together with Bukharin, Radek and Preobrazhensky.

B...: And who was the author of the basic text of these theses?

O...: The author of the basic text was Ossinsky.

VYSHINSKY: And who edited it?

O...: It was edited by all those participating, including Nikolai Ivanovich Bukharin.

B...: Then I should like to ask witness Ossinsky whether he was in Moscow on the eve of the October uprising.

O . . .: Yes, on the eve of the October uprising I was in Moscow.

B . . .: I should also like to know if witness Ossinsky was in Moscow during the October uprising.

THE PRESIDENT: What need is there for these questions?

B . . .: I need them for my defence, because later on I will have no opportunity to get answers to these questions.

VYSHINSKY: If the accused Bukharin states that he needs these questions for his defence and since, according to our laws, each accused has the right to defence in its full scope, I plead that this question be not ruled out.

B . . .: In this case I plead for putting again all the questions which the Court has ruled out before.

THE PRESIDENT: Accused Bukharin, do not engage in obstructing the work of the Court.

V . . .: If the accused Bukharin has need of putting all these questions for his defence, I, as Prosecutor, do not object to these questions being put here.

THE PRESIDENT: But the Court objects to these questions being put here, because they have no bearing on the case.

V . . .: I submit to the decision of the Court.

B . . .: I submit, too.

* * * * *

(Examination of Mantsev.)

MANTSEV: The attempt [an explosion on the premises of the Moscow Committee of the Communist Party] was directed against the Moscow Committee of the Communist Party.

VYSHINSKY: And was Bukharin the secretary of the Moscow Committee at that time?

M . . .: He was not the secretary.

V . . .: Was he present at this meeting of the Moscow Committee?

M . . .: In my opinion, he was not.

BUKHARIN: What do you mean, I was not present? I was contused during the explosion.

M . . .: It is possible he was there, I do not remember it.

* * * * *

(Examination of Yagoda.)

THE PRESIDENT: Have you any questions, Comrade Procurator?

VYSHINSKY: Of course. Hence, if we sum up your explanations, we may say the following: First — that you plead guilty to the fact that your participation in the underground work of the Rights was of long standing.

YAGODA: Yes.

V...: Second — that you plead guilty to having been one of the leaders of the underground "bloc of Rights and Trotskyites."

Y...: Yes, I do.

V...: Third — that, together with this bloc, you pursued the aim of overthrowing the Soviet government and restoring capitalism in the USSR.

Y...: Yes, I do. We set ourselves the task of seizing the Kremlin..

V...: That for the purpose of overthrowing the government you chose the method of an insurrection timed primarily for the outbreak of war. Is that so?

Y...: No, it is not so. An armed insurrection — that was nonsense. Only these babblers here could think of that.

V...: Well, what were you thinking of?

Y...: Of a "palace coup."

V...: That is to say, of a violent coup, carried through by a small group of plotters?

Y...: Yes, the same as they did.

V...: Timing it preferably for a military onslaught on the USSR by foreign powers, or did you have various plans?

Y...: There was one plan, namely, to seize the Kremlin. The time was of no importance.

V...: Was it your point of view that it was expedient in case of war to prepare and secure the defeat of the USSR?

Y...: That was the point of view of the bloc, and therefore it was mine too.

V...: Do you also admit being guilty of espionage work?

Y...: No, I do not admit being guilty of this activity.

V...: But you yourself have said that several spies were at work under your direct leadership.

Y...: Yes, I admit that.

V...: Did you know they were spies?

Y...: Yes, I did.

        •   •   •

V...: And do you admit being guilty of organizing and effecting terrorists acts: first — the murder of Comrade Kirov on the orders and instructions of the bloc?

Y...: I admit being guilty of complicity in the murder.

V...: Do you admit being guilty of complicity in the murder or in causing the death of Menzhinsky?

Y...: I do.

V...: Do you admit of being guilty of organizing the murder of Kuibyshev?

Y...: I do.

V...: Do you admit being guilty of the murder of Alexei Maximovich Gorky?

Y...: I do.

V...: I have no more questions.

THE PRESIDENT: Have Counsel for Defence any questions?

COUNSEL FOR DEFENCE KOMMODOV: Does the accused Yagoda confirm the testimony he gave at the preliminary investigation with reference to his meetings with Pletnev?

Y...: I said that.

K...: Is the same true as regards meetings with Kazakov?

Y...: I confirmed that.

K...: I have no more questions.

COUNSEL FOR DEFENCE BRAUDE: Who conceived the idea of death from disease?

Y...: I have said — Yenukidze.

BRAUDE: Allow me to ask you, what methods did you employ to secure Levin's consent to commit these terrorist acts?

Y...: In any case not such as he described here.

BRAUDE: You yourself went into detail about this at the preliminary investigation. Do you confirm this part of your testimony?

Y...: It is exaggerated, but that doesn't matter.

BRAUDE: I have no more questions.

* * * * *

(A portion of Bukharin's "last plea.")

I shall now speak of myself, of the reasons for my repentance. Of course, it must be admitted that incriminating evidence plays a very important part. For three months I refused to say anything. Then I began to testify. Why? Because while in prison I made a reevaluation of my entire past. For when you ask yourself: "If you must die, what are you dying for?"— an absolutely black vacuity suddenly arises before you with startling vividness. There was nothing to die for, if one wanted to die unrepented. And, on the contrary, everything positive that glistens in the Soviet Union acquires new dimensions in a man's mind. This in the end disarmed me completely and led me to bend my knees before the Party and the country. And when you ask yourself: "Very well, suppose you do not die; suppose by some miracle you remain alive, again what for? Isolated from everybody, an enemy of the people, in an inhuman position, completely isolated from everything that constitutes the essence of life. . . . [sic]" And at once the same reply arises. And at such moments, Citizens Judges, everything personal, all the personal incrustation, all the rancour, pride, and a number of other things, fall away, disappear. And, in addition, when the reverberations of the broad international struggle reach your ear, all this in its entirety does its work, and the result is the complete internal moral victory of the USSR over its kneeling opponents. . . .

The point, of course, is not this repentance, or my personal repentance in particular. The Court can pass its verdict without it. The confession of the accused is not essential. The confession of the accused is a medieval principal of jurisprudence. But here we also have the internal demolition of the forces of counter-revolution. And one must be a Trotsky not to lay down one's arms.

* * * * *

(A portion of Yagoda's "last plea.")

I want to correct the Procurator and make an objection on a part of the charges which he has made. . . . the Procurator is not right in considering me a member of the centre of the bloc. . . . I did not take part in the decisions of the bloc. . . . I was informed *post factum* . . . . Rykov . . . made the decisions.

. . . the Procurator announced it proved beyond doubt that I was a spy. This is not true. I am not a spy and have never been one. . .

It is not only untrue to say that I was an organizer but it is untrue to say that I was an accomplice in the murder of Kirov. I committed an exceedingly grave violation of duty . . . , but I was not an accomplice. . . .

My objections on these points are not an attempt to belittle the significance of my crimes. My defence would have no practical meaning here, because for each millionth part of my crimes, as the Procurator says, he wants my head. I staked my head and I surrender it, but I want to reduce my enormous debt to the Procurator. I know what my sentence will be, I have been awaiting it for a whole year. In the last hours or days of my life I do not want to play the hypocrite and say that I want to die. This is not true. I have committed heinous crimes. I realize this. It is hard to live after such crimes, it is hard to sit in prisons for tens of years. But it is terrible to die with such a stigma. Even from behind the bars I would like to see the further flourishing of the country which I betrayed.

Citizens Judges! I directed vast construction jobs — the canals. [See the document quoted on p.　.] Now these canals are the adornments of our era. I do not dare ask to be sent there even for the most arduous work. Citizens Judges! Our laws and our Court differ greatly from the laws and the courts of all bourgeois countries. . . . Our laws are based on a different principle, our Court is a different court. The Soviet Court differs from bourgeois courts in the fact that this Court, when trying a criminal case, does not base itself on laws as on a dogma, but is guided by revolutionary expediency. Our country is mighty, strong as never before, purged of spies, diversionists, terrorists and other scum, and I ask you, Citizens Judges, in passing your sentence on me, to consider whether there is revolutionary expediency in my execution now? . . . I address myself to the Court with the plea: forgive me if you can.

The Supreme Soviet of the USSR

According to the Stalin (1936) Constitution, the highest legislative body in the USSR is the bicameral Supreme Soviet. One chamber, the Union Soviet — elected in the proportion of one deputy for every 300,000 citizens, is charged with taking the federal view of matters brought before it; that is, of acting on behalf of the USSR as a whole. The other chamber is the Soviet of Nationalities which is charged with representing the views of the various national groups. Each Union Republic elects twenty-five deputies to this Soviet; each Autonomous Republic, eleven; each Autonomous Region, five; and each small national minority, one. The two chambers are co-equal; either may initiate legislation and both must consent to it. Certain powers are exercised jointly: for example, the election or appointment of the Presidium and the Council of Ministers. Some matters are presented in joint sittings, but each chamber also meets and acts separately. Both have parallel committees and commissions (e.g., of the Budget) which report to their respective Soviets.

The normal life of the Supreme Soviet is four years, although that of the first one (elected in December, 1937) was extended because of the war. The second Supreme Soviet was elected in 1946; the third, in 1950. There are two regular sessions each year. These vary in length but are usually less than a week. When the Supreme Soviet is not in session — and that is fifty or fifty-one weeks out of every year — the Presidium has full authority to issue decrees, ratify treaties, appoint and dismiss ministers and other officials. The Presidium also has the power to convene and to dissolve the Supreme Soviet, and to arrange elections to that body. The Presidium further has the power to declare martial law, and to interpret laws made by the Soviet even when that body is in session. The interim decrees, appointments, and dismissals have to be reported to and ratified by the Supreme Soviet. So far the Soviets have unanimously approved all actions taken by the Presidiums.

The brevity of the sessions, already noted; the size of the body; and the complexity of its agendas are all revealing as to the actual power and place of the Supreme Soviet. The first Supreme Soviet had 1,143 deputies; the second, 1,339; and the third, 1,317. The second session of the first Supreme Soviet had eight items on its agenda including: the budget, a complicated act establishing the judicial system, the election of a Supreme Court, and approval of numerous interim decrees and changes in personnel. These matters were all settled in eight working days. The first 1948 session of the Second Supreme Soviet occupied a total of six days. It dealt with the budget and with all interim edicts, appointments, and dismissals. These were typical sessions. The nature of the "debates" and actions may be judged from the material given below all of which is quoted from the authorized English version of the verbatim reports of the second session held in 1938.

Adopting the Federal Budget

At the first joint sitting of the two houses in the second (1938) session (10 August, 1938) "Comrade Zverev, People's Commissar of Finance of the USSR" presented a fourteen to fifteen thousand word report on the "Unified State Budget." The joint session then adjourned and the two houses considered the budget in their separate sessions. The matter was introduced in each chamber by a further report of some seven thousand words delivered by the Chairmen of the respective Budget Commissions. Each Soviet then devoted three sittings (11, 13, and 14 August) to "debates" on the budget. Fifteen deputies (out of 569) and two administrators spoke in the Union Soviet; fifteen deputies (out of 574) and one administrator spoke in the Soviet of Nationalities. Zverev and the respective Chairmen of the Budget Commissions then "replied to the debate." The speeches, all but one of which are quoted in full, are not quite typical because they contain certain criticisms. In fact, they were selected to illustrate the nature of the criticisms as well as the general character of the "debates."

Speech of A. F. Nikanorov of the Archangel Area and Region in the Union Soviet.

Comrades, members of the Supreme Soviet. The unified State Budget of the USSR for the year 1938, presented by the Government to the Second Session of the Supreme Soviet for consideration and approval, will unquestionably be approved and ratified by the Session of the Supreme Soviet. It will unquestionably be fully approved by the millions of the people of our great country. This Budget, both in its total, aggregating 125,184,200,000 rubles, and in its structure, is a truly popular Budget of the country of victorious socialism.

Our Budget is a striking manifestation of how, under the leadership of the Communist Party, under the leadership of our great Stalin, the Soviet people are firmly and confidently marching towards Communism.

The People's Commissar of Finance, in his report, and the deputies who spoke here were right in stressing the sharp distinction between the Budget of the Land of the Soviets, where the people are free, and the Budgets of the capitalist countries, where the working people are kept under the yoke of exploitation and oppression.

It is necessary, comrades, that we ourselves, the whole people and our class brothers abroad should remember that quite recently our country was under the yoke of an autocracy of landlords and capitalists. This found its reflection also in the Budget of tsarist Russia. In an article entitled, "Apropos of the State Revenue Roll," written in 1902, Validimir Ilyich Lenin analysed the Budget of the tsarist government drawn up by Witte and exposed the entire system of robbing the people. In discussing the fact that one of the items of revenue was foreign loans, Lenin showed that the tsarist Budget reflected the policy of enslaving a great country to foreign capital.

As to our Budget, not a single kopeck of its huge total goes into the pocket of any sort of capitalists, not a single kopeck goes to pay any loans advanced by foreign capitalists, as was the case in tsarist Russia.

In the same article Lenin showed what huge funds were assigned in the Budget for the maintenance of "personages of the imperial family."

At the same time all that the Budget of the Tsarist government provided for in expenditures through the Ministry of Public Education, which Lenin dubbed the "Ministry of Obscuration," amounted to 36,000,000 rubles. If the expenditures made through the various departments are included, the allocations for education comprised a little over 4 per cent of the entire Budget of tsarist Russia. At present we are expending 20,000,000,000 rubles, or 17 per cent of the Budget, on public education.

In those years in tsarist Russia all the schools, from lowest to highest, were attended by a little over 6,000,000 people, i.e., less than 50 for every 1,000 population. In 1938, however, in the USSR the elementary and intermediate schools are attended by 33,300,000 children, and approximately 2,000,000 students receive instruction in the higher educational establishments, training colleges, and schools for adults. And think, comrades, of all the people taking various kinds of courses! Here, for example, is our Archangel Region, which formerly was a place of exile for revolutionaries. In the city of Archangel alone there are 50,000 people, and in the region as a whole approximately 200,000 people who are studying.

I am deliberately comparing today's data with those referring to the years of the Russo-Japanese War. Today, when the Japanese military, not without the knowledge and approval of other imperialists, are trying to invade the Land of the Soviets, we may point to the vast distance which we have travelled under the leadership of the Party of Lenin and Stalin.

27,000,000,000 rubles for the People's Commissariat of Defence and the People's Commissariat of the Navy! A Budget aggregating 125,000,000,000 rubles! The moral and political unity of the 170,000,000 people of the Soviet Union.

These are our arguments, which shall serve as a stern warning to the aggressors.

It was with pride and joy that Lenin, after the revolution, announced to the delegates who attended the Congress of the Comintern that the Soviet state had accumulated 20,000,000 rubles in gold for the realization of an advance in industry. And in 1933 Comrade Stalin announced in his report to the January Plenum of the Central Committee of the CPSU that the Party had brought about not only the restoration of our industry, but also its rapid development, by using our internal resources, without usurious loans and credits from abroad.

Since then 350,000,000,000 rubles have been expended on strengthening the might of our country, on the development of industry, the collectivization of agriculture, the advancement of culture. We see the great victories of Socialist industrialization and of Socialist agriculture throughout our vast country, from end to end, from sea to sea.

In our Archangel Region, on the shores of the White, Barents and Kara Seas, in the regions of the Far North, Socialist life is seething like a hot spring, just as in every other part of our great country. This is attested to by our mechanized sawmills — as, for instance, the V. M. Molotov Mill — the Sulphate Works now under construction in Archangel, the paper mills, the 2,165 collective farms, representing 96.3 per cent of all peasant households in the region, the hundreds of mechanized timbering stations, the thousands of tractors, harvester combines and other agricultural machinery cultivating our fields.

We, the deputies to the Supreme Soviet from the Archangel Region, are of the opinion that the economic development of the North can and should be further advanced, and that it can and should be done more vigorously.

Timber is the principal resource of the Archangel Region. But the timber industry includes not only timber cutting and floating, but also the wood-chemical industry; however, the wood-chemical industry is still very little developed in our region. This is the result of the activity of the wreckers who for a long time had a hand in the administration of the region.

Valuable timber waste, which furnishes the raw material for chemical products and the production of furniture, remained unutilized in our region. Moreover, this waste represents a constant danger of causing fires. It is necessary to build not only large factories and enterprises, but also small factories and special shops for the utilization of this waste.

Timber is not the only item of wealth of the Archangel Region. We are also very rich in water. We have the greatest possibilities for the development of fisheries and of the canning industry. But these are very little developed. In some districts of the region, particularly in the extreme north, in Pechora, Bolshaya Zemlaya and Kanin-Timan districts, there are rich deposits of coal and other minerals. The Soviet tundra is not only a pasture for deer; it can become a base for the development of powerful industries. The working people of the Archangel Region — Russians, Nentsy and Komi — will do everything the Party and the Government demand in order to get the lights of Socialist industry to outshine the lights of the aurora borealis.

Under the conditions prevailing in the Archangel Region, agriculture occupies a comparatively small place in the economic life. But there are great possibilities for its development, since the harvest yields are fairly stable and high. The Archangel Region is the home of the fine Kholmogory breed of cattle, and we can achieve the introduction of this breed on a larger scale in other parts of the Soviet Union.

We are rich not only in an economic respect, but also in that we have remarkable people. There is not a single branch of economy in which we could not find people who are known not only in the Region, but throughout the country.

The enemies of the people tried to retard the development of our Region. They have been exposed by the organs of the People's Commissariat of Internal Affairs, directed by Nicolai Ivanovich Yezhov, and, on the whole, have been weeded out.

The capitalists are preparing to attack the Soviet Union. The working people of Archangel will never forget the hard labour prisons which the interventionists instituted on the islands of Mudyug and Yokanga in 1918–19, and in which many Soviet people perished. Like the whole Soviet people, the working people of our region — Russians, Nentsy, and Komi — will rise at a moment's notice to the defence of our sacred Soviet borders!

It will be absolutely necessary in the Budgets of the coming years to provide for an even more rapid development of the country of the North, for an even more rapid development of mechanization in timber cutting and floating. But in the current year some funds could also be provided for improvements in Archangel. The question of the utilization of timber waste should be tackled at once.

A few critical remarks concerning some People's Commissariats. These remarks are based on the experience of the work of the Budget Commission, of which I am a member.

First, with regard to the work of the People's Commissariat of Finance. When we discussed questions of estimates and plans, when we discussed special financial assessments, the officials of the finance organs showed that they knew their business. But when it came to the question of control, of checking up on how the finance organs are directing the carrying out of the Budget provisions, we established the fact that this work was unsatisfactory. The finance organs must draw from this very serious conclusions for themselves. We have impermissably big arrears in the collection of taxes from the rural population, particularly from the individual peasants. As for the collection of taxes from persons of the so-called liberal professions, it is particularly badly organized. In July 1938 the Budget Commission could not even get an answer to the question as to the sum of the arrears on this item in 1937.

The People's Commissariat of Finance has given an unsatisfactory account of itself in the work of developing the savings bank system. Most of the savings banks and the greatest part of the depositors are in the cities, while in the rural districts the savings bank system is very little developed.

The People's Commissariat of Finance has not been paying proper attention to the question of state insurance. With good work we should be able in the immediate future to double and treble the number of citizens insuring their lives and property.

The Government must demand that the People's Commissariat of Finance and other People's Commissariats should definitely improve their work in drawing up their Budgets. We cannot tolerate a situation when plans of financing are drawn up before the plans dealing with production, labour productivity, utilization of equipment, etc.

When the Budget Commission examined the Budget of the People's Commissariat of Agricultural Stocks, this Commissariat appeared in a very unfavorable light. We know that our country is very rich in grain, that in the rural districts there is plenty of grain and flour. We know that the population now wants to get a higher grade flour, that the population demands better work on the part of the trading organizations and the Commissariat of Agricultural Stocks. Instead of improving the work, the People's Commissariat of Agricultural Stocks proposed to the Budget Commission to curtail the plan of realization of flour, which also meant curtailment of receipts from the turnover tax. This was wrong, for the Budget Commission had information from a number of towns about difficulties in satisfying the demand for higher grade flour.

The shortcomings in the work of other People's Commissariats have already been mentioned. But it would be wrong, while criticizing the People's Commissariats, to pass by those shortcomings in the work of securing 100 per cent fulfillment of the Budget provisions for which we, the members of the Supreme Soviet, and the local Party and Soviet organizations are responsible. For instance, in our region the fulfillment of the Budget provisions in the first half of the current year was as follows: revenues 52.3 per cent, expenditures 49.3 per cent. At first glance, this seems not bad; but a closer scrutiny of the various items reveals that the revenue from local industry amounted to only 29 per cent of the estimate for the year. This is intolerable, and we, the leading workers of the region, are no less to blame for it than the workers of the People's Commissariats, for the Archangel Region has very extensive possibilities for the development of local industry.

A few words about the People's Commissariat of the Timber Industry. Its share in the Budget revenues is not a large one, but, as has been currently pointed out both in speeches and in the press, its work is unsatisfactory. We, the leading workers of the Archangel Region, cannot disclaim responsibility for the state of the timber industry. We are now bending our efforts to ensure the carrying out of the Government order about discarding log-floating on the Northern Dvina. Perhaps some of the comrades do not know what this log-floating represents. It means that the timber is floated not in rafts, but in single logs. On such a fine river as the Northern Dvina, these logs have caused great damage to our economy: steam boats have been smashed up through collisions with them, and an enormous amount of timber has been carried out into the White Sea. In 1932 approximately 2,000,000 cubic metres of timber drifted away into the sea. This year we shall make sure that our timber does not drift away into the White Sea.

Comrades, under the leadership of our Government, under the leadership of the Communist Party, the people of our country distribute the wealth they create along such channels as are necessary in the interests of Socialism. Consequently, the fulfillment of each item in the Budget depends upon all of us, upon every Soviet citizen. We members of the Supreme Soviet must remember Comrade Stalin's words about the duties of deputies and we shall have to improve our work for fulfillment of the provisions of the Budget.

Comrades, the approval of the unified state Budget for 1938 by the Supreme Soviet of the USSR will signify our full endorsement of the foreign and internal policy of the Soviet Government and the Communist Party. The approval of the state Budget by the Supreme Soviet will again demonstrate the unity and solidarity of the millions of the multi-national Soviet people, confidently marching towards communism under the leadership of our Party, under the leadership of the greatest man of our epoch — Comrade Stalin. (Applause.)

* * * * *

Speech of A. G. Smagina (Stalinabad City Area, Tadzhik SSR) in the Soviet of Nationalities.

Comrades, members of the Supreme Soviet. The state Budget of the USSR for 1938 submitted to the Session displays in bold relief the growing might of our Socialist country. Our Budget is evidence of tremendous victories in all spheres of Socialist construction. The Soviet people have won these victories under the leadership of the Bolshevik Party and our beloved leader, Comrade Stalin. (Applause.)

We are discussing the state Budget at a tense moment in the international situation. The fascists are becoming more brazen every day. The Japanese militarists are striving with might and main to involve Japan in a war with the Soviet Union. But the Japanese *samurai* have made a big mistake. Our heroic Workers' and Peasants' Red Army has taught them a good lesson. Our mighty Red Army is battle-tried, it defends the vital interests of the working people. It is invincible because it was formed and reared by the great leaders, Lenin and Stalin. (Loud and prolonged applause.)

Let the fascists and their hirelings be advised that our Red Army, led by one of Comrade Stalin's closest comrades, by the First Marshal of the Soviet

Union, Klim Voroshilov (loud applause) will make havoc of the enemy on his own territory. Comrades, I am working as an aviatrix in the civil air service. At the first summons of the Party and the Government I am ready together with the whole Soviet people to go to the defence of our country, and am prepared at any moment to change over to a war plane for the defence of the Soviet Union. (Prolonged applause.)

The moral and political unity of the Soviet people was made particularly evident to the world during the elections to the Supreme Soviet of the USSR and the Supreme Soviets of the Union and autonomous republics. Let the fascists and their hirelings be advised that all the Soviet people are united as never before around the Bolshevik Party and are infinitely devoted to Comrade Stalin, their leader and teacher. (Loud and prolonged applause.)

In the Budget, as is quite right, great attention is given to questions of defence of our country. There is no doubt that the Soviet of Nationalities will unanimously approve and sanction the 27,000,000,000 rubles which the Budget provides for the defence of the Land of Socialism.

Comrades, before the Great Socialist Revolution, the working people of Tadzhikistan were ruthlessly oppressed by the tsarist government and the Emir of Bokhara. The people of Tadzhikistan lived under a double yoke, in bondage and poverty. The working population of Tadzhikistan were prey to extortion and tyranny. Only one half of one per cent of the population could read and write. Tadzhikistan has been completely transformed in the two Stalin Five Year Plans. Scores of universities and intermediate schools have been opened. The republic has a total of 4,000 schools, attended by over 200,000 children. Over 250,000 adults are studying too, in the republic. Now 70 per cent of the population of Tadzhikistan have become literate. Expenditure on public education has increased from 34,000,000 rubles in 1932 to 219,000,000 rubles, the 1938 assignment. There was only one hospital in Tadzhikistan before the revolution, and even that was accessible only to *bais,* landowners, and mullahs. Now the republic has over 100 hospitals, and over 400 dispensaries for out-patients.

In the past Tadzhikistan had no industries or railways at all. Under the two Stalin Five Year Plans industrial development has made great headway in Soviet Tadzhikistan. I need only mention enterprises such as the "KIM" and "Nefteabad" oil fields, the Shurab collieries, the silkreeling mills, a giant cannery and many other industrial enterprises. Stalinabad, the capital of the republic, is being built up on a wide scale. The population of our towns is growing continually. For instance, since 1929 the population of Stalinabad has increased from 5,000 to 70,000.

I should like to call attention to the great victories Socialist agriculture has won in our republic. The peasantry of the Tadzhik SSR has taken the path of collective farming once and for all. 92 per cent of all peasant holdings in the republic have been collectivized. Agricultural machines have superseded the antediluvian *omach* and *ketman* on the fields of Tadzhikistan. The collective farmers of Tadzhikistan have made great progress in cotton cultivation. In 1937 the collective farmers picked 16 centners of cotton per hectare, whereas in 1934 the yield was 6.2 centners per hectare. On the basis of these economic achievements, the collective farmers have attained a cultured, prosperous life.

The friendship of the peoples of the whole Soviet Union is unbreakable. All our victories are due to a resolute application of the national policies of Lenin and Stalin; we have won them in a ruthless struggle against the Trotskyite, Bukharinite and bourgeois-nationalist fascist spies, diversionists and wreckers, who tried to thwart our victorious advance. The splendid men of the People's Commissariat of Internal Affairs, led by the Stalin People's Commissar, N. I. Yezhov (applause) discovered the enemies' dastardly plans in time and destroyed them.

Under the leadership of the Party of Lenin and Stalin, under the leadership of the Soviet Government and Vyacheslav Mikhailovich Molotov (applause) and Mikhail Ivanovich Kalinin personally (applause), with the help of the Great Russian people, Tadzhikistan has become a prosperous Soviet republic. The working people of Tadzhikistan have attained this happy and prosperous life as a result of the masterly leadership and constant care of Joseph Vissarionovich Stalin, the leader of peoples. (Loud applause. All rise.)

Comrades, conditions in Tadzhikistan are such that arterial roads are of great importance to the republic's economic life. In this year's Budget, the People's Commissariat of Finance of the USSR has made no provision even for repairs to existing roads. Therefore I ask that in the operation of the Budget, the People's Commissariat of Finance should find the necessary funds for repairs to arterial roads and for the construction of new roads, especially in the mountainous and frontier districts of our republic.

Comrades, the Budget of the Soviet Union, the Budget of all her republics, speak eloquently for the soundness of the national policy of the Party of Lenin and Stalin, and for the further economic and cultural progress of the peoples of the Soviet Union.

Under the leadership of Comrade Stalin (applause) the great strategist and tactician of the proletarian revolution, the leader of the working people, we shall go on boldly and confidently to new victories for Communism. (Applause.)

Speech of S. M. Ivanov (Ulan-Ude Rural Area, Buryat-Mongolian ASSR) in the Union Soviet. (Abridged.)

. . . I fully second the motion made by a number of deputies to approve the Budget of the USSR. A great part in all the successes which we have achieved in the past years was played by our finance system; for, unlike the Budgets of capitalistic countries, the primary purpose of our Soviet Budget is to advance the national economy of our country, to improve the material well being of the masses of the working people. It reflects the constant concern of the Bolshevik Party, the Soviet Government and Comrade Stalin personally for the flourishing of the former backward and downtrodden peoples, for raising their economy and culture to the level of the advanced peoples of the Soviet Union. Our Buryat-Mongolian ASSR furnishes a striking example of this. . . . [*There follows a review, partially statistical, of developments in this republic.*]

Soviet-Buryat Mongolia is a flourishing Socialist republic — a strong outpost of Socialism in the East. Under the leadership of the Bolshevik Party, and with the help of the Great Russian people, the peoples of Buryat-Mongolia, formerly doomed to extinction, have now obtained a happy and joyous life. . . . All our successes have been achieved under the leadership of the Party of Lenin and Stalin and the Soviet Government, with the daily help and attention of our great leader and teacher, the inspirer of our victories, Comrade Stalin (loud and prolonged applause) and his faithful associate, Comrade Molotov. (Loud and prolonged applause.) . . . [*After a brief reference to spies, wreckers, etc. who were caught "with the help of the glorious Soviet intelligence service," the speaker continued.*]

Comrades, I shall draw your attention to a number of defects and errors made by the People's Commissariat of Finance of the USSR, and the People's Commissariat of Finance of the RSFSR in drawing up the local Budgets. These Commissariats sometimes pay little attention to the distinguishing features of the remote republics, as in the case of Buryat-Mongolia. . . . First, I wish to point to the insufficient appropriations for the repair of school buildings and the purchase of school supplies. That is why many of our schools are badly repaired and ill-equipped. Secondly, I must draw the attention of the deputies to the fact that the People's Commissariat of Finance of the RSFSR and the Art Department do not provide sufficient funds for the development of our national art. . . . The most backward section of our work is in housing and municipal services. . . . the State Planning Commission and the People's Commissariat of Finance of the RSFSR are holding back the development of the municipal services, and our housing accommodations are hardly growing at all. This situation has obtained for a number of years. . . .

[The speaker briefly complained that the RSFSR Commissariat of Finance "did not take into consideration the special features of each republic," and did not give the governments of the autonomous republics any chance to amend or correct the proposed budgets in view of local knowledge and needs. He spoke specifically of the need for more attention to irrigation and transportation.]

A few words about the establishment of a fixed percentage of allocations from the Budget revenues, particularly the turnover tax. This year the People's Commissariat of Finance has changed the percentage of allocations from the revenue items of the Budget twice, and as a result placed us twice in financial difficulties.

I am confident that the Government of the USSR and the People's Commissariat of Finance will take these remarks into account. . . .

[The speaker endorsed the appropriation for defence ("We live in a capitalist encirclement.") and referred briefly to the international situation, especially to the Japanese threat. He pledged the support of the Buryat-Mongolians and asked Molotov to continue his policy of "resolution and firmness." The speech closed with the usual tributes to the CPSU (B).]

Long live the organizer and inspirer of the gigantic victories of Socialism — our great and wise, our own Comrade Stalin! (Loud and prolonged applause. All rise.)

* * * * *

I. I. Sidorov, Chairman of the Budget Commission of the Union Soviet, replied to the "debate" as follows.

Comrades, members of the Supreme Soviet. Inasmuch as all the deputies who spoke in the debate on the Budget expressed their agreement with the findings of the Budget Commission, and inasmuch as Comrade Zverev, People's Commissar of Finance of the USSR, in announcing the opinion of the Government, did not object to the majority of the amendments proposed and the criticisms made, the Budget Commission considers that its recommendations to increase the revenue side of the Budget by 1,553,775,000 rubles as against the draft submitted was fully and entirely justified.

The debate on the Unified State Budget was maintained on a high political level. Every deputy spoke in a statesmanlike way. The Unified State Budget of the USSR is a splendid Budget. It must be carried out both as regards revenue and expenditure in a Bolshevik way. A determined fight must be waged against violations of Budget discipline, and we must demand that all

People's Commissariats, departments, organizations, all citizens of our country fulfill their duties to the state Budget. And we, too, the members of the Supreme Soviet, must work hard to ensure that the provisions of the state Budget are carried out.

Comrades, the debate on the Unified State Budget has shown that all the items of revenue and expenditure meet with the unanimous approval of the deputies who have spoken and of the whole Soviet of the Union. Great enthusiasm and satisfaction are occasioned by the appropriation of 27,000,000,000 rubles for defence purposes, for the purpose of strengthening the military might of our Socialist country. This testifies to the ardent love of the working people for their native land, it testifies to the unanimous desire to strengthen the might of our Red Army, Navy and Air Force still further, it testifies to the moral and political unity of our people, and to the fact that the Soviet people in their millions are prepared to thoroughly smash any enemy on his own territory. (Prolonged applause.)

The fascists of Germany and Italy and the imperialists of Japan are trying to provoke us to war. The fascist agents within our country — Trotskyites, Bukharinites and bourgeois nationalists — have been smashed. The Soviet people are united more solidly than ever around the Bolshevik Party, around our leader and teacher, our great Stalin. (Loud applause.)

But, comrades, the fight is not over, it is still going on. We must therefore show even greater determination in rooting out and destroying the enemies of our people, no matter what mask they may hide behind. We declare to the fascists and the Japanese imperialists, and let them bear it well in mind, that we fully and entirely approve of the firm policy and practical acts of our Soviet Government, and that if we are subjected to military attack, our valorous Workers' and Peasants' Red Army will destroy the enemy on his own territory. Let the fascists know that war on us will end in the destruction of fascism. Communism will triumph all over the world! (Loud applause.)

Comrades, where, in what other country, does a Budget submitted by the government meet with such unanimous approval? There is no such country, nor can there be, under capitalist rule. It is possible only in our country, the country where Socialism is victorious, and where the Budget is like a mirror reflecting the vital interests of our population.

I call upon you to vote for and adopt such a Budget unanimously. (Prolonged applause.)

The work of the Session testifies to the unity of the Soviet people, to their love and devotion to the Soviet government and its leader, Vyacheslav Mikhailovich Molotov (loud and prolonged applause. All rise. Cries: "Long live Comrade Molotov!" "Hurrah for Comrade Molotov!") their love and devotion to our Bolshevik Party and its Leninist-Stalinist Central Committee, their love and devotion to the leader and teacher of all working people, the man who is leading us from victory to victory, our dear and great Stalin! (Loud applause and cheers. All rise. Cries: "Hurrah for Comrade Stalin!" "Hurrah for our leader and great teacher, Comrade Stalin!" "Long live our great Stalin!" Cheers.)

* * * * *

Zverev's "reply to the debate" in the Soviet of Nationalities.

Comrades, members of the Supreme Soviet. At the sittings of the Soviet of Nationalities and the Soviet of the Union we have had a comprehensive discussion of the draft Unified State Budget for 1938. The unanimous approval of the Budget bears witness to the fact that the proposed Budget reflects, both in the revenue and in the expenditure side, the great tasks that confront our country in the year 1938.

In discussing the Budget, the Chairman of the Budget Commission of the Soviet of Nationalities, Comrade Khokhlov, proposed some amendments to the draft submitted. One of the motions made by the Budget Commission of the Soviet of Nationalities is to increase the total revenues in the Budget by over 1,500,000,000 rubles, including an increase of 591,500,000 rubles from the turnover tax. An analogous motion . . . has been made by the Budget Commission of the Soviet of the Union. The Budget Commission of the Soviet of Nationalities has moved that the revenues in the Budget. be increased by 208,310,000 rubles from the profits tax on our economic organizations and industrial People's Commissariats. The Budget Commission has also moved to increase the revenues by 300,000,000 rubles through an increase in the receipts from state loan bonds purchased by the savings banks with the funds attracted in deposits from the population. The Budget Commission also proposes to increase the expenditures in the Budget by more than 1,500,000,000 rubles.

The Council of People's Commissars of the USSR has instructed me to state before the Session of the Supreme Soviet that it recognizes the expediency of the motions of the Budget Commissions for an increase in expenditures and revenues in the draft Budget submitted. With regard to the turnover tax, the Council of People's Commissars considers it possible to accept an increase in receipts not in the amount of 591,500,000 rubles, as proposed by the Budget Commission of the Soviet of Nationalities, but by 627,500,000 rubles as recommended by the Budget Commission of the Soviet of the Union.

The Budget Commission of the Soviet of Nationalities has raised the question of increasing the profits tax by 208,000,000 rubles. The Council of People's Commissars of the USSR is of the opinion that it is expedient and necessary to increase Budget revenue from the profits tax by 132,610,000 rubles.

The Council of People's Commissars of the USSR has no objections to the motion of the Budget Commission to increase the taxes and levies on the population by 30,000,000 rubles, and to increase the Budget revenues by attracting deposits to the savings banks. The improvement in the material well being of the working people, and the prosperity of the population both in the cities and in the countryside, create favourable conditions for the participation of the workers and all the working people in the work of the savings banks. The revenues that accrued from this source in the first half of the year amounted to 1,200,000,000 rubles. If the savings banks and finance organs work energetically, the 300,000,000 rubles which the Budget Commission refers to in its motion will undoubtedly accrue to the Budget revenue of the state. That is why the Council of People's Commissars considers it expedient to raise the Budget estimate of receipts from this source as well.

Nor has the Council of People's Commissars of the USSR any objection to increasing the estimates of receipts from the state social insurance fund by 75,000,000 rubles and from customs revenues by 250,000,000 rubles. Decisions adopted by the Council of People's Commissars of the USSR after the draft had been submitted to the Budget Commission fully ensure the receipts accruing to the Budget from customs revenues. As regards other revenues, the Council of People's Commissars considers it expedient to include in the Budget the sum of 122,094,000 rubles as additional revenue.

Beside the amendments to the draft Unified State Budget, remarks have been made by the Budget Commissions . . . , as well as by individual members of the Supreme Soviet, in criticism of the work of various economic People's Commissariats. Members of the Supreme Soviet have pointed out that some People's Commissariats, . . . have not been discharging their financial obligations to the state Budget, and have not been fulfilling their plans for the output of industry and the lowering of the cost of production. The Council of People's Commissars of the USSR has instructed me to inform the members of the Supreme Soviet that in the near future the Council of People's Commissars will take additional concrete measures to improve the financial and production activity of these People's Commissariats.

Members of the Supreme Soviet and the Chairman of the Budget Commission of the Soviet of Nationalities, Deputy Khokhlov, have also criticized the work of the People's Commissariat of Finance of the USSR. I fully agree with these critical remarks. Unquestionably there are still many deficiencies in the People's Commissariat of Finance.

Some members of the Supreme Soviet of the USSR have pointed out that the People's Commissariat of Finance is not sufficiently acquainted with the financial affairs of the Union republics, and has therefore committed mistakes in drawing up the Unified State Budget. I must state that when the People's Commissariat of Finance submitted the draft Unified State Budget to the Council of People's Commissars, the latter pointed out the mistakes and corrected the draft. However, the criticism to the effect that the People's Commissariat of Finance is not acquainted with the specific features of economy in the . . . various republics is justified. At the same time we must demand of the Councils of People's Commissars of the republics, and of the executive committees of the territories and regions, that in estimating their expenditures and filing their claims to the Union Budget they should approach the matter from the viewpoint of the interests of the state.

The work of drawing up the Budget for 1938 has shown that in some instances the statements and claims presented to the Union and republican organizations had been accepted without a critical analysis. It is this that explains the fact that at first the demands upon the Budget totaled 45,136,000,000 rubles, while now, after the Budgets of the various republics have been examined into by the Council of People's Commissars of the USSR, this part of the Budget, as you see, represents a sum of 34,747,000,000 rubles. Thus the claims of the Union republics had been exaggerated to the amount of 10,389,000,000 rubles. It is quite obvious that a situation like this cannot be tolerated in the future. It is necessary to conform to strict state discipline in putting claims to the Union Budget. Only that should be demanded which is actually needed. An impermissible attitude with regard to drawing up claims was displayed by the organizations of the Kirghiz SSR.

The state Budget of the Kirghiz SSR for 1937 totalled 235,000,000 rubles, and for 1938 this republic drew up a Budget in the amount of 617,000,000 rubles. The Council of People's Commissars of the USSR could not agree to this sum and, after an examination into the Budget, decided to allow Kirghizia the sum of only 312,844,000 rubles. The unfounded claims put in by the Kirghiz comrades show how in some instances the attitude to the Union Budget betrays a lack of consideration of the interests of the state.

Exaggerated claims had also been filed by the Tadzhik, Turkmen, Kazakh and Armenian SSRs and by a number of autonomous republics and regional executive committees. At the same time the exaggerated claims to expenditures were usually accompanied by a demand for an increase of revenues from Union sources, while the possibilities of the local sources were clearly underrated. Instead of mobilizing all forces to increase the sources of revenue, instead of bringing to light new possibilities and disclosing concealed resources, the People's Commissariats of Finance of the Union Republics followed the line of least resistance. They demanded an increase in the percentage of the allocations from the turnover tax in order thus to obtain the sums that would enable them to draw up the republican and local Budgets without a deficit.

The governments of the various Republics do not always show a critical attitude to the claims of the People's Commissariats and other institutions. In 1937 the expenditures on village reading rooms in the Kazakh SSR, as shown by the summary of the local Budgets, totalled 4,000,000 rubles, yet for 1938 the Republic filed a claim for 21,602,000 rubles. It acted in exactly the same way in regard to the expenditure on physical culture and on sports, which it raised to 890 per cent of the expenditure of the preceding year.

The People's Commissariat of Finance of the USSR is unquestionably in duty bound to improve its work and draw up its financial plans in conformity with the specific features of the various republics. But it is also necessary to enhance the sense of responsibility in dealing with Soviet state funds in the republics and regions. The workers in charge must demand only what is needed for the realization of the various measures, without putting in any extra claims.

The prompt collection of state taxes is the most important task of the finance bodies. However, there are many who fail to realize this. I have already pointed out that in some regions and republics the finance bodies have failed to organize the timely collection of taxes and levies on the population.

The situation as regards the utilization of the resources allotted for housing and municipal development is very bad. A checkup on the work of housing, municipal and public service development has shown that most of the republics are not fulfilling their plans. In the first half of the year the Tadzhik Republic completed only 17.3 per cent of the year's plan for housing, municipal and public service development, the Byelorussian Republic 22 per cent, the Kirghiz Republic 24.4 per cent, the Turkmen Republic 25.7 per cent, and the Kazakh Republic 26.5 per cent. The failure to fulfill the plans is explained by the fact that the local Soviets have not made the proper preparations for the construction work. Plans and estimates have not been drawn up on time, and in many cases the construction jobs have not been supplied with labour power.

The Central Municipal Bank and the Municipal Banks in the localities are not exercising proper control over housing, municipal and public service development. At best the managers of these banks read the statements of the amount of money drawn. But they do not fight to reduce the cost of construction and to make the builders keep within the estimates in their expenditures.

A serious deficiency in the Budget work is the poor state of accounting. The existing system of accounting with regard to the realization of the state and local Budgets does not provide an opportunity for a day-to-day control of the financial transactions of the Budget institutions and economic organizations. This system prevents the timely disclosure of violations of financial and Budget discipline. It will be necessary for the People's Commissariat of Finance of the USSR, together with the Central Administration of National Economic Accounting, to revise the forms of bookkeeping and statistical accountancy on the state Budgets and local Budgets. It is necessary to submit definite terms for and the order of submitting accounts.

The remarks of the Chairman of the Budget Commission and of members of the Supreme Soviet impose upon the People's Commissariat of Finance of the USSR the obligation of drawing the necessary conclusions and setting itself the immediate task of effecting a radical improvement in all spheres of finance work.

With the help which the People's Commissariat of Finance of the USSR receives from the Government and from Comrade Stalin, we will by all means accomplish the tasks set us in the Budget for 1938. (Applause.)

Voting on the Budget

The voting procedure was the same in both chambers. First, the budget was voted on section by section. Then the budget as a whole was voted on. Next the Budget Act was voted on article by article (there were ten articles in the Budget Act of 1938) and, finally, the vote was taken on the Budget Act as a whole. Here are typical motions and votes.

(Voting on sections of the Budget in the Union Soviet.)

ZVEREV: Expenditures on the People's Commissariat of Defence and the People's Commissariat of the Navy — 27,044,020,000 rubles.

CHAIRMAN: I shall take a vote on expenditures on the People's Commissariats of Defence and Navy in the amount of 27,044,020,000 rubles. Those in favor of the adoption of this sum, please raise their hands. Please lower your hands. Anybody against? No. Any abstentions? No. Adopted unanimously.

(Voting on articles — Soviet of Nationalities.)

ZVEREV: In Article 7 some editorial changes were made after the draft had been distributed. I shall read it in its final form. "Article 7. To note the unsatisfactory organization of the collection by the People's Commissariat of Finance of the USSR, and its local organs in 1937 of the legally established rural taxes and levies. To make it the duty of the People's Commissariat of Finance of the USSR and the local Soviet organs to adopt measures to improve the work of the finance bodies."

CHAIRMAN: Are there any remarks on Article 7?

VOICES: Adopt.

CHAIRMAN: Those in favor of adopting Article 7, please raise their hands. Please lower your hands. Anybody against? No. Any abstentions? No. Article 7 is adopted unanimously.

(Voting on the whole budget — Union Soviet.)

CHAIRMAN: . . . We have concluded the voting on the Union Budget section by section. I shall now take the vote of the Soviet of the Union on the Union Budget for 1938 as a whole. Those in favor of the adoption of the Union Budget as a whole, please raise their hands. Anybody against? No. Any abstentions? No. Adopted unanimously.

(Voting on the Budget Act — Soviet of Nationalities.)

CHAIRMAN: . . . I shall take a vote on the unified State Budget of the USSR (1938) Act as a whole. Those in favor of adopting this Act as a whole, please raise their hands. Please lower your hands. Anybody against? No. Any abstentions? No. The Unified State Budget of the USSR (1938) Act is adopted unanimously.

The following facts concerning the "debate" and vote on the budget in the first 1948 session of the Supreme Soviet show that the procedures followed in 1938 were not atypical. According to Soviet newspaper reports of the proceedings, forty-seven of the 1,339 deputies spoke on the Budget during the three days which were devoted to that subject. The press regarded only nineteen of these speeches as sufficiently important to merit reporting. Five of the nineteen speakers whose remarks were reported were federal (All-Union) officials. Six of the nineteen speakers specifically criticized the work of certain ministries; four, asked for larger appropriations for the speaker's area; and nine simply endorsed the budget as presented. There were no adverse criticisms reported in the press. At the conclusion of the "debate" the Finance Minister of the USSR (the title was changed in 1946) promised that all suggestions and criticisms would be duly considered. The budget as originally presented was then adopted unanimously by both chambers.

* * * * *

This material on the Supreme Soviet may be rounded out by some brief notes on the elections to that body. Candidates are nominated by six specified groups (including the CPSU(B) organizations). Only one candidate is presented for each place. No candidate opposed by the Party has ever been selected but not all candidates are Party members. Voting is by secret ballot on the basis of universal adult suffrage and no effort is spared to ensure mass participation in the election. In the first election (Dec., 1937), 96% of those qualified to vote did so. The corresponding percentages for the 1946 and the 1950 elections were, respectively, 99.7% and 99.8%. Virtually all the votes cast (99.2% in 1946, 99.73% in 1950) went to the official candidates. Ap-

proximately 76% of the deputies to the first Supreme Soviet were Party members. The figure for the second Supreme Soviet was 81%.

Rules of the Communist Party of the
Soviet Union (Bolshevik)

"Here in the Soviet Union, in the land of the dictatorship of the proletariat, that fact that not a single important political or organizational question is decided by our Soviet and other mass organizations without directions from the Party must be regarded as the highest [clearest] expression of the leading role of the Party." This statement by Stalin himself makes it absolutely clear that the Communist Party is not properly comparable to political parties in democratic countries. The CPSU (B) is the government-in-fact of the Soviet Union. The Party's own rules make this a matter of record. The following excerpts are from the rules "Adopted unanimously by the Eighteenth Congress of the CPSU(B)" which was held in March of 1939. There have been some changes in detail since that time, but no changes have been made in the sections quoted below. The source is: The Land of Socialism Today and Tomorrow. *Moscow: Foreign Languages Publishing House, 1939. Pp. 465–483* passim.

The Communist Party of the Soviet Union (Bolsheviks), . . . is the organized vanguard of the working class of the Union of Soviet Socialist Republics, the highest form of its class organization. In its activities the Party is guided by the theory of Marxism-Leninism.

The Party exercises the leadership of the working class, the peasantry, the intelligentsia, of the entire Soviet people, in the struggle for the consolidation of the dictatorship of the working class, for the consolidation and development of the socialist system, for the victory of communism.

The Party is the guiding nucleus of all organizations of the working people, both public and state, and ensures the successful construction of the communist society.

The Party is a united militant organization bound together by a conscious discipline which is equally binding on all its members. The Party is strong because of its solidarity, unity of will and unity of action, which are incompatible with any deviation from its program and rules, with any violation of Party discipline, with factional groupings, or with double dealings. The Party purges its ranks of persons who violate its program, rules or discipline.

The Party demands from its members active and self-sacrificing work in carrying out its program and rules, in fulfilling all decisions of the Party and its bodies, and in ensuring the unity of its ranks and the consolidation of fraternal international relations among the working people of the nationalities of the USSR as well as with the proletarians of all countries of the world.

I

Party Members, Their Duties and Rights

1. A Party member is one who accepts the program of the Party, works in one of its organizations, submits to its decisions, and pays membership dues.

2. It is the duty of a Party member:
   a) To work untiringly to improve his political knowledge and to master the principles of Marxism-Leninism;
   b) Strictly to observe Party discipline, to take an active part in the political life of the Party and the country, and to carry into practise the policy of the Party and the decisions of its bodies;
   c) To set an example in the observance of labour and state discipline, to master the technique of his work and constantly to improve his industrial or business qualifications;
   d) Constantly to strengthen the ties with the masses, promptly to respond to the needs and demands of the working people, and to explain to the masses the policy and decisions of the Party.

3. A Party member has the right:
   a) To take part in the free and business-like discussion at Party meetings or in the Party press of practical questions of Party policy;
   b) To criticize any Party worker at Party meetings;
   c) To elect and be elected to Party organs;
   d) To demand to be present in person whenever decisions are taken regarding his activities or conduct;
   e) To address any question or statement to any Party body, up to and including the Central Committee of the CPSU(B).

4. Members are admitted to the Party only individually. New members are admitted from among the candidate members who have been through the specified probationary period. Membership in the Party is open to conscientious and active workers, peasants and intellectual who are devoted to the cause of communism. Persons may join the Party on attaining the age of eighteen. . . . [*The detailed regulations about application and admittance to membership, expulsion from membership, and the status of candidate members are omitted since these have several times been altered since 1939.*]

III

Organizational Structure of the Party, Inner-Party Democracy

18. The guiding principle of the organizational structure of the Party is democratic centralism which signifies:
   a) The election of all leading Party bodies, from the highest to the lowest;

b) Periodical reports of the Party bodies to their Party organizations;

c) Strict Party discipline and subordination of the minority to the majority;

d) The absolutely binding character of decisions of higher bodies upon lower bodies.

19. : . . . a Party organization serving a given area is regarded as higher than any Party organization serving part of that area; and a Party organization serving a whole branch of work is regarded as higher than any Party organization serving part of that branch of work.

20. All Party organizations are autonomous in the decision of local questions, provided that their decisions do not conflict with the decisions of the Party.

. . .

25. The free and business-like discussion of questions of Party policy in individual organizations or in the Party as a whole is the inalienable right of every Party member and logically follows from inner-party democracy. Only on the basis of inner-party democracy is it possible to develop Bolshevik self-criticism and to strengthen Party discipline, which must be conscious and not mechanical. But wide discussion, especially discussion on an All-Union scale, of questions of Party policy must be so organized as to prevent it leading to attempts by an insignificant minority to impose their will upon the vast majority of the Party, or to attempts to form factional groupings which break the unity of the Party, attempts at splits which may shake the strength and firmness of the dictatorship of the working class. Therefore, a wide discussion on an All-Union scale can be regarded as necessary only if: (a) this necessity is recognized by at least several local Party organizations of the scale of a region or of a republic; (b) if there is not a sufficiently solid majority on the Central Committee of the CPSU(B) on important questions of Party policy; (c) if in spite of the existence of a solid majority on the Central Committee of the CPSU(B) advocating a definite standpoint, the Central Committee still deems it necessary to test the correctness of its policy by means of a discussion in the Party. Only compliance with these conditions can safeguard the Party against the abuse of inner-party democracy by anti-Party elements, only under these conditions is it possible to count on inner-party democracy benefitting the cause and on it not being used to the detriment of the Party and the working class. . . .

IV

Higher Party Organs

. . .

34. The Central Committee of the CPSU(B) sets up a Political Bureau for political work, an Organization Bureau for the general direction of organizational work, a Secretariat for current work of an organizational or executive nature, and a Party Control Commission to keep check on the way decisions of the Party and the Central Committee of the CPSU(B) are fulfilled.

35. The Party Control Commission: (a) Keeps a check on the way the decisions of the Party . . . are fulfilled by Party organizations and Soviet and economic bodies; (b) Investigates the work of local Party organizations; (c) Takes action against those who have violated the program or rules of the CPSU(B), or Party discipline.

36. . . . The Central Committee of the CPSU(B) directs the work of the central Soviet and public organizations through the Party groups within them. . . .

VIII

Primary Party Organizations

57. The primary Party organizations are the Basis of the Party. Primary Party organizations are set up in mills, factories, state farms, machine and tractor stations, and other economic establishments, in collective farms, units of the Red Army and Navy, in villages, offices, educational establishments, etc. where there are not less than three Party members. . . .

60. The primary Party organization connects the mass of the workers, peasants and intellectuals with the leading organs of the Party. Its task is:

a) To conduct agitational and organizational work among the masses for the carrying out of Party slogans and decisions, and to ensure the effective leadership of the factory press;

b) To recruit new members for the Party and to organize their political education;

c) To assist the district committee, city committee or political department in all its practical work;

d) To mobilize the efforts of the masses in the factories, state farms, collective farms, etc. for the fulfillment of the production plan, for the strengthening of labour discipline and for the development of socialist emulation and shock work;

e) To combat laxity and mismanagement in factories, state farms and collective farms, and to show a daily concern for the improvement of the cultural and living conditions of the workers and collective farmers;

f) To take an active part in the economic and political life of the country. . . .

IX

The Party and the Young Communist League

63. The Leninist Young Communist League conducts its activities under the guidance of the CPSÚ(B). The Central Committee of the YCL, as its leading body, is subordinated to the Central Committee of the CPSU(B). The activities of the local organizations of the YCL are directed and controlled by the appropriate republican, territorial, regional, city, and district organizations of the Party. . . .

XI

Party Groups in Non-Party Organizations

70. At all congresses and conferences and in all elected bodies of Soviet, trade union, cooperative and other mass organizations where there are not less than three Party members, Party groups are formed whose task it is to strengthen the influence of the Party in every respect and to carry out the Party policy among the non-Party people, to strengthen Party and state discipline, to combat bureaucracy, and tò keep a check on the way Party and Soviet directions are fulfilled. The group elects a secretary for its current work.

71, The Party groups are subordinated to the appropriate Party organizations. . . . In all questions the groups must strictly and unswervingly be guided by the decisions of the leading Party organs. . . .

Collective Troubles

Lacking access to the region of his study, and in the absence of anything like free and complete reporting the student of recent and contemporary Soviet affairs is forced to seek information wherever he can find it. Sometimes it turns up in what appear to be unlikely places. The following material is a case in point. The excerpts are selections from speeches on the "State Horse Tax on Individual Peasant Farms," delivered before the second (1938) session of the Supreme Soviet. They contain information on the following points, among others: policy, successes and failures of collectivization, private property, techniques of administration and of coercion, and the reality of power.

By way of a very brief background it may be pointed out that the forcible collectivization of agriculture during the Second Five Year Plan represents one of Stalin's greatest successes, his most dangerous gamble, and his most ruthless action. Lenin had tried but failed to accomplish the socialization, so-called, of agriculture. It had been one of the objectives of the First Five Year Plan, but it was not achieved then. Stalin recognized that he could not build "a socialized state" unless he could get the peasants — the majority of the Soviet people — into "socialized organizations." The continuance of his regime depended upon his doing so, but peasant opposition, though disorganized, was extremely strong. He spared no pains and no persons to win his gamble. Literally millions of peasants were deprived of their homes, their possessions, their families, their freedom, and their lives. By brutality combined with later concessions, Stalin won his gamble, collectivized agriculture, and saved his regime.

The material below indicates that the peasants were still fighting rear-guard actions in 1938 though the main struggle was then over. Statements in the Soviet press as late as 1950 indicated that peasant opposition to collectivization and "socialist discipline" still remained a serious problem.

The speeches are quoted from the official verbatim reports of the session.

(Speech of R. E. Melnikov (Smolensk Rural Area, Smolensk Region) in the Union Soviet.)

Comrades, members of the Supreme Soviet. I move that the Bill on the State Horse Tax on Individual Farms introduced by the Legislative Bills Commission of the Soviet of the Union be passed *in toto*.

This Bill is an expression of the Stalin policy of our Bolshevik Party and Government in the countryside, which is directed towards strengthening the collective farms in all ways, towards their further development and the transformation of all collective farms into Bolshevik collective farms and all collective farmers into prosperous farmers.

The Bolshevik Party, under the leadership of Comrade Stalin, has achieved historic victories in the bitter struggle against the most malicious enemies of the people. Agriculture has been reconstructed along Socialist lines on the basis of collective and state farms, on the basis of the introduction of modern machine technique into the process of agricultural production. Our Party, under the leadership of the great genius of toiling humanity, Joseph Vissarionovich Stalin, has solved the most difficult and complex problem of the Socialist revolution in our country.

The collective farm system in the countryside has conquered finally and irrevocably. The collective farm peasantry is a loyal, steadfast support of the Soviet power. The collective farms have inexhaustible opportunities for further increasing the harvest yields and carrying out Stalin's slogan of producing 7,000,000,000–8,000,000,000 poods of grain annually.

In his report at the Extraordinary Eighth All-Union Congress of Soviets, Comrade Stalin characterized our Soviet peasantry with exceptional vividness. He said: "Our Soviet peasantry is an entirely new peasantry. In our country there are no longer any landlords and kulaks, merchants and usurers to exploit the peasants. Consequently, our peasantry is a peasantry emancipated from exploitation. Further, our Soviet peasantry, the overwhelming majority, is a collective farm peasantry, i.e., it bases its work and wealth, not on individual labour and on backward technical equipment but on collective labour and up-to-date technical equipment. Finally, the farming of our peasantry is based, not on private property, but on collective property, which has grown up on the basis of collective labour.

"As you see, the Soviet peasantry is an entirely new peasantry, the like of which the history of mankind has never known before."

Comrades, the broad masses of the collective farm peasantry fully understand that their prosperous, cultured and happy life is inseparably linked up with the growth and consolidation of the national economy and the defensive power of the great Union of Soviet Socialist Republics. Therefore the peasant collective farmers manifest a high political level in their comprehension of state tasks. Therefore the collective farm peasantry considers honest Bolshevik fulfillment of all its obligations to the Soviet state its prime duty.

I should like to dwell on a few facts characterizing the tremendous changes which have taken place in agriculture in the Smolensk Region during the years of the Stalin Five-Year Plan periods. Before the revolution the overwhelming majority of the peasants in the old Smolensk Province owned but insignificantly small plots of land and eked out a miserable existence. Under pressure of landlord and kulak bondage the peasants abandoned the villages in search of remunerative work. Now 94.5 per cent of the peasant households in our region have united in collective farms and are therein building a happy, joyous and prosperous life. Thanks to the solicitude of the Bolshevik Party, the Soviet Government and our great Stalin personally, the collective farm peasantry of our Region has at its disposal modern agricultural technique. A total of 85 machine and tractor stations, 4,500 tractors, over 600 harvester combines, 1,750 flax pullers, complex threshing machines, tractor sowers and other agricultural machines are operating on the collective farm fields of the Smolensk Region. Modern agricultural technique has brought about fundamental changes in peasant labour, made it lighter and ensured a rapid expansion of the sown area, primarily of the area sown to the most important industrial crop in our region — flax. These successes forcefully demonstrate the brilliant results of the Stalin policy of collectivization of agriculture, achieved on the basis of the development and consolidation of the collective farm system.

The enemies of the people — the Right and Trotskyite traitors to their fatherland — having wormed their way into the leadership of what was formerly the Western Region, tried with all their might to retard the growth of the collective farms, used wrecking methods to disrupt collective farm economy, created conditions that were more favourable for the individual peasants than for the collective farmers. As a result of this hostile work the percentage·of collectivization of peasant households in the region remained on one and the same level for a long time.

On January 1, 1938, there were 29,000 individual farms in the region, or 6.4 per cent of the total number of farms. Of these individual farms, 11,394 owned horses, and many of the individual peasants used these horses not for agricultural work on their farms but for purposes of speculation and profiteering.

There were many cases in our region where as a result of the subversive activities of wreckers, as a result of the fact that local Soviet government organs in the region violated the decisions of the Party and the Government concerning non-collective farm peasants, the individual peasants were either not taxed at all or were taxed less than was due, not all the sources of income being estimated. For instance, in the Andreyevsky district of the Smolensk Region, the individual peasant Peter Belmachev owned two draught horses, large cattle [sic] and a large number of small livestock. All this property was incorrectly taxed. The amount of the tax was obviously underestimated, and even this reduced tax was systematically left unpaid.

For a number of years the local finance organs did not apply the measures required by law to compel this individual farm to carry out its obligations. In the village of Vertensk in the Duminich district, an individual peasant woman by the name of Senyushkina, who owned two horses, regularly used them not for her own agricultural work but for purposes of profiteering, engaging in carting and stacking bark. It is characteristic that in estimating the tax on Senyushkina's farm, the local organs took no account of this main source of income. The wrecking practice whereby the local Soviet organs tolerated cases of under-taxation with regard to individual farms had a harmful effect on the economic growth and consolidation of the collective farms and gave rise to unhealthy sentiments among some collective farmers.

Thanks to the exceptional sagacity of our great leader, Comrade Stalin, the glorious Soviet Intelligence service, headed by the Stalinite Commissar N. I. Yezhov, exposed and destroyed the hornets' nest of the Right and Trotskyite hirelings of fascism.

The Central Committee of the CPSU(B) and the Government rendered the Smolensk Region tremendous assistance, ensuring the successful elimination of the consequences of wrecking activities in agriculture.

The decisions of the Council of People's Commissars of the USSR and the Central Committee of the CPSU(B) adopted on April 19, 1938 — "On the

Prohibition of the Expulsion of Collective Farmers from Collective Farms," "On the Incorrect Distribution of Income in Collective Farms" and "On Taxes and Other Duties on Individual Peasant Farms" — played a big role in strengthening the collective farms and in rapidly eliminating the consequences of wrecking activities in agriculture.

These decisions vividly reflect the Stalinite solicitude for the collective farms and collective farmers.

In our Smolensk Region, 7,446 peasant farms entered collective farms during the first half of 1938.

It is our most important task to liquidate in a Bolshevik manner the consequences of wrecking activities in the agriculture of the region.

The Bill on the State Horse Tax on Individual Peasant Farms, which is up for adoption by the Session of the Supreme Soviet, meets the desires of the broad masses of collective farmers. This law will be a powerful weapon with which to suppress the profiteering carried on by the non-collective farm peasants. It will facilitate the still greater consolidation and development of Socialist agriculture, the further growth of a prosperous, cultured and happy life for the collective farm peasantry.

Comrades, we are all certain that our great Socialist fatherland will achieve wonderful new successes in all fields of Socialist construction in town and country. A guarantee of this is the fact that we are guided by the glorious Bolshevik Party, that we are being led from victory to victory by the great leader of toiling humanity, a man of the most profound wisdom and steel will — our own great Stalin. (Applause.)

* * * * *

(*Speech of A. S. Yezhov* (*Budyonny Area, Ordjonikidze Territory*) *in the Union Soviet. Somewhat abridged.*)

Comrades . . . I fully support the motion to pass the Bill. . . .

The collective farm system has been finally and irrevocably victorious. . . . As Deputy Ugarov said here, 93 per cent of the peasant households are united in collective farms. A total of 99 per cent of the sown area of the farms in our country belongs to the collective farms. . . .

Comrades, the Bill . . . is a document of great political importance. In our country only 7 per cent of the peasantry are on individual farms. But even this insignificant proportion of individual peasants demands serious attention. We cannot allow part of the working people — the individual peasants — to disregard Soviet laws. . . . We cannot permit individual farms to find themselves in more favourable conditions than the collective farmers.

At the plenum of the Leningrad Regional and City Committees of the CPSU(B) on October 10, 1934, the unforgettable Sergei Mironovich Kirov said: "If we want to complete the collectivization of our region, we must, first, actually ensure the advantage of the collective farmers over the individual peasants, and, second, compel the individual peasants to fulfill their state and social obligations as they should be fulfilled."

The facts are that some individual farms which own horses do not fulfill their state and social obligations from year to year. Thus . . . [in the district where I work as Party secretary] there are 625 individual farms. The majority of them own horses but from year to year fulfill neither their plans of agricultural work nor all their obligations to the state.

The enemies of the people who operated in the territory encouraged and cultivated this anti-state practice. Individual farms took absolutely no part in the repair work of our hospitals, schools, reading rooms and clubs, or in road construction, but they enjoyed the results of the work of the collective farmers. I am not opposed to the individual peasants using the schools, hospitals and roads built with the help of the collective farmers. They should enjoy all the benefits created in our country. But I am opposed to the practice of rotten liberalism on the part of some local officials in respect to those individual peasants who do not fulfill their social and state obligations. . . .

* * * * *

(Excerpts from the speech of A. I. Ugarov (Smolny Area, City of Leningrad) before a joint sitting of the two chambers of the Supreme Soviet, Party and Government leaders being present.)

. . . The Legislative Bills Commission . . . has charged me to report to you on the . . . Bill. Day by day the collective farm system in our country is gaining in strength. . . . The toiling peasants all over the world, languishing under the yoke of bourgeois, landlord and kulak exploitation, and burdened by imposts and taxes of all kinds, can see in the collective farm system in our country a great example of how life can be made new, free and bright. . . .

Our Constitution, as you know, permits the existence and operation of the small private economy of individual peasants and handicraftsmen, based on their personal labour and precluding the exploitation of the labour of others. We cannot, however, overlook the fact that the individual peasants indulge in economic practices which actually represent a circumvention of the Soviet laws and an infringement of the interests of the collective farmers and of the Soviet state. The economic activities of the individual peasants are sometimes of a nature that places the individual peasant farm in an advantageous position as compared with the collective farm — a state of affairs which is fundamentally at variance with the policy of our Communist Party and of our Soviet State. . . .

As far back as February 1933 . . . Comrade Stalin said that "one section of the individual peasants has become utterly corrupt and gone in for profiteering." The use of horses for profiteering purposes has become quite widespread. The individual peasants are sometimes known to purchase additional horses for the same profiteering purposes. In the Chernigov region . . . between August 1, 1937, and August 1, 1938, 938 horses were purchased by individual peasants. Of these, 718 horses are being used for carting and 167 in logging and peat extraction. . . . The incomes derived . . . amount to quite big sums . . . as much as 4,000–6,000 rubles a year, and sometimes even more, per farm. . . .

The widespread use of horses for profiteering undermines the discipline of the individual peasants as regards discharging all their duties to the state, furnishes them with an opportunity to evade the Soviet law, and has a decidedly bad influence on the less stable elements among the collective farmers. This state of affairs, comrades, cannot but have un undesirable effect on the remaining individual peasants as regards their joining collective farms.

It is in order to put a stop to the practice of individual peasants using their horses for profiteering, in order to improve the discipline of individual peasants as regards carrying out all their duties to the state, and in order to do away with the harmful influence which the individual peasants who have gone in for profiteering exert on the less stable elements among the collective farmers, that the Legislative Bills Commission has submitted to the Session the Bill on a State Horse Tax on Individual Peasant Farms. . . .

The Bill was adopted unanimously by both chambers of the Supreme Soviet. The new law went into effect immediately.

"AS THE TWIG IS BENT—"

Education, Soviet spokesmen iterate and reiterate, is a weapon of Communism. They have learned to use it with great effectiveness. One of their many devices is a rigid control over all textbooks used in their schools. Each textbook must have the approval of the Party leaders, and use of the approved text is mandatory. This makes textbooks an exceedingly important source of information about the direction in which the Soviet rulers are training their people. The following excerpts, touching on a variety of subjects, are from Soviet textbooks which were in use in the middle 1930s. They were selected for the very obvious reason that the men and women now rising toward places of power and responsibility in the Soviet system used these texts during their schooldays. The source of the first series of excerpts is: Gordon, F. First Grade Reader. (Approved by the Peoples' Commissariat of Education of the RSFSR.) Moscow: State Textbook Publishing House, 1935. Passim. The titles of the selections are those given in the Reader.

HOT LUNCHES AT SCHOOL

There goes the lunch bell. We must hurry. We must wash our hands. How good the hot soup smells! It will keep us warm all day. We will pass our plates. We will help to keep our table clean. We must not talk in the dining room. We get hot lunches everyday. All children in America do not get hot lunches. All children in England do not get hot lunches. Only the children in the Soviet Union get hot lunches in school everyday.

JIMMY — THE NEWSBOY

Jimmy is a little American boy. Jimmy is a newsboy. Jimmy sells newspapers on the street. Jimmy's father is a worker. He has not worked for a long time. Jimmy has many brothers and sisters. When their father does not work, they have nothing to eat. That is why Jimmy must work. That is why he cannot go to school.

TOM, THE NEGRO BOY

Tom is a little Negro boy. He lives in America. He must work on a big plantation. He must work very hard. He works very long hours. Tom's father works on the plantation, too. His mother works there, too. His brothers and sisters also work on the plantation. Tom has never gone to school. The schools in the South are for rich white people.

RED OCTOBER DAY

Red flags on October Day. Bright light on October Day. Over Soviet lands, to tell the world of worker's might, to tell the world of fearless fight, to call all workers to unite and struggle hand in hand. Red October Days are here. We are very busy in school. We are making banners for Red October Day. Mary has made the best banner. It says: "Long live the Red October!" We are making flags, too. John has a red flag. We are going to march in the parade. We will carry our banners. We will wave our flags. Red October is our holiday. We are Octoberites. We are the children of Red October.

THE RED TIE

Mary is a Pioneer. Mary has a red tie. Mary wears her tie to school everyday. The red tie has three corners. Do you know what they stand for? One corner stands for the *Pioneers,* one corner stands for the *Komsomols.* The third corner stands for the *Communist Party.* The Pioneers are the little brothers of the Komsomols. The Pioneer corner and the Komsomol corner can be tied in a knot. Have you a Pioneer tie?

JOSEPH STALIN

Comrade Stalin is known all over the world. Stalin is the son of a Georgian worker. Stalin was a very young boy when he began to work for the workers' cause. Stalin worked with Lenin. Stalin was sent to prison many times under the tsar. The last time he spent four years in exile. In the October revolution, he helped the workers to drive out the landlords and the capitalists. They did not give up at once. They tried to make things as they had been in the past. They began a war against the Soviets. In this war Stalin was the leader of the workers. Under his leadership the Red Army was successful. It defeated the enemy. At the same time, Stalin together with Lenin and other comrades began to build a new life. Lenin died, but the party which he helped to build, the Bolshevik Party, remained. It worked to help the workers create a new life. Stalin is its best leader and worker. We now have hundreds of new factories. There we make new machines, tractors, and airplanes. More peasants now live on the Kolkhozes. They work together. In the Kolkhozes, there are machines, schools, also nurseries for the little children. Now we have very few people who cannot read. The children and the grown-ups are studying. All the children must go to school. The workers and peasants stand for the land of the Soviets. The Red Army protects the land of the Soviets from its enemies. Its enemies are the landlords and capitalists of all countries. The friends of our Soviet country are the workers and peasants and the oppressed of all countries. From everywhere they send greetings to Stalin. We school children also send him our children's greetings.

Education in the Soviet Union means more than just a system of public schools. It includes every possible institution, agency, and means of communication. No possibility is overlooked. Social clubs, trade unions, collective farms, units of the armed forces, and so on and so on are all part of the educational system. So, also, are the movies, radio, television, the theatre, opera, the ballet, libraries, museums, and all printed material. Much attention is given to adult education — in fact, education in the Soviet way goes on almost literally from the cradle to the grave. The following selection is from a language textbook published by the Soviet government for the use of British and American workers who had immigrated or planned to emigrate to the USSR. There was a considerable number of such persons at the time the book was published. The selection was printed in Russian for the student to translate. The source is: A. I. Smirnitsky, et ali. Russian for English Speaking Workers. *Moscow: Cooperative Publishing Society of Foreign Workers in the USSR, 1933.*

BUILDING SOCIALISM, OUR UNIVERSAL TASK

Comrade Burns is an English worker. Comrades Green, and Davis, and I are American workers. You are Russian workers. We live and work in the

USSR. Workers and toilers of different nationalities are building here a new society, a socialist society. There are many workers of many nationalities in the USSR, but there is no national hostility here because in the USSR there is a real equality of national rights. Only in the USSR is there a real brotherhood of peoples.

We are foreign workers and you are Soviet workers, but building socialism in the USSR is our common task because building socialism in the USSR is the first stage of building socialism for the whole world.

* * * * *

The following selections are from a Soviet translation of a textbook prepared by M. Ovsyannikova and others for use in the lower schools. The source of the first excerpt is: Social Science. Part III. (*Moscow, 1935*), *pp. 42, 43. The second is from:* op. cit. Part I, *pp. 101, 102.*

#18. THE SIGNIFICANCE OF MARX AND ENGELS' DOCTRINE FOR THE INTERNATIONAL WORKERS' MOVEMENT

We are already acquainted with the life of those great revolutionaries Marx and Engels. They were friends and leaders of the workers and all toilers.

Not only did Karl Marx indicate to the working class its historical tasks but he also proved scientifically the inevitability of the downfall of capitalism and the creation of a communist society. The creation of a communist society, however, will only be possible when the power of the bourgeoisie and the power of capital has been overthrown.

Marx has proved that there is no other path to socialism than that of revolution. And that those who preach the peaceful path are enemies and deceivers of the toiling masses. Socialism is impossible without the overthrow of the power of the bourgeoisie. This is what Marx taught the workers.

But it is insufficient to overthrow the power of the bourgeoisie. It is also necessary to mercilessly crush any opposition of class enemies and to destroy the remnants of the capitalist class, tearing out capitalism by the roots. For scores and hundreds of years capitalism has been crippling and poisoning the consciousness of the people. It brought them up as its obedient slaves. It is necessary to tear out and burn out from the consciousness of the people these habits of slaves, and to reeducate them as conscious builders of a new communist society.

In order to accomplish all these tasks the working class must have their own workers' power. The proletariat must have its dictatorship, its proletarian state. The dictatorship of the proletariat is necessary in order to overthrow the power of the bourgeoisie, to crush its opposition, to retain in its hands the factories and mills, to develop and strengthen socialist forms and to build a classless society.

The victory of the proletarian revolution and the victory of socialism is impossible without the dictatorship of the proletariat. This is what Marx and Engels taught the working class of the whole world. *The doctrine of the proletarian dictatorship is the essence of Marxism.* He who comes forward against the dictatorship of the proletariat and against the armed violent overthrow of the capitalist class is against the teachings of Marx and is a traitor to the interests of the working class and an enemy of the proletariat.

Marx taught the workers that the dictatorship of the proletariat is necessary in order to prepare the transfer to a communist non-class society. The dictatorship of the proletariat represents the stepping stone from capitalism to communism, and whilst the communist society has not yet been established it is essential to strengthen by every means the dictatorship of the proletariat, not to weaken it. The interests of the proletarian revolution demand this.

Marx did not only prove that the class struggle between the bourgeoisie and the proletariat inevitably leads to the dictatorship of the proletariat; Marx likewise taught the workers that they cannot conquer without their own independent political party which would unite the most advanced, devoted conscious and disciplined members. *The victory of the workers' cause is impossible without a communist party armed with the advanced revolutionary theory.* All his life Marx taught this to the workers. He was the organizer and the leader of the first Communist Party, the Communist League and the International Workingmen's Association, the First International.

Marx at the same time pointed out to the proletariat their allies in the struggle against the bourgeoisie, the toiling peasantry. He studied the history of serfdom and servitude of the peasants and their struggles. Marx pointed out to the peasants that only under the guidance of the working class and its party could the peasantry liberate itself from servitude to the landowners and from ruin and poverty. Marx likewise taught the workers that their cause cannot conquer without a union with the peasantry, without a union with the oppressed peoples.

This is why Marx and Engels are great and famous. That is why we consider Marx and Engels as the great teachers and leaders of the working class of the entire world.

#74. THE CAUSE OF MARX, ENGELS, LENIN AND STALIN WILL CONQUER THROUGHOUT THE WORLD

Vladimir Ilyich Lenin continued the teachings of Marx and Engels. Lenin devoted his whole life to fighting against those who tried to distort the teachings of Marx and Engels and to render this teaching harmless for the bourgeoisie.

Lenin established the Communist Party, the Bolshevik Party, which led the working class of Russia to victory in October 1917. The working class, in union with the poor peasantry, has overthrown the power of the capitalists and has established its own power — the Soviet Power.

Lenin has done a great deal to strengthen this power of the Soviets. He has done a great deal to bring about a closer union between the workers and peasants.

Under the leadership of Lenin the Communist Party, followed by the workers and peasants of our country, is building a new socialist society.

Lenin organized the Communist International, under whose banner the revolutionary forces of the toilers of the world are now uniting.

Lenin died, but the cause begun by him is continued by his best pupil and follower, Conrade Stalin. Under his leadership our Communist Party is putting into effect the teachings of Marx and Lenin in the USSR. The Communist Party leads the working class and toiling peasantry of our country forward to the great struggle for socialism and is achieving victory after victory.

The toilers of the USSR have successfully fulfilled the First Five-Year Plan.

Our victories in socialist construction proved the correctness of the teachings of Marx, Engels, Lenin and Stalin. Our successes stand out as an example to the toilers of the whole world, an example of how to fight the capitalist enemy.

Under the banner of the Communist Parties in all countries the forces of the toilers are uniting. The Communist Parties of the whole world are preparing the workers to take over power.

Comrade Stalin is the leader of the Communist International, which unites and leads the struggle of the Communist Parties of the world.

The time is near when the toilers of all countries will overthrow the bourgeoisie and achieve their liberation.

The cause of Marx, Engels, Lenin and Stalin will conquer throughout the world.

A World to Win

Lenin and his colleagues believed that the revolution in Russia was only the first stage of a world-wide revolution. In fact, Lenin concluded his first speech after his return to Russia by hailing the world socialist revolution. He and his associates continued for some years to think that world revolution was impending and that a European socialist revolution was imminent. And they spent much thought, effort, and money to accelerate its coming. This was partly a reflection of their confidence in the Marxian "revelations," but it was also, in part, a reflection of general European developments immediately after the first world war. Discontent and unrest were almost every-

where apparent; riots and other disorders were common; mutinies and rebellions occurred in some countries; and there were full-scale revolutions which won temporary successes in Hungary and in Germany.

As a result of events in Germany in the Fall of 1918, the German Spartacist (Communist) leader, Karl Liebknecht, was released from jail. Lenin and his associates immediately ordered their ambassador in Berlin to present their congratulations to Liebknecht. The second sentence documents the statement that they believed the day of world revolution to be at hand. The message to the ambassador was handwritten on a sheet of notepaper. The original is in the Central Lenin Museum.

To the Russian Ambassador in Berlin

Convey our most ardent greetings to Karl Liebknecht. The release from prison of the representative of the revolutionary workers of Germany is a sign of a new epoch, the epoch of victorious socialism which is now beginning for Germany and for the whole world.

> On behalf of the Central Committee
> of the Russian Communist Party (Bolsheviks)
> Lenin, Sverdlov, Stalin